The Nimzo-Indian: 4 e3

Carsten Hansen

First published in the UK by Gambit Publications Ltd 2002

ISBN 1 901983 58 7

DISTRIBUTION:
Worldwide (except USA): Central Books Ltd, 99 Wallis Rd, London E9 5LN. Tel +44 (0)20 8986 4854 Fax +44 (0)20 8533 5821.
E-mail: orders@Centralbooks.com
USA: BHB International, Inc., 302 West North 2nd Street, Seneca, SC 29678, USA.

For all other enquiries (including a full list of all Gambit Chess titles) please contact the publishers, Gambit Publications Ltd, P.O. Box 32640, London W14 0JN.
E-mail: info@gambitbooks.com
Or visit the GAMBIT web site at http://www.gambitbooks.com

Edited by Graham Burgess
Typeset by John Nunn
Printed in Great Britain by The Cromwell Press, Trowbridge, Wilts.

10 9 8 7 6 5 4 3 2 1

Gambit Publications Ltd
Managing Director: GM Murray Chandler
Chess Director: GM John Nunn
Editorial Director: FM Graham Burgess
German Editor: WFM Petra Nunn

Contents

Symbols

+	check	Ech	European championship
++	double check	Echt	European team championship
#	checkmate	ECC	European Clubs Cup
!!	brilliant move	Ct	candidates event
!	good move	IZ	interzonal event
!?	interesting move	Z	zonal event
?!	dubious move	OL	olympiad
?	bad move	jr	junior event
??	blunder	wom	women's event
+–	White is winning	rpd	rapidplay game
±	White is much better	tt	team tournament
±	White is slightly better	sim	game from simultaneous display
=	equal position	corr.	correspondence game
∓	Black is slightly better	adv	advanced chess (man + machine)
∓	Black is much better	1-0	the game ends in a win for White
–+	Black is winning	½-½	the game ends in a draw
Ch	championship	0-1	the game ends in a win for Black
Cht	team championship	(n)	nth match game
Wch	world championship	(D)	see next diagram
Wcht	world team championship		

Foreword

Thanks for buying this book. It has taken a lot of effort and I have learned a lot while writing it. It is my sincere hope that you will feel you have learned something new through the study of the material that I have chosen to present to you.

My first experience with the Nimzo-Indian Defence came from the study of the Danish edition of Nimzowitsch's *My System*. At the time, I was rated no more than about 1100, and had already found my weapon as White, 1 c4, and a weapon against 1 e4, the Caro-Kann, 1...c6. Strictly speaking, *My System* was far too complicated for me at the time, but I enjoyed many of Nimzowitsch's examples and became fascinated with the Nimzo-Indian. Therefore my weapon against 1 d4 was found, and it served as my primary weapon along with the Queen's Indian until I hit a rating of about 1900-2000, when other openings such as the Benko Gambit started catching my interest.

But true love never dies, and my affinity with the Nimzo-Indian never died out either. I didn't study it with the same enthusiasm, and with White I did my best to stay clear of the Nimzo-Indian, because the thought of dealing with doubled c-pawns was just too much for me to handle, while the body of theory on the Capablanca (or Classical) System with 4 ♕c2 became too much to study.

While the 4 e3 Nimzo-Indian (also known as the Rubinstein System), certainly has a lot of theory to study as well, in this book we can also see that it doesn't have to be a difficult opening to play. You can easily pick a couple of lines, both as White and Black, and then build your Nimzo-Indian repertoire up around these lines and then get started with the opening.

Before I make it all sound too easy, I have to warn you that some lines are much more difficult to understand than others. I will particularly bring your attention to the Main Variation and the Reshevsky Variation, both of which are based on deep strategic understanding of the positions that arise; if you don't find the right plan, then you will quickly find yourself without counterplay in a rather depressing position. However, take a look at all of the lines and you will quickly get an idea about which lines appeal to you and which don't. Trust me: you don't have to know them all – nobody does.

The material in this book is mainly theory with some strategic commentary where relevant. This may make this book a little heavy to deal with for some players, and some of the moves may seem difficult to understand. If you run into such a move, ask your coach or a strong player you know if they can understand it. You can also set the position up on your chess computer (or program) and see if it agrees with the move or assessment mentioned in this book.

I have enjoyed writing this book, and it is my sincere hope that you will enjoy it too.

My sincere thanks to a number of people who have helped with this project: Stephanie Alexander for helping clear my mind and re-focus and motivate me, when needed; my brother, friend and language consultant, Bent Hansen; the people at ChessBase GmbH for supplying the chess world with great database and chess-playing programs – without these, being a chess-book author would be an even tougher job; and last but not least to the people at Gambit Publications for their trust in and patience with me. Particularly, the effort Graham Burgess and John Nunn have put into my books leaves me full of admiration.

Carsten Hansen
Torrance, California, September 2002

Bibliography

Printed Sources
Gligorić, *Play the Nimzo-Indian Defence* (Pergamon, 1985)
Pliester, *Rubinstein Complex of the Nimzo-Indian Defense* (ICE, 1995)
Taimanov, *Zashchita Nimtsovicha* (Fizkultura i Sport, 1985)
Kosten, *Mastering the Nimzo-Indian* (Batsford, 1998)
Emms, *Easy Guide to the Nimzo-Indian* (Gambit/Cadogan, 1998)
Nunn, Burgess, Emms & Gallagher, *Nunn's Chess Openings*
    (Gambit/Everyman, 1999)
Matanović et al., *ECO E* (Šahovski Informator, 1991)
Matanović et al., *Informator 1-83* (Šahovski Informator)
Khalifman, *Opening Repertoire for Black according to Karpov*
    (Chess Stars, 2001)

Electronic Sources
Mega Database 2000 (ChessBase, 1999)
The Week in Chess 1-399 (edited by Mark Crowther)
Starbase 2.33 (Federation Enterprise, 2000)
Megacorr 2 (Chess Mail, 2001)

1 Karpov Variation

1 d4 ♘f6 2 c4 e6 3 ♘c3 ♗b4 4 e3 0-0
5 ♘f3 d5 6 ♗d3 c5 7 0-0 dxc4 8 ♗xc4
cxd4 9 exd4 (D)

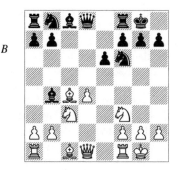

9...b6

This is the starting position of the
Karpov Variation. As we will see several times throughout this book, a particular line is rarely named after the
person who invented it, but rather after
the person who made it popular. The
Karpov Variation is certainly no exception. According to my database,
the position after Black's 9th move
first arose in two games played in the
Gothenburg 'B' tournament in 1920:
Euwe-Berndtsson Kullberg and P.Joh-
ner-Berndtsson Kullberg. In the second of these games Black showed
remarkably good understanding early
on in the game and obtained a good
position and never should have lost.

This variation enjoyed its first burst
of popularity in the latter part of the
1960s when a group of Hungarian

players, consisting of Portisch, Barcza,
Flesch and Lengyel, all played it with
some consistency. However, it was
only Karpov's emergence and his oc-
casional use of it that brought the line
into focus and caused it to be developed into a regular system of combating White in the 4 e3 Nimzo-Indian.

Before moving on to the regular
Karpov Variation, there are a number
of lines that are seen far less often, but
nonetheless deserve to be mentioned
in this context. They are:

a) 9...♕c7 usually transposes to
lines covered elsewhere, but one independent line is 10 ♕e2 ♘bd7 11 ♘b5
♕d8 12 a3 ♗e7 13 ♗f4 ♘e8 14 ♘c3
with an initiative for White, Reinder-
man-Garcia Paolicchi, Escaldes Z
1998.

b) After 9...♘c6, 10 a3 transposes
to Chapter 7, while 10 ♗g5 ♗e7 11
♖c1 b6 12 a3 ♗b7 13 ♕d3 ♖c8 14
♖fd1 ♘d5 15 h4 ♘xc3 16 ♖xc3 ♘a5
is fully adequate for Black, Ftačnik-
Maksimenko, Koszalin 1998.

c) 9...♗d7 10 ♗g5 ♗e7 11 ♕d3
♗c6 12 ♖ad1 ♘bd7 13 ♖fe1 ♖e8 14
♗b3 is quite pleasant for White, Sto-
cek-Krstić, Pula 2000.

d) 9...♗xc3 10 bxc3 and now:

d1) 10...♘bd7 11 ♗g5 transposes
to line 'e6'.

d2) 10...b6 11 ♗g5 will transpose
to one of the main lines of this chapter.

d3) 10...♕c7 11 ♗d3 (11 ♕e2 is a
popular alternative, but Black should

be able to neutralize White's initiative; for example, 11...♘bd7 12 ♗d2 b6 13 ♗d3 ♗b7 and play resembles what you will normally find in the Parma Variation – Line C in Chapter 2) 11...♘bd7 12 ♗g5 (after 12 ♗a3!?, Dolmatov-Flesch, Bucharest 1981 saw 12...♖e8?! 13 ♘d2 ♖d8 14 ♕f3 ±, but 12...♖d8!? is only a little better for White) 12...b6 13 ♖e1 ♗b7 transposes to note 'a' to Black's 11th move in Line B.

e) 9...♘bd7 *(D)* usually ends up transposing to one of this chapter's main lines after some 10th move by White and then 10...b6 by Black, but play can also go down independent paths:

e1) 10 ♕e2 transposes to note 'b' to Black's 9th move in Line C of Chapter 2.

e2) 10 ♗f4 ♘b6 11 ♗d3 ♗d7 12 ♗e5 ♗c6 13 ♘g5 ♘bd7 14 ♖c1 ♗xc3 15 ♖xc3 ♘xe5 16 dxe5 ♕d5 17 ♘f3 ♘e4 = Kuijf-de Boer, Dutch Ch (Hilversum) 1984.

e3) 10 a3?! ♗xc3 11 bxc3 ♕c7 12 ♕d3 (other moves can also be tried, but Black has 12...b6, which takes the play into the Karpov Variation with White having wasted a valuable tempo on a3, forcing the exchange on c3, which Black is likely to make without encouragement in any case) 12...e5 (Black can of course play 12...b6, but we look at a more independent line) 13 dxe5 ♘xe5 14 ♘xe5 ♕xe5 15 ♕g3 ♕xg3 16 hxg3 ♗e6 17 ♗xe6 fxe6 with equality, Spassky-Tal, Tbilisi Ct (4) 1965.

e4) 10 ♕b3 ♗e7 (10...♗xc3 11 bxc3 is what White is hoping for, while 10...♕a5 11 a3 ♗xc3 12 bxc3 should also be better for White) 11 ♖d1 ♘b6 12 ♗d3 ♘bd5 13 ♘e5 ♕b6 14 ♘xd5 ♘xd5 15 ♕c2 g6 16 ♕e2 ♗f6 17 ♗h6, and here 17...♗g7 18 ♗xg7 ♔xg7 19 ♖ac1, as played in the game Bitoon-Antonio, Philippine Ch (Quezon City) 2001, leaves White with the initiative, but 17...♖d8 leads to approximately equal chances.

e5) 10 ♕d3 a6 11 a4 b6 (11...♕a5 and 11...♘b6!? followed by ...♗d7-c6 have also been tried) 12 ♗f4 ♗b7 13 ♖ac1 ♖e8 14 ♖fd1 ♘f8 15 ♘e5 ♘g6 16 ♗g5 ♘xe5 17 dxe5 ♕xd3 18 ♗xd3 ♘g4 19 ♗f4 ♗c5 20 ♖c2 ♖ad8 21 h3 ♖d4 22 ♗xh7+ ♔xh7 23 ♖xd4 ♗xd4 24 hxg4 ♖c8 with an equal position, Tal-Polugaevsky, USSR Ch (Leningrad) 1974.

e6) 10 ♗g5 ♗xc3 (or 10...♕a5!? 11 ♖c1 ♗xc3 12 ♖xc3 b5 13 ♖a3 ♕b6 14 ♖b3 a6 15 a4 ♕c7 16 ♗d3 bxa4 17 ♖c3 ♕a5 with an equal position, Ljubojević-Korchnoi, Leon 1994) 11 bxc3 ♕c7 and here:

e61) 12 ♗d3!? ♕xc3 13 ♖c1 (13 ♖e1!?) 13...♕a5 14 ♘e5 ♘xe5 15 ♖c5 ♕a3 16 dxe5 ♕xc5 17 ♗xf6, and now 17...♖e8? 18 ♗xh7+! ♔xh7 19 ♕h5+ ♔g8 20 ♕g5 ♕f8 21 ♖d1! gave White a winning attack in Dolmatov-Speelman, Hastings 1989/90, but Black can defend with 17...gxf6!; e.g., 18 ♕g4+ ♔h8 19 ♕h4 f5 20 ♕f6+ ♔g8 21 ♖e1!? ♖e8 22 ♖e3 ♔f8 (22...♕c1+ 23 ♗f1 ♕xe3 could also be considered although it should also lead to a draw) and now 23 ♖h3 leads to a draw.

e62) 12 ♕e2 b6 13 ♖fc1 ♗b7 14 ♗d3 ♖ac8 15 c4 h6 16 ♗h4 (16 ♗d2!? ± Dautov) 16...♘h5 17 ♕e3 ♕f4 18 ♗g3 ♕xe3 19 fxe3 ♘xg3 20 hxg3 ± Čabrilo-Mirković, Belgrade 1991.

e63) 12 ♕d3 b6 13 ♗b3 (13 ♗h4 led to a better game for White in Gulko-Tatai, Rome 1988: 13...♘h5 14 ♘g5 ♘df6 15 ♗g3 ♕c6 16 ♗b5 ♕d5 17 ♗e5 ♗b7 18 f3 h6 19 c4 ♕d8 20 ♘h3 ±; Dautov has suggested the move 13...♗b7!? as an improvement, but White should still hold the better chances) 13...a5 (or 13...♗b7 14 ♖fe1 {14 ♗h4 ± Cu.Hansen} 14...♖ac8 15 ♖ac1 and now 15...♖fd8 16 ♕e3 ♕c6 17 c4 ± was G.Georgadze-Fossan, Gausdal 1992, but Dautov has suggested 15...h6 as an improvement, giving 16 ♗h4 ♘h5 17 ♗c2 ♘df6 with counterplay) 14 ♖ac1 a4 15 ♗c4! ♗b7 16 ♗b5 ♗c6 17 ♗xc6 ♕xc6 18 c4 h6 19 ♗f4 ± Anand-Adams, Groningen PCA 1993.

f) 9...a6 can also be considered. White has tried a number of moves, the most important of which are:

f1) 10 ♕e2 b5 11 ♗d3 ♗b7 12 a4 bxa4 13 ♖xa4 a5 14 ♗g5 ♘bd7 15 ♖d1 h6 16 ♗d2 ♕b6 with a pleasant game for Black, Gligorić-Hraček, Yugoslav Cht (Herceg Novi) 2001.

f2) 10 ♗d3 and now:

f21) 10...♘c6 11 ♗c2 ♗e7 12 a3 b5 13 ♕d3 ♗b7 14 ♗g5 (14 ♖e1!?

should be answered with 14...g6, since a move like 14...♖c8? can be met by 15 d5! exd5 16 ♗g5 g6 17 ♖xe7 ± Wells) 14...g6 15 ♖fe1 ♖c8 16 ♖ad1 ♘d5 17 ♗h6 ♖e8 18 ♘xd5 ♕xd5 19 ♕d2 ♕h5 20 ♗f4 ♗f6 = Fedorowicz-Yermolinsky, USA Ch (Salt Lake City) 1999.

f22) 10...b5 11 a4 (or 11 ♘e4 ♘bd7 12 ♗g5 ♗b7 13 ♖c1 ♗e7 14 ♘c5 ♘xc5 15 dxc5 ♖c8 16 b4 h6 17 ♗f4 ♘d5 = Acs-Asrian, Erevan jr Wch 2000) 11...bxa4 12 ♗g5 (12 ♖xa4 ♗e7 13 ♗g5 ♗b7 comes to the same thing) 12...♗b7 13 ♖xa4 ♗e7 14 ♕e2 a5 15 ♖d1 ♘a6 16 ♘e5 ♘b4 ½-½ Lanka-P.Schlosser, Austrian League 1997/8.

f3) 10 ♘e5 b5 11 ♕f3 ♕xd4!? (Psakhis has suggested 11...♕b6!?, a move which definitely deserves a test, whereas 11...♖a7 12 ♗d3 ♗b7 13 ♕h3 ♗xc3 14 bxc3 ♗e4 15 ♗g5 ♗xd3 16 ♕xd3 ♕d5 17 ♗xf6 gxf6 18 ♘g4 leaves White with the initiative, Ibragimov-Zagrebelny, St Petersburg 1997) 12 ♕xa8 ♕xe5 13 ♗e2 ♗xc3 14 bxc3 ♕xe2 15 ♕xb8 ♕c4 (or 15...♘d5 16 a4 ♘xc3 17 ♗a3 ♖e8 18 ♗b4 ♘d5 19 ♖ac1 ♗d7 20 ♕d6 ± Yakovich-Dreev, Russian Ch (Elista) 1995) 16 ♗a3 ♖e8 17 ♗b4 ♘d5 (Lautier-Salov, Wijk aan Zee 1997) and at this point White should opt for 18 ♖fe1 with fairly balanced chances.

f4) 10 a4 ♘c6 11 ♗g5 h6 12 ♗h4 (12 ♗e3 ♕a5 13 ♕b3 ♖d8 14 ♖fd1 ♘d5 15 ♘e4 ♕b6 16 ♕d3 ♗e7 17 b3 ♗d7 18 ♘g3 ♗e8 ½-½ Yusupov-Dautov, Bundesliga 1999/00) 12...♗e7 13 ♖e1 ♘d5 (13...♘h5 can be met by 14 ♗g3 ♘xg3 15 hxg3 ♗f6 16 d5 exd5 17 ♘xd5 with some initiative for

White, Lesiège-L.Johannessen, Bermuda 2002, while 13...♗d7 14 ♕e2 ♘h5 is more solid; e.g., 15 ♗xe7 ♘xe7 16 ♘e5 ♘f6 17 ♖ad1 ♕c7 18 ♗a2 ♖ad8 19 ♕d3 ♗c6 = Reinderman-Iordachescu, Ohrid Ech 2001) 14 ♗xe7 ♘cxe7 15 ♘xd5 exd5 16 ♗b3 ♗e6 17 ♘e5 ♘f5 with a better game for White, Krush-Barsov, Hastings 2001/2.

f5) 10 a3 ♗xc3 (10...♗e7?! 11 ♗a2 b5 12 d5! left White better in Dolmatov-Larsen, Amsterdam 1980) 11 bxc3 b5 12 ♗d3 ♕d5 13 a4 ♗b7 14 axb5 (14 ♕e2 ♖c8 15 ♗d2 ♘e4 16 ♗xe4 ♕xe4 17 ♕xe4 ♗xe4 = Ulybin-Kharitonov, Simferopol 1988) 14...axb5 15 ♖b1 ♗c6 16 ♖e1 ♘bd7 17 ♕e2 ♖a2 18 ♕f1 ± Aleksandrov-Kunte, Dubai 2001.

f6) 10 ♗g5 b5 and then:

f61) 11 ♗d3 ♗b7 (or 11...♗e7 12 ♕e2 ♗b7 13 a4 b4 14 ♘e4 ♘xe4 15 ♗xe4 ♗xe4 16 ♕xe4 ♘d7 17 ♗xe7 ♕xe7 18 ♖fc1 ♘f6 ½-½ Lesiège-Ashley, Bermuda 1997) 12 ♖c1 (after 12 ♕e2, 12...♗e7 is the previous bracket, while 12...♘bd7 transposes to note 'c12' to Black's 9th move in Line C of Chapter 2; 12 ♘e4 ♘bd7 13 ♖c1 h6 14 ♗h4 ♖c8 15 ♖xc8 ♕xc8 16 ♘xf6+ ♘xf6 17 ♘e5 ♗e7 is pleasant for Black, Sarwinski-Poluliakhov, Bydgoszcz 2001) 12...♘bd7 13 ♗b1 ♖c8 14 ♖e1 ♗e7 15 a3 ♖e8 16 ♕d3 ♘f8 17 ♖cd1 ♕b6 18 h4 ♖cd8 19 ♘e5 ♖d6 20 ♗e3 (I.Sokolov-Christiansen, Reykjavik 1998) and here Psakhis gives 20...♘d5!? 21 ♘e4 ♖dd8 = as Black's best.

f62) 11 ♗b3 ♗b7 12 ♕e2 (or 12 ♕d3 ♘bd7 13 ♖ad1 ♖c8 14 ♖fe1 ♕a5 15 ♗d2 ♖fd8 = Vladimirov-Barsov, Abu Dhabi 2001) 12...♗xc3 13 bxc3

♘bd7 14 ♘e5 ♕c7 15 ♘xd7 ♘xd7 16 ♕g4 ♔h8 17 ♖ae1 ♕xc3 18 d5 ♘f6 19 ♗xf6 ♕xf6 20 dxe6 ½-½ Balashov-Kharitonov, Pinsk 1993.

We now return to 9...b6 *(D)*:

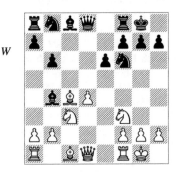

10 ♗g5

White has a number of alternatives:

a) 10 a3?! doesn't make a lot sense in the context of the Karpov Variation, as Black very often exchanges voluntarily on c3 or retreats his bishop to e7 without being prompted by White playing a3. Therefore, this move, despite being fully playable, must be considered a waste of time.

b) 10 ♕b3 ♗xc3 11 bxc3 ♕c7 12 ♗a3 ♖d8 13 ♘e5 ♘c6 14 ♘xc6 ♕xc6 15 ♖fd1 ♗b7 16 ♗f1 ♕c7 17 c4 ♖ac8 18 ♖ac1 leads to a tiny advantage for White, Agdestein-S.B.Hansen, Bundesliga 2000/1.

c) 10 ♕d3 ♗b7 11 ♗f4 ♘c6! 12 a3 ♗xc3 13 bxc3 ♖c8 14 ♗a2 ♘a5 15 ♖ac1 ♗e4 16 ♕e2 ♗b7 = Knaak-Garcia Palermo, Bucharest 1975.

d) 10 ♘e5 ♗b7 11 ♕d3 (11 ♗g5 is Line A) 11...♗xc3 12 bxc3 ♕c7 13 ♗a3 ♖e8 14 ♗b5 ♘c6 15 ♗xc6 ♗xc6 16 c4 ♗b7 = Larsen-Petrosian, Las Palmas 1975.

e) 10 ℤe1 ♗b7 11 ♗d3 (11 ♗g5 is Line B) 11...♘bd7 and now:

e1) 12 a3 (despite White scoring quite well with this move, I'm still of the same opinion as I expressed about 10 a3) 12...♗xc3 (12...♗e7 is also fully playable) 13 bxc3 ♕c7 14 c4 ℤfe8 15 ♗b2 ♕f4 16 ♕d2 ♘h5 17 ♗e2 ℤac8 18 ℤad1 ℤed8 19 g3 ♕xd2 20 ♘xd2 ♘hf6 is equal, Graf-J.Polgar, Ohrid Ech 2001.

e2) White has also tried 12 ♗d2; e.g., 12...ℤc8 13 ♕e2 ℤe8 14 ℤad1 ♗f8 (14...♗xc3!? 15 bxc3 ♘f8 16 ♘e5 ♘g6, intending ...♘d5, is worth a thought) 15 a3 ♕c7 16 ♘e5 ♘xe5 17 dxe5 ♘d5 18 ♘xd5 ♗xd5 19 ℤc1 ♕b8 = Donner-Ostojić, Wijk aan Zee 1969.

f) 10 ♕e2 generally transposes to other lines:

f1) 10...♘bd7 11 ♗g5 ♗b7 transposes to the note to Black's 11th move in Line D.

f2) However, after 10...♗b7 11 ♗f4 we reach independent territory that is harmless for Black: 11...a6 (Speelman's 11...♘c6, intending ...♘e7, is also worth remembering) 12 ℤac1 b5 13 ♗d3 ♘bd7 14 h3 ℤc8 15 ♘e4 ♕b6 16 ♘xf6+ ♘xf6 ½-½ Piket-P.H.Nielsen, Istanbul OL 2000.

10...♗b7 *(D)*

Both 10...♘bd7 and 10...♗xc3 will transpose to the main lines given below and therefore have no independent significance.

Here, White has the choice of the following moves:

A: 11 ♘e5	11	
B: 11 ℤe1	13	
C: 11 ℤc1	16	
D: 11 ♕e2	18	

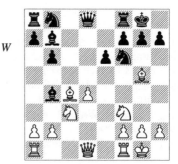

Two lesser lines:

a) 11 ♕d3 ♘bd7 12 a3 ♗xc3 13 bxc3 ♕c7 14 ♘d2 ℤac8 15 f3 ♗d5 16 ♗xd5 exd5 = Hübner-Van der Sterren, Munich 1988.

b) 11 ♗d3 usually ends up transposing to one of the main lines; e.g., 11...♘bd7 12 ℤc1 ℤc8 13 ℤe1 is Line B.

A)

11 ♘e5

This move isn't considered terribly problematic for Black. This is mainly due to it transposing to Line D or leading to an early draw. However, if Black stays away from the various transpositions, this line can be quite dangerous for him.

11...♗xc3

Alternatively:

a) 11...♘c6 12 ♗xf6 (after 12 ♘xc6 ♗xc6 13 ♕b3, *ECO* gives 13...♗e7 14 ℤad1 ± but also suggests 13...♕xd4!? and 13...♗xc3!?, both of which look solid enough for Black) 12...gxf6 (or 12...♕xf6 13 ♘d7 ♕h4 14 ♘xf8 ℤxf8 15 a3 ♗e7 16 d5 ♗d6 17 f4 exd5 18 ♘xd5 ♘e5, Krush-Wells, Hastings 2001/2, and now 19 g3! is better for White) 13 ♘xc6 (13 ♗a6!? ♗xa6 14

♘xc6 ♕d6 15 ♕g4+ ♔h8 16 ♕f3 f5 17 ♖fd1 ♗xc3 18 ♕xc3 ♖ac8 19 d5+ f6 with chances for both sides, Babula-Wells, Bundesliga 1998/9) 13...♗xc6 14 d5!? ♗xc3 15 dxc6 ♗xb2 16 ♕g4+ ♔h8 17 ♖ad1 ♕c7 18 ♗xe6 ♖g8 19 ♕h3, with an extra pawn and a continuing attack for White, G.Buckley-Kunte, London 2001.

b) 11...♗e7 12 ♕e2!? contains more venom than it appears: 12...♘c6 (not 12...♘d5 13 ♘xf7!) 13 ♗xe6 ♕xd4 14 ♘xf7 ♖xf7 15 ♖ad1 ♕e5 16 ♕xe5 ♘xe5 17 ♖fe1 ♘g6 18 ♘b5 with a better game for White, Hux-Spiegel, corr. 1987.

c) 11...♘bd7 12 ♘xd7 (12 ♕e2 ♗xc3 13 bxc3 transposes to Line D) 12...♕xd7 13 ♗xf6 gxf6 14 d5! ♗xc3 15 bxc3 ♗xd5 16 ♕g4+ ♔h8 17 ♕d4 ♖ac8? (17...♕d8! {Ftačnik} is a better move), Yusupov-Ivanchuk, Brussels Ct (3) 1991, and now 18 ♗a6! is best: 18...♖c5 19 ♕xf6+ ♔g8 20 ♖ad1! ♕c6 21 ♕g5+ ♔h8 22 ♕h6 ♔g8 23 ♖d4 ♗e4 24 ♗d3! ♗g6 25 ♗xg6 fxg6 26 ♖fd1 with an ongoing initiative for White.

12 bxc3 ♕c7 (D)

12...♘bd7 13 ♕e2 transposes to Line D.

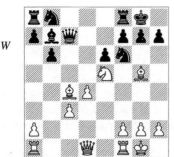

13 ♖c1

Again, there are some alternatives to look at:

a) 13 ♗d3 ♘bd7 14 ♘xd7 ♘xd7 15 ♖e1 ♖fe8 (15...♕xc3!?) 16 ♗e3 ♘f8 17 ♖g3 ♔h8 18 ♕h5 with a strong initiative for White, Reinderman-Douven, Breda 2001.

b) 13 ♗xf6 gxf6 14 ♕g4+ ♔h8 15 ♕h4 fxe5 16 ♕f6+ ♔g8 17 ♕g5+ with a perpetual. This line has been played many times, including no fewer than 22 times by Hungarian GM Laszlo Vadasz as either White or Black!

13...♘bd7 14 ♘xd7 ♘xd7 15 ♗b3

15 ♗d3!? also deserves attention: 15...♖fe8 16 ♕g4 ♘f8 17 ♖fe1 ♔h8?! (according to Psakhis, Black can obtain an equal position after 17...♖ac8!? 18 c4 ♕d6, which has a lot of truth to it) 18 c4 ♕d7 19 ♗f1 ♖ac8 20 c5 ♕a4?! 21 ♕d1 ♕xa2?? 22 ♗c4 ♕a3 (this gets a '??' from Psakhis, who recommends 22...♕b2, when 23 ♖e3 ♗d5 24 ♖b1 ♕xb1 25 ♕xb1 ♗xc4 26 cxb6 axb6 27 ♕xb6 ♖b8! is winning for Black, but missing that 23 ♖e2! is a little bit more than problematic for Black's queen; e.g., 23...♕b4 24 ♗d2 ♕a3 25 ♖a1 ♕b2 26 ♗e1 and the queen is a goner) 23 ♖e3 ♕a5 24 ♖a1 ♕b4 25 ♖a4 ♕b2 26 ♖b3 1-0 Li Shilong-Li Wenliang, Beijing 1997. The queen is trapped, so Black decided to call it a day.

15...♕c6

Black has to be careful, given that his kingside is short of defenders and White's two bishops are running rampant. In Sadler-Cooper, British League (4NCL) 1997/8, Black played very actively to maintain a reasonable position, only to collapse, despite White doing very little to encourage this: 15...e5 16 ♕g4 ♔h8 17 ♕h4 f6 18 ♗c2 e4 19 ♗d2 f5 20 ♗f4 ♕c6 21 c4 ♖ae8 22 ♗b3 e3?! (22...♘f6!?) 23 f3 ♘f6 24 ♖fe1 with a solid advantage for White, who won shortly.

16 ♕g4

Now:

a) 16...f5? (this very ugly move leaves the e6-pawn backward and dramatically weakens the dark squares; on the plus side, it has to be said that Black gets some compensation for his concessions through his control of the light squares, but this is by no means sufficient) 17 ♕g3 ♘f6 18 f3 ♔h8 19 ♖fe1 ♘d5 20 ♕e5 ♖ae8 21 c4 ♘b4 22 ♖cd1, Klundt-Jenke, Schwäbisch Gmünd 1990. By now, the ramifications of Black's poor decision regarding 16...f5? have come to show, as Black's position is unappealing and without any counterplay of substance.

b) A move like 16...♔h8, followed by ...b5, makes far more sense, and leaves White only slightly better.

B)

11 ♖e1 (D)

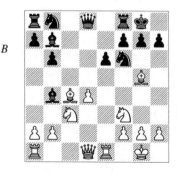

11...♘bd7

This is Black's natural set-up, but Black has two alternatives that also have to be considered carefully:

a) 11...♗xc3 12 bxc3 ♘bd7 13 ♗d3 ♕c7 14 c4 ♕d6 (14...♖ac8 15 a4 ♖fe8 16 a5 is very nice for White, Greenfeld-Kundin, Givatayim 1998) 15 ♘e5 (in Sher-Hellsten, Copenhagen 1996, Black quickly obtained a pleasant game after 15 ♗h4 ♗xf3 16 gxf3 g6 17 ♗f1 ♘h5 18 ♖c1 ♖ac8 19 a4 ♖c7 20 a5 ♖fc8 21 axb6 axb6 22 ♖b1 and here Black for some reason accepted White's draw offer; however, after 22...♖xc4! 23 ♗xc4 ♖xc4 Black is just better, the dynamism having gone from White's position) 15...♘xe5 16 dxe5 ♕c6 17 ♗f1 ♘e4 18 ♗e7 ♖fe8 19 ♗h4 h6 = Gligorić-Unzicker, Milan 1975.

b) 11...♘c6 12 ♗d3 (12 a3 ♗e7 will transpose to lines covered in Chapter 7; e.g., 13 ♕d3 is note 'f232' to White's 11th move of that chapter) 12...♗e7 13 a3 ♘d5 14 ♗e3 ♘xc3 15 bxc3 ♖c8 16 c4 ♘a5 17 ♘e5 ♗f6! is good for Black, J.Polgar-Karpov, Monaco rpd 1994. Black's well-coordinated forces apply just the right amount of pressure on the white c4-d4 pawn-phalanx to stop them in their tracks.

12 ♖c1

Or 12 ♗d3, and then:

a) 12...♗xc3 13 bxc3 transposes to note 'a' to Black's 11th move.

b) 12...♖c8 13 ♖c1 transposes to the main line.

c) 12...♗e7 13 ♕e2 ♖e8 14 ♖ac1 g6 15 ♗a6!? (played to weaken the light squares, in particular c6, on Black's queenside) 15...♗xa6 16 ♕xa6 ♔g7 (Baburin gives 16...♕c8!? 17 ♕d3 ♕b7 as an improvement for Black, but

White is still somewhat better) 17 ♖ed1 ♕b8 18 g3 ♗d6 19 ♗xf6+ ♘xf6 20 ♘b5 and White has a safe edge, B.Lalić-Hulak, Croatian Ch (Slavonski Brod) 1995.

12...♖c8 *(D)*

This appears to be Black's best option. The often seen 12...♗xc3?! is not as fortunate this time, since White can take back with the rook: 13 ♖xc3!? (13 bxc3 leads to more typical play) 13...♕b8 14 ♘e5! ♘xe5?! (14...♕d6 is probably safer) 15 ♖xe5 ♘e4? (15...♘d7 16 ♖e1 ♕d6 is given by Kantsler as '±', but truthfully, it cannot be much more than ±) 16 ♕g4! f5 17 ♗xe6+ ♔h8 18 ♗xf5 ♘xc3 19 bxc3 ♕c7 (Kumaran-Hellsten, Copenhagen 1996) and now 20 ♕h3 forces 20...♖xf5 21 ♖xf5 ♕c4 22 ♕e3 when White is much better.

13 ♗d3

13 ♕b3!? is a very important alternative:

a) 13...♕e7? 14 ♗d5!! (beautifully exploiting the various pins and the fact that the black queen is overburdened with defensive tasks) 14...♗a6 15 ♕a4 ♗xc3 16 bxc3 ± Browne-Ljubojević, Tilburg 1978.

b) 13...♗e7 was played by Kasparov against Kramnik in their London match. 14 ♗xf6 (14 ♘e5 ♘xe5 15 dxe5 ♘d7 =) and now:

b1) 14...♘xf6 15 ♗xe6 fxe6 (according to Kramnik, 15...♖c7 is the way to go, but in his analysis he did not mention Kantsler's suggestion of 16 ♘g5! fxe6 17 ♘xe6 '±') 16 ♕xe6+ ♔h8 17 ♕xe7 ♗xf3 18 gxf3 (Kramnik gives 18 ♕xd8 ♖cxd8 19 gxf3 ♖xd4 ±) 18...♕xd4 19 ♘b5 and now instead of 19...♕xb2? 20 ♖xc8 ♖xc8 21 ♘d6 ♖b8? (21...♖a8 is the only move) 22 ♘f7+ ♔g8 23 ♕e6! ♖f8 24 ♘d8+ ♔h8 25 ♕e7 1-0 Kramnik-Kasparov, London BGN Wch (10) 2000, Black should play 19...♕d2!? and after 20 ♖xc8 ♖xc8 21 ♘d6 ♖b8! 22 ♘e8 (White can consider 22 ♔g2 and 22 h4) 22...♖b7! 23 ♕e5 ♘g8 (Kramnik) and the chances are fairly level.

b2) 14...♗xf6 is given as interesting by Kramnik, whose analysis continues as follows: 15 ♘b5 ♗xf3 (15...♗g5 16 ♖c2! ♖a8 17 ♘d6 ♗xf3 18 ♕xf3 ♕f6 19 ♕b7 ±) 16 ♕xf3 a6 17 ♘a7 ♖c7 18 ♘c6 ♕c8! 19 ♗d3 (or 19 d5 exd5 20 ♗xd5 ♘e5! =) 19...♘b8 20 ♕e4 g6 21 ♕f4 ♖xc6 22 ♖xc6 ♘xc6 23 ♕xf6 =.

c) 13...♗a5 14 ♘e5 ♕c7 15 ♗xe6 fxe6 16 ♕xe6+ ♔h8 17 ♘f7+ ♖xf7 18 ♕xf7 ♖f8 19 ♕e7 (Knaak-Spasov, Sochi 1980) 19...♘g4! 20 f4 ♕c6 21 ♖e2 ♗xc3 22 ♖xc3 ♕d5 23 ♖d2 ♖f7 = (*ECO*).

d) 13...♗xc3 14 ♖xc3 h6 15 ♗h4 ♕e8! (this was first recommended by Brodsky in 1994; 15...♗xf3 and 15...♗d5 can also be considered) 16 ♕a3 (16 ♗b5!? ♖xc3 17 bxc3 a6 18

♗f1 ♕a8 19 ♘e5 ♘xe5 20 ♖xe5 ♘d5 21 c4 ♘f4 22 ♗g3 ♘g6 23 ♖e1 b5 and Black has almost equalized, Aagaard-Kumaran, London Drury Lane 1997) 16...a6 17 ♘e5 ♘xe5 18 dxe5 ♘e4 19 ♖xe4 ♗xe4 20 ♗e7 ♕d7 21 ♕d6 ♕a4 22 ♗b3 ♕b5 and Black is absolutely fine, Gormally-Wells, British Ch (Scarborough) 2001.

13...♖e8 *(D)*

The alternatives also have something to say for themselves:

a) 13...♗xc3 14 bxc3 ♕c7 and now:

a1) 15 ♗h4 ♕f4 (Black has also tried 15...♖fe8, 15...h6, 15...♕d6 and 15...♖fd8) 16 ♗g3 ♕g4 (16...♗xf3 allows White an edge: 17 ♗xf4 ♗xd1 18 ♖exd1 ♘b8 19 c4 ♘c6!, Flear-Tatai, Graz 1984, 20 ♗e2! ♖fd8 21 ♗e3 e5 22 dxe5 ♖xd1+ 23 ♖xd1 ♘xe5 24 c5 ± Lukacs/Hazai) 17 ♗e2 ♕f5 18 ♘d2 ♖fd8 19 ♘c4 ♘e8 20 ♗d3 ♕g5 21 ♕c2 ♘f8 22 f4 ♕d5 = Dvoretsky-Vasiukov, Frunze 1983.

a2) 15 c4 ♖fe8 16 ♕e2 h6! 17 ♗d2 ♗xf3 18 ♕xf3 e5 (Portisch-Karpov, Bugojno 1978) and here 19 d5 keeps the chances balanced.

b) 13...♗e7 14 ♕e2 (14 ♗b1 favoured Black after 14...♖e8 15 a3 ♘d5 16 ♗d2 ♘xc3 17 ♖xc3 ♖xc3 18 ♗xc3 ♘f6 ∓ in L.B.Hansen-Kalinichev, Bundesliga 1995/6) 14...♘d5 (14...h6 15 ♗d2 ♘d5 16 ♗b1 ♖e8 17 ♕d3 ♘f8 18 ♘e5 ♗g5 19 ♖cd1 ½-½ Psakhis-Bykhovsky, Israeli open Ch (Tel-Aviv) 2001) 15 ♕e4 (15 ♘xd5 ♗xg5 16 ♖xc8 ♗xc8 17 ♘b4 ♗b7 18 ♗e4 ♗e7 19 ♗xb7 ♗xb4 = Timman-Polugaevsky, Moscow 1981) 15...g6 16 ♕h4 ♗xg5 17 ♘xg5 ♘7f6 18 ♕h6 ½-½ Gligorić-Polugaevsky, Plovdiv

Echt 1983. There is plenty of play left in the position.

c) 13...♖c7!? (intending ...♕a8) 14 ♗f4 ♖c8 15 a3 ♗e7 16 ♕e2 ♘d5 17 ♘xd5 ♗xd5 18 ♖xc8 ♕xc8 19 ♖c1 ♕d8 = Zifroni-Tsesarsky, Israeli Cht 1999.

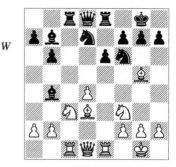

14 ♕e2

Other options:

a) 14 ♗b1 proved to be harmless in Hillarp Persson-Speelman, Copenhagen 1996: 14...b5 15 ♕d3 a6 16 a3 ♗xc3 17 ♖xc3 ♖xc3 18 ♕xc3 h6 19 ♗h4 ♕c8 20 ♕e3 ♕c6 21 ♖c1 ♕d5 ∓.

b) 14 ♗h4 ♗e7 (14...♘f8 is another possibility) 15 ♘e5 ♘xe5 16 dxe5 ♘d5 17 ♗xe7 ♕xe7 18 ♘e4 ♖xc1 19 ♕xc1 ♖c8 20 ♕b1 ♘f4 21 ♗f1 ♗xe4 22 ♕xe4 ♘d5 = Aleksandrov-Nisipeanu, Ohrid Ech 2001.

14...♗xc3

14...h6 also led to adequate play for Black in Spassky-Andersson, Buenos Aires 1979: 15 ♗h4 ♗e7 16 ♗a6 ♗xa6 17 ♕xa6 ♗b4 18 ♕xa7 g5 19 ♗g3 ♖a8 20 ♕b7 ♕c8 21 ♕xc8 ♖exc8 and Black won the pawn back.

15 bxc3 ♕c7 16 ♗h4

16 c4 transposes to note 'a2' to Black's 13th move.

16...♘h5

There are a few alternatives that deserve a glance:

a) 16...♕f4 17 ♗g3 ♕g4 18 ♘d2 ♕xe2 19 ♗xe2 ♖ed8 20 f3 and the bishop-pair ensures White a small but clear advantage, Scherbakov-Macieja, Polanica Zdroj 1996.

b) 16...♕d6!? 17 ♗a6 (17 ♘e5!? or 17 ♗g3 ♕a3, as played in Yagupov-Lastin, Moscow 1997, can also be considered) 17...♗xa6 18 ♕xa6 ♕b8 19 c4 ♕a8 (Gulko-Short, New York PCA Ct (4) 1994) 20 ♗xf6 ♘xf6 21 a4 ± Gulko.

17 ♕e3

White prevents the ...♘f4 fork. Other moves don't give White any hope of an advantage:

a) 17 ♗xh7+? ♔xh7 18 ♘g5+ ♔g6 19 g4 ♕f4! and White's game falls apart, Knaak-Sturua, Trnava 1980.

b) 17 ♘g5 g6! 18 ♕d2 ♗d5 19 f3 ♗c4 20 ♗b1 ♕f4 and Black's accurate play has completely neutralized any hopes White might have for an advantage, Psakhis-Hillarp Persson, Torshavn 2000.

17...♘df6 18 ♗g3

White didn't receive any reward for his aggressive approach in Gligorić-Browne, Novi Sad 1979: 18 ♘e5 ♘d5 19 ♕f3 ♘df4 20 ♗e4 ♗xe4 21 ♖xe4 f6! ∓.

18...♘xg3

½-½ Portisch-Andersson, Buenos Aires OL 1978.

C)

11 ♖c1 ♘bd7

Or:

a) 11...♗xc3 12 ♖xc3 (after 12 bxc3 ♘bd7 13 ♖e1 ♕c7 14 ♗d3 ♖ac8 we transpose to note 'a' to Black's 13th move in Line B) 12...♘c6 13 a3 ♖c8 14 ♗a2 ♘e7! 15 ♖xc8 ♕xc8 16 ♗xf6 gxf6 17 ♖e1 ♖d8 18 ♘h4 ♘g6! 19 ♕g4 f5 20 ♘xg6 hxg6 is very nice for Black, Illescas-Short, Wijk aan Zee 1997.

b) 11...♗e7 12 ♕e2 (12 ♖e1 ♘c6 13 ♗d3 ♘b4 14 ♗b1 ♘bd5 15 ♘e5 ♖c8 16 ♕d3 g6, Galliamova-S.Lalić, Pula wom Echt 1997, 17 ♗h6 ♖e8 18 f3 ±) 12...♘c6 13 ♖fd1 ♘b4 14 ♘e5 ♘fd5 15 ♗xe7 ♕xe7 16 a3 ♘f4 17 ♕g4 ♘bd5 18 ♘xd5 ♘xd5 19 ♗xd5 ♗xd5 20 ♖c3 ♖fc8 and Black can't be unhappy with his opening, R.Bjerke-Gausel, Gausdal 1995.

c) 11...♘c6 (D) bears a close resemblance to some of the lines in the Classical Variation (Chapter 7).

White has tried:

c1) 12 ♖e1 ♗e7 13 a3 transposes to line 'c32'.

c2) 12 ♗d3 ♘e7 13 a3 ♗xc3 14 bxc3 ♘g6 15 ♖e1 ♖c8 16 h4 ♕d6 17 ♘d2, and although Korchnoi-Gelfand, Biel 2001 ended quickly in a draw after 17...h6 18 ♗xf6 gxf6 19 ♗e4 ♗a6 20 ♗xg6 fxg6 21 ♕b3 (21 ♕g4!?) 21...♕d5 22 ♕c2 ½-½, I believe that

17...♘f4 and 17...♘d5 are better options for Black.

c3) 12 a3 ♗e7 (12...♗xc3 13 ♖xc3 ♖c8 14 ♗a2 ♘e7!? 15 ♖xc8 ♕xc8 16 ♘e5 ♘fd5 17 ♗xe7 ♘xe7 18 ♖e1 ♘d5 = Radjabov-Karpov, Buenos Aires 2001) and now:

c31) 13 ♗a2 ♘d5 14 ♗e3 ♘xc3 15 ♖xc3 ♗f6 16 ♕d3 ♕d6 17 ♖fc1 g6 18 h3 ½-½ Rashkovsky-Rodriguez Lopez, Ubeda 1999.

c32) 13 ♖e1 and now:

c321) 13...♖c8 14 ♗a2 ♘d5 15 ♗d2! ♘xc3 16 ♗xc3 ♗f6 (Speelman gives 16...♘b8!? 17 d5!? ♗xd5 18 ♗xd5 exd5 19 ♖e5 d4 20 ♘xd4 ♗f6 21 ♖e1 =) 17 d5 exd5 18 ♗xd5 ♗xc3 19 ♖xc3 (Speelman-Levitt, London 1992) and now, according to Speelman, Black should proceed with 19...♖c7 20 ♗e4 (20 ♖e2 ♖d7 21 ♖d2 ♘e5 =) 20...♕xd1 21 ♖xd1 ♖e8 22 ♘e5 ♖ce7 23 ♗xc6 ♗xc6 24 ♖xc6 ♖xe5, with a dead even endgame.

c322) 13...♘d5 14 ♗d2 ♘xc3 15 ♗xc3 ♗f6 16 d5 exd5 ½-½ Gligorić-Karpov, Tilburg 1977.

c33) 13 ♕d3 and now:

c331) 13...♘d5 14 ♗xd5! (14 ♗d2 is too tame: 14...♘xc3 15 ♗xc3 ♖c8 16 ♗a2 ♗f6 17 ♖fe1 ♘e7 18 ♘e5 ♗xe5 19 ♖xe5 ♘g6 20 ♖h5? {oops!} 20...♗xg2! and White is a pawn down for nothing, Lugovoi-Biriukov, St Petersburg 1998) 14...♗xg5 (14...exd5?! 15 ♗xe7 ♘xe7 16 ♖fe1 ♖c8 17 h4 h6 18 h5 is quite pleasant for White, Ivanchuk-Karpov, Linares 1991) 15 ♘xg5 ♕xg5 16 ♗e4 ♖fd8 17 ♗xh7+?! (17 ♕e3!? ♕h5 18 ♗f3 ♕f5! = Wells; 17 ♘e2!? ♘e5 18 ♗xh7+ ♔h8 19 ♕g3 ♕xg3 20 fxg3 ♔xh7 21 dxe5 ♗a6 22 ♖f2 ♖d7 with some compensation

for the pawn – Wells) 17...♔f8 18 ♗e4 ♖xd4 19 ♕e3 ♕xe3 20 fxe3 ♖d7 21 ♘b5 ♖c8 22 ♖fd1 ♘e5! 23 ♗xb7 ½-½ Ibragimov-Supatashvili, Ekaterinburg 1997.

c332) 13...♖c8 14 ♖fd1 ♘d5 15 ♗xd5 ♗xg5 16 ♘xg5 ♕xg5 17 ♗e4 h6 18 ♕e3 ♖fd8 = Portisch-Karpov, Milan 1975.

12 ♕e2

White's alternatives consist of:

a) 12 ♖e1 transposes to Line B.

b) 12 ♗d3 ♖c8 13 ♖e1 transposes to Line B.

c) 12 a3 is, in my humble opinion, not a move on which White should spend any time in this variation. In Neverov-Brodsky, St Petersburg 1995, Black slowly but surely equalized after 12...♗xc3 13 ♖xc3 ♕b8 14 ♗h4 ♗d5 15 ♗g3 ♕b7 16 ♗b5 ♖fc8 17 ♖xc8+ ♕xc8 18 ♕d2 ♕b7 19 ♖c1 ♖c8 =.

d) 12 ♕d3 ♖c8 13 ♗a6 ♗xa6 14 ♕xa6 ♗xc3 15 bxc3 ♕c7 16 c4 ♘e4 17 ♗e3 e5 18 dxe5 ♘xe5 = Kamsky-Speelman, New York PCA playoff 1994.

e) 12 ♗h4 ♖c8 13 ♗d3 ♗e7 14 ♕e2 ♘h5 15 ♗xe7 ♕xe7 16 ♗e4 ♘f4 17 ♕e3 ♗xe4 18 ♕xe4 ♘g6 = Beliavsky-Polugaevsky, USSR Ch (Moscow) 1983.

12...♖c8

Given that White is better in the main line, Black should look into the alternatives at this point:

a) 12...♕b8 13 ♖fd1 ♗xc3 14 bxc3 ♖c8 15 ♗d3 ♘d5 16 ♕d2 h6 17 ♗xh6! (17 ♗h4 ♕f4 is fine for Black) 17...gxh6 18 ♕xh6 (B.Lalić-Izeta, Benasque 1995) 18...♘f8! 19 ♕g5+ ♔h8 20 c4 ♘b4 21 ♘e5 and now

21...♕c7? is wrong due to 22 ♕f6+ ♔g8 23 ♗b1 (Giese) with nasty attack, but 21...♖c7!, intending ...♕d8, keeps things unclear.

b) 12...♗xc3 and now:

b1) 13 ♖xc3 ♕b8 14 ♗h4 ♕f4 15 ♗g3 ♕f5 (15...♕e4 has also been tried) 16 ♘e5 ♘xe5 17 dxe5 ♘e4 18 ♖e3 ♘xg3 19 hxg3 ♖fd8 = Iordachescu-Ibragimov, Minsk Z 2000.

b2) 13 bxc3 ♕c7 14 ♗d3 ♘g4 (14...♖ac8 15 ♖fe1 h6 16 ♗d2 ♖fe8 17 c4 ♗xf3 18 ♕xf3 e5 19 d5 ♘c5 20 ♗f1 with a little plus for White, Gligorić-Maksimović, Yugoslav Ch (Belgrade) 1999) 15 ♗e4 ♗xe4 16 ♕xe4 ♘gf6 17 ♕e2 and now:

b21) 17...h6 18 ♗d2 (18 ♗h4 ♖ac8 19 c4 ♖fe8 20 ♖fd1 ♘h5 21 ♗g3 ½-½ Moskalenko-P.H.Nielsen, Copenhagen 1995) 18...♕c6 19 c4 ♖fc8 20 ♖fe1 ♕a4 21 ♗f4 ♖c6 22 ♘e5 ♘xe5 23 ♗xe5 ♘d7 = Ljubojević-Ivanchuk, Monaco rpd 1996.

b22) 17...♖ac8 18 c4 ♕b7 19 ♖fe1 h6 20 ♗h4 ♕a6 = G.Georgadze-Kolev, Linares 1996.

b23) 17...♕b7 18 ♖fe1 h6 19 ♗xf6 ♘xf6 20 c4 ♖ac8 21 ♖c2 ♖c7 = Komarov-Psakhis, Andorra 1995.

13 ♘e5 ♕c7

This seems to be Black's best:

a) 13...h6?! 14 ♘xd7 ♕xd7 15 ♗xf6 gxf6 16 ♖fd1! ♕c6? (neither 16...f5 17 d5 nor 16...♗xc3 17 ♖xc3 looks pretty either, but after the textmove, it's over...) 17 ♕g4+ ♔h7 18 ♘d5! +– Taimanov-Browne, Wijk aan Zee 1981.

b) 13...♗e7!? 14 ♗a6!? (this little trick was first played as far back as the game Menchik – Milner-Barry, Margate 1939) 14...♗xa6 15 ♕xa6 ♖c7!

16 ♘b5?! (16 ♖fe1 may leave White with a slight advantage) 16...♘b8! 17 ♕a4 ♖xc1 18 ♖xc1 a6 19 ♘a7 ½-½ Gligorić-Petronić, Yugoslav Ch (Nikšić) 1997.

14 ♗b5 ♕d6 15 ♖fd1 ♗xc3 16 bxc3 ♕d5 17 f4 ♕d6 18 c4

± Beliavsky-Karpov, USSR Ch (Moscow) 1973.

D)

11 ♕e2 *(D)*

11...♗xc3

11...♘bd7 is one of those standard moves that will usually transpose to another line. In this position White has tried:

a) 12 ♖fd1 is note 'f' to White's 12th move in Line C2 of Chapter 2.

b) 12 ♖ac1 transposes to Line C.

c) 12 ♘e5 ♗xc3 13 bxc3 transposes to the main line.

12 bxc3 ♘bd7 13 ♘e5 ♕c7 14 ♘xd7

14 ♖ac1 is quite harmless; for example, 14...♘xe5 15 dxe5 ♘e4 16 ♗f4 ♖ac8 with a pleasant game for Black, Franić-B.Lalić, Croatian Cht (Makarska Tucepi) 1995.

14...♘xd7

14...♕xd7? allows White to ruin Black's kingside structure with 15 ♗xf6 gxf6 16 d5 ♗xd5 17 ♖ad1 ♖fd8 18 ♕g4+ ♔f8 19 ♗xd5 exd5 20 ♕h5 ± Vaiser-Polugaevsky, Sochi 1988. Black's position is a mess.

15 ♖ac1 *(D)*

15 ♖fc1 has been tested twice in encounters between Knaak and Möhring: 15...e5 (15...h6 16 ♗h4 ♕f4 17 ♗g3 ♕e4 18 ♕xe4 ♗xe4 ± Knaak-Möhring, Leipzig 1984) 16 ♗b3 ♕d6 17 ♕g4 exd4 18 cxd4 ± Knaak-Möhring, East Berlin 1987.

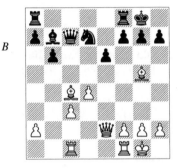

15...♕c6

I have chosen this as the main line since Gelfand used it recently, whereas none of the alternatives have stirred much interest at the highest levels. Alternatives:

a) 15...h6?! 16 ♗h4 (16 ♗d2 ♕c6 17 f3 a6 18 ♗d3 ♕d6 19 a4 ± Moiseev-Neikirkh, corr. 1985) 16...♖ac8 17 ♗b3 ♖fe8 18 a4?! (18 ♗g3 ♕c6 19 f3, followed by c4, is probably better) 18...♕d6 19 ♖fe1 ♕a3 20 ♕d1 e5? (this looks like the natural move, but it dramatically softens the a2-g8 diagonal, which Black should be very careful about; the correct move is 20...♘f8!?)

21 ♖a1 ♕b2 22 ♖b1 ♕xc3 23 ♕h5 ♖f8 24 ♗e7 ♕xd4 25 ♖bd1! (White is playing for mate) 25...♕c3 26 ♖e3! ♕c7 27 ♖g3 ♔h8 28 ♖xd7! ♕xd7 29 ♕xh6+! gxh6 30 ♗f6+ ♔h7 31 ♖g7+ ♔h8 32 ♖xf7+ ♔g8 33 ♖xd7+ 1-0 Reinderman-Van der Sterren, Dutch Ch (Rotterdam) 1999.

b) 15...♖fe8 16 ♖fe1 ♕c6 17 f3 ♖ec8 18 ♗d3 ♕d6 19 ♕f2 h6 20 ♗d2 ± Dokhoian-Rogers, Wijk aan Zee 1989.

c) 15...♖ac8 16 ♗d3 ♕c6 (Black's alternatives are 16...♖fe8?! 17 ♕g4 ♘f8 18 ♖fe1 ♘g6?! 19 ♗b5 ± Knaak-Enders, Dresden 1985, 16...e5 17 ♕g4!? ± intending ♗f5 and 16...h6 17 ♗d2, intending f3, ♖fe1, c4 and ♗c3, with good chances for White) 17 f3 ♕d6 18 ♕c2 h6 19 ♗h4 ♖fe8 20 ♗g3 ± Knaak-Vaiser, Szirak 1985.

d) 15...e5 16 ♗b3 and now:

d1) 16...h6!? 17 ♗h4 ♖ac8 18 ♕d2 (18 ♗c2 ♖fe8 19 ♖fe1, intending ♗g3 – Chekhov) 18...♕c6 19 f3 ♖fe8 20 ♖fe1 ♗a6 21 ♗g3 ♗c4 = Soffer-Tsesarsky, Givatayim 1997.

d2) 16...♖ae8 17 ♕g4 (17 ♕h5 ♕c6 18 ♕h3 ♘f6 {18...h6!? 19 ♗e3 ♘f6 can also be considered} 19 ♖fd1 ♘e4 20 ♗e3 ♘xc3 21 d5 ♕c8 22 ♕h5 and White has more than enough for the pawn, Lanka-Kohlweyer, Bundesliga 1996/7) 17...♔h8 18 ♕g3 f6 19 ♗d2 ♕c6 20 ♖fe1 f5 21 f3 f4 22 ♕f2 ♕g6 23 ♗c2 (Kindermann-Stanec, Vienna 1996) 23...♕f6 gives White a choice between 24 ♗e4!? ♗xe4 25 ♖xe4 ± and 24 ♕f1!?, intending ♕d3, with a better game for White.

e) 15...♕d6!? 16 f4?! (a positional error of some magnitude: the light squares are permanently weakened and another pawn is put on the colour of his own bishop; 16 f3!? is better) 16...♗d5 17 ♗d3 f5 18 ♖fe1 h6 19 ♗h4 ♘f6 20 ♕e5 ♕xe5 21 ♖xe5 ♗xa2 22 ♖a1 ♗d5 23 ♗xf5 exf5 24 ♗xf6 ♗e4 25 ♗h4 ♖f7 with better prospects in the endgame for Black thanks to his passed a-pawn and stronger bishop, Blehm-Tukmakov, Koszalin 1998.

16 f3 (D)

16...♖ac8 (D)
Or:

a) 16...♕d6 17 ♖fd1 (in the game Kobaliya-Kumaran, Moscow 1996, Black obtained a good position after 17 ♖fe1 ♖fc8 18 ♗d3 ♘f8 19 ♗d2 ♘g6 20 ♕e3 ♖d8 21 ♔h1 ♖ac8 22 ♗b1 ♗d5 23 ♕g5 ♖e8 24 ♕g4 f5 25 ♕g5 ♗c4 26 ♕e3 b5 27 ♕f2 ♘e7) 17...♖fe8 (Gelfand suggests 17...a6 18 a4 ♖fc8!?) 18 ♗b3 ♖ac8 19 ♗h4 ♕a3 20 c4 a5 (20...e5 21 ♖e1 a5!? can also be considered according to Gelfand) 21 ♕d2 (Gelfand-J.Polgar, Wijk aan Zee 1998) and here Gelfand gives 21...♗a6 22 ♖c3 ♕b4 23 ♖c2 ♕xd2 24 ♖dxd2 b5 25 cxb5 ♗xb5 =.

b) 16...a6 17 ♗d3 b5 18 c4 bxc4 19 ♗e4? (White is bit better after 19

♖xc4 ♕d6 20 ♖fc1) 19...♕b5 20 ♖b1 ♗xe4 21 ♖xb5 ♗d3 22 ♕b2 axb5 23 ♖d1 ♘b6 and Black is already clearly in command, Ravi-Prakash, Indian Ch (Nagpur) 1999.

17 ♗d3 ♕d6 18 ♖fd1 ♖fe8 19 ♕d2 ♘f8 20 ♗f4 ♕d7 21 ♗e3 b5 22 ♕e2 ♗c6 23 ♖b1 ♖b8 24 ♖b2 ♖b7 25 ♖db1 a6 26 c4 bxc4

½-½ Radjabov-Gelfand, Leon Echt 2001.

Conclusion

Generally speaking, Black is doing quite well in the Karpov Variation and I don't see why this should change. Looking at the individual main lines, if facing Line A, Black should try to transpose to Line D. Line B was the one Kramnik used with success against Kasparov in their 2000 match. Nonetheless, Black has several effective methods of countering this line and should equalize without too many headaches. The same can be said about Line C, which is fairly popular, but Black is OK. Finally in Line D, Black equalizes smoothly, as shown most recently by Gelfand.

2 Parma Variation and Related Systems

1 d4 ♘f6 2 c4 e6 3 ♘c3 ♗b4 4 e3 0-0
5 ♘f3 d5 6 ♗d3 c5 7 0-0 dxc4 8 ♗xc4
(D)

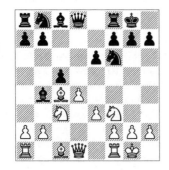

The chapter title mentions the Parma Variation, but we are going to look at a whole lot more than that. The lines in question are somewhat similar in some aspects, yet quite different overall.

Now:

A: 8...♕e7   23
B: 8...♗d7   26
C: 8...♘bd7   27

Line C is the Parma Variation.

Black has a number of other options:

a) 8...cxd4 9 exd4 is Chapter 1.

b) 8...a6 and now:

b1) 9 a4 cxd4 10 exd4 transposes to note 'f4' to Black's 9th move in Chapter 1.

b2) 9 ♕e2 ♘bd7 transposes to note 'c' to Black's 9th move in Line C.

b3) 9 a3 ♗a5 (9...cxd4 10 axb4 dxc3 11 ♕xd8 ♖xd8 12 bxc3 ♘e4 13 ♗b2 ♘d6 14 ♗e2 b5 15 ♘d2 ♗b7 16 c4 ± Portisch-Petrosian, Biel IZ 1976) 10 dxc5! (10 ♕e2 ♘bd7 and 10 ♗d3 ♘bd7 11 ♕e2 transpose to notes 'c42' and 'c424' respectively to Black's 9th move in Line C) 10...♗xc3 11 bxc3 ♕a5 12 a4 ♘bd7 13 c6 bxc6 14 ♕c2 c5 15 e4 ♕c7 16 ♖e1 ± Petrosian-Kuzmin, USSR Ch (Moscow) 1973.

b4) 9 ♗d3 cxd4 10 exd4 b5 11 ♘e4 ♘bd7 12 ♗g5 ♗b7 13 ♖c1 ♗e7 14 ♘c5 ♘xc5 15 dxc5 ♖c8 16 b4 h6 17 ♗f4 with better chances for White, Acs-Asrian, Erevan jr Wch 2000.

c) 8...♘c6 9 ♗d3 (9 a3 ♗xc3 10 bxc3 transposes to Line A of Chapter 6; 9 dxc5 ♕xd1 10 ♖xd1 ♗xc5 11 b3 a6 12 ♗b2 b5 13 ♗d3 ♘b4 ½-½ Savon-Kochiev, St Petersburg 1994) and here:

c1) 9...♕e7 transposes to note 'c' to White's 9th move in Line A.

c2) 9...cxd4 10 exd4 ♗e7 11 a3 b6 12 ♖e1 ♗b7 13 ♗c2 ♖c8 14 ♕d3 g6 15 ♗h6 ♖e8 16 ♖ad1 ♘d5 = ½-½ Najdorf-Gheorghiu, Mar del Plata 1971.

d) 8...b6 *(D)* usually transposes to other lines, mainly the Karpov Variation, but there are several independent possibilities:

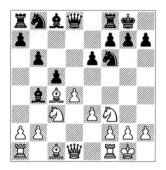

d1) 9 dxc5 ♕xd1 10 ♖xd1 ♗xc5 11 a3 ♗b7 12 b4 ♗e7 13 ♗b2 ♖c8 14 ♗b3 ♘bd7 ½-½ Korchnoi-Geller, Sousse IZ 1967.

d2) 9 ♗d2 cxd4 10 ♘xd4 ♗b7 11 ♕e2 ♘c6 12 ♘xc6 ♗xc6 13 ♖fd1 ♕e7 = Yusupov-Rozentalis, Groningen 1992.

d3) 9 ♕e2 and here:

d31) 9...♘bd7 transposes to Line C.

d32) 9...cxd4 10 exd4 transposes to note 'f' to White's 10th move in Chapter 1.

d33) 9...♗b7 and then:

d331) 10 dxc5 ♗xc3 11 bxc3 bxc5 12 ♗d3 ♗e4 13 ♖d1 ♕d5 14 c4 ♗xd3 15 ♕xd3 ♕xd3 16 ♖xd3 ♘bd7 ½-½ Politov-Serebriansky, corr. 1995.

d332) 10 ♖d1 and here:

d3321) 10...♘bd7 used to be considered a major error on account of 11 d5!, but Black doesn't need to lose immediately: 11...exd5 (11...♗xc3? 12 dxe6 ♗a5 13 exd7 ♕c7 14 e4 ♘xd7 15 ♘g5 +− Polugaevsky-Petrosian, USSR Ch (Leningrad) 1960) 12 ♘xd5 ♘xd5 13 ♗xd5 ♗xd5 14 ♖xd5 ♕c7 15 a3 ♗a5 and White has some initiative, but that's all, Lyrberg-Bezold, Wrexham 1994.

d3322) 10...♕e7 11 ♗d2 ♘bd7 12 a3 ♗xc3 13 ♗xc3 ♘e4 14 ♗e1 ♖fd8 15 ♖ac1 ± Spassky-Khasin, USSR Ch (Moscow) 1957.

d3323) 10...♕c8 11 ♗d2 cxd4 12 ♘xd4 ♘c6 13 ♘f3 ♕b8 14 ♗a6 ♗xa6 15 ♕xa6 ♖d8 = Lerner-Landa, Oberwart 1996.

d3324) 10...cxd4 11 ♘xd4 (11 exd4 ♘bd7 transposes to Line C2) 11...♕e7 12 ♗d2 ♘c6 13 ♘xc6 ♗xc6 14 a3 ♗c5 15 e4 e5 16 ♗g5 h6 17 ♗h4 ♗d4 is equal, Korchnoi-Kindermann, Zurich 1984.

d4) 9 a3 is another important option:

d41) 9...♗xc3 10 bxc3 ♕c7 (the alternatives 10...♗b7 11 ♗d3 ♘bd7 and 10...♘bd7 both transpose to note 'f2' to White's 9th move in Line C; 10...♗a6 11 ♗xa6 ♘xa6 12 ♕e2 ♕c8 13 e4 h6 14 ♗f4 ± Donner-Langeweg, Beverwijk 1966) 11 ♗d3 ♗b7 12 ♖e1 ♗e4 (or 12...♘bd7 13 e4 e5 14 ♗g5 with a slight advantage for White, Babula-Gallego, Panormo ECC 2001) 13 ♗xe4 ♘xe4 14 ♕d3 ♕b7 15 ♘e5 ♖d8 16 f3 ♘f6 (Knaak-Spassov, East Germany-Bulgaria 1982) and now ECO gives 17 ♕b5!? ♘bd7 18 ♘d3 ±.

d42) 9...cxd4 10 axb4 (10 exd4 is likely to transpose to Line C after 10...♗xc3 11 bxc3 ♗b7 followed by ...♘bd7) 10...dxc3 11 ♕xd8! (11 bxc3 is too slow: 11...♕c7 12 ♕b3 ♗b7 13 ♗e2 ♘bd7 14 h3 ♘e5 15 ♘xe5 ♕xe5 16 ♖d1 ♗d5 = Polugaevsky-Unzicker, USSR-West Germany 1960) 11...♖xd8 12 bxc3 *(D)* and here:

d421) 12...a5 13 ♗b2 ♗b7 14 ♗e2 ♘bd7 15 ♖fd1 ♖dc8 16 ♔f1! ♗d5 17 ♘d2 ♘e5 18 f3 ♘e8 19 e4 ♗c4 20 ♘xc4 ♘xc4 21 ♗xc4 ♖xc4 22 ♖d7

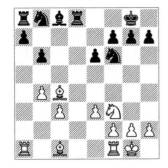

B

gives White a slight advantage, Yusupov-Rozentalis, Bundesliga 1995/6.

d422) 12...♗b7 13 ♗e2 (13 ♗b2 a6 14 ♗e2 b5 15 c4 ♘c6 16 cxb5 axb5 17 ♖xa8 ♖xa8 18 ♗xf6 gxf6 = Yusupov-Karpov, Tilburg 1993) and now:

d4221) 13...a5 14 ♗b2 ♘bd7 15 ♖fd1 axb4 16 cxb4 ± Stein-Kholmov, USSR Ch (Leningrad) 1963.

d4222) 13...a6 14 c4 ♘c6 15 ♗a3 ♘e4 16 ♖fc1 f6! 17 ♖ab1!? (17 h3 ♖ac8 18 ♖c2 ♔f7 19 ♖b1 ♘e7 = Yusupov-P.Nikolić, Munich 1994) 17...♖d7 (Engel-Glaser, corr. 1994) and now Glaser gives 18 c5!? bxc5 19 bxc5 ♔f7 20 ♘d4 ♘xd4 21 exd4 ♗d5 22 c6 ± as White's best option.

d4223) 13...♘c6 14 ♗b2 (14 ♗a3!? intending c4 can also be considered) 14...a6 15 ♖fd1 b5 (15...♘e4 transposes to line 'd423') 16 ♘d2 ♘e5 17 ♘b3 ♖xd1+ 18 ♖xd1 ♗d5 19 ♘a5 ♔f8 20 f3 ± Korchnoi-Szabo, Buenos Aires 1960.

d423) 12...♘e4 13 ♗b2 ♗b7 14 ♖fd1 ♘c6 15 ♗e2! a6 16 ♖xd8+ (16 ♘d4 and 16 ♘e1 have also been tried; both moves should provide a small advantage, but the exchange of rooks enhances White's advantage) 16...♖xd8 17 ♘d4! ♘xd4 18 cxd4 b5 19 ♖c1

♖c8 20 ♖xc8+ ♗xc8 21 f3 ♘d6 22 g4 and with two bishops and a mobile kingside pawn-majority against an immobile queenside majority, White has every chance of winning, Scherbakov-Prokopchuk, Perm 1997.

A)
8...♕e7 (D)

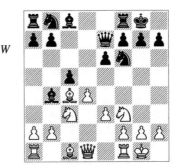

W

This move characterizes the Smyslov Variation, which, unlike most of the other named variations in the Rubinstein Nimzo, actually stems from the gentleman it is named after, Vasily Smyslov. He first played it in Gligorić-Smyslov, Bled Ct 1959, won by Black after an interesting endgame.

Black's idea is to keep White's dark-squared bishop restrained by not going for the exchange on d4. At the same time, Black will build up pressure against the d4-pawn by playing ...♖d8, ...♘c6 and even ...♗a5-b6. In some cases, Black also develops his light-squared bishop to c6 via d7 in order to prevent the white centre from moving forward.

It is not a very commonly played line; there are fewer than 200 games on my database.

9 a3

This move is played more than four times more frequently than the second most common move, 9 ♕e2. White's alternatives are:

a) 9 ♕d3 ♖d8 (9...♘bd7 10 a3 ♗a5 transposes to note 'b' to White's 10th move) 10 ♘e4 ♘xe4 11 ♕xe4 ♘d7 12 a3 ♗a5 13 dxc5 ♘xc5 14 ♕c2 ♗c7! 15 b4 ± Knaak-Taimanov, Jurmala 1978.

b) 9 ♗d2 ♖d8 10 a3 (10 ♕e2 transposes to line 'e3') 10...♗xc3 11 ♗xc3 ♘c6 12 ♕c2 cxd4 13 ♘xd4 ♗d7 14 ♖ad1 ♖ac8 15 ♘xc6 ♗xc6 with approximately equal chances, Prokopchuk-Lugovoi, Novgorod 1999.

c) 9 ♗d3 ♘c6 10 ♘e4 cxd4 11 exd4 h6 12 ♕e2 ♖d8 13 ♗e3 e5 14 dxe5 ♘xe5 15 ♘xe5 ♕xe5 16 ♘xf6+ ♕xf6 = Olafsson-O'Kelly, Dundee 1967.

d) 9 ♕c2 ♗d7 10 ♘e4 ♘xe4 11 ♕xe4 cxd4 12 ♘xd4 ♘c6 13 a3 ♗d6 ½-½ Cvetković-Bukić, Yugoslav Ch (Novi Travnik) 1969.

e) 9 ♕e2 is, as mentioned above, White most important alternative to 9 a3. After this Black has tried two different plans, both of which are outlined above:

e1) 9...♗d7 is similar to the Bronstein Variation – Line B.

e2) 9...♘c6 10 ♖d1 ♖d8 11 a3 ♗a5 transposes to note 'a31' to White's 10th move.

e3) 9...♖d8 10 ♗d2 cxd4 11 exd4 ♘c6 12 ♗e3 h6 13 ♖ac1 a6 14 ♖fd1 b5 15 ♗d3 ♗b7 = Darga-Ivkov, Amsterdam 1969.

9...♗a5 10 ♕c2

White again has a number of alternatives to consider:

a) 10 ♕e2 and here:

a1) 10...♖d8 11 ♗d2 transposes to note 'c1'.

a2) 10...♗d7 11 ♗d2 cxd4 12 exd4 ♘c6 (12...♗c6? 13 d5! ♗xc3 14 ♗xc3 ♘xd5 15 ♗xd5 ♗xd5 16 ♗b4 and White wins the exchange, Borisenko-Korchnoi, USSR Ch (Kiev) 1964) 13 ♗g5 ♗xc3 14 bxc3 ♕d6 15 ♗d3 ♘d5 16 c4 ♘f4 17 ♗xf4 ♕xf4 18 ♕e3 ♕xe3 19 fxe3 ± Sanguinetti-Szabo, Lugano OL 1968.

a3) 10...♘c6 and then:

a31) 11 ♖d1 ♖d8 12 ♖b1 ♗d7 13 ♗d2 ♗b6 14 dxc5 ♗xc5 15 b4 ♗d6 does not give White an advantage, Liberzon-Smyslov, Moscow 1963.

a32) 11 ♗d2 cxd4 12 exd4 ♖d8 13 ♗e3 ♗d7 14 ♖fd1 ♗e8 15 ♖ac1 ♖ac8 = Filip-Eliskases, Buenos Aires 1964.

b) 10 ♕d3 ♘bd7 (10...♖d8 11 ♘e4 a6 12 ♘xf6+ ♕xf6 13 ♕e4, Baumbach-A.Zaitsev, corr. 1971, 13...cxd4 14 exd4 h6 ± *ECO*) 11 ♘e4 (11 dxc5 ♘xc5 12 ♕c2 ♗xc3 13 ♕xc3 ♗d7 14 b4 ♘a4 15 ♕e5 ♖ac8 16 ♗b3 a6 17 h3, Krogius-Polugaevsky, Budapest 1965, and now 17...♗b5! equalizes) and then:

b1) 11...♗c7 was tested in one of the classic games in this line: 12 b4 ♘xe4 13 ♕xe4 ♘f6 14 ♕h4 cxd4 15 exd4 ♘d5! = Knaak-Smyslov, Berlin 1979, but White can obtain a better game with 12 ♘xf6+ ♕xf6 13 ♗d2!?; e.g., 13...b6 14 ♗c3 ♕g6 15 ♕xg6 hxg6 16 ♖fd1, as played in Tiemeyer-Dünhaupt, corr. 1972.

b2) 11...♗b6 12 ♘xf6+ ♕xf6 13 ♗d2 ♖d8 14 ♖ad1 cxd4 15 exd4 ♕g6 16 ♕b3 ♘f6 17 ♖fe1 with an initiative for White, Gligorić-Bukić, Yugoslavia 1970.

c) 10 ♗d2 and then:

c1) 10...♖d8 11 ♕e2 cxd4 goes against the basic strategy for Black: 12 exd4 (12 ♘xd4 ♗b6, Polugaevsky-Portisch, USSR-Hungary 1969, 13 ♘cb5 intending ♗b4 ± *ECO*) 12...♘c6 13 ♗e3 ♗xc3 14 bxc3 h6 15 ♘e5 ♘xe5 16 dxe5 ♘d5 17 ♗d4 b6 18 f4 ♗b7 19 f5 exf5 20 ♖xf5 and White has some initiative and a bishop-pair to compensate for his weakened pawn-structure, Van der Werf-G.Georgadze, Andorra 1997. Georgadze's 'inspiration' was provided by another game of his where he had been White.

c2) 10...♘c6 11 dxc5 ♕xc5 12 ♗a2 ♕h5 13 ♘e2 ♗xd2 14 ♕xd2 ♖d8 15 ♕c3 ♗d7 16 ♘g3 ♕b5 = Geller-Smyslov, Havana 1965.

d) 10 ♗d3 ♘bd7! 11 ♘e4 ♘xe4 12 ♗xe4 ♘f6 13 ♗c2 cxd4 14 exd4 h6 = Reshevsky-Najdorf, Santa Monica 1966.

10...♗d7 *(D)*

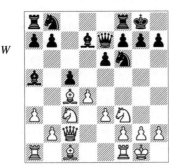

W

11 ♗a2

This standard move is seen in many lines in the Nimzo Rubinstein as well other lines in which White accepts an isolated pawn. The idea is to support the d5 advance as well as being able to

be switched to b1 to participate in an assault against Black's king.

a) 11 ♗d2 ♖c8 12 ♗a2 transposes to the main line.

b) 11 ♗d3 cxd4 12 exd4 ♗c6 13 ♘e5 ♖d8 14 ♗e3 h6 15 ♔h1 ♗e8 16 ♖fd1 ♘c6 = Beliavsky-Taimanov, Vilnius Z 1975.

c) 11 dxc5 ♕xc5 12 ♘e4 ♘xe4 13 b4 ♕h5 14 ♕xe4 ♗c6 15 ♕f4 ♗b6 = Gligorić-Smyslov, Bled Ct 1959.

d) 11 ♖d1 cxd4 12 exd4 ♖c8 13 ♗a2 h6 14 ♘e5 ♗e8 15 ♗b1 ♘bd7 16 ♖d3 ♘f8 17 ♕d1 ♔h8 18 ♗d2 ♗b6 = Belozerov-Yuferov, St Petersburg 1994.

11...♖c8

11...♘c6!? 12 dxc5 (Psakhis points to 12 ♘e5!? intending 12...cxd4 13 exd4 ♖c8 14 ♗g5 with chances of an attack) 12...♗xf3 13 gxf3 ♕xc5 14 b4 ♕g5+ 15 ♔h1 ♕h5 (Lugovoi-Taimanov, St Petersburg Ch 1998) and now Psakhis gives 16 bxa5!? as White's best, allowing 16...♕xf3+ 17 ♔g1 ♕g4+ with a perpetual check.

12 ♗d2 cxd4

Or 12...♗b6 13 ♖ad1 ♗c6 14 dxc5 ♗xc5 15 ♘d4 ♘bd7 16 ♘xc6 ♖xc6 ± Donner-Tatai, Solingen 1968.

13 exd4 h6

13...♗c6 allows 14 d5! ♗xc3 15 dxc6 ♗xd2 16 cxb7 ♕xb7 17 ♕xd2 ± Portisch-Gheorghiu, Skopje/Ohrid 1968.

14 ♖fe1 ♕d8 15 ♕d3 ♘c6 16 ♖ad1 ♗e8 17 ♗b1 ♘e7 18 b4 ♗c7 19 ♘e4 ♘ed5

Although the position after White's 17th is considered '±' by Taimanov, Black is doing fine at this point, and has equal chances, Letić-Brglez, corr. 1981.

B)

8...$\hat{a}$d7 *(D)*

This, the Bronstein Variation, was introduced by the legendary world championship challenger David Bronstein in the 24th Soviet Championship in Moscow 1957 in games against Furman and Petrosian. Both games ended in draws. The variation had its heyday in the last part of the 1960s, after which it more or less faded into obscurity until Yusupov used it to beat Rubinstein expert GM Rainer Knaak in 1991. Since then it has been played by several grandmasters, but it has never regained its former popularity.

9 $\mathbb{W}$e2

Let's consider White's alternatives:

a) 9 dxc5 $\hat{a}$c6! 10 $\hat{a}$b5 a6 11 $\hat{a}$bd4 $\hat{a}$xc5 12 b3 $\hat{a}$d5 13 $\hat{a}$xd5 $\mathbb{W}$xd5 14 $\hat{a}$b2 $\hat{a}$bd7 15 $\mathbb{Z}$c1 $\mathbb{Z}$ac8 = Furman-Bronstein, USSR Ch (Moscow) 1957.

b) 9 $\hat{a}$d3 $\hat{a}$c6 10 a3 cxd4 11 exd4 $\hat{a}$e7 12 $\mathbb{Z}$e1 $\hat{a}$bd7 13 $\hat{a}$c2 a6 14 $\mathbb{W}$d3 $\mathbb{Z}$e8 15 $\hat{a}$g5 g6 = Gligorić-Najdorf, Hollywood 1963.

c) 9 a3 and now:

c1) 9...cxd4 10 exd4 (10 axb4!?) 10...$\hat{a}$e7 11 $\hat{a}$b3 $\hat{a}$c6 12 $\hat{a}$c2 $\hat{a}$bd7

13 $\mathbb{W}$d3 $\mathbb{Z}$c8 14 $\hat{a}$g5 g6 15 $\mathbb{Z}$fe1 $\hat{a}$d5 with roughly equal chances, Fuhrmann-Gipslis, Berlin 1993.

c2) 9...$\hat{a}$xc3 10 bxc3 $\hat{a}$c6 11 $\mathbb{Z}$e1 (or 11 $\hat{a}$e5 $\hat{a}$d5 12 $\hat{a}$e2 cxd4 13 exd4!? $\hat{a}$e4 14 $\hat{a}$d3 $\hat{a}$d7 15 f4!? with an initiative for White, Pchlinski-Niewiadomski, corr. 1962) 11...$\hat{a}$bd7 12 $\hat{a}$d3 $\mathbb{W}$a5 13 $\hat{a}$b2 cxd4 14 exd4 (14 cxd4 $\hat{a}$e4 15 $\hat{a}$e5 $\hat{a}$xd3 16 $\hat{a}$xd7 $\hat{a}$xd7 17 $\mathbb{W}$xd3 $\mathbb{Z}$ac8 = Geller-Keres, Moscow Ct (2) 1962) 14...$\mathbb{W}$h5 15 $\hat{a}$e2 $\mathbb{W}$g6 16 $\hat{a}$f1 $\mathbb{W}$h5 = Martinez Acosta-Tullio, corr. 1976.

c3) 9...$\hat{a}$a5 10 $\mathbb{W}$e2 (both 10 $\hat{a}$e2 cxd4 11 $\hat{a}$exd4 $\hat{a}$c6 12 b4 $\hat{a}$xd4 13 $\hat{a}$xd4 $\hat{a}$c7 = Cherepkov-Taimanov, St Petersburg Ch 1997 and 10 $\mathbb{W}$d3 $\hat{a}$c6 11 $\hat{a}$e5 $\mathbb{W}$e7 12 $\mathbb{Z}$d1 $\mathbb{Z}$d8 13 $\mathbb{W}$c2 $\hat{a}$b6 14 dxc5 $\mathbb{Z}$xd1+ 15 $\hat{a}$xd1 $\mathbb{W}$xc5 = Ivkov-Garcia Gonzalez, Novi Sad 1976 fail to impress) 10...$\hat{a}$c6 11 $\mathbb{Z}$d1 $\hat{a}$bd7 (11...$\mathbb{W}$e7 transposes to the main line) 12 d5 (12 $\hat{a}$d2!? $\hat{a}$b6 ± Yusupov) 12...exd5 13 $\hat{a}$xd5 $\hat{a}$b6 14 $\hat{a}$xb6 (14 $\hat{a}$f4 $\mathbb{W}$c7 15 $\hat{a}$a2 $\mathbb{Z}$ae8 $\mp$ Knaak-Yusupov, Hamburg 1991) 14...$\mathbb{W}$xb6 15 $\hat{a}$e5 $\hat{a}$a4 16 $\mathbb{Z}$d3 $\mathbb{W}$c7 17 b3 $\hat{a}$xb3 18 $\mathbb{Z}$xb3 $\mathbb{W}$xe5 19 $\hat{a}$b2 with compensation for the pawn, but no more than that, Szabo-Kholmov, Leningrad 1967.

9...$\hat{a}$c6 10 $\mathbb{Z}$d1 $\mathbb{W}$e7 *(D)*

11 a3

White has a few other interesting possibilities:

a) 11 $\hat{a}$e5 $\mathbb{Z}$d8 and here:

a1) 12 a3 $\hat{a}$a5 13 dxc5 $\mathbb{Z}$xd1+ 14 $\hat{a}$xd1 $\mathbb{W}$xc5 15 $\hat{a}$xc6 $\mathbb{W}$xc6 16 b4 ± Taimanov-Reshevsky, Buenos Aires 1960.

a2) 12 $\hat{a}$d3 h6 13 $\hat{a}$c2 $\hat{a}$a5 14 $\mathbb{W}$c4 $\hat{a}$b6 15 a4 $\hat{a}$d5 16 $\hat{a}$xd5 exd5 17 $\mathbb{W}$d3 $\hat{a}$c6 18 $\hat{a}$xc6 bxc6 19 dxc5

W

&xc5 20 b3 &d6 21 &b2 &e5 = Portisch-Matanović, Sousse IZ 1967.

b) 11 &d2 &xf3 12 ♕xf3 ♘c6 13 &e1 cxd4 14 exd4 ♖ad8 15 ♕e3 &a5 16 &b5 ♘b4 17 ♖ac1 &b6 18 ♘a4 ♘bd5 19 ♕b3 &c7 with a pleasant game for Black, Neverov-Yusupov, Ohrid Ech 2001.

11...&a5

11...&xc3 12 bxc3 ♘bd7 13 a4 ♖fc8 14 &b3 ♕e8 15 c4 cxd4 16 exd4 ♘b6 17 a5 (Gligorić-Taimanov, Montilla 1977) 17...&xf3 18 gxf3 ♘bd7 19 f4 (*ECO*) gives White an advantage.

12 &d2

12 ♘e5 ♖d8 transposes to note 'a1' to White's 11th move.

12...&xf3

Vilela mentions that 12...♘bd7 13 dxc5 ♕xc5 14 ♘d4! is much better for White.

13 ♕xf3 ♘c6

Black can't venture 13...cxd4?! due to 14 exd4 h6 15 d5!, Najdorf-Schweber, Buenos Aires 1968.

14 dxc5 ♕xc5 15 &f1 ♕e7

Now White has tried:

a) 16 ♘e4 ♘xe4 17 ♕xe4 &xd2 18 ♖xd2 ♖fd8 19 ♖c2 ♖d5 ½-½ Donner-Kholmov, Havana 1965.

b) 16 g3!? and now 16...♖fd8?! 17 b4 ± was played in Boudy-Vilela, Cuban Ch (Sagua la Grande) 1981/2, but as pointed out in *ECO*, Black can improve with 16...♖ac8 with a minimal advantage for White.

c) 16 &e1 ♖ad8 17 ♖xd8 ♖xd8 18 ♖d1 ♖xd1 19 ♕xd1 ♕d7 20 ♕xd7 ♘xd7 with a somewhat better endgame for White, Sanguinetti-Matanović, Lugano OL 1968.

C)

8...♘bd7 (D)

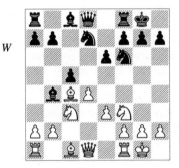

W

Here we have it, the Parma Variation, named after the Slovenian grandmaster Bruno Parma. Note that there are numerous ways for Black to transpose to the Karpov Variation by exchanging on d4, although some lines stay within the parameters of the Parma Variation despite the exchange of pawns on d4.

Black's plan depends mainly upon which basic set-up he chooses: either with ...a6 or with ...b6. In the former case, Black grabs space on the queenside, usually keeping the dark-squared bishop on the board and then opening the centre once he has finished developing. After the latter option, ...b6, Black will target the white centre by isolating the d-pawn and then blockading it, or, alternatively, exchange on c3 to take a closer look at the isolated pawn couple on c3 and d4.

9 ♕e2

White develops his queen to a safe square, clearing the way for the rook to transfer over to d1, where it can support the d-pawn's advance. Should Black exchange on d4, which frequently happens, the queen is ideally placed in supporting both a kingside attack and control over the centre.

a) 9 ♘e2 cxd4 (9...♘b6 10 ♗d3 cxd4 11 e4!? ♖e8 12 e5 ♘fd7 13 ♘exd4 ♘f8 14 ♗e4 ♘d5 15 ♕b3 with an initiative for White, Speelman-Kosten, English Ch (London) 1991) 10 ♘exd4 ♕e7 11 a3 ♗d6 12 ♘b5 ♗b8 13 ♗d2 a6 14 ♗b4 ♘c5 with equality, Beliavsky-Karpov, Reggio Emilia 1989/90.

b) 9 ♕d3 and here:

b1) 9...♕e7 10 a3 ♗a5 transposes to note 'b' to White's 10th move in Line A.

b2) 9...cxd4 10 exd4 transposes to note 'e5' to Black's 9th move in Chapter 1.

b3) 9...a6 10 a4 (10 a3 is also fairly harmless; e.g., 10...♗xc3 11 ♕xc3 b5 12 ♗d3 ♕b6 with chances for both sides – Taimanov) 10...♕a5! 11 ♗d2 ♖d8 12 ♖fd1 ♘b6 13 ♗b3 ♗d7 14 ♗c2 ♗c6 15 ♘e5 ♖ac8 16 ♗e1 cxd4 17 exd4 ♘bd5 ∓ Flear-Sax, Graz 1984.

c) 9 ♗d2 cxd4 (9...b6 10 ♕e2 transposes to note 'b' to White's 10th move) 10 exd4 (or 10 ♘xd4 a6 11 ♕e2 ♗d6 12 a4 ♘e5 13 ♗a2 ♗d7 14 ♖ad1 ♖c8 = Yusupov-P.Schlosser, Baden-Baden

1995) 10...b6 11 ♖c1 ♗b7 12 ♕e2 ♗xc3 13 ♗xc3 ♘d5 14 ♗d2 a6 15 ♗g5 ♘7f6 = Röder-Delchev, Aosta 2002.

d) 9 ♗d3 and here:

d1) 9...cxd4 10 exd4 b6 11 a3 transposes to line 'd432'.

d2) 9...a6 10 a4 (10 a3 ♗a5 11 ♕e2 transposes to note 'c424' to Black's 9th move) 10...♕e7 11 ♘e4 h6 12 ♘xf6+ ♕xf6 = Gligorić-Portisch, Buenos Aires OL 1978.

d3) 9...♕e7 10 ♘e5 ♖d8 11 ♕e2 ♘f8 12 a3 ♗a5 13 ♘c4 cxd4 14 exd4 ♗c7 15 ♖d1 ♘g6 = Renet-Mirallès, Paris 1987.

d4) 9...b6 (D) and here:

d41) 10 ♕e2 ♗b7 11 ♖d1 cxd4 12 exd4 transposes to Line C2.

d42) 10 ♖e1 ♗b7 11 a3 ♗a5 12 ♖b1 ♕e7 13 e4 h6 14 d5 ♗xc3 15 bxc3 c4 ½-½ Gligorić-Ribli, Plovdiv Echt 1983.

d43) 10 a3 cxd4 (10...♗xc3 11 bxc3 transposes to line 'f2') and here:

d431) 11 axb4 dxc3 12 bxc3 ♗b7 13 ♗b2 ♕c7 14 ♕e2 ♘g4 15 e4 ♖fd8 16 ♖fd1 ♘de5 = Korchnoi-Topalov, Batumi Echt 1999.

d432) 11 exd4 ♗xc3 12 bxc3 ♕c7 (12...♗b7 usually comes to the same thing) 13 ♗d2 ♝b7 14 ♖e1 ♜fe8 (or 14...♜ad8 15 ♘e5 ♞xe5 16 ♖xe5 ♜d5 with chances for both sides, Donner-Farago, Cienfuegos 1973) 15 ♘e5 ♜ad8 16 f4 ♞f8 17 ♕c2 ♞d5 18 f5 exf5 19 ♗xf5 (Gulko-Lobron, Manila IZ 1990) and at this point Gulko gives 19...♞g6! as equal.

e) 9 ♕b3 and here:

e1) 9...♕e7 10 ♖d1 ♞b6 11 ♗e2 cxd4 12 exd4 ♝d7 13 ♘e5 ♜ac8 14 ♘xd7 ♞fxd7 15 ♗f3 with a better game for White, Larsen-Andersson, Stockholm 1975.

e2) 9...b6 10 ♖d1 (10 d5 isn't as good; e.g., 10...♝xc3 11 dxe6, Vaiser-A.Petrosian, USSR 1973, 11...♝a5! 12 exd7 ♕xd7 13 ♖d1 ♕e7 = *ECO*) 10...♝b7 11 d5 ('±' Taimanov) 11...b5! 12 ♗xb5 exd5 13 ♘a4 ♜b8 14 a3 ♝a5 15 ♕c2 ♕e7 16 b3 ♜fc8! 17 ♗b2 d4! and Black is in charge, Sandkief-Palm, corr. 1978.

e3) 9...a6 10 a4 *(D)* (10 a3 is harmless: 10...♝a5 11 dxc5 ♘xc5 12 ♕c2 ♘cd7 13 b4 ♝c7 14 ♖d1 b5) and here:

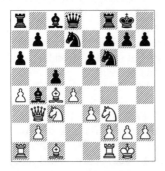

B

e31) 10...♜b8 11 ♖d1 ♕c7 12 ♗d2 b6 13 ♜ac1 ♝b7 14 ♗e2 ♝xc3 15 ♗xc3 ♘e4 16 ♗e1 ♝d5 17 ♕a3 ♕b7 18 ♘e5 ♘ef6 19 ♘xd7 ♘xd7 20 f3

cxd4 21 e4 ♗c6 22 ♜xd4 and White is better thanks to his bishop-pair, Portisch-Sax, Moscow 1990.

e32) 10...b6 11 d5 ♗xc3 12 dxe6 ♗a5 13 exd7 ♕xd7 14 ♖d1 ♕c7 15 ♗d2 = Petrosian-Simagin, Moscow 1966.

e33) 10...♗a5!? 11 ♖d1 cxd4 12 exd4 ♕b6! 13 ♕c2 ♕c7 14 ♗d3 (Portisch-Korchnoi, USSR-Rest of the World (Belgrade) 1970) and now 14...b6! 15 d5 ♗xc3 16 dxe6 ♗e5 17 exd7 ♗xd7 was given in the bulletin of the event.

e34) 10...♕e7 11 ♖d1 and now:

e341) 11...♗a5 12 ♕c2 cxd4 (Belov gives 12...♘b6!? as a better try) 13 exd4 ♘b6 14 ♗a2 h6 15 ♘e5 ♗d7 16 ♗b1 ± Tukmakov-Korchnoi, USSR Ch (Riga) 1970.

e342) 11...♜d8 12 ♗d3 (or 12 ♕c2 cxd4 13 exd4 ♘b6 14 ♗d3 h6 15 ♗f4 ♘bd5 16 ♗g3 ♗d7 17 ♗h4 ♜ac8 18 ♘xd5 exd5 19 ♕b3 a5 = Korchnoi-Bacrot, Albert (2) 1997) 12...♗a5 13 ♗d2 h6 14 ♜ac1 b6 15 ♘e4 ♗xd2 16 ♘fxd2 cxd4 17 exd4 ♗b7 18 ♜c7 ♜ab8 19 ♘xf6+ ♕xf6 20 ♗e2 ♕f4 21 ♕g3 ♕xg3 22 hxg3 = Beliavsky-Ribli, Belfort 1988.

e343) 11...♘b6 12 ♗e2 cxd4 13 exd4 h6 14 ♗f4 ♘bd5 15 ♗g3 b6 16 ♗h4 ♘f4 with approximately equal chances, Beliavsky-Razuvaev, Reggio Emilia 1995/6.

e344) 11...cxd4 12 exd4 ♘b6 13 ♗g5 ♘xc4 14 ♕xc4 ♗d7 (Portisch-Beliavsky, Frankfurt rpd 1998) 15 ♗xf6 gxf6 16 d5!? and White is clearly in control.

f) 9 a3 is also of some importance, although Black should not worry too much about this move:

f1) 9...♗a5 10 ♕c2 (10 ♕e2! a6 transposes to note 'c42' to Black's 9th move) 10...cxd4 11 exd4 ♗xc3 12 bxc3 b6 13 ♖e1 ♗b7 14 ♘e5 ♖c8 = Gligorić-Tal, Belgrade Ct (2) 1968.

f2) 9...♗xc3 10 bxc3 b6 11 ♗d3 ♗b7 and now:

f21) 12 ♗b2 ♕c7 13 c4 ♖ad8 14 ♖e1 ♗e4 15 ♗xe4 ♘xe4 16 ♖c1 ♖fe8 17 ♕c2 ♕b7 = Korchnoi-Gligorić, Buenos Aires OL 1978.

f22) 12 ♕e2 ♗xf3 13 ♕xf3 e5 14 ♗b2 ♕e7 15 ♕h3 ♖ad8 16 ♗f5 ♖fe8 17 ♖fd1 ♘f8 18 ♕g3 ♘g6 and in this position the knights are no worse than the bishops, and the position is approximately equal, Cifuentes-Piket, Dutch Ch (Amsterdam) 1996.

f23) 12 ♖e1 *(D)* and then:

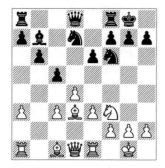

f231) 12...e5 13 e4!? ♕c7 (instead, 13...♕e7?! 14 ♗g5 ♕e6 15 a4 h6? led to a quick draw in Gerber-Landenbergue, Geneva 1995, but only because White missed 16 ♗xf6 ♕xf6 17 ♗b5, winning a pawn) 14 ♗g5! exd4 15 cxd4 cxd4 16 ♘xd4!? (after 16 e5?!, rather than 16...♘d5?! 17 ♖c1 ♘c5 18 ♘xd4 g6 19 ♗c4! ± Gulko-Hjartarson, Groningen PCA IZ 1993, 16...♗xf3! 17 ♕xf3 ♘xe5 18 ♕g3

♘h5! favours Black according to Psakhis) 16...♕e5!? (16...♖fe8?! 17 ♖c1 ♕e5 18 ♘f3 ♕a5 19 ♖c7 ± Babula-Votava, Czech Ch (Zlin) 1997) 17 ♘f3 ♕a5 18 ♗xf6 ♘xf6 19 e5 ♗xf3! 20 ♕xf3 ♖ae8 is unclear – Babula.

f232) 12...♗e4!? 13 ♗f1 (or 13 ♗xe4!? ♘xe4 14 ♕d3 ♘df6 15 c4 ♕c7 {Dautov gives 15...♕d7 16 ♗b2 ♖fd8 17 ♖ad1 ♖ac8 18 ♘e5 ♕b7 19 ♕b3 ±} 16 ♗b2 ♖fd8 17 ♖ac1 ♖ac8 and Black's chances are certainly not worse, Gligorić-Ljubojević, Belgrade 1979) 13...♕c7 14 ♘d2 (14 ♗b2!? may be better; e.g., 14...♖ad8 15 ♘d2 ♗b7 16 e4 ± Gligorić-Van Scheltinga, Enschede 1963) 14...♗g6 (14...e5 was tried in Petursson-Åkesson, Copenhagen 1995: 15 ♘xe4 ♘xe4 16 ♗b2 c4 17 f3 ♘d6 18 a4 ♘b7 19 e4 ♖fe8 20 ♗c1 ♘a5 21 ♗e3 a6 22 ♖b1 ♖ab8 23 ♕c2 with a position where I prefer White) 15 ♗b2 e5 16 e4 ♖ad8 (Hübner has suggested 16...cxd4!? 17 cxd4 exd4 18 ♗xd4 ♘c5 with chances for both sides as a possible improvement, but 19 ♗xf6 gxf6 20 ♕f3 ♖ad8 21 ♖ad1 ♕e5 22 ♘c4 may question this evaluation a bit, although White is no more than slightly better) 17 d5 ♘e8 18 c4 ♘d6 19 a4 ± Korchnoi-Hübner, Manila IZ 1990.

f233) 12...♘e4 13 ♗b2 ♕c7 (or 13...♖c8 14 c4 ♘d6 15 ♕e2 ♕e7 16 a4 a5 17 ♖ed1 ♖fd8 18 ♘d2 ♕g5 19 f4 ± Magerramov-Basin, Uzhgorod 1988) 14 c4 ♖ac8 15 ♕c2 ♘df6 16 ♘e5 ♖fd8 17 ♖ac1 ± Korchnoi-Ljubojević, Lucerne OL 1982.

f3) 9...cxd4 is also possible:

f31) 10 exd4 is really a Karpov Variation where White has wasted time with a3, which is normally not played in the Karpov Variation, un-less, of course, you don't know what you are doing! However, this line oc-curs relatively often by transposition from other lines, which explains why sometimes even GMs land up in this line with the white pieces. One possi-ble line is 10...♗xc3 11 bxc3 ♕c7 12 ♕e2 ♘b6 13 ♗d3 ♘bd5 14 c4 ♘f4 15 ♕e3 ♘xd3 16 ♕xd3 b6 17 ♗g5 ♘d7 = Gligorić-Filip, Amsterdam OL 1954. If you are worried about this line, study the lines in Chapter 1 for com-parison.

f32) 10 ♘b5 ♗e7 11 ♘bxd4 e5 12 ♘f5 (other knight moves have also been tried, but this is the sharpest and for that matter the only interesting move) 12...♘b6 13 ♘xe7+ ♕xe7 14 ♗e2 ♖d8 15 ♗d2 ♗g4 16 ♕e1 ♘bd5 17 ♖c1 ♘e4 18 ♗b4 ♘xb4 ½-½ Taimanov-Speelman, Leningrad 1984.

f33) 10 ♕xd4 ♗xc3 (or 10...♘b6 11 ♕xd8 ♖xd8 12 axb4 ♘xc4 13 e4 ♖d3! = Tal-Estrin, Lublin 1974) 11 ♕xc3 ♕c7 12 ♕b3 b6 13 ♗e2 ♗b7 is equal, Mecking-Korchnoi, Wijk aan Zee 1971.

f34) 10 axb4 dxc3 11 bxc3 ♕c7 *(D)* (after 11...b6, 12 ♕e2 transposes to note 'c3' to White's 10th move, but 12 ♗e2!? ♗b7 13 c4 ♕c7 14 h3 a5 15 ♗a3 axb4 16 ♗xb4 ♖xa1 17 ♕xa1 ♖a8 18 ♕b2 gives White a slight pull, Khalifman-Anand, New Delhi FIDE 2001) and now:

f341) 12 ♕e2 b6 (or 12...e5 13 e4 ♘b6 14 ♗d3 ♗e6 15 ♗e3 ♘fd7 16 ♖fc1 {Azmaiparashvili's 16 c4!? in-tending 16...♗xc4 17 ♖fc1 with com-pensation can also be considered} 16...♗c4 17 ♗xb6 ♘xb6 18 ♖a5 ♗xd3 19 ♕xd3 ♖fd8 ½-½ F.Portisch-Lukacs,

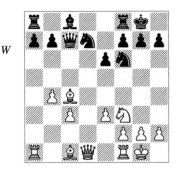

Hungarian Ch (Budapest) 1977) 13 ♗d2 ♗b7 14 ♗a6 ♗e4! 15 h3 ♖fd8 16 ♖fd1 ♘b8 17 ♗b5 a6 = Rogo-zenko-Ki.Georgiev, Skopje 2002.

f342) 12 ♗e2 ♕xc3!? (Kramnik mentions an alternative: 12...♘d5!? 13 ♗b2 ♘xc3 14 ♗xc3 ♕xc3 15 ♕d6 ♕c6! =) 13 ♗a3 ♘d5! 14 ♕b1 ♕f6 15 ♗d3 h6 16 b5 ♖d8 17 ♗b2 ♕e7 (Kramnik-Kasparov, London BGN Wch (12) 2000) and here Kramnik gives 18 ♗a3! ♕f6 19 ♗b2 = as best.

f343) 12 ♕b3 is currently White's best bid for an advantage, but even here it doesn't come easy:

f3431) 12...e5 13 ♗e2 e4 14 ♘d4 ♘e5 15 h3 ♗d7 16 c4 ♕c8 17 f4 (17 c5!?) 17...exf3 18 ♘xf3 ♘xf3+ 19 ♖xf3 ♗f5 20 ♗b2 ± Babula-Macieja, Czech Cht 2001.

f3432) 12...b6 13 ♗e2 ♗b7 14 ♖d1 (14 ♗b2 ♘g4 15 ♖fd1? {15 ♕c4!? =} 15...♗xf3 16 ♗xf3 ♕xh2+ 17 ♔f1 ♘de5 18 ♗xa8, Kallio-Anastasian, Batumi Ech 2002, and now Black's fastest win is 18...♕h4 19 g3 ♕h2 20 ♗g2 ♘f3) 14...♘e5 15 ♘xe5 ♕xe5 16 ♗d2 b5 17 c4 bxc4 18 ♕xc4 ♖fc8 19 ♕b5 ♕xb5 20 ♗xb5 = O.Rodri-guez-Estremera Panos, Spanish Ch 1993.

f3433) 12...♘b6 13 ♗e2 e5 14 ♖a5 (or 14 c4!? ♗e6 15 ♖a5 ♘fd7 16 ♘g5 ♗xc4 17 ♕c2 g6 18 f4 with compensation for the pawn, Timman-Keene, Reykjavik 1976) 14...♗e6 15 ♕c2 ♘bd7 16 c4 b6 17 ♖a6 (17 ♖a3 can also be considered; e.g., 17...♖fc8 18 ♗b2 ♗xc4 19 ♖c1 b5 20 ♗xc4 bxc4 21 ♖a5 with compensation for the pawn, but not much more than that, Lein-Rohde, USA Ch (Estes Park) 1986) 17...♖fc8 18 ♘d2 ♕b7 (18...♘b8 19 ♖a3 a5 20 ♗b2 ♘c6 21 b5 ♘e7 22 f4, Kramnik-Anand, Wijk aan Zee 2001, and here, according to Kramnik, Black should opt for 22...exf4!?, when 23 ♗xf6 gxf6 24 ♖xf4 f5 25 ♘f3 ♘g6 26 ♖d4 is unclear) 19 b5 (19 ♖a1 b5 20 c5 a5 21 ♖xa5 ♖xa5 22 bxa5 ♘xc5 23 ♕b2 ♕c7 = Babula-Ribli, Bundesliga 2001/2) 19...♘c5 20 ♖a3 a6 ½-½ Khalifman-Anand, Merida 2001.

We now return to the position after 9 ♕e2 *(D)*:

9...b6

Black has some other options:

a) 9...♕e7 10 a3 ♗a5 is similar to the Smyslov Variation, covered in Line A.

b) 9...cxd4 10 exd4 and here:

b1) 10...b6 followed by ...♗b7 will transpose to lines covered in Chapter 1.

b2) 10...a6 and now: 11 a4 is line 'c33'; 11 a3 transposes to line 'c411'.

b3) 10...♘b6 and then:

b31) 11 ♗d3 ♘bd5!? (11...♗d7 12 ♘e5 ♗c6 13 ♗g5 ♗e7 14 ♖ad1 ♘bd5 15 ♗b1 ± Smejkal-Hybl, Czechoslovak Ch (Prague) 1963) 12 ♗d2 ♗e7 13 ♖ad1 (13 ♘xd5 ♕xd5 14 ♗g5 ♗d7 15 ♘e5 ♗c6 16 ♘xc6 ½-½ Bets-Kholmov, Rovno 2000) 13...♘xc3 14 bxc3 b6 15 ♘e5 ♗b7 16 ♕e3 ♖c8 17 ♖fe1 ♘d7 18 ♕h3 f5 19 ♕e3 ♘f6 20 ♕e2 ♘e4 21 ♗xe4 fxe4 22 ♕g4 ½-½ Emms-Lalić, Maidstone 1994.

b32) 11 ♗b3 ♗d7 12 ♗g5 ♗c6 (or 12...♖c8 13 ♘e5 ♗e7 14 ♖fe1 ♘fd5 15 ♘xd5 ♗xg5 16 ♘xb6 axb6, Scherbakov-Kholmov, Pardubice 1996, 17 ♘xd7! ♕xd7 18 ♕g4 and in order to prevent d4-d5, Black has to play something like 18...♗d2 19 ♖ed1 h5 20 ♕h4 ♗h6 21 ♕xh5, which leaves White with a big advantage) 13 ♘e5 ♗e7 14 ♖ad1 ♘bd5 15 ♖fe1 ± Panno-Ja.Bolbochan, Buenos Aires 1965.

b4) 10...♕c7 11 ♘b5 ♕d8! 12 a3 ♗a5 13 b4 a6 14 ♘c3 ♗c7 15 ♗g5 h6 16 ♗h4 b5 ½-½ de la Riva-Magem, Terrassa 1995.

b5) 10...♗xc3 11 bxc3 ♕c7 (11...b6 should be compared with Chapter 1) and now:

b51) 12 ♗g5 transposes to note 'e62' to Black's 9th move in Chapter 1.

b52) 12 ♗b2 b6 13 ♗d3 ♗b7 14 c4 h6 15 ♘e5 ♘xe5 16 dxe5 ♕c6 17 f4 ♘d7 and Black is close to equal, Visier-Andersson, Las Palmas 1975.

b53) 12 ♗d2 b6 13 ♗d3 ♗b7 14 ♖ac1 ♖ac8 15 ♖fe1 ♖fd8 16 ♗g5 h6

17 ♗h4 ♖e8 18 ♗g3 ♕d8 19 ♗b5 ±
Karpov-Morozevich, Prague rpd 2002.

b54) 12 ♗a3 ♖e8 13 ♖ac1 (or 13
♘e5 a6 14 ♖ac1 b5 15 ♗b3 ♗b7 16 c4
♕a5 17 ♗d6 bxc4 18 ♕xc4 ♗d5 19
♕c7 ♕xc7 20 ♖xc7 ♗xb3 21 axb3 =
Lautier-Anand, Monaco Amber blindfold 1998) 13...b6 14 ♘e5 ♗b7 15 f4
♖ad8 16 ♗d3 ± Speelman-Richard-
son, British League (4NCL) 2001/2.

b6) 10...♖e8 11 ♖d1 (*ECO* claims
an edge for White after 11 a3, but this
is hardly likely as it will transpose
into a type of Karpov Variation after
11...♗xc3 12 bxc3 b6 in which White
has invested a tempo in playing a3,
while Black has spent one on the mod-
erately more useful ...♖e8; my feeling
is that it should be about equal) 11...a6
12 a4 b6 13 ♗g5 ♗b7 14 ♖ac1 ♘f8 15
♘e5 ♘g6 16 ♗d3 ♗e7 17 h4 with
chances for both sides, Pinter-Sunye,
Hastings 1980/1.

c) 9...a6 *(D)* is an important alternative. Now:

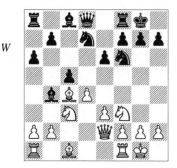

W

c1) 10 ♗d3 and then:

c11) 10...b5 11 a3 ♗a5 12 b4! cxb4
(12...cxd4 13 exd4 ♗b6 14 ♗g5 ♗b7
15 ♘e4 ♕b8 16 ♘c5 ± Vaganian-
Platonov, USSR 1971) 13 ♘xb5! (an

improvement over the older 13 axb4
♗xb4 14 ♘xb5 ♗b7 15 ♗a3 ♗xa3 16
♘xa3 ♘d5 17 ♕d2 ♘5b6 18 e4 ±
Danner-Kochiev, Reggio Emilia 1979)
13...♗b7 (or 13...b3 14 ♘d6 ♘d5 15
♗d2 ♗xd2 16 ♕xd2 ♘7f6 17 ♘c4
♗d7 18 a4! ♖b8 19 ♖fb1 ♕c7 20 ♘fe5
± Dautov) 14 ♘d6 ♗xf3 15 ♕xf3
♗c7 16 ♘b7! ♕e7 17 axb4 ± Gel-
fand-Epishin, Dos Hermanas 1994.

c12) 10...cxd4!? is possibly even
better: 11 exd4 b5 12 ♗g5 ♗b7 13
♖fd1 ♗e7 14 ♘e5 ♘d5 15 ♗d2 ♘xc3
16 bxc3 ♘xe5 17 ♕xe5 ♗f6 = Sigur-
jonsson-Larsen, Geneva 1977.

c2) 10 ♖d1 b5 11 ♗d3 (11 ♗b3
♗b7 12 ♗d2 cxd4 13 exd4 ♘b6 is
equal, Geller-Boleslavsky, USSR 1967)
11...♗b7 and then:

c21) 12 ♗d2 cxd4 13 exd4 ♘b6 14
♗g5 ♗e7 15 a3 ♘fd5 16 ♘e4 ♗xg5
and here 17 ♘fxg5?! ♘f4 18 ♕g4??
drops a piece: 18...♘xd3 19 ♖xd3
♗xe4 0-1 Iashvili-Dorfman, Oviedo
rpd 1992. After 17 ♘exg5 the chances
are approximately equal.

c22) 12 a4 c4 13 ♗c2 ♗xc3 14
bxc3 ♘e4 15 ♗b2 f5 16 ♘d2 ♘b6 17
axb5 axb5 18 f3 ♘xd2 19 ♕xd2 ♕g5
= Lyrberg-Kosten, San Sebastian 1995.

c3) 10 a4 prevents ...b5, but also
weakens White's queenside, in particular the b4 square. Then:

c31) 10...♕e7 11 ♘a2 ♗a5 12 dxc5
♗c7 13 b4 a5 14 ♗a3 axb4 15 ♗xb4
♘xc5 16 ♘c3 ♗a5 ½-½ T.Geor-
gadze-Razuvaev, USSR Ch (Vilnius)
1980.

c32) 10...b6 11 ♘a2 (11 d5!? is
worth a closer look: 11...♗xc3 12
dxe6 ♗a5 13 exd7 ♗b7 {13...♖xd7
14 ♖d1 ♕e7 15 b3 ±} 14 ♖d1 ♕e7 15
♗d2 ♗xd2 16 ♕xd2 ± Pinchuk-Lein,

Voronezh 1969) 11...♗b7 12 ♘xb4 cxb4 13 b3 ♘e4 14 ♗b2 a5 15 ♖fc1 ♕e7 16 ♖c2 ♖fc8 17 ♖ac1 h6 18 ♗d3 ♕d8 ½-½ Gligorić-Unzicker, West Berlin 1971.

c33) 10...cxd4 11 exd4 ♘b6 (or 11...♕a5!? 12 ♗d2 b6 13 ♖fe1 ♗b7 14 ♗b3 ♕h5 15 ♖ad1 ♖fd8 16 ♘e5 ♕xe2 17 ♖xe2 ♖ac8 with a pleasant game for Black, Zilberman-Vink, Dieren 2000) and here:

c331) 12 ♗b3 ♘bd5 13 ♘e4 ♗d7 14 ♗g5 ♗e7 15 ♘c5 ♗c6 16 ♘d3 ♕b6 17 ♗c4 ♖fc8 = Donner-O'Kelly, Utrecht 1961.

c332) 12 ♗d3 ♘bd5 13 ♘xd5 (13 ♗g5 ♗e7 14 ♖fe1 ♘b4 15 ♗c4 ♘fd5 16 ♗xe7 ♘xe7 17 ♘e4 ♘f5 leads to equality, Korchnoi-Shamkovich, Leningrad 1967) 13...exd5 14 ♗g5 (14 ♘e5!? has been suggested by Ftačnik, but 14...♖e8 should be fine for Black) 14...♕d6! 15 ♘e5 ♘e4 16 ♗f4 ♕e7! 17 f3 ♘d6 18 ♕f2 ♗f5! 19 ♗xf5 ♘xf5 20 ♘d3 ♗d6 21 ♖fe1 ♕d8 22 ♗xd6 ♕xd6 = Ivanchuk-Speelman, Reykjavik 1991.

c34) 10...♕c7 11 ♘a2 b5 12 ♗d3 ♗a5 (12...bxa4 13 ♘xb4 cxb4 14 ♖xa4 ± Portisch-Ardiansyah, Skopje OL 1972) 13 axb5 (13 b4 is best met with 13...♗xb4 14 ♘xb4 cxb4 15 e4 ♗b7 16 a5 e5 17 ♘xe5 ♘xe5 18 dxe5 ♕xe5 = Knaak-Enders, East Germany 1986) 13...axb5 14 ♗xb5 ♗b7 15 ♖d1 ♖fb8 (15...♖ab8?! is weaker: 16 dxc5 ♘xc5 17 b4 ♘g4 18 h3! ♗xf3 19 ♕xf3 ♕h2+ 20 ♔f1 ♕e5 21 ♕xg4 ± T.Georgadze-Balashov, USSR Ch (Vilnius) 1980/1) 16 h3 ♗b4 17 ♗xd7 ♘xd7 18 ♗d2 ♗xd2 19 ♕xd2 ♗xf3 20 gxf3 ♕b7 and Black has equalized, Karpov-Portisch, Moscow 1981.

c4) 10 a3 also has its points:

c41) 10...cxd4 and now:

c411) 11 exd4 ♗xc3 12 bxc3 b5 (12...♕c7 13 ♗b2 b5 14 ♗d3 ♘b6 = is quoted in *ECO* as being a game Reshevsky-Unzicker, but was in fact played in Turner-Bisguier, USA Ch (New York) 1957/8) 13 ♗d3 ♘b6 (13...♗b7 14 a4 ± Hort-Christiansen, Surakarta/Denpasar 1982) 14 ♘e5 ♗b7 15 ♗g5 (Reshevsky-Unzicker, Santa Monica 1966) and here Ftačnik correctly points out that 15...h6 16 ♗xf6 ♕xf6 17 f4 ♕e7 18 f5 exf5 intending ...f6 is Black's best.

c412) 11 axb4 dxc3 12 bxc3 ♕c7 13 ♗b2 (13 e4 isn't mentioned in *ECO*, but is nonetheless a good try for White as his bishops should promise him an advantage in the long term) 13...e5 14 e4 (14 ♗b3 e4 15 ♘d4 ♘e5 16 h3 with chances for both sides, Knaak-Enders, East German Ch (Nordhausen) 1986) 14...♘b6 15 ♗b3 ♗e6 (15...♗g4?! 16 ♖a5! ♖ac8 17 c4 ♘bd7 18 h3 is clearly better for White thanks to his bishops and spatial advantage, Evans-Reshevsky, USA Ch (New York) 1963/4) 16 ♗xe6 fxe6 and now 17 ♘d2 is given as unclear in *ECO*, but 17 ♖a5 ♕c4 18 ♕e3 ♘bd7 19 ♘d2 ♕c6 20 c4 leaves White with a solid plus.

c42) 10...♗a5 and now:

c421) 11 ♖d1 b5 12 ♗a2 ♗b7 13 dxc5 ♗xc3 14 bxc3 ♕c7 15 c4 ♘g4 with chances for both sides, Korchnoi-Tal, Budva 1967.

c422) 11 ♗a2 cxd4 12 exd4 ♗xc3 13 bxc3 b5 = Psakhis-Kasparov, USSR Ch (Frunze) 1981.

c423) 11 a4 ♕c7 (11...b6 12 ♖d1 ♗b7 13 d5 exd5 14 ♘xd5 ♘xd5 15

♗xd5 ♗xd5 16 ♖xd5 ♕c7 = Sarthou-Adams, Moscow FIDE 2001) 12 ♗d2 b6 13 ♗d3 ♗b7 14 ♖ac1 e5 15 ♘xe5 ♘xe5 16 dxe5 ♕xe5 = Gulko-Balashov, Vilnius Z 1975.

c424) 11 ♗d3! and then:

c4241) 11...b5 transposes to line 'c11'.

c4242) 11...♗c7 12 ♖d1 ♕e7 13 dxc5 ♘xc5 14 ♗c2 ♘cd7 15 e4 ♘e5 (Beliavsky-Balashov, Vilnius Z 1975) 16 ♗f4 ±.

c4243) 11...♕e7 12 ♘e4 ♗c7 13 ♘xf6+ ♘xf6 14 e4 e5 15 d5 b5 16 b3 ± Scheeren – Brinck-Claussen, Silkeborg 1983.

We now return to 9...b6 *(D)*:

W

White has two main options:

C1: 10 d5 35
C2: 10 ♖d1 39

Some minor alternatives:

a) 10 ♗d3 ♗b7 11 ♖d1 cxd4 12 exd4 transposes to Line C2.

b) 10 ♗d2 ♗b7 11 ♖fd1 cxd4 and then 12 ♘xd4?! is the note to White's 11th move in Line C2; 12 exd4 transposes to note 'b' to White's 12th move in Line C2.

c) 10 a3 cxd4 and here:

c1) 11 exd4 ♗xc3 gives Black a satisfactory form of the Karpov Variation (Chapter 1).

c2) 11 ♘b5 ♗e7 (11...d3 12 ♗xd3 ♗e7 13 ♖d1 ♗b7 14 e4 ♕b8 15 ♗g5 ♘c5 = Beliavsky-Ivanchuk, Reggio Emilia 1989/90) 12 ♘bxd4 ♗b7 13 b4 a6 14 ♗b2 ♗d6 15 ♖fd1 ♕e7 16 ♖ac1 b5 17 ♗d3 ♖ac8 = Onishchuk-Lautier, Moscow rpd 2002.

c3) 11 axb4 dxc3 12 bxc3 ♗b7 13 ♗b2 ♗xf3 14 gxf3 ♘e5 15 ♖fd1 ♘d5 16 ♗xd5 exd5 17 ♖d4 ♕d7 = Zaja-Ribli, Solin/Split 2001.

C1)

10 d5 *(D)*

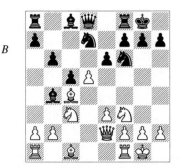

B

White throws the game headfirst into hair-raising complications, the outcome of which is still unclear.

10...♗xc3

This is pretty much forced as an exchange on d5 would leave the b4-bishop out in the cold, kept out by its own pawns on c5 and b6. On occasion, Black has tried 10...e5, which, however, is far from ideal: 11 e4 a6 (or 11...♗xc3!? 12 bxc3 a6 13 a4 ♘e8 14 ♗d3 ♘d6, Leverett-Goldin, Philadelphia 1994, 15 ♖b1!? and White is better thanks to his spatial advantage and Black's weak queenside pawns) 12 a4 ♘e8 13 ♘g5 ♗xc3 14 bxc3 ♘d6 15 f4 ♘xc4 16 ♕xc4 ± Tsamriuk-Kholmov, Makhachkala 1974.

11 dxe6 ♘e5

11...♗a5 has scored well for Black in practice, but is inferior from a theoretical point of view. White continues with 12 exd7 ♕xd7 13 ♖d1 ♕g4 (or 13...♕c7 14 e4 ♗e6 {14...♗b7 15 e5 ♖ae8 16 ♗f4 h6 17 h3 ♘e4 18 ♘h4 is much better for White} 15 ♗xe6 fxe6 and now instead of 16 e5, which left d5 to the black knight in N.Larsen-J.Andersen, corr. 1976, White should go for 16 ♘g5 ♖ae8 17 e5 ♘d5 18 ♕e4 g6 19 ♘xe6! +–) 14 h3 ♕h5 15 e4 ♗b7 16 e5 ♗xf3 17 gxf3 ♖ae8 18 ♗f4 ♕xh3 19 ♗h2 ± Gligorić-Matanović, Yugoslav Ch (Titograd) 1965.

12 exf7+

12 bxc3 gets mixed reviews: *ECO, NCO* and Gligorić give it as leading to equality, while Taimanov and Pliester claim an advantage for Black. Personally I tend to agree with the first group. 12...♘xf3+ 13 ♕xf3 ♗xe6 14 ♗xe6 fxe6 15 e4 *(D)* (15 ♕e2?! is weaker: 15...♕d7 16 f3 ♖ad8 17 ♕c4 ♕d5 18 ♕xd5 ♖xd5 and Black's better pawn-structure, his control over the d-file and White's weak c-pawn and bad bishop, leave Black clearly better, Woodhams-Parma, Buenos Aires OL 1978) and now:

a) 15...♕d7 16 ♗g5 ♕c6 (Chekhov suggests 16...♕a4!?) 17 ♗xf6 ♖xf6 18 ♕d3 ♖af8 19 ♖ad1, and now instead of 19...♖6f7?! 20 ♖d2 h6 21 ♖fd1 ♔h8 22 f3 ± as played in Gligorić-Unzicker, Moscow 1956, Black should try Chekhov's move 19...b5!?

intending ...a5 and ...b4, even if 20 e5!? looks better for White; for example, 20...♖g6 21 f3 ♕a6 22 ♖f2.

b) 15...♕e8!? is the move on which Pliester and Taimanov base their claim. The idea is to follow it up with ...♖d8 and then either ...♕c6 or ...♕g6, whichever is more effective. 16 ♗g5 (or 16 ♕e2!? ♖d8 17 f3 ♕h5 18 ♗f4 e5 19 ♗e3 ♔h8 {19...♕f7!? =} 20 ♕a6 ♖d7 21 a4 ± *Shredder 5-Nimzo 8*, Cadaques 2001) 16...♕g6 17 ♗xf6 ♕xf6 18 ♕xf6 gxf6 19 ♖fd1 ♖fd8 20 ♔f1 ♔f7 21 ♔e2 ♔e7 22 a4 = ½-½ Kouatly-Farago, Albena 1985.

c) 15...♕c7!? has only been tried once: 16 ♖e1 (16 ♗g5 ♕e5 17 ♗xf6 ♕xf6 transposes to line 'b') 16...♖ad8 17 ♗g5 h6 18 ♗h4 ♖d2 19 ♖ed1 ♕d7 and Black has at least equal chances, since the knight easily ends up becoming stronger than the bishop, Wells-Palac, Chartres 1990.

12...♔h8 13 bxc3 ♗g4 14 e4 *(D)*
14...♕e7

14...♘h5? invites trouble in through the front door. 15 ♗d5 and now:

a) 15...♗xf3 16 gxf3 ♕h4 17 f4! ♘xf4 18 ♗xf4 ♕xf4 19 ♕e3! ♕xe3 20 fxe3 ± Knaak-Sax, Thessaloniki OL 1988.

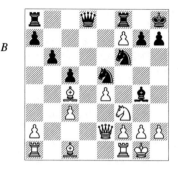

B

b) 15...♛f6 16 ♗g5 (16 ♕e3 is also effective: 16...♘xf3+ 17 gxf3 ♗xf3 18 ♕g5! ♖ad8 19 ♕xf6 ♘xf6 20 ♗g5 ♘xd5 21 ♗xd8 ♘xc3 22 ♖fe1, Kuuksma-Sadurskis, corr. 1968 and here 22...♖xd8!? 23 e5 ♘d5 24 ♖ad1! ♖f8 25 ♖d3 ♖xf7 26 ♖ee3 g5 27 ♖xf3 ♘f4 28 ♔f1 is better for White) 16...♕xg5 17 ♘xg5 ♗xe2 18 f4 ♘g6 19 ♖fe1 ♗d3 20 ♗xa8 ♖xa8 21 g3 ± Kraidman-Matanović, Netanya 1965.

c) 15...♕c8 16 ♔h1 ♗xf3 17 gxf3 ♕h3 18 ♖g1 ♘xf3 19 ♖g2 ♖ad8 20 c4 ♘h4 (20...♖xf7?? 21 ♗xf7 ♘h4 22 ♖g5 1-0 Savon-Jansa, Havana 1967) 21 ♖g3! (21 ♖g1?! ♘f3 22 ♖g2 ♘h4 23 ♖g1?! ½-½ Muir-Greenfeld, Haifa Echt 1989) 21...♘xg3+ 22 fxg3 ♘g6 23 ♗b2 with more than enough compensation for the exchange, Liavdansky-Estrin, USSR 1962.

15 ♖e1

This is the only move that offers White chances of an advantage. Other moves are harmless:

a) 15 ♗f4 ♘xc4 16 ♕xc4 ♕xe4 17 ♕xe4 ♘xe4 18 ♘e5 ♗h5 19 c4 ♗xf7 with equality, Geller-Pachman, Havana 1965.

b) 15 ♖d1 ♘xc4 16 ♕xc4 ♕xe4 17 ♕xe4 ♘xe4 18 ♖d3 ♗xf3 19 ♖xf3

♘f6 20 ♗g5 ♖xf7 = Portisch-Ljubojević, Montreal 1979.

15...b5

15...♗xf3?! is misguided as White's king will remain safe, while he will push the passed e-pawn forward with devastating effect. This was clearly illustrated in Portisch-Matanović, Zagreb 1965: 16 gxf3 ♘xc4 17 ♕xc4 ♖xf7 18 ♗g5 h6 19 ♗h4 g5 20 ♗g3 ♖af8 21 ♖ad1 ♘e8 22 e5!? ± ♖xf3 23 e6 ♔g8 24 ♖d7 ♕f6 25 ♗e5 ♕g6 26 e7+ ♖8f7 27 ♖d8 ♕c6 28 ♕e4 1-0. Black's position has collapsed.

16 ♗xb5 ♘h5

Or:

a) 16...♕e6? 17 ♘g5! ♗xe2 18 ♘xe6 ♗xb5 19 ♘xf8 ♖xf8 20 ♗a3 ± Knaak-Farago, Polanica Zdroj 1977.

b) 16...♖xf7!? and now:

b1) 17 ♗g5 ♕e6 18 ♕e3 ♗xf3 19 gxf3 and here:

b11) 19...♘h5 20 f4 ♕g4+ 21 ♔h1 ♘xf4 22 ♖g1 ♕f3+ 23 ♕xf3 ♘xf3 24 ♖g3 ♘xg5 25 ♖xg5 ♘h3 26 ♖f5 gave White a slight advantage in Miettinen-Huuskonen, corr. 1971.

b12) 19...♘fg4! is an improvement: 20 fxg4 ♘f3+ 21 ♔g2 (21 ♔h1? loses to 21...♕e5) 21...♕xg4+ 22 ♔h1 ♘xg5 with excellent chances for Black, who may even be better.

b2) In return, White may be able to improve with 17 ♗c4!?.

We now return to 16...♘h5 *(D)*:

17 ♗g5

Or:

a) In Knaak-Farago, Sochi 1980, White blundered with 17 ♗e8? in an attempt to keep the f-pawn, but after 17...♖axe8 18 fxe8♕ ♕xe8 19 ♗g5 ♘xf3+ 20 gxf3 ♗xf3 21 ♕d3 ♕e6 Black was winning.

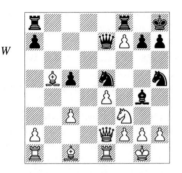

W

b) However, White can make a better attempt with 17 ♗c4, which has been played on several occasions, although even in this case Black seems to be doing fine:

b1) 17...♗xf3 18 gxf3 ♕f6 went well for Black in Aleksandrov-Naiditsch, Senden 1999: 19 ♗d5 ♘xf3+ 20 ♔g2 ♘xe1+ 21 ♕xe1 ♖ad8 and the weaknesses around White's king give Black sufficient counterplay. However, White can improve with 19 ♖d1!; e.g., 19...♘xf3+ and here it looks like both 20 ♔g2 and 20 ♔h1 lead to a better game for White.

b2) 17...♕f6 and then:

b21) 18 ♗d5? scores terribly for White: 18...♘xf3+ (18...h6 19 ♕e3 ♘xf3+ comes to the same thing, but 18...♖ad8?? loses to 19 ♗g5, Knaak-Vadasz, Trnava 1981) 19 gxf3 ♗xf3 20 ♕e3 h6 21 ♔f1 ♖ad8 (21...♖xf7, F.Portisch-Ribli, Hungary 1981, 22 ♗xf7 ♕xf7 23 ♗a3 ♖e8 24 ♖ad1 ♗xd1 25 ♖xd1 ♕xa2 26 ♗xc5 ♕c4+ 27 ♔g1 ♖xe4 28 ♖d4! = Sax) 22 ♗e6 (both 22 e5? ♕a6+ −+ Korchnoi-Sax, Skellefteå 1989 and 22 c4 ♖xd5 23 exd5 ♖xf7 −+ Gligorić-Parma, Yugoslav Ch (Vrbas) 1982 are disasters for White) and now:

b211) 22...♖xf7 23 ♗xf7 (23 ♗f5!?) 23...♕xf7 24 ♗a3 is unclear according to *ECO*. Black has at least a draw: 24...♕c4+ 25 ♔g1 ♕f7 26 ♔f1 with a repetition.

b212) However, 22...♕xe6!? 23 ♕xf3 ♘f6 24 ♔g2 ♖xf7 could easily become unpleasant for White.

b22) 18 ♗g5 ♗xf3 19 ♗xf6 ♗xe2 20 ♗d5 gxf6 21 ♗xa8 ♗d3 (21...♘f4!? 22 ♗d5 ♗d3 is the same) 22 ♗d5 ♘f4 (22...c4 can be met by 23 g3! ♘f3+ 24 ♔g2 ♘xe1+ 25 ♖xe1, when White's pawns are worth more than Black's piece) 23 ♖e3 ♘e2+ 24 ♔h1 ♘xc3 (24...c4 25 ♖e1 ♘xc3 26 ♗xc4 ♘xe4 27 ♖xe4 ♗xc4 28 f4 ♘d3 29 ♖e8 ♔g7 30 ♖1e3 ♖xf7 31 ♔g1!?, Knaak-Lukacs, East Berlin 1982, and here 31...a6! is given in *MegaBase*, and will lead to a draw after 32 ♖g3+ ♔h6 33 ♖h3+ ♔g6 34 f5+ ♔g5 35 ♖g3+ ♔h5) 25 f4 ♘g4 26 ♖g3 f5 27 exf5 ♘xd5 28 ♖xg4 ♖xf7 29 ♖e1 ♘f6 isn't without problems for White, although in the end it resulted in a draw in J.J.Kristensen-F.Kristensen, corr. 1993.

17...♕e6

17...♘xf3+ 18 gxf3 ♕xg5 19 fxg4 ♘f4 20 ♕f3 ♖xf7 21 ♗c4 ♖ff8 22 ♕g3 (22 ♔h1?! ♘g6 23 ♕g3 ♖f4 24 f3 ♖af8 gives Black excellent compensation for the pawn, Knaak-Farago, Polanica Zdroj 1974) 22...♘g6 23 ♖ad1 ♖f4 24 ♖d5 ♕h4 (24...♕xg4 25 ♕xg4 ♖xg4+ 26 ♔f1 ♘f4 27 ♖xc5 is much better for White) 25 ♕xh4 ♘xh4 26 ♖ed1 ♖xg4+ 27 ♔f1 ♖xe4 28 ♖d8+ ♖e8 29 ♖xa8 ♖xa8 30 ♖d7 ♖f8 31 ♗d5 ♘f5 32 ♔e2 1-0 (a bit premature) Ca.Hansen-S.Madsen, corr. 1975.

18 ♕e3 ♗xf3 19 gxf3 ♕xf7

Or:

a) 19...Xxf7 transposes to note 'b11' to Black's 16th move.

b) 19...♘xf7? 20 ♔h1 h6 21 ♗h4 is much better for White, Portisch-Kholmov, Budapest 1969.

20 ♗e2 (D)

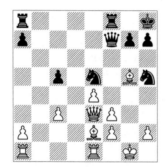

We have another interesting position on the board. Now:

a) 20...h6 21 f4 ♘xf4 22 ♗xf4 ♕xf4 and here:

a1) 23 Xad1 Xae8 24 Xd5 ♕h4 (or 24...c4 25 Xf1 ♘f3+ 26 ♗xf3 ♕xf3 27 Xd4 ♕g4+ 28 ♕g3 ♕e2 29 Xd7 Xg8 30 f3 ♕e3+ 31 ♕f2 ♕xc3 32 ♕d4 ♕xd4+ 33 Xxd4 with a better endgame for White, Gligorić-Jelen, Bled/Portorož 1979) 25 Xf1 ♘g6 (or 25...Xf4 26 f3 ± Gligorić-H.Olafsson, Lone Pine 1979) 26 ♗f3 ♘f4 27 Xxc5 ♘h3+ 28 ♔g2 ♘g5 29 Xxg5 hxg5 30 h3 Xf4 with chances for both sides, *Deep Fritz-Nimzo 8*, Cadaques 2001.

a2) 23 Xf1 Xab8 (23...♘g6 24 ♕xf4 ♘xf4 25 ♗c4 g5 26 Xad1 is better for White, Pitkanen-Palenius, corr. 1981) 24 Xab1 ♕xe3 25 fxe3 Xxf1+ 26 Xxf1 Xb2 27 Xf8+ ♔h7 28 ♔f1 Xb1+ 29 ♔f2 Xb2 30 ♔e1 Xb1+ 31 ♔d2 Xb2+ 32 ♔d1 Xxa2 33 Xe8 ♘f7 (33...♘g6

34 e5 is also better for White) 34 ♗c4 Xa1+ 35 ♔e2 ♔g6 36 h4 Xh1 37 Xe7 and White's advantage is steadily increasing, Van Oosterom-Hyldkrog, corr. 1998.

b) 20...Xae8 21 Xad1 h6 22 f4 hxg5 23 fxe5 ♘f4 24 ♕xc5 ♘h3+ 25 ♔g2 ♕e6 26 f3 ♘f4+ 27 ♔g1 ♕h3 28 ♕f2 ♘xe2+ 29 Xxe2 Xxf3 30 ♕xa7 Xef8 31 Xg2 X3f4 32 ♕d4 ♕f3 33 Xg3 ♕e2 34 Xh3+ ½-½ Lüsse-Hellström, corr. 1990. However, there is a lot to be analysed in this line and plenty of ideas that deserve to be tested.

C2)
10 Xd1 (D)

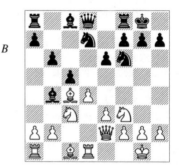

10...cxd4

Or:

a) 10...♗b7?! 11 d5 (11 ♗d2 transposes to note 'b' to White's 10th move in Line C) 11...exd5 (11...♗xc3 12 dxe6 ♗a5 13 exd7 ♕c7 14 e4 ♘xd7 15 ♘g5 +− Polugaevsky-Petrosian, USSR Ch (Leningrad) 1960) 12 ♘xd5 ♘xd5 13 ♗xd5 ♗xd5 14 Xxd5 ♕c7 15 a3 ♗a5 (Lyrberg-Bezold, Wrexham 1994) and now Pliester gives 16 ♕c2 as best, followed by either 17 b3 and ♗b2 or 17 b4!.

b) 10...♗xc3 11 bxc3 ♗b7 12 ♗d3 ♗e4 (Radev-L.Spasov, Pamporovo 1981) 13 ♗a6 ± *ECO*.

11 exd4

11 ♘xd4?! ♗b7 12 ♗d2 ♘e5 13 ♗b3 ♕e7 14 ♗e1 ♖fd8 gives Black a slight advantage, Petrosian-Parma, Bled 1961.

11...♗b7

After 11...♗xc3 12 bxc3 ♗b7 there are several possible transpositions: 13 ♗g5 is note 'f' to White's 12th move, while 13 ♗d3 is note 'a' to Black's 12th move.

12 ♗d3

Or:

a) 12 ♗b3 ♕c7 13 ♘b5 ♕b8 14 ♗g5 ♗d5 15 ♘e5 ♗xb3 with chances for both sides, Hort-Suba, Dortmund 1983.

b) 12 ♗d2 ♗xc3 (12...♖c8 13 ♗d3 transposes to the main line) 13 ♗xc3 (13 bxc3 ♕c7 14 ♗d3 ♖ac8 again transposes to the main line) 13...♘d5 14 ♗d2 ♖c8 15 ♖ac1 h6 16 ♗a6 ♖xc1 17 ♖xc1 ♕b8 = Haïk-Suba, Haifa Echt 1989.

c) 12 ♗f4 ♗xc3 13 bxc3 ♘d5 14 ♗d2 ♖c8 15 ♖ac1 ♕c7 16 ♗b5 a6 17 ♗xd7 ♕xd7 18 c4 ♘f6 19 ♘e5 ± Shabalov-Aagaard, Hamburg 1999.

d) 12 ♘e5!? ♗xc3 (12...♖c8 13 ♗g5 ♗xc3 14 bxc3 comes to the same thing) 13 bxc3 ♖c8 14 ♗g5 ♕c7 15 ♘xd7 ♘xd7 16 ♗b5 h6!? (16...♗d5 17 ♕g4 f5 18 ♕h3 ± Skembris-Beliavsky, Haifa Echt 1989; or 16...a6!? 17 ♗xa6 ♗xa6 18 ♕xa6 ♖a8 19 ♕d3 ♖a3 20 ♖dc1 ♖fa8 21 ♖c2 ± Aleksandrov-Gulko, Groningen FIDE 1997) 17 ♗e7 ♖fe8 18 ♗h4 a6 19 ♗g3 ♕d8 20 ♗xa6 ♗xa6 21 ♕xa6 ♖xc3 22 ♖ab1 ♕a8 23 ♕xa8 ♖xa8 24 d5 exd5

25 ♖xd5 ½-½ Illescas-Magem, Terrassa 1990.

e) 12 d5 is quite interesting:

e1) 12...exd5?! 13 ♘xd5 ♖e8 14 ♕c2! ♘xd5 15 ♗xd5 ♗xd5 16 ♖xd5 ♕e7 17 ♗g5 ♕e6 18 ♖ad1 ♘f6 19 ♖e5 ♕c8 20 ♕b3 ± Donner-Matanović, Leipzig OL 1960.

e2) 12...e5 13 ♗g5 ♗xc3 14 bxc3 ♖c8 15 ♗b5 e4 16 ♘d4 ♘e5 17 ♘f5 ♖c5 18 ♘g3 ♖xd5 19 ♘xe4 ± Howell-Kumaran, London 1993.

e3) 12...♗xc3 13 dxe6 ♗xf3 14 ♕xf3 (or 14 gxf3 fxe6 15 bxc3 ♕c7 16 ♗xe6+ ♔h8 17 ♗e3 ♘c5 18 ♗d5 ♘xd5 19 ♖xd5 ♘e6 = Gligorić-Unzicker, Leipzig OL 1960) 14...♘e5 15 exf7+ ♔h8 16 ♖xd8 ♘xf3+ 17 gxf3 ♖axd8 (capturing with the 'other rook', 17...♖fxd8?, is completely mistaken: 18 bxc3 ♖d1+ 19 ♔g2 ♘d7 20 f4! h6 21 ♗b2 ♖xa1 22 ♗xa1 ♖d8 23 ♗b2 g6 24 ♗d5 ± Donner-Karaklajić, Amsterdam 1965) 18 bxc3 ♖d7 (or 18...♘d5 19 ♗g5 ♖d7 20 ♖e1 h6 21 ♗xd5 ♖xd5 22 ♖e8 ♖xg5+ 23 ♔f1 ♖f5 24 ♖xf8+ ♔h7 with an equal endgame as tested several times, including Lukacs-Suba, Belgrade 1984) 19 ♗a3 ♖fxf7 20 ♗xf7 ♖xf7 21 ♖d1 ♖d7 22 ♖xd7 ♘xd7 and White's extra pawn is of no use, Portisch-Donner, Hamburg Echt 1965.

f) 12 ♗g5 ♗xc3 13 bxc3 ♕c7 *(D)* and here:

f1) 14 ♖ac1?! ♘g4! 15 d5 exd5 16 ♗xd5 ♗xd5 17 ♖xd5 ♖fe8 18 ♕d2 ♘df6 19 ♗xf6 ♘xf6 ∓ Neunhöffer-Ribli, Bundesliga 1985/6.

f2) 14 ♘d2 and then:

f21) 14...♖fe8 15 ♖ac1 e5 16 ♕d3 h6 17 ♗h4 ♖ac8 18 ♗g3 ♕d8 19 ♖e1 exd4 20 cxd4 with some initiative for

White, Mukhin-Kholmov, USSR Ch (Baku) 1972.

f22) Azmaiparashvili's 14...♘d5!? deserves a test, although after 15 ♖ac1 ♘f4 his '∓' evaluation is quite exaggerated; for example, 16 ♕g4!? ♘g6 (16...♘xg2? 17 ♗h6 g6 18 ♗f1! +−) 17 ♕g3 with chances for both sides.

f3) 14 ♗d3 ♕xc3 (Black can also consider the less risky 14...h6 15 ♗d2 ♖fe8 16 ♖e1 ♖ac8 17 ♖ac1 ♕d6 18 a4 ♖ed8 19 ♗a6 ♕d5 20 ♗xb7 ♕xb7 with approximately equal chances, Hübner-Suba, Manila OL 1992) 15 ♘e5 ♕a5 16 d5!? (16 ♕e3 ♖fe8! 17 a4 ♕d5 18 f3 ♘xe5! 19 ♕xe5 ♕xe5 20 dxe5 ♘d5 and White doesn't have enough for the pawn, Brilla Banfalvi-Bang, corr. 1988) 16...♗xd5 17 ♘xd7 ♘xd7 18 ♗b5 ♘c5? (this helps White box in the black queen, so 18...♘b8!? or possibly even 18...♘f6 should be considered) 19 ♗d2 ♕a3 20 ♖db1 a5 21 ♗c1 ♕c3 22 ♗b2 ♕b4 23 ♗xg7 and White has a much better endgame, Weiss-Farago, Austrian Cht 1998.

12...♖c8

Also to be considered:

a) 12...♗xc3 13 bxc3 ♕c7 14 c4 ♖fe8 15 ♗b2 ♕f4 16 ♕e3 ♕xe3 17 fxe3 ± Keres-Barcza, Budapest 1972.

b) 12...♖e8!? 13 ♗g5 ♗xc3 14 bxc3 ♕c7 15 ♖ac1 h6 16 ♗h4 ♘h5 17 ♗b5 is equal, Knaak-Suba, East Germany-Romania 1983.

c) 12...♘d5 13 ♗d2 ♗e7 14 ♖ac1 ♘xc3 15 bxc3 ♕c7 16 c4 ♗d6 17 ♗e4 ½-½ Petrosian-Kholmov, Moscow 1975.

13 ♗d2 ♗xc3

This exchange is quite common. Although the d-pawn now no longer is isolated, White has the hanging pawns on the c- and d-files, as well as the isolated a-pawn. These pawn weaknesses roughly balance White's bishop-pair.

Black has some alternatives that deserve a look, but not all are equally good.

a) 13...♖e8?! has been known for years to be inaccurate due to 14 ♘b5!; for example, 14...♗xf3 15 ♕xf3 ♗xd2 16 ♖xd2 ♖a8 17 ♘c3 ♖e7 18 ♖ad1 with better chances for White, Yusupov-Gschnitzer, Bundesliga 1992/3.

b) 13...♗e7?! should be met by 14 ♗a6!? ♕c7 15 ♖ac1 ♕b8 16 ♗xb7 ♕xb7 17 d5! ± according to *ECO*, but this has yet to be tried out.

c) 13...♗d6 14 ♘b5 (or 14 ♗g5 h6 15 ♗h4 ♕c7 16 ♘b5 ♕b8 17 ♘e5 {17 ♗g3!? is suggested in *Mega Database*} 17...♗xe5 18 dxe5 ♕xe5 19 ♘d6 ♕xe2 20 ♗xe2 ♖b8 21 ♗g3 ♗d5 22 ♖dc1 with full compensation for the pawn, Knaak-Pinter, East Germany-Hungary 1980) 14...♗b8 15 ♗g5 ♕e8 16 ♘e5 h6 17 ♘xd7 ♘xd7 18 ♗h4 f5 19 f3 ♘f6 20 ♗g3 ♖c6 21 ♖ac1 ± Knaak-Farago, Polanica Zdroj 1979.

d) 13...♘b8 isn't necessarily bad, but got Black into trouble in Korchnoi-Hübner, Biel 1984: 14 ♖ac1 ♘c6?!

(14...h6!?) 15 ♗g5 ♗e7 16 ♗xf6 ♗xf6 17 d5 exd5 18 ♗f5 ♖c7 19 ♘xd5 with an advantage for White.

14 bxc3 *(D)*

14 ♗xc3 has been played a few times: 14...♗xf3 15 ♕xf3 ♘d5 16 ♗d2 ♕h4 17 a3 ♘7f6 18 g3 ♕xd4 19 ♗b4 ♕xb2 20 ♖ab1 ♕e5 21 ♗xf8 ♔xf8 22 ♖bc1 and now instead of 22...♖c3?!, *Gandalf X-Fritz*, Paderborn 2002, Black should try 22...♖d8, keeping the rooks on with an interesting struggle to follow.

14...♕c7 15 ♖ac1

In Aleksandrov-Gulko, Groningen FIDE 1997, White tried 15 c4, but after 15...♖fe8, he got himself into minor difficulties with 16 ♖ac1?! (16 ♖e1 =) 16...e5! 17 ♘xe5 ♘xe5 18 dxe5 ♖xe5 19 ♗e3 ♖ce8 20 h3 ♕c6 and Black had the initiative.

15...♖fe8

15...♕d6 is given as '= Cebalo' in *ECO*, but it has been played on several occasions, including Polugaevsky-Korchnoi, USSR Ch (Tbilisi) 1959, in which White obtained a better game after 16 c4 ♖c7 17 ♕e3 ♖d8 18 h3 ♖dc8 19 ♗c3 ♖e8 20 ♗b2.

16 ♖e1 *(D)*

16 ♗b5 is also possible, but 16...a6 17 ♗xa6 ♗xa6 18 ♕xa6 ♖a8 19 ♕d3 ♖xa2 is even (*Megacorr2*). However, in the game Kluve-Portilho, corr. 1987, Black instead tried 16...♗c6 17 ♗xc6 ♕xc6 18 c4 ♘e4 19 ♗f4 ♘d6 20 ♘g5 (20 c5!? *MegaCorr2*) 20...f6 21 ♗xd6 ♕xd6 22 ♘e4 ♕e7 23 c5 with better chances for White.

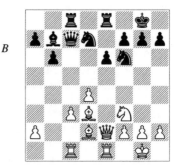

16...♕d6

Or:

a) 16...h6 17 h3 ♘d5 18 ♕e4 ♘f8 19 ♕h4 ♘e7 20 ♘e5 f6 21 ♘f3 ♘f5 = Pinter-Hulak, Lucerne OL 1982.

b) 16...♕c6 17 ♗b5 ♕d5 18 c4 ♕h5 19 ♘e5 ♕xe2 20 ♖xe2 ♖ed8 21 ♘xd7 ♘xd7 = Liberzon-Matanović, Moscow 1963.

17 ♗a6

White doesn't achieve anything with other moves:

a) 17 ♗b1 ♖c7 18 ♕d3 ♖ec8 19 ♘e5 ♘xe5 20 ♖xe5 ♕a3 ½-½ Dumitrache-Ionescu, Romanian Cht 2001.

b) 17 h3 h6 18 ♗b1 ♕d5 19 c4 ♕h5 = Scheeren-Ribli, Wijk aan Zee 1983.

17...♕d5 18 ♗xb7 ♕xb7 19 c4 ♕a6 20 ♖c2 h6 21 ♕d3 ♖ed8

White has at most a tiny pull, M.Gurevich-Chernin, Jurmala 1983.

3 ...♗a5 Systems

**1 d4 ♘f6 2 c4 e6 3 ♘c3 ♗b4 4 e3 0-0
5 ♗d3 d5 6 ♘f3 c5 7 0-0 ♘c6 8 a3**

In this chapter we discuss the following lines, of which the latter is more popular:

A: 8...♗a5 43
B: 8...dxc4 9 ♗xc4 ♗a5 49

In both cases, Black chooses to retreat his bishop to a5, rather than exchanging on c3. This retreat leaves the c5-pawn unprotected. White can often take this pawn, but Black will counter by exchanging on c3, leaving White with a disrupted pawn-structure on the queenside and with no means of protecting his newly acquired pawn advantage.

A)
8...♗a5 *(D)*

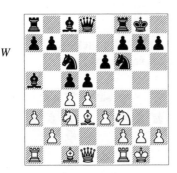

W

This was dubbed the Reykjavik Variation by Gligorić. The name stems from the famous 1st game in the 1972 world championship match between Spassky and Fischer in Reykjavik. The line was played many times before that particular game though, probably first in Landau-Flohr, Bournemouth 1939. But since the Spassky-Fischer game is the most famous game in this line, the name has some relevance.

9 cxd5!

This is considered White's best and is the reason why Black usually plays 8...dxc4 before retreating the bishop to a5. Several other moves are at White's disposal:

a) 9 h3 is quite tame: 9...dxc4 10 ♗xc4 ♕e7 (10...cxd4 11 exd4 should be compared with Line B) 11 ♕c2 ♖d8 12 ♖d1 a6 13 ♗d3 cxd4 14 exd4 h6 15 ♗e3 ♗d7 16 ♖ac1 ♗e8 with a pleasant game for Black, Djurić-B.Ivanović, Yugoslav Ch (Pljevlja) 1989.

b) 9 ♘e2 was the move Spassky played against Fischer. 9...dxc4 10 ♗xc4 and now:

b1) 10...cxd4 is probably best; e.g., 11 exd4 h6 12 ♗f4 ♗c7 13 ♗g3 ♗xg3 14 hxg3 ♕b6 15 b4 ♖d8 16 ♕d2 ♗d7 = Balashov-Langeweg, Wijk aan Zee 1973.

b2) 10...♗b6 (this is given an '!' by Gligorić, but this praise probably isn't justified) 11 dxc5 ♕xd1 12 ♖xd1 ♗xc5 13 b4 ♗e7 14 ♗b2 ♗d7! (this was Fischer's improvement over Spassky-Krogius, USSR Ch (Riga) 1958, which quickly went awry for Black after 14...b6 15 ♘f4 ♗b7 16 ♘g5 ♘d8 17 ♖ac1 h6? {17...♘c6!?} 18 ♘gxe6!

±) and now instead of 15 ♖ac1?! ♖fd8 16 ♘ed4 ♘xd4 17 ♕xd4 ♗a4 = Spassky-Fischer, Reykjavik Wch (1) 1972, White should try 15 e4! ♖fd8 16 e5 ♘e8 17 ♘g3 ♘c7 18 ♘e4 ± (Botvinnik).

b3) 10...♕e7 is suggested in *ECO*. Timman gave 11 dxc5 ♕xc5 12 ♗a2 ♖d8 13 ♕a4 b5 14 ♕h4 and now 14...b4 15 ♗d2 ±, although 14...♗b6 seems to improve.

c) 9 ♘a4 cxd4 10 exd4 dxc4 11 ♗xc4 h6 (11...♕d6 has also been tried) 12 b4 (12 ♕d3!? ♗c7 13 ♘c3 b6 14 ♖d1 ♗b7 15 b4 ♖c8 16 ♗b2 ♗b8 17 ♖ac1, Portisch-Browne, Amsterdam 1971, 17...♘e7! = Portisch) 12...♗c7 13 ♗b2 b6 (13...a6!? is interesting; e.g., 14 ♘c3 b5 15 ♗b3 ♘e7 16 ♕d3 ♗b7 looks pleasant for Black) 14 ♘e5 ♗b7 15 ♖c1 ♖c8 16 ♗b5 ♘e7 17 ♕e2 ♕d5 = Reshevsky-Levenfish, Leningrad 1939.

d) 9 dxc5 doesn't promise White anything: 9...♗xc3 10 bxc3 e5!? (the alternative 10...♕a5 is safer; e.g., 11 ♗b2 ♕xc5 12 ♕e2 ♘a5 13 ♘d2 dxc4 14 ♘xc4 ♘xc4 15 ♗xc4 e5 16 a4 ♖d8 = Uhlmann-Minev, Prague Z 1954) 11 ♘d2 (or 11 cxd5 ♕xd5 12 c4 ♕xc5 13 ♕c2 h6 14 ♗b2 ♗e6 = Bykov-Cherepkov, USSR 1957) 11...♗g4 12 ♕a4 d4! 13 ♘e4 ♘d7 (13...♘xe4 14 ♗xe4 ♗e2 15 ♖e1 d3 is also a possibility) 14 exd4 exd4 15 ♕c2 (15 cxd4!? ♘xd4 16 ♗e3 ♘e5 17 ♘d6 ♘xd3 18 ♗xd4 is more testing) 15...f5 16 ♘g3 f4 17 ♘e4 f3 18 g3 ♕e8 gives Black some compensation for the pawn, but it's not clear whether it is enough, Rivas-Nogueiras, Havana 1983.

e) 9 ♖b1 dxc4 10 ♗xc4 ♕e7 11 ♕c2 ♗d7 (11...cxd4 12 exd4 ♖d8 13

♖d1 is an interesting position; it looks like a typical IQP position, but the black bishop on a5 gives Black the unusual option of 13...♗b6, and chances are roughly balanced) 12 dxc5 (12 d5!? exd5 13 ♘xd5 ♘xd5 14 ♗xd5 also leaves White with a very slight initiative) 12...♕xc5 13 ♘e4 ♘xe4 14 b4 ♕h5 15 ♕xe4 ♗c7 16 ♗b2 with a space advantage for White, Szabo-Ivkov, Havana 1965.

f) 9 ♖e1 is according to Petursson best met by 9...dxc4 10 ♗xc4 a6, threatening ...b5. If White continues with 11 dxc5, Black can play 11...♗xc3; e.g., 12 bxc3 ♕xd1 13 ♖xd1 ♘e4 14 ♗b2 ♘a5 15 ♗e2 ♘xc5 16 c4 ♘a4 17 ♗e5 ♖e8 with a pleasant game for Black, Kluger-Troianescu, Bucharest 1954.

9...exd5

For some reason, there is no mention of 9...cxd4 in any of the books I have available. One possible line is 10 dxc6 dxc3 11 ♕c2 ♕c7 12 b4 ♗b6 13 ♕xc3 ♕xc6 14 ♕xc6 bxc6 15 ♗b2, with a better pawn-structure and development for White.

10 dxc5!

This is the only way White can make a bid for an advantage.

10...♗xc3 11 bxc3 *(D)*

11...♗g4

Black's main alternative, 11...♕a5, used to be considered inferior, but Swedish GM Hector seems to have brought the move back into business:

a) 12 ♖b1 ♕xc5 13 ♕c2 (13 ♖b5 ♕e7 14 c4 a6 15 ♖b1 dxc4 = Bronstein-Moiseev, USSR Ch (Moscow) 1951) 13...♗g4 14 ♖xb7 ♗xf3 15 gxf3 transposes to line 'b221'.

b) 12 ♕c2 and now:

b1) 12...♕xc5 will normally transpose to line 'c21' via 13 c4 dxc4 14 ♗xc4, but White can vary with 13 a4, which has scored very well. After 13...♖e8 14 ♗a3 ♕a5 White has two options:

b11) 15 ♖fb1 is theory's main line: 15...♕c7 (15...♘e5 16 ♘xe5 ♖xe5 17 ♗d6 ♖e6 18 ♖b5 ♕d8 19 ♗g3 ± Balogh-Cuadrado, corr. Wch 1950) 16 c4 dxc4 17 ♕xc4 ♗e6 18 ♕c2 ♗d5 19 ♗b2 ♕e7 20 ♗a3 (obviously 20 ♗xf6 has to be examined, since 20...♕xf6 21 ♗xh7+ ♔h8 22 ♗f5 leaves Black a pawn down; after 22...♗xf3 23 gxf3 ♘e5 24 ♕e4 ♖ad8 25 ♖d1 g6 26 ♗g4 b6, Black has some, but most likely not sufficient compensation, but this was hardly to the taste of Landau, who was a gifted tactician and loved to attack) 20...♕c7 21 ♖b5 and here instead of 21...♗xf3 22 gxf3 a6 23 ♖g5 h6 24 ♖g2, which gave White the desired kingside initiative in Landau-Flohr, Bournemouth 1939, Black should try the more solid 21...a6 22 ♖c5 ♖ad8; e.g., 23 ♖c1 ♕d6 24 ♖c3 ♕b8 with fairly level chances.

b12) 15 ♖ab1!? may actually be better: 15...♕c7 16 c4 dxc4 17 ♗xc4 ♗e6 18 ♗xe6 (18 ♗d3!? is also worth a try) 18...♖xe6 19 ♖fd1 with a solid

advantage for White, Timman-Kavalek, Amsterdam 1974.

b2) 12...♗g4!? is an idea that has been re-introduced by Hector:

b21) 13 a4?! ♗xf3 14 gxf3 ♖fe8 15 ♗a3 ♘e5 16 f4 ♖h5 (White has kept the pawn, but Black's initiative easily compensates for this) 17 f3 ♖e8 18 ♖ae1 d4! 19 cxd4 ♘xd4 20 ♕d1 ♘e6 and Black picks up another pawn; for example, 21 ♕c2 ♘xf4, F.Kristensen-Holmsgaard, corr. 1991.

b22) 13 ♖b1 ♗xf3 14 gxf3 and then:

b221) 14...♕xc5 15 ♖xb7 ♖ae8?! (15...♘e5 looks better; e.g., 16 ♗e2 ♕c8 17 ♖b4 ♕h3 and Black's initiative promises him some compensation) and now 16 a4? ♘e5 17 ♗e2 ♕c8! 18 ♖b4 ♕h3 followed by ...♖e6 gave Black a massive attack in P.M.Mortensen-Hector, Næstved 1988. However, 16 ♖b5 ♕d6 17 f4! makes it very difficult for Black to make any progress and therefore he is just a pawn down.

b222) 14...♘e5 15 ♖xb7 ♘xf3+ 16 ♔g2 ♘h4+ 17 ♔h1 ♕xc5 18 ♖b4 ♘g6 19 c4 ♘e5 with fairly balanced chances, Pyrich-J.Nielsen, corr. 1994.

b23) 13 ♘d4 and then:

b231) 13...♘e5 14 a4 ♖fd8 (another possibility is 14...♖fc8!?) 15 ♗a3 ♘xd3 16 ♕xd3 ♗d7 (not 16...♕xa4? losing to 17 c6!) 17 c6! (White very thematically sacrifices his useless extra pawn to open lines for his dark-squared bishop and disrupt Black's pawn-structure) 17...bxc6 18 ♗e7 ♖db8 19 ♗xf6 gxf6 20 ♖fc1 ± Bouwmeester-Smit, corr. 1967.

b232) 13...♕xc5 14 a4 ♖fc8 (after 14...♘xd4 15 cxd4 ♕xc2 16 ♗xc2

White has an obvious advantage) 15 ♘xc6 ♖xc6 16 ♗d2 ♗h5 17 ♖fb1 ♖c7 18 ♖b4 ♗g6 and Black has a very comfortable game, S.B.Hansen-Hector, Copenhagen 1991.

c) 12 c4 *(D)* and now:

c1) 12...♕c3 and then:

c11) 13 cxd5 ♕xa1 14 ♕c2 ♘a5 15 e4 ♗f5! (in Novotelnov-Smyslov, USSR Ch (Moscow) 1951, Black rammed his head against a wall with 15...♗d7 16 ♗b2 ♕a2 17 ♘d4 ♖fc8 18 ♖a1 ♖xc5 19 ♖xa2 ♖xc2 20 ♘xc2 +–) 16 ♗b2 ♕a2 17 ♘d2 ♘xe4 18 ♘xe4 ♕b3 (18...f6!? is more appetizing, although White clearly has enough for the exchange) 19 ♘f6+ gxf6 20 ♗xf5 ♕xc2 21 ♗xc2 ♔g7 ('=' Taimanov) 22 ♗c3 ♘c4 23 ♗d3 ♘e5 24 ♗f5 and despite being the exchange down, White has a lasting initiative in the endgame.

c12) 13 ♕c2!? ♕xc2 (13...♕xa1? 14 ♗b2 ♘b4 15 axb4 ♕a6 16 cxd5 is '±' according to Lim, but White is simply winning) 14 ♗xc2 dxc4 15 ♗b2 ('±' Lim) 15...♖d8!? 16 ♖fc1 ♖d5 17 ♗a4 ♘a5 18 ♗c3 ♖xc5 19 ♗b4 ♖h5 and White has yet to show an advantage.

c13) 13 ♖a2!? is probably White's best: 13...dxc4 14 ♗e2 ♕a5 15 ♗xc4 ♕xc5 16 ♖c2 and the two bishops should promise White the better prospects.

c2) 12...dxc4 13 ♗xc4 and then:

c21) 13...♕xc5 14 ♕c2 (14 ♕e2 ♘a5 15 ♗a2 ♗e6 16 ♗xe6 {16 ♗b2!?} 16...fxe6 17 ♘d4 ♕d5 18 ♖b1 a6 19 ♗b2 ♘c4 = Pachman-Zita, Czechoslovakia 1953) 14...♗e6 (14...♕h5 15 ♗b2 ♗g4 16 ♗e2 ♖ac8 17 ♕a4 ♘d5 18 h3 ± Lim-Gutierrez, Kikinda 1978) 15 ♗d3 ♕h5?! (15...♕xc2 16 ♗xc2 is called unclear by Lim, but nonetheless White is a tiny bit better thanks to his bishops) 16 ♗b2 ♖ac8 and now 17 ♕a4 ♗g4 18 ♕xg4 ♗xg4 19 ♘g5 gave White just a slight pull in Inkiov-Stojanović, Bor 1983, but the more direct 17 ♗xf6 gxf6 18 ♕b2 looks simply better for White.

c22) 13...♕c3 14 ♕b3 ♕xa1 (or 14...♕xb3 15 ♗xb3 ♘e4 = Keres) and now:

c221) 15 ♗b2 ♘a5 16 ♕c3 ♕xb2 17 ♕xb2 ♘xc4 18 ♕b4 ♗e6 19 ♘g5 ♗d5 (19...♘e5 20 ♘xe6 fxe6 21 ♕xb7 ♖fc8, intending ...♘c6 is unclear – Bronstein) 20 e4 a5 21 ♕c3 ♘xe4 22 ♘xe4 ♗xe4 23 ♕xc4 ♗c6 with a drawish endgame – Bronstein.

c222) The simple 15 ♗d2!? ♕xf1+ 16 ♗xf1 is English GM Peter Wells's idea, and may be better for White; e.g., 16...♘e4 17 ♗e1 ♘xc5 18 ♕c2 ♘e6 19 ♗d3 h6 20 ♗c3.

12 c4

Other moves:

a) 12 a4 is best met by 12...♕a5 since after 13 ♕c2, we have transposed to note 'b22' to Black's 11th move.

b) 12 ♗b2 ♘e5 13 c4 transposes to the note to White's 13th move.

c) 12 ♗e2 ♕e7 13 ♖b1 ♘e4 14 ♕c2 ♖ac8 15 ♗b2 ♘a5 16 ♗d3 ♖xc5 and although White later won in Stein-Tal, Kislovodsk 1966, Black has the initiative at this point.

d) 12 ♖b1 ♕c8 13 h3 ♗h5 14 ♗e2 ♖d8 15 ♗b2 ♘e4 16 ♘d2 ♗xe2 17 ♕xe2 ♘xc5 18 c4 d4 and Black already has the more comfortable position, Panno-Averbakh, Buenos Aires 1954.

e) 12 ♕c2 ♗xf3 13 gxf3 ♘e5 14 ♗e2 ♕c8 15 ♔h1 ♕xc5 with a good game for Black, Stein-Krogius, USSR 1960.

12...♘e5 *(D)*

This is almost universally played. Instead:

a) 12...dxc4 13 ♗xc4 ♕a5 14 ♗b2 gives White the better game.

b) 12...d4 is considered inadequate based on 13 ♗e2! (neither 13 exd4?! nor 13 ♖b1 offers White anything) 13...♘e4 (13...dxe3 14 ♗xe3 leaves White a pawn up, although it isn't easy to make effective use of it) 14 ♘xd4 ♘c3 15 ♕e1 ♘xe2+ 16 ♘xe2 ♕d3 17 f3 ♗e6 18 ♘f4 ♕xc4 19 ♗b2 ♕xc5 20 ♕g3! with a strong initiative for White, Vaganian-Shabanov, Daugavpils 1971.

13 cxd5

Nowadays this move is more popular than 13 ♗b2, which, however, is still given as the main line in *ECO*. Then 13...♘xf3+ (13...♘xc4 14 ♗xc4 dxc4 15 ♕xd8 ♖fxd8 16 ♗xf6 gxf6 17 ♖fc1 ♗e6 18 ♘d4 ♗d5 19 ♘f5 ± Taimanov-Flohr, USSR Ch (Moscow) 1955) 14 gxf3 ♗h3, with the following options:

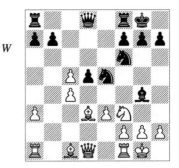

a) 15 ♔h1 dxc4 16 ♗xc4 ♗xf1 17 ♕xf1 ♕d2! 18 ♗xf6 gxf6 19 ♕h3 ♔h8 20 ♕f5 ♕c3 21 ♗d3 ♕xa1+ 22 ♗b1 ♕xb1+ 23 ♕xb1 ♖ab8 24 ♕f5 ♔g7 ½-½ Lengyel-Forintos, Budapest 1963.

b) 15 ♖e1 ♘e4! 16 ♗e5 ♕g5+ 17 ♗g3 ♘xg3 18 hxg3 dxc4 19 ♗xc4 ♕xc5 = Furman-Taimanov, USSR Ch (Kiev) 1954.

c) 15 cxd5 is an attempt to achieve more:

c1) 15...♘xd5 16 ♔h1 ♗xf1 17 ♕xf1 (Tal) gives White sufficient compensation for the exchange.

c2) 15...♘e4 16 f4 ♕xd5 (the alternative 16...♗xf1!? 17 ♗xe4 favours White) 17 ♕f3 ♕xd3 18 ♕xh3 also gives White the better chances according to Tal.

c3) 15...♕xd5 16 ♗xf6 gxf6 17 ♔h1 (not, of course, the tempting 17 ♗xh7+?? ♔xh7 18 ♕xd5 because of 18...♖g8+ 19 ♔h1 ♗g2+ 20 ♔g1 ♗xf3+) 17...♖fd8 (17...♖ad8 has no independent significance) 18 ♖g1+ ♔h8 and now:

c31) 19 ♗e2 ♕xd1 (19...♕xc5? 20 ♕a4 is very good for White) 20 ♖axd1 ♖xd1 21 ♗xd1 ♖c8 22 ♗b3 ♖xc5 23 ♗xf7 h6 and the active black pieces should enable Black to hold the draw, although in Portisch-Tal, Bled Ct (5) 1965, Black came very close to losing.

c32) 19 ♗e4 ♗g2+! (19...♛xc5 20 ♕b3 favours White) 20 ♔xg2 ♕g5+ 21 ♔h1 ♖xd1 22 ♖axd1 ♕xc5 23 ♖d5 and White's active pieces assure him the initiative, Beliavsky-Tal, Riga 1975.

c4) 15...♗xf1!? 16 ♗xf6 ♕xf6 17 ♗xf1 ♖fd8 18 e4 was given in the analysis to the stem game (Beliavsky-Tal) and tried out in Hesselbarth-Klatt, corr. 1987. After 18...♖ac8 (or 18...♕b2!?) 19 ♖b1 (19 ♖c1 ♕b2 20 a4 ♕a3 and either the c- or f-pawn falls) 19...♖xc5 20 ♖xb7 ♕g5+ 21 ♔h1 ♖c1 and Black is clearly in the driving seat. This may be why this line has fallen out of favour for White.

13...♗xf3

Or:

a) 13...♕xd5?! 14 ♗xh7+ ♔xh7 15 ♕xd5 ♘xf3+ 16 gxf3 ♘xd5 17 fxg4 ± Øgaard-Magnusson, Skopje OL 1972.

b) 13...♘xf3+?! 14 gxf3 ♗h3 15 e4 ♘d7 (15...♗xf1 16 ♗xf1 ♘d7 17 ♗e3 f5 18 ♗h3 fxe4 19 fxe4 is also pleasant for White, J.Rodriguez-Ferreira, Tucuman 1971) 16 ♔h1 ♗xf1 17 ♗xf1 ♘xc5 18 e5 ♕h4 19 ♗e3 b6 20 f4 and White's pawn-centre and bishop-pair give him a solid advantage, Donner-Pietzsch, Havana 1965.

14 gxf3 ♕xd5 15 ♗e2 ♕xc5

15...♕c6 16 ♗b2 ♖ad8 17 ♗d4 ♖fe8 18 ♖a2 ♖e7 19 ♖d2 ♖ed7 20 f4 ♘g6 21 ♗f3 ± Gustafsson-Reynolds, corr. 1981.

16 ♗b2 ♖ad8

Or 16...♖fd8 17 ♗d4 ♕e7 18 ♕c2 ♘c6 19 ♗b2 ♖d5 20 ♔h1 ♖c5 21

♕b3 ♕e6 22 ♕xe6 fxe6, with a drawable endgame for Black, Cu.Hansen-B.Pedersen, corr. 1978.

17 ♗d4 ♕c8!?

This is currently considered best. Other tries:

a) 17...♕e7 18 ♕c2 ♕e6 19 ♖fd1 b6 20 ♖ac1 ♖d5 21 ♗b2 ± Furman-Vladimirov, Gorky 1954.

b) 17...♕c6 18 ♔h1 ♕e6 19 ♕c2 (Bannik-Koblencs, Rostov-on-Don 1953) 19...♘c6 20 ♗c3 with at most a tiny advantage for White.

18 ♕b1

The older 18 ♕a4 is also playable, but OK for Black; for example, 18...♖d5 (18...♕f5!?) 19 f4 (19 ♗xe5 ♖xe5 20 f4 ♖c5 21 ♕xa7 ♘e4 gives Black good compensation for the pawn) 19...b5 (19...♕h3 also draws) 20 ♕b3 ♕h3 21 ♗xe5 ♘g4 22 ♗xg4 ♕xg4+ with a perpetual check, Antoshin-Krogius, Sochi 1964.

18...♖fe8 19 f4!?

In Tella-Lugovoi, Myyrmanni 1999, White clearly misunderstood the position, when he continued with 19 ♗xe5? ♖xe5 20 f4 ♖c5 21 ♗f3 b6 22 ♖d1 ♖xd1+ 23 ♕xd1 g6, when Black was clearly better; he controls the c-file, White has a weak a-pawn, loose king position and very little counterplay.

After the text-move (19 f4), Black has the following options:

a) 19...♖xd4?! 20 exd4 ♘c6 21 ♗f3 ♘xd4 22 ♕xb7 ♕f5 23 ♖ae1 ♖f8 24 ♗g2 ± Schekachev-Dizdar, Paris 1996.

b) 19...♘c4?! 20 ♗xf6 ♘d2 21 ♕b2 gxf6 22 ♖fd1 ±.

c) 19...♕h3 20 ♕xb7 ♖d5 21 f3 ♖xd4 22 exd4 ♘g6 23 ♗c4 ♘xf4 24

♕xf7+ ♔h8 25 ♖a2 ± Jelen-Dizdar, Portorož 1987.

d) 19...♘g6!? is a suggestion by Wells:

d1) 20 ♗f3 and now:

d11) 20...♘h4?! 21 ♕xb7 ♖d7 22 ♕xc8 ♘xf3+ 23 ♔g2 ♘h4+ 24 ♔h3 ♖xc8 25 ♔xh4 is much better for White – Wells.

d12) 20...b6!? 21 ♗xf6 gxf6 transposes to line 'd2'.

d13) 20...♘xf4! seems to be a better option for Black; e.g., 21 ♗xf6 ♘h3+ 22 ♔g2 gxf6 23 ♕xb7 ♕f5 24 ♕b1! (24 ♖ac1? ♔h8! is devastating, while 24 ♖ad1 ♔h8 25 ♖xd8 ♖xd8 is comfortable for Black) 24...♖d3 25 ♕b4 ♘g5 26 ♕g4 ♕g6 with fairly level chances.

d2) 20 ♗xf6 gxf6 21 ♗f3 b6 has been given as unclear, but 22 ♖c1 ♕h3 23 ♗g2 ♕g4 24 h3 looks more pleasant for White.

B)

8...dxc4 9 ♗xc4

9 axb4 cxd4 10 ♗xc4 transposes to the note to White's 10th move in Chapter 7.

9...♗a5 *(D)*

This is called the Larsen Variation. 9...♗xc3 10 bxc3 transposes to Line A of Chapter 6, while 9...cxd4 is Chapter 7.

The Larsen Variation was not in fact invented by Larsen, but first played in the 1930s. Only in 1964 did Larsen take up the line in his game against Kølvig in the Danish Championship. Later on he used it in games against Taimanov, Gligorić, Reshevsky and finally Portisch in their Candidates match in 1968, before putting it to rest.

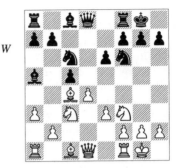

In not dissimilar fashion to the Reykjavik Variation (Line A), Black maintains pressure on the c3-knight and retains the option of ...♗xc3 if White decides to play dxc5 at some point.

It has the added benefit of not allowing White to exchange on d5 and thereby leave Black with an IQP.

Often Black enters the Larsen variation by playing 7...dxc4 8 ♗xc4 and only then 8...♘c6. The point behind this move-order is that it avoids White's extra option of 9 axb4.

10 ♕d3

This move has several points:

1) The otherwise standard move, 10...♗b6 now has little effect because of 11 ♖d1.

2) White prepares to put pressure on Black's kingside by ♗a2-b1.

However, White has a wide selection of other moves to choose from:

a) 10 ♘a4 cxd4 11 exd4 transposes to note 'c' to White's 9th move in Line A.

b) 10 ♘e2 transposes to note 'b' to White's 9th move in Line A.

c) 10 ♗d3 and now:

c1) 10...♗b6 11 dxc5 ♗xc5 12 b4 ♗e7 13 ♗b2 a6 14 ♖c1 ± Najdorf-Reshevsky, Buenos Aires 1953.

c2) 10...a6 11 ♘e4 cxd4 12 exd4 h6 13 b4 ♗c7 14 ♗b2 ♘d5 15 ♖e1 b6 16 ♖c1 ± Smyslov-Najdorf, Buenos Aires 1970.

c3) 10...♕e7 11 ♘e4! (note this idea: White exchanges the main defender of the black kingside, while getting more room for his own pieces – this idea occurs with some frequency in this and other lines) 11...♘xe4 (11...cxd4?! is worse: 12 b4 ♗b6 13 b5 ♘d8 14 ♘xf6+ ♕xf6 15 exd4 ± Portisch-Langeweg, Amsterdam 1969) 12 ♗xe4 ♗b6 13 dxc5 ♕xc5 14 b4 (Reshevsky-Burger, New York 1969) and here 14...♕e7 leaves White with only a little plus.

c4) 10...cxd4 (the most important move) 11 exd4 and then:

c41) 11...h6 12 ♗c2 ♗c7 13 ♖e1 ♖e8 14 ♗e3 b6 15 ♕e2 ♗b7 16 ♖ad1 ♘e7 17 ♘e5 ♘ed5 18 ♗c1 ± Taimanov-Mecking, Palma de Mallorca IZ 1970.

c42) 11...♗b6 12 ♗e3 ♘d5 (or 12...h6 13 ♗c2 and now not 13...♘g4? 14 ♕d3 g6 15 ♗b3 ± Taimanov-Parma, Vinkovci 1970, but 13...♕e7 followed by 14...♖d8, which seems to improve convincingly):

c421) 13 ♗g5 f6 14 ♗e3 ♘ce7 (14...♘xe3 15 fxe3 e5 is unclear according to *ECO*) 15 ♕c2 and now instead of 15...♘xe3 16 fxe3, which favoured White in Polugaevsky-Karpov, Moscow Ct (1) 1974, 15...♔h8! has been recommended, as 16 ♗xh7?? loses to 16...f5, and otherwise Black has equalized.

c422) 13 ♘xd5 exd5 (13...♕xd5 is also fully playable: 14 ♕c2 ♕h5 15 ♖ad1 ♗d7 16 ♗e2 ♕g6 17 ♕xg6 hxg6 = Reshevsky-Parma, Netanya 1971)

14 h3 ♘e7 (14...h6 15 ♗c2 ♘e7 16 ♘e5 ♗f5 17 ♗b3 ♕d6 = Furman-Gipslis, Moscow 1970) 15 ♗g5 (15 ♕c2!?) 15...f6 16 ♗d2 ♗f5 17 ♗b4 ♗xd3 18 ♕xd3 ♖e8 19 ♖fe1 ♕d7 and Black has effortlessly equalized, Gligorić-Karpov, Hastings 1971/2.

d) 10 ♗a2!? *(D)* and now:

d1) 10...cxd4 11 exd4 ♗b6 12 ♗e3 ♘d5 13 ♕e2 (Gligorić mentions 13 ♘xd5 exd5 14 ♕d3! without giving an evaluation, but White must be a bit better) 13...♘ce7 14 ♖ad1 is according to Taimanov better for White, Taimanov-Parma, USSR-Yugoslavia 1973.

d2) 10...♕e7!? (this resembles the Smyslov Variation, which is Line A of Chapter 2) 11 ♕c2 ♗xc3 (11...cxd4 12 exd4 ♖d8 13 ♗e3 a6 appeals more to me) 12 ♕xc3 cxd4 13 exd4 ♕d6 (13...♖d8!?) 14 ♗g5 ♘e4 15 ♕d3 ♘xg5 16 ♘xg5 ± Garcia Palermo-Armas, Bayamo 1985.

d3) 10...a6 and now:

d31) 11 ♘e2 cxd4 12 ♘exd4 ♘xd4 13 ♘xd4 ♗c7 14 ♗d2 ♗d6 is OK for Black, Taimanov-Karpov, USSR Ch (Moscow) 1973.

d32) 11 ♘a4 cxd4 12 exd4 h6 13 ♗f4 ♗c7 14 ♗xc7 ♕xc7 15 ♕e2 ♖d8 is quite comfortable for Black, Polu-gaevsky-Karpov, Moscow Ct (3) 1974.

d33) 11 ♗b1 and here:

d331) 11...♗b6 12 ♕c2 (12 dxc5 ♕xd1?! {12...♗xc5!?} 13 ♖xd1 ♗xc5 14 b4 ♗e7 15 ♗b2 b5 16 ♘e4 ♗b7 17 ♘xf6+ gxf6 18 ♖d7 ♖fd8 19 ♗xh7+ ♔xh7 20 ♖xb7 ± Lukacs-Lechtynsky, Stara Zagora Z 1990) 12...g6 (Polu-gaevsky mentioned 12...cxd4 13 exd4 ♘xd4? 14 ♘xd4 ♗xd4 15 ♗g5 +−) 13 dxc5 ♗xc5 14 b4 ♗e7 (*ECO* suggests 14...♗d6!?, but here too White seems to have the more pleasant game; e.g., 15 ♖d1 ♕e7 16 ♗b2 e5 17 ♘g5 with a grip on the central light squares) 15 ♗b2 e5 16 ♖d1 and White's better coordinated pieces promise him the better chances, Polugaevsky-Karpov, Moscow Ct (5) 1974.

d332) 11...♕e7 12 ♕c2 ♗c7 13 ♖d1 and now:

d3321) 13...g6 14 dxc5 ♕xc5 15 ♘d5 ♕xc2 16 ♘xf6+ ♔g7 17 ♗xc2 ♔xf6 18 b4 ± Garcia Palermo-Garcia Martinez, Havana 1985. This is normally the only line given here.

d3322) However, 13...♖d8 seems somewhat more logical, not allowing the ♘d5 trick and activating the rook. White may still be a little better after 14 dxc5 ♕xc5 15 ♖xd8+ ♘xd8 16 b4 ♕d6 17 ♗b2 ♘c6, but it surely isn't much.

d4) With 10...♗b6 Black forces White to make a decision regarding his d-pawn:

d41) 11 d5 exd5 12 ♘xd5 ♗g4 (12...♘xd5 13 ♗xd5 leaves White with a slight pull) doesn't offer White anything.

d42) Therefore White has to go for 11 dxc5 ♗xc5 12 b4:

d421) 12...♕xd1 13 ♖xd1 ♗e7 is not mentioned in any books I have come across, yet in practice Black has had few problems drawing, although in theory he should be a little worse; e.g., 14 ♗b2 b6 15 e4 ♖d8 16 ♖xd8+ ♗xd8 17 e5 ♘e8 18 ♖d1 ♗b7 19 ♖d7 ♗c8 20 ♖d1 ♗b7 21 ♖d7 ♗c8 22 ♖d2 ♗b7 23 ♗b1 ♘e7 ½-½ Polugaevsky-F.Olafsson, Las Palmas 1974.

d422) 12...♗d6 13 ♗b2 ♕e7 14 ♕c2 ♗d7 15 ♖fd1 (Polugaevsky gives 15 ♘e4 ♘xe4 16 ♕xe4 as slightly better for White, which is quite true, since Black will have a hard time freeing himself from White's grip on the position) 15...♘e5 and now:

d4221) 16 ♘g5 ♖ac8 (Polugaev-sky-Karpov, Moscow Ct (7) 1974) and now 17 ♕e2 is best, although Black has equalized.

d4222) The more direct 16 ♘xe5 ♗xe5 17 f4!? was successfully tried out in Tinelli-Capuano, corr. 1978: 17...♗b8 (17...♗xc3 18 ♗xc3 ♖fc8 19 ♖ac1 ♘d5 20 ♗xd5 exd5 21 ♕f2 also leaves White better thanks to the opposite-coloured bishops) 18 ♗b1 ♖c8 19 ♕d3 (19 g4!?) 19...g6 20 g4 (20 ♘e4!? is possibly better) 20...♗e8?! (20...♗c6 is more active and better) 21 g5 ♘h5 22 ♕d4 f6? (22...e5!?) 23 ♘e4 e5 24 gxf6 1-0.

To conclude the coverage of the 10th move options, it seems like 10 ♗a2!? is an excellent alternative to the main line.

10...a6 *(D)*
11 ♖d1

White has some interesting alternatives at his disposal:

a) 11 a4 ♗d7 12 dxc5 ♕e7 13 e4 ♕xc5 14 ♗e3 ♕h5 and here:

W

a1) 15 ♗f4 ♖ac8 16 ♖ac1 ♖fd8 is slightly better for Black, Portisch-Larsen, Poreč Ct (3) 1968.

a2) Euwe suggested 15 ♘e2!? as a possible improvement, but 15...♘e5 16 ♘xe5 ♕xe5 still looks comfortable for Black.

b) 11 dxc5 is harmless against correct play from Black: 11...♕xd3 12 ♗xd3 ♗xc3 13 bxc3 ♖d8 (Ftačnik prefers 13...♘a5 14 ♖b1 ♖d8 and gives 15 ♗c2 ♗d7 16 a4 ♗e8 = but 15 ♘e5!? may be more problematic) 14 ♗c2 ♖d5 15 a4 ♖xc5 16 ♗a3 ♖xc3 17 ♖fc1 ♔h8 18 ♘g5 ♘d8 19 ♗e7 h6 20 ♗xf6 gxf6 21 ♘e4 ♖c4 22 ♘xf6 ♔g7 with an equal endgame, Portisch-Furman, Madrid 1973.

c) 11 ♘e4 b5 12 ♘xf6+ (12 ♗a2 c4 13 ♘xf6+ ♕xf6 14 ♕e4 ♗b7 15 ♗b1 g6 16 ♘e5 ♖fc8 17 ♘d7 ♕e7 18 ♘c5 ♖a7 19 ♘xb7 ♖xb7 = Thorsteins-H.Olafsson, Icelandic Ch (Gardabaer) 1991) 12...♕xf6 (Larsen has suggested 12...gxf6, which may be playable, but I don't like the look of it) 13 ♕e4 ♗b7 14 ♗d3 g6 15 dxc5 and Black can now play:

c1) 15...♖fd8 16 ♗e2 b4 17 ♕f4 (17 ♗d2!? is also possible) 17...♕e7 18 ♘g5 bxa3 19 bxa3 ♗c7 20 ♕h4 h5

and Black has sufficient compensation for the pawn, Donner-Polugaevsky, Amsterdam 1972.

c2) 15...♘b4!? 16 ♕e5 (16 ♕xb7 ♘xd3 is better for Black) 16...♕xe5 17 ♘xe5 ♘xd3 18 ♘xd3 ♖fd8 19 ♘e5 ♗c7 20 ♘f3 (the knight gets a bit of exercise before getting exchanged) and here:

c21) 20...♗xf3 21 gxf3 a5 22 ♖b1 b4 23 e4 ♖d3 24 axb4 axb4 25 ♗e3 ♗e5 26 ♖fc1 f5 (Timman-Tal, Hastings 1973/4) is given as '=' everywhere, which probably is true, but all the chances are on White's side, although Black's active pieces should secure the draw. For those who don't feel convinced by this, 20...a5 is the move...

c22) 20...a5!? 21 ♘d4 ♖d5 22 c6 ♗c8 23 ♗d2 e5 24 ♘f3 ♗g4 and a draw was soon agreed in Gligorić-Unzicker, Ljubljana 1969.

11...b5 12 ♗a2 c4

Other options:

a) 12...♗b6 and now:

a1) 13 ♕e2 cxd4 14 exd4 ♘xd4 15 ♘xd4 ♗xd4 16 ♗e3 e5 17 ♗xd4 exd4 18 ♕e5 ♖e8 19 ♖xd4 ♕b6 20 ♕d6 (Pytel-Adamski, Poland 1974) 20...♕xd6 21 ♖xd6 ♗b7 gives White control over the d-file, but that is about it, and the position is roughly equal.

a2) 13 h3 ♗b7 (13...c4 14 ♕e2 ♕e8 was suggested by Keres) 14 dxc5 ♕xd3 15 ♖xd3 ♗xc5 16 b4 ♗e7 is equal, Korchnoi-Polugaevsky, USSR Ch (Moscow) 1973.

a3) 13 ♕c2 c4 14 ♕e2 ♕e8 (since White's aim is to build up in the centre, this is the perfect reply, since Black can now meet e4 with ...e5) 15 b3 cxb3 16 ♗xb3 ♗b7 17 e4 e5 18

dxe5 ♘xe5 19 ♘xe5 ♕xe5 20 ♗b2
♗d4 (Portisch-Polugaevsky, Palma de
Mallorca IZ 1970) and now Boleslavsky gives 21 ♗d5 ♗xc3 (Taimanov
gives 21...♘xd5 22 ♖xd4 ♘xc3 23
♗xc3 '±', but after 23...♖ac8 24 ♕b2
♖fe8, Black should be doing OK) 22
♗xc3 ♕xc3 23 ♗xb7 ♖a7 as equal,
which seems to be true.

b) 12...♗b7 and then:

b1) 13 ♗b1 and here:

b11) 13...cxd4 looks natural but is
effectively met by 14 exd4 ♘e7 15
♘g5 ♘g6 16 h4! with an attack, Ani-
kaev-Shabanov, USSR 1969.

b12) 13...c4 is untried. Then 14
♕e2 ♕e8 15 ♗d2 ♗b6 transposes to
note 'c2' to White's 14th move.

b13) 13...♘e7 14 ♕e2 (14 dxc5 is
best met by 14...♗xc3 15 ♕c2 ♕a5 16
♕xc3 ♕xc3 17 bxc3 ♖fd8 =) 14...cxd4
15 exd4 ♕c7 16 ♗d2 ♗xc3 17 ♗xc3
♘ed5 with a comfortable game for
Black, Gligorić-Karaklajić, Novi Sad
1955.

b2) 13 dxc5 ♗xc3 14 ♕c2 ♕e7 15
♕xc3 ♖fd8 (15...♘e4 16 ♕c2 ♘xc5
17 e4 ♖fc8 18 ♗f4 ± Reshevsky-
Damjanović, Netanya 1969) 16 ♗d2
♘e4 17 ♕c2 ♘xc5 18 e4 (18 ♗e1 offers less: 18...♘a4! 19 ♖ac1 ♖xd1 20
♖xd1 ♖c8 21 ♗b1 g6 22 ♕e2 ♕f6 =
Portisch-Larsen, Poreč Ct (7) 1968 –
Larsen's last game with the variation
that bears his name) 18...♖ac8 19 ♗g5
f6 20 ♗e3 ♘d7 (Pomar's suggestion
20...♘a4 also leaves White better after
21 ♕e2 ♔h8 22 ♖dc1) 21 ♕e2 and
White is better thanks to his bishop-
pair and the weak e6-pawn, Portisch-
Pomar, Las Palmas 1972.

We now return to the position after
12...c4 *(D)*:

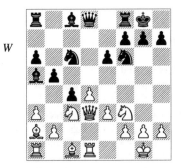

13 ♕e2

Or 13 ♕c2!? ♗b7 14 ♗b1 ♘e7 15
♕e2 ♗xc3 (15...♘ed5!? may be better;
e.g., 16 ♘a2 ♗c7 or 16 ♘xd5 exd5
with a decent game for Black) 16 bxc3
♘e4 17 ♗b2 ♘g6 18 ♖e1 f5 19 f3 ♘g5
20 a4 and White's pieces are slowly
coming to life with a better game,
Panno-Bronstein, Buenos Aires 1968.

13...♕e8 *(D)*

By the way, 13...♗b7?! doesn't do
Black any good: 14 e4 ♗xc3 15 bxc3
♘e7 16 ♗b1 ♘g6 17 ♗c2 and White
has the type of centre that Black should
strive to prevent, Gligorić-Ilievsky,
Skopje/Ohrid 1968.

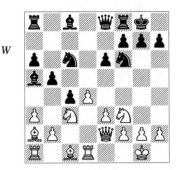

I love this move (13...♕e8), even
though that may sound somewhat silly.

However, this calm way of meeting White's central build-up is in the true spirit of Nimzowitsch.

14 e4

This is what Black's previous move prepared to meet. Other options:

a) 14 ♗b1 e5 15 d5 ♗xc3 16 bxc3 ♘a5 (16...e4 also looks attractive; e.g., 17 ♘d2 ♘a5 18 a4 ♕e5 19 ♗a3 ♖e8 with a pleasant game for Black) 17 e4 ♘b3 18 ♖a2 ♘xc1 19 ♖xc1 ♗g4 = Gligorić-Tal, Belgrade Ct (8) 1968.

b) 14 h3 e5 15 d5 ♘d8 16 e4 ♘b7 17 ♗b1 ♘d7 18 ♗c2 ♘d6 with a good game for Black, Reshevsky-Larsen, Lugano OL 1968.

c) 14 ♗d2!? ♗b6 (now 14...e5? is bad on account of 15 dxe5 ♘xe5 16 ♘d5 ± according to Taimanov) 15 ♗b1 *(D)* (or 15 b3 cxb3 16 ♗xb3 ♗b7 17 ♗e1, Portisch-Haag, Hungarian Ch (Budapest) 1968/9, 17...♖c8 = Taimanov) and now:

B

c1) 15...e5? is again wrong: 16 dxe5 ♘xe5 17 ♘e4 ♘xe4 18 ♗xe4 ♘c6 19 ♘g5! h6 (Portisch-Larsen, Poreč Ct (1) 1968) and here White should continue 20 ♕f3! ♗d7 21 ♗h7+! ♔h8 22 ♗c3, with an unpleasant position for Black:

c11) 22...hxg5? 23 ♖xd7! ♔xh7 24 ♕h5+ ♔g8 25 ♕xg5 +− Shamkovich.

c12) 22...♖d8 23 ♗f6! Shamkovich.

c13) 22...f6 23 ♗g6 ♕xg6 24 ♖xd7 ♕xg5 25 ♕xc6 ± Shamkovich.

c14) 22...♗a5 23 ♗e4 ♗xc3 24 ♖xd7 ♕xd7 25 ♗xc6 ♕e7 26 bxc3 ± (Taimanov).

c15) 22...♗d8 (best) 23 ♖xd7 ♕xd7 24 ♗e4 ♗xg5 25 ♗xc6 ♕c8 26 h4 ♗e7 27 ♗xa8 ♕xa8 28 ♕g4 f6 29 ♕e6 with a better game for White.

c2) 15...♗b7!? 16 ♘e4 (16 a4 ♘a5 = Larsen) 16...♘xe4 17 ♗xe4 f5 18 ♗c2 e5 is analysis by Euwe, who evaluates it as equal. This was given a test in Prieditis-Prokopp, corr. 1970: 19 dxe5 ♘xe5 20 ♘xe5 ♕xe5 21 ♗c3 ♕e6 (21...♕e8 looks more solid) 22 ♕h5 g6 23 ♕h6 ♖f7 24 ♖d2 ♕c6 25 ♕h3 ♖d8 26 ♖ad1 and White had the better prospects due to Black's loose king position.

14...e5 15 d5 ♘d4!? *(D)*

Another idea is 15...♘d8, intending ...♘d7 and ...♘b7 followed by either ...♘d6 or a knight to c5, as in note 'b' to White's 14th move.

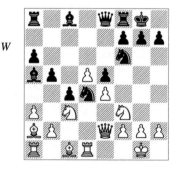

W

16 ♘xd4 exd4 17 ♖xd4 ♕e5

This move is considered better than 17...♗b6, when 18 ♗e3 ♘g4 19 e5! favours White:

a) 19...♕xe5 20 ♖xg4 ♗xg4 21 ♕xg4 ♗xe3 22 fxe3 ♕xe3+ 23 ♔f1 ♖ae8 (Knaak-Lechtynsky, Halle 1981) and here 24 ♕g3 has been recommended as leading to a better game for White.

b) Accepting White's exchange sacrifice by 19...♘xe3 doesn't make it any easier for Black: 20 ♕xe3 ♗xd4 21 ♕xd4 ♗f5 22 d6 with a truly unpleasant position for Black.

18 ♗e3 ♘g4 19 f4 ♕b8 20 ♖ad1 *(D)*

Now we have reached a very critical position for the Larsen Variation. Black can pick up an exchange to compensate for White's strong centre, but the question is whether it is enough. Black has tried the following moves:

a) 20...♘xe3 21 ♕xe3 ♗b6 22 ♗b1 a5 23 ♘xb5 (23 e5 ♗g4 24 ♖1d2 b4 is quite double-edged) 23...♗c5 24 a4

B

♗d7 25 e5 ♗xb5 26 axb5 ♕xb5 with chances for both sides, Gligorić-Gheorghiu, Skopje/Ohrid 1968.

b) 20...♗b6 21 ♗b1 ♖e8 22 e5 ♘xe3 23 ♕xe3 ♗b7 24 ♔h1 ♗xd4 25 ♖xd4 ♕a7! and now instead of 26 ♕e4?! g6 27 ♕e3?! (27 f5!?) 27...♖ad8! 28 ♘e4 ♗xd5 29 ♘f6+ ♔f8 30 ♗e4 ♗c6! 31 f5 ♕xd4 32 ♕h6+ ♔e7 and 0-1, Øgaard-Wade, Skopje OL 1972, White should try 26 ♕d2 ♖ad8 27 ♘e4 ♕b6, with a complicated game and chances for both sides.

4 Nimzowitsch Variation

1 d4 ♘f6 2 c4 e6 3 ♘c3 ♗b4 4 e3 0-0 5 ♘f3 d5 6 ♗d3 c5 7 0-0 ♘c6 8 a3 ♗xc3 9 bxc3 b6 *(D)*

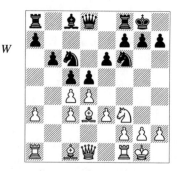

W

This position characterizes the Nimzowitsch Variation. The name is again something I have adopted from Gligorić, who acknowledges that the main contributor to this line in its early years really was the Estonian GM Paul Keres. However, since Keres helped develop so many lines, Gligorić thought that it made sense to name it after Nimzowitsch, who first employed this line in a game against Réti in Berlin 1928.

Black's plan is to play ...♗a6 and thus force the exchange of the light-squared bishops, hoping to make it more difficult for White to play e4. However, White has a fairly clear path to a safe advantage and therefore this method of playing has fallen out of favour.

10 cxd5!

It has been established that this is the most accurate way for White to continue. Other continuations leave White empty-handed:

a) 10 ♕c2 ♗a6 11 cxd5 ♗xd3 12 ♕xd3 ♕xd5 13 c4 ♕d6 (13...♕e4 is also fine, Muñoz-F.Olafsson, Reykjavik 1957) 14 ♖d1 ♖fd8 15 ♗b2 e5 is equal, Sanchez-Averbakh, Stockholm IZ 1952.

b) 10 a4 ♗a6 (this is again the simplest) 11 cxd5 ♗xd3 12 ♕xd3 exd5 13 dxc5 bxc5 14 ♗a3 c4 15 ♕c2 ♖e8 with equality, Vlagsma-Simutowe, Netherlands-Yugoslavia 1949.

c) 10 ♘e5 (this is similar to the main line, but it gives Black more options) 10...♗b7 11 f4 ♘a5 12 cxd5 ♕xd5 (in the main line Black only has ...exd5 available) 13 ♕e2 cxd4 14 exd4 ♘b3 and Black is OK, Keres-Averbakh, Zurich Ct 1953.

10...exd5 11 ♘e5!?

This is White's most popular move. However, two other moves are played with some frequency and score reasonably well for White:

a) 11 a4 c4 (11...♕c7 transposes to note 'a' to Black's 11th move in Line B of Chapter 5; this is probably Black's best option) 12 ♗c2 ♗g4 (Bondarevsky mentions that 12...♘e4 can be met by 13 ♗xe4! dxe4 14 ♘d2 f5 15 ♗a3 ♖f6 16 f3 exf3 17 ♖xf3 ±) 13 ♕e1 ♘e4 (this is better than 13...♖e8? 14 ♘h4 ♗h5 15 f3 ♗g6 16 ♘xg6 hxg6 17 e4 ± Taimanov-Botvinnik, USSR

Ch playoff (5) (Moscow) 1952 and 13...♗xf3 14 gxf3 ♕d7 15 ♔g2 ♘h5 16 ♖g1 f5 17 ♔h1 ± Taimanov) and now:

a1) After 14 ♘d2? Euwe gave 14...♘xd2? 15 ♗xd2 f5 16 f3 ♗h5 17 e4 fxe4 18 fxe4 ♖xf1+ 19 ♕xf1 ♗g6, claiming equality, even though 20 exd5 then works well for White. However, this doesn't matter as 14...♘xc3! 15 f3 ♘b4! is very strong.

a2) Therefore White should prefer 14 ♗xe4 dxe4 15 ♘d2.

b) With 11 ♗b2 White intends to open the centre with 12 dxc5 bxc5 13 c4, but after 11...c4 White's dark-squared bishop looks a bit silly on b2. 12 ♗c2 and now:

b1) 12...♘e7 13 ♘d2 ♖e8 14 ♖e1 ♗f5 15 f3 ♗xc2 16 ♕xc2 ± Najdorf-Reshevsky Buenos Aires (10) 1952.

b2) 12...♗g4 13 ♕e1 and then:

b21) 13...♘e4 14 ♘d2 ♘xd2 (or 14...♗f5 15 f3 ♘xd2 16 ♕xd2 ♗xc2 17 ♕xc2 followed by e4 with a small plus for White) 15 ♕xd2 ♗h5 16 f3 ♗g6 17 e4 ♕d7 18 ♖ae1 ± is a position that was reached twice by Petrosian as Black in the 1953 Candidates Tournament in Zurich. In the 2nd round he held Reshevsky to a draw and the same result came about in the 15th round against Smyslov. However, Petrosian needed to use all his phenomenal defensive skills; Black is clearly worse at this point.

b22) 13...♗xf3 14 gxf3 ♕d7 (the move 14...♘h5 was analysed by Bronstein, who recommends that White refrain from a quick e4, but rather prepares it with f4, f3, ♕f2, ♖ae1, ♗c1, ♔h1 and only then e4) 15 ♔g2 ♖ae8 16 ♖g1 ♘h5 17 ♕f1 f5 18 ♔h1 and now, rather than 18...f4 19 e4 ± Sverdlovsk-Novosibirsk, cities corr. 1954, Black should play 18...g6, which limits White to a slight advantage.

11...♕c7

This is Black's most solid option. Black forces White to make a decision regarding his knight on e5 and simultaneously tries to control White's upcoming central advance. Other moves:

a) 11...♘e7?! intending ...♗f5 appears logical, but is well met by 12 a4 c4 13 ♗b1 ♗f5 14 ♘c6! ±.

b) 11...♘xe5?! 12 dxe5 ♘g4 (or 12...♘d7 13 f4 c4 14 ♗c2 ♘c5 15 a4 ♗b7 16 ♗a3 ♕e7 17 a5 f6 18 ♕b1! ± Gligorić-Pomar, Beverwijk 1967) 13 f4 f5 14 h3 ♘h6 15 ♖a2 ♗e6 16 ♖d2 ♕e7 17 ♗e2 ♖ad8 18 ♗f3 ♕f7 19 c4 ± Van Oosterom-Kramer, corr. 1991-3.

c) 11...♗b7!? and now:

c1) 12 ♗b2 (intending 12...♖e8 13 ♘xc6 ♗xc6 14 c4 ±) 12...c4 13 ♘xc6 ♗xc6 14 ♗c2 ♖e8 15 a4 a5 (15...♕d7 can also be considered) 16 ♕e2 ♕e7 17 ♖fe1 g6 18 f3 ± Yusupov-Lobron, Munich 1992.

c2) 12 ♘xc6 ♗xc6 and then:

c21) 13 a4 ♕d7 14 ♕c2 and now, rather than 14...♘e4 15 f3 ♘f6 16 ♗f5 ± Najdorf-Sliwa, Leipzig OL 1960, 14...♖fe8 is OK for Black according to Yusupov.

c22) Taimanov's 13 dxc5!? bxc5 14 ♕c2 intending c4 is interesting.

c23) 13 f3 and here Taimanov gave 13...♖e8 14 ♖a2 ♕d7 15 ♖b2 ♖ac8 16 ♕e1 ±, but Yusupov's suggestion 13...♕d7!? is quite interesting. Black intends to follow up with ...♖ac8, ...cxd4, ...♗b5, followed by doubling rooks on the c-file. White's best reply seems to be something like 14 ♖a2, hoping to enter Taimanov's analysis after 14...罩fe8, but Black can possibly play 14...奧b5 with a decent game.

12 ②xc6

12 f4 is met by 12...②e7 13 f5 奧b7 14 奧d2 ②c8 15 奧e1 ②d6 = Ståhl-berg-Sämisch, Dresden 1936.

12...豐xc6 13 f3 a5

Other move don't give Black much joy:

a) 13...②e8 14 e4 cxd4 15 cxd4 豐c3 16 罩b1 豐xd4+ 17 含h1 and now:

a1) 17...dxe4? just loses material: 18 奧xe4 豐xd1 19 罩xd1 罩b8 20 奧f4.

a2) 17...②d6 18 exd5 奧f5 19 奧xf5 ②xf5 20 豐xd4 ②xd4 21 罩d1 ± Por-tisch-Pomar, Palma de Mallorca 1966.

a3) 17...奧b7 can be considered, although White has more than enough compensation for the pawn after 18 奧b2 豐c5 19 罩c1 豐d6 20 exd5 豐xd5 21 罩e1; e.g., 21...罩d8 22 豐a4.

b) 13...奧e6 14 豐e1 ②d7 15 罩a2 (15 e4 f5! is OK for Black according to Bronstein) 15...f5 16 h3 c4 17 奧b1 b5 18 g4 ②b6 19 罩g2 豐d6 20 豐h4 with a strong kingside initiative for White, Taimanov-Bagirov, Tbilisi 1957.

c) 13...奧b7 14 a4 豐d7 15 豐e1 罩fe8 16 豐h4 奧c6 17 g4 h6 18 奧f5 ± Geller-Sliwa, Gothenburg IZ 1955.

14 豐e2 *(D)*

If White allows the exchange of light-squared bishops, then Black has no problems; e.g., 14 a4 奧a6 15 奧xa6 罩xa6, Lindblom-Persitz, Leipzig OL 1960.

14...奧b7

Black has to limit White's activity in the centre and attempt to prevent

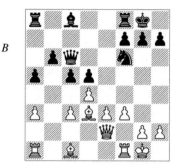

B

White from playing e3-e4. Two other moves:

a) 14...c4 15 奧c2 b5 16 豐e1 (although *ECO* gives this as played in Rabar-Petrosian, Belgrade 1954, White actually played the premature 16 e4 in that game and was soon willing to set-tle for a draw) 16...罩e8 17 豐h4 g6 18 g4 罩b8 19 奧d2 with a better game for White, Simchen-König, corr. 1982.

b) 14...罩a7!? 15 罩b1 (15 e4!? is another idea) 15...c4 16 奧c2 罩e7 17 奧d2 b5 and at this point rather than 18 罩be1 奧b7 19 豐d1 豐d6 = Vuković-Puc, Yugoslav Ch (Ljubljana) 1960, White should play 18 豐e1, intending 豐h4 and g4 with a better game.

15 a4 c4 16 奧c2 罩fe8 17 豐f2 豐e6 18 豐h4 g6 19 奧d2

Gligorić-Persitz, Hastings 1968/9. This position is generally considered slightly better for White. Black is wait-ing for White to commit himself, but with plans such as a kingside attack with g4, h4 and mobilization of all the forces on the kingside, the central e4 advance, and pressure on the b-pawn, White has all the chances.

5 Khasin Variation

1 d4 ♘f6 2 c4 e6 3 ♘c3 ♗b4 4 e3 0-0
5 ♘f3 d5 6 ♗d3 c5 7 0-0 ♘c6 8 a3
♗xc3 9 bxc3 ♕c7 (D)

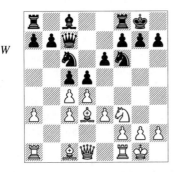

W

This variation is not very different
from the Nimzowitsch Variation,
which is covered in Chapter 4. The
main difference is that with 9...♕c7
Black prevents White from conduct-
ing the advantageous plan from the
previous chapter (10 cxd5 exd5 11
♘e5).

The Khasin Variation is also sometimes called the Pawn-Roller Variation, given that White builds up a
strong centre with f3 and e4. The central theme in this line is that Black tries
to limit White's advantage in the centre and ideally blockade it, before setting his own trump, the queenside
pawn-majority, in motion. White either builds up in the centre as mentioned above or initiates a kingside
attack with f3 and g4. The success for
either side very much depends on how
well each player conducts his own
strategy while preventing the opponent from proceeding with his.

10 cxd5!

Moves like 10 ♗b2, 10 ♕e2, 10
♖e1, 10 a4, 10 h3 and 10 ♕c2 can
transpose to lines covered in Chapter 6
after 10...dxc4 11 ♗xc4, but Black can
also attempt to side-step the transpositions:

a) 10 ♕c2 ♘a5 and now:

a1) Against 11 cxd5?! Black has
the important *zwischenzug* 11...c4!;
e.g., 12 ♗e2 exd5 13 ♘d2 ♗g4 (this
move was branded as inaccurate in
ChessBase Magazine, where 13...♖e8
was recommended, citing amongst
others the following line as proof: 14
♗f3 g6 15 e4 dxe4 16 ♘xe4 ♘xe4 17
♗xe4 ♘b3 18 ♖a2 {18 ♖b1!? ♕d6 19
♗h6 can also be tried} 18...♘xc1 19
♖xc1 ♕f4 '∓', but White can continue
20 ♗d5; for example, 20...♖e2 21
♕xe2 ♕xc1+ 22 ♕f1 ♕xc3 23 ♕xc4
♕xc4 24 ♗xc4 with approximately
equal chances) 14 ♗xg4 ♘xg4 15 g3
f5 ∓ Geller-Petrosian, Amsterdam Ct
1956.

a2) 11 ♘e5 dxc4 (or 11...b6 12
cxd5 exd5 13 f3 c4 14 ♗f5 ♘c6 15
♘g4 ♕e7 = J.Rodriguez-Panno, Havana 1969) 12 ♘xc4 ♘xc4 13 ♗xc4
♗d7 (13...cxd4 is also playable: 14
cxd4 ♗d7 15 ♕e2 ♖ac8 16 ♗d3 ♗a4
17 ♖b1 and now instead of 17...♗c2?,
Chandler-Blackstock, Brighton 1979,
Black can keep the chances equal with

17...♖fd8) 14 ♗d3 cxd4 15 exd4 (15 cxd4 ♕xc2 16 ♗xc2 ♖fc8 is of course without problems for Black) 15...♖ac8 and now, instead of 16 c4? ♗b5 with a slight advantage for Black, Prokhorovich-Averbakh, USSR Ch (Sverdlovsk) 1957, 16 ♗d2 is about equal.

b) 10 ♗b2 ♘a5?! 11 cxd5 exd5 (11...c4 usually transposes to line 'b2' after 12 ♗c2 exd5 13 ♘e5, but if White tries to take advantage of the move-order by playing 12 d6??, he loses a piece after 12...♕b6, Uhlmann-Milić, Gotha 1957) 12 ♘e5 (12 ♘d2?! can be met by 12...♖e8, or 12...♘g4 forcing 13 ♘f3) and now:

b1) 12...b5 does not have the best reputation, but *ECO*'s 'refutation' isn't exactly clear: 13 a4 (13 ♗xb5?? ♖b8 –+) and now:

b11) 13...b4 14 cxb4 (14 ♖c1! gives Black fewer options and should be preferred) 14...cxb4 15 ♖c1 ♕d6? (15...♕b6!? ±) 16 ♖c5 ± Cherepkov-Reshko, Leningrad 1963.

b12) *ECO* gives 13...♘c4 a '?', offering 14 ♗xc4 bxc4 15 ♗a3 and now 15...♘e4(?) 16 f3 +–, but 15...♖e8! is OK for Black (16 ♗xc5 ♘e4).

b2) 12...c4 13 ♗c2 and now:

b21) 13...♘c6 14 ♘xc6 (Taimanov's suggestion 14 f4!? is also worth a look, although I think 14...♘e7?!? intending ...♗f5 is an adequate reply; after 15 f5 ♖e8 16 g4 ♘c6 Black should not be worse) 14...♕xc6 15 f3 ♖e8 16 ♕d2 ♗d7 17 ♕f2 ♕b6 18 a4 ± Geller-Nikitin, Kislovodsk 1966.

b22) 13...♘e4! 14 f3 ♘d6 15 h3 (15 a4 f6 16 ♘g4 ♖e8! is given as unclear by Piket) 15...♗f5 (Piket gives 15...♖e8 as better: 16 ♖e1 f6 17 ♘g4 ♗f5 18 ♗xf5 ♘xf5 19 e4 with chances

for both sides) 16 a4 f6 17 ♘g4 ♖fe8 18 ♗a3! (Piket-Aleksandrov, Istanbul OL 2000) 18...♗xc2 19 ♕xc2 h5 20 ♘xf6+ gxf6 21 ♕g6+ ♕g7 22 ♕xg7+ ♔xg7 23 ♗xd6 ♖xe3 24 ♖ae1 ♖ae8 25 ♔f2 ♖xe1 26 ♖xe1 ♖xe1 27 ♔xe1 with a drawn endgame according to Piket.

b3) 12...b6!? 13 f3 ♗b7 14 e4 (this looks premature; 14 ♖e1!? preparing e4 seems to be a better way to proceed) and then:

b31) 14...dxe4 15 fxe4 and now 15...♗xe4 16 ♖xf6 gxf6 17 ♗xe4 fxe5 18 ♕g4+ ♔h8 19 ♕f5 f6 20 ♗xa8 ♖xa8 21 ♕xf6+ ♕g7 is at least equal for Black, while 15...♘xe4!? 16 ♕g4 ♕c8 is also sufficient for Black; e.g., 17 ♗xe4 ♕xg4 18 ♗xh7+ ♔xh7 19 ♘xg4 cxd4 20 cxd4 ♘c4 ∓.

b32) 14...c4 15 ♗c2 ♘b3 (15...dxe4 16 fxe4 and now 16...♗xe4 17 ♖xf6 ♗xc2 18 ♕xc2 gxf6 19 ♕f5 ♕e7 20 ♘d7 gives White compensation for the exchange, and 16...♘xe4 17 ♕g4 gives him compensation for the pawn) 16 ♗xb3 cxb3 17 ♕xb3 dxe4 18 fxe4 ♘xe4 19 ♖ad1 ♘c5 20 ♕c2 (20 ♕a2!? prevents 20...f6 and probably keeps an edge; for example, 20...♘a4 21 ♗a1; 20 ♖xf7 leads to an even endgame after 20...♖xf7 21 ♕xf7+ ♕xf7 22 ♘xf7 ♘a4! 23 ♘d6 ♘xb2 24 ♖d2 ♘a4 25 ♘xb7 ♖b8 26 ♘d6 ♘xc3) 20...f6 is equal, Lugovoi-Pushkov, Elista 2001.

c) 10 h3 ♖d8?! 11 cxd5 (11 ♕e2!? ♘a5?! {11...b6 and 11...dxc4 are both better} 12 cxd5 exd5 13 ♘e5 ♗e6 14 f4 ♖ac8 15 ♖b1 ♗d7 16 ♗d2 ♗a4 17 ♗e1 ♖d6 18 g4 favours White, Ibragimov-Luther, Athens 1993) 11...exd5 is similar to note 'c' to White's 11th move, although Black here rarely plays 11...♖d8 as the rook really doesn't belong on the closed d-file; e.g., 12 ♘d2 b6 13 ♖e1 ♗b7 14 ♗b2 cxd4 15 cxd4 ♘a5 16 ♖c1 ♕e7 (Ovseevich-Tolnai, Budapest 1999) 17 ♕a4 intending ♗c3 gives White a slight advantage.

10...exd5 *(D)*

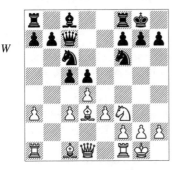

W

This is first major branching point in Khasin's Variation. The main lines are:

A: 11 ♘h4   63
B: 11 a4   69

There are several alternatives, but few of them offer White any real prospects of an advantage:

a) 11 dxc5 has long been considered inadequate: 11...♗g4 (11...♘e5 is also playable) 12 ♗e2 ♖fd8 (in the game Vaïsser-Brenninkmeijer, Hilversum 1993, White obtained an advantage after 12...♘e4 13 ♗b2 ♖ad8 14 c4 dxc4 15 ♕c2 ♗xf3 16 gxf3 due to his bishop-pair) and now, rather than 13 a4?! ♘e4 14 ♕c2 ♘xc5 ∓ Filip-Korchnoi, Curaçao Ct 1962, White should continue 13 ♗b2!? intending 13...♘e4 14 c4 dxc4 15 ♕c2 as in Vaïsser-Brenninkmeijer.

b) 11 ♘e1 and now:

b1) 11...c4 12 ♗c2 ♗g4 (Schwarz gives 12...♘g4 13 g3 f5 =) 13 f3 ♗h5 14 g4 ♗g6 15 ♘g2 ♘e7 16 ♗d2 is slightly better for White, Ježek-Ragozin, Marianske Lazne 1956.

b2) 11...♖e8 seems to accommodate White's plans of e4 less; e.g., 12 f3 ♗d7 13 g4 h6 14 ♘g2 ♖ac8 15 ♖a2 (Baragar-B.Hartman, Ottawa 1984) 15...♘a5 (15...cxd4 16 cxd4 ♘a5 is also worth considering) 16 ♘f4 cxd4 (or perhaps even 16...g5!?, when 17 ♘g2 cxd4 18 cxd4 b5 19 ♕e1 ♘c4 is a bit messy, but probably favourable for Black) 17 cxd4 b5 and Black shouldn't be any worse.

c) 11 h3 is not a very useful move and substantially weakens White's kingside structure, in particular the dark squares when White has to play both f3 and e4. Then:

c1) 11...♖d8?! transposes to note 'c' to White's 10th move.

c2) 11...♘e7 12 dxc5 ♕xc5 and instead of 13 a4 ♖e8 14 ♗a3 ♕xc3 15 ♘d4 ♗d7 16 ♕b1 with compensation for the pawn, Balashov-Dizdar, Berlin 1988, *ECO* gives 13 ♕c2 intending c4 as clearly better for White.

c3) 11...b6 12 a4 ♖e8 13 ♘d2 ♘a5 14 ♗b2 c4 (14...♗b7!?) 15 ♗c2 ♘e4 16 ♘xe4 dxe4 17 f3 ♗f5 18 ♕e1 ♗g6 19 f4 f5 20 g4 and White is in control, Iskusnykh-Balashov, Moscow 1996 (the exact move-order was 10 h3 b6 11 cxd5 exd5).

c4) 11...♖e8 12 a4 (12 dxc5 ♘a5 13 a4 ♕xc5 is fine for Black, Lukacs-Hölzl, Austrian League 1996/7) and now:

c41) 12...♘e4 13 ♗xe4 ♖xe4 14 dxc5 is possibly better for White.

c42) 12...♘e7 is best met by 13 dxc5!? ♕xc5 14 ♕c2 ♗d7 15 ♗a3 ♕c7 16 c4, when although the chances are roughly balanced, the open position suits White's bishop-pair.

c43) 12...c4 13 ♗c2 (13 ♗b1 does not seem particularly logical; in Ekström-Pelletier, Swiss Ch (Pontresina) 2000, Black obtained a pleasant game after 13...♕a5 14 ♖a3 ♘e7 15 ♘e5 ♗f5 16 ♗xf5 ♘xf5 17 ♕c2 ♘d6) 13...♘e4 (13...♕a5!?, as in Ekström-Pelletier, is definitely also worth a thought) 14 ♗xe4 dxe4 15 ♘d2 ♗f5 16 ♘xc4 ♘xd4 17 cxd4 (at first glance 17 ♕xd4 seems to work out fine for White but after 17...♖ad8 18 ♕xa7 ♕xc4 19 ♕xb7 ♖d6 20 ♕b5 ♕c8 Black's threats against the white kingside more than compensate for the pawn deficit, Stojanović-Abramović, Niš 1996) 17...♕xc4 18 ♗a3 ♗d7 = Gligorić-Stojanović, Nikšić 1996.

c5) 11...c4 (D) obliges White to make a decision regarding his bishop:

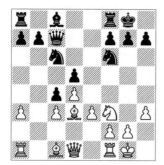

W

c51) In Keres-Evans, Munich OL 1958, White proceeded with 12 ♗b1 and after 12...♖e8 13 ♘d2 b5 14 ♖e1 ♘e4 (14...♗d7 15 e4 dxe4 16 ♘xe4 ♘d5 17 ♗d2 is pleasant for White) 15

♘xe4 dxe4 16 a4 ♖b8 17 axb5 ♖xb5 both sides had chances; Black's are based on a possible kingside initiative.

c52) 12 ♗c2 and now:

c521) 12...♘e7 is quite logical: Black wants to exchange the light-squared bishops with ...♗f5 and, with those out of the way, more easily contain White's central pawn-break. After 13 ♘e5 ♗f5 14 f3 ♗xc2 15 ♕xc2 ♘h5 (15...♘c6 16 ♘g4 ♘h5 17 e4 f5 18 exf5 ♘g3 19 ♖e1 ♘xf5 20 ♗g5, O.Rodriguez-Dizdar, Barcelona 1991, 20...♕d6!? prevents 21 ♗f6 and leaves White with only a faint initiative) 16 a4 f6 17 ♘g4 f5 18 ♘e5 ♘c6 19 ♘xc6 ♕xc6 and Black has solved his opening problems, Rechlis-Maksimović, Berlin 1988.

c522) 12...♖e8 13 ♘d2 ♗d7!? (or 13...b5 14 ♕f3 {14 ♖e1!?} 14...♗b7 15 ♗b2 ♖e7 16 ♖fe1 ♖ae8 = Beliavsky-Byrne, Moscow 1975) and then:

c5221) 14 f3? is answered with 14...♗xh3! 15 ♔f2 (15 gxh3 ♕g3+ 16 ♔h1 ♕xh3+ 17 ♔g1 ♕g3+ 18 ♔h1 is not met with 18...♘g4 19 fxg4 ♖e6, as given by Heemsoth, due to 20 ♖f5!, but by 18...♖e6! threatening 19...♘g4) 15...♖xe3! 16 ♘e4 (neither 16 ♔xe3 ♕g3! nor 16 gxh3 ♕h2+ 17 ♔xe3 ♖e8+ is especially appealing to White) 16...♖xe4 17 ♗xe4 ♕h2! –+ Zawisz-Vorobil, corr. 1987.

c5222) 14 ♖e1!? also prepares e4, but without weakening the kingside further. Although I prefer White, the chances are probably about even.

d) 11 ♗b2 doesn't seem particularly obvious, putting the bishop behind friendly pawns. Then:

d1) 11...♘a5?! transposes to note 'b' to White's 10th move.

d2) 11...c4 12 ♗c2 ♗g4 (12...♖e8 has also been tried) 13 ♕e1 ♗h5 (or 13...♗xf3 14 gxf3 ♕d7 15 ♔g2 ± Yusupov) 14 ♘h4 ♘g4 15 g3 ♗g6?! (15...♖fe8 ± Pliester) 16 ♘xg6 hxg6 17 f3 ♘f6 18 ♕f2 and the white centre soon starts rolling, Yusupov-Almasi, Altensteig 1993.

d2) 11...♗g4 12 ♕e1 ♗xf3 (other options include 12...c4, 12...♗h5 and 12...♖fe8) 13 gxf3 ♕d7 14 ♔h1 (14 ♔g2!?) 14...♕h3 15 ♕d1 cxd4 16 cxd4 ♕h4 = Karpman-Magerramov, Podolsk GMA 1989.

e) 11 ♘d2 is scoring phenomenally for White, but this isn't because of the opening. Black has tried:

e1) 11...♘g4 12 g3 c4 13 ♗b1 f5 14 ♖e1 ♖e8 (14...♗e6 15 f3 ♘f6 16 a4 ♕a5 17 ♕c2 ♖f7 18 ♗a3 ♖d8 19 ♗a2 and White's position contains more dynamic potential, Rivas-Eslon, Seville 1992) 15 ♘f1 ♗e6 16 ♖a2 ♕d7 17 f3 ♘f6 18 h3 h5 19 ♖h2 ♘e7 = Taimanov-Osnos, St Petersburg 1995.

e2) 11...c4 12 ♗c2 ♘g4 13 g3 f5 14 a4 ♕a5 15 ♖a3 ♗d7 16 ♖e1 ♖ae8 17 ♘f1 ♘f6 18 f3 ♖f7 19 ♗d2 ♕c7 20 ♖a1 g6 = Nenashev-Gavrikov, Bad Wiessee 2000.

e3) 11...♖e8 12 ♖e1 ♗g4 13 f3 ♗h5 14 ♘f1 b6 (14...♗g6!?) 15 g4 ♗g6 16 ♖a2 ♗xd3 17 ♕xd3 ♖ad8 18 ♖g2 with some initiative for White on the kingside, Tepper-Monner, corr. 1999.

A)

11 ♘h4 *(D)*

Like a lone ranger, the knight heads out on the flank to lead the white forces forward. White's idea is to play f3, ♖a2-e2 and then e4 or g4. At first, the results with this plan were quite

B

encouraging for White, but nowadays Black's chances are considered fully adequate. Now:

A1: 11...♘e7!?   64
A2: 11...♕a5!   67

Other moves:

a) 11...♗d7 12 f3 ♖fe8 transposes to line 'c24'.

b) 11...b6 12 f3 ♖e8 13 ♖a2 ♗b7 14 g4 ♘d7 15 ♘f5 ♘e7 16 ♘g3 ♘c8 17 e4 ♘d6 18 e5 ♘c4 19 f4 with an initiative for White, Barbero-Ricardi, Argentine Ch (Buenos Aires) 1985.

c) 11...♖e8 and now:

c1) 12 a4 c4 13 ♗c2 ♕a5 14 ♕e1 ♘e4 15 ♗b2 ♕d8?! (15...f6!? 16 f3 ♘g5 is better) 16 f3 ♘d2 17 ♕xd2 ♕xh4 18 e4 ± Lugovoi-Acs, Budapest 1997.

c2) 12 f3 gives Black four reasonable options:

c21) 12...♘e7 13 g3 transposes to note 'a' to Black's 12th move in Line A1.

c22) 12...b6 transposes to line 'b'.

c23) 12...♘a5 13 ♖a2 cxd4 14 cxd4 ♘c4 15 ♖e2 b5 16 e4 dxe4 17 fxe4 ♗g4 18 ♘f3 ♕b6 19 ♔h1 ♖ac8 20 ♖ee1 ± Donner-Troianescu, Havana 1971.

c24) 12...♗d7 13 ♖a2 ♕a5 14 ♗d2 ♕b6 15 ♕b1 ♘a5 (Korchnoi's suggestion 15...♕xb1!? was given a try in Nitsche-Schuetz, Canada 1987: 16 ♖xb1 b6 17 ♘f5 g6 18 ♘g3 ♖ac8 19 ♔f2 ♔g7 with about even chances) 16 ♖b2 ♕d6 17 ♗c1 ♖ac8 18 ♘f5 ♗xf5 19 ♗xf5 ♖c7 with approximate equality, Donner-Korchnoi, Amsterdam 1972.

A1)
11...♘e7!? 12 g3!?
This little move opens a retreat-square for the h4-knight and thereby avoids it being exchanged for its black counterpart. Otherwise:

a) White has to avoid 12 f3? g5, when he loses a piece.

b) 12 ♗b2 ♖e8 13 a4 ♗e6 14 ♖c1 c4 15 ♗c2 ♕d7 ∓ Petrosian-Averbakh, USSR 1974.

c) 12 ♖a2 ♘g6 13 ♘xg6 hxg6 14 f3 ♗f5 15 ♗e2 ♖ac8 16 g4 ♗d7 17 ♖b2 b6 18 ♗a6 ♖ce8 19 ♗d3 ♕c6 = Yusupov-A.Sokolov, Riga Ct (12) 1986.

d) 12 a4 is more popular than the above options, but nonetheless Black should be doing alright:

d1) 12...b6 13 ♗a3 ♗e6 14 ♖c1 ♖fd8 15 ♕e2 ♘g6 16 ♘xg6 hxg6 17 c4 dxc4 18 ♗xc4 ♗xc4 19 ♖xc4 ♖d5 20 dxc5 bxc5 21 ♖fc1 ± Knaak-Lerner, Thessaloniki OL 1988. Black's c-pawn is under pressure.

d2) 12...c4?! is premature: 13 ♗c2 (13 ♗b1!? intending ♖a2-e2 and f3 is probably best) 13...♖e8 (13...♘g6 leads to a better game for White: 14 ♘f5 ♘e4 15 ♗xe4 dxe4 16 ♕h5!? ♗e6 17 f3 exf3 18 ♕xf3 ± Blackstock-Ornstein, Budapest 1977) 14 ♕e1 (planning f3,

when he will be able to meet ...g5 with ♕g3; however, 14 g3!? is probably better, while 14 ♗a3 transposes to line 'd3') 14...♔h8!? 15 ♗a3 g6 16 g3 (16 ♘f3!? ♘c6 17 ♕b1 h6 18 ♖e1 followed by e4 is another interesting idea) 16...♗h3 17 ♘g2 ♘f5 18 ♗c1 ♖e7 19 ♗a3 ♖ee8 ½-½ Unzicker-Byrne, Haifa OL 1976.

d3) 12...♖e8 13 ♗a3 c4 14 ♗c2 and now:

d31) 14...♗d7!? has only been tried once: 15 ♕e1 ♘g6 (15...♔h8!?) 16 ♘f5 ♘e4 17 ♘g3 ♘xg3 18 hxg3 ♘e7 19 ♕b1 g6 ½-½ Donner-Geller, Wijk aan Zee 1975. However, White is a little better after 20 e4 dxe4 21 ♗xe4 ♗c6 22 ♗xc6 ♕xc6 23 ♗xe7 ♖xe7 24 ♕b5.

d32) 14...♘g6 15 ♘f5 ♘e4 gives White two interesting possibilities:

d321) 16 ♗xe4 ♖xe4 17 ♘d6!? (the older continuation 17 ♘g3 is only considered sufficient for equality by *ECO*, but after 17...♖e8 18 ♕h5 ♕c6 19 a5 ♘f8 20 f3 ♗e6 21 e4 White has the better chances, Panno-Korchnoi, Palma de Mallorca 1969) 17...♖e6 18 ♘xc8 ♖xc8 19 ♕h5 ♖d8 20 ♖fb1 ♖b6 21 ♕d1 ♖xb1 22 ♖xb1 ♕d7 23 ♖b5 with an initiative for White in the endgame, G.Georgadze-Bjerke, Gausdal 1992.

d332) 16 ♕h5 and then:

d3321) 16...♘xc3 17 ♘g3 b5 (or 17...♕c6 transposing to 'd3322') 18 ♗b4 ♘xa4 19 ♕xd5 ♗d7 20 ♗xa4 bxa4 21 ♖fc1 ± Knaak-Tischbierek, Berlin 1989.

d3322) 16...♕c6 17 ♘g3 ♘xc3 (17...♘f6 also leads to a better game for White: 18 ♕d1 b6 19 ♕d2 ♗b7 20 f3 ± Anton-Vlaud, corr. 1989) 18 ♗b2

♘e4 19 ♘xe4 dxe4 20 d5 ♕d6 21 ♗d4 and although Black is a pawn ahead, White's bishop-pair and better coordination provide him with ample compensation, Knaak-Zilbershtein, Tallinn 1979.

d3323) 16...♗xf5! 17 ♕xf5 ♖ad8 18 ♗b4 ♘e7! = Tischbierek.

d333) 16 ♘g3 is better according to Tischbierek. 16...♘xc3 17 ♕h5 ♕c6 transposes to 'd3322' without allowing 16...♗xf5.

d4) 12...♘g6 13 ♘f5 (exchanging on g6 robs White's position of its dynamism) 13...♖e8!? (13...c4 14 ♗c2 ♘e4 15 ♘g3 f5 16 ♘e2 ♗d7 has been considered equal since Donner-Parma, Beverwijk 1964) 14 f3 ♗d7 (Black refuses to close the centre with ...c4 and thereby leaves his intentions open; White is struggling to find a plan) 15 ♖a2 ♖ac8 16 ♔h1 ♘e7 17 ♘g3 ♘c6 18 ♗d2 h5!? 19 ♖e1 g6 with chances for both sides, Muir-Motwani, British Ch (Plymouth) 1989.

We now return to 12 g3!? (D):

12...♗h3!?

Other moves include:

a) 12...♖e8 13 f3 ♘g6 14 ♘f5 (14 ♘g2 may also be worth a thought)

14...♗xf5 (14...♘e7!?) 15 ♗xf5 ♘e7 16 ♗b1 ♘c8 17 ♖a2 ♘d6 18 ♖e2 ♖ac8 19 a4 ♕a5 20 ♖fe1 (Baragar-Ehlvest, Zagreb IZ 1987) and here Ftačnik gives 20...♕xc3 21 ♗b2 ♕c4 as unclear, although 22 dxc5 ♕xc5 23 ♗d4 ♕c6 24 ♗xf6 gxf6 25 ♕d4 leaves White with a pull.

b) 12...c4 kicks the bishop:

b1) 13 ♗b1 ♘e4!? (13...♘g6 14 ♘g2 ♘e4 15 ♕e1 ♘d6 16 a4 ± Berger-Pachman, Amsterdam IZ 1964) 14 ♕e1 ♕a5 (14...♗h3 15 ♘g2 ♕a5 is also worth considering) 15 ♗b2 ♕b6 16 ♖a2 f5 with about even chances, Khodos-A.Zaitsev, USSR Ch (Erevan) 1962.

b2) 13 ♗c2 ♘g6 14 ♘g2 ♘e4 15 ♗b2 (15 ♕e1? should be avoided due to 15...♗f5, threatening ...♘xg3 and 16 g4 is answered with 16...♘g5! ∓ Hybl-Pachman, Prague 1963) 15...f5 16 f3 ♘d6 17 a4 ♗d7 18 ♗a3 ♖ac8 19 ♕d2 and while Black has prevented e4 for now, the white position contains more dynamic potential, Portisch-Rubinetti, Palma de Mallorca IZ 1970.

c) 12...♘g6 13 ♘g2 (Pliester mentions 13 ♘f5 ♘e4 14 ♗xe4 dxe4 15 ♕h5 as deserving attention) 13...♘e4!? (13...♗h3 14 ♖e1 transposes to note 'b2' to Black's 13th move) 14 c4 (the slower 14 ♗b2 suggests itself, but Black is doing fine after 14...♖e8 15 f3 ♘d6 followed by ...♕c6 with excellent control over White's centre) 14...cxd4 15 cxd5 ♘c3 16 ♕h5 ♕d7 (16...♖d8!?), Howell-King, British Ch (Plymouth) 1989, and here 17 ♘f4!? leaves White with a slight advantage.

13 ♖e1

13 ♘g2?! has scored well in practice, but Black can obtain a good game

with 13...♗f5 14 f3 ♗xd3 15 ♕xd3 ♖ac8 16 ♗d2 ♖fe8 17 ♖a2 ♘c6 18 ♗e1 ♕b6, Gligorić-Larsen, Milan 1975.

13...♕d7

Or:

a) 13...c4 14 ♗c2 (14 ♗f1?! is positionally wrong; after 14...♗xf1 15 ♖xf1 ♘e4 16 ♗b2 f5 Black is simply better, Hjartarson-Byrne, Reykjavik 1982) 14...♘e4 (or 14...b5 15 f3 ♗d7 {15...♘g6!?} 16 e4 dxe4 17 ♗f4 ♕b6 18 fxe4 ± Brilla Banfalvi-Napolitano, corr. 1975) 15 ♗b2 f5 16 ♘g2 g5 17 f3 ♘f6 18 a4 ♗xg2 19 ♔xg2 ± Balashov-Gulko, USSR 1975.

b) 13...♘g6 can easily transpose to the main line.

b1) However, according to Pliester, it gives White a chance to play 14 ♘f5, since 14...♘e4 15 ♗xe4 dxe4 16 ♕h5 is pleasant for White. However, 14...♕d7! immediately questions this idea; e.g., 15 ♕f3 c4 (not 15...♗g4? due to 16 ♘h6+ with an advantage for White) 16 ♗c2 ♕e6, leaving White with nothing better than 17 ♘h4, after which both 17...♘xh4 and 17...♗g4 18 ♕g2 ♘e4 19 ♗xe4 dxe4 are very good for Black.

b2) 14 ♘g2 c4 15 ♗c2 (15 ♗f1?! ♘e4 16 ♗d2 ♖ae8 17 ♖a2 ♖e7 18 ♕e2 ♖fe8 19 f3 ♘xd2 20 ♕xd2 h5 with a better game for Black, Boleslavsky-Uusi, Minsk 1957) 15...♘e4 16 ♗b2 ♖ae8 17 ♕e2 is given in *ECO* as slightly better for White on account of Gligorić-Averbakh, Yugoslavia-USSR (Belgrade) 1961, but in the game Bensi-Casalgrandi, corr. 1990, Black won in spectacular style after 17...♗xg2 18 ♔xg2 f5 19 f3 (19 a4!?) 19...♘g5 20 ♕d2 ♕d7 21 h4?! ♘xf3! 22 ♔xf3 f4 23 ♔g2 and here 23...fxe3

is strongest; e.g., 24 ♖xe3 ♘xh4+ with a continuing attack.

14 f3 ♘g6 15 ♘g2 cxd4

The immediate 15...♗f5!? is also worth looking into. White has then tried:

a) 16 ♗xf5 ♕xf5 17 g4 ♕c8 18 g5 ♘e8 19 a4 ♘d6 20 ♗a3 ♘f5 (another idea is 20...♘c4!?) 21 ♗xc5 ♖e8 22 e4 ♘fh4 and Black has more than enough for the pawn, Knaak-Averbakh, Polanica Zdroj 1976.

b) 16 ♗f1 h5!? (preventing g4; *ECO* only mentions 16...cxd4 17 g4! ♗e6 18 cxd4 ♘e8 19 h4 ± Shashin-Osnos, USSR 1980) 17 ♖a2 ♖ac8 18 ♖b2 (18 a4!? cxd4 19 cxd4 is about equal) 18...♖c7 19 ♗d2 c4 20 a4 ♖e8 and with total control over White's possible breaks, Black has a comfortable position, Weiss Nowak-Balashov, W.Berlin 1988.

16 cxd4 ♗f5 17 ♗f1

Or:

a) 17 g4 looks fairly logical. After 17...♗xd3 18 ♕xd3 ♖ac8 19 ♗d2 ♖fd8 20 ♖ec1 h5 the chances are fairly balanced.

b) 17 ♗b2 ♗xd3 18 ♕xd3 ♖ac8 19 ♖ac1 ♖xc1 20 ♖xc1 ♖c8 with an equal position, Thorsteins-Hjartarson, Reykjavik 1992.

17...♖ac8

The older move 17...♖fc8 is also perfectly reasonable: 18 ♖a2 ♕c6 (18...h5!? is again an interesting idea) 19 ♗d2 ♗c2 20 ♕a1 ♕d7 21 ♖c1 ♗a4 22 ♖b2 ♖xc1 23 ♕xc1 ♖c8 and despite White's bishop-pair the position is approximately equal, Gligorić-Averbakh, Yugoslavia-USSR (Rijeka) 1963.

18 ♖a2

ECO's suggestion 18 g4!? ♗c2 19 ♕d2 ♖c7 20 ♗b2 ♖fc8 was tried out in Gignac-Hampl, corr. 1992: 21 ♖ac1 ♕a4 22 ♕b4 ♕xb4 23 axb4 with fairly balanced chances.

18...♖c7 19 g4

Or 19 ♗d2 ♖fc8 20 ♗b4 ♗c2 21 ♕d2 ♗b3 22 ♖b2 ♗c4 and it's clear that Black has solved his opening problems, Zsinka-T.Tolnai, Hungary 1993.

19...♖fc8

Now:

a) 20 ♗d2?! ♗c2 21 ♕a1 ♗b3 22 ♖b2 ♗c4 23 a4 h5 24 gxh5 ♘xh5 ∓ Adelaide jr Wch 1988.

b) 20 gxf5 ♖xc1 21 ♕xc1 ♖xc1 22 ♖xc1 is better, with a continued complicated struggle ahead.

A2)
11...♕a5! *(D)*

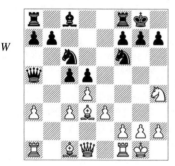

By forcing White to protect the c3-pawn with the bishop, Black prevents White from continuing his plan as outlined above. 11...♕a5 is an idea of Makarychev's, and has replaced the more traditional moves in this position.

12 ♗b2

This is White's most popular choice, but the results don't seem to vindicate this. Other moves include:

a) 12 ♕e1 ♖e8 13 ♗b2 transposes to the main line.

b) 12 ♕c2? c4 forces White to give up his control of the b1-h7 diagonal and leaves Black with a pleasant game.

c) 12 ♖b1 is a suggestion by Goldstern. The idea is to meet 12...♕xc3 with 13 ♖b5, but 12...c4 (12...a6!? is also worth a thought) 13 ♗f5 ♕xc3 14 ♖b5 (14 ♗xc8?! ♖fxc8 15 ♖xb7 ♖ab8 is pleasant for Black) 14...♗xf5 15 ♘xf5 b6 16 ♗b2 ♕d3 is fine for Black.

d) 12 ♗d2 and here:

d1) 12...c4 and then:

d11) 13 ♗b1 ♘e4 14 ♗e1 (14 f3!? ♘xd2 {14...♘d6 15 e4 ±} 15 ♕xd2 f5 16 e4 = is possibly better) 14...♕d8 15 g3 ♗h3 16 ♘g2 f5 17 f3 ♗xg2 18 ♔xg2 ♘d6 19 ♗d2 b5 with a better game for Black, Knaak-Tischbierek, Rostock 1984.

d12) 13 ♗c2 ♘e4 14 f3 ♘xd2 15 ♕xd2 ♕d8 16 g3 ♗h3 17 ♖fb1 (taking advantage of the light-squared bishop not occupying this square) 17...♖b8 18 a4 a6 19 ♖b2 ♖e8 20 ♖ab1 ♘a5 21 ♕f2 with a more pleasant game for White, Lesiège-Onishchuk, Koszalin 1999.

d2) 12...♘e4!? 13 ♗e1 c4 and here:

d21) 14 ♗b1 ♕d8 15 g3 (15 ♕c2 has the interesting point that 15...♕xh4 16 f3 ♕h6 17 fxe4 ♕xe3+ 18 ♗f2 ♕xe4 19 ♕xe4 dxe4 20 ♗xe4 gives White ample compensation for the pawn, Ezhov-Vershenkov, Orel 1992, and is best met by 15...f5 16 f3 ♘d6, when the queen-bishop line-up is a bit misplaced) 15...♗h3 16 ♘g2 f5 17

Ξa2 ♕d7 18 f3 ♘f6 19 Ξaf2 Ξfe8 20 ♗d2 Ξe7 21 Ξe1 ♗xg2 22 ♔xg2 Ξae8, intending ...♘d8-f7-d6 with total control over the white centre, A.Schneider-Shereshevsky, Budapest 1991.

d22) 14 ♗c2 ♕d8 (14...♘xc3 15 ♕h5 g6 can lead to a quick draw following 16 ♘xg6 hxg6 17 ♗xg6 fxg6 18 ♕xg6+ with a perpetual, but best is 16 ♕h6 ♘e2+ 17 ♔h1 ♕b6 18 Ξb1 ♕a6 19 ♗d1 c3 {19...♕xa3? loses to 20 ♘f3!} 20 ♗xe2 ♕xe2 21 ♗xc3 ±) 15 g3 ♗h3 16 ♘g2 f5 17 f3 ♘d6 18 ♗d2 ♕d7 with chances for both sides, Lesiège-Spraggett, Branton 2001.

12...Ξe8

12...c4 has not fared as well; e.g., 13 ♗c2 ♘e4 14 ♕e1 ♕d8 15 f3 ♘d2 (15...♘f6!?) 16 ♕xd2 ♕xh4 17 e4 ♗e6 18 Ξae1 with a clear initiative for White, Lautier-Kramnik, Monaco Amber blindfold 1997.

13 ♕e1

The alternatives are:

a) 13 ♕c1?! ♗d7 14 ♘f5 ♕c7 15 ♘g3 ♘a5 16 ♕d1 Ξad8 17 Ξe1 ♘e4 ∓ Portisch-Beliavsky, Amsterdam 1990.

b) 13 Ξe1 c4 (13...♗d7 14 f3 ± Kramnik) 14 ♗c2 ♘e4 15 Ξc1 (Kramnik suggests 15 ♕h5!?, but moves like 15...♘f6!? 16 ♕f3 ♘e4!? and 15...g6!? 16 ♕h6 with the possibility of daring to take on c3, are fine for Black) 15...♕d8 16 g3 g5 17 ♘g2 g4! ∓ Lautier-Kramnik, Tilburg 1997.

13...♕d8

Or 13...♗d7 14 f3 ♘e7 15 c4 ♕xe1 16 Ξfxe1 dxc4 17 ♗xc4 ♘ed5 18 ♗xd5 ♘xd5 19 e4 ♘f4 (19...♘e7!?) 20 dxc5 Ξac8 (Sadler-Ehlvest, Groningen FIDE 1997) 21 ♗d4!?, intending 21...♘e6 22 c6!? ±.

14 Ξd1

Or:

a) 14 ♘f5?! ♘e4 (14...♗xf5!? 15 ♗xf5 ♘e4 ∓ Gavrikov) 15 ♘g3 ♘xg3 16 hxg3 (Milov-Gavrikov, Biel 1995) and Gavrikov gives 16...♕g5!, intending 17 dxc5 ♗f5 18 ♗e2 ♕e7, as best.

b) 14 f3? is even worse because 14...♕e7 15 ♗c1 cxd4 16 cxd4 ♘xd4 costs White a pawn.

14...cxd4 15 cxd4 ♘e4 16 f3 ♘d6

Black's idea is to play ...f5 with excellent control over White's main break e4. Also, the knight may head to c4 at some point.

Obviously White cannot sit passively and let this happen...

17 g4!?

This position is quoted as '±' in ECO, but things are not that clear just yet.

17...♗d7 18 ♘g2

18 ♕g3 ♕e7 19 Ξde1 ♘a5 20 ♗c3 ♘dc4 21 ♗b4 ♕g5 22 ♘g2 Ξac8 and now instead of 23 h4 ♕d8 24 ♕f2 ♗b5 with the better game for Black, Sitchev-Van Oosterom, corr. 1988-92, White should try 23 ♗xa5 ♘xa5 24 ♕d6 ♗e6 25 ♕b4 b6 26 ♗b5 with chances for both sides.

18...♘a5 19 ♕e2 Ξc8 20 e4 ♘ac4 21 ♗a1 ♗a4 22 Ξde1 ♗b5

Vaiser-Makarychev, USSR 1982. Here Makarychev gives 23 a4 ♗xa4 24 ♘f4 with compensation for the pawn for White. Pliester in reply suggests 24...dxe4 25 fxe4 ♕g5 26 e5, after which both 26...♗d7 and 26...f6 appear adequate for Black. However, even better for Black is 24...♗c6!, which more or less forces 25 e5, and then 25...♕g5 26 ♘h5 ♗d7!. While the white centre is not as loose as in

Pliester's line, his position contains less dynamic potential and in particular the a1-bishop lacks a purpose.

B)
11 a4 *(D)*

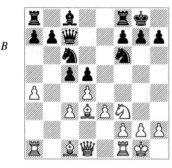

As 11 ♘h4 has shown unsatisfactory results for White after 11...♕a5, White has had to look in new directions for a way to obtain an advantage in Khasin's Variation. As we have seen in several examples, it often pays off for Black if he waits with ...c4 until he is certain that he can prevent the white centre from rolling forward. Therefore, White has taken a liking to 11 a4 as it forces Black to make a quick decision about his c-pawn and so prevents Black from keeping the central tension.

11...♖e8
Or:

a) The little tried 11...b6 is possible; e.g., 12 ♗a3 (12 h3 transposes to note 'c3' to White's 11th move) 12...♘a5 13 ♘e5 ♖e8 14 f3 ♗b7 15 ♖a2 ♖ad8 with equal chances according to *ECO*, Borisenko-Vasilchuk, USSR 1956, but this line needs to see more action before its true value can be established.

b) Although 11...c4 is played quite often, it plays right into White's hands. After 12 ♗c2, Black has tried:

b1) 12...♗g4 13 ♕e1 (13 ♗a3 ♖fe8 transposes to note 'a' to Black's 13th move) 13...♗xf3 14 gxf3 ♕d7 15 ♔h1!? (after 15 ♕e2 ♖fe8 16 ♔h1 ♕h3 17 ♖g1 ♘h5 18 e4 ♖e6 19 ♗e3 ♘e7, Black's chances are no worse, Azmaiparashvili-Vaganian, Manila OL 1992) 15...♖fe8 (15...♕h3!? 16 ♕d1 ♘h5 17 e4 ♖ad8 {17...dxe4 18 fxe4 ♕xc3? 19 ♖a3 ♕xd4 20 ♕xh5 +−} 18 ♖g1 ± Georgadze) 16 ♖g1 ♘h8 17 ♕f1 g6 18 ♕g2 ♘h5 19 e4 ♘e7 20 ♗h6 ♕e6 21 ♖ab1 b6 22 ♕g4!? is much better for White, G.Georgadze-Dydyshko, Bundesliga 1997/8.

b2) 12...♖e8 13 ♘d2 (13 ♗a3 transposes to the main line; 13 ♘h4 ♘e7 transposes to note 'd2' to White's 12th move in Line A1) 13...♗g4 (13...♘e7 14 ♗a3 ♗f5 has also been tried) 14 f3 ♗h5 15 ♖e1 ♖ad8 (15...♕a5!? 16 ♗b2 ♖ad8 was suggested by Ftačnik) 16 ♘f1 ♗g6 17 ♘g3 (17 g4 is answered by 17...♗xc2 18 ♕xc2 h5 – Ftačnik) 17...♕a5 18 ♗d2 a6 19 e4 dxe4 20 fxe4 (20 ♘xe4!? ♘d5 21 ♕b1!? is an interesting way to steer clear of the draw) 20...♘h5 21 ♘f1 ♘f6 and a draw was soon agreed upon in Kamsky-Salov, Sanghi Nagar FIDE Ct (7) 1995.

12 ♗a3
White proceeds with his plan, forcing Black to push the c-pawn. Alternatives include:

a) 12 ♘h4 transposes to note 'c1' to Black's 11th move in Line A.

b) 12 h3 transposes to note 'c4' to White's 11th move.

12...c4 13 ♗c2

13 ♗e2 is hardly an alternative; without contesting control of the important e4-square, White is left without an active plan.

13...♘e4

Black has two other options of some merit:

a) 13...♗g4 14 ♕e1 and then:

a1) 14...♕d7 15 ♘h4 ♗h5 (15...g5 16 f3 ♗e6 17 g4!? h5?! {17...♘a5!? ±} 18 ♘f5 ♔h8, Li Wenliang-Hakki, Calcutta 2001, 19 h4! ♘h7 20 hxg5 ♖g8 21 f4 +−) 16 ♗f5 ♕c7 17 f3 g5 18 g4 ♗g6 19 ♘xg6 hxg6 20 ♗b1 ♔g7 21 ♖a2 ♖h8 with chances for both sides, Babula-Lauber, Bundesliga 1996/7.

a2) 14...♗h5 15 ♘h4 and here:

a21) 15...♖e6?! 16 f3! ♖ae8 17 e4! dxe4 18 fxe4 ♘g4! 19 g3 ♘f6 20 ♖b1!? ♘xe4 21 d5 ♖e5 22 dxc6 ♘g5 23 cxb7! ± Yusupov-Hjartarson, Munich 1993.

a22) 15...♘g4?! 16 g3 ♗g6 (Black didn't have much fun with 16...♘h6?! in Neverov-Anka, Berlin 1995: 17 f3 ♕d7 18 e4 f5 19 ♗c1! fxe4 20 ♗xh6 gxh6 21 fxe4 dxe4 22 ♕e3 and the black position was falling apart) 17 ♘xg6! (17 ♗d1 ♕d7 18 ♘xg6 hxg6 19 ♖a2, Korchnoi-Illescas, Buenos Aires 1993, and here Pliester's 19...g5! 20 ♖e2 ♘f6 21 f3 g4! secures Black a pleasant game) 17...hxg6 18 ♕d2! (18 ♕e2 ♕d7 19 h3 ♘f6 = Geller-Matanović, Bled 1961) and here:

a221) 18...f5?! 19 ♖ae1 ♘f6 20 f3 ♕d7 (20...♖e6 21 g4 fxg4 22 e4! leaves White with the initiative – Dautov) 21 g4! fxg4 22 ♗xg6 ♘e7 23 ♗xe8 ♖xe8 24 ♗xe7 ♖xe7 25 ♕g2 with a big advantage for White, Yusupov-Lobron, Munich 1994.

a222) 18...♖e6?! 19 e4! (Dautov gives 19 ♖ae1 as less effective due to 19...♖ae8 20 e4 {'?' Dautov, but '!' Yusupov} 20...dxe4 21 d5 ♘ce5 22 ♗xe4 ♘xh2! 23 ♔xh2 ♘g4+ and now 24 ♔h1 ♖xe4 25 ♖xe4 ♖xe4 26 f3 ♘e3 27 ♖e1 ♕xg3 28 fxe4 ♕h4+ 29 ♔g1 ♕g3+ with a perpetual, but 24 ♔g1! improves; for example, 24...♖xe4 25 ♖xe4 ♖xe4 26 d6! ±) 19...dxe4 20 d5 ♖d8? (20...♘ce5 21 ♗xe4! ♖d8 22 ♗g2 ♘f6 23 ♕d4 ±; 20...e3 21 fxe3 ♖xe3 22 ♗c5! ♖e5 23 ♕f4 ±) 21 ♕e2 and White wins a piece, Van der Sterren-Renet, Linares Z 1995.

a223) 18...♘f6!? 19 f3 ♘a5 20 ♖ae1 (20 ♖ab1!?, forcing a decision on the queenside before proceeding in the centre, seems the right way to go) 20...♘b3 21 ♕d1 ♕c6 (21...♕a5!? may improve; e.g., 22 ♗xb3 ♕xc3 23 ♗xc4 ♖xe3! or 22 ♗b4 ♕xa4 23 e4 a5 24 ♗d6 ♖e6 25 ♗f4 ♕b5) 22 ♗xb3 cxb3 23 ♕xb3 ♖ac8 24 ♗b4 b6 25 a5 ♕b5 26 ♕a2 bxa5 27 ♗xa5 ♖e6 with some, but not fully adequate, compensation for the pawn, Beliavsky-I.Sokolov, Budva 1996.

a23) 15...♕d7 16 f3 ♕e6 17 ♗c1 ♗g6 (this is the plan behind Black's previous moves; he hopes to make the e4 advance more difficult to achieve) 18 ♘xg6 hxg6 (Matveeva-A.Marić, Belgrade wom 1996) 19 ♖b1 b6 20 ♕h4 ♕e7 21 ♖e1 soon followed by e4 with a better game for White.

a3) 14...♗xf3 15 gxf3 ♕d7 16 ♔g2 (16 ♔h1!? ± Yusupov) 16...♘h5 17 ♕d1 g6 18 ♖g1 is slightly better for White, Garcia Martinez-Troianescu, Leipzig OL 1960.

b) 13...♕a5!? was introduced by Norwegian GM Jonathan Tisdall. It hasn't been tried out that much just yet. White has replied:

b1) 14 ♕e1 ♘e4 and the f3-knight is in way. After 15 ♗b2 ♕d8 16 ♖b1 ♗f5 17 ♗a3 b6 18 ♘d2 (Norri-Veingold, Finnish Cht 1997/8) 18...♕g5 Black has a slight initiative.

b2) 14 ♕c1 ♗g4 (14...♕d8?! 15 ♘d2 b6 16 ♖e1 {16 ♕b1!? g6 17 e4 ±} 16...♗a6 17 e4 dxe4 18 ♘xe4 ♘xe4 19 ♗xe4 ♕f6 20 ♖e3 ♗b7 21 ♕c2 g6 22 ♖ae1 ± Kanko-Veingold, Vantaa 1999) 15 ♕b2 (15 ♖e1!? is worth investigating closer, while 15 ♗d6?! left Black better in Bjerke-Tisdall, Gausdal 1996: 15...♖ad8 16 ♗g3 ♘e4 17 ♗xe4 dxe4 18 ♘e5 ♘xe5 19 ♗xe5 ♗e2) 15...♕c7 16 ♖ae1 ♘e4 17 ♗xe4 ♖xe4 18 ♘d2 ♖ee8 19 e4 ♘a5 20 ♕b5 with an initiative for White, Kanko-Veingold, Helsinki 1998.

We now return to 13...♘e4 *(D)*:

14 ♗xe4

By surrendering the light-squared bishop, White hopes to be able to push the e4 advance through more easily, using the tempi he will gain through the exchange.

14 ♕e1 keeps the bishop for now and intends to proceed with 15 ♘h4 in classical fashion. However, Black has been able to neutralize this line:

a) 14...♕d8!? (preventing ♘h4) 15 ♗xe4 ♖xe4 16 ♘d2 ♖e8 17 f3 ♕a5 18 ♗b2 b5! 19 axb5 ♕xb5 = Bannik-Averbakh, USSR Ch (Riga) 1958.

b) 14...♕a5!? 15 ♗b2 ♕d8! 16 ♗xe4 ♖xe4 17 ♘d2 ♖e8 18 f3 ♗f5! 19 e4 ♗g6 (intending 20...f5 21 e5 f4 with control over the b1-h7 diagonal), Lugovoi-Greenfeld, St Petersburg-Beersheba 1998, and now Greenfeld gives 20 ♕g3!? as best; the chances are about even.

14...♖xe4 15 ♘d2 ♖e8

Or 15...♖h4!? 16 g3 (16 f4, which was once used in a correspondence world championship game, is best met with 16...♗f5) 16...♖h6, and then:

a) 17 f3 ♗h3 18 ♖f2 ♖g6 19 ♔h1 ♖e8 20 e4 (20 ♖e2!? Pliester) 20...dxe4 21 fxe4 ♘a5 22 ♕e2 ♘b3 and Black has solved his opening problems, Azmaiparashvili-Ljubojević, Leon 1994.

b) 17 e4 and here:

b1) 17...♕a5? 18 ♖e1 ♗e6 (or 18...♕xc3 19 exd5 +− Almasi) 19 ♖e3! dxe4 20 ♘xe4 ♕h5 21 h4! ± Kamsky-Z.Almasi, Groningen 1995.

b2) 17...♕d7?! 18 ♕e2! ♕h3 19 f3! ± Almasi.

b3) 17...♗h3 18 ♖e1 ♕d7 19 exd5 ♕xd5 20 ♕f3 ♗e6 21 ♖ab1 ± Heigl-Schulze, corr. 1996.

b4) 17...♗e6!? (Almasi) 18 ♖e1 ♕d7 19 ♖e3 (Thompson-Nalepa, corr. 1996) 19...f5! = intending 20 e5 f4 with excellent control over the light squares.

16 e4

White has also tried some moves to prepare this advance, but with less success:

a) 16 ♖e1?! ♗f5 17 f3 ♗d3 18 e4 ♕a5 ∓ Arlandi-Komarov, Reggio Emilia 1997/8.

b) 16 ♕c2 ♗e6 17 ♖ab1 ♖ad8 18 f3 ♕d7 (M.Bengtson-G.Shahade, Framingham 2001) 19 e4 f5 20 e5 f4 =.

16...♗e6

16...dxe4!? was introduced in Lautier-Kramnik, Monaco Amber rpd 1998: 17 ♖e1 ♗f5 18 ♘xc4 ♖ad8 19 ♘e3 (Komarov suggested 19 ♕e2!? as a possible improvement) 19...♗c8 20 ♕h5 ♕a5 21 ♕xa5 ♘xa5 22 d5 b6 23 ♗b4 ♘b7 24 a5 f5 =.

17 ♖e1 *(D)*

This is White's most popular move, but two other moves deserve attention:

a) 17 e5 ♕a5 (Dautov gives the move 17...♗f5!?, continuing 18 f4 ♕a5 19 ♗b2 ♕b6 20 ♗a3 ♕a5 = but 18 ♕f3!? seems to improve) 18 ♕c2 g6?! (18...♕d8 19 f4 g6 20 f5 ♗xf5 21 ♖xf5 gxf5 22 ♕xf5 ♖e6 23 ♖f1 gives White enough compensation for the exchange – Dautov) 19 ♘f3 ♗f5 20 ♕d2 ♘d8 21 ♗b4 ♕c7 22 h3, intending 23 g4 ± Van der Sterren-Cifuentes, Dutch Ch (Amsterdam) 1996.

b) 17 ♕f3 ♕a5 18 ♗c5 ♖ad8 19 ♖fb1 dxe4 20 ♕g3 ♗d5 21 ♖b5 ♕a6 22 ♘f1 ♘a5 23 ♘e3 ♘b3 24 ♖e1 ♗e6 25 ♗b4 (Babula-Arlandi, Portorož 1998) 25...f6 with chances for both sides.

After the text-move (17 ♖e1), Black can consider the following moves:

a) 17...♕a5!? is an untried suggestion by Komarov. He continues 18

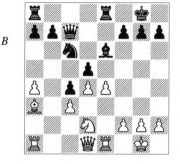

B

♕c2 dxe4 19 ♘xe4 ♗f5 without giving an evaluation.

b) 17...♘e7 18 ♗xe7 ♖xe7 19 ♘f1 dxe4 20 ♖xe4 ♗f5 21 ♖xe7 ♕xe7 22 ♘e3 ♗d3 23 a5! is slightly better for White, G.Georgadze-Arlandi, San Marino 1998.

c) 17...dxe4 18 ♘xe4 ♗d5 19 ♘d6!? (or 19 ♕g4 ♖e6 20 ♖e3 ♘e7!? 21 ♘g3 ♘g6 22 ♘f5 ♖ae8 23 ♖ae1 ♕f4 = Lautier-Gelfand, Groningen FIDE 1997) 19...♖ed8 20 ♘f5 ♗e6 21 ♘e3 (21 ♕f3!?) 21...f5 22 ♕f3 ♕a5 23 ♖ec1 ♖ac8 24 ♕g3 ♕c7 ½-½ Gligorić-Komarov, Yugoslavia 1998.

d) 17...♕d7 18 f3 (18 ♕f3!? Kacheishvili) 18...b6 (Kacheishvili gives 18...f5!? 19 e5 f4! 20 ♖b1 ♗f5 21 ♖b5 ♘d8 22 ♕c1 ♘e6 as interesting) 19 ♖b1 ♖ab8 20 ♘f1 ♘a5 21 ♖b5! a6 22 ♖b2 ♘b3 23 ♘e3 (Sturua-Kacheishvili, Georgian Ch 2000) and now 23...♕xa4 24 ♗d6 ♖bd8 25 ♗c7 ♖d7 26 exd5 ♖xc7 27 dxe6 fxe6! 28 ♘xc4 ♕xc4 leads to an equal endgame according to Kacheishvili.

6 Main Variation

The *Main Variation* is a name that has been carried over from book to book and is nowadays quite misplaced for all three lines that are covered in this chapter as they are really not the main variations any longer and haven't been for some time now – and are not likely to be so for some time to come.

1 d4 ♘f6 2 c4 e6 3 ♘c3 ♗b4 4 e3 0-0 5 ♗d3 d5

The three lines that fall under the heading of this chapter are 6 ♘f3 c5 7 0-0 ♘c6 8 a3 ♗xc3 9 bxc3 dxc4 10 ♗xc4 ♕c7, 6 a3 ♗xc3+ 7 bxc3 c5 8 cxd5 exd5 9 ♘e2 and 6 a3 ♗xc3+ 7 bxc3 dxc4 8 ♗xc4 c5 9 ♘e2. Of these lines, the first is by far the most popular.

We discuss these lines according to the following scheme:

A: 6 ♘f3 c5 7 0-0 ♘c6 8 a3 ♗xc3
   9 bxc3 dxc4 10 ♗xc4   73
B: 6 a3 ♗xc3+ 7 bxc3   89

A)

6 ♘f3 c5 7 0-0 ♘c6 8 a3 ♗xc3 9 bxc3 dxc4 10 ♗xc4 *(D)*

10...♕c7

This line used to be tremendously popular, hence the name 'Main Variation'. That is not so any longer due to the amount of theory mainly Black has to acquaint himself with, whereas White's task is much easier, having a selection of several interesting moves, although many lead to fairly balanced positions.

B

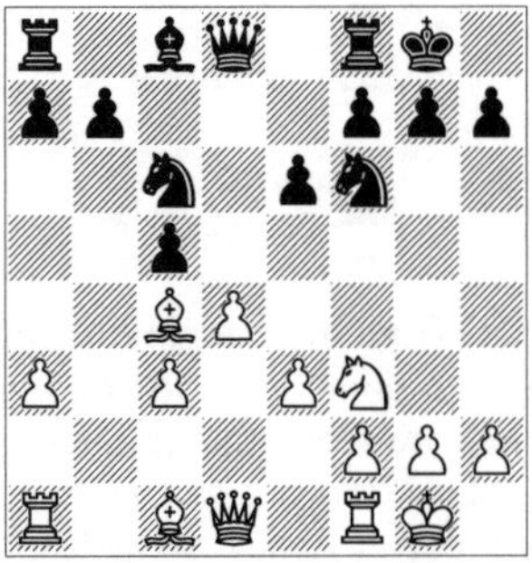

Black has a few alternatives that are seen quite rarely:

a) 10...♕e7?! 11 a4 b6 12 ♖e1 ♗b7 13 e4 h6 14 d5 ♖fd8 15 ♗d3 ♘a5 16 c4 ♘e8 17 ♗b2 ± Portisch-Miles, Tilburg 1981.

b) 10...♕a5?! 11 ♕c2 ♗d7 12 e4 cxd4 13 cxd4 ♖ac8 14 e5 ± Kozma-Papapostolou, Leipzig OL 1960.

c) 10...♘a5?! 11 ♗a2 b6 12 ♕e2 ♘e4 13 ♗b2 ♗b7 14 ♘e5 c4 15 f3 ± Ståhlberg-Weissgerber, Bad Nauheim 1936.

d) 10...b6 11 ♖e1 ♗b7 12 e4 cxd4 13 cxd4 h6 14 ♗b2 with a better game for White, Portisch-Rozentalis, Debrecen Echt 1992.

After 10...♕c7 *(D)*, we have the biggest choice of moves for White at any point in the Rubinstein Nimzo-Indian:

A1: 11 ♗e2   75
A2: 11 ♗d3   77
A3: 11 ♗a2   83
A4: 11 ♗b2   86
A5: 11 ♗b5   87

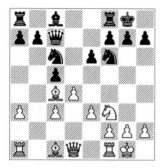

Aside from these main line moves, there are a number of sidelines, some of which are seen quite frequently:

a) 11 e4?! was a speciality of the Finnish player Ilmari Niemelää, but it isn't any good: 11...♘xe4 12 ♗d3 ♘f6 13 ♗g5 ♘e7 14 ♗xf6 gxf6 15 ♘d2 f5 ∓ Niemelää-Gislasson, Moscow OL 1956.

b) 11 ♕e2?! e5 and here:

b1) 12 dxe5 ♘xe5 13 ♘xe5 ♕xe5 14 ♗b2 (14 f3 ♗d7 is pleasant for Black, Fraguela-Byrne, Torremolinos 1976) 14...♘g4 15 g3 ♕h5 16 f3 ♘e5 17 ♗d5 c4 18 ♗xc4 ♘xc4 19 ♕xc4 ♗e6 leaves Black with sufficient compensation for the pawn, Richter-Blazi, Bavaria 1995.

b2) 12 d5 e4 13 dxc6 ♗g4 (or 13...♘g4!? 14 ♘e5 ♘xe5 15 ♗d5 bxc6 16 ♗xe4 ♗e6 with light-squared compensation – Pliester) 14 cxb7 ♕xb7 15 ♕b2 ♕xb2 16 ♗xb2 exf3 17 h3 ♗h5 ∓ Chandler-Hübner, Biel 1987.

b3) 12 ♗b5 e4 13 ♗xc6 bxc6 14 ♘e5 ♘d5 = Husari-Tischbierek, Novi Sad OL 1990.

b4) 12 h3 e4 13 ♘d2 ♘a5 14 ♗a2 b6 15 a4 ♖e8 16 ♗a3 ♗d7 = Krush-de Firmian, San Francisco 1999.

c) 11 h3 and then:

c1) After 11...e5, 12 ♗a2 transposes to Line A3, and 12 ♗b2 to Line A4.

c2) 11...♖d8 12 ♗a2 b6 (12...e5 transposes to note 'a' to Black's 12th move in Line A3) 13 ♖e1 ♗b7 14 e4 ♘e7 15 ♗b1 h6 16 ♗d3 ♖ac8 17 ♗d2 ♘g6 = Gelfand-Beliavsky, Munich 1994.

d) 11 a4 doesn't do much to challenge Black either:

d1) 11...e5 12 ♗a3 e4 13 ♘d2 b6 14 ♕c2 ♘a5 15 ♗e2 ♖e8 16 dxc5 bxc5 17 c4 ♗g4 18 ♗d1 ♖ab8 19 h3 ± Panno-Ivkov, Copenhagen jr Wch 1953.

d2) 11...♖d8 12 ♗a3 b6 13 ♕e2 ♗b7 14 ♖fd1 ♖ac8 15 ♖ac1 ♘a5 16 ♗d3 ♕c6 17 ♗b5 ♕c7 = Fyllingen-Dydyshko, Års 1999.

d3) 11...b6 12 ♗a3 ♗b7 13 ♖e1 (or 13 ♗e2 ♖fd8 14 ♕c2 ♘a5 15 dxc5 bxc5 16 c4 ♗e4 17 ♕c3 ♖ab8 = Najdorf-Reshevsky, Zurich Ct 1953) 13...♖fd8 14 ♕e2 ♖ac8 15 ♗a2 ♘a5 16 ♘e5 ♗d5 with a pleasant game for Black, Cifuentes-Komarov, Benasque 1996.

e) 11 ♖e1 e5 12 d5 ♘a5 (12...e4?! 13 dxc6 exf3 14 ♕xf3 ♗g4 15 ♕g3 ♕xc6 16 e4 has been known as clearly better for White since Reshevsky-Euwe, Zurich Ct 1953) 13 d6 ♕d8 14 ♘xe5 ♘xc4 15 ♘xc4 ♗e6 16 ♘b2 ♘e4 17 f3 ♘xd6 18 e4 ♘c4 = Panno-Szabo, Buenos Aires 1955.

f) 11 ♕c2 and now:

f1) 11...♗d7 12 ♗d3 ♖ac8 13 c4 cxd4 14 exd4 ♘a5 15 ♗g5 = Inkiov-Nikolac, Rome 1984.

f2) 11...b6 12 ♗d3 ♘a5 13 c4 ♗b7 14 ♘e5 ♘c6 15 ♗b2 cxd4 16 exd4 ♖fd8 = Aleksandrova-Ovseevich, Alushta 1999.

f3) 11...e5 and now:

f31) 12 ♗a2 is note 'b' to White's 12th move in Line A3.

f32) 12 ♗e2 transposes to Line A1.

f33) 12 ♗d3 transposes to Line A2.

f34) 12 ♘xe5 ♘xe5 13 dxe5 ♕xe5 14 f3 ♗e6 (14...♘d5!?) 15 ♗xe6 ♕xe6 16 e4 ♖fd8 17 ♗e3 ♕c4 18 ♖fd1 b6 = Tsevremes-Nikolaidis, Kavala 2001.

f35) 12 ♗b5 e4 (12...cxd4 13 cxd4 exd4 14 ♘xd4 ± *ECO*) 13 ♘g5 (or 13 ♗xc6 ♕xc6 14 ♘e5 ♕c7 15 f3 exf3 16 ♖xf3 ♘g4 17 ♘xg4 ♗xg4 18 ♖g3 ♗h5 19 c4 with equality, A.Schneider-C.Horvath, Debrecen 1988) 13...a6 14 ♗c4 ♘a5 15 ♗a2 ♗f5 16 f3 ♖ac8 17 fxe4 ♗g6 (H.Olafsson-Zaltsman, Reykjavik 1982) 18 ♕f2 ♘xe4 19 ♘xe4 ♗xe4 20 ♕f4 with about equal prospects.

A1)
11 ♗e2 *(D)*

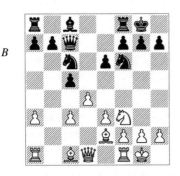

So, what is White up to with this move? Well, he wants to play d5 in reply to ...e5, and then preferably follow up with c4 with plenty of space for his bishops. Black, on the other hand, wants to play ...e5-e4 and, if possible, prevent White from playing d5, in which case White will be suffocating behind his pawn-chain.

11...e5

Black moves ahead with his plan. A couple of alternatives:

a) 11...♗d7 12 ♗b2 ♖fd8 13 ♗d3 ♗e8 14 ♕e2 ♘e7 15 ♘e5 ♖ac8 16 e4 ♘g6 with about even chances, Lukacs-Barczay, Hungarian Ch (Budapest) 1978.

b) 11...♖d8 tries to prevent White's aspirations by keeping the pressure on White's centre. Now:

b1) 12 ♕c2 e5 transposes to the main line.

b2) 12 ♗b2 e5 13 ♕c2 again transposes to the main line.

b3) 12 c4?! ♕b6! 13 ♕c2 cxd4 14 exd4 ♘xd4 15 ♘xd4 ♕xd4 16 ♖d1 ♕b6 17 ♗e3 ♕c7 18 ♖xd8+ ♕xd8 19 ♗f3 ♕c7 and White has insufficient compensation for the pawn, Van Beers-Kolev, Istanbul OL 2000.

12 ♕c2

Or:

a) 12 ♗b2 transposes to note 'c' to White's 12th move in Line A4.

b) 12 h3 e4 13 ♘d2 ♘e7 14 ♗b2 transposes to note 'b1' to Black's 13th move in Line A4.

c) 12 d5 is in accordance with White's plan. Now:

c1) 12...♖d8 and here:

c11) 13 e4 ♘e7 14 ♕c2 ♘g6 15 c4 ♘e8 16 ♗b2 ± O'Kelly-Donner, Havana 1964.

c12) 13 c4 e4 14 ♘d2 ♘e5 15 f4 exf3 16 gxf3 gives White a slight advantage, Gligorić-Ljubojević, Bugojno 1982.

c2) 12...e4 and then:

c21) 13 dxc6 ♘g4 14 g3 exf3 15 ♗xf3 ♘e5 16 ♗g2 ♘xc6 = Plachetka-Prandstetter, Bratislava 1983.

c22) 13 ♘e1 ♘e5 14 f4 exf3 15 gxf3 ♗h3 16 ♖f2 (16 ♘g2 ♖ad8, Knaak-Timoshchenko, Polanica Zdroj 1976, 17 c4 b5 18 e4 and here *Schach-Archiv* gives 18...♘xc4 19 ♗xc4 bxc4 20 ♗f4 ♕d7 21 ♕c2 with a pleasant game for White, but 18...bxc4!? improves) 16...♖ad8 17 e4 (Burgalat-Cataldi, corr. 1984) 17...h6 18 ♘d3 ♘xd3 19 ♕xd3 with chances for both sides – Sakharov.

12...♖d8

Black aims to exert as much pressure as possible against the white centre. Other moves include:

a) 12...e4 13 ♘d2 ♗f5 14 ♘b3 cxd4 15 cxd4 ♖ac8 16 ♕d1 ± Brophy-Agrain, corr. 1995.

b) 12...♗g4 13 d5! ♘a5 14 e4 ♘e8 15 ♖b1 ± Knaak-Prandstetter, Bratislava 1983.

c) 12...♖e8!? 13 ♗b2 ♗d7 14 ♖fd1 e4 15 ♘d2 ♗g4 16 ♘f1 ♗xe2 17 ♕xe2 ♘a5 = Giddins-Kaspi, Tyniste ECC 1999.

13 ♗b2

This odd-looking move is aimed at the eventual opening of the centre. White also has the possibility of opening it immediately by 13 dxe5 ♘xe5. Then:

a) 14 c4 ♘xf3+ 15 ♗xf3 ♘g4 16 ♗xg4 ♗xg4 17 f3 ♗e6 with a pleasant game for Black, Rumiantsev-Kondratiev, USSR Cht (Riga) 1968.

b) 14 ♘e1 c4! 15 f3 ♕c5 16 ♖f2 b6 = Gipslis-Szabo, Tallinn 1969.

13...♗g4

If Black doesn't fancy the kind of play that develops in the main line, he

can also try 13...e4 14 ♘d2 ♗f5 (not 14...♗g4?, as played in Khalifman-Kveinys, Liepaja rpd 2001, because White can win a pawn by 15 ♘xe4) 15 ♘b3 cxd4 (15...c4!? 16 ♗xc4 ♘g4 17 g3 ♘ce5 18 ♗e2 ♘d3 19 ♘d2 ♕b6 20 ♖ab1 ♕h6 gives Black compensation for the pawn, Van der Sterren-Onishchuk, Bundesliga 2000/1) 16 cxd4 ♖d6 17 ♖fc1 ♖e8 18 ♘c5 ♕e7 and now 19 ♕b3 ♘d8 ½-½ was Piket-Kramnik, Dortmund 2000. However, it seems the right time to activate the dark-squared bishop by 19 a4 followed by ♗a3, when White should be better.

14 dxe5 ♘xe5 15 c4 ♘xf3+ 16 gxf3 ♗h3

Dropping the bishop back with 16...♗h5 leaves White better after 17 ♖fe1 ♗g6 18 ♕c3 ♘e8 19 e4 f6 20 ♕e3 ± Lutikov-Aronson, USSR 1957.

17 ♖fd1 ♕c6

17...♖xd1+ leads to a better game for White: 18 ♖xd1 ♖d8 19 ♖b1 (or 19 ♖c1 ♕c6 20 ♔h1 ♕e6 21 e4 h6 22 ♖g1 ± Taimanov-Kholmov, USSR Ch (Erevan) 1962) 19...♕c6 20 ♔h1 ♗g4 (20...h6 21 ♖g1 ♕e6 22 ♕c3 ♔f8 23 e4 b6 24 ♕e3 with an initiative for White, Yusupov-Van der Sterren, Bundesliga 1997/8) 21 ♔g2 (or 21 e4!? ♗h3 22 ♖g1 with an interesting struggle ahead) 21...♗c8 22 ♖g1 b6 23 ♕c3 ♕e6 24 ♔h1 ♔f8 and Black should be able to neutralize the white pressure, Vaïsser-Kolev, Elista OL 1998.

18 ♕c3 ♘e8 19 ♔h1 ♗e6 20 ♖g1 f6 21 ♖g3 ♖d7 22 ♖ag1 ♖ad8 23 ♗c1 ♗f5 24 e4 ♗g6

Black has somewhat the better position, Khalifman-Kramnik, Linares 2000.

A2)
11 ♗d3 *(D)*

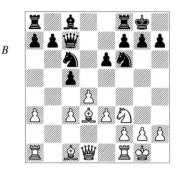

White removes his bishop from any potential hassle from being opposite the black queen. On d3, the bishop points in the direction of the black king. The problem with the d3-square is that after Black's next move, 11...e5, White is forced either to exchange on e5 or to play e4 at some point.

11...e5

11...♖d8 12 ♕c2 e5 transposes to note 'c' to Black's 12th move.

12 ♕c2

12 dxe5 (12 ♘xe5 ♘xe5 13 dxe5 ♕xe5 is the same) 12...♘xe5 13 ♘xe5 ♕xe5 14 ♕c2 and now 14...♗g4 is note 'b' to Black's 12th move and 14...♖d8 transposes to line 'c2' of that note.

12...♖e8

With this move, Black forces White to make the decision that I mentioned above. Black also has a selection of other moves to choose from:

a) 12...♕e7 (this move is similar to 12...♖e8 in so far as it forces White to decide what to do with his centre) 13 dxe5 ♘xe5 14 ♘xe5 ♕xe5 *(D)* and now:

a1) 15 ♖e1 is best answered with 15...♖d8, when 16 f3 transposes to line 'a51'.

a2) 15 c4? (this looks pretty stupid, but as we shall see in the coverage of this line, it is a fairly common idea that often wins White the initiative; here, however, it doesn't...) 15...♘g4 16 f4 ♕xa1 17 ♗b2 ♘xe3 18 ♕c3 ♕xb2 19 ♕xb2 ♘xf1 is much better for Black, J.Cooper-R.Smith, Welsh U-18 Ch (Swansea) 1970.

a3) 15 e4? c4! 16 ♗e2 ♕xe4 17 ♕xe4 ♘xe4 18 ♗xc4 ♘xc3 19 ♖e1 ♗d7 20 ♗d2 ♖fc8 is slightly better for Black, Mecking-Avarez del Monte, Rio Hondo 1966.

a4) 15 f4 has mainly been tried out in correspondence games, but White has only proved the tiniest of edges: 15...♕e7 16 c4 ♖e8 17 ♖e1 ♘e4 18 ♗b2 ♗f5 19 ♗e5 f6 20 ♗xe4 ♗xe4 21 ♕xe4 fxe5 22 f5 ♖ad8 23 ♖ed1 ♔h8 with equality according to Taimanov, but White surely seems more comfortable in this position with the central position of his queen and Black's light-squared weaknesses.

a5) 15 f3 ♖d8 (15...♗d7 transposes to line 'b31' and 15...♗e6 to 'b32') and then:

a51) 16 ♖e1 ♗d7 17 a4 ♗c6 18 e4 ♘d5 19 ♗d2 ♘f4 = Gligorić-Evans, Dallas 1957.

a52) 16 e4 c4 17 ♗e2 ♕c5+ 18 ♔h1 ♗e6 19 ♗f4 ± Ketzscher-Jordan, corr. 1973.

b) 12...♗g4 13 ♘xe5 (totally harmless is 13 ♘g5 h6 14 ♘e4 ♘xe4 15 ♗xe4 exd4 16 cxd4 cxd4 17 exd4 ♕d6 = Ilivitsky-Taimanov USSR Ch (Kiev) 1954) 13...♘xe5 14 dxe5 ♕xe5 *(D)* and now:

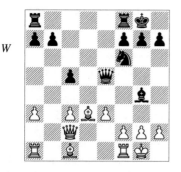

b1) 15 f4?! ♕e7 16 c4 ♖ad8 17 a4 ♖d6 18 ♖a3 ♖fd8 19 e4 ♕d7 with an invasion on the d-file, F.Portisch-Rigo, Kecskemet 1985.

b2) 15 ♗b2 ♖fd8 (15...c4!?) 16 c4 ♕d6 17 ♗f5 ♗xf5 18 ♕xf5 ♕e6 19 ♕xe6 fxe6 20 ♗xf6 gxf6 21 ♖fd1 ½-½ Lilienthal-Ragozin, USSR Ch (Kiev) 1954.

b3) 15 f3 makes a lot of sense. The black bishop is kicked away and the g4-square is guarded by the f-pawn. Now:

b31) 15...♗d7 and here:

b311) 16 ♖e1?! ♗a4! (taking the important d1-square away from White) 17 ♕b2 ♖ad8 18 ♗f1 b6 19 c4 ♕e6 20 ♕c3 ♘d7 with a better game for Black, Furman-Antoshin, USSR Ch (Moscow) 1955.

b312) 16 a4 ♖fe8 17 e4 c4 18 ♗e2 (Petrosian-Spassky, Moscow Wch (20) 1966) 18...♕c5+ 19 ♔h1 ♖ad8 gives White a slight advantage.

b313) 16 e4 c4 17 ♗e2 ♕c5+ 18 ♔h1 ♖fe8 19 ♖e1 ♗c6 20 ♗f1 b5 21 ♗e3 ♕e7 22 ♕f2 ± Furman-Tolush, USSR 1955.

b32) 15...♗e6 16 f4 (less problematic for Black is 16 e4 c4 17 ♗e2 ♕c5+ 18 ♔h1 ♘d7 19 a4 ♕c7 20 ♗a3

♘c5 = Botvinnik-Euwe, Amsterdam OL 1954) 16...♕d6 17 ♖d1 ♕e7 18 c4 and here, instead of 18...b5? 19 cxb5 c4 20 ♗f1 ♕c5 21 a4 ± Taimanov-Darga, Hastings 1955/6, Black should play 18...♗g4 19 ♖e1 ♖ad8 20 e4 ♕d6 21 ♗f1 ♕d4+ 22 ♗e3 ♕xe4 23 ♕f2 with a small but clear advantage for White according to Taimanov.

c) 12...♖d8 is another option:

c1) 13 h3 ♕e7 14 ♘xe5 ♘xe5 15 dxe5 ♕xe5 16 ♗b2 ♗xh3! (forcing a draw) 17 gxh3 ♕g5+ 18 ♔h2 ♘g4+ 19 ♔h1 ♕h4 20 ♔g2 ♕g5 21 ♔h1 ♕h4 with a draw by repetition, Van der Sterren-Sturua, Istanbul OL 2000.

c2) 13 dxe5?! is completely harmless, since Black has not even wasted a move forcing White to do this, so *ECO*'s '±' is misplaced in this line. 13...♘xe5 14 ♘xe5 ♕xe5 15 f3 ♗e6 is equal.

c3) 13 ♖e1 ♗g4 14 ♘xe5 ♘xe5 15 dxe5 ♕xe5 16 f3 ♗d7 17 a4 ♖ac8 18 e4 c4 19 ♗f1 ♘d5 20 ♗d2 ♘b6 offers chances for both sides, Murdzia-Aleksandrov, Sas van Gent jr Ech 1992.

c4) 13 ♗b2 and here:

c41) 13...h6?! 14 h3 ♕e7 15 ♘xe5 ♘xe5 16 dxe5 ♕xe5 17 c4 ♕e7 18 ♖ad1 ± Bronstein-Hörberg, Amsterdam OL 1954.

c42) 13...♗g4 and now:

c421) 14 ♘xe5 ♘xe5 15 dxe5 ♕xe5 16 c4 ♕d6 17 ♗f5 ♗xf5 18 ♕xf5 ♕e6 19 ♕xe6 fxe6 20 ♗xf6 gxf6 21 ♖fd1 ½-½ Lilienthal-Ragozin, USSR Ch (Kiev) 1954.

c422) 14 ♘g5 h6 15 ♘e4 ♘xe4 16 ♗xe4 ♗e6 17 f4 exd4 18 cxd4 cxd4 19 ♗xd4 f5 20 ♗xc6 ♕xc6 and although White has some initiative, it is easily neutralized, Szabo-O'Kelly, Budapest 1952.

We now return to 12...罩e8 *(D)*:

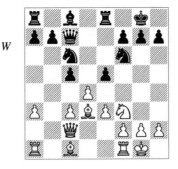

Now:

A21: 13 e4 79
A22: 13 ②xe5 81

Or 13 ②g5 h6 14 ②e4 ②xe4 15 &xe4 exd4 16 cxd4 cxd4 17 exd4 豐d6 18 &xc6 bxc6 ½-½ Taimanov-Tolush, Leningrad Ch 1957.

A21)

13 e4

For those who don't like the positions for White where he has to exchange knight and pawn, this is the only proper choice for White here.

13...c4

Or:

a) 13...&g4 14 ②xe5 ②xe5 15 dxe5 豐xe5 16 f4 豐e7 17 c4!? ②xe4 18 &b2 and White's forces on the long diagonals pointing towards Black's king more than compensate for the sacrificed pawn, Rajković-Hort, Hastings 1972/3.

b) 13...exd4 14 cxd4 and here:

b1) 14...cxd4 15 ②xd4 ②g4 16 ②f3 豐a5 17 &b2 ②ge5 18 ②xe5 ②xe5

and now, instead of 19 &xe5?! as in Bradvarević-Jović, Vrnjačka Banja 1962, White should play 19 罩fc1 since 19...②xd3 20 豐xd3 leaves opposite-coloured bishops on the board, thus favouring the one with the initiative, in this case White.

b2) 14...&g4 has received renewed attention in the last couple of years since Kasparov's sensational 28-move loss to Ivan Sokolov in 1999. Now:

b21) 15 e5 &xf3 16 exf6 ②xd4 17 &xh7+ 當h8 18 fxg7+ 當xg7 19 &b2 罩ad8 *(D)* and then:

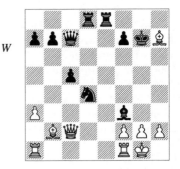

b211) 20 罩fc1?! 罩h8 (20...罩e2 21 &xd4+ 罩xd4 22 豐c3 豐f4 23 豐xf3 豐xf3 24 gxf3 當xh7 25 罩xc5 罩dd2 ∓ Tsesarsky) 21 豐xc5 豐xc5 22 罩xc5 當xh7 23 &xd4 罩hg8 24 &e5! 罩xg2+ 25 當f1 罩g6 with equality, Langeweg-Kuijpers, Dutch Ch (Leeuwarden) 1980.

b212) 20 &f5 罩e2 21 &xd4+ 罩xd4 22 豐c3 &d5 23 罩fe1 with at most a minimal advantage for White according to Wells.

b213) 20 gxf3 罩h8 21 當h1 and here:

b2131) 21...罩xh7 22 罩g1+ 當h8 23 罩g3 豐e5 24 罩ag1 罩h4? (24...豐h5 25

🗲1g2 f6 26 ♕c4 ♕f7, Porath-Ståhlberg, Amsterdam OL 1954, 27 ♕xc5 ♘e2 28 ♕g5 ♘xg3+ 29 fxg3 🗲d6 30 🗲c2 and here Wells's analysis ends, but Black seems to be able to defend with 30...♕f8 31 ♕f5 🗲hd7 32 ♗e5 🗲d1+ 33 ♔g2 🗲1d2+ and a draw is likely) 25 ♕c1?! (Tsesarsky mentions 25 f4! ♕h5 26 f3! ±) 25...♔h7?? (25...♕h5! = Kasparov) 26 ♕b1+ ♔h8 27 ♕f1 ♕e6 28 ♕g2 1-0 I.Sokolov-Kasparov, Wijk aan Zee 1999.

b2132) 21...♔f8!? (this move appears to be much better than Kasparov's move above) 22 ♕e4 f5 (22...f6!? 23 ♕h4 🗲xh7 24 ♕xf6+ ♔e8 25 🗲fe1+ ♔d7 26 h4 🗲f8 27 🗲e7+ 🗲xe7 28 ♕xf8 with chances for both sides, Endzelins-Bouwmeester, corr. 1984) 23 ♕h4 🗲xh7 24 ♕f6+ ♔e8 25 🗲fe1+ ♔d7 26 🗲e5 ♔c8 27 ♗xd4 cxd4 28 ♕xf5+ ♔b8 and since the black king has found safety on the queenside, Black takes control of the game.

b22) 15 ♕xc5 and now:

b221) 15...♘xe4 16 ♗xe4 🗲xe4 17 ♘g5 🗲xd4 (Black faces more problems after 17...🗲e7 18 ♕c2 g6 19 ♘e4 ♗f5 20 ♘f6+ ♔g7 21 ♕d2 ♔xf6 22 d5 🗲d8 23 ♗b2+ ♘e5 24 f4 ♕c5+ 25 ♗d4 🗲xd5 26 fxe5+ ♔e6 27 ♗xc5 🗲xd2 28 ♗xe7 ♔xe7 29 🗲f2 with a fairly clear edge for White, Kazić-Majstorović, corr. 1954) 18 ♗b2 🗲f4 19 🗲ae1 h6 20 ♘e4 ♗e6 21 ♕c3 🗲g4 22 f4 ♕b6+ 23 ♔h1 ♕b3 24 ♕xb3 ♗xb3 25 h3 and White has more than sufficient compensation for the pawn, Leserer-Matt, corr. 1982.

b222) 15...♗xf3 16 gxf3 ♕d7 and here:

b2221) 17 ♗e3 can lead to an early draw after 17...♘xe4 18 ♗xe4 🗲xe4

19 fxe4 ♕g4+, as in Gauba-Schott, corr. 1993.

b2222) 17 ♗b2 ♘xe4 18 ♗xe4 🗲xe4 19 🗲fe1?! (19 fxe4 ♕g4+ is a draw like above), Tobies-Glasewald, corr. 1986, and here Black can secure an advantage with 19...🗲e6! 20 🗲xe6 fxe6!.

14 ♗xc4 exd4 15 cxd4 *(D)*

15 🗲e1 is not a threat to Black, who can achieve a good game by continuing 15...♗g4 16 ♘g5 ♘e5 17 ♗b5 ♗d7 18 ♗xd7 (Dittmann-F.Olafsson, Reykjavik U-26 Wcht 1957) and now 18...♘fxd7 is simplest, leaving Black just better.

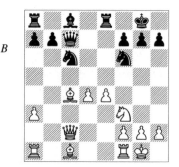

15...♘a5

Or:

a) 15...♘xe4? 16 ♗d3 ♘f6 17 ♗g5 ♕d6 18 ♗xf6 ♕xf6 19 ♗xh7+ ♔h8 20 d5 ♘e5 21 ♗e4 ± Hudovski-Dajnko, corr. 1977.

b) 15...🗲xe4?! 16 ♗d3 🗲e7 (the alternative 16...🗲e8 transposes to line 'a') 17 ♗g5 (Rogers suggests 17 d5!? ♘xd5 18 ♗xh7+ ♔h8 19 ♗g5 with an uncomfortable task ahead for Black) 17...♗g4!? 18 ♗xf6 gxf6 19 ♗xh7+ ♔g7 20 ♗e4 🗲ae8 (Gölz-Rellstab, Gotha 1957) and here 21 ♘d2!? ♘xd4

22 ♕xc7 ♖xc7 leaves the chances balanced.

16 ♗d3

16 ♘d2 ♘xe4 17 ♗xf7+ ♕xf7 18 ♘xe4 ♗f5 19 ♕a4 ♖xe4 20 ♕xa5 ♖xd4 and Black has nothing to worry about, Gil.Gonzales-Pellegrino, corr. 1971.

16...♕xc2 17 ♗xc2 ♘xe4 18 ♖e1 ♗f5

18...♘d6!? 19 ♗f4 ♘ac4 20 ♗b3 ♗f5 21 ♘e5 ♗e6 22 ♘d3! ♖ad8 23 ♘c5 ♗c8 (I.Rogers-Solomon, Sydney 1999) and now Rogers gives 24 ♗g5!? as best; e.g., 24...f6 25 ♗f4 ♔h8 26 d5 or 24...♖xe1+ 25 ♖xe1 ♖f8 26 ♗f4 b6 27 ♘d3 ±.

19 ♗f4

Rogers suggested 19 ♗a4!?; a sample line of his analysis runs 19...♘c6 20 ♗b2 ♖ad8 21 ♘e5 ♘xe5 22 dxe5 ♖f8 23 ♗c2! ♘g3 24 ♗d1! ♘e4 25 g4 ♗g6 26 f4 f5 ±.

19...♘d6 20 ♗a4 b5 21 ♗xd6 bxa4 22 ♖xe8+ ♖xe8 23 ♖e1 ♖xe1+ 24 ♘xe1 f6 25 f3

Although White has a slight edge in this endgame, it quickly led to a draw in Kiprov-Yudovich Sr, corr. 1972.

A22)

13 ♘xe5 ♘xe5 14 dxe5 ♕xe5 15 f3 *(D)*

15...♗d7

15...♗e6 is an interesting alternative:

a) 16 e4 ♖ad8 (or 16...c4 17 ♗e2 ♕c5+ 18 ♔h1 ♘d7 19 ♗f4 b5 20 ♖fd1 f6 with equality, Portisch-Spassky, Geneva Ct (4) 1977) 17 ♗e2 b6 18 a4 ♗d7 19 ♖d1 ♗c6 20 ♖xd8 ♖xd8 21 ♗e3 h6 ½-½ Korchnoi-Spassky, Leningrad 1974.

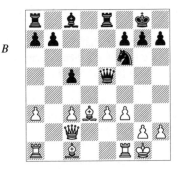

b) 16 ♖e1 ♖ad8 17 ♖b1 ♕d5! (17...c4 is less accurate: 18 ♗f1 b6 19 e4 ± Hort-Spassky, Reykjavik Ct (2) 1977) 18 ♗b5 ♗f5 19 e4 ♘xe4 20 ♗xe8 ♘d6 21 ♕e2 = Gligorić-F.Olafsson, Bad Lauterberg 1977.

16 a4

White has to show some care to avoid ending up in trouble. Two inferior moves:

a) 16 ♖e1?! ♗a4! (16...♖ad8 17 a4 ♗c6 18 e4 transposes to the main line) 17 ♕b2 ♖ed8 18 ♗f1 b6 ∓ Sanguinetti-Redolfi, Argentine Ch (Buenos Aires) 1958.

b) 16 e4?! c4 (16...♖ad8 17 a4 transposes to the main line) 17 ♗e2 ♘d5!? (17...♕c5+ and 17...♗c6 are two alternative moves that have been tried out) 18 ♗xc4 ♘xc3 19 ♗e3 ♖ac8 20 ♕b3 ♗a4! 21 ♗xf7+ ♔f8 ∓ (Beliavsky).

16...♖ad8

Black has to play actively to avoid slowly being pushed backwards off the board. That can easily happen if White gets time to activate his bishop-pair. Some alternatives:

a) 16...♖ac8 17 ♖e1 and now:

a1) 17...♖ed8?! 18 e4 ♘d5 19 ♗d2 ♘b6 20 a5! c4 21 axb6 cxd3 22 ♕xd3

♗e6 23 ♕e3 axb6 24 ♖eb1! ♕c5 25 ♕xc5 bxc5 26 ♗e1! and White has clearly the better chances in the endgame, due to Black's weak queenside pawns, Yusupov-Ivanchuk, Brussels Ct (3) 1991.

a2) 17...h6 18 e4 ♘d5 19 ♗d2 ♘f4 20 ♗f1 c4? (a positional error as Black now loses control over the g1-a7 diagonal; 20...b6 ± is correct – Yusupov) 21 ♗e3 ♕c7 22 ♕d2 ♘e6 23 ♗xc4 ♕xc4 24 ♕xd7 ♘c5 25 ♕b5 is much better for White, Yusupov-Ljubojević, Belgrade 1991.

a3) 17...♗c6 18 e4 ♘d5 19 ♗d2 ♘f4 (Lugovoi-Goldin, Russian Ch (Elista) 1996) 20 ♗f1 ± (Kantsler).

a4) 17...c4 18 ♗f1 ♕a5 19 e4 ♘d5 20 ♗d2 ♘b6 21 ♗e3 ♘xa4 22 ♗d4 b5 23 ♕d2 with compensation for the pawn, but no more than that, Makariev-Landa, Sochi 1992.

b) 16...♗c6 17 ♖e1 (17 e4 ♖ad8 transposes to the main line) 17...h5 (17...♖ad8 18 e4 again transposes to the main line) 18 e4 ♘d5 19 ♗d2 ♘f4 20 ♗f1 h4 21 ♗e3 ♖ad8 22 ♖ad1 b6 = Gligorić-Averbakh, Portorož IZ 1958.

17 e4

Black has more or less completed his development, while White is still struggling to find the right squares for his pieces and is trying to avoid handing the initiative over to Black. Some alternatives:

a) 17 ♖e1 ♗c6 18 e4 transposes to the main line.

b) 17 ♖a3 ♗c6 18 c4 ♖d6 19 a5 ♖ed8 20 ♖e1 h6 21 ♗f1 ♘h5 22 ♕c3 ♕e7 with approximately equal prospects, Hort-Miles, Amsterdam 1981.

17...♗c6 *(D)*
18 ♖e1

18 ♗c4 is an important alternative:

a) 18...h5 19 a5 h4 20 h3 (White prefers to weaken his dark squares rather than softening the g2-e4 pawn chain by allowing ...h3; e.g., 20 ♕b3 ♖d7 21 ♗e3?! h3 22 g3? ♘xe4! and White's game is falling apart) 20...♖e7 21 ♖e1 ♘h5 22 ♗e3 b5 23 axb6 axb6 with chances for both sides, Lugovoi-Landa, Russian Ch (Elista) 1996.

b) 18...b6 19 ♗d2 ♖d7 and now not 20 ♗e3? (Gligorić-Filip, Portorož IZ 1958) 20...♘xe4!, but 20 ♖fd1 with equality.

c) 18...♖d7 19 ♖e1 (or 19 ♕b3 ♖ed8 20 ♖a2 ♘h5 21 g3 ♘xg3 22 hxg3 ♖d2 = Portisch-Spassky, Geneva Ct (10) 1977) 19...♘d5 (19...♖ed8?! 20 ♗e3 h6 21 a5 ♘h5 22 ♕c1 g5 23 ♕a3 ± Beliavsky-Korchnoi, Wijk aan Zee 1984) 20 ♗d2 ♘f4 21 ♖ad1 ♖ed8 22 ♗xf4 ♕xf4 23 ♖xd7 ♖xd7 24 ♗d5 ♕c7 ½-½ Babel-Filutowski, corr. 1992-4.

18...♘d5 19 ♗d2

19 ♖a3 can again be considered; e.g., 19...♖d7 20 ♗f1 ♘f4 21 ♗e3 ♖ed8 22 ♖aa1 ♘e6 23 ♕b3 h5 24 a5 and White is perhaps a little bit better, Panno-Van Riemsdijk, São Paulo Z 1972.

19...♘f4

19...♘b4!? is also worth a thought.

20 ♗f1

Here Black faces an important decision:

a) 20...♖d6 allows White to relieve himself from some of the pressure through exchanging a set of rooks: 21 ♗e3 ♖ed8 22 ♖ed1! h5 23 ♖xd6 ♖xd6 24 ♖d1 ♖g6 25 ♕d2 and White's army is finally playing together as an orchestra, thus giving him an advantage, Donner-Knaak, Amsterdam 1974.

b) 20...g5 21 ♗e3 h5 22 a5 ♖e6 (Yusupov-Beliavsky, Munich 1994) and here Beliavsky claims a better game for White with 23 ♕f2! b6 24 axb6 axb6 25 ♖a6 ♗e8 26 ♖b1 ♖dd6 27 ♖a8.

c) 20...c4 21 ♗xf4 (neither 21 ♗xc4 ♘h3+ 22 gxh3 ♕c5+ nor 21 ♗e3 ♘d3 22 ♗xd3 cxd3 23 ♕d2 ♕a5 24 ♖a2 f5 25 exf5 ♕xf5 = Donner-Sosonko, Dutch Ch (Leeuwarden) 1978, makes a lasting impression) 21...♕xf4 22 ♖ad1 ♕e5 23 ♗xc4 ♕c5+ 24 ♖d4 ♖xd4 25 cxd4 ♕xd4+ 26 ♔h1 ♖d8 27 ♕b3 ♖d7 28 h3 g5! 29 e5 ♔g7 and although White holds the initiative at this point, Black secured a draw much later through accurate defence in Bacrot-Sosonko, Cannes 1996.

A3)

11 ♗a2 *(D)*

11...e5

Black has tried a few other moves, but these have the unfortunate characteristic of favouring White:

a) 11...♖d8 12 ♗b2 h6 13 ♕e2 b6 14 e4 a5 15 ♖fe1 ♗a6 16 ♕c2 cxd4 17 cxd4 ± Shipov-R.Bagirov, Moscow 2002.

B

b) 11...b6 and here:

b1) 12 ♖e1 e5 13 e4 cxd4 (better than 13...♗g4?! 14 dxc5! bxc5 15 h3 ♖ad8 16 ♕e2 ♗xf3 17 ♕xf3 ± Kasparov-Kramnik, Linares 1997) 14 cxd4 exd4 15 ♗g5 ♗g4 16 ♗xf6 gxf6 17 h3 ♗xf3 18 ♕xf3 ♕e5 and Black has no reason to worry, Knaak-C.Horvath, Dresden 1988.

b2) 12 ♕e2 e5 13 d5 e4 14 ♘d2 ♘e5 15 c4 ♘eg4 16 f4 exf3 17 gxf3 ♘e5 18 ♔h1 ± Furman-Kondratiev, Leningrad 1952.

12 h3

It is quite important for White not to let Black pin the f3-knight in this line, where the light-squared bishop that could break the pin is parked over on a2. Alternatives:

a) 12 d5?! e4 13 dxc6 ♗g4 (or 13...exf3 14 ♕xf3 ♗g4 15 ♕g3 ♕xc6 16 f3 ♗e6 17 c4 ♖fd8 18 ♗b2 ♘e8 = Kožul-Dizdar, Croatian Ch (Slavonski Brod) 1995) 14 h3 ♖ad8 15 ♕a4 b5 16 ♕xb5 exf3 17 ♕xc5 fxg2 18 ♔xg2 ♗e2 and White is facing difficulties, I.Watson-Chandler, British Ch (Morecambe) 1981.

b) 12 ♕c2 and here:

b1) 12...♗g4 13 dxe5 (13 ♘xe5 is harmless; for example, 13...♘xe5 14

dxe5 ♕xe5 15 f3 ♗e6 16 ♗xe6 ♕xe6
17 e4 ♖fd8 18 ♗e3 b6 is equal, Simić-
Chekhov, Yugoslavia-USSR 1976)
13...♘xe5 14 ♘e1 ♖ad8 15 f3 ♗d7!
16 c4 ♗c6 17 ♗b2 (Pliester suggests
17 e4!? as a possible improvement)
17...♖fe8 18 ♗c3 ♕e7 19 ♕e2 ♘fd7
20 ♘c2 f5 21 ♖ad1 ♘b6 and Black
holds the better prospects, A.Schnei-
der-Barczay, Hungarian Ch (Budapest)
1980.

b2) 12...e4 13 ♘d2 ♗f5 14 f3 ♖ae8
15 a4 ♕d7 16 fxe4 ♘xe4 17 ♘xe4
♖xe4 18 ♕f2 ♗g6 19 ♗a3 ♖fe8 20
♗xc5 b6 21 d5 ♘e5 and Black has
somewhat the better chances, A.Schnei-
der-Ki.Georgiev, Plovdiv Echt 1983.

12...e4
This pawn-push has become the
main line, but it is quite committal and
Black's obligation to keep it well-
protected can prove to be a liability.
Black can also consider:

a) 12...♖d8 13 ♘g5 ♖d7 14 ♕c2
cxd4 15 cxd4 exd4 16 ♗b2 h6 17 ♘f3
d3 18 ♕c4 b5 19 ♕h4 ♕d6 20 ♖fd1 is
slightly better for White, Djurić-Raj-
ković, Yugoslavia 1983.

b) 12...b6 13 d5 (13 ♕c2?! e4 14
♘g5 ♗a6 15 ♖d1 ♖ae8 ∓ Gelfand-
Korchnoi, Horgen 1994) 13...e4 14
dxc6 exf3 15 ♕xf3 ♗a6 (15...♕e5!?
16 e4! ♕xe4 17 ♕xe4 ♘xe4 18 ♖e1
♘xc3 19 ♗c4 a6 20 a4 ± Korchnoi) 16
c4 ♖ae8 17 ♗b2 ♘e4 18 ♖ad1 ♕xc6
19 ♕f4 ± Volzhin-Aleksandrov, Køge
1997.

c) 12...♗f5 13 d5 ♖ad8 14 ♕e2
♘e7 15 c4 ± Simagin-Khasin, USSR
Ch (Tallinn) 1965.

13 ♘h2 (D)
From h2, the knight not only supports the pawn-break with the f-pawn,

but is also ready to jump into action
via g4.

13 ♘d2 has proved much less effective; e.g., 13...♖e8 14 ♗b2 ♗f5 15
♕e2 ♖ad8 16 ♘b3 b6 17 c4 ♕e7 18
♖ac1 a5 19 dxc5 ½-½ Stanec-Slutsky,
Kazan ECC 1997.

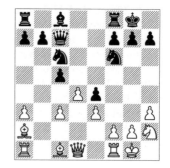

13...♗f5
While I have kept this move as the
main line, it is clear that it is no longer
Black's main preference. The idea behind the move is to keep the e4-pawn
firmly protected, but current practice
has shown that this is far from Black's
most effective plan. Other options for
Black:

a) 13...♘e7 14 ♕e2 ♗d7 15 c4 ♘f5
16 ♗b2 ♘e8 17 ♖fd1 with a comfortable advantage for White, Ibragimov-
Rubinetti, São Paulo 1991.

b) 13...♕e7 is a speciality of Log-
inov's: 14 a4 (14 ♗b2 ♖d8!?, intending
...♘e5 {Kantsler}, is also acceptable
for Black) 14...♗e6 15 ♗a3 ♗xa2 16
♖xa2 b6 17 ♕e2 ♖fc8 18 c4 ♘a5 with
equality, Iskusnykh-Loginov, Kazan
1995.

c) 13...b6 is another recent dis-
covery that has been serving Black
quite well. The idea is that White has

vacated the f1-a6 diagonal, so Black may as well take charge of it. Then:

c1) 14 f4 ♗a6 15 ♖f2 ♗d3 16 dxc5 bxc5 17 c4 ♖fd8 18 ♗b2 ♗xc4 19 ♕c1 ♗xa2 20 ♗xf6 gxf6 21 ♖fxa2 ♕e7 and Black is by no means worse, Knaak-Tischbierek, East German Ch (Stralsund) 1988.

c2) 14 c4 ♖d8 15 ♗b2 (15 d5 also favours White – Knaak) 15...cxd4 16 exd4 ♘e5! 17 d5 ± Knaak-Schmitt-diel, Dortmund 1990.

d) 13...♘a5 14 f3 (14 ♗b2 b6 15 c4 ♗f5 16 ♕e2 ♘d7 17 ♖ac1 ♖ad8 18 ♖fd1 ♖fe8 = Scherbakov-Kholmov, Russia Cup (Ekaterinburg) 1997; 14 ♘g4 ♗xg4 15 hxg4 c4 16 a4 ♖fe8 17 ♖b1 ♖ac8 18 ♖b5 a6 = Pieniazek-Luther, Koszalin 1997) and now:

d1) 14...cxd4? 15 cxd4 ♗e6 16 d5! ♕e5 17 ♖b1 ♗d7 18 ♗b2 ♕g5 19 ♕d2 b6 20 ♗xf6 +− Knaak-J.Horvath, Szirak 1985.

d2) 14...c4!? 15 ♗b1 ♖e8 16 ♖a2 ♗f5! 17 ♕e1 ♘d5 18 g4 ♗g6 19 f4 f6 20 f5 ♗f7 with chances for both sides, Knaak-Luther, Bad Lauterberg 1991.

d3) 14...b6! 15 ♕e2 ♗e6 16 ♘g4 ♘xg4 17 fxg4 ♕c6 18 ♕d1 ♖ad8 19 a4 ♘c4 and Black is by no means any worse, Sturua-Tiviakov, Bugojno 1999.

14 ♘g4!

White doesn't achieve anything by continuing 14 ♗b2 ♖ad8 15 ♕e2 ♖d6 (15...♗g6!? is a suggestion of Bondarevsky's) 16 ♖fd1 ♖fd8 17 a4 b6 = Reshevsky-Larsen, Dallas 1957.

14...♘xg4

It is best for Black to exchange knight for knight here. 14...♗xg4 15 hxg4 h6 16 ♖b1 ♖ad8 17 f4 exf3 18 ♕xf3 ± Danner-J.Horvath, Budapest 1986.

15 hxg4 ♗g6 16 a4

Or 16 ♕e2 ♘a5 17 a4 b6 18 dxc5 bxc5 19 ♗d5 ♖ad8 20 c4 ♘c6 21 ♗a3 ± Yudovich Jr-Strand, corr. 1958-9.

16...♖fd8 *(D)*

16...♖ad8 17 ♕e2 ♖fe8 (17...b6 leads to even greater problems: 18 ♗a3 ♔h8 19 ♖ad1 ♖fe8 20 ♗c4 f5 21 ♗b5 fxg4 22 ♕xg4 ♖d5 23 ♕g3 and Black's position is falling apart, Scherbakov-Kupreichik, Aalborg 1993) 18 ♗a3 b6 19 ♗c4 ♘a5 20 ♗a6 f6 21 ♖ad1 ± Knaak-Ki.Georgiev, E.Germany-Bulgaria (Sofia) 1986.

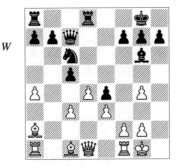

W

17 ♕e2

This is not White's only attractive possibility:

a) 17 ♗a3 b6 (or 17...♘e5 18 ♗xc5 b6 19 ♗b4 a5 20 ♗a3 ♕xc3 21 ♕c1 ♕xc1 22 ♖fxc1 ♘xg4 23 ♖ab1 ±) 18 ♕e2 ♖d7 19 ♗c4!? h6 20 ♖ad1 ± Volzhin-Skvortsov, Russian Ch (Elista) 1996.

b) 17 f4 exf3 18 ♕xf3 ♖d7 19 ♗a3 c4!? (19...cxd4 20 exd4 ♘a5 21 ♖ae1 h6 22 ♖e5 ♖c8 23 g5 ± Markauss-Fechner, corr. 1990) 20 e4 ♖e8 21 ♖ae1 h6 22 g5 hxg5 23 ♕g4 ♘a5 24 e5 ± Markauss-Kharlamov, corr. 1988-90.

17...♘e7

17...b6 18 ♗a3 ♔h8 (18...♘a5 19
♖fd1 c4 20 ♖ab1 f6 21 d5 ± Knaak-
Luther, East German Ch 1987) 19 ♖ad1
(Lombard-Unzicker, Zurich 1975)
19...cxd4 20 cxd4 f6 intending ...♗f7
± (R.Marić).

**18 f4 exf3 19 ♕xf3 ♘c6 20 ♗a3
b6 21 ♗d5 ♖ac8 22 ♖ad1 ♘a5 23 e4**

With the bishop-pair and a beautiful pawn-centre, White has the better
prospects, Anton-Berndt, corr. 1977.

A4)

11 ♗b2 *(D)*

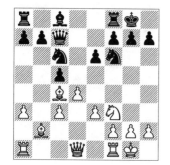

11...e5

11...♖d8 has a terrible track record
after 12 ♕e2; e.g., 12...b6 13 e4 ♗b7
14 ♗d3 ♘e7 15 ♘e5 ± Levenfish-
Kan, USSR Ch (Leningrad) 1937, but
12...e5 should improve considerably.

12 h3

Or:

a) 12 dxe5?! ♘xe5 13 ♗e2 ♖d8 14
♕c2 ♘fg4 15 ♘xe5 ♕xe5 16 g3 ♗f5
17 ♕c1 (G.Georgadze-Lesiège, Elista
OL 1998) 17...♕e4 18 c4 f6 is better
for Black.

b) 12 ♖c1 doesn't make a lot of
sense: 12...♗f5 (12...♗g4!?) 13 ♗b5

e4 14 ♗xc6 ♕xc6 15 ♘e5 ♕c7 =
Lapienis-Salm, corr. 1989.

c) 12 ♗e2 and here:

c1) 12...♖d8 13 ♕c2 transposes to
Line A1.

c2) 12...e4 13 ♘d2 ♗f5 (13...♖d8
14 ♕c2 transposes to the note to
Black's 13th move in Line A1) 14 c4
♖fe8 15 d5 ♘e5 16 ♖e1 ♗g6 17 a4
♖ab8 18 ♖a3 ♘fd7 19 f4 exf3 20 gxf3
f6 21 f4 ♘f7 22 ♗g4 f5 23 ♗f3 and
White is comfortably better, Flear-
Spassky, London 1986.

c3) 12...♗g4 13 dxe5 ♘xe5 14 c4
♘xf3+ 15 ♗xf3 ♖fd8 16 ♕e2 ♗xf3
17 ♕xf3 ♘e8 18 h4 ♕e7 19 h5 h6 20
♖fd1 b6 21 ♕g4 and White's bishop is
stronger than the black knight, Yusu-
pov-Ehlvest, Riga Tal mem 1995.

12...e4

Or:

a) 12...♖d8 13 ♗a2 ♕e7 14 ♘g5
♖f8 15 d5 ♘a5 16 c4 with a solid advantage for White, Gligorić-Van Scheltinga, Dublin 1957.

b) 12...b6 13 ♕e2 ♗b7 14 ♗a2 e4
15 ♘d2 ♖ad8 16 ♖ad1 and now,
instead of 16...♕c8?! 17 d5! ♗a6 18
c4 ♘xd5 19 ♘xe4, when all White's
pieces have awoken, Cherepkov-Spas-
sky, USSR Ch (Moscow) 1961, Black
should continue 16...♕e7, preventing
White from playing d5.

c) 12...♗f5 and now:

c1) 13 ♗b5 e4 14 ♘h4 ♗e6 15 c4
cxd4 16 exd4 a6 17 d5 axb5 18 ♗xf6
gxf6 19 dxe6 bxc4 20 ♕g4+ ♔h8 21
♕xe4 fxe6 22 ♕xc4 = Bennborn-
Nabel, corr. 1999.

c2) 13 ♕e2 ♖fe8 14 ♖fd1 ♖ad8 15
a4 e4 16 ♘d2 ♘d5 17 ♘b3 cxd4
(Hort-King, Bundesliga 1985/6) 18
cxd4 leaves White with the upper hand.

13 ♘d2

13 ♘h2 is also interesting, but Black obtains a pleasant position after 13...b6 14 ♖c1 ♘a5 15 ♗a2 ♗a6 16 c4 cxd4 17 ♗xd4 ♕c6 18 ♘g4 ♘d7, Franić-Palac, Zadar 1995.

13...♘a5

Or:

a) 13...♗f5 14 ♘b3 b6 15 ♕e2 ♖ad8 16 a4 ♘e7 17 ♘d2 ♘g6 18 f4 exf3 19 ♕xf3 is quite pleasant for White, Najdorf-Rubinetti, Buenos Aires 1970.

b) 13...♘e7 and then:

b1) 14 ♗e2 gives White an edge: 14...cxd4 15 cxd4 ♗e6 16 ♕b1 ♗d5 17 ♖c1 ♕d7 18 a4 ♖fc8 19 a5 ± Brinck-Claussen – Kolarov, Lugano OL 1968.

b2) 14 ♗b3!? b5? (this is a big misunderstanding that allows White to open the position for his bishops; a safer and better choice is 14...♗f5, followed by development of the rooks to the c- and d-files) 15 c4! ♗e6?! 16 cxb5 ♗xb3 17 ♕xb3 +− Maresca-Pellegrini, corr. 1984.

14 ♗a2 c4

14...♗f5 15 c4 ♖fe8 16 d5 ♘d7 17 f4 exf3 18 ♕xf3 ♗g6 19 h4!? with an initiative for White, Kramnik-Tiviakov, Wijk aan Zee 2001.

15 f3

Or 15 a4 ♖e8 16 ♗a3 ♗e6 17 ♖b1 b6 18 ♕c2 ♗d5 19 ♖b5 with an ongoing initiative for White, Prasad-Mishra, Indian Ch (Nagpur) 2002.

15...♗xh3

15...♕c6 isn't any good: 16 ♗b1 ♕b5 17 ♖a2 ♕g5 18 fxe4 ♗xh3 19 ♕f3 ± Casas-Lombardy, Argentina 1957.

16 ♘xe4 ♘xe4 17 fxe4 ♕g3 18 ♕f3 ♕xf3 19 ♖xf3

± Cherepkov-Tseshkovsky, USSR Ch (Alma-Ata) 1968.

A5)

11 ♗b5 (D)

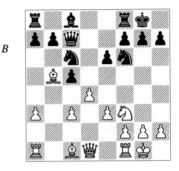

B

11...a6

There are various alternatives for Black:

a) 11...♘a5 12 ♗d3 c4 13 ♗c2 b6 14 e4 ♘b3 15 ♖b1 is slightly better for White, R.Garcia-Rosetto, Mar del Plata 1966.

b) 11...b6?!, although played several times by strong GMs, is of questionable value:

b1) 12 ♕e2 ♗b7 13 e4 e5 14 d5 ♘a5 15 ♘h4 ♗c8 16 ♖d1 ♘e8 17 f4 ♘d6 18 ♗d3 f6 19 ♖b1 ♕e7 with a pleasant game for Black, Marzolo-Belozerov, Tallinn jr Ech 1997.

b2) 12 ♖e1 ♗b7 13 e4 ♘e7 14 ♗d3 ♘d7 15 g3 ♖fd8 (15...♖ad8!? 16 ♗f4 ♕c8 17 a4 ± Knaak) 16 ♗f4 ♕c6 17 a4! ♘f8 18 h4 ♕e8 19 a5 ± Ivanchuk-Tiviakov, Linares 1995.

c) 11...♗d7 and here:

c1) 12 ♕e2 a6 13 ♗d3 e5 14 ♘xe5 ♘xe5 15 dxe5 ♕xe5 16 f4 ♕e7 17 e4 c4 18 ♗c2 ♗f5 ½-½ Szabo-Padevsky, Moscow OL 1956.

c2) 12 Rb1 Da5 (still untried, but apparently best) 13 Ad3 Ac6 14 De5 Ae4 15 f3 Axd3 16 Wxd3 Dc6 = (Taimanov).

c3) 12 a4 is the move seen most frequently:

c31) 12...Da5 13 Aa3 b6 14 De5 Axb5 15 axb5 Rfd8 16 Wf3 ± Kuuksmaa-Axelson, corr. 1968.

c32) 12...Rfd8 13 Aa3 b6 14 We2 Da5 15 Rac1 Axb5 16 axb5 ± Kuzmin-Estevez, Leningrad IZ 1973.

c33) 12...b6 13 Re1 a6 14 Af1 Rfc8 15 Aa3 Da5 16 De5 Ae8 17 Ad3 ± Geller-Matanović, USSR-Yugoslavia (Zagreb) 1958.

c34) 12...a6 and here:

c341) 13 Ad3 e5 14 Wc2 Rfe8 15 Dxe5 Dxe5 16 dxe5 Wxe5 17 f3 (Chinch-Deforel, corr. 1989) 17...Rad8 18 e4 Ae6 =.

c342) 13 Ae2 Rfd8 14 Aa3 e5 15 Wc2 cxd4 16 cxd4 exd4 17 Ae7 Rdc8 18 Axf6 gxf6 19 We4 (Lerner-Zaichik, USSR 1978) 19...Wd6 20 Rad1 We6 21 Wh4 and White has the initiative (Tal).

d) 11...Rd8 and now:

d1) 12 Wc2 Ad7 13 a4 Rac8 14 Aa3 cxd4 15 exd4 Ae8 = Gligorić-Matanović, Yugoslav Ch (Kragujevac) 1959.

d2) 12 Ab2 a6 13 Ad3 e5 14 Wc2 Ag4 15 Dxe5 Dxe5 16 dxe5 Wxe5 = Geller-Averbakh, USSR Ch (Leningrad) 1960.

d3) 12 Re1 a6 13 Ad3 e5 14 Wc2 Ag4 15 Dxe5 Dxe5 16 dxe5 Wxe5 17 f3 Ae6 18 Af1 (O'Kelly-Secchi, corr. 1959) 18...b5!, intending ...Ac4, with equal chances – Taimanov.

12 Ad3

Two alternatives:

a) 12 Axc6 is quite harmless for Black: 12...Wxc6 13 Re1 b5 14 De5 Wc7 15 e4 Ab7 16 f3 Rfc8 17 Ae3 cxd4 18 cxd4 Dd7 19 Dd3 Wc2 = Speelman-Tiviakov, Kropotkin 1995.

b) 12 Ae2 e5 and now:

b1) 13 Ab2 Rd8 14 Wc2 Ag4 15 dxe5 Dxe5 16 c4 Dxf3+ 17 gxf3 Ah5 (or 17...Ah3 18 Rfb1 We7 19 Kh1 We6 20 Rg1 Af5 21 Wc3 Ag6 = Lautier-Yermolinsky, Wijk aan Zee 1997) 18 Rfd1 Dd7 19 Rd2 Df8 20 Rad1 f6 21 Ac3 Af7 22 f4 Rxd2 23 Wxd2 ± Malaniuk-Tiviakov, Kropotkin 1995.

b2) 13 Wc2 Ag4 14 d5 Da5 (not 14...Dxd5? on account of 15 Dg5 Df6 16 Axg4 h6 17 De6! fxe6 18 Axe6+ ± Chekhov) 15 e4 c4 (Iskusnykh-Balashov, Elista 1995) and now 16 Ae3 leaves White better – Chekhov.

12...e5 13 Wc2 (D)

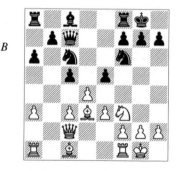

13...Re8

The threat of ...e4 now forces White to make a decision about the centre. Other tries include:

a) 13...Rd8 14 Ab2 Ag4 15 Dg5 h6 16 Dge4 Dxe4 17 Axe4 Ae6 (Szabo-Gligorić, Buenos Aires 1955) 18 Rfd1 ±.

b) 13...b5 14 e4! exd4 15 cxd4 c4 16 ♗e2 ♖e8 17 d5 ♘e5 18 ♗b2 ♘xf3+ 19 ♗xf3 ♗g4 20 d6 ♕c6 21 ♗xg4 ♘xg4 22 h3 ♘e5 23 ♖ad1 ± Timman-Lutz, Wijk aan Zee 1995.

14 e4!? *(D)*

This is clearly White's most interesting choice. The alternative 14 ♘xe5 ♘xe5 15 dxe5 ♕xe5 is worth looking into, but Black should be OK: 16 f3 ♗d7 (16...b5 17 ♖e1 ♗b7 18 e4 c4 19 ♗f1 ♘d5 20 ♗d2 ♘f4 is equal, Petrosian-Averbakh, Portorož IZ 1958) 17 ♖b1 ♗c6 18 ♖e1 ♖ad8 19 ♗f1 ♘d7 20 e4 ± Kamsky-Tiviakov, Groningen 1995.

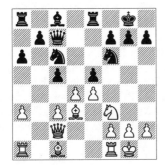

14...exd4

14...c4 hasn't been played since the early 1960s and for a good reason, as it leaves it up to White to play for a win: 15 ♗xc4 exd4 16 cxd4 ♘a5 17 ♘e5 ♗e6 18 ♗d3 ♕xc2 19 ♗xc2 ♖ac8 20 ♗d3 ♘b3 21 ♖b1 ♘xd4 22 ♖xb7 with better chances for White due to Black's weak a-pawn, Bronstein-Filip, Portorož IZ 1958.

15 cxd4 ♗g4 16 e5

16 ♕xc5 ♘xe4 17 ♗xe4 ♖xe4 is about even, Vaïsser-Kacheishvili, Erevan OL 1996.

16...♗xf3 17 exf6 ♘xd4 18 ♗xh7+ ♔h8 19 fxg7+ ♔xg7 20 ♗b2 ♖ad8

Farago-Dely, Budapest 1965. Now 21 ♗f5!? is White's best, with chances for both sides.

B)

6 a3 ♗xc3+ 7 bxc3 *(D)*

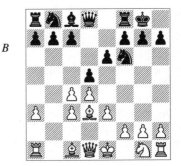

Now:

B1: 7...c5   90
B2: 7...dxc4   94

Other possibilities are seen on occasion:

a) 7...b6 8 cxd5 exd5 9 f3 c5 10 ♘e2 ♗a6 11 0-0 transposes to note 'b' to White's 11th move in Line B1.

b) 7...♘bd7?! 8 cxd5 exd5 9 ♘e2 ♖e8 10 0-0 ♘f8 11 f3 c5 12 ♘g3 cxd4 13 cxd4 a6 14 ♕d2 ± Euwe-Steiner, Groningen 1946.

c) 7...e5 8 cxd5 (8 ♘e2 is also seen now and then, but Black obtains a pleasant position after 8...e4 9 ♗c2 dxc4 10 ♘g3 ♖e8 11 0-0 ♗g4 12 ♕e1 c5 13 ♖b1 ♕c7 14 a4 ♘c6 15 ♖b5, Suba-Chandler, London 1990, when Rogers's 15...b6 is best) 8...♕xd5 9 f3 exd4 10 cxd4 c5 11 ♘e2 cxd4 12 ♘xd4 ♘c6 13 ♘xc6 ♕xc6 14 0-0 ±

Furman-Kholmov, USSR Ch (Leningrad) 1963.

d) 7...c6 reminds me of a Semi-Slav, but with the dark-squared bishop missing: 8 ♘e2 b6 9 cxd5 cxd5 10 0-0 ♗a6 11 f3! ♗xd3 12 ♕xd3 ♕c8 13 e4 ♕a6 14 ♕e3 ± Ibragimov-Rausis, Linares 1997.

B1)
7...c5
This is the natural follow-up.
8 cxd5
8 ♘e2 dxc4 9 ♗xc4 transposes to Line B2.
8...exd5
This recapture with the pawn is played almost exclusively, but the two alternative captures are also available to Black:

a) 8...♘xd5 can be met by 9 c4 ♘f6 10 ♘f3 ± (Botvinnik) or 9 ♘e2 followed by 0-0 and e4, with an advantage for White.

b) 8...♕xd5 9 ♘f3 (9 ♕f3 used to be considered the best move, but in Milov-Ki.Georgiev, Groningen FIDE 1997, Black showed how to equalize: 9...cxd4 10 ♕xd5 ♘xd5 11 cxd4 b6 12 ♗d2 ♗a6 13 ♗xa6 ♘xa6 14 ♘f3 ♖fc8 =) 9...b6 (or 9...cxd4 10 exd4 ♘bd7 11 c4 ♕a5+ 12 ♗d2 ♕c7 13 0-0 ± Kotov-Yanofsky, Groningen 1946) 10 ♕e2 cxd4 11 cxd4 ♗b7 12 0-0 ♘bd7 13 ♗b2 ♖ac8 14 ♖fc1 h6 15 ♗c4 ♕f5 16 a4 ± Gelfand-Rozentalis, Tilburg 1992.

9 ♘e2 (D)
Or 9 f3:

a) 9...b6 10 ♘e2 is note 'a' to White's 10th move.

b) 9...♘c6 10 ♘e2 ♖e8 transposes to note 'd23' to Black's 9th move.

c) 9...♖e8 10 ♘e2 b6 (10...♘c6 is again note 'd23' to Black's 9th move) 11 0-0 and now 11...♗a6 transposes to note 'b2' to White's 11th move and 11...♘c6 to note 'd232' to Black's 9th move.

B

9...b6
This is Black's most natural move and was also Capablanca's choice in his famed loss to Botvinnik in Rotterdam (AVRO) 1938. Black supports his c5-pawn while preparing ...♗a6 to exchange off White's strong bishop. Alternatives include:

a) 9...♖e8 10 0-0 will transpose to other lines; e.g., 10...♘bd7 11 f3 ♘f8 transposes to note 'b' to Black's 7th move in Line B, 10...♘c6 is line 'd23' and 10...b6 11 f3 ♖e8 transposes to note 'a' to Black's 10th move.

b) 9...♗g4 10 0-0 (10 f3 leads to similar positions) 10...♗h5 11 ♖b1 ♕c7 12 f3 ♗g6 13 ♘f4 ♘c6 14 g4 ♖ad8 15 ♖b2 ♖fe8 (Sadler-Abramović, Oberwart 1990) 16 g5! ♘h5 17 ♘xg6 fxg6 18 f4 ♘e7 19 f5 ± Abramović.

c) 9...c4?! is a bit premature in my book; Black will want to wait to make this decision for some time as he may be able to open the c-file and use it to his own advantage. After 10 ♗c2, Black has tried:

c1) 10...♗g4?! 11 f3 ♗h5 12 ♘g3 ♗g6 13 0-0 ♖e8 14 ♗xg6 hxg6 15 ♕c2 ♘c6 16 ♗d2 ± with e4 to follow soon, Bozić-Simonović, Yugoslav Ch (Zagreb) 1946.

c2) 10...♘c6 (or 10...♖e8 11 0-0 ♘c6) 11 0-0 ♖e8 12 f3 b5 13 ♘g3 h5 (13...♗e6? is worse: 14 e4 ♘d7 15 f4 f6? 16 exd5 ♗xd5 17 ♗xh7+ +− Henley-Gunawan, Surakarta 1982) 14 ♘h1 (Romanovsky gives 14 e4!? h4 15 ♘h1 dxe4 {15...h3!?} 16 fxe4 ♘xe4 17 ♕f3, when Black's position is falling apart) 14...♘a5 15 ♘f2 ♗b7 16 ♖e1 ± and White is ready to play e4, Petrosian-Troianescu, Budapest 1952.

d) 9...♘c6 (D) is another popular way of meeting White's set-up. Now:

d1) 10 f3 usually transposes to line 'd23' via 10...♖e8 11 0-0.

d2) 10 0-0 and now:

d21) 10...b6 11 f3 ♖e8 transposes to line 'd232'.

d22) 10...♗g4 11 f3 ♗h5 12 ♖b1 ♖b8 (or 12...b6 13 ♘f4 ♗g6 14 g4 with an initiative for White, Reshevsky-Fischer, Los Angeles (11) 1961) 13 ♘f4 ♗g6 14 ♘xg6 hxg6 15 a4 ♖e8 16 ♖e1 ± B.Lalić-Garcia Ilundain, Andorra 1993.

d23) 10...♖e8 11 f3 (11 a4 ♗d7 12 ♘g3 ♖c8 13 ♗a3 cxd4 14 cxd4 ♘a5 15 ♘f5 ± Aleman-J.Enevoldsen, Helsinki OL 1952) and here:

d231) 11...♕c7 12 ♘g3 ♗d7 13 ♖a2 ♖ac8 14 ♖e2 ♕b6?! (14...cxd4 15 cxd4 ♘a5 ± Moiseev) 15 ♔h1 cxd4 16 cxd4 ♘a5 17 ♖b2 is much better for White, Vaganian-Balashov, Leningrad 1977.

d232) 11...b6 12 ♖a2 ♘a5 (12...♗b7 13 g4 c4 14 ♗b1 ♘a5 15 ♘g3 ♘b3 16 g5 ♘d7 17 e4 leaves White with a strong kingside initiative, Kacheishvili-Jenni, Linares 2001) 13 ♘g3 ♗b7 14 ♖e2 ♖c8 15 ♔h1 cxd4 16 cxd4 ♘c4 17 e4 ± M.Gurevich-Agzamov, USSR Ch (Riga) 1985.

d233) 11...♖b8 12 ♖f2 ♕c7 13 g4 b5 14 ♘g3 is slightly better for White, Hoeksema-Sosonko, Dutch Ch (Eindhoven) 1993.

d234) 11...♗d7 12 ♘g3 ♕c7 (the alternative 12...♕a5?! didn't fare well in Petrosian-Ljubojević, Nikšić 1983: 13 ♕d2! ♕a4 14 ♖b1 ♘a5 15 ♗c2 ♕c4 16 ♗d3 ♕a4 17 e4 ±) 13 ♖a2 h6 14 ♖e2 ♖ad8 15 ♗b2 b5 16 e4 cxd4 17 cxd4 ♕b6 18 ♗b1 ♗c8 19 ♖d2 ± ECO.

10 0-0

Or:

a) 10 f3 and now 10...♗b7 11 0-0 transposes to note 'c' to Black's 10th move, while 10...♗a6 11 0-0 is note 'b' to White's 11th move.

b) 10 a4 ♖e8 (10...♗a6?! 11 ♗a3 ♕c8 12 0-0 ♖e8 13 ♘g3 ♗xd3 14 ♕xd3 c4 15 ♕c2 g6 16 ♖ac1 ± Spassky-Yukhtman, USSR 1952) 11 0-0 ♕c7 12 ♗a3 ♘bd7 13 ♘g3 ♗b7 14 ♖c1 ♖ad8 = Stoltz-Kaila, Helsinki 1947.

10...♗a6 (D)

Black continues in accordance with his initial game-plan; his hope is that if White achieves the e4 advance, White's pressure on the kingside will be less of a threat with the light-squared bishops off the board. Otherwise:

a) 10...♖e8 11 f3 (11 a4 transposes to note 'b' to White's 10th move) and now 11...♗a6 transposes to note 'b2' to White's 11th move and 11...♘c6 to note 'd232' to Black's 9th move.

b) 10...♘c6 11 f3 ♖e8 is again note 'd232' to Black's 9th move.

c) 10...♗b7 11 f3 ♘c6 12 ♘g3 ♖e8 13 ♕d2 ♕d7 14 ♗b2 ♖ad8 15 ♖ad1 ± Kramer-Lange, Baarn 1949.

11 ♗xa6

Rather than awaiting the inevitable, White exchanges the bishops immediately to misplace Black's queen's knight somewhat. The alternatives also have some merit:

a) 11 ♘g3 ♗xd3 12 ♕xd3 ♘c6 13 ♗b2 ♘a5 14 ♖ad1 cxd4 15 cxd4 ♖e8 16 f3 ♘c4 17 ♗c1 ♘d6 18 ♖fe1 h5!? 19 ♘f5 ♘xf5 20 ♕xf5 ♕d7 = Høi-Tolnai, Budapest 1989.

b) With 11 f3, White continues his central build-up, a choice that has found many followers:

b1) 11...♗xd3 12 ♕xd3 and here:

b11) 12...♖e8 13 ♘g3 transposes to line 'b23'.

b12) 12...♘c6 13 e4 (13 ♘g3 ♖e8 is again line 'b23') 13...cxd4 14 cxd4 ♕d7 15 ♗g5 ♘e8 16 ♖ac1 ♘d8 17 ♗d2 ♘c7 18 ♗b4 ♖e8 19 e5 ± Cvitan-Čabrilo, Lugano 1984.

b13) 12...♘bd7 13 ♘g3 ♖e8 14 ♖a2 ♖c8 15 ♖e2 ♗e6 16 ♗b2 h5!? 17 e4! h4 18 ♘f5 ± Balashov-Groszpeter, Minsk 1982.

b2) 11...♖e8 maintains the pressure towards the e4-square. Now:

b21) 12 ♗xa6 ♘xa6 transposes to note 'c4' to White's 12th move.

b22) 12 ♖a2 ♕c8 13 ♗b1!? ♘c6 14 ♖e1 ♗c4 15 ♖b2 ♕a6 16 a4!? ♖ad8 17 g4! ♘d7 18 ♘f4 ♘f8 19 ♖g2 and White's chances are somewhat to be preferred, Gulko-Campora, San Roque 1996.

b23) 12 ♘g3 ♗xd3 (or 12...♕c8 13 ♗xa6 ♘xa6 14 ♕d3 ♕b7 15 ♖a2 ♖e6 16 ♖e2 ♖ae8 17 ♖fe1 h5 = Beliavsky-Short, Linares 1990) 13 ♕xd3 ♘c6 and then:

b231) 14 ♖a2 ♕d7 (or 14...♖c8 15 ♖e2 ♖c7 16 ♗b2 ♘d7 17 e4 ± Ragozin-Taimanov, USSR Ch (Moscow) 1948) 15 ♖e2 ♖ad8 16 ♗b2 h5 (or 16...♖e6 17 ♖d1 cxd4 18 cxd4 ♘e8 19 e4 ♘e7 20 e5 ♖c8 21 f4 g6 22 f5 with a strong initiative for White, Khalifman-Bologan, Prague rpd 2002) 17 ♖d1 h4 18 ♘f5 c4 19 ♕c2 ♘e7 20 ♘xe7+ ♖xe7 21 e4 dxe4 22 fxe4 ♖de8 with chances for both sides, Milov-Campora, Andorra 2001.

b232) 14 ♗b2 and here:

b2321) 14...♘a5 15 e4 ♘c4 16 ♗c1 cxd4 17 cxd4 ♘d7 18 e5 f6 19 f4 fxe5 20 fxe5 ♘f8 21 ♖a2 ± Lin Ta-Rogers, Shah Alam Z 1990.

b2322) 14...cxd4 15 cxd4 h5!? 16 ♖ae1 g6 17 e4 h4 18 ♘e2 ♘h5 19 e5 ♘e7 20 g4! ± Korchnoi-Tolnai, Austrian Cht 1996.

b2323) 14...♖c8 15 ♖ae1 (15 ♖ad1 is an interesting alternative; for example, 15...h5 16 e4 c4 17 ♕c2 g6 18

罝fe1 h4 19 ②f1 ②h5 20 鬱d2 gives
White an initiative, Grabliauskas-Djur-
huus, Copenhagen 1998) 15...鬱c7 16
e4 cxd4 17 cxd4 ②a5 18 e5 ②d7 19
罝e2 g6 20 f4 鬱c4 21 鬱f3 favours
White, Bareev-Matychenkov, USSR
Cht (Naberezhnye Chelny) 1988.

b2324) 14...c4!? 15 鬱d2 b5 16
罝ae1 a5 17 e4 b4! 18 e5 ②d7 (Aver-
bakh-Donchenko, USSR 1970) 19 ②f5
b3 is unclear – Kasparov.

11...②xa6 *(D)*

12 鬱d3

White continues to prepare the e4
central break. Alternatives include:

a) 12 ②b2? was Botvinnik's choice
in the famed game against Capablanca:
12...鬱d7 13 a4 罝fe8? (Kasparov gives
13...cxd4 14 cxd4 罝fc8, intending
...罝c4 and ...罝ac8, when Black holds
the initiative) 14 鬱d3 c4? (14...鬱b7!
was Botvinnik's recommendation) 15
鬱c2 ②b8 16 罝ae1 ②c6 17 ②g3 ②a5
18 f3 with an initiative for White, Bot-
vinnik-Capablanca, Rotterdam (AVRO)
1938.

b) 12 鬱a4 鬱c8 13 ②b2 ②e4 14
罝ad1 b5 15 鬱c2 罝e8 16 ②f4 鬱c6
with chances for both sides, Ribeiro-
Pomar, Skopje OL 1972.

c) 12 f3 and here:

c1) 12...②b8 13 鬱d3 罝e8 14 ②g3
transposes to note 'b23' to White's
11th move.

c2) 12...②c7 13 ②g3 罝e8 14 罝e1
鬱d7 15 e4 dxe4 16 fxe4 ②b5 17 ②b2 ±
Vaganian-Antoshin, USSR Ch (Riga)
1970.

c3) 12...鬱d7 13 ②g3 cxd4 (*ECO*
suggests 13...罝ad8!?) 14 cxd4 罝fe8
15 鬱d3 ②c7 16 a4 ②e6 17 ②d2 ±
Arencibia-Agdestein, Gausdal jr Wch
1986.

c4) 12...罝e8 13 ②g3 ②c7 14 鬱d3
②e6 15 ②b2 罝c8 16 罝ad1 鬱c7 17
罝c1 g6 18 e4 c4 19 鬱d2 鬱f4 20 鬱f2
鬱h4 = Radjabov-Mateo, Biel 2000.

12...②c7

Or 12...鬱c8 13 ②b2 (13 f3 罝e8 14
②g3 transposes to Beliavsky-Short in
note 'b23' to White's 11th move)
13...cxd4 14 cxd4 ②c7 15 罝fe1 鬱d7
16 f3 罝fe8 ± Reshevsky-Fine, New
York 1941.

13 f3

White continues in line with the
standard plan. There are two other options:

a) 13 dxc5!? bxc5 14 c4 罝b8 (or
14...dxc4 15 鬱xc4 鬱d5 = Fine-Stein-
er, USA 1940) 15 罝a2 鬱e7 16 cxd5
②cxd5 17 罝c2 罝fc8 18 ②g3 鬱c7 19
e4 ②f4 20 鬱f3 ②g6 21 ②b2 罝b6
(Suba-Sax, Manila OL 1992) 22 罝fc1
±.

b) 13 ②g3 鬱d7 14 f3 (14 a4!?)
14...鬱b5 15 鬱d2 鬱c6 (15...cxd4 16
cxd4 ②e6 =) 16 ②b2 罝fe8 17 罝ae1
罝ad8 18 鬱f2 ②d7 19 e4 with a better
game for White, Szabo-Hort, Budapest 1973.

13...鬱e8

Two alternatives:

a) 13...罝e8 14 ♘g3 ♘e6 15 ♗b2 ♕d7 16 罝ae1 ± Tomić-Szabo, Vinkovci 1970.

b) 13...♕d7 14 e4 ♕b5 15 ♕xb5 ♘xb5 16 a4 ♘c7 17 exd5 罝fe8 18 d6 (Vaiser-Oll, Tallinn rpd 1983) 18...罝xe2 19 dxc7 cxd4 20 cxd4 ♘d5 =.

14 a4 ♕c6 15 c4 cxd4 16 cxd5 ♕xd5 17 e4 ♕d7 18 ♕xd4

Now Lilienthal-Benkö, Budapest-Moscow 1949 continued 18...♘e6 19 ♕f2 罝fd8 20 ♗b2 ± but, as suggested in *ECO*, Black can equalize with 18...罝fd8 19 ♕f2 罝ac8 20 ♗b2 ♘ce8 =.

B2)
7...dxc4 8 ♗xc4 c5 (D)

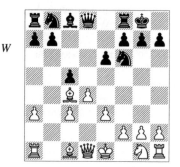

9 ♘e2

This version of the Main Variation is largely harmless since White lets Black do pretty much what he wants in the centre. Alternatives include:

a) 9 ♘f3 is likely to take us to Line A (9...♘c6 10 0-0 transposes immediately) and may be White's best move.

b) 9 ♗b2 has been a favourite of Milov's. Now:

b1) 9...♕c7 10 ♗d3 b6 (10...e5?! 11 dxe5 ♕xe5 12 ♘f3 ♕e7 13 c4 ♘c6

14 ♕c2 ± Milov-Lutz, Saint Vincent Ech 2000) 11 e4 (11 ♕e2 ♘c6 12 e4 e5 13 d5 ♘a5 14 h3 c4 15 ♗c2 ♘d7 is quite comfortable for Black, Petrosian-Najdorf, Buenos Aires 1979) 11...e5 12 d5 c4 13 ♗c2 ♘bd7 14 ♘e2 ♘c5 15 ♘g3 b5 16 0-0 a5 17 ♗c1 罝a6 18 罝b1 ♗d7 19 f4 and White has a sizeable advantage, Milov-J.Polgar, Buenos Aires 2000.

b2) 9...♕a5!? has become an important alternative in recent years:

b21) 10 ♕d2 ♘bd7 11 罝c1 b5 12 ♗d3 ♗b7 13 ♘f3 罝ac8 is better for Black, Milov-Tiviakov, Buenos Aires 1996.

b22) 10 ♘e2 cxd4 11 exd4 b6 12 0-0 ♗a6 13 ♗d3 ♗xd3 14 ♕xd3 ♘bd7 15 c4 罝ac8 16 罝fc1 ♕a4 17 ♘g3 罝fd8 and a draw was soon agreed upon in Yusupov-Z.Almasi, Dortmund 1998.

b23) 10 ♘f3 cxd4 11 exd4 b6 (11...♘bd7 12 0-0 e5 13 罝e1 exd4 14 ♘xd4 ♘e5 15 ♗b5 ♕c7 16 ♕e2 ♘g6 17 c4 ♗g4 18 f3 gives White a slight pull, Balashov-Osnos, Moscow 1972) 12 0-0 (12 a4 ♗a6 13 ♘d2 罝c8 14 ♗xa6 ♕xa6 15 c4 ♘bd7 16 0-0 ♕a5 17 罝e1 罝c7 18 罝e3 罝ac8 = Milov-Lautier, Biel 1996) 12...♗a6 13 ♗d3 罝c8 14 罝c1 ♗xd3 15 ♕xd3 b5 16 ♘d2 ♘bd7 = Milov-Granda, Buenos Aires 1996.

9...♕c7

This is Black's most popular choice; he prepares ...e5. Other moves with the same idea have also been tried:

a) 9...♘bd7 10 0-0 e5 11 a4 ♕c7 12 ♗a2 b6 13 ♗a3 ♗a6 14 c4 罝fe8 15 d5 e4 16 ♘g3 ♕e5 17 ♕c2 ♕g5 18 罝ae1 h5 with chances for both sides, Fradkin-Luther, Sverdlovsk 1989.

b) 9...b6 10 0-0 ♕c7 11 ♗d3 ♗a6 (11...e5!? – Pliester) 12 e4 ♗xd3 13 ♕xd3 ♘bd7 14 ♗g5 ♕c6 15 ♘g3 h6 16 ♗d2 ♖ad8 17 ♕e2 ♔h8 18 e5 ♘g8 with chances for both sides, Damljanović-Lukacs, Belgrade 1984.

c) 9...e5 and then:

c1) 10 0-0 and here: 10...♘bd7 is line 'a'; 10...♘c6 transposes to line 'd43'; 10...♕c7 11 ♗d3 transposes to the main line.

c2) 10 ♗a2 ♕c7 11 f3 (*ECO*'s 11 0-0 ♘c6 12 d5 is about even) 11...♖d8 12 d5 e4! 13 0-0 ♘bd7 14 fxe4 ♕e5 15 ♗b1 ♘xe4 16 ♕c2 f5 17 c4!? ♘d6 18 ♔h1 ♖e8 19 ♘g3 ♘b6 with better chances for Black, Agdestein-Chandler, Haninge 1988.

d) 9...♘c6 (*D*) is very direct and prepares ...e5. Now:

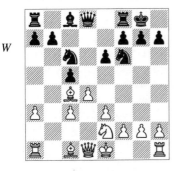

W

d1) 10 a4 ♕c7 11 ♕c2 b6 12 ♗d3 ♘a5 13 ♗a3 ♗b7 14 dxc5 bxc5 15 c4 ♘c6 16 0-0 ♘e5 = Boudy-Filip, Polanica Zdroj 1976.

d2) 10 ♘g3 e5 11 d5 ♘a5 12 ♗a2 and now:

d21) 12...♘e8!? (aiming for d6 to block White's passed d-pawn and control the c4-square *á la* Nimzowitsch) 13 e4 ♘d6 14 0-0 f6 15 f4 ♗d7

(Milov-Psakhis, Haifa 1995) and now, according to Dautov, White should continue 16 ♗e3!? b6 17 fxe5. He then gave 17...fxe5 18 ♕h5 ♘ac4 19 ♗xc4 ♘xc4 20 ♗g5 ♖xf1+ 21 ♖xf1 ♕e8 22 ♕h4 ♘xa3 23 ♘h5 with compensation for the pawn, which in my opinion is rather substantial; the threat is ♗f6 with a strong attack. However, 17...♘ac4! improves: 18 ♗xc4 ♘xc4 19 ♕e2 ♘xe5 20 ♗f4 ♖e8 and Black is doing fine.

d22) 12...♗d7 13 c4 b5 14 cxb5 ♗xb5 15 f3 (15 e4!? ♘b7, intending ...♘d6, is fine for Black), Milov-Alterman, Israel 1997, 15...e4! and now Alterman gives the following lines: 16 ♗b2 ♘c4! 17 ♗xc4 ♗xc4 18 ♗xf6 ♕xf6 19 ♖c1 ♗d3 20 fxe4 c4 with compensation, and 16 fxe4 ♖e8 17 ♗b1 ♖b8! 18 ♗c2 h5 19 ♕f3 ♘c4 with an initiative.

d3) 10 f4 was played in the interesting pairing Larsen-Gligorić, Lone Pine 1979. Incidentally, Larsen is an expert on the black side in the Nimzo-Indian and Gligorić on the white side of the Rubinstein. After 10...b6 11 0-0 ♗b7 12 ♘g3 ♘a5 13 ♗d3 cxd4 14 cxd4 ♖c8 15 ♖f2 ♘c4 16 a4 ♖e8 17 ♖c2 ♕d5 18 ♕e2 ♘d6 Black controlled the centre and had the better chances.

d4) 10 0-0 is quite a popular alternative:

d41) 10...♕e7!? was suggested by Botvinnik, who continued his analysis 11 ♗a2 ♖d8 12 ♕e1 e5 13 ♗b2 cxd4 14 cxd4 exd4 15 ♘xd4 ♘xd4 16 ♗xd4 ♗e6 with even chances, but improvements seem possible; e.g., 13...♗e6!? and 12...b6!? both look very interesting for Black.

d42) 10...♕c7 11 ♗b2 (other possibilities are 11 ♗a2 and 11 ♗d3) 11...♖d8 (11...e5 transposes to line 'd4342') 12 ♗a2 b6 13 ♖e1 ♗b7 14 ♘g3 ♖d7 15 ♕e2 ♖ad8 16 ♖ad1 ± Petrosian-Korchnoi, Velden Ct (14) 1980.

d43) 10...e5 *(D)* and now:

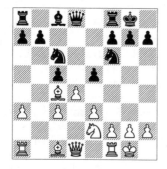

d431) 11 ♗a2 ♗e6! 12 ♗xe6 fxe6 13 ♕b3 ♕d5 14 c4 ♕d7 15 dxe5 ♘xe5 16 ♗b2 ♕d3 17 ♘c1 ♕xb3 18 ♘xb3 ♘xc4 19 ♗xf6 ♖xf6 ½-½ J.O.Fries Nielsen-Cu.Hansen, Esbjerg 1985.

d432) 11 a4 ♕c7 12 ♗a2 ♖d8 13 d5 e4 14 f4?! (14 ♘f4 is a safer option for White) 14...c4! 15 ♗xc4 ♗g4 16 ♖f2 (Pomes-Psakhis, Terres Catalanes 1996) 16...♘e7! 17 ♗b3 ♘exd5 and White's position is falling apart.

d433) 11 ♖b1 ♕c7 12 ♗a2 ♖d8 13 ♕c2 b6 14 ♘g3 (Speelman-Karpov, Linares 1991) and here Pliester gives 14...♗a6 as best, while Ftačnik suggests 14...♗e6!? 15 ♗xe6 fxe6, which he believes is equal.

d434) 11 ♗b2 *(D)* is the main continuation:

d4341) 11...♕d6 12 f3 ♖d8 13 ♖c1 ♗e6 14 ♗xe6 fxe6 15 ♕e1 ♖ac8 16

♕g3 b6 with a pleasant game for Black, Flear-Lau, Bundesliga 1983/4.

d4342) 11...♕c7 12 ♗a2 (12 ♗d3 transposes to the main line; 12 ♖c1 ♘a5 13 ♗a2 ♖d8 14 ♘g3 ♗e6 15 ♗xe6 fxe6 16 ♕e2 c4 is slightly better for Black, Ermenkov-Kindermann, Baden-Baden 1985) 12...♖d8 13 ♕c2 ♗g4 14 ♖ad1 e4 15 f3 exf3 16 gxf3 ♗e6 17 c4 cxd4 18 ♘xd4 ♘xd4 19 ♗xd4 ♘e8 20 ♖c1 ½-½ Chandler-Kavalek, Bochum 1981.

d4343) 11...♗f5 12 ♘g3 (12 f3?! is inaccurate: 12...♕b6 13 ♕d2 ♘a5 14 ♗a2 ♗e6 15 dxe5 ♗xa2 16 exf6 ♖fd8 ∓ Høi-Romanishin, Plovdiv Echt 1983) 12...♗e6 13 ♗xe6 fxe6 14 ♕e2 ♖f7 15 dxe5 ♘xe5 16 c4 ♕c7 17 ♖ad1 ± Sadler-Motwani, Ostend 1991.

d4344) 11...♖e8 12 ♕c2 ♕c7 13 d5 ♘a5 14 ♗a2 c4 15 e4 ♘d7 16 ♗c1 ♘c5 17 ♗e3 ♗d7 with chances for both sides, Bagirov-Agzamov, Telavi 1982.

d4345) 11...♕e7 12 ♘g3 (or 12 a4 ♖d8 13 ♗a3 b6 14 ♕c2 ♘a5 15 ♗a2 ♗a6 16 ♖fe1 ♘c4 17 ♗xc4 ♗xc4 and Black is doing well, Høi-Sigurjonsson, Reykjavik 1982) 12...♖d8 13 d5 e4 14 ♗a2 (Gulko-Koepcke, Los Angeles 1987) 14...♗g4 15 ♕d2 c4 16 ♗xc4 ♗e6 = Pliester.

d4346) 11...♗e6! 12 ♗xe6 fxe6 13 ♕b3 ♕d5 14 ♕a2 (14 c4 leads to a pleasant game for Black after 14...♘a5 15 cxd5 ♘xb3 16 ♖ad1 exd4 17 dxe6 ♖ae8 18 exd4 ♖xe6 19 ♘c1 ♘xd4 20 ♗xd4 cxd4 21 ♖xd4 ♖c8, as in Grosz-peter-Ehlvest, St John 1988) 14...♕xa2 15 ♖xa2 ♖ac8 (15...♘a5!? is given as equal in *ECO*, but in fact Black even has the better chances) 16 ♗a1 ♘a5 17 dxe5 ♘g4 18 c4 ♘xc4 19 a4 (Vag-anian-Ehlvest, Tallinn 1983) 19...♖fd8 20 ♘f4 ♔f7 21 ♖c2 ♘a5 22 h3 ♘h6 = *ECO*.

10 ♗d3 *(D)*

With this move, White supports his central aspirations. Instead, 10 ♗a2 isn't difficult for Black to deal with:

a) 10...e5 transposes to note 'c2' to Black's 9th move.

b) 10...♖d8 11 0-0 e5 12 ♗b2 (12 f3!?) 12...♗e6!? 13 ♗xe6 fxe6 14 ♕b1!? (Golubović-Abramović, Tivat open 1995) and now 14...♘bd7 looks best; e.g., 15 ♕a2 c4 and Black should be OK.

c) 10...b6 11 0-0 ♗a6 and now:

c1) 12 ♗b2 ♘c6 13 ♖c1 ♘a5 14 c4 ♖fd8 15 ♕c2 cxd4 16 ♘xd4 ♖ac8 17 ♘f3 ♕e7 ∓ Høi-Øgaard, Gausdal Z 1987.

c2) 12 ♖e1 ♘c6 13 ♘g3 ♖fd8 14 ♗b2 (14 ♘h5 ♘xh5 15 ♕xh5 ♘a5 16 d5, Aleksandrov-Itkis, Kishinev 1998, 16...e5 17 e4 ♗c4 = Psakhis) 14...♘a5 15 a4 (or 15 ♗b1 ♖ac8 16 e4 ♘c4 17 ♗c1 cxd4 18 cxd4 e5! 19 d5 ♘e8 20 ♗d3 ♘ed6 21 ♕e2 b5 with an equal position, Marin-Dokhoian, Budapest 1988) 15...♗c4 16 ♗xc4 ♘xc4 17 ♕e2 ♘a5 18 e4 ♖ac8 is comfortable for Black, Ki.Georgiev-Hjartarson, Lina-res 1988.

B

10...e5

With this move, play takes on a character similar to that of Line A. Some alternatives:

a) 10...b6 11 0-0 transposes to note 'b' to Black's 9th move.

b) 10...♘c6 11 f4?! (the alternative is 11 0-0 e5 transposing to the main line) 11...b6 12 0-0 ♗b7 13 ♘g3 (13 e4 ♘a5 14 e5 ♕c6 15 ♖f3 ♘e4 is pleasant for Black – Pliester) 13...♖ad8 and now, instead of 14 e4? as played in Konings-Pliester, Enschede 1992, White should play 14 ♖b1, but Black is fine nonetheless after 14...♘a5 15 ♖b2 ♗c6.

11 0-0

Other moves have proved harmless:

a) 11 e4?! cxd4 12 cxd4 exd4 13 0-0 ♘c6 14 h3 ♖e8 15 ♘g3 ♘e5 16 ♗f4 ♗d7 17 ♗xe5 ♕xe5 18 f4 ♕a5 19 e5 ♘d5 20 ♕h5 h6 and White has some, but not quite adequate, compen-sation for the pawn, Lein-Hjartarson, Reykjavik 1990.

b) 11 dxe5 ♕xe5 12 ♕c2 ♗e6 13 ♘g3 c4 14 ♗e2 ♘bd7 15 0-0 ♘c5 16 f4 ♕c7 17 e4 ♘b3 18 ♖b1 ♕c5+ 19 ♔h1 ♗g4 and Black is having a good time, Hort-Sosonko, Hastings 1975/6.

11...♘c6 *(D)*

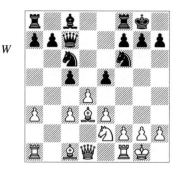

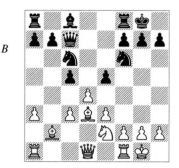

The best way for Black to continue. Other moves favour White:

a) 11...b6 12 ♘g3 ♘bd7 13 e4 cxd4 14 cxd4 exd4 15 ♗g5 h6 16 ♖c1 ♕b8 17 ♗h4 ± Greenfeld-Shrentzel, Beersheba 1988.

b) 11...e4 12 ♗c2 ♘c6 13 f3 cxd4 14 cxd4 exf3 15 ♖xf3 and at this point 15...♗g4 was met by 16 ♖xf6! gxf6 17 ♕d3 with a strong attack in Keene-Toth, Rome 1979.

12 ♗b2 (D)

This move looks more than a little odd, but the idea is to avoid getting an isolated d-pawn.

A similar idea lies behind 12 ♕c2 ♗e6 13 ♘g3 (now White gets the isolated d-pawn anyway, but other moves haven't proved too successful either) 13...cxd4 14 cxd4 exd4 15 ♗b2 ♖ac8 16 exd4 ♕f4 with a pleasant game for Black, Ibragimov-Dizdar, Budapest ECC 1996.

12...e4

12...♖d8 is another move to consider. After 13 ♘g3 exd4 14 cxd4 cxd4 15 ♕c2 ♕d6 16 ♖ad1 ♗g4 17 f3 ♗e6 18 exd4, Black has to be careful not to end up in serious trouble; e.g., 18...h6 19 d5 ♘xd5 20 ♗h7+ ♔f8 (20...♔h8 can lead to a draw; e.g., 21

♘h5 f6 22 ♘xg7 ♔xg7 23 ♕g6+ ♔h8 24 ♗g8!? ♗f5 25 ♕xf5 ♔xg8 26 ♕g6+ ♔f8 27 ♕xh6+ with a perpetual check) 21 ♘h5 and now Black blundered in Sadler-Wilder, London 1988 with 21...♘e5? 22 f4 ♘g4 23 ♗xg7+. He should instead have tried 21...f6, although 22 ♕g6 ♖d7 23 ♖fe1 isn't particularly inspiring.

13 ♗b1 ♘a5 14 ♗a2 c4 15 ♘f4 b6

Black has a fun alternative in 15...g5!? 16 ♘h5 ♘g4 17 ♘g3 h5, although after 18 f3, the black king may be in a bit too much danger.

16 a4 ♖e8 17 ♖e1 ♗b7 18 ♗a3 ♘d5 19 ♗b4 (D)

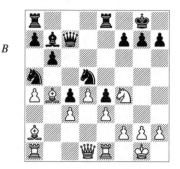

White has the better game, Sadler-Chandler, London Lloyds Bank 1991.

7 Classical Variation

1 d4 ♘f6 2 c4 e6 3 ♘c3 ♗b4 4 e3 0-0 5 ♘f3 d5 6 ♗d3 c5 7 0-0 ♘c6 8 a3 dxc4 9 ♗xc4 *(D)*

9 axb4 cxd4 10 ♗xc4 transposes to the note to White's 10th move.

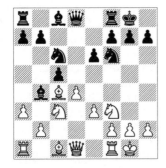

9...cxd4 10 exd4

White has a reasonable alternative in 10 axb4 dxc3:

a) 11 bxc3 is harmless: 11...♕c7 12 ♕b3 (or 12 ♗e2 b6 13 ♗b2 ♗b7 14 ♕b3 a5 15 ♕c4 ♕b8! 16 ♕h4 ♘e5 = Mecking-Larsen, Palma de Mallorca IZ 1970) 12...b6 13 ♖d1 ♗b7 14 ♗e2 (Stein-Ivkov, USSR-Yugoslavia 1963) 14...a5 = *ECO*.

b) 11 b5 ♕xd1 (11...♘e7!? is a possible alternative) 12 ♖xd1 c2 13 ♖d2 ♘b4 14 ♘e5 (14 ♖a4!? ♘bd5 15 ♗d3 ♗d7 16 e4 ♘c7 17 ♖b4 ♖fd8 18 ♘e5 leaves White somewhat better) 14...a6 15 f3 ♘fd5 16 e4 ♘b6 17 ♗e2 axb5 (17...a5!?) 18 ♖xa8 ♘xa8 19 ♗xb5 is slightly better for White, Yusupov-Kamsky, Tilburg 1993.

c) 11 ♕xd8 ♖xd8 12 bxc3 should be equal, but Black has to be careful that White's bishop-pair doesn't fully wake up: 12...b6!? (12...♘e4 13 b5 ♘e7 14 ♗b2 ♔f8 15 ♗e2 f6 16 ♖fd1 ± Polugaevsky-Gipslis, USSR 1969) 13 ♗b2 ♗b7 14 ♗e2 a6 15 ♖fd1 ♖xd1+ 16 ♖xd1 (Schmaus-Dünhaupt, corr. 1970) and here 16...b5 is necessary, as White will otherwise continue 17 c4 with both a spatial edge and the bishop-pair. According to Taimanov, White will then send his knight to a5 via d2-b3 with an advantage.

We now return to 10 exd4 *(D)*:

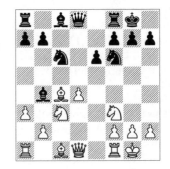

This is the basic position of the Classical Variation, which despite its name that oozes of grand games played by equally grand masters, is seen very rarely and has never been particularly popular at any level.

According to my database, this position was first reached in the game J.Berger-W.Paulsen, Nuremberg 1883, but through an entirely different move-order. The first game with a Nimzo move-order was Montgomerie-Alexander, Stockholm OL 1937.

10...♗e7

The bishop belongs here, although a few other moves have also been tried:

a) 10...♗a5!? bears a resemblance to lines covered in Chapter 3 and is a noteworthy idea. 11 ♗g5 (11 ♕d3!?) 11...h6 12 ♗e3 ♘e7 13 ♕d3 ♘ed5 14 ♘e5 (Frost-Pau, corr. 1991) and now 14...♗c7!? is equal.

b) 10...♗xc3 11 bxc3 and then:

b1) 11...♕a5 12 ♕e2 (12 ♕e1 b6 13 ♗g5 ♘d5 14 ♗d3 ♗a6 15 c4 ♕xe1 16 ♖fxe1 ± Eingorn) 12...♕xc3 13 ♗d2 ♕c2 14 ♗d3 ♕a4 (14...♕b3!? was suggested by Darga) 15 ♖fc1 ♘xd4 16 ♘xd4 ♕xd4 17 ♗b4 ♗d7 (17...♖e8!?) 18 ♗xf8 ♖xf8 19 ♗b5 ♗xb5 20 ♕xb5 ± Boleslavsky-Petrosian, USSR Ch (Moscow) 1957.

b2) 11...♕c7 12 ♕e2 b6?! (Black should try 12...♘a5 13 ♗d3 ♕xc3) 13 ♗d3 h6 14 c4 ♗b7 15 ♗b2 ♖fe8 16 ♖fe1 ± Gligorić-Bachtiar, Havana OL 1966.

11 ♖e1

This is White's most popular choice, but he has tried many other moves over the years:

a) 11 ♗d3 b6 12 ♖e1 transposes to the main line.

b) 11 d5 exd5 12 ♘xd5 ♘xd5 13 ♕xd5 ♕xd5 14 ♗xd5 ♗d7 15 ♗g5 ♗xg5 16 ♘xg5 h6 17 ♘f3 ♖ac8 ½-½ Antoshin-Estrin, Moscow 1955.

c) 11 ♗e3!? is reasonably interesting despite *ECO*'s dismissal of the move as leading to prompt equality: 11...a6 12 d5 (12 ♗a2 b5 13 d5 will come to the same thing) 12...exd5 13

♘xd5 b5 14 ♗a2 ♗e6 (14...♘xd5 15 ♗xd5 ♗b7 and now 16 a4 ♕d6 = Bronstein-Fuchs, Gotha 1957 is given in *ECO*, but 16 ♖c1!? is more interesting; e.g., 16...♘a5 17 ♗xb7 ♘xb7 18 ♗d4 ♖e8 19 ♖e1 with a small positional plus for White) 15 ♗b6 ♕b8 16 ♘xe7+ ♘xe7 17 ♗d4 ♗xa2 18 ♗xf6 gxf6 19 ♖xa2 ± Furman-Korchnoi, Bucharest 1954.

d) 11 ♗f4 a6 12 ♗a2 b5 13 d5 (13 ♖e1 b4 {13...♗b7!? Taimanov} 14 ♘a4 bxa3 15 bxa3 ♗xa3 16 ♕c2 ♘xd4 17 ♘xd4 ♕xd4 18 ♗e5 ♕b4 with chances for both sides, Ragozin-Chekhover, Moscow 1935) 13...exd5 14 ♘xd5 ♘xd5 15 ♗xd5 ♗b7 16 ♘e5 ♘xe5 (Taimanov notes that 16...♖c8? loses to 17 ♘d7 ♖e8 18 ♗xf7+ ♔xf7 19 ♕d5+ ♔g6 20 g4) 17 ♗xb7 ♖a7 18 ♗e4 ♕xd1 19 ♖axd1 ♘c4 20 ♗c1 and although White has a very slight plus at this point, it is insufficient to make anything out of and a draw was soon agreed in Bronstein-Boleslavsky, Moscow Ct playoff (3) 1950.

e) 11 ♗g5!? and now:

e1) 11...♘d5 12 ♗xd5 (12 ♗xe7 ♘cxe7 13 ♕d3 ♘xc3 14 bxc3 ♘g6 15 ♖fe1 ♗d7 16 ♘e5 ♖c8 is equal, Filip-Urbanec, Czechoslovak Ch (Prague) 1954) 12...♗xg5 (according to *ECO*, 12...exd5 equalizes, but after 13 ♗xe7 ♘xe7 14 ♕b3 followed by ♖fe1 and ♖ac1, White has a definite initiative) 13 ♗xc6 bxc6 14 ♘xg5 ♕xg5 15 ♕e2 ± F.Petersen-Golombek, Varna OL 1962.

e2) 11...a6 12 ♗a2 (12 ♕d3 transposes to line 'f13') 12...b5 13 ♕d3 transposes to line 'f132'.

e3) 11...h6 12 ♗h4 b6 13 ♕d3 ♗b7 14 ♗a2 ♘h5 15 ♗g3 ♘xg3 16

hxg3 ♗f6 17 ♖ad1 ♘e7 = Bogdanov-Arbakov, Berne 1994.

f) 11 ♕d3 *(D)* and here:

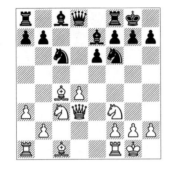

f1) 11...a6 and then:

f11) 12 ♗a2 b5 13 ♗g5 transposes to line 'f132'.

f12) 12 ♗b3 e5!? 13 d5 ♗g4 14 ♗e3 ♗xf3 15 gxf3 ♘d4 16 ♗xd4 exd4 17 ♕xd4 ♗d6 = 18 ♖ae1 ½-½ Scherbakov-Fokin, Ekaterinburg 1997.

f13) 12 ♗g5 and now:

f131) 12...♘d5 13 ♘e4 (13 ♗xd5 exd5 14 ♗xe7 ♘xe7 15 ♖fe1 ♗f5 16 ♕d2 ± Alatortsev-Kan, Moscow 1950) 13...♗xg5 14 ♘exg5 g6 (14...♘f6 was suggested by Taimanov, but 15 ♘e5 leaves White with the initiative) 15 ♖ac1 ♘a5 16 ♗a2 ♗d7 17 ♕d2 with a solid advantage for White, Taimanov-Golombek, Stockholm IZ 1962.

f132) 12...b5 13 ♗a2 (13 ♗b3 ♗b7 14 ♗c2 g6 15 ♗h6 ♖e8 16 ♖ad1 ♖c8 17 ♕e2 ♘a5 with a pleasant game for Black, Fedorowicz-Dlugy, New York (6) 1984) 13...♗b7 (13...b4 14 ♘a4 ♕a5 15 ♗b1 g6 16 ♘c5 ♖d8 17 ♖c1 ♘d5 and now rather than the established 18 ♕e4, which allows the reply 18...♗xg5 19 ♘xg5 bxa3 20 ♖xa3?! ♕d2, Palmasson-Minev, Reykjavik

1957, White should play 18 ♘xe6 ♗xe6 19 ♖xc6 bxa3 20 ♗xe7 ♘xe7 21 ♖c3 ±) 14 ♖ad1 (14 ♗b1 g6 15 ♖d1 ♘a5 16 ♗a2 ♘d5 = Taimanov) 14...♖c8 15 ♖fe1 b4 (both 15...♘d5 16 ♘xd5 ♗xg5 17 ♘b6 ♘b4 18 axb4 ♗xf3 19 ♕xf3 ♕xb6 20 ♕g4, Bondarevsky-Sokolsky, USSR Ch (Moscow) 1950, and 15...♖e8? 16 ♗xf6 ♗xf6 17 d5 exd5 18 ♖xe8+ ♕xe8 19 ♘xd5 ♗d8 20 ♖e1 ♕f8 21 ♕f5, Portisch-Bilek, Hungarian Ch (Budapest) 1975, are much better for White) 16 ♘a4 bxa3 17 bxa3 ♘a5 18 ♗b1 g6 19 ♘e5 ♘d5 20 ♗h6 ♖e8 21 ♕h3 (21 ♕f3 ♘f6 =) 21...♗g5 22 ♗xg5 ♕xg5 23 ♘xf7 ♔xf7 24 ♕xh7+ ♔f6 (Jakab-Koneru, Budapest 2001) and now 25 ♘c5 puts the most pressure on Black.

f2) 11...b6 *(D)* and now:

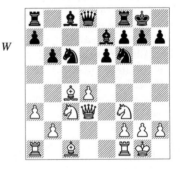

f21) 12 ♗b3 a5! 13 ♖d1 ♗a6 14 ♕c2 ♖c8 15 ♗f4 ♘a7 16 ♗e5 ♘b5 17 ♘g5 h6 18 ♗xf6 hxg5 = Jaracz-Macieja, Polish Ch (Warsaw) 1995.

f22) 12 ♖e1 ♗b7 13 ♗a2 ♖c8 14 ♗g5 ♖c7 15 ♖ad1 ♖d7 16 ♗b1 g6 17 ♗h6 ♖e8 18 ♗a2 (Najdorf-Giardelli, Buenos Aires 1975) 18...♗f8 19 ♗g5 ♗g7 =.

f23) 12 ♗g5 ♗b7 and then:

f231) 13 ♖ad1 ♖c8 14 ♖fe1 ♘d5 (Black has to stop White from playing d5; if not, something like this can happen: 14...♕c7? 15 ♗a2 ♖fd8 16 d5! ♘xd5 17 ♗xd5! h6 18 ♗xh6! gxh6 19 ♖xe6! fxe6 20 ♕g6+ ♔f8 21 ♕xh6+ ♔e8 22 ♕xe6 ♕f4 23 ♕g6+ ♔d7 24 ♘b5! ♕f6 25 ♗e6++ ♔xe6 26 ♘g5+ ♔e5 27 ♕e4# (1-0) Sarwinski-Przewoznik, Poznan 1986) 15 ♗xd5 exd5 16 ♕f5 (16 ♗xe7 ♘xe7 17 ♘e5 is somewhat better for White) 16...g6 17 ♕xd5 (17 ♕f4!? avoids the forcing sequence that follows and is better for White) 17...♕xd5 18 ♘xd5 ♗xg5 19 ♘xg5 ♖fd8 20 ♘e7+ ♘xe7 21 ♖xe7 ♖xd4 22 ♖de1 ♗xg2! and the game quickly fizzles out in a draw, Pinter-H.Olafsson, Brønshøj 1985.

f232) 13 ♖fe1 h6 14 ♗e3 (or 14 ♗f4 ♗d6 15 ♗xd6 ♕xd6 16 d5 exd5 17 ♘xd5 ♘xd5 18 ♗xd5 ♘d8 with an equal position, Balashov-Makarychev, Minsk 1979) 14...♗d6! (in elegant fashion, Black reorganizes his pieces to limit White's initiative) 15 ♖ad1 ♘e7 16 ♗c1 ♖c8 17 ♗a2 ♘ed5 and Black has at least equalized, Yudasin-Seirawan, Biel IZ 1993.

11...b6

Or:

a) 11...♗d7 12 ♗a2 ♖c8 13 ♕d3 ♖e8 14 ♗b1 (14 ♘e5 can also be played) 14...g6 15 ♗a2 a6 (Geller's 15...♕a5 seems to leave White slightly better after 16 d5 exd5 17 b4 ♕d8 18 ♘xd5 ♗e6 19 ♘xe7+ ♖xe7 20 ♕xd8+ ♖xd8 21 ♗b2 ♘e8 22 ♗xe6 ♖xe6 23 ♖xe6 fxe6 24 ♖e1 – a long variation, but fairly forced; 15...♕b6!? may also be worth looking into) 16 ♗h6 ♕a5?! (16...♗f8 and 16...♘g4 look safer) 17 d5 exd5 18 ♘xd5 (Gligorić-Pomar,

Nice OL 1974) 18...♗e6 19 ♘xe7+ ± Geller.

b) 11...a6 (D) and here:

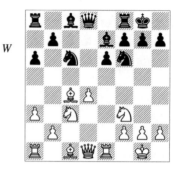

b1) 12 ♗d3 b5 13 ♗c2 ♗b7 14 ♕d3 g6 15 ♗h6 ♖e8 16 ♖ad1 ♖c8 17 ♗b1 b4 18 ♘e4 ♘xe4 19 ♖xe4 ½-½ Smyslov-Flesch, Szolnok 1975.

b2) 12 ♗g5 b5 and then:

b21) 13 ♗b3 ♗b7 14 ♕d3 b4 15 ♘a4 bxa3 16 bxa3 ♘a5 (Tsesarsky gives 16...♕a5 as better, but his analysis is flawed: 17 ♗xf6 ♗xf6 18 ♘c5 ♕c7 19 ♖ab1 ♖ab8 and here he continues with 20 ♗c2, but 20 d5! exd5 21 ♗xd5 is very unpleasant for Black) 17 ♗c2 g6 18 ♖ab1 ♗c6 19 ♘c3 ♕d6 20 ♘e5 (Peker-Tsesarsky, Petah Tiqwa 1997) 20...♖fc8 21 a4 ♗d5 ∓ Tsesarsky.

b22) 13 ♗d3 ♗b7 14 ♗c2 ♖c8 15 ♕d3 g6 16 ♖ad1 b4 17 ♘a4 ♘d5 18 ♘c5 ♗xg5 19 ♘xb7 ♕e7 = Pachman-Golombek, Saltsjöbaden IZ 1952.

b23) 13 ♗a2 ♗b7 (13...♖a7!? intending ...♖d7, ...♗b7 and ...♕a8 is another plan worth considering) 14 ♕d3 b4 15 ♘a4 bxa3 16 bxa3 ♘a7 17 ♖ad1 ♘b5 18 ♗b1 g6 19 ♘e5 ♗d5 20 ♘c5 (Gild.Garcia-Am.Rodriguez, Thessaloniki OL 1984) 20...♘g4 21

&xe7 &xe5 22 &xe5 &xe7 = Tsesarsky.

b3) 12 &a2 and now:

b31) 12...&d5?! 13 &e4 b6 14 &d3 &a7 15 &b1 g6 16 &a2 (we have already seen this standard ploy several times; the idea is to induce Black to weaken his dark squares, whereupon White can go back to pushing for the d5 advance) 16...&d7 17 &h6 &e8 18 &ad1 &b7 19 h4 with an attack for White, Farago-Flesch, Budapest 1976.

b32) 12...b5?! 13 d5! exd5 14 &xd5 &xd5 15 &xd5 &b7 16 &h5 &d6 17 &g5 &ad8 18 &xe7 &xe7 19 &g5 &g6 20 &xh7+ &xh7 21 &xh7 &xh7 22 &xe7 &d5 23 &xd5 &xd5 24 g3 ± Benjamin-Dlugy, USA Ch (Estes Park) 1985.

b33) 12...&d6 13 &e3 (13 &e4 &xe4 14 &xe4 &d8 15 h4 &f6 16 &g5 h6 17 &xf6 &xf6 18 &e2 b5 19 &e5 ± Gligorić-Savić, Herceg Novi 2001) 13...b5 (13...&d8!? doesn't allow White to push the d-pawn and is therefore safer) 14 &c1 &b7 15 d5! exd5 16 &c5 &d7 17 &xd5 &xd5 18 &xd5 &xc5 19 &xc5 ± Brodsky-Berg, Copenhagen 1994.

12 &d3

An alternative is 12 &f4 &b7 13 &a2 &c8 14 &d3 &d7 15 &ad1 &d5 16 &b1 g6 17 &h6 &fe8 18 &e4 with a slight advantage for White, Najdorf-Reshevsky, Buenos Aires 1953.

12...&b7 13 &c2 *(D)*

13...&e8

Other tries:

a) 13...&d6 14 &d3 g6 15 &g5 &fd8 16 &ad1 &h5 17 &c1 (White has to look into 17 d5!? exd5 18 &xd5 &xg5 19 &xg5 &e5 20 &c3 &ac8 21 &c7 &c6 22 &xc6 &xc6 23 &b5 with

an ongoing initiative) 17...&f8 18 &g5 &e7 19 &c1 &f8 20 &g5 ½-½ Yusupov-Hübner, Dortmund 1997.

b) 13...&c8 14 &d3 g6 (14...&e8? transposes to the note to Black's 14th move) 15 &h6 &e8 16 &ad1 and now:

b1) 16...a6 17 &b3 (Gligorić-Panno, Palma de Mallorca IZ 1970) and now according to Gligorić Black should play 17...&a5 18 &a2 &xf3 'with equality', but 19 &xf3 leaves White with all his pieces coordinated perfectly and a d5 advance looming constantly; e.g., 19...&f8 20 &g5 &e7 21 d5! or 19...&c4 20 d5!.

b2) 16...&f8 17 &g5 &e7 18 &a4 a6 19 &xf6 &xf6 20 d5 exd5 21 &xe8+ &xe8 22 &xd5 &d8 23 h4 (23 b4?! led to a quick win for White in Brinck-Claussen – May, corr. 1978, but Black is simply a pawn up after 23...&xb4! 24 axb4 &xa4) 23...&f8 24 &g5 b5 25 &b3 &a5 26 &a2 &c4 27 &e3? (this is pushing the envelope quite a bit too much; correct is 27 &xc4 bxc4 28 &e4 with roughly equal chances) and now instead of 27...h6, as played in Tarjan-Browne, USA Ch (Mentor) 1977, Byrne/Mednis give 27...&xg5 28 hxg5 &xb2 29 &d7 &xd1 30 &g4 and now continue with

30...♘c3 31 ♘h6+ ♔g7 32 ♕d4+ f6 33 ♕d7+ ♔h8 34 ♘f7+ and a draw by perpetual check, but Black can do even better with 30...h5! —+.

14 ♕d3 g6 *(D)*

14...♖c8? is a well-known mistake: 15 d5! exd5 16 ♗g5 ♘e4 17 ♘xe4 dxe4 18 ♕xe4 g6 19 ♕h4 ♕c7 (19...h5 is best met with 20 ♗b3 ♖c7 21 ♖ad1 ♖d7 22 ♕e4 +— Kaloskambris-Skalkotas, Greek Ch 1976) 20 ♗b3 h5 21 ♕e4 ♔g7 22 ♗xf7 ♔xf7 23 ♗h6 ♕d6 24 ♕c4+ ♔f6 25 ♖ad1 and White wins, Petrosian-Balashov, Leningrad 1974.

W

15 h4

Other moves don't promise White any advantage:

a) 15 ♗h6 ♖c8 transposes to note 'b' to Black's 13th move.

b) 15 ♗f4 ♖c8 16 ♖ad1 ♘a5 17 ♘e5 (17 ♗a4 is a suggestion of Bagirov's, but Yusupov claims an advantage for Black after 17...♗c6 18 ♗xc6 ♘xc6 19 ♕a6 ♘d5 20 ♘xd5 ♕xd5)

17...♘d5 18 ♗d2 ♘xc3 19 ♗xc3 ♗d5 20 ♗a4 ♖f8 21 ♘d7 ♖e8 22 ♘e5 ½-½ Mecking-Polugaevsky, Lucerne Ct (4) 1977.

15...♖c8

15...♕d6 16 ♗g5 ♖ad8 17 ♖ad1 ♕b8 18 ♗b3, and now 18...a6? 19 d5! ♘a5 20 dxe6!! ♘xb3 21 exf7+ ♔xf7 22 ♕c4+ ♔g7 23 ♘e5! gave White a massive attack in Yusupov-Lobron, Nussloch 1996. However, Black may be able to maintain the balance with Ftačnik's idea 18...♘a5!?; e.g., 19 ♗a4 ♗c6.

16 ♗g5 ♘d5 17 ♖ad1 ♗xg5 18 ♘xg5 ♘xc3 19 bxc3

T.Georgadze-Makarychev, USSR Ch (Vilnius) 1980. Georgadze gives 19...♘e7! 20 c4 ♘f5 21 g3 'unclear' as best.

Conclusion

If this line makes you think of the Karpov Variation, which is covered in Chapter 1, it's for a good reason, as they are similar in several ways. The problem for Black in this line is that the c6-knight blocks the light-squared bishop when it's developed to b7, making White's d5 advance a more potent threat.

In the main line it seems like Black can maintain the balance, but he has to be ready to defend accurately for some time to be rewarded with equality. However, White may be able to obtain an advantage by deviating with 12 ♗f4, or, a move earlier, with 11 ♕d3.

8 Averbakh Variation

**1 d4 ♘f6 2 c4 e6 3 ♘c3 ♗b4 4 e3 0-0
5 ♘f3 d5 6 ♗d3 c5 7 0-0 ♘bd7** *(D)*

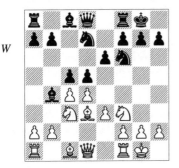

This position characterizes the Averbakh Variation.

This line was first played in the game P.Johner-Stähelin, Berne 1932, which was won by White. Later the line was developed by Ragozin and Averbakh, after which it gained some popularity. This popularity peaked twice, in the early 1950s and the late 1960s. Since then this line has only been played on rare occasions by top GMs.

Black's idea with 7...♘bd7 is double-edged. Ideally, he wants to exchange pawns on d4 and c4 and then transfer the d7-knight to d5 via b6. Secondly, the knight can also drop back to f8, assisting in the defence of the black king.

Our main lines are now:

A: 8 a3 105
B: 8 cxd5 107

In addition to the two main moves, White has the following less critical lines at his disposal:

a) 8 ♘e2 ♕e7 9 ♕c2 b5!? 10 b3 bxc4 11 bxc4 dxc4 12 ♗xc4 ♗b7 with equality, Ravinsky-Ragozin, Moscow Ch 1942.

b) 8 ♕e2 a6 and now:

b1) After 9 a3, 9...♗a5 is best, transposing to note 'c' to White's 9th move.

b2) 9 ♖d1 ♕e7 10 ♗d2 dxc4 11 ♗xc4 b5 12 ♗d3 ♗b7 13 a3 ♗a5 14 ♖ac1 ♗b6 15 ♗b1 ♖ac8 = Krogius-Bondarevsky, Leningrad 1949.

c) 8 ♗d2 was a favourite of Levenfish's. Now 8...cxd4 (or 8...dxc4 9 ♗xc4 transposing to note 'c' to White's 9th move in Line C of Chapter 2) 9 exd4 dxc4 10 ♗xc4 transposes to note 'c' to White's 9th move in Line C of Chapter 2.

A)

8 a3 *(D)*

8...♗a5

Alternatively:

a) 8...dxc4?! 9 axb4! (9 ♗xc4 transposes to note 'f' to White's 9th move in Line C of Chapter 2) 9...cxd4 10 ♗xh7+! ♘xh7 11 ♕xd4 ♘b6 12 ♕xd8 ♖xd8 13 e4 ♗d7 14 ♗e3 ♘f6 15 ♘e5 ± Taimanov-Barcza, Havana 1967.

b) 8...cxd4?! 9 ♘xd5! exd5 10 axb4 dxc4 11 ♗xc4 ♘b6 12 ♗b3 dxe3 13 ♗xe3 ♘bd5 14 ♗c5 ♖e8 15 ♖e1 ♖xe1+ 16 ♕xe1 b6 17 ♗d4 ♗b7 18 ♖d1 with a strong initiative for White, Tal-Tolush, USSR Ch (Riga) 1958.

c) 8...♗xc3 9 bxc3 and now:

c1) 9...dxc4 10 ♗xc4 transposes to note 'f2' to White's 9th move in Line C of Chapter 2.

c2) 9...♕c7!? (Black is playing a Khasin Variation with the knight on d7 instead of c6) 10 cxd5 exd5 11 ♘h4 (11 a4!?) 11...♖e8 12 f3 ♘f8 13 ♖a2 ♗d7 14 g4 ♕a5 with chances for both sides, W.Schön-B.Lalić, 2nd Bundesliga 1995/6. This line clearly needs more testing before a clear evaluation of its merits can be given.

9 ♕c2

Or:

a) 9 cxd5 exd5 transposes to Line B.

b) 9 ♗d2 and now:

b1) 9...cxd4 10 exd4 dxc4 11 ♗xc4 a6 12 a4 b6 13 ♕e2 ♗b7 14 ♖fd1 ♖e8 15 ♘e5 ♗xc3 16 ♗xc3 ♘d5 with equality, Gligorić-Averbakh, Titovo Užice 1966.

b2) 9...a6 and then:

b21) 10 ♖c1 dxc4 11 ♗xc4 b5 12 ♗a2 cxd4 (Parma gives 12...♗b6!? in *ECO*) 13 exd4 ♗b7 with chances for both sides, F.Olafsson-Ortega, Havana OL 1966.

b22) 10 ♕e2 ♗c7 11 ♖ac1 dxc4 12 ♗xc4 b5 13 ♗a2 cxd4 14 exd4 ♗b7 15 ♗g5 h6 16 ♗h4 ♗f4 with a double-edged position, Spassky-Gheorghiu, Winnipeg 1967.

b23) 10 b3 ♗c7 11 ♕c2 b6 12 cxd5 exd5 13 e4 dxe4 14 ♘xe4 (14 ♗xe4 ♘xe4 15 ♘xe4 cxd4 16 ♖fc1 ♗b8 17 ♘xd4 ♗b7 is also fine for Black) 14...♗b7 15 dxc5 ♗xe4 16 ♗xe4 ♘xe4 17 ♕xe4 ♘xc5 ½-½ Toran-Ivkov, Malaga 1968.

c) 9 ♕e2 a6 (9...dxc4 10 ♗xc4 a6 transposes to note 'c42' to Black's 9th move in Line C of Chapter 2; 9...cxd4 10 exd4 dxc4 11 ♗xc4 ♗xc3 12 bxc3 is similar to note 'b5' to Black's 9th move in Line C of Chapter 2; the difference is that here the pawn is on a3) with the following options:

c1) 10 cxd5!? is possible.

c2) 10 ♖b1 is rather harmless; e.g., 10...dxc4 11 ♗xc4 b5 12 ♗d3 ♗b7 13 b4 (Geller-Szabo, Budapest Ct 1950) 13...cxd4!? 14 exd4 ♗c7 (*ECO*) is at least equal for Black.

c3) 10 a4 ♕e7 (Black should prefer 10...dxc4 11 ♗xc4 transposing to note 'c423' to Black's 9th move in Chapter 2) 11 ♗d2 (11 ♖d1 is also an interesting idea) 11...♗c7 12 cxd5 exd5 (Bilek-Smyslov, Moscow 1967) 13 ♖ad1 ♕d6 14 ♖fe1 ± Dolmatov.

c4) 10 dxc5 should be harmless: 10...♗xc3 11 bxc3 ♘xc5 12 ♗c2 ♗d7 (12...♘ce4 13 cxd5 ♘xc3 14 ♕d3 ♘cxd5 15 ♖d1 gives White sufficient compensation for the pawn) 13 cxd5 exd5 14 c4 dxc4 15 ♕xc4 ♗b5 16 ♕xc5 ♖c8 17 ♕f5 g6 18 ♕f4 ♖xc2 (18...♗xf1?! is playing with fire in view of 19 ♗b2 ♘h5 20 ♕h6 with excellent compensation for the exchange)

19 ♘d4 ♗xf1 20 ♘xc2 (Smyslov-Averbakh, Moscow Ch 1946) 20...♕d5 =.

c5) 10 ♖d1 ♗e7 (10...dxc4 11 ♗xc4 transposes to note 'c421' to Black's 9th move in Line B of Chapter 2) 11 ♗d2 ♗c7 12 cxd5 exd5 13 e4 cxd4 14 ♘xd5 ♘xd5 15 exd5 ♕xe2 16 ♗xe2 ± Gheorghiu-Tal, Moscow 1967.

d) 9 a4 dxc4 10 ♗xc4 cxd4 11 exd4 ♕c7 12 ♕e2 ♘b6 13 ♗d3 ♘bd5 14 ♘b5 ♕b8 15 ♘e5 (Furman-Butnoris, USSR Ch (Kharkov) 1967) 15...a6 16 ♘a3 ♘b4 with equality according to Petrosian and Suetin.

e) 9 ♖b1 ♕e7 (9...dxc4 is also possible) 10 ♗d2 dxc4 11 ♗xc4 b6 (Taimanov-Averbakh, USSR 1962) 12 dxc5 = Parma.

9...dxc4

9...a6 has been proved better for White after 10 b3!? ♗c7 (10...dxc4 and 10...♗xc3 have also been tried) 11 ♗b2 b6 (11...♕e7 12 cxd5 exd5 13 e4!? dxe4 14 ♘xe4 ♘xe4 15 ♗xe4 ♘f6 16 ♖fe1 ± Kondratiev-Bostatis, USSR 1967) 12 cxd5 exd5 13 e4 dxe4 14 ♗xe4 ♘xe4 15 ♘xe4 ± Furman-Taimanov, Baku 1951.

10 ♗xc4 cxd4

The alternative 10...♕e7 has been tried on a few occasions: 11 dxc5 ♕xc5 12 ♘a4 (12 ♗xe6!? deserves an extra look) 12...♕c7 13 ♕e2 a6 14 b4 b5 15 bxa5 (Portisch-Langeweg, Wijk aan Zee 1968) 15...bxc4 =.

11 exd4 ♗xc3 12 bxc3

12 ♕xc3 gave White nothing in Gligorić-Tal, Belgrade Ct (4) 1968: 12...b6 13 ♗f4 ♗b7 14 ♕d3 ♘h5 15 ♘g5 ♘df6 16 ♗e5 h6 17 ♘h3 ♘g4 with approximately equal chances.

12...b6

12...♕c7 is also worthwhile; e.g., 13 ♗d3 e5!? 14 ♗e3 e4 (or 14...exd4 15 cxd4 ♕xc2 16 ♗xc2 ♘b6 = Dolmatov) 15 ♗xe4 ♘xe4 16 ♕xe4 ♕xc3 17 ♖fc1 (Gligorić-Gipslis, Moscow 1967) 17...♕a5 18 ♗d2 ♕a6 19 ♗b4 ♘f6 20 ♕h4 ♖e8 = Dolmatov.

13 ♖e1

Of White's alternatives, 13 ♗d3 appears most critical: 13...♗b7 14 ♕e2 ♕c7 15 ♗d2!? (15 c4?! ♖ac8 16 ♗d2 ♗xf3 17 ♕xf3 e5 gives Black excellent play, Cvetković-Gipslis, Kapfenberg Echt 1970) 15...♖fe8 16 ♖fe1 ♖ad8 17 ♘e5 ♘xe5 18 ♕xe5 ♕xe5 19 ♖xe5 ♘d7 20 ♖e3 with a very slight pull for White in the endgame, Anton-Fechner, corr. 1977.

13...♗b7 14 ♘e5 ♖c8 15 ♗d3

15 ♘xf7!? is interesting: 15...♖xf7 16 ♗xe6 ♘f8 (16...♕e7!?) 17 ♗xf7+ (17 ♗xc8 ♕xc8 18 f3 is possibly better) 17...♔xf7 (Lehtinen-Karjalainen, corr. 1972) and now 18 ♗e3 is best.

15...♘xe5 16 ♖xe5 ♕c7 17 c4 ♕c6

Now:

a) 18 f3, which led to victory for White in Giertz-Gauba, corr. 1977, is best met by 18...♗a6, when the c-pawn is bound to fall.

b) After 18 ♖g5 (Gligorić-Tal, Belgrade Ct (2) 1968), both 18...♘e4 and 18...h6 lead to satisfactory play for Black.

B)

8 cxd5 exd5 *(D)*

8...cxd4?! forces a clearly better position on White: 9 exd4 exd5 10 ♗g5 ♗xc3 11 bxc3 ♕c7 12 ♖c1 ± Parma-Barcza, Varna OL 1962.

9 a3

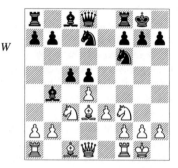

W

This aggressive move has caused people to abandon the Averbakh Variation. White's alternatives, while interesting, are less of a problem for Black:

a) 9 ♘e5?! ♖e8 10 ♘xd7 ♗xd7 11 dxc5 ♗xc5 = F.Portisch-Haag, Hungarian Ch (Budapest) 1966.

b) 9 ♘e2 (Pliester) 9...c4 10 ♗c2 ♗d6 =.

c) 9 ♗d2 ♖e8 10 a3 (or 10 ♖c1 a6 11 b3 ♘f8 = Panno-Gligorić, Buenos Aires 1955) 10...♗xc3 (10...♗a5?! 11 dxc5 ♘xc5 12 ♗b5! ± Alster-Ujtelky, Czechoslovak Ch (Bratislava) 1955) 11 ♗xc3 c4 12 ♗c2 ♘e4 13 ♗e1 ♘b6 14 b3 ♗g4 15 h3 ♗h5 with a pleasant game for Black, Bronstein-Gligorić, Belgrade 1954.

d) 9 ♕b3 ♗xc3! (not 9...♘b6?! 10 ♘e2!? a5 11 dxc5 ♘bd7 12 ♕c2 ♘xc5 13 ♗xh7+ ♘xh7 14 a3 ♘a6 15 axb4 ♘xb4 16 ♕b3 ± Korchnoi-Tal, Moscow Ct (4) 1968) 10 ♕xc3 c4 (or 10...b6?! 11 dxc5 ♘xc5 12 b4 ♘ce4 13 ♗xe4 ♘xe4 14 ♕d4 ± Filip-Botvinnik, Moscow OL 1956) 11 ♗c2 b6 12 ♘e5 ♗b7 13 b3 b5 14 f3 (Parma gives 14 a4 as better) 14...♘b6 15 ♗b2 ♘e8 16 e4 ♘d6, with a pleasant game for Black, Donner-Damjanović, Havana 1968.

9...♗a5

This was Black's original intention, which has now gone into disfavour thanks to Gligorić's idea below. Therefore attention has turned to 9...♗xc3 10 bxc3:

a) 10...♖e8 11 ♘d2 ♕c7 12 a4 b6 13 ♖e1 ♘f8 14 f3 ± Farago-Barczay, Szolnok 1975.

b) 10...c4 11 ♗c2 ♖e8 and here:

b1) 12 a4 ♘e4 13 ♗xe4 dxe4 14 ♘d2 b6 15 f3 (Timman gives 15 ♘xc4 ♗a6 16 ♘d6 ♗xf1 17 ♘xe8 ♗xg2 as good for Black, while Ftačnik suggested both 15 ♗a3 and 15 ♕e2 as alternatives) 15...♗b7 16 fxe4 ♗xe4 17 ♘xe4 ♖xe4 18 ♖a2 ♘f6 19 ♖af2 ♕d6, with the centre blocked and a better game for Black, Timman-Yusupov, Linares Ct (3) 1992.

b2) 12 ♘d2 ♕a5 (12...b5 seems less accurate; after 13 a4 bxa4 14 ♗xa4 ♗b7 15 ♖e1 ♕c7 16 f3 a5 17 ♗c2 g6, Van der Sterren-Piket, Amsterdam 1994, 18 e4 gives White a solid advantage) 13 ♗b2 ♘b6 (13...b5 14 ♖e1 ♗b7 15 f3 ♘b6 16 ♖c1 ± F.Olafsson-Barcza, Prague Z 1954) 14 ♖e1 ♗d7 15 a4 ♘e4 16 ♘f1! f5 17 f3 ♘f6 18 ♗a3!? (or 18 h3 h5 19 ♘g3 g6, Petrosian-Debarnot, Las Palmas 1975, 20 h4 ±) 18...♕xc3 19 ♕b1 ♕a5 20 ♗b4 ♕a6 21 a5 ♘c8 22 ♗xf5 ♗xf5 23 ♕xf5 ♘e7 (Cvitan-Vyzhmanavin, Manila OL 1992) and now Pliester gives 24 ♕h3! ♘c6 25 ♗c3 followed by ♘g3 and e4 as much better for White.

10 b4! *(D)*

Or:

a) 10 ♘e5 has proved fairly harmless; e.g., 10...cxd4 11 exd4 ♗xc3 12 bxc3 ♕c7 13 ♘xd7 ♗xd7 14 ♕c2

萱fe8 15 f3 h6 ½-½ Donner-Korchnoi, Wijk aan Zee 1968.

b) 10 &d2 is also insufficient for an advantage; e.g., 10...a6 11 dxc5 ②xc5 12 &e2 ②ce4 13 ②xe4 dxe4 14 ②d4 = Szabo-Balanel, Moscow OL 1956.

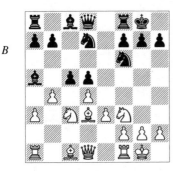

B

10...cxb4 11 ②b5!

White sacrifices a pawn to activate his queenside. The combination of control over the a3-f8 diagonal, access to d6 with the b5-knight and the pressure along the a- and b-files very much resembles the play Black occasionally obtains in the Benko Gambit. White has at least enough compensation for the pawn.

11...②e4!?

This move has so far only been used in correspondence games, but with reasonable results for Black. Other moves, on the other hand, have not shown much merit:

a) 11...bxa3? 12 &xa3 萱e8 13 ②d6 萱e6 14 ②g5 is very problematic for Black.

b) 11...②b8 12 axb4 &xb4 13 萱xa7 (13 ②xa7 is also good) 13...萱xa7 14 ②xa7 &e6 15 ≝a4 ≝b6 16 &a3 &xa3 17 ≝xa3 ± Tukmakov-Tal, Sochi 1970.

White has better piece coordination and a superior pawn-structure.

c) 11...a6 is Black's most popular way of meeting White's aggression, but Black has yet to receive any reward; in my database the score is 6/6 in White's favour: 12 ≝b3 bxa3 (note that after 12...axb5, 13 axb4 regains the piece back; 12...≝e7 13 &d2 ②e4 14 &xb4 &xb4 15 ≝xb4, Gligorić-Yanofsky, Lugano OL 1968, 15...≝d8 16 ②c3 ②df6 17 萱fc1 ±) 13 ②d6 (D) and now:

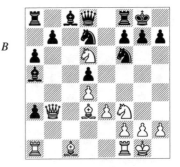

B

c1) 13...≝b6 14 ≝xb6 &xb6 15 &xa3 &d8 (removing White's access to f5 with 15...g6 is probably Black's best, although White still has a solid advantage after 16 萱fc1) 16 萱fb1 &e7 17 ②xc8 &xa3 18 ②b6 ②xb6 19 萱xb6 &e7 20 萱xb7 ± F.Portisch-Barlov, Wijk aan Zee 1985.

c2) 13...&c7 14 &xa3 &xd6 15 &xd6 萱e8 16 萱fc1 and then:

c21) 16...≝b6 17 ≝a3! ②e4 18 &f4 ②f8 19 萱ab1 ≝d8 20 &c7 ≝e7 21 ≝b3 ②e6 22 &e5 ≝d8 23 &xe4 dxe4 24 ②d2 is much better for White, Pinter-Gheorghiu, Baile Herculane Z 1982. The other knight makes its way to d6 via c4.

c22) 16...♖e6 17 ♗f4 h6 18 h3 ♘f8 19 ♗c7 ♕e8 20 ♘e5 and White's pressure on Black's centre and queenside more than compensates for the pawn deficit, Gligorić-Andersson, West Berlin 1971.

c23) 16...♘e4!? is an untested continuation, but maybe deserves a try; e.g., 17 ♗c7 (17 ♕xd5? ♘df6 –+) 17...♕e7 18 ♗f4 (18 ♕xd5? ♘xf2! is unfortunate for White) 18...♘df6 19 ♘g5!? and while White has compensation for the pawn, Black should not be very badly off.

12 axb4 ♗b6 13 ♕b3 ♘df6 14 ♘e5 (D)

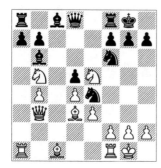

14...♖e8!?

Or:

a) 14...♗d7?! 15 f3 ♗xb5 16 ♗xb5 ♘g5 17 ♘d7 (17 ♗d3!?) 17...♘xd7 18 ♕xd5 ♘e6 19 ♗xd7 ♘c7 20 ♕f5 g6 21 ♕h3 ± Baumbach-Dünhaupt, corr. 1968.

b) 14...♗e6 15 f3 a6 16 fxe4 (16 ♘a3 and 16 ♕b1!? both improve for White), Rickers-Krezdorn, corr. 1987, 16...dxe4! 17 ♗c4 axb5 18 ♖xa8 bxc4 19 ♖xd8 cxb3 20 ♖xf8+ ♔xf8 21 ♗b2 ♘d5 may be tolerable for Black.

15 f3 ♘d6 (D)

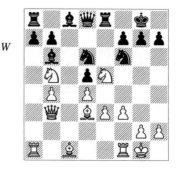

Now:

a) 16 ♘c3 ♗f5 17 ♗e2 ♖c8 18 ♗d2 (18 ♖d1 should be slightly better for White), Brilla Banfalvi-Idema, corr. 1983, and now Black can try 18...♗xd4!? 19 exd4 ♕b6 20 ♗e3 ♖xe5 21 ♘a4 ♖xe3 22 ♕xe3 ♕xb4, with chances for both sides.

b) 16 ♗d2 gives White an advantage: 16...♗e6 17 ♖a2 ♖e7 18 ♘xd6 ♕xd6 19 b5 ♖c7 20 ♗b4, Sv.Pedersen-J.Steiner, corr. 1978-87.

Conclusion

The Averbakh Variation hasn't been a popular choice for Black for many years. As we have seen above, Black can be satisfied with his position in Line A, but he faces some awkward problems in Line B.

9 Delayed Fianchetto Variation

1 d4 ♘f6 2 c4 e6 3 ♘c3 ♗b4 4 e3 0-0 5 ♘f3 d5 6 ♗d3 c5 7 0-0 b6 *(D)*

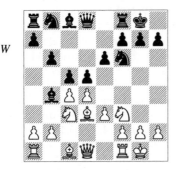

This approach has never been particularly popular, but nonetheless it deserves to be discussed. If allowed, Black would like to play ...♗a6 to exchange off the light-squared bishops.

8 cxd5

White has to adopt this aggressive approach to take advantage of Black's set-up. Otherwise:

a) 8 ♕e2 is harmless: 8...cxd4 9 exd4 ♗a6 10 ♗g5 ♗xc3 11 bxc3 ♗xc4 = Lombardy-Keres, Zurich 1961.

b) 8 a3 ♗xc3 (8...cxd4 9 axb4 dxc3 10 bxc3 dxc4 11 ♗xc4 ♕c7 = Kavalek-Tolush, Polanica Zdroj 1964) 9 bxc3 and then:

b1) 9...dxc4 10 ♗xc4 ♕c7 11 ♗d3!? ♗b7 12 ♖e1 cxd4 13 cxd4 ♗e4 14 ♗xe4 ♘xe4 15 ♕d3 ± Garcia Gonzales-Mateo, Bayamo 1984.

b2) The line 9...cxd4 10 cxd4 ♗a6 = is credited to Taimanov, but was played in Nilsson-Pietzsch, Varna OL 1962.

b3) 9...♗a6 and then:

b31) 10 ♘e5 ♘bd7 11 ♕a4 ♕c8 12 cxd5 ♗xd3 13 ♘xd3 exd5 14 ♗b2 ♖e8 15 ♘f4 c4 16 ♖ae1 b5 with chances for both sides, Reshevsky-Forintos, Skopje 1970.

b32) 10 cxd5 ♕xd5 (or 10...exd5 transposing to note 'c' to White's 9th move) 11 ♗xa6 ♘xa6 12 ♕e2 ♕b7 13 ♗b2 ♖ac8 14 ♖fe1 ♘e4 = Zsinka-Ikonnikov, Budapest 1991.

8...exd5 *(D)*

9 dxc5

Or:

a) 9 ♗d2 ♗g4 (9...♗a6!? as suggested in *ECO* is also worth attention) 10 a3 ♗xc3 11 ♗xc3 c4 12 ♗e2 ♘c6 with equality, Gligorić-Keres, Bled Ct 1959.

b) 9 ♘e2 c4 10 ♗c2 ♖e8 11 ♘e5 ♗d6 12 b3 cxb3 (12...b5!?) 13 ♗xb3 ♘bd7 14 f4 with some initiative for

White, Atalik-Bogdanovski, Pula Echt 1997.

c) 9 a3 ♗xc3 10 bxc3 ♗a6 and here:

c1) 11 dxc5 bxc5 12 ♗xa6 ♘xa6 13 c4 dxc4 14 ♕a4 ♘c7 15 ♕xc4 ♕d5 16 ♕c2 ♘e6 = Geller-Keres, USSR 1962.

c2) 11 ♗xa6 ♘xa6 12 ♕a4 (or 12 ♕d3 ♘c7 13 c4 ♘e6 14 ♗b2 dxc4 15 ♕xc4 ♖c8 with fairly level chances, Szabo-Keres, Amsterdam Ct 1956) 12...♕c8 (as after 12 ♕d3, Black can also consider 12...♘c7 here) 13 ♗b2 c4?! (this move is generally a bad idea in this line if White can potentially activate his bishop; instead, a solid move like 13...♖e8 is perfectly good) 14 ♘d2 (or 14 ♕c2 ♖e8 15 ♖fe1, Salov-Hjartarson, Reykjavik 1991, 15...♘e4!? 16 a4 ♘b8! 17 ♘e5 ♘c6 18 ♘xc6 ♕xc6 19 ♗a3 ♖e6 with counterplay – Pliester) 14...♖e8 15 ♖fe1 and now instead 15...♘e4?! 16 ♘f1 h5 17 f3 ♘d6 18 ♖e2, when White keeps the initiative, Semkov-Petursson, Thessaloniki OL 1988, Black should try something like 15...♖b8!? or 15...♘c7!? with a perfectly reasonable position.

d) 9 ♘e5!? (D) is another approach for White:

d1) 9...♖e8 and here:

d11) 10 ♗d2 ♗a6 11 ♗xa6 ♘xa6 12 ♕a4 ♕c8 13 ♖ac1 ♕b7 14 ♕c6 ♖ab8 = Portisch-Spassky, Geneva Ct (14) 1977.

d12) 10 ♗b5!? is a recent idea of Sadler's. After 10...♖e6 11 ♘e2 a6 12 ♗a4 c4 13 ♘g3 (13 ♘f4!?) 13...♗b7 14 f4 b5 15 ♗c2 ♘bd7 16 ♗d2 ♗f8 17 ♕f3 White has a kingside initiative, Sadler-Nickoloff, Elista OL 1998.

d13) 10 ♘e2!? c4?! (Dolmatov gives 10...♕c7!? as better) 11 ♗c2 ♗d6 12 f4 b5 13 ♘g3 ♘bd7?! (Gulko suggests 13...♗b7!? as a better option) 14 ♕f3 (in *Informator*, Gulko gives 14 e4!? as an interesting possibility, but after 14...♘b6 15 ♘c6 ♕c7 16 e5, Black can improve on Gulko's 16...♘fd7 with 16...♘g4!?) 14...♗b7 15 ♗d2 ♗f8?! (15...♘f8!? Gulko) 16 a4 b4 17 a5 ♖c8 18 a6 ♗a8 19 ♘f5 with a strong initiative for White, Korchnoi-Gulko, Novgorod 1995.

d2) 9...♗b7 is also popular:

d21) 10 ♘e2 c4 11 ♗c2 ♘bd7 12 f4 b5 (Portisch-Sanguinetti, Biel IZ 1976) 13 ♘g3! ± *ECO*.

d22) 10 ♗d2 ♘c6 (10...cxd4 11 exd4 ♘c6 and now according to Pliester 12 ♕a4 and 12 ♗g5 are White's most critical options) 11 a3 ♗xc3 12 ♗xc3 ♖e8 (12...♘xe5?! 13 dxe5 ♘e4 14 ♗xe4 dxe4 15 ♕g4 ♕e7 16 ♖fd1 ♕e6 17 ♕h4 ♗d5 18 ♖d2 is very pleasant for White, Gligorić-Szabo, Yugoslavia-Hungary 1960) 13 ♘xc6 ♗xc6 14 dxc5 bxc5 15 b4! d4 16 exd4 cxd4 17 ♗b2 ♕d5 18 f3 ♘g4!? 19 ♕d2 (19 ♗e4? ♕e5!) 19...♘e3 20 ♖fc1 with a solid advantage for White due to his bishop-pair, Gligorić-Ljubojević, Belgrade (10) 1979.

d3) 9...♗xc3 10 bxc3 ♗a6 and then:

d31) 11 ♗a3 ♖e8 12 ♖c1 ♗xd3 13 ♕xd3, and now 13...♕c8 14 c4 left Black struggling due to his lack of development in Szabo-Lengyel, Miskolc 1963. Black has to play 13...c4, which is normally dubious in this line, but here Black is doing OK.

d32) 11 ♗xa6 ♘xa6 12 a4 ♖e8 13 ♕f3 ♕c8 14 ♗b2 ♕e6 15 ♕e2 ♘c7 with equality, Farago-Forintos, Budapest 1968.

d33) 11 f3 attempts to build up a rolling centre, as seen frequently in the Rubinstein Nimzo-Indian. Here, however, Black can obtain equality after 11...♗xd3 12 ♕xd3 ♖e8 13 ♕f5 ♘bd7 14 ♘d3 ♕c8 15 ♘f2 b5 16 e4 ♘f8, as in Garcia Gonzales-F.Olafsson, Novi Sad 1976.

9...bxc5 *(D)*

Taking back with the bishop makes less sense in this position, as Black is too far behind in development to obtain enough counterplay to compensate for the isolated pawn.

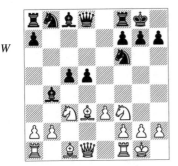

10 ♘e2

10 ♘a4 has scored reasonably for White, but shouldn't worry Black, as he can challenge the knight and equalize after 10...♘bd7 11 b3 ♘b6 12 ♘b2 ♗g4, Smyslov-Keres, Bled Ct 1959.

10...♗g4

Or:

a) 10...♘c6 11 b3 ♗g4 transposes to the main line.

b) 10...♗b7 (or 10...♘bd7 11 b3 ♗b7) 11 b3 ♘bd7 12 ♗b2 ♗a5 13 ♘g3 g6 14 ♖c1 ♖c8 15 ♖c2 ♕e7 16 ♕e2 ♖c7 17 ♖fc1 ♖fc8 (Gligorić-Szabo, Moscow OL 1956) 18 ♗a3 (Pliester) with a pull for White.

11 b3 ♘c6 12 ♗b2 d4!?

An active alternative is 12...♘e4?!, which has mainly been tested in correspondence chess games: 13 ♕c2 ♗xf3 14 gxf3 ♘d2 (Dalko-Tolush, corr. 1962) and here White does best to continue with 15 ♖fd1! ♘xf3+ 16 ♔g2 ♘ce5 17 ♖xh7+ ♔h8 18 a3 ♗a5 19 ♕xc5, when Black has to find compensation for the pawn(s) (19...♔xh7 20 ♗xe5 ♘xe5 21 ♖xd5).

13 exd4 ♗xf3 14 gxf3 ♘xd4 15 ♘xd4 cxd4 16 ♗xd4 *(D)*

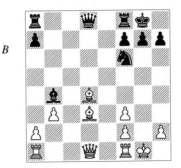

Obviously Black cannot now play 16...♕xd4?? on account of 17 ♗xh7+ winning the queen.

16...♕d6

Instead of building up on the king-side, Black seeks to activate his pieces to control the central squares.

The older continuation 16...♘h5 is best answered with 17 ♔h1 ♕h4 18 ♗e5! ♖fe8 19 ♗g3, when Black does not have sufficient compensation for the pawn, Taimanov-Limbos, Luxembourg 1963.

17 ♗e3 ♖ad8 18 ♗c4 ♕e5 19 f4 ♕e4 20 ♕e2 ♖fe8 *(D)*

Black has now activated his major pieces. Doubtless feeling uncomfortable, White allowed Black to force a repetition of moves in Levitt-Grosz-peter, Copenhagen 1988: **21 ♖ad1 ♕g6+ 22 ♔h1 ♖xd1 23 ♖xd1 ♕e4+ 24 ♔g1 ♕g6+ 25 ♔h1 ♕e4+** ½-½.

W

Conclusion

The Delayed Fianchetto Variation isn't seen very often, but according to the lines considered above, Black is doing reasonably OK. White's best chances at present spring from 9 ♘e5!?.

10 Reshevsky Variation

**1 d4 ♘f6 2 c4 e6 3 ♘c3 ♗b4 4 e3 0-0
5 ♘e2 (D)**

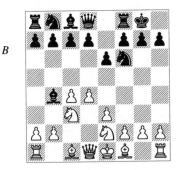

This is the starting position of the Reshevsky Variation.

Just like many other lines in the Nimzo-Indian, the Reshevsky Variation is not named after the inventor of the line, but after the man who popularized it. The originator of this line was Rubinstein himself, who played set-ups with an early ♘e2 against all of Black's 4th move options. The idea with the early ♘e2 is to prevent Black from giving White doubled c-pawns. Only after kicking the b4-bishop away will White move his knight on to greener pastures.

According to my database, Reshevsky used this line in 19 games, scoring a very respectable 76% (+11 =7 −1). His first game in this line was his encounter with Botvinnik at the AVRO tournament in 1938, while the last came against Smagin at Palma de Mallorca

1989, with an amazing gap of 51 years in between.

The Reshevsky Variation is a fairly slow variation, in which the action only starts after an initial manoeuvring phase. With his knight move to e2, White signals that he doesn't want to take on a pawn-structure with doubled pawns and that he is often even willing to spend an extra tempo getting his misplaced knight to a more active square. At lower levels, these signals can indicate that the player with the white pieces is uncomfortable with pawn-structures such as backward or isolated pawns compensated by better piece coordination or something of that kind.

5...d5

Black challenges White in the centre, both a logical and a correct response to White's somewhat passive set-up. Other options include:

a) 5...b6 is certain to transpose to lines in Chapter 11.

b) 5...d6 6 a3 ♗xc3+ 7 ♘xc3 e5 8 ♗e2 a5 9 0-0 ♘c6 10 b3 ♗f5 11 ♗b2 ± Lugovoi-Torok, Harkany 1993.

c) 5...♘e4 is supposed to be bad for Black, but he has done reasonably well here: 6 ♕c2 (or 6 ♗d2 ♘xd2 7 ♕xd2 d5 8 a3 ♗e7 9 cxd5 exd5 = Iliushin-Mchedlishvili, Erevan jr Wch 1999) 6...f5 7 a3 ♗xc3+ 8 ♘xc3 ♘xc3 (8...♕f6!? 9 ♗d3 ♘xc3 10 ♕xc3, Sollars-J.C.Diaz, Siegen OL 1970, and now 10...b6!? has yet to be tried) 9

♕xc3 d6 10 g3 ♕e7 11 ♗g2 and White has the bishop-pair and can open the position at will, Euwe-Henneberger, Zurich 1934.

d) 5...c5 6 a3 and now:

d1) 6...♗xc3+ 7 ♘xc3 cxd4 8 exd4 d5 transposes to note 'a' to Black's 8th move in Line B11 of Chapter 17.

d2) 6...cxd4 7 axb4 (7 exd4 transposes to Line A of Chapter 17) 7...dxc3 8 ♘xc3 d5 9 cxd5 exd5 (or 9...♘xd5 10 ♘xd5 ♕xd5 11 ♕xd5 exd5 12 ♗d2 ± Botvinnik-Najdorf, Moscow OL 1956) 10 ♗e2 ♘c6 11 b5 ♘e7 12 0-0 ♘f5 13 ♖a4 ♗e6 14 g4 ♘d6 15 f4 ± Beliavsky-Inkiov, Thessaloniki OL 1988.

e) 5...b5 is an entertaining gambit invented by the colourful Vitolinš. White can obtain an advantage after 6 cxb5 a6 7 ♘f4 (7 ♘g3 ♗b7 8 ♗d2 axb5 9 ♘xb5 ♗e7 10 ♘c3 c5 11 dxc5 ♗xc5 12 ♖c1 ♘a6 13 a3 ♗e7 14 b4 ♘c7 15 ♕b3 ± Petkević-Vitolinš, Riga 1985) 7...♗b7 8 bxa6 ♘xa6 9 ♗d3 d6 (9...c5!?) 10 0-0 e5 11 ♘h5 and Black does not have enough compensation for the pawn, Karl-Boog, Swiss Cht 1991.

f) 5...♖e8 6 a3 (6 g3 d5 7 ♗g2 dxc4 8 0-0 c6 is fine for Black, G.Georgadze-Bacrot, Groningen FIDE 1997) 6...♗f8 *(D)* and here:

f1) 7 g3 d5 8 b3 (8 cxd5 exd5 9 ♗g2 c6 10 0-0 ♘a6 11 b3 ♗f5 12 ♖a2 ♕d7 13 f3 h5 = Panczyk-Volzhin, Polish Cht (Wisla) 1998) 8...♘c6 9 ♗g2?! (Lautier gives 9 cxd5 exd5 10 ♗g2 ♘e7! 11 0-0 ♘f5 12 ♘f4 c6 = as best) 9...dxc4 10 bxc4 ♘a5 11 c5 (Lautier-Grünfeld, Palma de Mallorca 1989) 11...e5! 12 0-0 exd4 13 exd4 c6 14 ♘f4 ♗f5 ∓ Lautier.

W

f2) 7 e4 and here:

f21) 7...e5? is approved in *ECO*, but as far back as 1937, Cecil Purdy had shown the way for White: 8 dxe5 ♘g4 9 ♘g3 ♕h4 10 ♗e2 d6 11 ♘b5 ♘a6 12 exd6 (Purdy-Crowl, corr. 1937) and now Podgaets gave 12...♖d8, intending ...c6 as equal, but after 13 c5! ♘xc5 14 ♕d5 ♘e6 15 ♕h5! Black is clearly struggling.

f22) 7...d6 8 ♗g5 ♘bd7 9 f3 c6 10 ♕d2 a5 11 b3 e5 12 d5 ♗e7 13 ♗e3 h6 = Prudnikova-Ovchinikova, Russian wom Ch (Elista) 1995.

f23) 7...d5 8 e5 ♘fd7 9 cxd5 (9 c5 b6 10 b4 a5 11 ♖b1 axb4 12 axb4 bxc5 13 bxc5 ♘c6 14 ♗e3 ♗a6 15 f4 f6 with a pleasant game for Black, Tran Ngoc Thach-Torre, Vung Tau Z 2000) 9...exd5 10 ♗e3 (after 10 ♘xd5?! c5! Black regains the pawn with good play, while 10 f4 c5 11 g3 cxd4 12 ♘xd4 ♘c6 13 ♗g2 ♘dxe5 14 fxe5 ♖xe5+ gives Black a strong initiative to compensate for the sacrificed piece, Karasev-Gipslis, USSR 1975) 10...c5 11 f4 ♘c6 12 dxc5 ♗xc5 13 ♗xc5 ♘xc5 14 b4 ♘e6 15 ♘xd5 ♘ed4! = Nemet-Dizdar, Liechtenstein 1988.

f3) 7 d5, with a wide choice for Black:

f31) 7...e5 8 ♘g3 a5 9 ♗e2 ♘a6 10 0-0 ♘c5 11 b3 g6 12 h4 ± M.Gurevich.

f32) 7...d6 8 g3 (8 ♘g3 doesn't give White any advantage: 8...a5 9 ♗e2 ♘bd7 10 e4 exd5 11 cxd5 ♘c5 12 f3 c6 and Black is in the driving seat, Damaso-Piket, Lisbon 2001) 8...exd5 (or 8...♘bd7 9 ♗g2 a5 {9...♘e5 10 0-0 c5!? can also be considered} 10 0-0 ♘c5 11 b3, N.Nikolić-Pikula, Herceg Novi 2001, 11...exd5 12 cxd5 ♗d7 with fairly even chances) 9 cxd5 c5 10 dxc6 bxc6 11 ♗g2 d5 12 0-0 ♘bd7 13 ♘d4 ♗b7 14 ♖e1 c5 = G.Georgadze-Bacrot, Groningen FIDE 1997.

f33) 7...a5 and now:

f331) 8 ♘g3 ♘a6 9 ♗d3 (9 ♖b1 is endorsed in *ECO*, but 9...exd5 10 cxd5, Pytel-Vyzhmanavin, Leningrad 1984, 10...♘c5!? is fine for Black; e.g., 11 b4 axb4 12 axb4 ♘ce4 13 ♘cxe4 ♘xe4 with about even chances) 9...♘c5 10 ♗c2 exd5 11 cxd5 c6 12 0-0 b5 13 e4 ♗a6 and Black has a pleasant game, Goldin-Shabalov, Cali 2001.

f332) 8 g3 ♘a6 9 ♗g2 ♘c5 10 b3 c6 11 0-0 (Vyzhmanavin-Salov, Jurmala 1983) 11...cxd5 12 cxd5 e5 with a pleasant game for Black.

f34) 7...exd5 8 cxd5 c5 (8...a5!? 9 ♘g3 ♘a6 10 ♗e2 ♘c5 11 0-0 ± M.Gurevich-Shabtai, Tel-Aviv 1989) 9 ♘g3 (9 g3 d6 10 ♗g2 ♘bd7 11 0-0 a6 12 h3 g6 with a pleasant version of a Modern Benoni for Black, Benitah-Nikolac, Portorož 1998) 9...d6 10 ♗e2 a6 (10...g6 11 0-0 ♗g7 12 e4 a6 13 ♗g5 b5 14 ♕d2 ♘bd7, M.Gurevich-Moskalenko, Lvov 1985, 15 ♕f4 ±) 11 a4 ♘bd7 (11...g6 12 0-0 ♘bd7 13 e4 h5! 14 ♗g5 ♗g7 with chances for both sides, Bagirov-Dydyshko, USSR

1984) 12 0-0 g6 13 f4 h5 14 ♗f3 ♗g7 and Black is at least equal, Guliev-Brodsky, Nikolaev 1995.

f4) 7 ♘g3 d5 (7...d6 is also possible) 8 ♗d3 (8 ♗e2 also leads to a balanced game) 8...b6 9 0-0 ♗b7 10 b4 ♘bd7 11 ♗b2 g6 with fairly even chances, Karsa-Bischoff, Clichy 1993.

We now return to 5...d5 *(D)*:

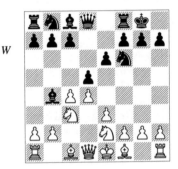

6 a3

This is in accordance with White's set-up. Clearly the knight doesn't want to remain on e2 forever, so the bishop has to be forced away.

In my opinion, 6 cxd5 is a clear misunderstanding, as it gives Black more options than he has available after 6 a3. That said, one of the greatest specialists in the Reshevsky Variation, Mikhail Gurevich, has played 6 cxd5 several times with very good results. In response, Black has two options:

a) 6...♘xd5 7 ♗d2 (7 a3 ♗e7 transposes to Line A, while 7 e4 ♘b6 8 g3 c5 9 a3 cxd4 10 axb4 dxc3 11 ♕xd8 ♖xd8 12 bxc3 e5 is fine for Black, Guliev-Belikov, Moscow 1996) 7...♘f6 8 ♘g3 c5 9 a3 ♗xc3 10 bxc3 ♘c6 11 f4 b6 is equal, Lerner-Osnos, USSR 1981.

b) 6...exd5 is the most popular continuation:

b1) 7 a3 will often transpose back to the main line, but it allows Black some extra options. If White wanted this line, he should have played 6 a3, since now Black has 7...♗d6 (7...♗e7 transposes to Line B) 8 b4 ♘bd7 9 ♘g3 ♘b6 10 ♗d3 c6 11 0-0 ♖e8 12 ♖e1 a5 with full equality, Fedorowicz-Browne, New York 1984.

b2) 7 g3 makes more sense:

b21) 7...♗g4 8 ♗g2 ♕d7 9 0-0 c6 (Kharitonov gives 9...♗xe2 10 ♘xe2 ♖e8 as unclear) 10 f3!? ♗h3 11 ♗xh3 ♕xh3 12 ♕b3 ♗xc3 13 bxc3 ♕d7 14 c4 ± Bönsch-Smagin, Dresden 1985.

b22) 7...♖e8 8 ♗g2 and here:

b221) 8...c6 transposes to line 'b231'.

b222) 8...♗f8 9 0-0 c6 10 ♘f4 (10 f3 is met with 10...c5!, which is an often-seen idea in this system; however, ...c5 should only be played once White has played f3) 10...♘a6 11 b3 ♘c7 12 ♗b2 b6 13 ♖c1 ♗b7 14 ♖c2 g6 = Shulman-Brodsky, Nikolaev 1995.

b23) 7...c6 8 ♗g2 and now:

b231) 8...♖e8 and then:

b2311) 9 ♕c2 is a speciality of Israeli GM Boris Avrukh. In Avrukh-Roiz, Israeli Ch (Ramat-Aviv/Modin) 2000, Black equalized after 9...♘a6 10 0-0 ♗f8 11 a3 ♘c7 12 ♗d2 ♘e6, but 9...g6!?, intending 10...♗f5 with control over e4, looks even better.

b2312) 9 0-0 ♗f5 (9...♗f8 transposes to line 'b222') 10 ♘f4 ♘a6 11 ♘d3 ♗f8 12 a3 ♘c7 13 f3 h6 with a pleasant game for Black, Karasev-Platonov, USSR Ch (Riga) 1970.

b232) 8...♘a6 9 0-0 ♗f5 10 f3 ♖e8 11 g4 ♗g6 12 ♘f4 ♘d7 13 ♖f2 ♘b6

with chances for both sides, Bönsch-Hübner, Munich 1990.

b233) 8...♗d6 9 0-0 ♖e8 10 f3 c5 11 b3 ♘c6 12 ♕d2 b6 13 ♗b2 ♗a6 and Black has a pleasant game, Shirov-Kamsky, Monte Carlo Amber rpd 1995.

6...♗e7

This seems at present the most logical response to 6 a3. Two other possibilities have been tried:

a) 6...♗xc3+?! plays into White's hands: 7 ♘xc3 b6 8 b4! dxc4 (8...c5?! 9 dxc5 bxc5 10 cxd5 cxb4 11 axb4 exd5 12 ♗e2 ± Reshevsky-Van den Berg, Amsterdam 1970) 9 ♗xc4 ♗b7 10 0-0 (Milan-McLardy, corr. 1969) 10...♕d6!?, intending 11 f3 a5 12 b5 c5 with chances for both sides.

b) 6...♗d6 7 c5 (the aimless 7 cxd5 exd5 transposes to note 'b' to White's 6th move, and is what Black is hoping for; 7 ♘g3 c5 {7...c6 8 c5 ♗e7 is line 'b2'} 8 dxc5 ♗xc5 9 ♗e2 a5 is similar to a Queen's Gambit Accepted with the colours reversed and the white knight misplaced on g3: 10 0-0 ♘c6 11 cxd5 exd5 12 ♘b5 ♗e6 13 ♕a4 ♕b6 = Chernin-Aseev, USSR Ch (Lvov) 1984) 7...♗e7 and here:

b1) 8 ♘f4 b6 9 b4 is line 'b323'.

b2) 8 ♘g3 c6 (8...b6 9 b4 is line 'b322') 9 f4 b6 10 b4 transposes to line 'b31'.

b3) 8 b4 and now:

b31) 8...c6 9 f4 b6 (9...a5 10 ♗d2 b6 11 ♘a4 ♘bd7 12 ♘ec3 ♗a6 13 ♗xa6 ♖xa6 is about even, Volkov-Aleksandrov, Krasnodar 1998) 10 ♘g3 a5 11 ♗d2 ♘fd7 12 ♗e2 ♗a6 13 0-0 f5 14 ♕b3 ♗xe2 15 ♘gxe2 ♕c8 16 ♖ab1 ♕a6 17 b5 (Raičević-Kudrin, Valjevo 1984) and now 17...♕c8!?

looks best ; e.g., 18 cxb6 ♘xb6 19 a4
♘c4 or 18 bxc6 ♘xc6 19 cxb6 ♘xb6!
– in both cases Black has every reason
to be pleased with his position.

b32) 8...b6 *(D)* and then:

b321) 9 ♖b1 c6 10 ♘g3 a5 11 ♗e2
axb4 12 axb4 bxc5 13 dxc5 (13 bxc5
e5! is equal), Epishin-Bühler, Geneva
2001, 13...e5! with a pleasant game for
Black.

b322) 9 ♘g3 c6 10 ♗d2 bxc5 11
bxc5 e5! 12 ♗e2 g6 13 0-0 (Illescas-
Morozevich, Madrid 1996) and now
13...e4 is best according to L.B.Han-
sen, leaving the chances just about
balanced.

b323) 9 ♘f4 and then:

b3231) 9...c6 10 ♘d3 ♗a6!? (the
continuation 10...♘bd7 11 ♗e2 a5 12
♗d2 is given by M.Gurevich in *ECO*,
who continues with 12...axb4, but
12...♘e4!? is interesting; for example,
13 ♘xe4 dxe4 14 ♘f4 bxc5 15 bxc5
e5 with chances for both sides) 11 f4
♘e4 12 ♗b2 bxc5 13 ♘xe4 dxe4 14
♘xc5 ♗xf1 15 ♖xf1 (Fauland-Hölz,
Graz 1991) and now 15...a5!? sends
White searching for equality.

b3232) 9...a5 10 ♗b2 (10 ♖b1
axb4 11 axb4 c6 12 ♗e2 ♘bd7 13 0-0

♗a6 14 ♗b2 ♕c7 ½-½ Supatashvili-
Brodsky, Perm 1997) 10...axb4!? 11
axb4 ♖xa1 12 ♕xa1 ♘c6 13 ♘d3 bxc5
14 bxc5 (Ragozin-Konstantinopolsky,
USSR Ch (Tbilisi) 1937) 14...♗d7!?,
intending 15...♕a8, should leave Black
with equal chances.

We now return to 6...♗e7 *(D)*:

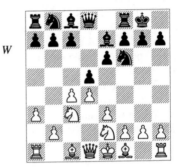

7 cxd5

Or:

a) 7 c5 b6 (7...a5!? has also been
tried) 8 b4 bxc5 9 bxc5 c6 10 f4 ♗a6 is
equal, Davidović-Farago, Dortmund
1986.

b) 7 ♘g3 is a reasonably popular
choice, but not one against which
Black should experience any trouble
equalizing:

b1) 7...c6 is a little too timid: 8
♗d3 b6 9 0-0 ♗b7 10 ♕e2 ♘bd7 11
♖d1 ♕c7 12 e4 ± I.Sokolov-Grün-
berg, Budapest 1986.

b2) 7...b6 8 cxd5 exd5 9 ♗d3 and
now:

b21) 9...c5 10 dxc5 bxc5 11 0-0 g6
12 e4!? and now, instead of 12...♘bd7?!
13 exd5 ♘b6 (Nenashev-Gogolis,
Khania 1994) 14 ♗h6 ♖e8 15 ♗b5
♗d7 16 d6 ±, Black should continue
12...d4, even if White is better after 13

e5 dxc3 14 exf6 ♗xf6 15 bxc3 ♗xc3 16 ♗h6.

b22) 9...♖e8 10 0-0 ♗a6 11 b4 ♗xd3 12 ♕xd3 ♗f8 13 ♗b2 a6 14 ♖ac1 with only a slight initiative for White, Adianto-Zaw Winlay, Dubai 1996.

b3) 7...♘bd7 8 ♗d3 dxc4 9 ♗xc4 e5 = Boleslavsky.

b4) 7...dxc4 8 ♗xc4 c5 9 0-0 cxd4 10 exd4 ♘bd7 11 ♗f4 ♘b6 12 ♗d3 ♗d7 13 ♗e5 ♗c6 14 ♕e2 ♘bd5 with an equal position, Mikenas-Sishkin, USSR 1960.

b5) 7...c5 and here:

b51) 8 cxd5 exd5 transposes to note 'b4' to White's 8th move.

b52) After 8 dxc5 the position resembles one from the Queen's Gambit Accepted, but with colours reversed:

b521) 8...dxc4 9 ♕c2 (9 ♕xd8 is nothing for Black to worry about; e.g., 9...♖xd8 10 ♗xc4 ♗xc5 11 b4 ♗e7 12 ♗b2 ♘bd7 13 ♘b5 a6 14 ♘d4 ♘b6 15 ♗b3 ♗d7 with a better game for Black, Forintos-Csom, Hungarian Ch (Budapest) 1981) 9...♗xc5 10 ♗xc4 ♘bd7 11 0-0 b6 12 ♖d1 ♗b7 13 b4 ♗e7 14 ♗b2 a5 = Piket-Adams, Wijk aan Zee 2001.

b522) 8...♗xc5 9 b4 ♗e7 (9...♗d6!?) 10 ♗b2 dxc4 11 ♕c2 b5!? 12 ♘xb5 a5 13 ♗xc4 axb4 14 0-0 bxa3 15 ♗xa3 ♗xa3 16 ♖xa3 ♖xa3 17 ♘xa3 with equality, Razuvaev-Gulko, Tashkent 1984.

c) 7 ♘f4 *(D)* is another popular choice, but here too Black has several satisfactory continuations:

c1) 7...b6 8 cxd5 ♘xd5 (8...exd5 has been played on several occasions with equally good results) 9 ♘cxd5 exd5 10 ♗e2 ♗b7 11 ♗f3 c6 12 0-0

B

♘d7 13 ♕c2 ♘f6 = Norri-Wiedenkeller, Finland-Sweden 1989.

c2) 7...dxc4 is another line that has served Black well even if other books on the Nimzo-Indian have scorned it. 8 ♗xc4 and here:

c21) 8...♘c6 doesn't strike one as very logical, putting the knight in front of the c-pawn, but the idea is to play ...e5 after proper preparation; e.g., 9 ♘d3 a6 10 0-0 ♕d6 11 ♕e2 (Hort-Kostro, Luhačovice 1971) 11...b5 12 ♗a2 ♖d8 13 ♘f4 ♗b7 leads to interesting play.

c22) 8...c5 9 0-0 ♘c6 (9...cxd4, 9...a6 and 9...♘bd7 are all worthy alternatives) 10 dxc5 ♗xc5 11 b4 ♗d6 12 ♘ce2 ♕e7 13 ♘g3 ♖d8 14 ♕e2 ♘e5 and Black has a slight initiative, Paasikangas-Veingold, Jyväskylä 1998.

c3) 7...a5 8 b3 c6 9 ♗e2 ♘bd7 10 cxd5 ♘xd5 11 ♘cxd5 exd5 12 0-0 ♗d6 = Botterill-T.Petrosian, Hastings 1977/8.

c4) 7...c6 is Black's main continuation:

c41) 8 cxd5 exd5 transposes to note 'd4' to White's 8th move in Line B.

c42) 8 h3 ♘bd7 9 cxd5 ♘xd5 10 ♘fxd5 exd5 11 ♗d3 ♘f6 12 ♕c2 ♖e8 13 g4 g6 14 ♗d2 c5 and Black is

taking control over the action, Korchnoi-Gelfand, Lvov 2000.

c43) 8 b4 ♘bd7 9 c5 b6 10 ♘d3
♕c7 11 f4 a5 12 ♗d2 ♗a6 13 ♗e2
♘e4 14 ♘xe4 dxe4 = Keene-Anders-
son, Reykjavik 1972.

c44) 8 ♗e2 ♘bd7 9 cxd5 ♘xd5 10
e4 ♘xc3 11 bxc3 e5 12 ♘h5 ♕a5 13
♗d2 g6 14 ♘g3 (Kourkounakis-Tivia-
kov, Gausdal 1992) and here 14...h5!?
looks like an interesting idea.

c45) 8 b3 ♘bd7 9 ♗b2 (9 ♗d3
♗d6! 10 ♗b2 = *ECO*) 9...♖e8 10 ♕c2
dxc4 11 ♗xc4 e5 12 dxe5 ♘xe5 13
♗e2 ♗d6 14 0-0 ♕e7 15 b4 ♗g4 =
Mestel-Arnason, Esbjerg 1984.

c46) 8 ♗d2 ♘bd7 9 cxd5 exd5
(9...♘xd5!? is an interesting option
Kharitonov gives, among others: 10
e4 ♘xf4 11 ♗xf4 e5 12 dxe5 ♕c7
with compensation for the pawn) 10
♗d3 ♗d6 11 ♕f3 ♖e8 12 g4 ♕e7 13
g5 ♘e4 14 h4 b5 with chances for both
sides, Morović-I.Rogers, Spanish Cht
(Cala Galdana) 1994.

c47) 8 ♗d3 and now:

c471) 8...b6 9 0-0 ♘bd7 10 ♖e1
♗b7 11 cxd5 cxd5 12 ♕e2 a6 13 ♗d2
♗d6 14 ♖ed1 ♖e8 = Edzgveradze-
Kiseliov, Moscow 1996.

c472) 8...dxc4 9 ♗xc4 ♘bd7 10
0-0 (10 ♘d3 c5 11 ♗a2 b6 12 0-0 ♗b7
13 ♕e2 ♕c7 14 ♗d2 ♖ac8 15 ♖ad1
♕b8 = Christiansen-Benjamin, USA
Ch (Chandler) 1997) 10...e5 11 ♘fe2
(after 11 dxe5?! ♘xe5 12 ♗e2 ♗f5 13
b4 ♕c7 14 ♗b2 ♖ad8 15 ♕c1 ♗d6
Black is in control, Hon Kah Seng-
Polugaevsky, Thessaloniki OL 1984)
11...exd4 12 exd4 (12 ♘xd4 ♘e5 13
♗e2 c5 14 ♘f3, S.Bekker Jensen-
Stojanovski, Copenhagen 1997, and
now 14...♘xf3+ 15 ♗xf3 ♕c7 16 ♘d5

♘xd5 17 ♗xd5 ♗f6 secures a pleasant game for Black) 12...♘b6 13 ♗b3
♗f5 14 ♘g3 ♗g6 15 ♗f4 ♘fd5 16
♘xd5 ♘xd5 17 ♗c1 ♕b6 and again
Black is enjoying himself, R.Gonza-
lez-Browne, Los Polvorines 1980.

c473) 8...♘bd7 9 cxd5 (9 0-0 dxc4
10 ♗xc4 transposes to line 'c472')
9...♘xd5 (9...exd5 is note 'd422' to
White's 8th move in Line B; 9...cxd5
is also possible) 10 e4 ♘xf4 11 ♗xf4
e5!? 12 dxe5 ♕c7 13 ♗g3 ♘xe5 and
White has nothing to brag about, Pet-
ursson-H.Olafsson, Gausdal 1986.

We return to 7 cxd5 *(D)*:

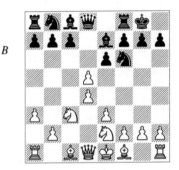

Now:
A: 7...♘xd5   121
B: 7...exd5   124

A)
7...♘xd5 8 ♕c2
Or:

a) 8 e4 ♘xc3 (both 8...♘f6 and
8...♘b6 are worthwhile alternatives;
the intention is to follow up with 9...c5
and after 10 d5 exd5 11 exd5 play
around the white d-pawn) 9 ♘xc3 (9
bxc3 c5 10 ♘g3 ♕c7 11 ♗b2 ♖d8 12
♗d3 ♘c6 13 ♘e2 ♖b8 14 0-0 b5 with a
pleasant game for Black, Levitt-Parker,

British League (4NCL) 1999/00) 9...c5 10 d5 exd5 11 ♘xd5 ♘c6 12 ♗c4 ♗f6 13 0-0 ♗d4 14 ♗e3 ♗e6 15 ♗xd4 ♘xd4 16 b4 b6 17 ♖c1 f5! = Torre-Korchnoi, Lucerne OL 1982.

b) 8 ♘xd5 exd5 and now:

b1) 9 ♘f4 c6 10 ♗d3 ♘d7 11 ♕c2 ♘f6 12 ♗d2 a5 13 f3 ♖e8 14 0-0 ♗d6 = G.Georgadze-Pogorelov, Mondariz 1997.

b2) 9 g3 ♘d7 (or 9...a5!? 10 ♗g2 c6 11 0-0 ♘a6 12 ♕c2 ♘c7 13 ♗d2 ♘b5 14 f3 ♘d6 = Zaja-Avrukh, Pula 2000) 10 ♗g2 ♘f6 11 0-0 ♗d6 12 ♘c3 c6 13 b4 a6 14 ♖e1 ♖e8 = Reshevsky-Botvinnik, Amsterdam 1938.

c) 8 ♗d2 ♘xc3 (8...♘d7 9 g3 {9 ♕c2 transposes to the main line} 9...♘5f6 10 ♗g2 c5 11 0-0 cxd4 12 exd4 ♘b6 13 ♗f4 ♘fd5 14 ♕d3 ♗d7 15 ♘xd5 ♘xd5 16 ♗xd5 exd5 ½-½ Kovačević-Palac, Nova Gorica 2002) 9 ♘xc3 c5 10 dxc5 ♗xc5 11 ♘e4 ♗e7 12 ♗c3 ♘c6 = Taimanov-Karpov, Leningrad IZ 1973.

d) 8 g3 is a fairly popular move, but Black has always scored reasonably well against it. He has four main options:

d1) 8...♘d7 9 ♗g2 ♘xc3 10 ♘xc3 (10 bxc3!?) 10...e5 11 0-0 exd4 12 exd4 ♘f6 and now, instead of 13 d5 a6 14 h3 ♗d6 = O.Rodriguez-Suba, Cala Galdana 2001, White should opt for 13 ♗f4; e.g., 13...♗d6 14 ♕d2 and Black still has some problems finishing his queenside development.

d2) 8...c5 9 ♗g2 ♘xc3 10 bxc3 ♘d7 (10...♘c6 has also been tried on many occasions) 11 0-0 ♕c7 12 a4 ♖b8 13 e4 b6 14 ♗e3 ♗b7 (14...♗a6!?) 15 ♕c1 ♖bc8 = Hort-Brunner, Bundesliga 1988/9.

d3) 8...b6 9 ♗g2 ♗b7 10 e4 ♘xc3 11 bxc3 ♘c6 12 0-0 ♘a5 = Wexler-Korchnoi, Buenos Aires 1960.

d4) 8...♘xc3 9 ♘xc3 c5 and here:

d41) 10 dxc5!? used to be considered quite tame until Mikhail Gurevich managed to put some fire back into it. After 10...♕xd1+, Gurevich's new idea is 11 ♔xd1! (11 ♘xd1 ♗xc5 12 ♗g2 ♗e7 13 ♗d2 ♘d7 14 b4 ♖b8 = will only inspire the most docile of us, Bagirov-Krogius, USSR Ch (Leningrad) 1960) 11...♗xc5 12 ♗g2. Then:

d411) 12...♘d7 allows White an edge: 13 ♗d2 ♗e7 14 ♔c2 ♖b8 15 ♖hd1 b5 16 e4 a5 17 ♗f4 ♗b7 18 ♗d6!? ♗xd6 (M.Gurevich-Wells, Escaldes Z 1998) and here Gurevich gives 19 e5! as best; e.g., 19...♗xe5 20 ♗xb7 ♗xb7 21 ♖xd7 ♘c6 22 ♖a7 ± or 19...♖b6 20 exd6 ♗b7 21 ♗xb7 ♖xb7 22 b4 ±.

d412) 12...♘c6 13 ♔c2 e5!? 14 b4 ♗b6 15 ♗b2 ♗e6! 16 ♗d5 (16 ♖ad1 ♖ac8 17 ♔b1 ♗b3 18 ♖d7 ♖fd8 19 ♖xb7 ♖d2 with counterplay – Gurevich), M.Gurevich-Ligterink, Dutch Cht 1998, and here 16...♘d4+!? looks like the simplest path to equality: 17 exd4 exd4 18 ♗xe6 (18 ♘a4 d3+ 19 ♔xd3 ♗xd5 20 ♘xb6 axb6 =) 18...dxc3 19 ♗xc3 fxe6 20 f4 = Gurevich.

d42) 10 d5 ♗f6 (10...exd5 11 ♘xd5 ♘c6 12 ♗g2 ♗e6 13 0-0 ♕d7 14 e4 ♗xd5 15 exd5 ♘d4 and now, instead of 16 b4 ½-½ Dzindzichashvili-Polugaevsky, Reykjavik 1990, 16 ♗e3!? ♗f6 17 ♕d3 may be more interesting for White thanks to his passed pawn and bishop-pair) 11 ♗g2 ♗xc3+ 12 bxc3 exd5 and now:

d421) 13 ♕xd5 ♕e7 14 ♖b1? (14 0-0 is better, but after 14...♘c6 Black is also quite comfortable) 14...♘c6 15 0-0 ♗e6 16 ♕h5 ♖ad8 ∓ Shaked-Kramnik, Tilburg 1997.

d422) Winants suggests that 13 ♗xd5 may be better and gives the line 13...♗h3!? 14 ♗xb7 (14 ♗xf7+ ♔xf7 15 ♕h5+ ♔g8 16 ♕xh3 ♕d3 with compensation for the pawn) 14...♘d7 15 ♕h5 (15 ♗xa8 ♕xa8 16 f3 ♘e5 17 ♔f2 ♖d8 18 ♕e2 ♘g4+ 19 ♔e1 ♘e5 20 ♔f2 ♘g4+ =) 15...♖b8 16 ♕xh3 ♖xb7 17 0-0 ♕f6, when Black has ample light-squared compensation for the pawn.

8...♘d7 *(D)*

Or:

a) 8...♘f6 9 g3 c5 10 ♗g2 ♘c6 11 dxc5 ♗xc5 12 b4 ♗d6 13 0-0 e5 14 ♖d1 ♕e7 15 b5 leaves White with a very pleasant game, Sliwa-Gipslis, Riga 1959.

b) 8...♘xc3 9 ♘xc3 ♘d7 (9...c5 10 dxc5 ♗xc5 11 ♗e2 ♗d7 12 0-0 ♕e7 13 b4 ♗b6 14 ♗b2 ± Ghitescu-Langeweg, Beverwijk 1967) 10 ♗e2 c5 11 dxc5 ♗xc5 12 b4 ± Taimanov.

9 g3

This deployment of the light-squared bishop looks like White's most natural set-up, but other moves are possible:

a) 9 b4 a5 10 b5 c5 11 bxc6 bxc6 = (Furman).

b) 9 ♘g3 ♘xc3 (or 9...c5 10 ♗d3 ♘5f6 11 0-0 b6 12 dxc5 ♘xc5 13 ♗e2 ♗b7 14 b4 ♘cd7 15 ♗b2 a5 is equal, Spassky-Smyslov, Amsterdam Ct 1956) 10 bxc3 c5 11 ♗d3 ♘f6 12 0-0 ♕c7 13 c4 h6 14 ♗b2 ♗d7 15 ♖ac1 (L.B.Hansen-Tiviakov, Istanbul OL 2000) 15...cxd4 16 exd4 ♖fd8 =.

c) 9 e4 ♘xc3 10 ♘xc3 c5 11 d5 ♘b6 (11...♗f6!? 12 dxe6 fxe6 13 f4 ♗d4 14 e5 ♘b6 15 ♗d3 ♕h4+ 16 g3 ♕h3 17 ♘e4 h6 18 ♘d6 ♗d7 is level, G.Georgadze-Schlosser, Bundesliga 1997/8) 12 dxe6 ♗xe6 13 ♗e2 ♗f6 (13...f5!? is also satisfactory for Black, M.Gurevich-Hauchard, Belgian Cht 1997) 14 0-0 a6 15 f4 ♗d4+ 16 ♔h1 f6! 17 ♖d1 ♖c8 and here Psakhis prefers the black position, G.Georgadze-Salov, Elista 1998.

d) 9 ♗d2 and here Black can equalize in several ways:

d1) 9...♘xc3 10 ♘xc3 e5 11 d5 ♘f6 12 e4 ♗d7 13 ♗b5 ♗xb5 14 ♘xb5 ♕d7 15 ♘c3 ♗c5 with an equal position, Slutsky-Tiviakov, Amsterdam 1956.

d2) 9...♘5f6 10 g3 (10 ♖d1 b6 11 ♘f4 ♗b7 12 ♗e2 c5 is also perfectly OK for Black, Volkov-Korchnoi, Batumi Echt 1999) 10...e5 11 ♗g2 exd4 12 ♘xd4 ♘e5 13 0-0 (Garcia Palermo-Suba, Dortmund 1985) 13...c5 14 ♘f5 ♗xf5 15 ♕xf5 ♕xd2 16 ♖ad1 ♕xb2 17 ♕xe5 ♖ae8 18 ♖b1 = Garcia Palermo.

d3) 9...c5 10 ♘xd5 exd5 11 ♘f4 cxd4! 12 ♘xd5 dxe3 13 ♘xe3 ♘f6 14 ♗d3 ♗e6 = Petrosian-Korchnoi, Velden Ct (2) 1980.

9...♘xc3 10 bxc3

10 ♘xc3 is completely harmless, as demonstrated most recently in Corral Blanco-Topalov, Spanish Cht (Cala Galdana) 1999: 10...e5 11 ♗g2 exd4 12 exd4 ♗f6 13 ♗e3 ♘b6 14 0-0 c6 15 ♖ad1 ♗g4 16 f3 ♗e6.

10...c5 11 ♗g2 ♕c7

11...♖b8!? was first tried out in M.Gurevich-Motwani, Ostend 1991: 12 e4 e5 13 0-0 b5!? 14 ♖d1 ♕c7 15 dxe5 ♘xe5 16 ♘f4 ♗g4 (Gurevich gives 16...♗b7 17 ♘d5 ♗xd5 18 ♖xd5 ♖fd8 19 ♗f4 ♖xd5 20 exd5 ♗d6 as equal) 17 ♖e1 c4 18 ♘d5 ♕d7 19 ♗f4 ♘d3! with chances for both sides.

12 0-0

Since Black is doing quite well after this move, White should consider the alternatives carefully:

a) 12 a4 ♖b8 13 a5 b5 14 axb6 axb6 15 0-0 b5 with fairly balanced chances, M.Gurevich-Petursson, Wijk aan Zee 1990.

b) 12 ♕b3 ♘b6 13 0-0 ♗d7 14 a4 cxd4 15 cxd4 ♖ab8 16 ♗d2 ♕c4 is equal, Polugaevsky-Averbakh, USSR Ch (Tbilisi) 1959.

12...♖b8 13 c4 cxd4 14 exd4 b6 15 ♗f4 ♗d6 16 ♗xd6 ♕xd6 17 ♖fc1 ♗a6 18 ♕a4

18 c5? is worse: 18...bxc5 19 dxc5 ♘xc5 20 ♕xc5 ♕xc5 21 ♖xc5 ♗xe2 22 ♖c7 a6 and although White managed to draw in Rustemov-P.H.Nielsen, Copenhagen 2001, at this point Black is a pawn up for no compensation.

18...♗b7

Now, instead of 19 ♕xa7? ♗xg2 20 ♔xg2 ♕c6+, which left White scrambling to save his queen in Zilberman-Taimanov, USSR 1979, White should play 19 ♗xb7 ♖xb7 20 ♖ab1 ♖c8 with about even chances.

B)
7...exd5 (D)

W

8 g3
Or:

a) 8 h3 ♖e8 (8...c5, 8...♘bd7 and 8...c6 are perfectly good alternatives) 9 g4 c6 10 ♗g2 ♘a6 11 0-0 ♘c7 12 ♘g3 h6 13 ♗d2 ♘e6 14 b4 a5 15 ♕b3 ♗d6 and Black has at least equalized, Züger-Kindermann, Vienna 1986.

b) 8 ♘g3. Although I think the knight is better placed on g3 (compared to f4, as in line 'd') where it aids the central e4 advance and can jump to f5, it is also a target after a later ...h5. Now:

b1) 8...c6 9 ♗d3 ♖e8 10 b4 transposes to line 'c53'.

b2) 8...♖e8 9 ♗e2 (9 ♗d3 c6 10 b4 is again line 'c53') 9...♗e6 (9...a5!?) 10 b4 c6 11 0-0 ♘bd7 12 f3 a5 and White already has to show some care to avoid ending up worse, A.Shneider-Tsiganova, Kuopio 1992.

b3) 8...a5 9 ♗d3 ♖e8 10 0-0 c6 11 ♗d2 ♘a6 12 ♘ce2 ♗d6 13 ♕c2 (Nenashev-Podgaets, USSR Army Ch (Odessa) 1991) and now 13...h5!?, to chase the g3-knight, looks like an interesting possibility.

b4) 8...c5 9 dxc5 (9 ♗e2 ♘c6 10 0-0 cxd4 11 exd4 ♗e6 12 b4 ♖c8 13 ♕d3 ♘e4 14 ♘cxe4 ½-½ Karpov-Byrne, Montilla 1976) 9...♗xc5 and here the two critical lines are:

b41) 10 ♗e2 ♘c6 11 0-0 (11 b4 ♗d6 12 ♗b2 ♗e5 13 ♘a4 ♗xb2 14 ♘xb2 a6 15 0-0 ♖e8 = D.Gurevich-Leitão, Cali 2001) 11...♗e6 (11...d4!? 12 ♘a4 ♗d6 13 b4 ♗e5 14 ♖b1 dxe3 15 ♗xe3 ♘d4 led to easy equality in Pfeiffer-Wade, Leipzig OL 1960) 12 b4 ♗d6 (12...d4 13 ♘a4, Lilienthal-Larsen, Moscow 1962, 13...♗d6 is unclear according to *ECO*) 13 ♘b5 ♗e5 14 ♘d4 ♘xd4 15 exd4 ♗c7 = Camara-Najdorf, Mar del Plata 1969.

b42) 10 b4 d4! 11 bxc5 (11 ♘a4? dxe3 12 ♕xd8? {12 ♘xc5? exf2+ 13 ♔e2 ♗g4+ is very unfortunate for White} 12...exf2+ 13 ♔e2 ♗g4+ is also the end for White) 11...dxc3 12 ♕c2 ♕a5 13 ♖b1 ♗d7 (Euwe-Alekhine, The Hague Wch (17) 1937) and here the only proper way for White to continue the battle is 14 ♘e2; e.g., 14...♘a6 15 ♕xc3 ♕xc3+ 16 ♘xc3 ♘xc5 with roughly equal chances.

c) 8 b4 *(D)* is another popular choice, but here too Black should be able to equalize without too many worries:

c1) 8...♖e8 9 ♘g3 ♘bd7 10 ♗d3 c6 transposes to line 'c534'.

c2) 8...♗f5 allows White to pick up a tempo by threatening to kick the bishop with the knight: 9 ♘g3 ♗g6 10 f4 (this seems like the logical follow-up, but a more conservative approach, such as 10 ♗e2, may be even better) 10...h6 (another idea is 10...♕d7; e.g., 11 ♗e2 a5 12 b5 ♖e8 13 0-0 h6 with chances for both sides) 11 f5 ♗h7 12

B

♗d3 c6 13 0-0 ♗d6 and Black's problems are over, Schlagenhauf-S.Johannessen, Gausdal 1986.

c3) 8...b6 9 ♘f4 c6 10 ♗d3 ♗d6 11 ♘fe2 (11 0-0 ♗xf4!? 12 exf4 ♗a6 = Hecht) 11...♖e8 12 ♘g3 c5 13 ♘b5 ♗xg3 14 hxg3 a6 15 ♗xh7+ (Hecht gives 15 ♘c3 cxd4 16 ♘e2 dxe3 17 ♗xe3 ♘bd7 ∓) 15...♘xh7 16 ♕h5 axb5 17 ♕xh7+ ♔f8 18 ♕h8+ ♔e7 19 ♕xg7 ♖g8 20 ♕h7 (G.Georgadze-Adams, Groningen FIDE 1997) and here 20...c4!? 21 e4 ♗e6 22 ♖h5 ♘c6 (Hecht) enables Black to start consolidating.

c4) 8...♘bd7 9 ♘g3 ♘b6 (9...♖e8 10 ♗d3 c6 is yet another transposition to 'c534') 10 ♗d3 g6!? (preventing ♘f5; 10...c6 11 0-0 ♘e8 12 b5 ± Salov-Gavrikov, USSR Ch (Minsk) 1987) 11 0-0 a5 12 b5 ♗d6 13 ♘ce2 a4 14 ♕c2 ♕e7 with a complicated game and approximately level chances, Van Beek-Kishnev, Antwerp 1998.

c5) 8...c6 (the most popular line) 9 ♘g3 and now:

c51) 9...♘e8 10 ♗d3 ♘d6 (targeting e4 and c4) 11 0-0 f5 12 f3 ♗e6 13 ♘ge2 ♘d7 14 b5 ♘b6 15 bxc6 bxc6 16 ♘a4 ♘xa4 17 ♕xa4 ♕d7 = Marin-Sax, Warsaw Z 1987.

c52) 9...b5!? is an intriguing idea. It seems best for White to continue with 10 &xd2 a5 11 bxa5 &xa5 and now:

c521) 12 ♕b3 ♘a6 13 ♘b1 (13 a4 h5!? 14 &d3 h4 15 ♘f5 &xf5 16 &xf5 b4 17 ♘a2 c5 and Black is better) 13...b4 14 &xa6 &xa6 15 ♘f5 c5 and with White's king stuck in the centre and his development not quite in place, Black has the better chances, Mamedova-Papaioannou, Korinthos 1999.

c525) 12 a4 b4 (12...bxa4 13 ♘xa4 &a8 =) 13 ♘a2 c5 14 dxc5 &xc5 15 ♘xb4 d4 16 ♘d3 dxe3 17 fxe3 &e8 and Black's attacking chances compensate for the material deficit, Mamedova-Prudnikova, Warsaw wom Ech 2001.

c53) 9...&e8 10 &d3 *(D)* and then:

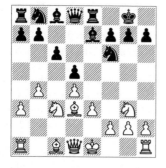

c531) 10...b5?! 11 &d2 ♘bd7 12 a4 &xb4 13 axb5 c5 14 0-0 c4 15 &c2 a5 16 bxa6 &xa6 17 &xa6 &xa6 18 ♕a1 ± Reshevsky-Taimanov, Zurich Ct 1953.

c532) 10...a5 11 b5 c5 12 0-0 ♘bd7 13 ♘f5 (13 &b2 cxd4 14 exd4 is given as slightly better for White by Byrne/Mednis, but frankly speaking I

don't see any advantage for White after 14...♘b6) 13...&f8 14 dxc5 ♘xc5 15 ♘d4 &g4 16 &e2 &xe2 17 ♘cxe2 ♘ce4 18 ♘f4 &d6 and Black's piece activity compensates for the isolated pawn, Tolk-Chuchelov, Antwerp 1999.

c533) 10...&d6 11 0-0 and then:

c5331) 11...♘bd7 has been tried, but White appears to be able to obtain an edge in several ways; for example, 12 ♕c2!? ♘f8 13 b5 &d7 14 a4 &c8 15 &a3 &b8 16 &fc1 ♘g4 17 ♘f1 ♕g5 18 ♕d2 ± Nenashev-Antonio, Asian Cht (Singapore) 1995.

c5332) 11...♕c7!? 12 &d2 ♘bd7 13 &c1 a6 14 ♕b3?! (14 &e1!?) 14...h5! 15 &fe1 h4 16 ♘f1 ♘g4 17 f4 ♘df6 and Black is in control, Chiburdanidze-Xu Yuhua, Batumi rpd 2001.

c534) 10...♘bd7 11 0-0 (11 &d2 is best met with 11...b6 12 0-0 &b7 13 f3 c5! 14 ♘ce2 &f8 15 &b1 c4 16 &c2 g6 17 ♘c3 h5!, when Black has taken charge of the game, Stoll-Bouwmeester, corr. 1985) and now:

c5341) 11...&d6 is line 'c5331'.

c5342) 11...♘b6 12 b5 c5 13 dxc5 &xc5 14 ♘a4 (14 ♕c2!?) 14...♘xa4 15 ♕xa4 d4 16 ♕c2 &b6 17 e4 ♘g4 18 h3 ♘e5 with balanced chances, Shulman-Lautier, Ohrid Ech 2001.

c5343) 11...b5 12 &d2 ♘b6 13 a4 a6 = Gligorić-Reshevsky, New York 1952.

d) 8 ♘f4 *(D)* is also seen relatively often. On f4, the knight doesn't support the otherwise traditional e3-e4 break in the centre, but White hopes to discourage counterplay with ...c5, as the black d-pawn may then become vulnerable. Black has tried:

d1) 8...&e8 usually transposes to 'd421' via 9 &d3 c6.

d2) 8...a5 9 ♗d3 c6 transposes to 'd423'.

d3) 8...b6 9 ♗d3 ♗b7 10 0-0 ♗d6 11 ♘ce2 (11 ♕f3!? gives White the better chances) 11...a5 12 ♗d2 ♘bd7 13 ♖c1 c5 with about even chances, Lubiensky-Petrosian, Tbilisi 1949.

d4) 8...c6 is Black's most solid choice. Then:

d41) 9 ♗e2 a5 10 f3 ♖e8 11 0-0 ♗f8 12 ♗d3 ♘a6 13 ♔h1 ♘c7 leaves Black with a pleasant game, Zayats-Gorbatov, Moscow 1992.

d42) 9 ♗d3 is the natural square for this bishop. Now:

d421) 9...♖e8 10 0-0 and then: 10...♘bd7 is 'd4223'; 10...a5 is 'd423'; 10...♗d6 is 'd424'.

d422) 9...♘bd7 and here:

d4221) 10 ♗d2 ♗d6 11 ♕f3 ♖e8 12 g4 ♕e7 13 g5 ♘e4 14 h4 b5 with double-edged play, Morović-I.Rogers, Spanish Cht (Cala Galdana) 1994.

d4222) 10 g4 ♗d6 11 ♕f3 ♗xf4 12 ♕xf4 ♖e8 13 g5 ♘h5 14 ♕f3 g6 with a complicated struggle ahead, Hernando-Pogorelov, Mondariz Balneario 1999.

d4223) 10 0-0 ♖e8 (10...♘b6 11 f3 c5 is also OK for Black, S.Bekker Jensen-L.Johannessen, Oropesa del

Mar U-18 Wch 1998) 11 f3 (11 b4 ♗d6 12 ♕c2 ♘f8 13 ♗d2 ♗d7 14 b5 ♗xf4 15 exf4 cxb5 16 ♘xb5 ♘e4 is equal, Ashley-Onischuk, Wijk aan Zee 2000) 11...♘f8 12 ♗c2 (or 12 b4 ♘g6 13 ♘fe2 a5 14 ♖b1 axb4 15 axb4 ♗e6 = Evans-Unzicker, Buenos Aires 1960) 12...♘e6 13 e4 dxe4 14 ♘xe6 ♗xe6 15 fxe4 ♗g4 16 ♕d3 ♗h5 17 ♗f4 ♗g6 and although White has a nice centre, the chances are about equal, Irzhanov-Ehlvest, St Petersburg 1994.

d423) 9...a5 10 0-0 (10 h3 ♘a6 11 0-0 ♘c7 12 ♕c2 ♘e6 13 ♘fe2 ♗d6 = Bu Xiangzhi-Lengyel, Budapest 1999) 10...♖e8 (10...♘a6 is also fine for Black; e.g., 11 f3 ♘c7 12 ♕e1 c5 13 ♕f2 ♘e6 14 ♘fe2 ♗d7 15 g4 ♕b6 = Polugaevsky-Tal, USSR Ch (Riga) 1958) 11 ♗d2 (11 f3 ♘a6 12 ♕c2 g6 13 g4 ♘c7 14 ♕g2 b5 15 ♗d2 ♘e6 = Reshevsky-Evans, USA Ch (New York) 1958/9) 11...♘bd7 12 f3 ♗d6 13 ♔h1 ♗xf4 14 exf4 ♕b6 15 ♗e1 and now, instead of 15...♘f8 16 ♕d2 ♘g6 17 f5 ♘e7 18 g4 ± ♕xd4? 19 ♗f2 ♕e5 20 ♗g3 ♕d4 21 ♖fe1 with a strong initiative for White, Najer-Fedorovsky, Swidnica 1999, Black should play 15...♕c7!? 16 ♕c1 ♕d6 followed by ...c5.

d424) 9...♗d6 10 0-0 ♖e8 11 ♕c2 b6!? (11...♘bd7 12 f3 ♘f8 13 ♕f2 ♘e6 14 ♘fe2 c5 15 ♗d2 cxd4 16 exd4 a6 17 ♖ad1 ± Lerner-Kaiumov, Beltsy 1979) 12 b4 (12 e4 dxe4 13 ♘xe4 ♘xe4 14 ♗xe4 g6 is about even) 12...♗a6!? 13 b5 ♗b7 14 ♗b2 cxb5 15 ♗xb5 (15 ♘xb5 ♗xf4 16 exf4 ♘c6 17 ♖ad1 = Psakhis) 15...♘c6 16 ♕f5 a6! (Nikolaidis-Guseinov, Pula 1997) and here White should play 17 ♗d3

♘e7 18 ♕g5 (Psakhis) with chances for both sides.

8...c6

Black has tried numerous other moves at this point. Here are some of the more important lines:

a) 8...♗f5 9 ♗g2 c6 transposes to note 'b' to Black's 9th move.

b) 8...♘bd7 9 ♗g2 ♘b6 (9...c6 transposes to note 'c' to Black's 9th move) 10 0-0 (there are two good alternatives: 10 ♕c2 ♖e8 11 0-0 a5 12 b3 ♗f8 13 ♖d1 g6 14 f3 followed by e4 ± M.Gurevich-Polacek, Philadelphia 1989; 10 ♕d3 a5 11 a4 c6 12 0-0 ♘bd7, Botvinnik-Lilienthal, Absolute USSR Ch (Leningrad/Moscow) 1941, 13 f3 ± Fine) and now:

b1) 10...a5 11 a4 ♖e8 12 b3 ♗f5 13 h3 h6 14 g4 ♗h7 15 f4 ♘e4 16 f5 ♘xc3 17 ♘xc3 ± Torre-Peters, Hastings 1980/1.

b2) 10...♖e8 11 b3 ♗f5 (11...a5 12 a4 transposes to 'b1') 12 f3 c5 13 g4 ♗g6 14 ♘f4 cxd4 15 exd4 ♖c8 16 ♘xg6 hxg6 17 ♕d3 ♗d6 and Black is doing just fine, Vera-Chandler, Novi Sad OL 1990.

c) 8...♖e8 9 ♗g2 with a further branch:

c1) 9...c6 transposes to note 'd' to Black's 9th move.

c2) 9...♗f8 10 0-0 c6 transposes to note 'd5' to Black's 9th move.

c3) 9...a5 10 0-0 c6 (10...♗f8 11 ♕c2 ♘a6 12 ♗d2 c6 13 ♖ad1 b5 14 ♗c1 g6 is fine for Black, Narciso Dublan-Z.Almasi, Pamplona 2001/2) 11 f3 ♘a6 12 ♗d2 ♘c7 13 ♗e1 ♗f8 14 ♕d2 ♘d7 15 ♗f2 ♘b6 and Black has obtained a decent position without too many difficulties, Gyimesi-Portisch, Hungarian Cht 1995.

d) 8...♗g4 9 ♗g2 ♕d7 10 h3 (10 0-0 c6 11 f3 ♗h3 12 ♘f4 ♗xg2 13 ♔xg2 ♘a6, Ward-Chandler, British Ch (Southampton) 1986, 14 e4!? and 10 f3!? ♗h3 11 ♗xh3 ♕xh3 12 ♘f4 ♕d7 13 e4 are both worthwhile alternatives) 10...♗xe2 11 ♕xe2 c6 12 0-0 ♘a6 and then:

d1) 13 b4 is harmless: 13...♘c7 14 ♖b1 ♘b5 (14...b5!? can, as we have seen before, be tried out in positions like this) 15 ♕d3 ♘xc3 16 ♕xc3 ♘e4 = Groszpeter-L.Bronstein, Lucerne OL 1982.

d2) 13 ♗d2 ♘c7 14 g4 ♖fe8 15 ♕d3 ♗d6 16 ♖ad1 ♖ad8 17 b4 ♘b5 and Black has a comfortable position, Agzamov-Beliavsky, USSR Ch (Moscow) 1983.

e) 8...a5 9 ♗g2 usually just transposes to other lines:

e1) 9...c6 transposes to the main line.

e2) 9...♖e8 10 0-0 c6 transposes to note 'd6' to Black's 9th move.

e3) 9...♘a6 10 0-0 ♖e8 (10...c6 transposes to the main line) and now pretty much any white move will be answered with 11...c6, transposing to lines you will find below.

9 ♗g2 (D)

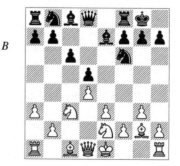

9...a5

With this popular move, Black prevents White from playing on the queenside, leaving the kingside his only point of attack, limiting the area needing attention to a bare minimum. Still, Black has a handful of reasonable alternatives:

a) 9...♗d6 10 0-0 a5 11 b3 ♖e8 12 ♖a2 ♘a6 13 h3 ♘c7 14 ♘f4 (Taimanov-Bellin, Hastings 1975/6) is given as slightly better for White, but with 14...♘e6!?, intending ...♘xf4, Black is definitely not any worse.

b) 9...♗f5 is a common and logical choice for Black. Now:

b1) 10 f3 is best met by 10...c5, but this has yet to be tried. In Chernin-Smyslov, Reggio Emilia 1986/7, Black instead chose 10...♕c8, but after 11 g4 ♗d7 12 ♘f4 ♘a6 13 g5 ♘e8 14 h4 ♘d6 15 e4 White held the upper hand.

b2) 10 0-0 ♕d7 (10...♖e8 is line 'd3'; 10...a5 is note 'b' to Black's 10th move; 10...♗d6 11 f3 ♖e8 12 e4 dxe4 13 fxe4 ♗xe4 14 ♖xf6 ♗xg2 15 ♖xd6 ♕xd6 16 ♔xg2 ♘d7 ± was originally given by Petrosian in his notes to Petrosian-Timman, Bugojno 1982) 11 f3 h5!? 12 e4 dxe4 13 fxe4 ♗g4 14 ♗e3 ♘h7 15 ♕e1! ♘g5 16 ♘f4 and White has a slight advantage, M.Gurevich-Cekro, Germany Cup 1996.

c) 9...♘bd7 10 0-0 ♖e8 (10...♘e8 11 b3 f5 12 ♗b2 ♘df6 13 ♘c1 ♗e6 14 ♘d3 ♗f7 15 ♘e5 ± Kärner-Spassky, Tallinn 1975) 11 h3 ♘f8 12 b4 a6 13 ♘f4 ♘g6 14 ♘xg6 (ECO gives 14 ♘d3 as '±'; this is arguably an improvement, but 14...♗f5, intending 15 g4 ♗c8!, playing for dark-squared weaknesses on the kingside, is fine for Black) 14...hxg6 15 g4 ♗d6 16 f3 a5

and Black is firmly in control, Torre-Unzicker, Wijk aan Zee 1981.

d) 9...♖e8 10 0-0 *(D)* and now Black has a wide choice:

B

d1) 10...♘bd7 transposes to line 'c'.

d2) 10...♗d6 11 ♕c2 ♘bd7 12 b4 ♘f8 13 f3 a5 14 ♖b1 axb4 15 axb4 ♘e6 16 e4 ± Kasparov-Lechtynsky, Baku 1980.

d3) 10...♗f5 11 f3 c5 (the logical response to the softening of the g1-a7 diagonal) 12 dxc5 ♗xc5 13 ♘d4 (13 g4!?) 13...♗g6 14 ♘ce2 ♘c6 with a good game for Black, Landenbergue-Peptan, Biel 1998.

d4) 10...♘a6 11 h3 (ECO mentions 11 h3 h5 12 f3 ±) 11...♘c7 12 g4 h6 13 ♘g3 ♗d6 14 f4 a5 15 ♕f3 ♘e6 16 ♘f5 ♗c7 17 ♗d2 b6 and again Black has obtained a pleasant position, Machelett-P.Schlosser, Bundesliga 1994/5.

d5) 10...♗f8 (note that Black can obtain this position with an extra tempo after 5...♖e8 6 a3 ♗f8 7 g3 d5 8 cxd5 exd5 9 ♗g2 c6 10 0-0, which obviously is OK for Black) 11 b4 (or 11 h3 b6 12 ♘f4 ♗b7 13 b4 b5!? 14 ♘d3 a5 and Black is doing quite well,

S.Kasparov-Tissir, Tanta City 2001)
11...h5!? 12 f3 a5 13 b5 c5 14 ♘f4
♗e6 with a double-edged position, Qi
Jingxuan-Abramović, Asia-Yugoslavia
1984.

d6) 10...a5 and here:

d61) 11 f3 c5! 12 g4 h6 13 ♕e1
♘c6 14 ♕f2 ♖b8! 15 ♘g3 b5 is another example for Black on how to
counter the f3 set-up; Black is better,
Wessman-Lalić, Novi Sad OL 1990.

d62) 11 ♘f4 ♗d6 12 h3 ♘a6 13 b3
♘c7 14 ♘ce2 ♘e6 15 ♘d3 ♘g5 16
♘ef4 ♕b6 with a roughly level position, Guliev-Kharitonov, St Petersburg
1994.

d63) 11 h3 and now:

d631) 11...♗d6 12 g4 h6 13 f4
♘a6 14 ♘g3 b5 15 ♕f3 b4 16 axb4
axb4 17 ♘ce2 ♘e4 18 ♘xe4 dxe4 19
♕f2 ± Kasparov-Lerner, USSR Ch
(Minsk) 1979.

d632) 11...♘bd7 12 ♕c2 ♘f8 13
♗d2 ♘e6 14 ♖ad1 ♘g5 15 g4 h6 16
♗c1 b5 and Black has comfortably
equalized, M.Gurevich-Geller, USSR
Ch (Moscow) 1985.

e) 9...♘a6 10 0-0 and now:

e1) 10...♗g4 11 f3 ♗h5 12 ♘f4
♗g6 13 ♘xg6 hxg6 14 b4 ♘c7 15 e4
a5 16 ♖b1 axb4 17 axb4 ♘e6 18 e5
♘d7 and although White has more
space, Black's position is fully playable,
Guliev-Hraček, Stare Mesto 1992.

e2) 10...♘c7 and here:

e21) 11 ♘f4 a6 12 b4 ♘b5 13
♘xb5 axb5 14 ♗b2 ♗f5 15 f3 ♗d6 16
♖e1 ♖e8 and Black has a good game,
Ramayrat-Larsen, New York 1986.

e22) 11 h3 a6 12 a4 a5 13 b3 ♘a6
14 g4 ♘e8 15 ♘g3 ♘d6 16 ♘ce2 ♘b4
17 ♗a3 f5 and Black is in control,
Torre-Larsen, Bugojno 1984.

e23) 11 f3 supports both the e4 and
g4 advances, but even so Black can
equalize with 11...c5 12 dxc5 (12 ♗d2
b6 13 ♗e1 ♖e8 14 ♕d2 ♗a6 15 ♗f2
cxd4 16 exd4 ♗d6 = Gyimesi-Epi-
shin, Pärnu 1996) 12...♗xc5 13 b4
♗d6 14 ♕d3 ♖e8 15 ♖d1 ♕e7 16
♘d4 ♗d7 17 ♗d2 ♖ac8 is roughly
equal, Saidy-Unzicker, Venice 1969.

10 0-0 *(D)*

10...♘a6

Some alternatives:

a) 10...♖e8 transposes to note 'd6'
to Black's 9th move.

b) 10...♗f5 11 f3 ♘a6 12 e4 dxe4
13 fxe4 ♗g4 14 h3 ♗xe2 15 ♘xe2
♘c7 16 ♗e3 ± M.Gurevich-Tsigan-
ova, Aaland/Stockholm 1997.

c) 10...♘bd7 11 h3 b5 12 g4 ♗a6
13 ♖e1 b4 14 ♘a4 bxa3 15 bxa3 ♘b6
= Mascariñas-Flesch, Lvov 1981.

11 f3

Alternatives:

a) 11 ♘f4 ♘c7 12 f3 c5 13 ♘a4
♘a6 14 g4 ♗d7 15 ♘c3 ♗c6 16 ♘ce2
♕b6 = Lutikov-Tal, USSR Ch (Tbilisi) 1959.

b) 11 h3 ♘c7 12 g4 ♘fe8 13 ♘g3
♘d6 14 f4 f5 15 b3 ♘ce8 = Henley-
Farago, Hastings 1982/3.

c) 11 ♕c2 ♖e8 12 ♖d1 g6 13 f3 c5 (13...♘c7 14 e4 ♘e6 is also noteworthy) 14 ♔h1 cxd4 15 exd4 (15 ♘xd4!? looks more appealing to me) 15...♘c7 16 ♘f4 ♗d6 = Grotnes-Ernst, Gausdal 1992.

11...c5

This standard way of challenging White's central build-up should be familiar by now. Note that Black should not play ...c5 until White has committed himself to playing f3. Two interesting alternatives:

a) 11...b5!? 12 g4 h6 13 ♗d2 ♖e8 14 ♗e1?! b4 15 axb4 ♘xb4 16 ♗g3 ♗a6 ∓ Volke-P.Schlosser, Bundesliga 1994/5.

b) 11...♘c7 12 ♗d2 ♘fe8 13 ♕c2 b5 14 ♖ad1 ♗a6 15 ♖fe1 ♘e6 16 ♗c1 ♖c8 with a complicated struggle ahead, Summerscale-Aagaard, London 1997.

12 g4

With the e4 advance prevented, this move is the logical follow-up. Other moves include:

a) 12 b3 ♖e8 13 ♖a2 ♗f8 14 g4 h6 15 ♘g3 ♘c7 16 h3 ♗d7 = Anikaev-A.Petrosian, USSR 1976.

b) 12 dxc5 ♗xc5 13 ♘d4 ♖e8 14 ♕d3 ♗f8 15 ♗d2 ♘c5 16 ♕c2 ♗d7 = Groffen-Chuchelov, Belgian Cht 1998.

12...h6 13 ♗d2 ♖e8 14 ♗e1 *(D)*

Now, Black has done well with the following options:

a) 14...♘c7 15 ♗f2 b6 16 ♖e1 ♘e6 17 ♕d2 ♗d6 18 ♖ad1 ♗b7 favours Black, Bronstein-Bareev, Rome 1990.

B

b) 14...♗d7 15 h3 ♘c7 16 ♗f2 b5 17 e4 cxd4 18 ♗xd4 dxe4 19 fxe4 ♗c6 and Black has seized the initiative, Kjeldsen-Dokhoian, Århus 1991.

Conclusion

Of White's options on move 7, only 7 cxd5 offers him any realistic chance of obtaining an advantage.

Line A (7...♘xd5) is much livelier than Line B and therefore this will be the choice for people who are playing for a win or like dynamic positions as Black. Even so, the end result is a fairly balanced position. In Line B, the majority of the sidelines as well as the main line lead to equal chances, but the player with superior understanding of the positions that occur in this line will often score very well here. One of the specialists in this line, Mikhail Gurevich, is an excellent example of this. A study of his games in this line is warmly recommended.

11 Fischer Variation and Related Systems

1 d4 ♘f6 2 c4 e6 3 ♘c3 ♗b4 4 e3 b6 5 ♘e2 (D)

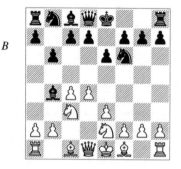

B

The name Fischer Variation only applies to the lines where Black employs 5...♗a6 against 5 ♘e2. It was Rubinstein himself who first used 5 ♘e2 back in 1925 in a game against Rabinovich in the Moscow tournament. Rubinstein lost the game, but that didn't deter him from using it again on a few other occasions. Later, Reshevsky and in particular Botvinnik as well as Portisch and Gligorić took the line up. As usual in the lines with an early ♘ge2 for White, the idea is avoid doubled c-pawns, which so many people dread having to look after.

As you will see below, Black has developed no fewer than four systems to meet this set-up. Each has its own characteristics, from the strikingly bold to the solid and somewhat passive.

In addition Black occasionally plays 5...0-0, but it generally ends up transposing to variations considered in Line B.

A)

5...c5 (D)

W

This system, which only truly shows its face after 6 a3 ♗a5, has been advocated by Romanishin in particular, who brought it back from obscurity in the late 1970s, and Psakhis, who has introduced a number of new ideas for Black in this highly provocative system.

Therefore, I name it the Romanishin/Psakhis Variation. In addition, the American GM Dmitri Gurevich has also been a fierce advocate for Black's side.

While I'm fascinated by the boldness of Black's idea, I have always had my doubts about the correctness of this variation, but so far Black has been able to hold his own.

When you think about the problems Black typically has if he wishes to play for a win, this variation comes across as a very interesting option. I say this because both sides on every move from move 6 or 7 and onwards have to make an independent decision. The positions we come across in this line don't resemble anything else we encounter in the Nimzo-Indian; the pieces are developed to odd squares and the plans are completely different. No wonder they appeal to creative players such as Psakhis and Romanishin, amongst others.

6 a3

This is played almost exclusively, but two minor alternatives need to be mentioned:

a) 6 ♘g3 ♗b7 7 a3 ♗xc3+ (obviously, Black can also play 7...♗a5, transposing to note 'e' to White's 7th move) 8 bxc3 d6 9 f3 ♘bd7 10 e4 ♕c7 11 d5 0-0-0 with approximately equal chances, Gamundi Salamanca-Romanishin, Zaragoza 1996.

b) 6 d5!? and now:

b1) 6...0-0 7 a3 ♗a5 8 g3 exd5 9 cxd5 d6 10 ♗g2 ♗a6 11 ♗d2 ♖e8 12 ♕c2 ♕c8 13 ♖b1 ♗xc3 14 ♗xc3 ♘bd7 15 ♖d1 ± led to a better game for White in I.Sokolov-Romanishin, Biel 1988.

b2) 6...exd5 7 cxd5 and now, as mentioned by Sokolov, Black can consider 7...♗a6, which has yet to be tested, or 7...♗b7 8 a3 ♗a5, which transposes to note 'c' to White's 7th move.

6...♗a5

Other moves are rarely seen and lead to a better game for White:

a) 6...cxd4 7 exd4 ♗e7 8 d5 gives Black a bad version of the Reshevsky Variation (Chapter 10).

b) 6...♗xc3+ 7 ♘xc3 and now:

b1) 7...0-0 8 ♗e2 ♗b7 9 d5 exd5 10 cxd5 ♖e8 11 0-0 ♗a6 12 e4 ♗xe2 13 ♕xe2 d6 14 ♗f4 ± Ibragimov-Anastasian, Ubeda 2001.

b2) 7...♗b7 8 d5 d6 9 e4 0-0 10 ♗g5 ♖e8 11 ♗e2 h6 12 ♗e3 exd5 13 exd5 with a better game for White, Donner-Bouteville, Munich OL 1958.

b3) 7...cxd4 8 exd4 0-0 9 ♗e2 ♗b7 10 0-0 ±.

We now return to 6...♗a5 (D):

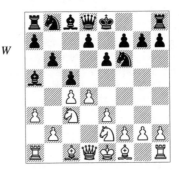

7 ♖b1

White goes straight for trapping the caged-in bishop, but as we shall see, it is nearly impossible to trap it. White has tried numerous other ideas, which include:

a) 7 ♘f4 is harmless: 7...♘c6 8 ♗d3 e5 9 ♘h5 0-0 10 0-0 ♗xc3 11 bxc3 ♖e8 12 ♘xf6+ ♕xf6 and Black has fully equalized, O.Rodriguez-Rivas, Spanish Cht (Cala Galdana) 1994.

b) 7 f3 0-0 8 d5 ♗a6 9 ♘g3 exd5 10 cxd5 ♗xf1 11 ♖xf1 b5 12 ♔f2 a6 13 e4 d6 = Milov-Agopov, Oslo 2002.

c) 7 d5 exd5 (or 7...0-0 8 ♗d2 ♗a6 9 ♕a4 ♗xc3 10 ♘xc3 exd5 11 cxd5 ♗xf1 12 ♔xf1 d6 = Mancini-Inkiov, Le Touquet 2001) 8 cxd5 ♗b7 (the alternative 8...♗a6!? can also be considered) and now instead of 9 d6? ♘e4 10 f3 ♘xc3 11 bxc3 ♕h4+ 12 ♔d2 0-0, when Black is as good as winning, Vogel-Slobodjan, 2nd Bundesliga 1995/6, White should try 9 ♗d2 0-0 10 ♘f4 with chances for both sides.

d) 7 ♕a4 and now:

d1) 7...♘a6 8 ♗d2 (8 ♖b1 transposes to note 'f' to White's 8th move) 8...0-0 9 ♘g3 ♗b7 (9...cxd4 has also been tried) 10 f3 ♕e7 11 ♗d3 ♕d6 12 b4 cxb4 and here instead of 13 ♘ce4 ♘xe4 14 ♘xe4 ♕e7 15 c5! ♗c6 16 ♕b3 f5 17 ♘f2 ♘xc5 18 dxc5 bxc5 with chances for both sides, Webb-Õim, corr. 1985, White can consider 13 ♘b5!?, although 13...♕e7 14 ♖b1 bxa3 15 ♗xa5 bxa5 16 ♕xa5 a2 17 ♕xa2 ♘b4 18 ♕a3 a5 seems to be fairly level.

d2) 7...♘c6 and then:

d21) 8 ♗d2 cxd4!? (Romanishin also mentions 8...0-0!? 9 d5 exd5 10 cxd5 ♘e5 11 ♘g3 ♗xc3 12 ♗xc3 d6 13 ♗e2 ♖e8 followed by ...♗d7 with a good game for Black) 9 exd4 ♗xc3 10 ♗xc3 ♘e4 11 d5 ♘xc3 12 ♘xc3 ♘e5 (Zaja-Romanishin, Croatia 1993) 13 dxe6 fxe6 14 ♗e2 0-0 15 0-0 with chances for both sides – Romanishin.

d22) 8 g3 ♘e4 9 ♗g2 ♘xc3 10 ♘xc3 ♗xc3+ 11 bxc3 ♗b7 12 0-0 ♕c7 13 ♖d1 0-0 14 e4 e5 = Dydyshko-Psakhis, Minsk 1986.

e) 7 ♘g3 is a favourite of British GM Jonathan Levitt, but Black should not have many problems here either: 7...♗b7 8 ♗d2 0-0 9 ♗d3 (9 ♖b1 ♘a6 transposes to the main line) 9...cxd4 (9...♗xg2 has yet to be refuted – or played for that matter; 9...d5 10 cxd5 cxd4 11 exd4 ♗xc3 12 bxc3 ♕xd5 13 f3 ♗a6 is fine for Black, Sashikiran-Nenashev, Calcutta 1997) 10 exd4 ♗xc3 11 ♗xc3 (11 bxc3?! d5 12 0-0 dxc4 13 ♗xc4 ♘c6 14 ♕e2 ♘a5 15 ♗a2 ♖c8 16 ♖fc1 h6 17 ♖ab1 ♕d7 gives Black excellent control over the light squares on the queenside, Levitt-Psakhis, Moscow 1988) 11...d5 12 c5 (Pliester suggests 12 b3!?, but I think Black should be pleased after 12...dxc4 13 bxc4 b5!? intending 14 cxb5 ♗xg2 15 ♖g1 ♗d5 with a better game for Black) 12...♘e4 13 ♕c2 ♕h4 14 0-0 f5 15 ♘xe4 dxe4 16 ♗c4 ♗d5 17 ♗xd5 exd5 18 ♕b3 ♕d8 = Levitt-Romanishin, Groningen 1990.

f) 7 ♗d2 is White's second most popular choice. He is again targeting the a5-bishop. Given that there isn't an immediate threat to the bishop, Black has tried a number of replies:

f1) 7...♗b7? is unfortunate and is promptly punished by 8 b4 cxb4 9 ♘b5 ♕e7 10 ♘c7+ ♔d8 11 ♘xa8 bxa3 12 ♗xa5 bxa5 13 ♖b1 ♔c8 14 ♕b3 +− Starc-P.Meyer, Austrian Cht 1997.

f2) 7...♘a6 8 ♘g3 0-0 9 ♗d3 d5 10 cxd5 cxd4 11 exd4 ♗xc3 12 bxc3 ♕xd5 13 ♕e2 ♘c7 14 ♘e4 ± Kharlov-Jaracz, Biel 1997.

f3) 7...♘c6 8 d5 exd5 9 cxd5 ♘e5 10 ♘g3 0-0 11 ♗e2 d6 12 0-0 a6 13 e4 ♖e8 14 ♕c2 ♗d7 (Beliavsky-Grosar, Slovenian Ch (Griže) 1996) 15 h3! ± Beliavsky.

f4) 7...♗a6 8 ♕a4 ♗xc3 9 ♘xc3 0-0 10 dxc5 bxc5 11 ♗e2 d5 12 cxd5 ♗xe2 13 ♘xe2 ♘xd5 14 0-0 ♕d6 15 ♖ab1 ♕a6 = Korchnoi-Van der Wiel, Amsterdam 1987.

f5) 7...0-0 *(D)* is the main line. Now White can try:

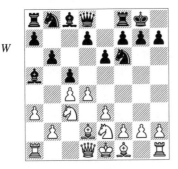

f51) 8 ♖b1 and now 8...♕e7 is note 'c3' to Black's 7th move, while 8...♘a6 transposes to the main line.

f52) 8 ♘f4 ♗xc3 9 ♗xc3 ♘e4 10 ♕c2 ♘xc3 11 ♕xc3 cxd4 12 ♕xd4 ♘c6 13 ♕c3 ♗a6 = Chevallier-Psakhis, Metz 1994.

f53) 8 ♕c2 ♗a6 9 dxc5 bxc5 10 ♘g3 d5 11 ♗e2 ♗xc4 12 ♗xc4 dxc4 (Bagirov-Romanishin, Riga 1981) and now Bagirov gives 13 ♘ce4! ♘c6 14 0-0 ♘xe4 15 ♘xe4 ♕d3 16 ♕xd3 cxd3 17 ♗xa5 ♘xa5 18 ♘xc5 ♖fd8 19 ♖fd1 d2 20 b4 ♘c4 21 ♖a2 with equality.

f54) 8 ♘g3 ♗b7 transposes to line 'e'.

f55) 8 d5 and then:

f551) 8...d6 9 ♘g3 exd5 10 cxd5 ♗b7 11 e4 ♖e8 12 ♗b5 ♘bd7 13 0-0 ♗xc3 14 ♗xc3 ♘xe4 and here, instead of the greedy 15 ♗xg7?! ♔xg7 16 ♕g4+ ♔h8 17 ♕xd7 ♕xd7 18 ♗xd7 ♘xg3 19 fxg3 ♖e7 with a better endgame for Black, Granda-Psakhis, Aruba 1992, according to Psakhis White should play 15 ♘f5! g6 16 ♘h6+ ♔f8 17 ♕f3 ♕e7!? 18 ♗c6!? ♗xc6 19 dxc6 and here 19...♘b8 is easiest.

f552) 8...♗a6 9 ♘f4 ♖e8 10 ♗d3 ♗xc3 11 ♗xc3 exd5 12 ♘xd5 ♘xd5 13 cxd5 ♗xd3 14 ♕xd3 ♕g5 15 0-0 d6 = Illescas-Wells, Linares Z 1995.

f553) 8...exd5 9 cxd5 (or 9 ♘xd5 ♘xd5 10 cxd5 ♗xd2+ 11 ♕xd2 ♗a6 = D.Gurevich-Murey, Beersheba 1982) 9...d6 10 ♘g3 a6 11 ♗e2 b5 12 0-0 ♘bd7 is equal, Kharlov-Garcia Palermo, Cañete 1994.

g) 7 g3 ♗b7 (7...♘c6 leads to a better game for White after 8 ♗g2 ♗xc3+ 9 ♘xc3 ♗a6 10 ♕a4 ♕c8 11 0-0 0-0 12 ♖d1 ♖b8 13 ♘b5, Ibragimov-Nenashev, Komotini 1993) 8 d5 and now:

g1) 8...♘e4 9 ♗d2 ♘xd2 10 ♕xd2 d6 11 ♗g2 ♘d7 12 0-0 ♗xc3 13 ♘xc3 e5 14 f4 ± Jelen-Grosar, Slovenian Ch 1992.

g2) 8...b5 9 ♗g2 bxc4 and here:

g21) 10 e4 exd5 (10...0-0 11 0-0 is line 'g22') 11 exd5 d6 12 0-0 0-0 13 ♗f4 ♕b6 (13...♘a6 intending ...♘c7 has been suggested by Serper) 14 ♕a4 ♗xc3 15 ♘xc3 ♘bd7 16 ♖fd1 ♖fe8 17 ♕xc4 (Ibragimov-Cebalo, Bled 1995) 17...♘e5!? with a pleasant position for Black.

g22) 10 0-0 0-0 11 e4 d6 (11...exd5 12 exd5 is line 'g21') 12 h3 exd5 13

exd5 ♘bd7 14 ♗f4 ♘e5! 15 ♗xe5 dxe5
16 ♕a4 ♗xc3 (both 16...♗a6!? and
16...♕b6 look appealing for Black) 17
♘xc3 ♕b6 18 ♖fd1 ♕b3 19 ♖d2 ♖fd8
= Kacheishvili-Shariyazdanov, Roque
Saenz Pena 1997.

g3) 8...exd5 9 ♗g2 ♗a6 10 b4 (or
10 cxd5 ♗xc3+ 11 ♘xc3 0-0 12 b4?!
{12 f4!? Horvath} 12...♗c4 13 f4 d6
14 bxc5 bxc5 15 ♔f2 ♘bd7 16 ♖e1
♖b8 17 e4 ♕a5 18 ♖e3 ♗b3 19 ♕e2
♘b6 ∓ Shirov-I.Sokolov, Pardubice
1994) 10...cxb4 11 axb4 ♗xb4 12
♗xd5 ♘xd5 13 ♕xd5 0-0 14 ♕xa8
♕f6 and now:

g31) 15 ♗d2? ♘c6 16 ♕xf8+
♗xf8 17 ♖xa6 and now Black can obtain a winning position with Marin's
17...♘b4! (rather than 17...♘e5?? 18
♖xa7?? {18 ♘d4! ♘xc4 19 ♘d1 +−}
18...♘d3+ 19 ♔d1 ♘xf2+ 20 ♔c2
♘xh1 −+ Ki.Georgiev-Wojtkiewicz,
Odorheiu Secuiesc Z 1995), which is
surprisingly difficult to meet.

g32) White should play 15 0-0!;
e.g., 15...♘c6 16 ♕xf8+ ♔xf8 17
♖xa6 ♗xc3 18 ♖d1 ±.

We now return to the position after
7 ♖b1 *(D)*:

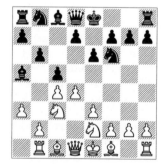

7...♘a6

Black continues his series of artifi-
cial-looking moves, but obviously he
is forced to deal with the immediate
threat of 8 b4.

The main alternative, 7...♕e7, also
has an artificial appearance:

a) 8 d5 exd5 9 cxd5 0-0 10 ♘f4
♘e4!? 11 ♗d2 ♗xc3 12 bxc3 ♕h4!
13 g3 ♕f6 14 ♕c2 ♘xd2 15 ♕xd2 d6
with chances for both sides, Shul-
man-Dydyshko, Minsk 1995.

b) 8 ♕a4 ♘c6 (8...♘a6 transposes
to note 'f2' to White's 8th move) 9
♗d2 ♗xc3 10 ♗xc3 ♘e4 11 dxc5
bxc5 12 g3 0-0 13 ♗g2 f5 14 0-0 with
an equal position, O'Kelly-Puc, Belgrade 1952.

c) 8 ♗d2 looks like a careful move
that isn't meant to harm anybody, but
in conjunction with b4 and ♘b5, it can
cause severe problems for Black if he
is not constantly alert:

c1) 8...♘c6 9 d5! (9 ♘g3 immediately doesn't cause many worries for
Black: 9...cxd4 10 exd4 ♗xc3 11 ♗xc3
d5 12 ♗d3 dxc4 13 ♗xc4 ♘d5 = Garcia Gonzalez-Romanishin, Cienfuegos
1977) 9...♘e5 10 ♘g3 again looks
trivial, but as De Boer gives, 10...♗xc3
11 ♗xc3 d6 ± is forced, since White is
threatening to trap the bishop; e.g.,
10...0-0? 11 d6! ♕xd6 12 b4! cxb4 13
♘b5! (didn't I warn you earlier on?)
13...♘d3+ 14 ♗xd3 ♕xd3 15 axb4
♕xc4 16 bxa5 +− G.Georgadze-Zan-
giev, St Petersburg 1996.

c2) 8...♘a6 9 ♘g3 (9 d5 0-0 10
♘g3 transposes to line 'c33') 9...0-0
10 ♗d3 ♗b7 11 0-0 d6 12 ♕e2 ♖fe8
13 d5 ♗xc3 14 ♗xc3 ♘b8 15 e4
♘bd7 16 f4 ± Watanabe-Dgebuadze,
Rotterdam 1998.

c3) 8...0-0 and here:

c31) 9 b4 cxb4 10 axb4 ♗xb4 11 ♖xb4 ♕xb4 12 ♘d5 and now:

c311) 12...♘xd5 13 ♗xb4 ♘xb4 14 ♘c3 ♘8c6!? 15 ♗e2 d5 16 0-0 dxc4 17 ♗xc4 with no more than a small plus for White, Züger-Sharif, Val d'Aoste 1988.

c312) 12...♕a3!? 13 ♘xf6+?! (13 ♗b4 looks better) 13...gxf6 14 ♘f4 ♔h8 15 ♗d3 and then:

c3121) Shipov recommends playing 15...♖g8, but his analysis is flawed: 16 ♕h5 ♖g7 17 ♕h6 ♕a1+ 18 ♔e2 ♕xh1 19 ♗xh7 and now he calls 19...♗a6(?) unclear, but this loses to 20 ♘h5!. However, Black can improve with 19...♕xh2!! 20 ♕xh2 ♖xh7 21 ♘h5 ♗a6, when he is somewhat better.

c3122) 15...f5 (Nenashev-Orlov, St Petersburg 1995) should be met by 16 g4'!' ♗b7 17 gxf5 ♗xh1 18 ♕h5 with an attack according to Shipov, but 18...e5! seems to stop the white attack cold. White badly needs an improvement if he is to continue playing 9 b4.

c32) 9 d5 ♗a6 10 ♘f4 e5 11 ♘h5 ♗xc3 12 ♗xc3 ♘xh5 13 ♕xh5 d6 14 ♗d3 with a pull for White, Milovanović-Teofilović, Djakovo 1994.

c33) 9 ♘g3 ♘a6 10 d5 (10 ♗d3 cxd4 11 exd4 ♗xc3 12 bxc3 d5 13 0-0 dxc4 14 ♗xc4 ♘c7 15 a4 ± Dzindzichashvili-D.Gurevich, New York 1983) and here:

c331) 10...♗b7 11 ♗e2 exd5 12 cxd5 ♘c7 and now White went for 13 b4 cxb4 14 axb4 ♗xb4 15 ♖xb4 ♕xb4 16 ♘ce4 in Vaiser-Rashkovsky, Sverdlovsk 1984, which could have been met by 16...♕xe4 17 ♘xe4 ♘xe4 with chances for both sides – *ECO*. Instead, Stetsko suggests 13 ♗f3!, which should leave White a little better.

c332) 10...♘c7 11 ♕f3 ♗xc3 12 ♗xc3 (Korchnoi-D.Gurevich, Pasadena 1983) 12...d6 13 ♗xf6 ♕xf6 14 ♕xf6 gxf6 15 ♘e4 ♘e8 16 dxe6 ± de Boer.

c333) 10...d6 11 ♕f3 ♗b7 12 ♗d3 ♘d7 13 ♕e2 ♘e5 = Norri-Kochiev, Tampere 1996.

c4) 8...♗xc3 is the radical way to avoid having to worry about the a5-bishop later. Despite it going against all logic, White has a hard time proving an advantage: 9 ♘xc3 (or 9 ♗xc3 ♗b7 10 b4?! {10 dxc5!? and 10 f3!? are better tries for White} 10...♘e4 11 ♗a1 cxb4 12 axb4 ♕h4 13 ♘g3 ♘xg3 14 fxg3 ♕e4 ∓ Franić-Kurajica, Kastel Stari 1997) 9...♗b7 10 b4 cxd4 11 exd4 ♘e4 12 ♘xe4 ♗xe4 13 ♖b3 ♘c6 14 ♖e3 d5 and although White has the initiative right now, Black has excellent chances of equalizing completely, Handke-Lanzani, Charleville 2000.

c5) 8...♗a6 9 ♕a4 (or 9 b4 cxb4 10 axb4 ♗xb4 11 ♖xb4 ♕xb4 12 ♘b5 ♕e7 13 ♘c7+ ♔d8 14 ♘xa8 ♗c4 15 ♘c3 ♗xf1 16 ♖xf1 d5! 17 ♘b5 ♕b7 18 ♘d6 ♕e7 19 ♘b5 ♕b7 20 ♘d6 ♕e7 21 ♘b5 ½-½ Onishchuk-Rogozenko, Skopje 2002) 9...cxd4 (Shoron-D.Gurevich, Denver 1985) 10 ♘xd4 ♗xc3 11 ♗xc3 0-0 (Gurevich) with approximately equal chances.

We now return to 7...♘a6 *(D)*:

8 ♗d2

While this is White's most frequently chosen move, it isn't clear that it is best. White's alternatives are:

a) 8 d5 ♗b7 and then:

a1) 9 ♗d2 0-0 transposes to note 'c5' to White's 9th move.

a2) 9 g3 b5 10 ♗g2 bxc4 11 0-0 ♗xc3 12 ♘xc3 ♘xd5 13 ♘xd5 exd5

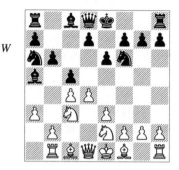

14 ♗xd5 ♕b6 15 ♕f3 ♗xd5 16 ♕xd5 (Bu Xiangzhi-P.Carlsson, Athens jr Wch 2001) 16...♕c6!? 17 ♕xc4 d5 18 ♕d3 =.

b) 8 f3 and here:

b1) 8...0-0 9 d5 d6 10 e4 exd5 11 cxd5 ♘h5 (11...♖e8!? and 11...♘d7!? are worth looking into) 12 g4!? ♕h4+ 13 ♔d2 ♘f6 14 ♕e1 ♕xe1+ 15 ♔xe1 ♘d7 16 ♔f2 ♘e5 17 ♘b5 ♖d8 18 ♘g3 and thanks to Black's poorly coordinated pieces and the pawn weakness on d6, White holds the better chances, Aleksandrov-Romanishin, Nikolaev Z 1995.

b2) 8...♗b7 9 e4 0-0 10 d5 exd5 11 cxd5 ♖e8 12 g3 b5 13 ♗g2 b4 14 axb4 ♘xb4 15 0-0 ♗a6 = Shulman-Nisipeanu, Erevan OL 1996.

c) 8 ♘f4 0-0 9 ♗d3 d6 (or 9...♗b7 10 0-0 ♗xc3 11 bxc3 ♗e4 12 f3 ♗xd3 13 ♘xd3 ♕c8 14 ♕a4! ♘b8 15 e4, Groszpeter-D.Gurevich, Bourgoin-Jallieu 1982, 15...d6 16 ♗f4 ♘e8! with chances for both sides – D.Gurevich) 10 0-0 ♗xc3 11 bxc3 ♗b7 12 f3 e5 13 ♘e2 e4 14 fxe4 ♗xe4 15 ♘g3 ♕e7 16 ♖f4 ♗xd3 17 ♕xd3 ♖ae8 = Groszpeter-Adamski, Copenhagen 1989.

d) 8 g3 ♗b7 (8...♘e4 lands Black in some trouble: 9 ♗g2 ♗b7 10 d5

♗xc3+ 11 ♘xc3 ♘xc3 12 bxc3 0-0 13 0-0 e5 14 f4 with a passive defence ahead for Black, Muir-Ward, British Ch (Plymouth) 1989) 9 d5 and now:

d1) 9...exd5 10 ♗g2 ♖b8 11 cxd5 b5 12 0-0 b4 (Paramos Dominguez-Campos Moreno, Santiago 1995) 13 ♘e4!? ♘xe4 14 ♗xe4 0-0 15 ♕c2 g6 16 ♘f4 ±.

d2) 9...b5 10 ♗g2 bxc4 11 0-0 ♗xc3 (11...0-0 12 e4 d6 13 ♗g5 h6 14 ♗xf6 ♕xf6 15 ♕a4 ♗b6 16 dxe6 ♕xe6 17 ♘f4 ± Paramos Dominguez-G.Georgadze, Mondariz 1997) 12 ♘xc3 exd5 13 ♘xd5 ♘xd5 14 ♗xd5 ♕b6 15 ♕f3 ♗xd5 16 ♕xd5 0-0 17 ♕xc4 ♕e6 = M.Gurevich-Rashkovsky, USSR Ch (Kiev) 1986.

e) 8 ♘g3 ♗b7 (D) (8...0-0 has also received some airtime: 9 ♗d3 d5 10 cxd5 cxd4 11 exd4 ♗xc3+ 12 bxc3 exd5 13 0-0 and White has a solid advantage due to his bishop-pair and Black's misplaced knight on a6, Nenashev-Kaiumov, Tashkent 1992), with the following options for White:

e1) 9 ♗d2 cxd4?! (9...0-0 is better, and transposes to the main line) 10 exd4 ♗xc3 11 bxc3 h5 12 h4 ♖c8 13 ♕a4 ♖a8 14 ♗g5 ♕c8 15 f3 ♘c7 16

♗d3 ♗c6 17 ♕c2 ± Lautier-J.Polgar, Cannes 2001.

e2) 9 f3 0-0 10 ♗d2 (10 e4!? should be met with the flexible 10...d6!?) and now:

e21) 10...cxd4 11 exd4 ♗xc3 12 bxc3 and then:

e211) 12...d5 13 cxd5 and here 13...♕xd5 14 ♗d3 transposes to the main line, but Black may be able to improve by 13...exd5!? intending ...♘c7 and ...♗a6 to liquidate White's bishop-pair and immobilize his pawns.

e212) 12...d6 13 ♗d3 ♘b8 14 0-0 ♘bd7 15 f4 ♕c7 16 f5 e5 17 ♘h5 ♖ac8 18 d5!? (Rechlis gives 18 ♘xf6+ ♘xf6 19 ♗g5 ♘e4 20 ♗xe4 ♗xe4 21 ♕g4 f6!, when Black has neutralized White's initiative) and now instead of 18...♖fe8? 19 ♗e3! ♕d8 20 ♗g5! ♔h8 21 ♕e1 ♕c7 22 ♘xf6 gxf6 23 ♗e3 ± Rechlis-Psakhis, Tel-Aviv 1992, Black should play 18...♕c5+ 19 ♔h1 e4 20 ♘xf6+ ♘xf6 21 ♗e2 ♗a6 22 ♖b4 e3 (Rechlis) with approximately equal chances.

e22) 10...d5!? is the newer move. Then:

e221) 11 b4 cxb4 12 ♘a4?! (Psakhis gives 12 ♘a2!? b3 13 ♖xb3 ♗xd2+ 14 ♕xd2 ♖c8 15 c5 ♘b8 = as White's best) 12...♕e7! 13 c5! bxa3 14 ♗xa5 bxa5 15 ♗xa6 ♗xa6 16 ♕b3 e5! 17 ♕xa3 ♘h5! 18 ♘xh5 exd4 19 ♘f4 ♖fe8 20 ♖d1 and now, instead of the terrible 20...♕g5?? 21 ♖xd4 1-0 Kacheishvili-Sax, Pula Echt 1997, Psakhis gives 20...♕e5! 21 g3 g5! 22 ♘g2 dxe3 23 ♘c3 d4 24 ♘e4 g4! and Black wins.

e222) 11 cxd5!? cxd4 12 exd4 ♗xc3 13 bxc3 exd5 14 ♔f2 ♘c7 15 h4 ♘ce8 16 h5 ♘d6 17 ♗d3 ♖c8 18 ♕a4

a6 with no more than a minimal pull for White, Neverov-Kholmov, Pardubice 2001.

e3) 9 ♗d3 ♗xc3+ (for those who like balancing on a tightrope, there is also 9...h5!?; e.g., 10 d5 exd5 11 ♘f5 ♕b8! 12 cxd5 g6 13 ♘g3 ♘xd5, Vaïsser-Serper, Novosibirsk 1993, and according to Serper, White should continue 14 0-0! ♗xc3 15 e4! ♗e5!? 16 exd5 h4 17 ♘e4! ♘c7! with an unclear position, and it indeed looks that way: Black has to get his pieces developed and his king into safety and White has to prove his position is worth a pawn) 10 bxc3 ♗xg2 11 ♖g1 ♗b7 12 e4 d6 13 ♘h5 ♘xh5 14 ♕xh5 ♕f6 15 ♖g2 e5 16 d5 with compensation for the pawn, Korchnoi-Timman, Ubeda rpd 1997.

f) 8 ♕a4 is a popular choice, but also one that shouldn't scare Black. Again White adds support to the possible b4 advance. Black has tried:

f1) 8...♗xc3+?! 9 ♘xc3 0-0 10 ♗e2 ♗b7 (D.Gurevich-Yermolinsky, USA Ch (Parsippany) 1996) and now Yermolinsky gives 11 d5!, with the continuation 11...exd5 12 cxd5 ♘c7 13 e4 a6 14 0-0 b5 15 ♕c2 d6 16 b4 ±, but Black may be able to improve with 11...♘c7!?; for example, 12 e4 b5! with chances for both sides.

f2) 8...♕e7 and here:

f21) 9 ♗d2 ♗b7 10 ♘g3 0-0!? (10...♗xc3?! 11 ♗xc3 cxd4?! 12 exd4 0-0 13 ♗d3 ♘c7 14 0-0 ± Lautier-Beliavsky, Belgrade 1997) 11 ♗d3 ♗xg2 12 ♖g1 ♗c6 13 ♕d1 g6 14 d5 ♗b7 15 ♔f1 ♘e8 16 e4 ♘g7 17 ♕f3 b5 18 h4 ♘c7 19 h5 with compensation for the sacrificed pawn, Conquest-Fedorchuk, Ohrid Ech 2001.

f22) 9 dxc5! ♘xc5 10 ♕d1 ♗xc3+ 11 ♘xc3 0-0 (an old piece of analysis by Swedish GM Harry Schüssler, in which 9 dxc5! was first recommended, continued 11...♗b7 12 f3 0-0 13 ♗e2 ♖fd8 14 b4 ♘a6 15 0-0 d5 16 cxd5 ♘xd5 17 ♘xd5 ♖xd5 18 ♕a4 ♘c7 19 e4 and White has a clear advantage) 12 f3 ♘h5 13 b4 ♘b7 14 ♕d2 f5 15 ♗d3 ♘d6 16 0-0 ♘f7 17 f4 ♗b7 18 e4! is also much better for White, Garcia Gonzalez-Csom, Havana 1985.

f3) 8...♗b7!? (D) looks like Black overlooked White's threat of b4, but he is covered:

f31) 9 b4 ♗c6! 10 b5 (10 ♘b5 cxb4 11 f3 0-0 12 ♗d2 bxa3 13 ♗xa5 bxa5 14 ♕xa3 ♘b4 also fails to impress – Black is better, Tataev-Fradkin, Moscow 1992) 10...♗e4 11 ♖b2 cxd4 12 exd4 ♘c7 13 ♗d2 ♗b7 14 ♘f4 a6 15 bxa6 ♗xa6 and Black has obtained a comfortable game by very simple means, Aleksandrov-Nenashev, Frunze 1989.

f32) 9 f3 ♖c8 10 ♗d2 ♗c6 11 ♕c2 0-0 12 ♘g3 cxd4 13 exd4 ♗xc3 14 ♗xc3 ♘c7 and now instead of the positional blunder 15 b4? b5! 16 c5 ♘fd5 17 ♗d2 f5, which left Black with good

control over the entire position in Sambuev-Shariyazdanov, St Petersburg 2001, White should continue 15 ♗d3!? d5 16 b3 with chances for both sides.

f33) 9 ♗d2 further targets the a5-bishop, but once again Black is prepared for the challenge:

f331) 9...♕e7 transposes to line 'f21'.

f332) 9...♗c6 10 ♕d1 (the alternative 10 ♕c2 0-0 11 ♘g3 ♕e7 12 d5 ♗b7 13 ♗d3 exd5 14 cxd5 g6 15 ♕a4 ♖ac8 16 0-0 h5 17 ♖fd1 offers White better chances, S.Maksimović-Galliamova, Subotica wom IZ 1991) 10...d5!? 11 cxd5 exd5 12 ♘g3 ♗xc3 13 bxc3!? ♘c7 14 f3 0-0 15 ♗d3 ♕d7 16 0-0 ♗b5 17 ♗f5 ♘e6 18 ♖e1 ♗a4 19 ♕e2 ♖fe8 20 ♕f2 is approximately equal according to Gavrikov, although I tend to prefer White's chances, Gavrikov-Wirthensohn, Swiss Ch 1997.

8...0-0 (D)
Or:
a) 8...♗b7!? 9 d5 transposes to note 'c5' to White's 9th move.
b) 8...♕e7 transposes to note 'c2' to Black's 7th move.

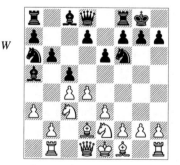

9 ♘g3

This move is based on a few ideas. First of all, White has to complete his development and the knight is in the way. Secondly, from g3 the knight supports the f4-f5 pawn push; thirdly, the knight helps to control the important e4-square. Nevertheless, White has some alternatives that merit a closer look:

a) 9 dxc5 bxc5 10 ♘f4 ♗b7 11 ♗d3 d5 12 cxd5 exd5 13 0-0 ♗c7 14 ♘ce2 ♕d6 15 ♘g3 g6 with chances for both sides, Dzuban-Serper, USSR Cht (Azov) 1991.

b) 9 ♘f4 shouldn't worry Black:

b1) 9...♗xc3 10 ♗xc3 ♘e4 11 ♖c1 ♗b7 12 ♗e2 ♕g5 13 ♗f3 ♘xc3 14 ♖xc3 ♗xf3 15 ♕xf3 ½-½ Timoshchenko-Psakhis, Sverdlovsk 1987.

b2) 9...♗b7 10 ♗d3 (10 d5 transposes to line 'c5') 10...cxd4 11 exd4 ♗xc3 12 ♗xc3 (12 bxc3?! is mistaken on account of 12...♗e4 13 0-0 ♕c8 14 ♕a4 ♗xd3 15 ♘xd3 ♘e4, when White is struggling with his inferior pawn-structure, Tisdall-Brynell, Gausdal 1995) 12...d5 13 cxd5 ♘xd5 14 ♘xd5 ♕xd5 ½-½ Gyimesi-Sax, Hungarian Ch (Budapest) 1995.

b3) 9...cxd4! 10 exd4 ♗xc3 11 ♗xc3 d5 and here:

b31) 12 ♘h5?! (this lunge isn't justified by the position and lands White in trouble) 12...♗b7 13 cxd5 ♘xd5 14 ♕g4 g6 15 ♗d2 f5 16 ♕g3 f4 17 ♘xf4 ♘xf4 18 ♗xf4 ♕xd4 19 ♗e3 ♕e4 and despite his weak dark squares, Black is clearly in the driving seat thanks to his lead in development and better coordinated pieces, I.Sokolov-Gabriel, Bad Godesberg 1999.

b32) 12 ♕f3 is better; for example, 12...♗b7 13 ♗d3 ♘c7 =.

c) 9 d5 is another important possibility, even though this is the kind of pawn-push Black hopes for, as the d-pawn will often be left stranded on d5, separated from White's other forces. Black has now tried:

c1) 9...♕e7 10 ♘g3 transposes to note 'c33' to Black's 7th move.

c2) 9...♗xc3 10 ♘xc3 exd5 11 cxd5 ♘c7 12 ♗d3 d6 13 0-0 ♘g4 14 ♗e2 ♕h4 15 h3 ♘f6 16 ♗e1 ♕h6 with chances for both sides, Letreguilly-Petran, Budapest 1995.

c3) 9...exd5 10 cxd5 (White doesn't obtain any advantage after 10 ♘xd5 either; e.g., 10...♗xd2+ 11 ♕xd2 ♘c7 12 ♘ec3 ♘fxd5 13 cxd5 d6 14 ♗e2 f5 = Ermenkov-Wojtkiewicz, Budapest Z 1993) 10...d6!? (10...♗b7 is best met by 11 e4; for example, 11...♖e8 12 f3 d6 13 ♕a4 ♗xc3 14 ♘xc3 ♘c7 15 ♗e2 with a slight advantage for White) 11 f3 (11 ♘f4 ♗xc3 12 ♗xc3 ♘c7 13 ♗e2 ♗b7 14 ♗xf6 ♕xf6 15 0-0 ♕e7 16 ♗f3 f5 17 ♘e2 ♕e5 with a distinct initiative for Black, Shulman-Palac, Pula Echt 1997) 11...♖b8 12 ♘f4 ♗xc3 13 ♗xc3 ♖e8 14 ♔f2 ♘c7 15 e4 a5 16 ♗e2 ♖a8 17 a4 ♗d7 18 g4 b5 19 h4 b4 and it is anyone's game, Maksimenko-V.Gurevich, Simferopol 1991.

c4) 9...♖e8!? deserves more tests. The idea behind this move is that White cannot play 10 e4 as 10...exd5 11 exd5 d6 lands him in an unpleasant pin, and after 10 f3 exd5 11 cxd5 b5 12 e4 b4 13 ♘b5 ♕b6 14 ♘g3?! ♗b7 15 ♘f5?!, as played in Nenashev-Kiseliov, Prague 1990, Black can seize the initiative by 15...♘xe4! 16 fxe4 ♖xe4+ 17 ♔f2 c4+ 18 ♗e3 ♖xe3 19 ♘xe3 ♕xb5.

c5) 9...♗b7 10 ♘f4 (10 e4 exd5 11 exd5 is advocated by Lautier, whose analysis continues 11...♖e8 12 f3! intending ♔f2, ♘f4 and ♗d3 ±, but 11...♕e7!? can be considered, while 11...♘g4 12 f3 ♘e5 13 ♘f4 ♕f6 14 ♔f2 ♗xc3 15 bxc3 ♘c7 is pleasant for Black, Jelen-Grosar, Ljubljana 1992) 10...♗xc3 11 ♗xc3 ♘e4 12 ♕c2 ♘xc3 13 ♕xc3 ♘c7 14 ♖d1 (Lautier-Psakhis, Paris 1989) 14...d6 15 ♗d3 (15 ♗e2 e5 16 ♘d3 b5 and Black is in command, Jelling-P.H.Nielsen, Danish League 1994/5) 15...e5 =.

c6) 9...d6 has scored well for Black:

c61) 10 f3?! exd5 11 ♘xd5 ♘xd5 12 cxd5 ♗xd2+ 13 ♕xd2 ♘c7 14 ♘g3 f5 is better for Black, Guliev-Shariyazdanov, Tula 1999.

c62) 10 ♘f4?! hands Black the initiative: 10...♗xc3 11 ♗xc3 e5 12 ♘e2 (12 ♘h5!? =) 12...♘e4 13 f3 ♘xc3 14 ♘xc3 ♘c7 15 ♕d2 f5 16 f4 ♗d7 17 ♗e2 exf4 18 exf4 ♕h4+ 19 g3 ♕h3 leaves White with a very uncomfortable position, Kasparov-Romanishin, USSR Ch (Minsk) 1979.

c63) 10 ♘g3 ♗xc3 (10...exd5 11 cxd5 is similar to line 'c3') 11 ♗xc3 exd5 12 cxd5 ♘c7 13 e4 (after 13 ♗c4 b5 14 ♗a2 c4!? {Pliester suggests 14...♗b7!?} 15 e4 ♖e8 16 ♗xf6 ♕xf6 17 0-0 ♗d7 Black has solved his opening problems) 13...♖e8 14 ♗xf6 ♕xf6 15 ♗e2 ♗d7 16 0-0 ♗b5 17 ♗xb5 ♘xb5 with a comfortable game for Black, Lautier-Romanishin, Polanica Zdroj 1991.

We now return to 9 ♘g3 *(D)*:

9...♗b7

With 9...d5!?, Black can obtain a position that somewhat resembles the Karpov Variation and is OK for Black:

B

a) 10 dxc5 bxc5 11 ♗d3 d4 12 ♘ce4 dxe3 13 ♘xf6+ ♕xf6 14 fxe3 ♗xd2+ 15 ♕xd2 ♖d8 16 ♖f1 ♕h4 17 ♖f4 ♕e7 leaves White's position disorganized, Nenashev-Nasybullin, USSR Cht (Azov) 1991.

b) 10 cxd5 cxd4 11 exd4 ♗xc3 12 bxc3 ♕xd5 (12...exd5 is also a worthwhile option for Black: 13 ♗e2 ♘c7 14 ♗f4 ♘e6 15 ♗e3 ♕c7 16 ♕d2 ♘e8 17 0-0 ♘d6 18 ♗f4 ♘e4 19 ♘xe4 ♕xf4 20 ♕xf4 ♘xf4 21 ♘g3 ♘xe2+ 22 ♘xe2 ♗a6 with a pleasant endgame for Black, Arlandi-Palac, Montecatini Terme 1997) 13 ♗e2 ♗b7 14 f3 ♘c7 15 ♗f4 ♕a5 16 ♕d2 ♘cd5 17 ♗d6 and now instead of 17...♘xc3 18 ♖b2 ♘fd5 19 ♗xf8 ♖xf8 20 ♖b3 ♖c8 21 ♘e4 ♖c6 (Bernal Moro-Gomez Esteban, Spanish Cht (Cordoba) 1995) 22 ♘xc3 ♖xc3 23 ♖xc3 ♘xc3 24 ♕b2!, when Black doesn't have sufficient compensation for the exchange, Black should continue 17...♖fd8 18 ♗b4 ♕a4 19 c4 ♘xb4 20 axb4 b5 21 c5 ♗c6, when he is by no means worse.

10 ♗d3 *(D)*

This is by far White's most popular move. Only one of the alternatives is important:

a) 10 d5? is no good: 10...♗xc3! 11 ♗xc3 exd5 12 cxd5 ♘xd5 13 ♗xg7 ♔xg7 14 ♘f5+ ♔h8 15 ♘d6 ♗c6 16 ♗xa6 ♕e7 17 ♘f5 ♕e5 18 ♗d3 ♘f4! and White's position falls like a house of cards, Magerramov-Psakhis, Klaipeda 1988.

b) 10 b4? is another tempting but inferior move, as indicated by Psakhis, who gives the line 10...cxb4 11 ♘ce2 ♕e7! 12 ♕b3 bxa3! 13 ♗xa5 bxa5 14 ♕xb7? ♖ab8 −+.

c) 10 f3!? transposes to note 'e2' to White's 8th move.

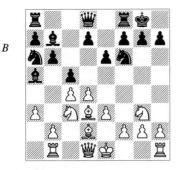

B

10...d5

This is the most popular of Black's four principal options. Black declines the offer of the g2-pawn and instead challenges White in the centre. The other options are:

a) 10...♗xg2 is still untried at top level and probably for a good reason. Pliester gives 11 ♖g1 ♗b7 12 d5!?, which definitely needs a test. A sample line is 12...g6 13 h4 exd5 14 cxd5 ♗xc3 15 bxc3 ♘xd5 16 c4 ♘dc7 17 h5 ♕f6 18 ♘f5 ♔h8!? 19 ♖c1 +−. This by no means represents best play from both sides, but illustrates the dangers that can await Black.

b) 10...cxd4 11 exd4 ♗xc3 and now:

b1) 12 bxc3 is harmless for Black. 12...d5 and now:

b11) 13 c5 is usually considered somewhat better for White, based on 13...♘b8 14 ♗g5 ♘bd7 15 ♗b5 ♕c7 16 ♗xd7 ♘xd7 17 ♗e7 ♖fe8 18 ♗d6, when 18...♕d8 19 0-0 ♗c6 20 f4 gave White some initiative in Knaak-Gabriel, Altensteig 1993. However, the alternative 18...♕c6!, targeting the weak light squares in White's camp, makes far more sense; Black follows up with 19...♗a6 with a better game.

b12) 13 0-0 dxc4 14 ♗xc4 ♘b8 15 ♖e1 ♕d6 16 a4 ♘bd7 17 ♗d3 ♖ac8 18 a5 ♖fe8 19 axb6 axb6 20 ♘h5 (20 f3!?) 20...e5 21 ♘xf6+ ♘xf6 is equal, Knaak-Psakhis, Baden-Baden 1992.

b2) 12 ♗xc3! d5 13 b3 and then:

b21) 13...dxc4 14 bxc4 ♗xg2? (accepting the g2-pawn this time doesn't appear to be a health-conscious decision this time either) 15 ♖g1 ♗b7 16 ♘h5! g6 17 d5! and now: 17...♘xh5 18 ♕xh5 ♕e8 19 ♕h6 e5 20 f4 ♘c5 21 ♗c2 ♘d7 22 f5 +−; 17...e5 18 ♕f3 ♘xh5 19 ♕xh5 ♕d6 20 f4 ♕xa3?! 21 ♔d2 ♖fe8 22 ♗xg6 hxg6 23 ♖xg6+ ♔f8 24 ♕g5 ♕a2+ 25 ♖b2 ♕xb2+ 26 ♗xb2 fxg6 27 ♕f6+ ♔g8 28 fxe5 +−; 17...♘d7 18 ♕d2 exd5 19 ♕h6 ♕e7+ 20 ♔d2 f6 21 ♖xg6+ hxg6 22 ♕xg6+ and soon game over.

b22) 13...♕c8 14 0-0 dxc4 15 bxc4 ♕c6 16 f3 ♖fd8 17 ♕e2 ± Graf-Forintos, Deizisau 2001.

c) 10...♗xc3 11 bxc3 d5 12 cxd5 exd5 13 ♕e2 ♘c7!? (13...c4 is also playable) 14 dxc5 ♘e6 15 cxb6 axb6 16 ♗c1 d4!? 17 cxd4 ♖e8, threatening both ...♘f4 and ...♘xd4, gives Black sufficient compensation for the pawns, Edzgveradze-Landa, Mlada Boleslav 1994.

11 cxd5

Or:

a) 11 ♕e2 cxd4 12 exd4 ♗xc3 13 bxc3 transposes to note 'b12' to Black's 10th move.

b) 11 0-0 cxd4 12 exd4 and then:

b1) 12...♗xc3 13 bxc3 dxc4 14 ♗xc4 ♖c8 15 ♕e2 ♘b8 (15...♘c7!?) 16 ♗d3 ♖e8 (16...♕d6!?) 17 ♖fe1 ♘bd7 (Edzgveradze-Zhu Chen, Kishinev wom IZ 1995) 18 f3 ±.

b2) Black has probably shied away from 12...dxc4 13 ♗xc4 ♕xd4 because of 14 ♗xa6 ♗xa6 15 b4, but this may be unjust since after 15...♖ad8 16 ♗e1 ♕e5 17 ♕b3 ♗xf1 18 ♘xf1 ♗xb4 19 ♕xb4 ♖d3 Black has the better chances.

11...cxd4 12 exd4 ♗xc3 13 bxc3 ♕xd5 14 f3

White has tried 14 ♕e2 on several occasions, but with limited success:

a) 14...♘c7 15 f3 ♖fd8 (15...e5?! 16 ♗c4 ♕c6 17 dxe5 ♖fe8 18 f4 ♖ad8 19 0-0, Lautier-Beliavsky, Ubeda rpd 1997, and Black's best continuation is 19...♕xg2+ 20 ♕xg2 ♗xg2 21 ♔xg2 ♖xd2+ 22 ♔h3 ♘fd5 23 ♘e4 ♖c2 24 ♖f3 ± according to Lautier) 16 0-0 ♘ce8 17 ♘e4 ♖ac8 18 ♕f2 ♕h5 19 ♖b5 ♖d5 20 g4 ♘xe4 21 ♗xe4 ♕h3 22 ♗xd5 ♗xd5 23 ♖bb1 h5 and Black has good compensation for the exchange, Vaiser-Cebalo, Cannes 1990.

b) 14...♘b8 15 f3 ♕a2 and here:

b1) 16 ♘e4 ♘xe4 17 fxe4 ♗a6! 18 0-0 ♗xd3 19 ♕xd3 ♕xa3 20 ♕g3 f6! 21 ♗f4 e5! 22 dxe5 ♕c5+! 23 ♔h1 ♘c6 is slightly better for Black, Nenashev-Psakhis, Moscow 1992.

b2) 16 0-0!? ♕xa3 17 ♘e4 ♘xe4 18 fxe4 e5 19 ♖f5 exd4 20 cxd4 ♘c6 (Lomineishvili-Bagaturov, Schwäbisch Gmünd 1998) and now 21 ♕e3!? is the best way for White to proceed; after 21...♕d6 22 d5 ♘e7 23 ♖g5 White has compensation for the pawn, but not much more than that.

We now return to 14 f3 *(D)*:

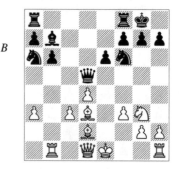

Black has tried several things here:

a) 14...♘b8 15 ♘e4 ♘bd7 16 0-0 ♕c6 17 ♕e1 ♘xe4 18 fxe4 left White obviously better in De Souza-Leitão, São Paulo 1998 due to his bishop-pair and better centre.

b) 14...♘c5 15 ♗c2 ♘cd7 16 0-0 ♗a6 17 ♖e1 ♖ac8 18 ♘e4 ± Mohota-Ravi, Calcutta 2002.

c) 14...♘c7!? 15 ♘e4 ♕d8 16 0-0 h6 17 ♕e2 ♖c8 18 ♖bd1 ♘fe8 19 ♔h1 f5!? (the beginning of a light-square strategy equivalent to the one we saw in note 'a' to White's 14th move) 20 ♘g3 b5!? 21 ♘h5 a6 22 a4 ♗c6 23 ♘f4 ♖f6 24 axb5 axb5 25 c4 bxc4 26 ♗xc4 ♕d7 27 ♘d3 ♗d5 28 ♘e5 ♗xc4 29 ♕xc4 ♕d5 and although White still has the initiative, Black's position is defensible, Epishin-Cebalo, St Vincent 2001.

d) 14...e5!? 15 ♗g5 exd4 (Black can also consider 15...♕a5!?) 16 ♗xf6 and now:

d1) 16...♕e6+?! 17 ♕e2 ♘c5 18 ♗xh7+ ♔xh7 19 ♕xe6 fxe6 20 ♗xd4 ♘d3+ 21 ♔d2 ♗a6 22 ♘e4 e5 23 ♗e3 ♖fd8 24 ♗g5 ♖d5 25 ♔e3 gives White an extra pawn and good winning prospects, which he quickly exploited in Epishin-Vezzosi, St Vincent 2001.

d2) 16...gxf6!? and then:

d21) 17 cxd4?! ♖fe8+ 18 ♔f1 ♖ad8 and White's position is far from easy to play; e.g., 19 ♘e2 ♘c5! 20 dxc5 ♗a6! or 19 ♘f5 ♘c5! 20 ♘h6+ ♔g7 21 ♘f5+ ♔h8!. In both cases, White is clearly in trouble.

d22) 17 ♗e4!? ♕e6 18 cxd4 f5 19 d5 ♗xd5 20 ♕xd5 fxe4 21 ♕xe6 fxe6 22 ♘xe4 ♖ad8 and the chances are approximately equal.

B)

5...♗b7 *(D)*

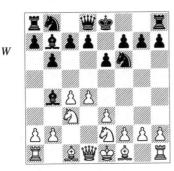

This move looks somewhat passive, at least in comparison with the alternatives. However, in classic Nimzo-Indian Hypermodern style, it invites White to push his pawns forward in the centre, leaving them and the squares around

them vulnerable. This line isn't very popular nowadays as White seems to be able to obtain a small positional advantage with best play from both sides.

6 a3 ♗e7

This retreat constitutes the main line in the present system, but there are other options for Black:

a) 6...♗d6 is a relatively recent arrival. White has tried:

a1) 7 ♕c2 c5 8 f3 ♘c6 9 dxc5 bxc5 is fine for Black.

a2) 7 b3 0-0 8 ♘g3 c5 9 ♗b2 cxd4 10 ♕xd4 ♗e7 11 ♖d1 ♘c6 12 ♕f4 ♕b8 with a hedgehog position that is perfectly OK for Black, Vaïsser-Wells, Antwerp 1993.

a3) 7 ♘g3 h5!? challenges White's knight immediately: 8 f3 h4 9 ♘ge4 ♗e7 10 ♘xf6+ ♗xf6 11 e4 d5 (another idea is 11...e5!?) 12 cxd5 exd5 13 e5 ♗e7 14 f4 c5 = De Souza-Slipak, Buenos Aires 1998.

a4) 7 ♕d3 c5 8 e4 cxd4 9 ♘xd4 0-0 10 ♘db5 ♗e5 11 f4 ♗xc3+ 12 ♘xc3 ♘c6 (12...d5!?) 13 e5 ♘e8 14 ♘e4 ♕h4+ 15 ♕g3 (B.Kristensen-Popović, Saint John 1988) 15...♕xg3+!? looks fine for Black; e.g., 16 ♘xg3 ♘d4 17 ♖b1 f6 or 16 hxg3 h6 17 ♗d2 ♘d4 18 ♗d3 ♘b3 19 ♖d1 d5!? in both cases with a satisfactory game for Black.

b) 6...♗xc3+ 7 ♘xc3 *(D)* (the highly unusual 7 bxc3 d5 8 ♘g3 0-0 9 f3 ♘bd7 10 cxd5 exd5 11 ♗d3 ♖e8 12 0-0 c5 13 a4 ♘f8 14 ♖a2 ♖c8 15 ♖e2 ♘e6 16 ♖fe1 gave White a pleasant position in Lilienthal-Kellner, corr. 1982) and now:

b1) 7...d6 8 d5 0-0 9 ♗d3 ♘bd7 10 0-0 a5 11 b3 ♕e7 12 ♗b2 ± Feick-Münder, 2nd Bundesliga 1987/8.

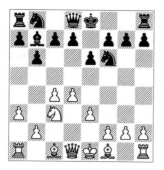

B

b2) 7...c5 8 d5 d6 9 e4 ± Donner-Boutteville, Munich OL 1958.

b3) 7...♘e4 and now:

b31) 8 ♕c2 transposes to Line D2.

b32) White can seek independent territory with 8 ♘xe4 ♗xe4 9 ♕g4 ♗g6 10 ♗e2 ♘c6 11 ♗d2 ♘a5 12 ♗c3 h5 13 ♕g3 h4 14 ♕g4 ♖h7 (Gligorić-Stoltz, Prague 1946) and here 15 0-0 ♘b3 16 ♖ae1 is just a shade better for White.

b4) 7...0-0 is a popular sideline:

b41) 8 f3 d5 9 cxd5 exd5 10 ♗d3 c5 11 0-0 ♘c6 12 ♘e2 ♖e8 = Tisdall-Rivas, Stockholm 1988.

b42) 8 b4 c5!? 9 bxc5 bxc5 10 d5 exd5 11 cxd5 d6 12 ♗e2 ♘bd7 13 0-0 ♕e7 14 ♖b1 ♘b6 15 ♗f3 ♖ab8 with equality, Van Seters-Thorsteinsson, Skopje OL 1972.

b43) 8 d5 and now:

b431) 8...d6 9 ♗d3 ♘bd7 10 0-0 ♘e5 11 ♗e2 ♗a6 12 b3 exd5 13 ♘xd5 c6 14 ♘f4 ± Handke-Mönch, Fürth 1999.

b432) 8...c6 9 e4 cxd5 10 exd5 exd5 11 cxd5 ♕e7+ 12 ♗e3 ♕e5 13 ♗c4 ♖c8 14 ♗a2 ♗a6 15 ♕d4 d6 16 ♕xe5 dxe5 17 f3 ♘bd7 18 0-0-0 and White is slightly better, Benjamin-Adianto, San Francisco 1991.

b433) 8...♕e7 9 ♗e2 exd5 (9...d6 10 0-0 c6 11 dxe6 ♕xe6 12 b3 ♘bd7 13 ♗b2 ♘e5 14 ♕d4 c5 15 ♕d2 ♖ad8 = Euwe-Capablanca, Amsterdam (3) 1931) 10 cxd5 c6 11 ♗f3 ♕e5 12 dxc6 dxc6 13 0-0 ♘bd7 (Åkesson-Kostić, Valjevo 1984) 14 ♕c2 ♖ad8 15 b4 leaves White with a minimal advantage.

b434) 8...exd5 9 cxd5 c6 10 ♗c4 cxd5 11 ♘xd5 ♘c6 12 0-0 ♘e5 13 ♘xf6+ ♕xf6 14 ♗e2 = Furman-Levenfish, USSR Ch (Moscow) 1948.

b44) 8 ♗d3 d5 (Black has also tried 8...d6, but 9 0-0 c5 10 d5 e5 11 e4 h6 12 b4 ♘bd7 13 ♗e3 gives White the better chances, G.Georgadze-Pozubszki, Bad Wörishofen 1998) and here:

b441) 9 0-0 a5 10 b3 ♘bd7 11 ♗b2 ♘e4 12 ♕c2 ♘xc3 13 ♗xc3 ♕h4 14 cxd5 exd5 and Black has a comfortable game, Raičević-Bebchuk, Belgrade 1988.

b442) 9 cxd5 exd5 10 0-0 (10 b4 transposes to line 'b552') 10...c5 (or 10...♘bd7 11 b3 ♘e4 12 ♘e2 c5 13 ♗b2 ♖c8 14 ♖c1 ♕e7 15 ♘f4 cxd4 16 ♗xd4 ± Larsen-Korning, Danish Ch (Århus) 1959) 11 dxc5 bxc5 12 b4 ♘bd7 13 ♗b2 ♕e7 14 ♘a4 c4 15 ♗c2 ♗c6 16 ♘c3 ± Averbakh-Infantozzi, Montevideo 1954.

b5) 7...d5 and now:

b51) 8 ♗d3 0-0 transposes to line 'b44'.

b52) 8 b3 0-0 9 ♗b2 ♘bd7 10 ♗d3 and now:

b521) 10...c5 (Black turns down the pawn, trusting his higher-rated opponent) 11 0-0 ♕e7 12 ♕e2 dxc4 13 bxc4, and here 13...e5?! 14 d5 e4 15 ♗c2 ♗a6 16 a4 ♖fe8 17 ♘b5 gave

Black an unsatisfactory position in the game M.Gurevich-Gelashvili, Korinthos 1998, but 13...罝fd8 improves; then the chances should be approximately equal.

b522) 10...dxc4 11 bxc4 桌xg2 wins the g-pawn, and I fully believe that Black should be able to get away with this, even though White has some chances on the g-file combined with the a1-h8 diagonal.

b53) 8 桌e2 0-0 9 0-0 ⵕbd7 10 b4 dxc4 11 桌xc4 c5 12 桌b2 cxb4 13 axb4 ± Bu Xiangzhi-N.Nogueira, Lisbon 2000.

b54) 8 b4 0-0 9 cxd5 ⵕxd5?! (Black should prefer 9...exd5 ±) 10 ⵕxd5 ৩xd5 11 f3 ৩g5 12 ৩c2 罝c8 13 e4 ৩e7 14 桌e3 ± Donner-Spassky, Santa Monica 1966. White has the bishop-pair and the better centre.

b55) 8 cxd5 and now:

b551) 8...ⵕxd5 9 ⵕxd5 (9 桌d3 0-0 10 e4 ⵕxc3 11 bxc3 and now both 11...c5 and 11...f5 have some merit; the chances are about even) 9...exd5 10 b4 c6 11 桌d3 桌a6 12 0-0 桌xd3 13 ৩xd3 ⵕd7 = Savchenko-Anastasian, Tbilisi 1989.

b552) 8...exd5 9 b4 (9 桌d3 a5 10 0-0 桌a6 11 桌xa6 ⵕxa6 12 f3 c5 = Toth-Korchnoi, Swiss Cht 1997) 9...0-0 10 桌d3 ⵕbd7 (another approach by Black is 10...c5 11 bxc5 bxc5 12 ⵕe2 c4 13 桌c2 ⵕc6 14 0-0 ⵕa5 15 f3 罝b8 16 罝b1 罝e8 17 ⵕc3 ± Vaiser-Utasi, Szirak 1985) 11 0-0 c5 12 bxc5 bxc5 13 罝b1 桌c6 14 桌f5 罝e8 15 dxc5 ⵕxc5 16 罝b4 ৩e7 17 桌b2 罝ab8 18 ⵕe2 ± Gligorić-Andersson, Wijk aan Zee 1971.

We now return to the position after 6...桌e7 (D):

7 d5

White accepts Black's invitation to plough forward in the centre, which also appears to be White's only chance for an advantage in this line. Other moves are pretty harmless:

a) 7 ⵕg3 h5!? 8 d5 h4 9 ⵕge4 ⵕxe4 10 ⵕxe4 b5 11 ৩d4 bxc4 12 桌xc4 桌f6 13 ⵕxf6+ ৩xf6 14 ৩xf6 gxf6 ∓ Kärner-Kengis, Tallinn 1982.

b) 7 f3 d5 8 cxd5 exd5 9 ⵕg3 0-0 10 桌d3 c5 11 0-0 罝e8 12 ⵕf5 桌f8 = Bogoljubow-Keres, Hamburg 1943.

c) 7 b4 a5 8 b5 d6 (8...d5!? Kengis) 9 ⵕg3 h5!? 10 桌e2 h4!? 11 桌f3 (Speelman-Kengis, London 1991) and now 11...d5!? 12 ⵕge2 ⵕe4 (Kengis) gives chances for both sides.

d) 7 ⵕf4 and now:

d1) 7...d6 8 d5 e5 9 ⵕd3 c6 10 e4 0-0 11 g3 (11 桌e2 makes more sense) 11...cxd5 12 exd5 a6 13 ⵕb4 ৩c7 14 桌e2 ⵕbd7 with a pleasant game for Black, Van Beek-Ikonnikov, Dieren 2000.

d2) 7...d5 8 cxd5 exd5 9 桌b5+ c6 10 桌e2 0-0 11 0-0 ⵕbd7 12 桌f3 桌d6 = O.Rodriguez-Sisniega, Buenos Aires OL 1978.

d3) 7...0-0 8 桌d3 (or 8 桌e2 d5 {8...d6 is also OK for Black} 9 cxd5

exd5 10 ♗f3 c6 11 0-0 ♗d6 12 b4
♗xf4 13 exf4 ♖e8 14 ♖e1 ♖xe1+ 15
♕xe1 a5 16 b5 cxb5 17 ♘xb5 ♘c6 =
Efimov-Karpov, San Giorgio rpd 1995)
8...d6 9 0-0 ♘bd7 10 b3 ♖e8 11 ♗b2
♗f8 12 ♗c2 e5 = Kharlov-Liogky,
Cappelle la Grande 1999.

7...0-0 (D)

Black has five minor alternatives:

a) 7...d6 8 ♘g3 0-0 transposes to
the main line.

b) 7...a5?! 8 e4 e5 9 ♘g3 0-0 10
♗d3 ♘e8 11 h4 ♘a6 12 ♘f5 ♘c5 13
♗c2 ♘d6 14 ♘xd6 ♗xd6 15 ♗e3 ±
Lilienthal-Kotov, USSR Ch (Moscow)
1945.

c) 7...b5 8 dxe6 fxe6 9 ♘xb5 0-0
10 ♘g3 c5 11 f3 d5 12 ♗d3 (Grigor-
ian-Kupreichik, USSR Ch (Moscow)
1976) and now 12...♘bd7 13 cxd5
exd5 14 0-0 (*ECO*) is relatively best,
although White is clearly better.

d) 7...exd5 8 cxd5 0-0 9 g3 ♖e8 10
♗g2 c6 11 0-0 ♗f8 12 b4 a5 13 b5
cxb5 14 ♘xb5 ♘a6 15 ♗b2 is slightly
better for White, Yusupov-Onishchuk,
Bundesliga 1998/9.

e) 7...e5 8 ♘g3 g6 9 ♗d3 d6 10 f4
♘bd7 11 f5 with more space and
better chances for White, Reshevsky-
G.Kramer, New York 1951.

8 ♘g3

This move is White's most popular
choice, but he frequently tries two different approaches:

a) 8 g3 can be met with 8...b5!.
White's best then appears to be 9 ♘f4
bxc4 10 ♗xc4 exd5 11 ♘cxd5 c6 12
♘xf6+ ♗xf6 13 0-0 d5 = Korchnoi-
Kengis, Berne 1996.

b) 8 e4 and here:

b1) 8...d6 and then:

b11) 9 g3 c6 10 dxe6 fxe6 11 ♘d4
♗c8 12 ♗h3 e5 13 ♗xc8 ♕xc8 14
♘f5 ♕e6 15 ♗g5 gives White a slight
advantage, Ståhlberg-Marini, Mar del
Plata 1947.

b12) 9 ♘g3 ♘bd7 10 ♗e2 c6 11
0-0 ♖e8 transposes to note 'b21' to
Black's 9th move.

b2) 8...exd5 9 cxd5 ♖e8 (9...d6?!
10 ♘g3 c6 11 ♗c4 ♘bd7 12 0-0 ♘e5
13 dxc6 ♗xc6 14 ♗a2 ♕d7 15 ♖e1
½-½ Sosnicki-Grabarczyk, Polish Ch
(Ksiaz) 1998; White is comfortably
better at this point though) 10 g3 ♗c5
11 ♗g2 ♘g4 12 0-0 ♕f6 (Najdorf-
Balinas, Lugano OL 1968) and here
13 ♕e1 keeps the balance.

b3) 8...♖e8 and now:

b31) 9 g3?! b5! 10 cxb5 (after 10 b3
bxc4 11 bxc4 Suba gives 11...♘a6 as
'unclear', but 11...♗c5!? may be even
better for Black – the threat of 12...♘g4
leaves White struggling) 10...♘xe4 11
♘xe4?! (11 ♗g2 ♘xc3 12 ♘xc3, Kar-
asev-Ornstein, Albena 1976, 12...a6!
13 0-0 ♕c8 ∓ Ornstein) 11...exd5 12
♘d2 d4 13 f3 d3 14 ♔f2 dxe2 15
♗xe2 a6! with the initiative and a clear
advantage for Black, Marin-Suba, Romanian Ch 1985.

b32) 9 ♘g3 exd5 10 cxd5 ♗d6 11
f3 ♘h5!? 12 ♘xh5 ♕h4+ 13 g3 ♕xh5

and Black is doing fine, Vehre-Blumenfeld, corr. 1986.

8...d6

Or:

a) 8...b5 9 dxe6 fxe6 10 ♘xb5 transposes to note 'c' to Black's 7th move.

b) 8...a5 9 ♗e2 ♘a6 10 0-0 ♖e8 11 e4 exd5 12 cxd5 ♗c5 13 ♗f4 gives White a slight advantage, Verdier-Conquest, French Cht 1995.

c) 8...♗d6 9 f4 b5 10 dxe6 fxe6 11 ♘xb5 e5 is messy, but Black should have sufficient compensation for the pawn, Kuligowski-Helmers, Reykjavik 1982.

d) 8...♖e8 9 ♗e2 ♗f8 10 e4 d6 11 0-0 ♘bd7 12 ♗e3 c6 13 ♕d2 ♖c8 (13...exd5!? 14 exd5 cxd5 15 cxd5 ♖c8 with counterplay – Kramnik) 14 dxe6! fxe6 15 f4 ♕e7 16 ♖ad1 ♖cd8 17 ♔h1 ♕f7 18 ♕c2 ♔h8 19 b4 e5 with chances for both sides, Kasparov-Kramnik, Moscow (10) rpd 2001.

9 ♗e2 (D)

White often plays 9 e4, but it has little independent significance; for example, 9...c6 10 ♗e2 transposes to the main line, while 9...♘bd7 10 ♗e2 is note 'b1' to Black's 9th move.

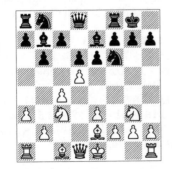

9...c6

This is played most frequently. The subsequent play will often take on the character of the Hedgehog Variation of the Symmetrical English. Black's alternatives include:

a) 9...♖e8!? is sort of a Romanian speciality:

a1) 10 e4 ♘bd7 11 0-0 transposes to line 'b21'.

a2) 10 0-0 ♗f8 11 e4 c6 12 dxe6 ♖xe6 13 f4 ♘bd7 14 b4 a6 15 ♖a2 b5 16 ♖d2 ♕c7 and Black has equalized, Supatashvili-Ionescu, Elista OL 1998.

b) 9...♘bd7 and now:

b1) 10 e4 and then:

b11) 10...c6 11 0-0 a6 (11...♖e8 is line 'b21') 12 ♗e3 ♖e8 transposes to line 'b213'.

b12) 10...♖e8 11 0-0 is line 'b21'.

b2) 10 0-0 ♖e8 and now:

b21) 11 e4 c6 (11...♗f8 transposes to note 'd' to Black's 8th move; 11...a6 12 ♗e3 ♖c8 13 ♖c1 c6 14 dxc6 {Gavrikov gives 14 dxe6 fxe6 15 f4 as unclear} 14...♖xc6 15 b4 ♕a8 16 ♕b3 ♖cc8 17 ♖fd1! ♗f8 {17...♘xe4? 18 ♘cxe4 ♗xe4 19 ♘xe4 ♕xe4 20 ♗f3 ♕f5 21 ♗b7 ± Gavrikov} 18 f3 ♕b8 19 ♗f1 ♗a8 with approximately equal chances, Yrjölä-Gavrikov, Turku 1988) and then:

b211) 12 ♗f4 cxd5 13 cxd5 e5 14 ♗e3 g6 15 ♗h6 ♗f8 16 ♗xf8 ♖xf8 17 b4 ± Sriram-Annageldiev, Asian Ch (Calcutta) 2001.

b212) 12 dxe6 fxe6 13 h4!? a6 (13...d5!?) 14 h5 h6 15 ♗f4 ♕c7 16 ♕d2 ♗f8 17 ♖ad1 e5 18 ♗e3 with a better game for White, Knaak-Foisor, Bad Wörishofen 1992.

b213) 12 ♗e3 a6 13 dxe6 (13 ♖c1 ♗f8 {13...♖c8 is line 'b12'} 14 b4 g6 15 ♗g5 h6 16 dxc6 ♗xc6 is equal, De

Resende-Vescovi, San Vernardo 1999) 13...fxe6 14 ♕c2 c5 15 ♖ad1 ♕c7 16 f4 ♗f8 17 ♗d3 ± M.Gurevich-Foisor, Cappelle la Grande 1999.

b22) 11 f4!? c6 12 dxe6 fxe6 13 ♗f3 ♕c7 14 b3 (Stoica gives 14 b4 as slightly better for White, which may or may not be true, but 14...d5!? looks fully playable for Black) 14...♖ad8! 15 ♗b2 d5! 16 cxd5 exd5 17 ♔h1 ♗a6 with a pleasant game for Black, Hort-Stoica, Porz ECC 1991.

10 e4

10 ♗f3 is also playable, but doesn't amount to anything after 10...♕c7 (or 10...♕c8!? Ionescu) 11 0-0 ♘bd7 12 e4 ♖fe8 13 ♗f4 ♘e5 14 ♗e2 ♗f8 (Ionescu gives 14...♖ac8! followed by ...♕b8 as the most accurate) 15 ♖c1 (Suba-Ionescu, Romanian Ch 1987) 15...♖ac8 16 dxc6 ♗xc6 17 ♘d5 ♕d8 18 ♘xf6+ ♕xf6 19 ♕d2 ♕e7 = Ionescu.

10...cxd5

Or:

a) 10...exd5 11 cxd5 cxd5 transposes to the main line.

b) 10...♖e8 11 0-0 ♘bd7 transposes to note 'b21' to Black's 9th move.

c) 10...♘bd7 is note 'b11' to Black's 9th move.

d) 10...♘a6!? 11 0-0 ♘c7 12 dxc6 ♗xc6 13 ♗f4 ♕d7 14 b4 ♖fd8 15 ♕b3 b5 (this looks a bit premature, but it may be difficult for White to take advantage of this fact) 16 ♖fd1 bxc4 17 ♗xc4 a6 18 ♖d2 ♘b5 19 e5 ♘xc3 20 exd6 ♘cd5 21 dxe7 ♕xe7 and Black's chances are by no means worse, Chekhov-Kengis, Moscow 1986.

11 cxd5 exd5 12 exd5 ♘a6 *(D)*

12...♖e8?! 13 0-0 ♘bd7 14 ♘f5! (14 ♗f4 g6 15 ♖c1 a6 16 a4 ♗f8 17

♖e1 ♖c8 = Ehlvest-Khalifman, Kuibyshev 1986) 14...♗f8 15 ♗f4 ♘e4 16 ♗b5! a6 17 ♕g4 ♔h8 18 ♘xe4 ♖xe4 19 ♗xd7 ♕xd7 20 f3! ± M.Gurevich-Khalifman, USSR Ch (Minsk) 1987. White threatens ♗xd6!.

13 0-0 ♘c7 14 ♗f3

The more aggressive 14 ♘f5!? sacrifices a pawn, which Black is fairly happy to pick up: 14...♘fxd5 15 ♘xd5 ♗xd5 16 ♗f4 ♘e6 17 ♗g3 ♗b7 18 ♖e1 (18 ♘xe7+ ♕xe7 19 ♗xd6 ♕g5 20 ♗f3 ♗xf3 21 ♕xf3 ♖fd8 22 ♖ad1 ♖ac8 = Nisipeanu/Stoica) 18...d5 and now instead of 19 ♗f3 ♖e8! ∓ Manolache-Berescu, Romanian Ch (Targoviste) 2001, Nisipeanu and Stoica give 19 ♗d3 with compensation for the pawn.

14...♕d7 15 ♗e3

15 ♖e1 ♖fe8 16 ♗f4 ♗f8 17 ♕d2 ♖xe1+ 18 ♖xe1 ♖e8 = Lerner-Gavrikov, Beltsy 1981.

15...♖fe8 16 ♖c1 ♖ac8 17 ♕d4 ♗a6 18 ♖fd1 ♘b5 19 ♘xb5 ♗xb5

Black has fully equalized, Knaak-T.Horvath, Hungary 1986.

C)

5...♗a6 *(D)*

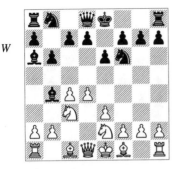

Finally we reach the Fischer Variation. In the early years of this line, the 1950s, it was mainly Prins, Keres and Smyslov who employed this variation – notably, Smyslov used it several times in his matches against Botvinnik for the world championship, just like Bronstein first did in 1951 with great success.

It wasn't until 1965 that Fischer took up this line, but he used it on several occasions, with good results.

Black's idea is to play ...d5 and exchange the light-squared bishops and then play on the light squares.

White now has two main lines:

C1: 6 ♘g3   151
C2: 6 a3   160

In addition, White has two quite rarely played lines, which nonetheless deserve a look:

a) 6 ♘f4 0-0 7 ♗d3 c5 8 0-0 cxd4 9 exd4 ♗xc3 10 bxc3 ♕c7 11 ♕f3 ♘c6 12 c5 ♗xd3 13 ♘xd3 ♘a5 = Ilivitsky-Keres, USSR Ch (Moscow) 1952.

b) 6 ♕a4 c5 7 a3 ♗xc3+ 8 ♘xc3 0-0 and here:

b1) 9 d5!? exd5 (9...♕e7 10 f3 exd5 11 cxd5 ♗xf1 12 ♔xf1 d6 13 ♔f2 ♘bd7 14 ♖f1 a6 15 e4 b5 16 ♕c2

♘e5 and Black should be doing OK, Speelman-Timman, Linares 1991) 10 cxd5 ♗xf1 11 ♔xf1 d6 12 f3 ♘bd7 13 e4 a6 14 g3 ♘e5 15 ♔g2 ♘fd7 16 ♕c2 c4 and Black is doing fine, Johannessen-Brynell, Oslo 2001.

b2) 9 dxc5 bxc5 10 ♗e2 d5 11 0-0 ♕d7 12 ♕xd7 ♘bxd7 13 cxd5 ♗xe2 14 ♘xe2 exd5 15 b4 ♖fb8 16 bxc5 ♘xc5 is equal, Suba-Franco, Cordoba 1995.

C1)
6 ♘g3 *(D)*

This move was first used by Reshevsky.

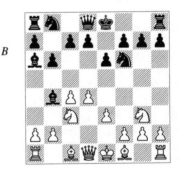

Black has two main lines to choose from, each leading to very different play:

C11: 6...0-0   152
C12: 6...♗xc3+   156

Or:

a) 6...d5?? is an accident that has happened more than once, most recently in Kaminik-Lukov, Cappelle la Grande 1996; the GM gave up after 7 ♕a4+ b5 8 ♕xb4 bxc4 9 b3 c5 10 ♕xc5 ♘bd7 11 ♕a3 ♕c8 12 ♗d2 ♘b6 13 e4 ♗b7 1-0.

b) 6...♘c6 7 ♗d2 0-0 8 ♕a4 ♗b7 9 ♗e2 d5 10 cxd5 ♘xd5 11 0-0 ♘xc3 12 bxc3 ♗e7 13 c4 ♘b8 14 ♗c3 c5 15 d5! with the better game for White, G.Georgadze-Rodriguez Lopez, La Coruña 1996.

c) 6...c5 7 d5 exd5 (7...0-0 8 e4 transposes to note 'b' to Black's 7th move in Line C11) 8 cxd5 ♗xf1 9 ♔xf1 0-0 10 e4 transposes to note 'b1' to Black's 7th move in Line C11.

d) 6...h5 is an idea that typically pops up in positions like these, where the knight can be chased away. White can play:

d1) 7 ♗d3 allows the pawn-push 7...h4 (*ECO* also mentions 7...♗xc3+!? 8 bxc3 h4) 8 ♘e2 h3 9 g3 ♗b7 10 0-0 ♗f3 11 ♕c2 ♘c6 12 a3 ♗xc3 13 ♘xc3 0-0 14 ♖e1 ♗g2 with chances for both sides, Smejkal-Hort, Luhačovice 1971.

d2) 7 h4! ♗b7 (7...♗xc3+ 8 bxc3 d5 9 ♕f3 ♗b7 10 ♗d3 c5 11 cxd5 ♕xd5 12 e4 ♕d8 13 ♗g5 is much better for White, Gligorić-Rubinetti, Palma de Mallorca IZ 1970) 8 ♗d2 (or 8 ♕d3 d5 {8...c5!? *ECO*} 9 cxd5 exd5 10 ♕c2 c5 11 a3 cxd4 12 axb4 dxc3 13 bxc3 ♘bd7 14 ♘f5 0-0 15 ♗b2! with a slight advantage for White, Knaak-Bronstein, Tallinn 1979) 8...♗d6!? (or 8...a6 9 ♕c2 d5 10 cxd5 ♘xd5 11 ♘xd5 ♗xd2+ 12 ♕xd2 ♕xd5 13 ♖c1 ± Geller-Keres, USSR Ch (Tbilisi) 1959) 9 ♘ge2 (after 9 ♖h3!?, rather than 9...a6?! 10 d5!? ± Cherepkov-Al.Ivanov, Minsk 1985, Black should try 9...g6!? 10 f3 ♗e7 targeting our friend on h4) 9...c5 10 ♕c2 ♘c6 11 a3 cxd4 12 exd4 ♖c8 13 b4 a5 with a reasonable game for Black, Obodchuk-Onishchuk, Poikovsky 2002.

C11)
6...0-0 (D)

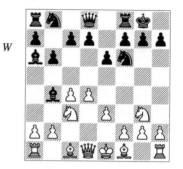

7 e4

White has a few alternatives:

a) 7 ♗d3 c5 (7...d5 8 cxd5 ♘xd5 9 ♘ge2 c5 10 ♗xa6 ♘xa6 11 a3 ♗xc3+ 12 bxc3 ♕d7 = Mamedova-C.Foisor, Warsaw wom Ech 2001) 8 0-0 cxd4 9 exd4 d5 10 cxd5 ♗xd3 11 ♕xd3 ♘xd5 12 ♘h5 ♘c6 13 ♕g3 g6 14 ♘xd5 exd5 is equal, Lautier-Hraček, Groningen FIDE 1997.

b) 7 ♕b3 c5 8 dxc5 bxc5 9 ♗e2 ♘c6 10 0-0 ♘a5 11 ♕c2 ♗xc4 12 ♗xc4 ♘xc4 13 ♘ce2 d5 14 a3 ♗a5 15 b3 ♘d6 16 ♕xc5 ♘fe4 with an equal position, Panno-Van der Sterren, Wijk aan Zee 1978.

7...♘c6

Black has several interesting alternatives:

a) 7...d6 8 ♗d2 (8 ♗d3 c5 9 d5 transposes to line 'b32') 8...c5 9 a3 ♗a5?! (Bronstein gives 9...♗xc3 10 ♗xc3 ♘c6 as Black's best, although 11 d5!? may be considered) 10 d5 exd5 11 cxd5 ♗xf1 12 ♔xf1 ♘bd7 13 h4 ♖e8 14 f3 ± ½-½ Reshevsky-Keres, Zurich Ct 1953.

b) 7...c5 8 d5 and now:

b1) 8...exd5 9 cxd5 ♗xf1 10 ♔xf1 d6 11 ♗f4 ♖e8 12 f3 ♗xc3 13 bxc3 ♘fd7! and now instead of 14 ♗xd6?! ♕f6 15 ♗xb8 ♖axb8 16 ♕c2 ♘e5 17 ♔f2 c4 18 ♖hb1 b5 19 ♔g1 ♘d3 with good compensation for the pawn, Lautier-Leitão, New Delhi FIDE 2000; according to Leitão White should play 14 h4! intending h5, ♘f5 and ♖h3 ±.

b2) 8...♖e8 9 f3 d6 10 ♗e2 exd5 11 cxd5 ♗xc3+ (11...♗xe2 12 ♘gxe2 b5 13 0-0 a6 14 a4!, Korchnoi-Short, Madrid 1995, and now 14...♗xc3!? 15 bxc3 ♘bd7 leaves White with only a minimal advantage – Korchnoi) 12 bxc3 ♗xe2 13 ♘xe2 ♘bd7 14 0-0 b5 15 ♘g3 ♕b6 16 ♗g5 h6 17 ♗f4 ♘e5 = Mchedlishvili-Istratescu, Ohrid Ech 2001.

b3) 8...d6 and then:

b31) 9 ♗e2 exd5 10 exd5 ♗xc3+ 11 bxc3 ♘fd7 12 0-0 ♘e5 13 f4 ♘xc4 14 f5 f6 15 ♗xc4 ♗xc4 16 ♖f4 b5 17 ♖g4 ♖f7 18 ♗f4 ♕e7 with somewhat better chances for Black, Iashvili-Alterman, Formia 1994.

b32) 9 ♗d3 ♘bd7 10 ♗f4 and here 10...♗xc3+ 11 bxc3 ♘e5 12 ♗xe5 dxe5 13 0-0 gave White a solid advantage in Shaked-Bunzmann, Budapest 1997, but 10...exd5 11 cxd5 ♗xd3 12 ♕xd3 ♗xc3+ 13 bxc3 ♖e8 14 f3 ♘e5 is fine for Black.

c) 7...d5 8 cxd5 (8 e5!? ♘e4 9 ♘gxe4 dxe4 10 a3 {10 ♗e3 c5 11 a3 is slightly better for White – Veličković} 10...♗xc3+ 11 bxc3 ♘c6 12 h4 f6 13 ♕c2 ♘a5 14 ♕xe4 f5 15 ♕f4 ♗xc4 leads to a balanced position, Kjeldsen-Brynell, Denmark-Sweden 1998) 8...♗xf1 (8...♗xc3+ 9 bxc3 ♗xf1 10 ♔xf1 transposes to line 'c1') 9 ♔xf1 and then:

c1) 9...♗xc3 10 bxc3 exd5 11 e5 (11 ♗g5 '±' is given by Euwe) 11...♘e4 and now:

c11) 12 ♕g4 ♕d7 13 ♘f5 g6 14 ♘h6+ ♔g7 15 ♕h4 ♕d8 16 ♕h3 f5 17 exf6+ ♘xf6 18 ♗g5 ♕d7 19 ♗xf6+ ♖xf6 ½-½ Psakhis-Panchenko, Sochi 1987.

c12) 12 f3 ♘xg3+ 13 hxg3 f5 14 exf6 ♕xf6 15 ♖h5 (or 15 ♕d3 h6 16 ♗a3 ♖e8 17 ♖h5 ♕c6 18 g4 ± Makarov-Raetsky, USSR Cht (Naberezhnye Chelny) 1988) 15...c6 16 ♕d3 ♕g6 17 ♕xg6 hxg6 18 ♖e5 ♘d7 19 ♖e6 ♖f6 20 ♖e2 ± Gligorić-Hecht, West Berlin 1971.

c2) 9...exd5 10 e5 ♘e8 11 ♕b3 (11 ♕g4 ♔h8 12 ♘ge2, Vaiser-Wilde, West Berlin 1988, 12...c5 is fairly balanced) 11...♗xc3 12 bxc3 c5 13 ♗a3 ♘a6 (Rogers-Brynell, Malmö 1993) and here Rogers gives 14 ♖e1 ±.

8 ♗d3

Two other moves also look interesting:

a) 8 ♗g5 h6 9 h4 is the kind of chess all of us like to play once in a while. Black has three options:

a1) 9...e5?! 10 a3 ♗e7 11 d5 ♘d4 12 ♘f5 ♘xf5 13 exf5 e4 14 ♗e3 ♗c5 15 g4 ♗xe3 16 fxe3 ♘h7 17 ♕c2 ♖e8 18 0-0-0 ± Ornstein-Eisterer, Vienna 1986.

a2) 9...d6 10 a3 ♗xc3+ 11 bxc3 hxg5 12 hxg5 ♖e8 13 gxf6 ♕xf6 14 ♘h5 ♕h6 15 ♖h3 with a strong initiative for White, Handke-M.Becker, 2nd Bundesliga 1999/00.

a3) 9...hxg5!? used to be considered a major error, but Black has recently revived it: 10 hxg5 g6 11 e5 ♘h7 12 ♕g4 ♘xg5 13 ♘ge4 ♔g7 14 ♘xg5 ♖h8 15 ♖xh8 ♕xh8 16 ♕f4

♖f8 17 ♕f6+ ♔g8 18 ♕xh8+ ♔xh8 = Hedman.

b) 8 e5 ♘e8 9 ♕a4 ♗b7 10 ♗d3 ♘xd4 11 ♕xb4 c5 (11...♗xg2 is fun to analyse; one line goes 12 ♗xh7+ ♔xh7 13 ♕xf8 ♘c2+ 14 ♔d1 ♘xa1 15 ♘ce4 with a dangerous initiative for White) 12 ♕a4 ♗xg2 13 ♗e4 ♗xe4 14 ♘cxe4 ♘f3+ 15 ♔f1 ♘xe5 16 f4 ♘g6 and with three pawns for the bishop, Black has excellent compensation, Lautier-Wahls, Dortmund 1989.

We now return to the position after 8 ♗d3 (D):

8...e5

At this juncture, only one Black's alternatives is of any use:

a) 8...♘xd4? can be met with both 9 e5 followed by ♗xh7+ as well as 9 ♕a4, winning material.

b) 8...d5? 9 cxd5 ♗xd3 10 ♕xd3 exd5 11 e5 ♘e4 12 a3 ♗xc3+ 13 bxc3 f5 14 ♘e2 ♘a5 15 h4 ♘b3 16 ♖b1 ♘xc1 17 ♖xc1 f4 18 ♕f3 ♕e7 19 c4 ± Portisch-Spassky, Moscow 1967.

c) 8...♘a5!? 9 ♗g5!? and then:

c1) 9...h6? (Black weakens his kingside without any purpose at all) 10 h4! d6 (10...♗e7 is now too late;

the kingside is already weakened: 11 ♗xf6! ♗xf6 12 e5 ♗e7 13 ♕g4 with a strong initiative and clearly better chances for White) 11 ♘h5 hxg5 12 hxg5 ♘xe4 13 ♗xe4 ♕xg5 14 f4 ♕h6 and now 15 ♕f3, as played in Knaak-Adorjan, Szirak 1985, does win, but 15 ♘f6+! is even more effective, since 15...♕xf6 is met by 16 ♗h7+ ♔h8 17 ♗g6+ ♔g8 18 ♖h8+ ♔xh8 19 ♕h5+ ♔g8 20 ♕h7#.

c2) The correct 9...♗e7!, as given by *ECO*, completely fits the bill. Now 10 e5 ♘e8 11 ♗xe7 ♕xe7 12 b3 c5 13 0-0 cxd4 14 ♗e4 ♖d8 15 ♕xd4 d5 gives Black a fully satisfactory position, while 10 ♗xf6!? ♗xf6 11 e5 ♗e7 12 ♕e2 ♗b7 13 0-0 f5 14 exf6 ♗xf6 leads to chances for both sides.

9 d5

White has, or so it seems at first sight, an interesting option in 9 0-0 on account of 9...exd4 10 ♘d5! with excellent compensation and 9...♘xd4 10 ♕a4 ♗xc3 11 bxc3, attacking Black's pieces on a6 and d4. However, Black has a clever riposte in 11...♘e6!, as 12 ♕xa6 is met by 12...♘c5, winning the piece back with a better game. White can instead pick up an exchange with 12 ♗a3, but after 12...♗b7 13 ♗xf8 ♕xf8 14 ♕c2 ♘f4, Black has more than adequate compensation; for example, 15 ♖fe1 (Vegh-Wahls, Tapolca 1986) 15...♕c5 with a positional advantage for Black – the exchange is of no importance, as White has nowhere to make it count.

9...♗xc3+

9...♘a5 10 ♕e2 ♗xc3+ 11 bxc3 transposes to the note to Black's 10th move.

10 bxc3 ♘e7

10...♘a5 is also possible, but after 11 ♕e2, Black has to be a little careful:

a) 11...d6? leads to disaster for Black: 12 ♗g5! h6 13 ♗d2! (White has the target on the kingside that he needs in order to break through) 13...♘d7 14 ♘f5! ♕f6? (14...♔h7 is better, but White will open the kingside to his advantage with g4-g5) 15 h4! ♘c5 16 ♗g5! hxg5 17 hxg5 ♕xg5 18 ♕h5! ♘xd3+ 19 ♔f1 ♕xg2+ 20 ♔xg2 ♘f4+ 21 ♔f3 1-0 (on account of 21...♘xh5 22 ♘e7+ ♔h7 23 ♖xh5#) Krüger-Iskov, Dortmund 1978.

b) 11...♘e8!? *(D)* is Black's correct move. Then:

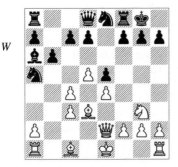

b1) 12 c5 ♗xd3 13 ♕xd3 bxc5 (or 13...♘b7!? 14 cxb6 ♘c5 15 ♕e2 axb6 with a pleasant position for Black) 14 ♕b5 c6 15 dxc6 d6 16 0-0 ♕b6 17 ♕a4 ♘xc6 18 ♘f5 ♖c8 19 ♖d1 ♕c7 20 ♖d3 ♘e7 21 ♘e3 c4 and although White has some compensation for the pawn, it shouldn't be sufficient, Halldorsson-Bensiek, corr. 1988.

b2) 12 ♗a3 d6 13 0-0 c5!? (in Sadler-K.Arkell, London 1991, Black played more passively: 13...♘f6 14 f4 ♘d7 15 f5 f6 16 ♘h5 ♘c5 17 ♗xc5!

bxc5 18 g4 ♖b8 19 h4 with an attack for White) 14 ♘f5 g6 15 ♘e3 ♘g7 16 f4 f6 17 ♗c1 ♕d7 18 f5 g5 19 h4 gxh4 20 ♔f2 h5! 21 ♖h1 ♔f7 22 ♖xh4 ♔e7 23 ♗d2 ♖f7 24 ♖g1 ♕a4 and Black has a perfectly defensible position, Kooskinen-Smit, corr. 1983.

b3) 12 f4 f6 13 0-0 (13 ♘f5!?) 13...♘d6 14 fxe5 fxe5 15 ♖xf8+ ♕xf8 16 ♗a3 ('±' Anton) 16...g6! 17 ♖f1 ♕e7 18 c5!? ♗xd3 19 ♕xd3 ♘db7! 20 d6!? cxd6 21 cxb6 axb6 22 ♖b1! ♕e6 23 ♖xb6 ♘c6! 24 ♖xb7 ♖xa3 (Anton-Smit, corr. 1990) and now White's best chance to win the game lies in 25 ♕d5!, as suggested by Anton. Possibly best is 25...♖xc3, when play could continue 26 ♖xd7 ♕xd5 27 exd5 ♖c1+ 28 ♘f1 ♘b4 29 ♖xd6 e4!? 30 ♖d8+ ♔f7 31 d6 ♘c6 32 ♖d7+ ♔e6 33 ♖xh7 ♔xd6, and Black should no longer be able to lose.

We now return to 10...♘e7 *(D)*:

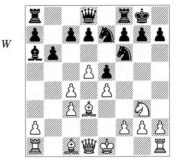

11 0-0

Or:

a) 11 f4 d6 12 fxe5 dxe5 13 0-0 ♘d7 14 ♗a3 ♘c5 15 ♘f5 ♘xf5 16 ♖xf5 ♕d6 17 ♕f3 f6 18 ♕e3 ♖f7 19 ♖f2 ♖d8 20 ♖b1 with an initiative for White, but Black's position is solid and he should be able to defend, Stra-schewski-Lisak, corr. 1988.

b) 11 h4 d6 12 h5 h6 13 ♗e3 (13 ♘f1 c6 14 ♘e3 ♔h8 15 ♕e2 ♖c8 16 ♗d2 cxd5 17 cxd5 ♗xd3 18 ♕xd3 ♘d7 gives Black a fully satisfactory position, Knaak-Wahls, Biel 1996) 13...♘d7 14 ♕d2 ♕c8 (instead of this provocative move, Psakhis recom-mends 14...♘c5!? 15 ♗e2 f5 with a nice position for Black) 15 ♗xh6!? gxh6 16 ♕xh6 ♘c5 17 ♗e2 ♕d8 18 ♘f5 (as Psakhis mentions, 18 ♖h4!? ♗c8 19 ♗g4!? looks quite dangerous for Black, but no win is apparent; e.g., 19...f6 20 ♗f5 ♗xf5 21 ♘xf5 ♘xf5 22 ♖g4+ ♔f7 23 ♕h7+ ♔e8 24 exf5 ♕e7 25 ♖g7 ♖f7 26 ♕h8+ ♔d7 27 ♕xa8 ♖xg7 28 ♕c6+ {Psakhis} with a perpetual check) 18...♘xf5 19 exf5 ♘e4! 20 ♖h3 f6 21 ♕g6+ ½-½ Khal-ifman-Emelin, St Petersburg 1998.

c) 11 ♗g5!? ♘e8 and now:

c1) 12 c5? ♗xd3 13 d6 cxd6 14 cxd6 ♘xd6 15 ♕xd3 ♘b7 ∓ Knaak-Ligterink, Jurmala 1978.

c2) 12 a4!? f6 13 ♗e3 ♕c8 14 0-0 ♘d6 15 ♕e2 ♘b7 16 f4 d6 17 fxe5 dxe5 18 c5 ♗xd3 19 ♕xd3 bxc5?! (Black should consider 19...♖d8 20 ♖ad1 bxc5 21 ♕c4 ♘d6 22 ♕xc5 c6 23 c4 cxd5 24 cxd5 ♕d7 with a solid position) 20 a5 a6 21 ♖ab1 ♖f7 22 ♖f2 ♘xa5 23 ♗xc5 ♘b7 24 ♗a3 ♘d6 25 c4 with a good initiative for White, Sadler-Wahls, Bundesliga 1999/00.

c3) 12 h4!? f6 13 ♗e3 c5 14 h5 ♘d6 15 ♕e2 ♖c8!? (an improvement over 15...f5? 16 ♗g5! h6 17 exf5!! +– Knaak-Reeh, Balatonbereny 1987) 16 a4 ♘b7 17 f4 ♘a5 18 f5 ♕e8 19 ♔d1 h6 20 ♔c2 ♖b8 (threatening ...♘c8-d6, targeting the c4-pawn) 21 ♘f1

♘xf5 22 exf5 e4 23 ♘d2 exd3+ 24 ♕xd3 ♘xc4! with a better game for Black, Velker-Bougiovanni, corr. 1994. White should probably have tried to play h6, before Black got to play ...h6 first.

11...d6 12 a4

Other moves have also failed to produce any advantage:

a) 12 f4 exf4 13 ♗xf4 ♘d7 14 ♕h5 ♘g6 15 e5 dxe5 16 ♗e3 e4 17 ♘xe4 ♕h4 18 ♕xh4 ♘xh4 19 ♗f4 ♖ac8 with equality, Levitt-Wahls, Bundes-liga 1987/8.

b) 12 ♗g5 ♘d7 13 ♕g4 f6 14 ♗e3 ♘c5 15 ♗xc5 bxc5 16 ♖fb1 ♕c8 is equal, Petrosian-L.Schneider, Skara Echt 1980.

12...♘d7 13 a5 c6

Black starts his counterplay imme-diately so as not to become a sitting duck when White starts his kingside initiative.

14 axb6 axb6 15 ♗g5 ♘c5 16 ♗e2 ♕c7 17 f3 ♖fc8 18 ♗xe7

A necessary and good decision: with the pawn-structure becoming more and more static, the role of the bishop-pair has played itself out and White instead sets his eyes on another target, the d5-square.

18...♕xe7 19 ♘f5 ♕f8 20 dxc6 g6 21 ♘e3 ♖xc6 22 ♘d5 ♔g7

Black has equalized, Sadler-Wahls, Bundesliga 1998/9.

C12)

6...♗xc3+ 7 bxc3 (D)
7...d5

Black immediately focuses on the a6-f1 diagonal in an attempt to ex-change off the light-squared bishops and prevent White from castling.

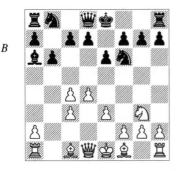

B

7...0-0 has also been tried: 8 e4 ♘e8 9 ♗d3 ♘c6 10 0-0 (10 ♗a3?! d6 11 ♕a4 ♘a5 12 0-0 c5 13 e5 ♕c7 14 ♖fd1 f5 15 f4 ♖f7 16 ♖ac1 g6 17 ♗e2 dxe5 18 fxe5 ♖c8 19 ♘f1 ♕d7! ∓ Cebalo-Djurić, Vršac 1983) 10...♘a5 11 f4!? ♗xc4 12 f5 gave White interesting attacking chances in Platonov-Tseshkovsky, USSR Ch (Alma-Ata) 1968.

8 ♗a3

Or:

a) 8 cxd5 ♗xf1 9 ♔xf1 (9 ♘xf1 looks more natural but is quite time-consuming; for example, 9...♕xd5 10 f3 0-0 11 ♘g3 ♕c4 12 ♕b3 ♕a6 13 c4 c5 14 dxc5 bxc5 15 ♗b2 ♘bd7 with equality, Gamundi Salamanca-Franco, Cordoba 1995) 9...♕xd5 (9...exd5 10 ♗a3 ♕c8 11 ♕e2 ♕a6 12 ♕xa6 ♘xa6 13 ♖c1 ♔d7 leads to equality, Zayats-Dragomaretsky, Minsk 1998) 10 ♕d3 ♘bd7 (10...♘c6 11 e4 ♕d7 12 ♗g5 ♘g8 13 ♔e2 f6 14 ♗c1 ♘ge7 is also equal, Gligorić-Portisch, Torremolinos 1961) 11 e4 ♕a5 12 e5?! (Timman gives 12 f3 followed by ♔f2 as the best continuation for White, offering roughly equal chances) 12...♘d5 13 c4 ♘b4 14 ♕b3 ♘c6 15 ♗b2 0-0 16 ♗c3 ♕a6 17 ♕b5 ♕b7! with better

chances to Black, thanks to his lead in development and White's loose pawn-structure, Gligorić-Portisch, Wijk aan Zee 1975.

b) 8 f3 0-0 (*ECO* suggests 8...dxc4 9 e4 ♕d7 with chances for both sides) 9 cxd5 ♗xf1 10 ♔xf1 exd5 11 ♔f2 c5 12 ♖e1 ♘c6 13 a4 ♖c8 14 ♗a3 ♘a5 15 ♔g1 ♖e8 = Gligorić-R.Rodriguez, Manila 1968.

c) 8 ♕f3 is White's principal alternative to the main line. Now 8...0-0 9 cxd5 (here 9 ♗e2 is harmless due to 9...c5 10 0-0 ♘c6 11 cxd5 ♗xe2 12 ♕xe2 exd5 13 ♕b5 ♕c8 14 ♗a3 ♖e8 15 ♖ac1 ♘a5 = Levitt-Wells, British Ch (Swansea) 1987, while 9 e4?! asks for trouble: 9...dxe4 10 ♘xe4 ♘xe4 11 ♕xe4 ♕d7!! 12 ♗a3 ♖e8, Portisch-Fischer, Santa Monica 1966, and now Ftačnik gives 13 0-0-0 as best, although 13...♘c6 is quite pleasant for Black) and here:

c1) 9...exd5 10 ♗xa6 ♘xa6 11 ♕e2 ♕c8 12 f3!? (12 0-0 c5 13 f3 ♘c7 14 e4 ♕a6 15 ♕xa6 ♘xa6 16 e5 ♘d7 17 ♘f5 ♖fe8 18 f4 ♘c7 19 ♖b1 ♖ed8 20 ♗a3 ± Levitt-K.Arkell, British Ch (Plymouth) 1989) 12...♖e8 13 0-0 h5?! (13...c5!?) 14 ♕d3 c5 15 ♗d2 ♘c7 16 e4 h4 17 ♘f5 dxe4 18 fxe4 ♘xe4 and then:

c11) 19 ♖ae1 ♘xd2 20 ♕xd2 ♖xe1 21 ♕xe1 ♕e6 22 ♕xh4 ♘d5 (Donner-Pachman, Amsterdam 1967) and now 23 ♕g4! makes decisive material gains.

c12) 19 ♖f4! ♘xd2 20 ♕h3 g6 21 ♘h6+ ♔g7 22 ♖xf7+ ♔h8 23 ♕xh4 ♕d8 24 ♕h3 ♕g5 25 ♘g8+ ♔h5 26 ♕xh5+ gxh5 27 ♘f6 is winning for White.

c2) 9...♕xd5 10 e4 (*D*) and here:

B

c21) 10...♕b7 11 ♗e2 ♗xe2 12 ♕xe2 c5 13 0-0 (13 ♗g5!?) 13...♕a6 14 ♕xa6 ♘xa6 15 ♗a3 ♖fc8 with an equal position, Lombard-Larsen, Biel IZ 1976.

c22) 10...♕a5 and here:

c221) 11 e5 ♗b7 12 ♕d3 ♘e4 13 ♘xe4 ♗xe4 14 ♕xe4 ♕xc3+ 15 ♔d1 ♖d8 16 ♗d3 ♕xa1 17 ♔e2 ♕xa2+ 18 ♗d2 ♘c6 19 ♕xc6 ♕b2 20 ♕e4 g6 and the position is still unresolved, P.Littlewood-Christiansen, Hastings 1981/2.

c222) 11 ♗e2 ♗xe2 12 ♘xe2 ♘bd7 (12...c5 13 0-0 cxd4 14 cxd4 ♘bd7 15 a4 ♖fc8 16 ♕d3 ♕b4 17 f3 ♕c4 18 ♕xc4 ♖xc4 gives Black adequate play, Brunner-Huss, Swiss Ch 1992) 13 0-0 c5 14 ♘g3 cxd4 15 cxd4 ♖ac8 16 e5 (16 ♗f4, as suggested by Ftačnik, is well answered by 16...e5) 16...♘d5 17 ♕g4 ♔h8 18 ♘h5 ♖g8 19 ♕f3 f5 20 exf6 ♘7xf6 21 ♘xf6 ♘xf6 and Black's chances are by no means worse, Sadler-Brunner, Altensteig 1992.

c223) 11 ♗xa6 ♕xa6 12 ♗g5!? (12 ♘e2 ♘bd7 13 0-0 c5 14 ♘g3, Kuuksmaa-Koskinen, corr. 1984, 14...cxd4 15 cxd4 ♖fc8 16 e5 ♘d5 17 ♘e4 ♘f8 18 ♘d6 ♖c7 19 ♗d2 ♖d8 is given as

unclear in *ECO*) 12...♘bd7 13 ♕e2! and now:

c2231) 13...♕xe2+?! (this leads to an endgame that is slightly uncomfortable for Black) 14 ♔xe2 c5 15 a4! ♖fc8 16 ♖hc1 (16 ♖hb1!? was suggested by Ftačnik and may well be more accurate) 16...♔f8 17 f3 ♘e8 18 ♗f4 cxd4 19 cxd4 ♔e7 20 ♘f1 ± Knaak-Wahls, Baden-Baden 1992.

c2232) Knaak gives 13...♕a3 14 ♖c1 c5 15 0-0 with chances for both sides as Black's best.

8...♗xc4

Black has some alternatives that deserve a closer look:

a) 8...h5 and now, rather than 9 ♕a4+ ♕d7 10 ♕xd7+ ♔xd7 11 cxd5 exd5 = Øgaard-Larsen, Manila 1975, Larsen points out that 9 h4 ♗xc4 10 ♗xc4 dxc4 11 e4 ♘c6 12 ♕a4 is somewhat better for White.

b) 8...dxc4 makes White's last move a true pawn sacrifice. After 9 ♗e2 (9 e4 ♕d7 10 ♗e2 is line 'b1') 9...♕d7, we have:

b1) 10 e4 ♘c6 11 0-0 0-0-0 12 ♕c2 h5 13 ♖fd1 ♘e7 (13...h4 14 ♘f1 ♘a5 15 ♗b4 ♕c6 16 f3 ♘h5 17 ♘e3 ♘f4 18 ♗f1 gives White compensation for the pawn, Najdorf-Donner, Wijk aan Zee 1971) 14 ♗c1 ♖dg8 15 ♘f1 g5 16 ♘e3 ♗b7 17 f3 g4 18 ♘xc4 with a better game for White thanks to his two bishops and more space, Graf-Cvek, Mitropa Cup (Leipzig) 2002.

b2) 10 ♗f3 ♘d5 was played in Ornstein-Hecht, Cienfuegos 1975. *ECO* then gives 11 ♕c1 followed by e4 with compensation for the pawn as White's best.

9 ♗xc4 dxc4 *(D)*

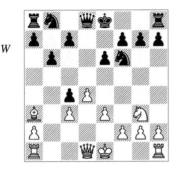

10 0-0

Or:

a) 10 e4 ♕d7 11 0-0 transposes to the main line.

b) 10 ♕a4+ is the choice for those who don't fancy playing the gambit without the light-squared bishops, or who like endgames: 10...♕d7 11 ♕xc4 ♕c6 (11...h5?! 12 h4 ♘c6 13 e4 0-0-0 14 ♕e2 ♔b8 15 ♗c1! is much better for White, Gligorić-Speelman, Lucerne OL 1982) 12 ♕xc6+ ♘xc6 and now:

b1) 13 ♖c1 0-0-0 14 c4 transposes to line 'b31'.

b2) 13 ♔e2 ♘a5 14 ♗b4 ♘c4 15 ♔d3 ♘b2+ 16 ♔c2 ♘c4 = led shortly to a draw in H.Olafsson-King, Dortmund 1988.

b3) 13 c4 0-0-0 (13...♘a5 14 ♖c1 ♖c8 15 e4 c5 16 d5 0-0 17 0-0 ± Spassky-Szabo, Amsterdam 1973) and then:

b31) 14 ♖c1 ♔b7 15 ♔e2 ♖d7 and here:

b311) 16 f3 ♖hd8 17 ♗b2 (Timman-Korchnoi, Dortmund 1994) and Ftačnik gives 17...h6 18 ♖hd1 ♘e8 19 ♘e4 f5 as unclear.

b312) 16 ♖hd1 ♖hd8 17 ♗b2 ♘e8 18 f4 g6 19 h4 ♘a5 20 e4 ♘d6 21 c5

♘dc4 22 ♗c3 f5 and Black has solved his opening problems; the position is about equal, Kjeldsen-Danielsen, Danish League 1998/9.

b313) 16 ♗b2 ♖hd8 17 f3 ♘e8 18 ♘e4 h6 19 ♘d2 f6 20 h4 e5 21 d5 ♘b8 22 e4 c5 with a defensible position for Black, although also rather boring as only White has any chances of winning, Lugovoi-Emelin, St Petersburg Ch 1995.

b32) 14 ♔e2 ♖d7 (14...♔b7 15 f3 ♖d7 16 h4 ♖hd8 17 ♖hd1 ♘a5 18 ♖ac1 c5 19 ♗b2 cxd4 20 ♗xd4 ♘e8 21 ♘e4 ♘c6 22 ♗c3 is slightly better for White, Gulko-Rechlis, Oz.com blitz 2000) 15 ♖hd1 (15 ♖ac1 ♔b7 transposes to line 'b31') 15...♖hd8 16 ♖ac1 ♘e7 17 e4 ♘g6 18 ♗b2 c5 19 d5 e5 20 f3 ♘e8 21 h4!? f6 (21...♘xh4 22 ♗xe5 f6 23 ♖h1 g5 24 ♗c3 ♘xg2 25 ♘h5 ♖f7 26 ♖cg1 ♘h4 27 f4 is much better for White) 22 h5 ♘f4+ 23 ♔f2 ♘d6 and although Black should be able to defend this, White has the initiative and can keep pressing and pressing, leaving Black with rather dull prospects, Nenashev-Klarenbeek, Khania 1993.

10...♕d7

This has become Black's standard way to hold the pawn. Two other tries:

a) 10...♕d5 doesn't have any independent importance since after 11 e4, 11...♕b5 transposes to the main line, whereas the greedy 11...♘xe4? lands Black in trouble after 12 ♕g4 ♘xg3 13 ♕xg7 ♘xf1 14 ♕xh8+ ♔d7 15 ♖xf1 ± Christiansen.

b) 10...h5!? has only been tried out once, by the adventurous Vasily Emelin: 11 ♕f3 (11 ♕a4+ ♕d7 12 ♕xc4 h4 13 ♘e2 ♕c6 is absolutely fine for

Black) 11...♕d5 12 e4 ♕g5 13 ♖fe1 ♘c6 14 ♖ab1 h4 15 ♘f1 h3 16 g3 ♕a5 17 ♘e3 ♕xc3 18 ♗b2 ♘xd4 19 ♕d1? ♕xe1+! 0-1 Norri-Emelin, St Petersburg 1997. This line deserves further tests.

11 e4

11 ♖b1!? has achieved good results: 11...h5 (or 11...♘c6?! 12 ♕e2 ♘a5 13 ♗b4 ♘b7 14 ♕xc4 ♘d6 15 ♕d3 ♕c6 16 ♗xd6 cxd6 17 c4 ± Singleton-Clarke, corr. 1981) 12 h4 ♕c6 (Yudasin recommends 12...♘c6 followed by ...0-0-0) 13 e4 ♘bd7 14 d5! ♕b7?! (according to Lautier, Black should play 14...exd5, even though 15 exd5 ♕xd5 16 ♖e1+ ♔d8 17 ♕a4 ♖e8 18 ♖ed1 ♕e6 19 ♖b2!, threatening both ♖bd2 and ♖e2, gives White more than sufficient compensation for the pawns) 15 dxe6 fxe6 16 ♕a4 0-0-0 17 ♕xc4 ± Lautier-P.Nikolić, Wijk aan Zee 1997. If White doesn't manage to find an advantage in the main line, this seems like the way to go.

11...♕b5 (D)

11...♘c6 12 ♕e2 h5 13 e5 (ECO gives 13 ♖fd1!? and 13 ♖fe1!? intending ♘f1-d2 as alternatives) 13...♘d5, Kozma-Pachman, Czechoslovak Ch (Luhačovice) 1968, 14 ♕xc4 ♘a5 15 ♕d3 ♕a4 16 ♗c1 0-0-0 with chances for both sides according to Hort.

12 ♖b1!?

This is currently the critical move. Other tries include:

a) 12 ♕c2 ♘c6 13 ♖fe1 0-0-0 14 ♖eb1 ♕a5 15 ♗b4 ♕g5 16 ♕e2 h5 17 ♘f1 h4 18 f3 ♘h5 19 ♕xc4 ♘f4 20 ♖b2 = Vaïsser-Rechlis, Tel-Aviv 1992.

b) 12 d5 ♘bd7 13 dxe6 fxe6 (Szabo-Hort, Wijk aan Zee 1973) 14 f4 0-0-0 15 ♗e7 ♖de8 16 a4 gives

W

White enough compensation for the pawn – Trifunović.

c) 12 f4 ♘bd7 13 ♕c2 ♕a6 14 ♕b2 h5 is still unresolved, Cebalo-de Firmian, Vršac 1983.

d) 12 ♕f3!? ♘bd7 (Christiansen-de Firmian, USA Ch (Greenville) 1983) 13 ♖fe1!? intending ♘f5 ± ECO.

12...♕a6 13 ♗b4 ♘c6

13...♘bd7 is interesting; 14 a4 c5 15 ♗a3 0-0 16 f4 ♖ad8 17 f5 e5 18 d5 ♖b8 19 ♗c1 b5 was good for Black in Dearing-Pritchett, Scottish Ch (Oban) 1996. White needs an improvement in this line, but an obvious one doesn't spring to mind; for example, 14 d5 0-0-0 doesn't seem to do the trick.

14 a4 0-0-0 15 ♕e2 h5 16 h4

Now:

a) 16...♖h6?! is both clumsy and slow; after 17 ♖fe1 ♖g6 18 ♘f1 ♔b7 19 ♘d2 e5 20 d5 ♘a5 21 ♗xa5 ♕xa5 22 ♕xc4 ♕a6 (Plachetka-Skrobek, Warsaw 1983) White should play 23 ♕a2 with an ongoing initiative.

b) The untried 16...♖dg8!? (Pliester) is better, when I don't see any obvious route to an advantage for White.

C2)

6 a3 (D)

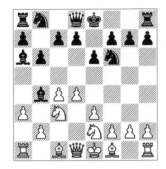

B

This move was Botvinnik's choice in his encounters with both Bronstein and Smyslov in their world championship matches in the 1950s. It leads to more strategically complicated play than 6 ♘g3 and gives the better player room to outplay his opponent, whereas Line C1 was more of a hunt for the initiative. Black has two options:

C21: 6...♗xc3+ 161
C22: 6...♗e7 166

C21)
6...♗xc3+ 7 ♘xc3 d5 *(D)*

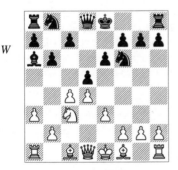

W

8 b3
Although this is by far White's most popular move, he also has a number of alternatives:

a) 8 g4?! looks like White forgot to exchange on d5 or that he failed to notice that Black didn't play 6...♗e7; after 8...♗xc4 9 ♗xc4 (relatively best is 9 g5 ♘e4 10 ♘xe4 ♗xf1 11 ♖xf1 dxe4 12 ♕g4 ♕d5 ∓) 9...dxc4 10 e4 c5 (Ortega-Akopian, Linares 1996) 11 g5 ♘fd7 12 ♗e3 0-0 Black has the better game.

b) 8 ♕a4+ c6 9 ♕b4 ♕e7 10 ♕xe7+ ♔xe7 11 b3 c5 12 dxc5 bxc5 13 ♗e2 ♖c8 is equal, Kelečević-Farago, Sarajevo 1983.

c) 8 cxd5 ♗xf1 9 ♔xf1 exd5 has been played on several occasions:

c1) 10 g3 0-0 11 b4 c6 12 ♔g2 ♘bd7 13 a4 a6 = Mecking-Rubinetti, Buenos Aires 1970.

c2) 10 f3 0-0 (10...c5!? *ECO*) 11 b4 ♖e8 12 ♖a2 ♘c6 = Tukmakov-Timman, Reykjavik 1972.

c3) 10 ♕f3 0-0 11 g4?! (in this line, this familiar pawn-push is a clear mistake as White doesn't have sufficient firepower to back it up; solid and better is 11 g3 intending ♔g2, although this is only equal) 11...♖e8 12 ♔g2 c5 13 dxc5 ♘c6 14 ♖d1 ♘e5 and White's position doesn't look very attractive any more, Wilder-Weinstein, USA 1977.

d) 8 b4 and then:

d1) 8...0-0 9 ♕f3 transposes to line 'f22'.

d2) 8...dxc4 9 ♕f3 c6 10 b5 ♗b7 11 ♗xc4 ♕c8 12 ♕g3 0-0 13 ♗b2 a6 14 bxa6 ♗xa6 = Murshed-Agzamov, Calcutta 1986.

d3) 8...♗xc4 9 ♗xc4 dxc4 10 ♕e2 ♕d7 (10...c5 11 dxc5 bxc5 12 ♕xc4 cxb4 13 axb4 0-0 14 0-0 ♘bd7 15 ♗b2 ♘e5 16 ♕b5 ♕b8 = Bass-Vladimirov, Graz 1981) 11 ♕xc4 ♕c6 12

♕xc6+ ♘xc6 13 ♗b2 (13 ♔e2 0-0-0
14 ♖d1 ♔b7 15 ♗b2 ♖d7 16 ♖ac1
♖hd8 ½-½ Rechlis-Bischoff, Berne Z
1990; there is plenty of play left in this
position and as White I would continue) 13...0-0-0 14 ♖c1 ♔b7 15 ♘e2
a5 16 b5 ♘a7 17 a4 c6 18 bxc6+ ♘xc6
19 f3!? with an initiative for White,
Kaspi-Rechlis, Israeli Cht 1999.

e) 8 ♗e2 0-0 (after 8...♗xc4 9 ♗xc4
dxc4 10 ♕a4+ ♕d7 11 ♕xc4 ♕c6 12
♕xc6+ ♘xc6 13 b4 0-0-0 14 ♗b2
White has a tiny pull due to his bishop
and spatial advantage, Ibragimov-Pav-
lović, Ilioupolis 1995) 9 cxd5 (9 b3
transposes to the main line) 9...♗xe2
10 ♕xe2 exd5 11 0-0 c5?! (Wells's
11...♖e8!? looks correct) 12 dxc5 bxc5
13 ♖d1 ♘c6 14 ♕f3 ♕a5 15 ♗d2
(Wells mentions 15 b4!? as a promising alternative) 15...♘e5 16 ♕f5 ♕c7
17 b4! favours White, Bu Xiangzhi-
Sutovsky, Shenyang 1999.

f) 8 ♕f3 (D) and here:

f1) 8...c6 9 b3 0-0 and now:
f11) 10 g4!? is aggressive:
f111) 10...♘bd7?! 11 g5 ♘e8 12
cxd5 ♗xf1 13 dxc6 ♗a6 14 cxd7 ♘d6
15 ♗b2 ♕xd7 gives Black some, but
not totally adequate, compensation

for the pawn, Gaprindashvili-Ehlvest,
Philadelphia 2001.

f112) 10...dxc4 11 bxc4 e5!? looks
like the best way to counter White's
kingside attack.

f12) 10 ♗b2 ♗b7 11 ♗e2 ♘bd7
12 0-0 ♖b8 13 cxd5 ♘xd5 14 e4 ♘xc3
15 ♕xc3 ± Kharlov-Akopian, Bastia
rpd 1999.

f2) 8...0-0 gives White a handful of
options:

f21) 9 b3 c6 transposes to line 'f1'.
f22) 9 b4 ♗b7 10 ♗e2 ♘bd7 11
♗b2 c5 12 ♖d1 cxb4 13 axb4 ♕e7 14
♗a3 a5 15 ♖b1 ♗a6 is pleasant for
Black, Hort-Seul, Essen 2000.

f23) 9 g4 c6 10 g5 ♘e8 11 cxd5
cxd5 is fully satisfactory for Black,
Pähtz-Bischoff, Bundesliga 1990/1.

f24) 9 cxd5 ♘xd5 10 ♗xa6 ♘xa6
11 0-0 c5 12 ♘xd5 ♕xd5 13 ♕xd5
exd5 14 dxc5 ♘xc5 = Kharlov-Suls-
kis, Bastia rpd 1999.

f25) 9 ♗e2 c5 10 dxc5 bxc5!? (the
alternative 10...♘bd7 11 cxd5 ♗xe2
12 ♕xe2 ♘xc5 is also fine for Black,
Taimanov-Spassky, USSR Ch (Baku)
1961) 11 cxd5 ♗xe2! 12 ♔xe2 exd5
13 ♖d1 ♘c6 14 ♘xd5 ♘xd5 15 ♖xd5
♕b6 and White's exposed king provides Black excellent compensation
for the pawn, Khasin-Sloth, corr. 1975.

8...0-0
Alternatively:

a) 8...♘c6 and now both 9 ♗e2 0-0
and 9 a4 0-0 10 ♗e2 transpose to the
main line.

b) 8...c5 9 a4 cxd4 (9...♘c6?! gets
Black into trouble: 10 ♗a3 cxd4 11
♘b5 ♘e4 12 cxd5 dxe3?! 13 f3 ♘e5
14 fxe4 ♕h4+ 15 g3 ♕f6, Avrukh-
Manor, Israeli Cht 2000, 16 ♖a2! +–)
10 exd4 0-0 11 ♘b5 ♘c6 12 ♗b2 ♖e8

13 ♗e2 e5 14 dxe5 ♘xe5 = Ojanen-Khasin, corr. 1981.

9 ♗e2

Alternatives:

a) 9 ♕f3 c6 transposes to note 'f1' to White's 8th move.

b) 9 ♗b2 ♘c6 10 cxd5 (10 ♖c1 ♘a5 11 ♘b1 dxc4 12 bxc4 c5 13 ♘d2 cxd4 14 exd4 ♖e8 is of course OK for Black, Savon-Emelin, St Petersburg 1997) 10...♗xf1 11 dxc6 ♗xg2 12 ♖g1 ♗d5! (12...♗xc6? 13 d5! will cause Black problems with all of White's available firepower aimed at g7) 13 ♕e2 ♘e8 14 e4 ♗xc6 15 0-0-0 with compensation for the pawn, Pähtz-Portisch, Bad Wörishofen 1992.

c) 9 ♗d3 and now:

c1) 9...dxc4 10 bxc4 ♘c6 and now 11 ♕e2 e5 12 d5 ♘a5 13 ♗b2 ♖e8 14 e4 ♘d7 15 ♘b5 ♘c5 is fully playable for Black, but as Pliester points out, 11 ♘b5 to meet 11...♘a5 with 12 ♗d2 may be more accurate, although Black probably will go for 11...e5!? instead.

c2) 9...c5 10 dxc5 dxc4 11 bxc4 bxc5 12 0-0 ♘c6 13 ♘b5 ♘e5 14 ♗e2 ♕b8 15 ♗b2 ♖d8 16 ♕c2 ♘eg4 17 g3 ♗b7 with chances for both sides, Shirov-Sutovsky, Tilburg 1996.

d) 9 a4 is an important alternative. Now Black has tried:

d1) 9...♕d7 10 ♗e2 ♘c6 transposes to note 'c' to Black's 10th move.

d2) 9...c5 10 ♗a3 dxc4 11 bxc4 ♘c6 12 ♘b5 ♗b7 13 ♗e2 ♘e4 14 ♗f3 (Botvinnik-Smyslov, Moscow Wch (13) 1957) 14...♘a5 is about equal.

d3) 9...♘c6 10 ♗d3 (10 ♗e2 transposes to the main line, while 10 ♗a3 transposes to the note to White's 11th move) 10...dxc4 11 bxc4 e5 12 d5 e4?! (12...♘a5!? =) 13 ♗e2 ♘e5 14 ♕d4 is

slightly better for White, Godard-Lepelletier, Gonfreville 1999.

9...♘c6 *(D)*

Or:

a) 9...dxc4 10 bxc4 ♘c6 and then: 11 0-0 is note 'a' to White's 10th move; 11 ♕c2 is note 'c' to White's 10th move; 11 ♘b5 is note 'd' to White's 10th move; 11 a4 transposes to the main line.

b) 9...♘bd7 has received some attention from the young German Dimitrij Bunzmann. A recent game went 10 0-0 c5 11 a4 ♖e8?! (Avrukh gives 11...♗b7 12 ♗a3 ♖e8 13 ♖c1!? as better, although probably still slightly favouring White) 12 ♘b5! cxd4 13 exd4 e5 14 ♘d6! ♖f8 (after 14...♖e6?! 15 ♘xf7 ♔xf7 16 cxd5 White wins material – Avrukh) 15 ♗a3 exd4 16 ♕xd4 ± Avrukh-Bunzmann, Biel 1999.

c) 9...♕d7 10 ♗b2 (this appears best, although 10 0-0 is more popular) 10...dxc4 11 bxc4 ♘c6 12 ♕a4 ♘a5 13 ♕xd7 ♘xd7 14 ♘b5 ♖fc8 15 ♗c3 ± Barle-Pritchett, Pula 1975.

d) 9...c5 10 dxc5 bxc5 11 0-0 ♘bd7 12 a4 ♗b7 13 ♗a3 ♕b6 14 ♖b1 ♘e5 15 cxd5 ♘xd5 16 ♘xd5 ♗xd5 17 ♕c2 is slightly better for White, Ulko-Sorokin, St Petersburg 2000.

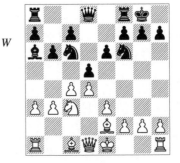

10 a4

As we have seen several times above, this is a typical plan for White in this type of position. He opens a diagonal for his dark-squared bishop and start a queenside initiative. Other moves include:

a) 10 0-0 dxc4 (10...♘a5 11 ♖b1 c6?! {11...c5!? =} 12 a4 ♕e7 13 ♗d2 ♖fe8 14 ♕e1! ± Hort-Lombardy, Reykjavik 1978) 11 bxc4 ♘a5 promises Black equal chances; e.g., 12 ♕a4 ♕e8 13 ♕b4 e5, Irzhanov-Huss, Moscow OL 1994.

b) 10 cxd5 ♗xe2 11 ♘xe2 ♕xd5 12 ♘f4 ♕b5 13 ♕d3 ♕xd3 14 ♘xd3 ♘a5 15 ♖b1 c5!? 16 dxc5 ♖fd8 17 ♔e2 ♘e4 18 ♗d2 ♘b7 19 cxb6 ♘xd2 20 ♔xd2 axb6 and Black has of course fully equalized, Heinemann-P.Schlosser, Bundesliga 1990/1.

c) 10 ♕c2 and now Black can improve over 10...e5?! 11 cxd5 ♗xe2 12 dxc6 ♗a6 13 dxe5 ♘g4 14 ♕f5 ± Supatashvili-Anastasian, Protvino Z 1993 with 10...dxc4 11 bxc4 ♘a5 12 ♘a4 ♗b7.

d) 10 ♘b5 dxc4 11 bxc4 ♘a5 12 ♗d2 c6 13 ♗xa5 bxa5 14 ♘c3 c5 = Botvinnik-Smyslov, Moscow Wch (7) 1957.

10...dxc4

This may actually be an inaccurate move-order, as White has an additional option on his next move that may cause Black headaches. Line 'c' should be the move-order of preference:

a) 10...♘a5 11 ♗a3 (11 ♘b5 does nothing for White: 11...c6 12 ♘a3 c5 13 ♘b5 cxd4 14 exd4 ♘e4 15 ♗b2 ♖c8 16 ♖c1 ♗xb5 17 axb5 ♕e7 18 0-0 ♕b4 19 f3 ♘d6 and Black is in control, M.Gurevich-Tukmakov, USSR Ch (Riga) 1985) 11...♖e8 12 0-0 ♖c8 13 ♘b5 ♘e4 14 f3 ♗xb5 15 fxe4 ♗a6 16 exd5 exd5 17 ♗g4 ♖b8 18 ♕f3 ♘xb3!? 19 ♕xf7+ ♔h8 20 ♕h5 h6 (M.Gurevich-Liu Dede, Jakarta 1996) 21 ♖ae1! ♘d2!? 22 ♖f7 ♘xc4 23 ♕g6 ♕g5 24 ♕xg5 hxg5 25 ♗e7 (Gurevich) and White has the initiative.

b) 10...♖e8 11 0-0 (or 11 ♗b2 ♘a5 12 0-0 c6 13 ♖b1 ♕c8 14 cxd5 ♗xe2 15 ♕xe2 cxd5 16 ♘b5 ♕d7 17 ♖fc1 ♖ec8 = ½-½ Zilberman-Soffer, Rishon le Zion 1992) 11...dxc4 12 bxc4 ♘a5 13 ♘b5 c6 14 ♘a3 e5 15 ♗b2 exd4 16 exd4 ♘d5 = Shabalov-Burnett, St Paul 2000.

c) 10...♕d7 11 0-0 and now:

c1) 11...dxc4 12 bxc4 transposes to note 'a' to White's 12th move.

c2) 11...♖fd8 12 ♗b2 (12 ♘b5 ♘a5 13 ♗b2 dxc4 14 bxc4 c6 15 ♘a3 c5 16 dxc5 ♕e7 17 ♕c2 ♕xc5 18 ♖fd1 ♗b7 = Aleksandrov-Akopian, New Delhi FIDE 2000) 12...♘a5 13 ♘b5 c6 14 ♘a3 ♕e7 (14...dxc4 is probably superior; e.g., 15 ♘xc4 ♘xc4 16 bxc4 ♖ac8 {16...c5 17 d5! ±} followed by ...c5 =) 15 ♗c3 ♖ab8 16 ♕c2 dxc4 17 ♘xc4 (17 b4!?) 17...♘xc4 18 bxc4 c5 19 a5 b5 = Boersma-Timman, Dutch Ch (Leeuwarden) 1981.

We now return to the position after 10...dxc4 *(D)*:

11 bxc4

As mentioned above, White may have something even better. Fischer once recommended 11 ♗a3, when after 11...♖e8 White has:

a) 12 ♗xc4 ♗xc4 13 bxc4 ♘a5 14 ♕e2 ♕d7 15 0-0 ♕c6 and Black is calling the shots, Vezzosi-Zaja, Reggio Emilia 2001/2.

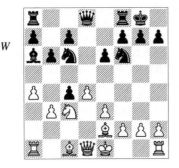

W

b) 12 b4!? ♘e7 and now 13 0-0 ♘ed5 14 ♖c1 c6 15 ♗f3 b5 16 a5 ♕c7 left Black a clear pawn up in Evans-Fischer, USA Ch (New York) 1965. Instead Fischer recommended 13 b5 ♗b7 14 0-0, which Pliester surprisingly claimed had yet to be tested, although his countrymen gave it a test in Schouten-Timman, Dutch Ch (Leeuwarden) 1975: 14...♘ed5 15 ♕c2 ♘xc3 16 ♕xc3 ♘e4 17 ♕c2 ♕g5 18 f4 ♕g6 19 ♗xc4 ♖ac8 20 ♖ac1 c5 and Black had a fully satisfactory position.

c) 12 bxc4 ♘a5 (12...e5 13 d5 ♘a5 14 ♘b5 ♗xb5 15 axb5 ♘b7 16 ♗b4 ♘d7 17 ♖a3 ♘bc5 18 ♕a1 ± Avrukh-Barsov, Antwerp 1999) 13 ♘b5 and now:

c1) 13...c6 14 ♘d6 ♖e7 15 0-0 (theory holds 15 e4 ♖d7 16 e5 to be better for White, but in *Gambit Tiger-Nimzo*, Cadaques 2001, it was proved that it isn't so clear: 16...♘e8 17 ♕c2 ♘xd6 18 exd6 c5 19 dxc5 bxc5 20 0-0 ♖xd6 with a better game for Black) 15...c5 16 e4! ♖d7? (16...♕xd6 17 e5 ♕d8 18 exf6 ♖d7! is critical) 17 e5 ♘e8 18 dxc5 bxc5 19 ♗xc5 ♗xc4 20 ♖b1 ♖c8 21 ♘xc8! ♖xd1 22 ♘e7+ ♔h8 23 ♖fxd1 +– Bielecki-Skrobek, corr. 1977.

c2) 13...♗b7 14 0-0 ♘e4 15 ♗b4 a6 16 ♘a3 c5 17 ♗xa5 bxa5 18 ♕d3 ♕c7 19 ♗f3 f5 and Black has got over the worst, Zaja-Hulak, Croatian Ch playoff (Zagreb) (4) 2000.

11...♕d7

Traditionally theory has condemned both of Black's alternatives, but it appears things are not as clear as was once thought:

a) 11...e5 12 d5 ♘a5 13 ♗a3 ♖e8 14 ♘b5 ♕d7 15 0-0 ('±' *ECO*) 15...c6 16 dxc6 ♕xc6 17 ♕c2 ♘b7 18 ♖ac1 ♖ec8 19 ♕b2 ♕e6 20 ♖fd1 ♘c5 = A.Marić-Polaczek, Biel 1992.

b) 11...♘a5 and now:

b1) 12 ♘b5 and then:

b11) 12...♕d7 13 ♗d2 (13 0-0 c6 14 ♘a3 c5 15 ♗b2 ♖fd8 is similar to the main line) 13...c6 14 ♘a3 ♘b7 15 0-0 c5 16 ♗c3 cxd4 17 exd4 ♖ac8 18 ♘b5 (Lugovoi-Eismont, Balatonbereny 1993) and here 18...♘d6!? is best; for example, 19 d5 ♘fe4 20 ♗b4 ♖fd8 21 ♕d4 ♘c5 with approximately equal chances.

b12) 12...c6 13 ♘a3 c5 14 ♘b5 (or 14 ♗d2 ♘c6 15 dxc5 bxc5 16 0-0 ♕e7 17 ♗f3 ♗b7 = Rivas-Franco, Pamplona 1994/5) 14...♗b7 15 0-0 a6 16 ♘a3 ♗c6 17 ♗b2 ♕d7 18 dxc5 ♕xd1 19 ♗xd1 bxc5 and Black has equalized, M.Gurevich-Vladimirov, Batumi rpd tt 2001.

b2) 12 ♗a3 ♖e8 13 ♘b5 and now Black may be able to improve over 13...c6 14 ♘d6 ♖e7 15 0-0 ± Donner-Kupper, Venice 1967, with 13...♗b7 14 0-0 a6 15 ♘c3 ♖c8 intending ...c5, but this deserves a closer look before being tested in practice.

We now return to the position after 11...♕d7 *(D)*:

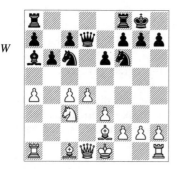

12 ♘b5

This is the only move that keeps Black under pressure. The alternatives shouldn't keep Black up at night:

a) 12 0-0 ♖fd8 13 ♗b2 ♘a5 14 ♘b5 should be compared with the main line.

b) 12 ♗a3 ♖fd8 13 0-0 e5 14 d5 ♘a5 15 ♘b5 ♗b7 16 f4 e4 17 ♗b2 c6 = Høi-Hamann, Copenhagen Ch 1980.

c) 12 ♗b2 ♘a5 13 ♘b5 c6 14 ♘a3 ♖fd8 15 0-0 ♖ac8 16 ♗d3 ♕e7 17 ♕c2 c5 = Lutsko-Brodsky, Nikolaev Z 1993.

12...♖fd8

Or:

a) 12...♘a5 transposes to note 'b11' to Black's 11th move.

b) 12...♗b7 13 f3 ♖fd8 14 0-0 ♘a5 15 ♕c2 c6 16 ♘a3 c5 17 dxc5 bxc5 = D.Gurevich-Kopec, Boston 1988.

13 ♗b2 ♘a5 14 ♕c2 c6 15 ♘a3 ♕e7 16 0-0 c5

White now has two options, neither of which has produced any advantage for White:

a) 17 ♘b5 ♗b7 18 ♗a3 (18 f3?! a6 19 ♘a3 ♘c6 20 ♖fd1 cxd4 21 exd4 ♘xd4!, Goormachtigh-Mikhalchishin, Sas van Gent 1990, and now Ivanchuk gives 22 ♗xd4 ♖xd4 23 ♖xd4 ♕c5 24

♕b2! ♖d8 25 ♖ad1 e5 26 a5! ♖xd4 27 ♖xd4 exd4 28 ♕xb6 ♕xb6 29 axb6 ♘d7 30 ♘c2 =) 18...♘c6 19 ♖fd1 a6 20 ♘c3 ♘b4 21 ♕b3 a5 22 ♘b5 h6 23 ♗b2 ♖ac8 24 f3 = Botvinnik-Smyslov, Moscow Wch (21) 1957.

b) 17 ♖fd1 ♗b7 18 ♗c3 ♘c6 19 ♕b2 ♘e4 20 ♗e1 ♕g5 21 ♗f1 with roughly equal chances, Adla-L.Bronstein, Argentine Ch (Buenos Aires) 1986.

C22)
6...♗e7 *(D)*

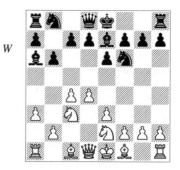

Rather than giving up the bishop-pair and helping White with his development (don't forget that on e2 the knight blocks in the light-squared bishop), Black withdraws his bishop to e7. For players who have to win as Black, this is by far the most interesting continuation. However, this line also provides excellent chances for White to grab the initiative from the opening and carry it over to the middlegame.

7 ♘f4

In one of the first games featuring 5...♗a6, Botvinnik preferred 7 ♘g3. After 7...d5 (7...h5 8 ♗d3 h4 9 ♘ge2 h3 10 g3 d5 11 cxd5 ♗xd3 12 ♕xd3 exd5 13 0-0 ♘c6 14 b4 ♕d7 15 ♗d2 a5 16 b5 ♘d8 17 f3 ± Sunye-Sisniega, Santa Catalina 1987) we have:

a) 8 b3 0-0 9 ♗e2 c5 10 0-0 ♘c6 = Kristinsson – Brinck-Claussen, Varna OL 1962.

b) 8 ♕a4+ c6 9 cxd5 ♗xf1 10 ♘xf1 ♘xd5 11 ♗d2 ♘xc3 12 ♗xc3 ♕d5 13 f3 ♗h4+ 14 ♔e2 0-0 15 g3 ♗e7 and Black has a pleasant position, Shapiro-Ashley, New York 1989.

c) 8 cxd5 ♗xf1 9 ♘xf1 (White can also take with king or rook, but neither promises White any chance of an advantage) 9...exd5 (9...♘xd5 can also be considered, although White can claim an edge after 10 ♘g3 ♘xc3 11 bxc3 ♘c6 12 0-0 0-0 13 ♕g4 ♖e8 14 e4, Garcia Padron-Sisniega, Santa Catalina 1987) 10 ♘g3 ♕d7 (in Hrivnak-Veselovsky, Moravian Cht 1999, Black chose a somewhat different continuation: 10...0-0 11 0-0 ♖e8 12 ♗d2 ♕d7 13 ♖c1 c6 14 ♕f3 ♘a6 15 ♖fd1 ♘c7 16 ♗e1 ♘e6 =) 11 ♕f3 ♘c6 12 0-0 g6 13 ♗d2 0-0 14 ♘ce2 h5! 15 ♖fc1 h4 16 ♘f1 ♘e4 and Black has equalized, Botvinnik-Bronstein, Moscow Wch (17) 1951.

7...d5

This move is the correct response to White's knight jump to f4: Black immediately starts to create counterplay. Other moves are somewhat passive:

a) 7...d6 8 b4 (8 d5 and 8 ♗d3 are also considered better for White) 8...c6 9 ♗b2 0-0 10 ♗e2 e5 11 ♘h3 ♘bd7 12 0-0 ± Henley-Benjamin, USA Ch (Berkeley) 1984.

b) 7...0-0 and now:

b1) 8 b4 ♗b7 9 ♗e2 a5 10 b5 d6 11 ♗f3 ♕c8 12 0-0 ♘bd7 13 ♗b2 ♖e8

14 ♖c1 is slightly better for White, Izeta-Ubilava, Elgoibar 1998.

b2) 8 e4 d6 9 ♗e2 ♘bd7 10 0-0 c6 11 d5 cxd5 12 cxd5 ♗xe2 13 ♕xe2 e5 14 ♘d3 ± Reshevsky-Bisguier, New York 1957.

8 cxd5

Other moves have failed to produce an advantage, but nonetheless deserve a closer look:

a) 8 ♕b3 c6 9 cxd5 exd5 10 ♗xa6 ♘xa6 11 ♕a4 ♘b8 12 0-0 0-0 13 ♗d2 ♗d6 14 ♘ce2 ♕c7 15 ♖ac1 ♖c8 = Aleksandrov-Emelin, Moscow 2002.

b) 8 ♕f3 c6 and now:

b1) 9 b3 is fairly tame and shouldn't cause Black any headaches: 9...♗d6 10 ♗b2 0-0 11 ♗d3 ♕e7 12 0-0 ♖e8 13 ♖fd1 ♗b7 14 cxd5 exd5 15 b4 b5 16 ♖e1 ♘e4 = Van der Wiel-Timman, Sarajevo 1984.

b2) 9 cxd5 cxd5 10 ♗xa6 ♘xa6 11 0-0 0-0 12 ♗d2 ♕d7 (Janda-Kozak, Dečin 1995) and now 13 ♖fc1!? looks like the right move.

c) 8 b3 0-0 and here:

c1) 9 ♕f3 c6 10 ♗b2 ♗d6 transposes to line 'b1'.

c2) 9 ♗d3 c5 10 cxd5 cxd4 11 ♗xa6 ♘xa6 12 ♕xd4 ♘c5 13 ♖b1 ♗d6 14 dxe6 ♗xf4 15 ♕xd8 ♖fxd8 16 exf4 ♘d3+ 17 ♔e2 ♖ac8 18 ♗d2 (Shariyazdanov-Belozerov, Ekaterinburg 1996) and here Black can go for 18...fxe6 19 ♖hd1 ♘g4 20 f3 ♖xc3! 21 ♗xc3 ♘xf4+ 22 ♔e1 ♘xg2+ 23 ♔e2 ♘f4+ 24 ♔e1 ♘g2+ with a perpetual check.

c3) 9 ♗e2 c6 10 0-0 ♘bd7 11 ♗b2 was played in Arencibia-Canda, Bayamo 1989, and now 11...dxc4!? 12 bxc4 e5 13 dxe5 ♘xe5 would have led to an equal position.

c4) 9 ♗b2 ♗b7 10 ♗d3 ♘bd7 11 0-0 c6 12 ♕e2 ♗d6 13 ♘h5 ♕e7 14 e4 (Høi-Kristiansen, Danish Ch (Odense) 1980) and here Høi gives 14...dxc4!? 15 ♗xc4 e5 with chances for both sides.

8...♗xf1 *(D)*

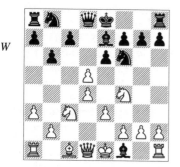

9 ♔xf1

The piece sacrifice 9 dxe6 has often been dismissed, but the game Hillebrand-Heide, corr. 1968 seems to prove the dismissal premature: 9...♗a6 10 exf7+ ♔xf7 11 e4 c5 (11...♗c4!? is as yet untried; then 12 e5 ♘c6 13 ♗e3! ♔g8 14 exf6 ♗xf6 is a bit messy, even though I tend to prefer White's chances) 12 e5 (*ECO* only discusses the merits of 12 ♕b3+; e.g., 12...c4 13 ♕d1 ♘c6 14 ♗e3 ♗d6 15 e5 ♘xe5 16 dxe5 ♗xe5 17 ♘fd5 ♖e8 18 ♘xf6 ♕xf6 with better chances for Black, Lombardy-Keres, Mar del Plata 1957) 12...♕xd4 ('∓' Taimanov) 13 e6+ ♔f8 14 ♕f3 ♘c6 (14...♕e5+ 15 ♗e3 g5 16 ♘fe2 ♗xe2 17 ♔xe2 ♘c6 18 ♕xc6 ♔g7 19 ♖ad1 is also better for White) 15 ♕xc6 ♖d8 16 ♕f3 ♗d6 17 ♗e3 and White was simply a pawn up. Given the importance of this (re-)discovery, it would be interesting to see it

tested by top players. For now we will have to wait and see what the future will bring.

9...♘xd5

In 9...exd5 Black has an equally important alternative that has been the battleground for some of the most interesting games in the Fischer Variation. 10 g4 (10 ♕f3 will normally transpose to line 'c2'; e.g., 10...c6 11 g4 g5 12 ♘h5 ♘xh5 13 gxh5) and here:

a) 10...c6!? 11 g5 ♘e4!? (11...♘fd7 was once considered obligatory, as in the stem game of 10 g4, Botvinnik-Smyslov, Moscow Wch (2) 1954: 12 h4 ♗d6 13 e4 dxe4 14 ♘xe4 ♗xf4 15 ♗xf4 0-0 16 h5 with a dangerous attack for White) 12 h4 ♗d6 13 ♕g4 (13 ♕f3!?) 13...♕d7! 14 ♕xd7+ ♘xd7 15 ♘fe2 (R.Bagirov-Allahverdiev, Baku 1998) and now 15...h6! leaves Black with the better chances.

b) 10...0-0!? 11 ♕f3 (11 g5 ♘e4 12 ♘cxd5 ♗xg5 13 ♕c2 ♘f6 14 h4 ♗h6 15 ♘xf6+ ♕xf6 is fine for Black, P.Wells-Pigott, British Ch (Morecambe) 1981) 11...c6 12 ♖g1 ♘a6 13 ♗d2 ♘c7 14 ♖e1 ♖e8 15 g5 ♘e4 16 ♘xe4 dxe4 17 ♕xe4 ♗xg5 18 ♕g2 ♗h6 = Lutsko-Emelin, Tallinn 2001.

c) 10...g5 11 ♘h5 (11 ♘d3 is less threatening: 11...h5 12 gxh5 ♖xh5 13 ♘e5 c6 14 ♕f3 ♕c8 15 h3 ♘bd7 is equal, Filip-Pachman, Prague Z 1954) 11...♘xh5 12 gxh5 *(D)* and the tension grows. Black has tried:

c1) 12...♖f8 13 ♕f3 c6 14 e4 dxe4 15 ♕xe4 f5 16 ♕e2 (White can also play 16 ♕e5! and after 16...♘d7, the reply 17 ♕e6 gives White the better game) 16...f4 17 ♕e4 ♕d7 18 h4! gxh4 19 ♗xf4 ♕f5 20 ♖e1 ♕xe4 21

B

♖xe4 ± Sundararajan-Peralta, Erevan jr Wch 1999.

c2) 12...c6 13 ♕f3 ♘a6 (13...♖f8 is line 'c1') 14 e4 ♘c7 and now:

c21) 15 ♖g1 h6 16 h4 is given as better for White in *ECO*, but this evaluation was questioned in Manes-Walters, corr. 1984: 16...dxe4 17 ♕xe4 ♕d7 18 hxg5 ♕h3+ 19 ♔e1 0-0-0 and Black's lead in development more than compensates for the small material deficit.

c22) 15 h4 h6 16 hxg5 hxg5 17 ♗d2 ♔f8 18 ♖e1 (18 e5!? is better), Lukov-Thormann, Bulgaria 1980 and now Black should opt for 18...dxe4! 19 ♕xe4 ♕d7 with chances for both sides.

10 ♘cxd5

White has two interesting alternatives:

a) 10 e4 ♘xf4 (10...♘xc3 is also possible) 11 ♗xf4 0-0 12 ♖c1 ♕d7 13 ♕a4 c6 14 ♖d1 ♕b7 15 d5 (15 g3!?) 15...cxd5 16 exd5 ♗f6 17 ♘b5 ♘d7! and Black has a small lead in development, Grotnes-Inkiov, Gausdal 1990.

b) 10 ♕f3 c6 11 g3 0-0 12 ♔g2 ♘d7 13 ♖d1 ♘xc3! (13...♕c7 14 e4 ♘xc3 15 ♕xc3 ♖ac8 16 ♗e3 ♕b7 17 f3 ♖fe8 18 ♖ac1 ♗f8 19 b4 is slightly

better for White, D.Gurevich-H.Olafsson, Reykjavik 1982) 14 bxc3 ♕c7 (intending 15 e4 e5) equalizes.

10...exd5 (D)

W

11 ♕h5

Other moves are harmless:

a) 11 ♕a4+ c6 12 ♗d2 ♕d7 13 ♗b4 ♗d6 14 ♖e1 f5 = Moiseev-Veselovsky, USSR 1980.

b) 11 ♕f3 c6 12 b4 a6 13 ♗b2 ♘d7 14 ♖c1 ♖c8 15 g3 0-0 16 ♔g2 b5 = Moskalenko-Utemov, Moscow 1994.

11...♗g5

11...c6 12 ♘e6 g6 13 ♕e5 ♗f6 14 ♘xd8+ ♗xe5 is another fascinating option; White now has two moves:

a) 15 ♘xf7 ♔xf7 16 dxe5 ♘d7 17 f4 ♘c5 18 b4 ♘e4 19 ♗b2 ♔e6 20 ♔e2 h5 21 ♖hc1 c5 22 ♖ab1 (intending to penetrate by means of ♗a1, bxc5 and ♖b7) 22...g5 23 ♖f1 ♖af8 24 fxg5 ♖fg8! (Timman-Hübner, Montreal 1979) and now Hübner gives 25 ♖f4! ♖xg5 26 g3 h4 27 g4 h3 ±.

b) 15 ♘xc6 ♘xc6 16 dxe5 ♘xe5 17 ♗d2 ♔e7 18 ♗c3 (18 ♔e2 ½-½ was Unzicker-Korchnoi, Johannesburg 1980, but in the final position, White still has a slight edge to work with) 18...f6 19 ♔e2 ♔e6 20 ♖hd1 ♖hd8 21

置d4 f5 22 置ad1 ± Rechlis-Adams,
Manila IZ 1990; however, this is not
the type of position you can expect to
win against Adams from!

12 ②e6

12 e4 is a more aggressive line, but
Black nonetheless still equalizes after
12...奧xf4 13 奧xf4 ②c6 14 置c1 (according to Pliester, White should look
into 14 exd5 ②e7 15 置e1 0-0 16 d6
cxd6 17 奧g5 f6 18 豐e2, but 18...fxg5!
19 豐xe7 豐xe7 20 置xe7 置ac8 is just
better for Black) 14...②e7 15 奧xc7
豐d7 16 exd5 0-0! 17 d6 ②f5 18 豐f3
置ac8 19 豐c6 置fd8! 20 豐xd7 置xd7 21
置d1 ②xd6 22 奧xd6 置xd6 23 壺e2
置c2+ 24 置d2 置xd2+ 25 壺xd2 置xd4+
½-½ Saeed-Timman, Taxco IZ 1985.

12...g6 13 豐xg5 fxe6 14 豐e5

14 豐xd8+?! is mistaken, as illustrated in the game M.Remmler-Inkiov,
Avoine 1995: 14...壺xd8 15 奧d2 ②c6
16 壺e2 壺d7 17 置ac1 a5 and Black's
knight is much better than White's
lame bishop.

**14...壺d7 15 豐g7+ 壺c8 16 奧d2
②c6 17 置c1 壺b7 18 壺e2 豐e7 19
豐xe7 ②xe7**

½-½ Corral Blanco-Vallejo Pons,
Spanish Cht (Barcelona) 2000.

D)

5...②e4 (D)

This move dates back to the game
Rubinstein-Kashdan, Hamburg OL
1930. The line doesn't have a name as
such, which tempts me to dub it the
American Variation, due to Kashdan
playing it first and then through the efforts of Santasiere, Bisguier and nowadays de Firmian. Nowadays this line
is employed with some frequency by
Kuzmin, Andersson, Korchnoi, Ward,

Timman, Cu.Hansen and Adams. These
are not players you would normally be
able to fit into the same group since
their playing styles and temperaments
are very varied.

The line bears some resemblance to
the Dutch Variation, while many of the
positions that arise have some similar-
ities to those found in the 4 豐c2 lines,
which for obvious reasons are not covered here. Black's idea is to exchange
some minor pieces to make it easier
for himself to control the e4-square.
Here we have two main lines:

D1: 6 奧d2   171
D2: 6 豐c2   174

White also has the following options:

a) 6 a3?! 豐h4 7 ②g3 奧xc3+ 8
bxc3 b7 9 奧d3 f5 10 0-0 0-0 11 豐e1
②c6 12 f3 ②d6 with a pleasant game
for Black, Speelman-de Firmian, Brussels rpd 1992.

b) 6 豐b3 c5 7 a3 奧a5 8 f3 奧xc3+
9 bxc3 ②d6 10 e4 ②c6 11 豐a4 (Paa-
sikangas-Kärner, Finnish Cht 1994)
11...cxd4 12 cxd4 豐h4+ 13 g3 (13
②g3 ②xd4 is also fine for Black)
13...②f6 14 豐b3 e5 15 奧b2 奧a6 with
a good game for Black.

c) 6 f3 is a reasonably popular side-line. Black has two principal answers:

c1) 6...♗xc3+!? is called dubious in *ECO*. After 7 bxc3 ♘d6 8 ♘g3 ♘c6 (*ECO* quotes 8...♗a6?! 9 ♕a4 ♕h4 10 ♗d3 ♘f5 11 ♗xf5 exf5 12 0-0 ♕f6 13 e4 ♘c6 14 ♕a3! ♕xc4 15 ♖e1 ± Meulders-Winants, Belgian Ch 1983) 9 e4 ♗a6 10 e5?! (Pliester mentions that Black should aim for a position such as the one that would arise after 10 ♕a4 ♘a5, but in fact White should prefer this, since after 11 c5 he is perfectly OK) 10...♘xc4 11 ♗d3 ♘6a5 12 0-0 ♗b7 (12...d5!?) 13 ♕e2 ♗d5 favours Black, Fedorowicz-Ward, Cannes 1988.

c2) 6...♘xc3 7 bxc3 (*D*) (7 ♘xc3?! exchanges another set of minor pieces while still ending up with doubled pawns, easing Black's task tremendously: 7...♗xc3+ 8 bxc3 ♘c6 9 e4 ♗a6 10 ♕a4 ♕h4+ 11 g3 ♕h5 12 ♔f2 ♕a5 with an easy game for Black, even though White still has plenty to play for, J.Lauridsen-Ward, Copenhagen 1997) and here:

c21) 7...♗d6 8 e4 ♘c6 9 e5 (9 ♘g3? ♕h4 10 e5 ♘xe5 11 dxe5 ♗xe5 12 f4 ♗xc3+ 13 ♗d2 ♗xa1 14 ♕xa1

0-0 ∓ Muir-Monier, Thessaloniki OL 1984) 9...♗e7 10 ♘g3 ♗a6 11 ♗d3 ♘a5 12 ♕e2 d5 13 cxd5 ♗xd3 14 ♕xd3 ♕xd5 = Burger-Bisguier, New York 1969.

c22) 7...♗e7 and now:

c221) 8 ♘g3 ♘c6 (or 8...h5!? 9 ♗d3 h4 10 ♘e4 ♘c6 11 0-0 ♗a6 12 f4 ♘a5 13 f5 exf5 14 ♖xf5 g6 15 ♖f2 0-0 = Ashley-Adams, New York 1996) 9 ♗d3 ♗a6 (9...h5 can again be considered; e.g., 10 0-0 h4 11 ♘e4 ♗a6 12 ♕e2 ♘a5 13 ♘d2 d5 14 cxd5 ♗xd3 15 ♕xd3 ♕xd5 16 c4 ♕d7 with approximately equal chances, Yusupov-Handke, Altenkirchen 2001) 10 0-0 ♘a5 11 ♕e2 d5 (in Shirov-Adams, Las Palmas 1994, Black was slightly worse off after 11...c6 12 f4! d5 13 cxd5 ♗xd3 14 ♕xd3 exd5 15 f5) 12 cxd5 ♗xd3 13 ♕xd3 ♕xd5 14 f4 (Pomes-Narciso, Spanish Cht (Cala Galdana) 2001) 14...♕c4 15 ♕c2 0-0 gives Black a good game.

c222) 8 e4 ♘c6 9 ♘g3 ♗a6 10 ♗d3 ♘a5 11 ♕e2 d6 (or 11...0-0 12 0-0, Evans-Santasiere, USA Ch (New York) 1951, 12...c5 13 d5 e5 {13...d6!?} 14 ♘f5 ♗g5 ± Schwarz) 12 0-0 ♕d7 13 ♖b1 h5! 14 ♖e1 h4 15 ♘f1 c5 16 ♗e3 ♖c8 17 ♘d2 e5 18 f4 ♗f6! and Black has solved his opening problems, I.Sokolov-D.Johansen, Manila OL 1992.

D1)
6 ♗d2 ♘xd2

No other move makes sense for Black at this point; despite White's dark-squared bishop being restricted by his own pawns at the moment, it is the right piece to eliminate.

7 ♕xd2 (*D*)

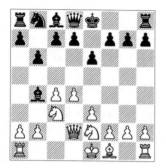

B

7...0-0

Black's alternatives also deserve attention:

a) 7...d5 8 cxd5 exd5 9 a3 ♗e7 10 g3 (10 ♘f4 is another option) 10...c6 11 ♗g2 0-0 12 0-0 ♘d7 13 ♕c2 ♘f6 14 ♘f4 g6 15 ♕a4 ♕d6 16 ♖ac1 and White has a slight pull, M.Gurevich-Enders, Eger 1987.

b) 7...f5 8 g3 ♗b7 9 d5 0-0 10 ♗g2 ♕f6 11 0-0 e5 12 a3 ♗xc3 13 ♘xc3 d6 14 ♘b5 ♖f7 15 b4 and White has somewhat the better prospects, Aleksandrov-Yerotsky, Minsk 2000.

c) 7...♗a6 8 a3 and here:

c1) 8...♗xc3 9 ♘xc3 (9 ♕xc3 0-0 10 b4 {10 ♘f4 has also been tried} 10...d6 11 ♘f4 ♘d7 12 ♗e2 ♗b7 13 0-0 ♕g5 14 f3 e5 15 ♘h3 exd4 16 ♕xd4 ♕e5 = Taimanov-Zsinka, Budapest 1982) 9...d5 10 b4 dxc4 11 b5 ♗b7 12 e4 a6 13 ♗xc4 0-0 14 0-0 axb5 15 ♗xb5 ♕e7 16 a4 ♖d8 17 ♕e3 with a better game for White; Black has a hard time getting active counterplay, Hübner-de Firmian, Manila IZ 1990.

c2) 8...♗e7 9 ♘f4 ♗g5 (9...♘c6 10 b4 ♗b7 11 ♗e2 0-0 12 0-0 a5 13 b5 ♘b8 14 ♘d3 ± Knaak-Plachetka, Trnava 1983) 10 ♘h5 g6 11 ♘g3

(D.Gurevich-Christiansen, Estes Park 1984) and here Gurevich recommends playing 11...0-0!? followed by ...f5, leaving White only slightly better, an evaluation that may well be a matter of taste.

d) 7...♗b7 8 a3 (or 8 d5!? ♘a6 9 a3 ♗xc3 10 ♘xc3 ♘c5 11 ♖d1 a5 12 b4 axb4 13 axb4 ♘a6! 14 ♘b5 0-0 15 ♗e2, Shirov-Adams, Leon 1995, and here Shirov gives 15...exd5!? 16 cxd5 ♕e7 17 d6 cxd6, intending 18 ♘xd6 ♗xg2 19 ♖g1 ♗h3 20 ♕d4 g6 with an unclear position) and now:

d1) 8...♗e7 and then:

d11) 9 ♘f4 ♗g5!? 10 ♗d3 0-0 11 0-0 (O.Rodriguez-I.Sokolov, Barcelona 1992) and now Sokolov gives 11...d5 as Black's best. His analysis continues 12 cxd5 ♗xf4 13 exf4 (13 dxe6 ♗d6 14 exf7+ ♔h8) 13...exd5 '='. Although my computer prefers White in this position, I tend to like Black's chances due to White's weakened pawn-structure.

d12) 9 0-0-0 ♘c6 10 ♔b1 ♘a5 11 ♘f4 ♗a6 12 c5 ♗xf1 13 ♖hxf1 0-0 14 b4 ♘c4 15 ♕a2 d5 16 cxd6 ♘xd6 leaves Black with a good game, Suba-Luce, London 1990.

d13) 9 e4!? has been given as slightly better for White by I.Sokolov, but after 9...0-0 10 g3 c5 (10...f5 is possible) 11 d5 exd5 12 ♘xd5 ♘c6 13 ♗g2 (Wessman-Wedberg, Stockholm 1990) 13...♗f6 Black is doing OK. Even 9...f5 can be considered.

d14) 9 d5 0-0 10 g3 d6 (10...c5 11 ♗h3 e5 12 f4 exf4 13 gxf4 d6 14 0-0-0 ♖e8 15 ♘g3 ± Szabo-Botvinnik, Oberhausen Echt 1961) 11 ♗g2 (not 11 ♘d4?! c5 12 ♘c2 f5 13 e4 fxe4 14 ♘xe4 exd5 15 cxd5 ♘d7 16 ♗g2 b5, when Black is firmly in control, K.Arkell-Crouch, Lichfield 2000) 11...♘d7 12 0-0 e5 13 f4 f5 (13...♘f6 and 13...♖e8 can also be considered; they are less radical than the text-move and not as committal, but also rather more passive) 14 e4 exf4 15 ♘xf4 ♗g5 16 exf5 ♖xf5 17 ♕c2 ± Jelen-Grosar, Slovenian Ch 1992.

d2) 8...♗xc3 9 ♘xc3 0-0 10 ♗d3 (10 d5 is a less radical approach: 10...d6 11 ♗e2 ♘d7 12 0-0 ♕e7 13 f4 ♖ae8 14 ♖ae1 e5 15 f5 ± Pein-Ward, Haringey 1988) 10...♗xg2 11 ♖g1 ♗f3 12 e4 ♔h8 13 ♕e3 ♗h5 14 ♖g5 g6 15 ♔d2 f6 16 ♖g3 ♘c6 17 ♖ag1 e5 18 d5 ♘d4 19 ♘e2 c5 20 ♘xd4 exd4 21 ♕h6 with an initiative to compensate for the pawn, Sadler-Adams, London 1989.

8 a3

Other tries include:

a) 8 d5 was tested in Speelman-Korchnoi, New York rpd 1995: 8...♘a6 9 a3 ♗e7 10 b4 ♗f6 11 ♖d1 exd5 12 ♘xd5 ± but Black may instead try 8...e5 9 a3 ♗e7 10 ♘g3 a5 11 ♗d3 ♘a6 with chances for both sides.

b) 8 ♘g3!? worked out extremely well for White in Shabalov-de Firmian, Philadelphia 1995, where Black continued 8...♖e8?!, a move which doesn't make a lot of sense; after 9 ♗d3 g6 10 h4 h5 11 e4 d5 12 e5 ♘c6 13 ♘xh5!, Black was already busted. However, Black can easily improve with 8...♗b7; e.g., 9 a3 ♗xc3 10 ♕xc3 f5 with equal chances.

8...♗e7 *(D)*

In Petrosian-Kurajica, Banja Luka 1979, Black went for 8...♗xc3 9 ♘xc3 f5?! (Petrosian gave 9...d6!? intending ...♗b7 and ...♘d7 ±) 10 ♗d3 d6 11

0-0 ♘d7 12 f4 ♘f6 13 d5 ♖e8 14 ♖ae1 ±.

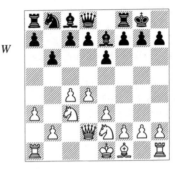

9 ♘f4

White's set-up and development plan follow those you will see for White in the Reshevsky Variation. Other moves fail to make a good impression:

a) 9 d5 and here:

a1) 9...♗a6 10 ♘g3 d6 11 ♗e2 e5 12 e4 ♗g5 13 ♕c2 g6 14 b4 ♗c8 15 ♗d3 a5 16 0-0 ♘a6 17 ♖ab1 h5 ½-½ Lautier-Short, Leon Echt 2001.

a2) 9...e5 10 ♘g3 (or 10 g3 d6 11 ♗g2 ♘d7 12 0-0 h5!? 13 f4 h4 14 ♖ae1 a5 15 b3 ♗a6 16 ♕c2, Shaked-Adams, Tilburg 1997, and here Adams gives 16...♘f6 as best, intending 17 fxe5 ♘g4; the chances are about even) 10...d6 11 ♗d3 f5 12 0-0 g6 13 f4 ♘d7 14 ♘ce2 h5 15 e4 h4 16 ♘h1 ♘c5 and Black has no reason to complain, Shirov-de Firmian, Tilburg 1993.

a3) 9...exd5 10 cxd5 c5 11 d6 ♗f6 12 ♘d5 ♘c6 13 ♘g3 g6 14 h4 ♗b7 15 h5 ♘a5! with a complicated struggle ahead, Knaak-Bischoff, Bavaria ECC 1991.

b) 9 g3 and now:

b1) 9...♗b7 10 d5 transposes to note 'd14' to Black's 7th move.

b2) 9...♗a6 10 ♘c1 (or 10 b3 c6 11 d5 ♗f6 12 ♖c1 exd5 13 cxd5 c5 14 ♗g2 d6 15 b4 ♘d7 = Høi-Kristiansen, Danish Ch (Tønder) 1993) 10...c6 11 ♗e2 ♗b7 12 0-0 d5 13 cxd5 exd5 14 b4 ♘d7 15 ♘d3 ♘f6 16 ♗f3 ♖e8 is equal, Vaïsser-Korchnoi, Pula Echt 1997.

b3) 9...d5 10 cxd5 exd5 11 ♘f4 c6 12 b4 a6 13 ♗g2 ♗d6 = Speelman-Korchnoi, Biel IZ 1993.

9...d6

Black may also consider:

a) 9...♘c6 is altogether too passive a set-up: 10 ♗e2 a5 11 0-0 d6 12 ♗f3 ♗d7 13 b3 and White is comfortably better, as Black will have a hard time generating counterplay, Franco-Sunye, Lucerne OL 1982.

b) 9...c5!? is an interesting way to liven the position up somewhat: 10 ♗d3 cxd4 11 exd4 ♘c6 12 ♘fe2 ♗b7 13 0-0 ♖c8 14 b4 d6 with approximately chances, Garcia Vicente-Izeta, Benasque 1993.

10 ♗e2 ♗b7

10...a6 11 0-0 ♘d7 12 b4 ♗b7 13 ♖ab1 ♖e8 14 ♘d3 ♗f8 15 ♖fd1 g6 16 ♘e1 ♘f6 17 ♘f3 d5 and Black has equalized without too many difficulties, G.Nikolić-Bischoff, Biel 1995.

11 0-0 ♘d7 12 ♖fd1

In the game Sadler-Larsen, London 1989, White tried 12 d5 instead, but after 12...e5 13 ♘d3 ♔h8 14 b4 f5 15 f4 ♗a6 16 ♘b5 ♗f6 17 ♖ac1 ♗c8 18 fxe5 ♗xe5 19 ♘xe5 ♘xe5 20 ♘d4 a5 21 ♖f4 axb4 22 axb4 ♗d7, Black had once more equalized.

12...♗g5 13 b4 ♕e7 14 ♖ac1 ♗h6 15 ♗f1 g6 16 ♕c2 c6

½-½ Aleksandrov-Ehlvest, Polanica Zdroj 1997. Black has equalized,

but there is of course plenty of play left in this position.

D2)

6 ♕c2 *(D)*

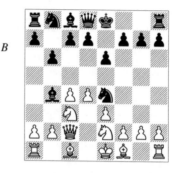

White immediately attacks the renegade knight. In this way he keeps his bishop-pair, unlike in Line D1.

6...♗b7

6...f5 is a major alternative:

a) 7 a3 ♗xc3+ 8 ♘xc3 ♗b7 transposes to the note to Black's 8th move.

b) 7 g3?! ♘xc3 8 ♘xc3 ♗b7 9 d5 b5! 10 ♗g2 bxc4 11 0-0 0-0 12 ♖d1 e5 13 ♗f1 d6 14 ♗xc4 ♘d7 15 ♘a4 ♗a5 16 b4 ♗b6 with chances for both sides, Donner-Timman, Wijk aan Zee 1975.

c) 7 f3 ♘xc3 8 ♘xc3 ♗b7 9 ♗d2 ♕h4+ 10 ♔d1 0-0 11 ♘b5 ♗xd2 12 ♕xd2 ♖d8 13 ♔c2 d6 14 ♖e1 ♘d7 15 ♗d3 a6 16 ♘c3 ♕f6 and Black obviously has no problems at all, Krutti-Bergström, York 2000.

d) 7 ♘f4 c5! 8 ♗d3 cxd4 9 exd4 (Timman mentions 9 ♗xe4!? fxe4 10 exd4 0-0 11 ♕xe4 ♘c6 followed by ...♗a6 and Black has compensation for the pawn) 9...♘xc3 10 bxc3 ♗d6 11 ♕e2 (11 0-0 followed by ♖e1 is better according to Timman) 11...0-0 and here White must avoid 12 h4?! ♗b7 13 ♔f1 (Salov-Timman, Amsterdam 1996) 13...♕c7! ∓ (Timman); instead, 12 0-0 is roughly equal.

7 a3

White has also tried:

a) 7 ♘g3?! ran into trouble in the game Bareev-Zsinka, Næstved 1988: 7...♕h4! 8 ♗d3 f5 9 0-0 ♗xc3 10 bxc3 0-0 11 ♘e2 ♖f6 12 ♗xe4? ♗xe4 13 ♕d1 ♗f3!! 0-1 (due to 14 gxf3 ♖h6 15 ♖e1 ♕xh2+ 16 ♔f1 ♕h3+ or 14 ♖e1 ♖g6 15 g3 ♕xh2+! and game over).

b) 7 f3 ♘xc3 (7...♗xc3+ 8 bxc3 ♘d6 9 ♘g3 ♕h4 10 ♗d3 ♗a6 {the alternative 10...f5!? is given as better for Black by Pliester, but that is somewhat exaggerated; after 11 0-0 0-0 12 ♖b1 White seems to be doing OK} 11 ♕a4 f5 12 0-0 0-0 13 ♗a3 ♗b7 14 c5 ± Taimanov-Levin, USSR Ch (Kharkov) 1967) and now:

b1) 8 ♘xc3 ♕h4+! 9 ♕f2 ♗xc3+ 10 bxc3 ♕xf2+ 11 ♔xf2 c5 12 dxc5 bxc5 13 ♖b1 ♗a6 14 ♖b3 ♘c6 with a pleasant game for Black, Litinskaya-Ignachenko, corr. 1986.

b2) 8 bxc3 ♗e7 (8...♗d6!? can also be considered; e.g., 9 e4 ♘c6 10 ♘g3?! {better is 10 e5 ♗e7 – Sloth} 10...♕h4, Brglez-Sloth, corr. 1970, and here 11 ♕f2 ♗xg3 12 ♕xg3 ♕xg3+ 13 hxg3 ♗a6 = is White's best – Sloth) 9 ♘g3 ♘c6 (9...h5!? deserves a closer look) 10 ♗d3 ♗a6 11 0-0 ♘a5 12 ♕e2 d5 13 cxd5 ♗xd3 14 ♕xd3 ♕xd5 15 e4 ♕c4 16 ♕e3 g6 ½-½ Benjamin-de Firmian, Los Angeles 1987.

c) 7 ♘f4!? *(D)* is White's most notable alternative; he gives up on the idea of preventing Black from giving

him a doubled pawn and instead fights for the initiative. Now Black has tried:

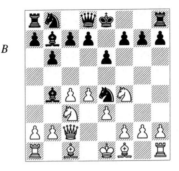

B

c1) 7...♗xc3+ 8 bxc3 f5 9 ♗d3 ♕h4 10 0-0 g5 11 ♘e2 g4 12 ♘g3 ♘g5 13 e4 f4 14 ♗xf4 ♘f3+ 15 gxf3 gxf3 16 ♔h1 ♕xf4 17 e5 ± Scherbakov-I.Sokolov, Ljubljana ECC 1995.

c2) 7...f5 8 ♗d3 ♕h4 (8...0-0 is line 'c4') 9 0-0 ♗xc3 10 bxc3 g5 and now instead of 11 ♘e2 ♘f6! 12 f3 ♖g8 13 d5 g4 14 ♘d4 gxf3 15 ♘xf3 ♕h5 16 ♗a3 exd5!? 17 ♗xf5 dxc4 18 e4 ♘c6 with chances for both sides, Lautier-Wedberg, Harplinge 1998, Lautier gives a thumbs up to 11 f3!? ♘f6 12 g3! ♕h6 13 ♘g2 ♕g6 14 d5 ♘a6 15 ♗a3 ±.

c3) 7...♘xc3 8 bxc3 ♗d6 9 e4 e5 10 ♘d5 ♘c6 11 ♗e3 exd4 12 cxd4 ♘b4 13 ♕b3 ♘xd5 14 cxd5 ♕e7 and the chances are about even, Kastanieda-Yuferov, Moscow 1995.

c4) 7...0-0 8 ♗d3 f5 (8...d5!? 9 0-0 ♘f6 10 cxd5 exd5 11 ♗d2 ♗d6 12 e4?! dxe4 13 ♘xe4 ♘xe4 14 ♗xe4 ♗xe4 15 ♕xe4 ♘d7 16 ♖ac1 ♘f6 ∓ Cruz Lopez-Gomez Esteban, Basque Ch 1995) 9 0-0 and here:

c41) 9...♘xc3 10 bxc3 ♗d6 11 ♖b1 ♗xf4 (after 11...c5! 12 e4, as played in

Scherbakov-Kiseliov, Russian Ch (Elista) 1994, Scherbakov believes Black should play 12...cxd4 13 exf5 ♕f6 with chances for both sides) 12 exf4 ♖f6 13 ♗e3 ♖h6 14 f3 ♘c6 15 c5 ♕h4 16 g3 ♕h5 (I.Sokolov-Korchnoi, New York 1996) and now Sokolov gives 17 ♖f2!? ♘e7 18 ♖bf1 ♘d5 19 ♗c1 intending a3 and c4 with a small plus for White.

c42) 9...♗xc3!? 10 bxc3 c5 11 f3 ♘d6 is a suggestion of Pliester's. Emms continues by giving 12 e4 ♘c6 13 d5 ♘e5 and 12 ♗a3 ♘a6 13 e4 ♕g5; in both cases Black has good reason to be happy with his position.

7...♗xc3+

7...♘xc3 can also be tried; Guliev-Kiseliov, Vladivostok 1994 continued 8 axb4 ♘xe2 9 ♗xe2 ♕g5 10 ♗f1 ♕h4 11 ♗d2 ♗e4 12 ♕d1 ♘c6 with chances for both sides.

8 ♘xc3

White can sidestep the next exchange on c3 through 8 bxc3; e.g., 8...♕h4 9 ♘f4 0-0 10 ♗d3 f5 11 0-0 g5?! (11...c5!? is probably better) 12 f3 ♘f6 13 g3 ♕h6 14 ♘g2 ♘c6 (Grigorian-Kuzmin, USSR 1974) and now 15 e4 fxe4 16 fxe4 seems to leave White with the better game.

8...♘xc3

8...f5 is a popular alternative; White has several ways to meet it:

a) 9 b4 0-0 10 ♗b2 d6 11 d5 ♘xc3 12 ♕xc3 e5 13 ♗d3 c6 = Franco-Izeta, Pamplona 1993/4.

b) 9 b3 d6 10 ♗b2 0-0 11 0-0-0 (11 d5 ♘xc3 12 ♕xc3 e5 13 f4 ♘d7 14 ♗d3 ♕h4+ 15 g3 ♕h6 = Korchnoi-Botvinnik, USSR 1960) 11...♘d7 12 f3 ♘xc3 13 ♕xc3 ♕e7 14 ♔b1 (G.Georgadze-Kurajica, Bosnia 1998) and here

14...e5!? 15 d5 f4 16 ♗d3 ± is the best Black can hope for – Georgadze.

c) 9 d5 ♘xc3 10 ♕xc3 and now:

c1) 10...♕f6 11 ♕xf6 gxf6 12 ♗e2 a5 13 ♗d2 ± Norri-Hentunen, Espoo 1993.

c2) 10...0-0 11 dxe6 dxe6 12 b3 ♕e7 13 ♗b2 ♘d7 14 0-0-0 ♘f6 15 f3 ♖ad8 16 ♗e2 ± Korchnoi-Markland, Hastings 1971/2.

c3) 10...♕e7 11 dxe6 (11 b4 can be met with 11...a5; for example, 12 dxe6 dxe6 13 c5 axb4 14 axb4 ♖xa1 15 ♕xa1 ♗d5 16 ♗b5+ c6 17 ♗e2 0-0 and Black is doing well, Avrukh-Grosar, Pula 2000) 11...dxe6 12 b3 ♘d7 13 ♗b2 e5 14 0-0-0 0-0-0 15 b4 ♖he8 16 f3 ♕h4 and now rather than 17 ♕e1?! ♕h6!, when Black has the better chances, I.Sokolov-Cu.Hansen, Groningen 1991, 17 c5!? is best according to Sokolov; his analysis ends in equality.

9 ♕xc3 *(D)*

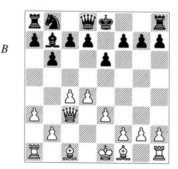

9...0-0

Before milling further down the main line, let's look at Black's alternatives:

a) 9...f5 10 d5 transposes to note 'c' to Black's 7th move.

b) 9...♕f6 10 b3 d6 11 ♗b2 ♘d7 12 ♕c2 ♕g6 13 ♕xg6 hxg6 14 f3 ♔e7 15 ♔f2 g5 = Øgaard-Sloth, Esbjerg 1978.

c) 9...♕h4 doesn't have the best reputation, but this may not be entirely justified. White has two replies:

c1) 10 b4 and then:

c11) 10...d6 11 ♗b2 ♘d7 12 c5 ♗d5 13 cxd6 cxd6 14 ♗b5?! ♔e7 15 ♖c1?! and here Korobov-Bar, Moscow 2002 concluded 15...♖hd8 16 ♗xd7 ♖xd7 17 0-0 ♗xg2 18 ♔xg2 ½-½. Black can instead try 15...♖hc8!, which looks like an error, but appears to work out well: 16 ♕xc8 ♖xc8 17 ♖xc8 ♗xg2 18 ♖g1 ♕xh2 19 ♖xg2 ♕xg2 20 ♖c7 ♕g1+ 21 ♔e2 ♕g4+ 22 ♔d2 (22 ♔e1 ♕f5 23 d5 ♕b1+ 24 ♗c1 a6 isn't any better for White) 22...♕f5 23 ♖xd7+ ♔e8! 24 ♗c6 ♕xf2+ 25 ♔c3 ♕xe3+ 26 ♔c2 a5 and thanks to his pawn-mass and White's not particularly coordinated pieces, Black has the better prospects. A long variation, and improvements are quite possible, but fascinating nonetheless.

c12) 10...0-0 11 ♗b2 f6 12 ♖d1 ♗e4 13 d5 ♖e8 14 dxe6 dxe6 15 b5 a6 with a complicated struggle ahead, Korchnoi-Short, Bundesliga 1998/9.

c2) 10 b3 d6 (10...0-0?! is weaker on account of 11 ♗b2 f6 12 d5! exd5 13 ♖d1! d4 14 ♖xd4 ♕h5 15 ♗e2 ♕g6 16 ♖g4 ± I.Sokolov-Korchnoi, Novi Sad OL 1990) and then:

c21) 11 ♗b2 ♘d7 12 d5 and now:

c211) 12...♘f6!? 13 ♗d3 exd5 14 cxd5 ♗xd5 15 ♕xc7 (15 ♗b5+ ♔d8 16 0-0-0 {Ftačnik} 16...c6 17 ♗c4 ♔d7 with chances for both sides) 15...0-0 16 ♕xd6 ♘e4! (Ftačnik gives 16...♖ad8 17 ♗xf6 gxf6 18 ♕g3+ ♕xg3 19 hxg3

♗xg2 20 ♗xh7+ ♔g7 21 ♖h2 ♗d5 with counterplay, although White can claim the better chances with 22 ♗c2) 17 ♗xe4 ♕xe4 18 ♕g3 ♕g6 19 ♕xg6 hxg6 20 0-0 ♗xb3 with equal chances in the endgame.

c212) 12...0-0-0!? 13 ♗e2 exd5 14 cxd5 ♘c5 15 0-0 ♗xd5 16 b4 ♘a4 17 ♕d4 ♕xd4 18 ♗xd4 c5 ∓ Kaspi-Bar, Israeli Ch (Ramat-Aviv/Modiin) 2000.

c22) Ftačnik gives 11 c5 dxc5 12 dxc5 0-0 13 ♗b2 f6 as unclear, but White can continue 14 ♕c4; for example, 14...♕xc4 15 ♗xc4 ♔f7 16 0-0 may leave White with a minimal pull.

We now return to 9...0-0 *(D)*:

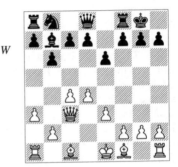

10 b4

Or:

a) 10 f3?! runs into some trouble: 10...♕h4+ 11 ♔e2 (11 g3?! has been played on several occasions, but after 11...♕h5 12 e4 f5 13 ♗g2 fxe4 14 fxe4, Farago-Kuzmin, Polanica Zdroj 1977, 14...d6! followed by ...♘d7-f6 Black has the better chances – Kuzmin) 11...f5 12 g3 ♕h5 13 ♗g2 d6 14 ♔f2 ♘d7 15 ♖f1 c5 16 ♔g1 and after completing castling by hand, White has equalized, Korzubov-Cu.Hansen, Copenhagen 1984.

b) 10 ♕c2 ♛h4 11 b4 a5 12 b5 d6 13 ♗b2 ♘d7 with chances for both sides, Ravi Sekhar-Kuzmin, Bangalore 1981.

c) 10 b3 and then:

c1) 10...♛h4?! transposes to Sokolov-Korchnoi in note 'c2' to Black's 9th move.

c2) 10...d5 11 ♗b2 ♘d7 12 ♗e2 dxc4 13 d5 ♛g5 14 h4 ♛f6 15 dxe6 fxe6 16 ♕xf6 (Øgaard-Kuzmin, Reykjavik 1978) and now 16...♘xf6 17 ♗xc4 ♗d5 leaves the chances even.

c3) 10...d6 11 ♗b2 and here:

c31) 11...♛h4 12 d5 e5 13 g3 ♛e4 14 ♖g1 ♘d7 15 ♗d3 ♛g4 16 ♕c2 f5 17 h4 a5 = Aleksandrov-Moiseenko, Ohrid Ech 2001.

c32) 11...♘d7 12 d5 (12 0-0-0 f5 13 f4? {13 f3 = Emms} 13...♘f6 14 ♖g1 ♕e7 15 ♗e2 ♗e4 and with his control over the e4-square, Black has the advantage, Remlinger-de Firmian, New York 1987) 12...f6 13 ♖d1 ♕e7 14 ♗e2 f5 15 0-0 ♖f6 16 f4 ♘c5 17 ♗f3 ♖h6 18 g3 ♖e8 = G.Georgadze-Kurajica, Benasque 1996.

c33) 11...♛f6! 12 ♕c2 (12 f3 ♘d7 13 ♗e2?! {Emms gives 13 0-0-0!? as equal} 13...♛h4+ 14 g3 ♛h6 15 0-0-0 f5 16 ♔b1 ♖ae8 17 ♔a1 a5 18 ♖dg1 e5 leaves Black in charge, Shulman-Cu.Hansen, Stockholm 1996) 12...♛h6 (12...♛g6 13 ♗d3 f5 14 f3 ♛h6 15 ♕e2 ♘d7 ± Tisdall-Sloth, Gladsaxe 1983) 13 0-0-0 ♘d7 14 ♔b1 f5 15 f3 ♖ae8 (Townsend-Ward, British League (4NCL) 2001/2) and here 16 h4 is best, although 16...♘f6 is perfectly fine for Black.

10...d6

This popular move may not even be Black's best. Two alternatives:

a) 10...d5 11 ♗b2 ♘d7 12 ♖c1 ♖c8 13 c5 c6 14 ♗d3 ♘b8 15 a4 ± J.Fernandez-Kuzmin, Budapest 1976.

b) 10...a5!? has been tried out a few times by Markland; e.g., 11 ♗b2 axb4 12 axb4 ♖xa1+ 13 ♗xa1 ♛h4! 14 d5 f6 15 dxe6 dxe6 16 ♕d4 ♛xd4 17 ♗xd4 ♘c6 18 ♗c3 ♖a8 and Black has no problems at all in the endgame, Sterud-Markland, corr. 1982.

11 ♗b2 (D)

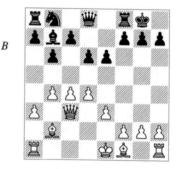

11...f5

Again, it is not wholly clear whether this is Black's best move. Alternatives include:

a) 11...♘d7?! 12 c5! is problematic for Black: 12...bxc5 (Emms also gives 12...♗d5 13 c6 ♘f6 14 f3, threatening e4) 13 dxc5 ♘f6 14 ♖d1 e5 15 c6 ♗c8 16 ♗d3 ♘g4 17 h3 ♛h4 18 0-0 ♘f6 19 ♕c2 ♗e6 20 f4 ± Conquest-Crawley, British Ch (Blackpool) 1988.

b) 11...♛h4!? is the first of three queen moves I will look at in this position. 12 d5 e5 13 ♗d3 (13 g3 is best met by 13...♕e4!; e.g., 14 ♖g1 c6 15 dxc6 ♘xc6 with chances for both sides) 13...c6 14 e4 f5 15 exf5 cxd5 16 cxd5 ♗xd5 17 0-0 ♘c6 18 f4 ♘d4 with a good game for Black, Franco-Lima, Salamanca 1989.

c) 11...♕g5!? has only been tried once: 12 h4 ♕g4 13 ♖h3 f5 (13...a5!?) 14 f3 ♕h5 15 ♔f2 ♘d7 16 c5 ♗d5!? 17 cxd6 cxd6 18 ♕c7 ♘f6 with a good game for Black, P.Rosell-Sutela, corr. 1995.

d) 11...♕f6!? needs thorough testing by strong players, as its only appearance so far at GM level told us little about its merits: 12 h4 ♘d7 ½-½ Bu Xiangzhi-Moiseenko, Moscow 2002. Emms instead analysed 12 c5!?, giving the line 12...dxc5 13 dxc5 ♕xc3+ 14 ♗xc3 bxc5 15 bxc5 ♘d7 16 ♗a5 ♘xc5 17 ♗b4 ♘b3 18 ♖b1 c5 19 ♗c3 c4 20 ♗xc4 ♖fc8 21 ♗xb3 ♖xc3 =.

We now return to the position after 11...f5 (D):

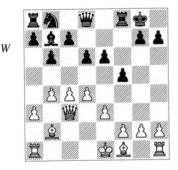

12 d5!?

Or:

a) 12 h4?! ♘d7 13 c5 ♗d5! 14 c6 ♘f6 15 f3 ♕e8 16 ♖c1 ♕g6 17 ♕d2 f4 18 e4 ♗xe4! 19 ♕xf4 ♗d3 with a better game for Black, Vaiser-de Firmian, Moscow 1989.

b) 12 0-0-0 ♘d7 13 d5 e5 14 f3 a5 15 ♔b1 ♕e7 (Black can also consider 15...axb4 16 axb4 ♖a4 17 ♗d3 ♕a8 intending ...b5) 16 ♗e2 ♘f6 17 ♖d2 ♔h8 18 ♖hd1 ♕f7 with chances for both sides, Sashikiran-Handke, Biel 1999.

12...e5 13 c5!?

This highly aggressive approach seems to be White's best bid for an advantage, although 13 ♗d3 is more popular: 13...c6 14 0-0 cxd5 15 f4 ♘d7 16 cxd5 ♗xd5 17 ♗c4 ♗xc4 18 ♕xc4+ ♔h8 19 ♖ad1 ♕e7 20 ♕c6 exf4 21 exf4 ♘f6 = Rossiter-Ward, Oakham 1994.

13...bxc5 14 bxc5

Now:

a) In J.Horvath-T.Horvath, Balatonbereny 1988, Black went completely wrong with 14...f4? 15 c6 ♗a6 16 exf4 ♖xf4 17 ♗c1 ♖g4 18 ♗e3 ♗xf1 19 ♔xf1 ♘a6 20 g3 with a solid advantage for White thanks to Black's unhappy knight on a6.

However, as Emms points out Black has two other options that are worth looking into:

b) 14...♗xd5 15 ♖d1 ♗f7 (Emms) 16 f4 ♕e7 17 cxd6 cxd6 18 fxe5 dxe5 19 ♕xe5 ♕xe5 20 ♗xe5 ♘c6 with approximately equal chances.

c) 14...♗a6!? 15 ♗xa6 ♘xa6 16 c6 ♘c5 17 ♕c2 ♖b8 with an unclear position – Emms. This evaluation too seems to be correct as, for example, 18 ♗xe5 doesn't lead to anything; e.g., 18...♘b3 19 ♖b1 dxe5 20 ♖xb3 ♕xd5 21 ♖xb8 ♖xb8 22 0-0 e4 with equal chances.

12 Dutch Variation

1 d4 ♘f6 2 c4 e6 3 ♘c3 ♗b4 4 e3 b6 5 ♗d3 ♗b7 *(D)*

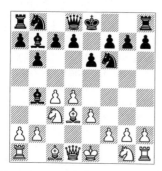

6 ♘f3

In connection with the main line, there are a few lines that deserve attention:

a) 6 f3 often ends up transposing to the Sämisch Variation, but play can also develop independently: 6...c5 (other moves have been tried at this point, such as 6...0-0, 6...d5, 6...♘h5 and 6...♗xc3+, but in each case White generally obtains a better game) 7 ♘e2 (7 a3 ♗xc3+ 8 bxc3 is the Sämisch Variation, which is not the subject of this book) and now:

a1) 7...0-0 8 0-0 cxd4 9 exd4 d5 10 cxd5 ♘xd5 and Black has a pleasant game, Einarsson-H.Olafsson, Reykjavik 1996.

a2) 7...cxd4 8 exd4 0-0 9 ♗g5 ♗e7 10 0-0 d5 11 cxd5 ♘xd5 12 ♗xe7 ♕xe7 is equal, Ilić-Romanishin, Belgrade 1988.

a3) 7...♘c6 8 0-0 cxd4 9 exd4 d5 10 cxd5 ♘xd5 11 ♘xd5 (11 ♕a4 0-0 =) 11...♕xd5 12 ♗f4 ♗e7! = Capablanca-Kan, Moscow 1935.

b) 6 ♘e2!? is far more interesting:

b1) 6...c5!? can be tried.

b2) 6...0-0 7 0-0 (7 a3 ♗xc3+ 8 ♘xc3 {8 bxc3 is another Sämisch} 8...d5 9 cxd5 exd5 10 0-0 ♗a6 11 ♗xa6 ♘xa6 12 ♕d3 ♘b8 13 b4 with a little plus for White, Paramos-Vehi Bach, Zaragoza 1994) 7...d5 8 cxd5 ♘xd5 9 e4 ♘xc3 10 bxc3 ♗e7 11 c4 ♘d7 12 ♗b2 e5! = Gelfand-Akopian, Cap d'Agde rpd 1996.

b3) 6...♗xg2 7 ♖g1 is the critical line:

b31) 7...♗e4 8 a3 (this makes it a real gambit, but after 8 ♗xe4 ♘xe4 9 ♖xg7 ♘xf2 10 ♕c2 ♕h4 11 ♘g3 both 11...♗f8, as in Szilagyi-Florian, Hungarian Ch (Budapest) 1946, and 11...♘d3+ 12 ♕xd3 ♗f8 leave Black with a sizeable advantage) 8...♗xc3+ 9 ♘xc3 ♗xd3 10 ♕xd3 ♘h5 11 e4 ♘c6 (11...g6 12 ♗g5 f6 13 ♗h6 gives White sufficient compensation for the pawn) 12 ♗e3 (12 ♗g5 f6 13 ♗e3 ♘e7 14 0-0-0 d6 15 f4 ♕d7 16 ♔b1 g6 17 d5 0-0-0 and White is fighting to show compensation for the pawn, Paramos Dominguez-Vehi Bach, Barcelona 2000) 12...d6 13 0-0-0 ♘e7 14 c5 g6 15 cxd6 cxd6 16 ♔b1 and White has adequate compensation for the pawn, Dzindzichashvili-de Firmian, New York 1996.

b32) 7...♗f3 8 ♕c2 (8 ♖g3 ♗h5 9 e4 ♘c6 10 f3 ♗g6 ∓ Zsinka-Chernyshov, Zalakaros 1995; 8 ♖xg7 ♗xc3+ {or 8...♘g4!? 9 h3 ♗xc3+ 10 bxc3 f5! and the rook is trapped – Emms/*Fritz*} 9 bxc3 ♘e4 10 ♕c2 ♕h4 = V.Georgiev-Genov, Bulgarian Ch (Plovdiv) 1999) 8...♘h5 (8...g6 is another good move) 9 ♗d2 (9 ♗e4 ♗xe4 10 ♕xe4 ♘c6 11 d5 ♘e7 ∓ Agrest-Zsinka, Oberwart 1993) 9...♕h4 10 0-0-0 ♘c6 11 ♖df1 ♗d6 12 ♘b5 ♗xh2 with a few extra pawns for Black, J.Eriksson-Brynell, Rönneby 1998.

We now return to 6 ♘f3 *(D)*:

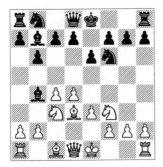

6...♘e4

Otherwise:

a) 6...0-0 is the subject of Chapters 13 and 14.

b) 6...♕e7 7 0-0 ♗xc3 8 bxc3 d6 9 ♘d2 e5 10 e4 ♘bd7 11 ♖e1 0-0 12 ♘f1 ♖fe8 13 ♘g3 with an initiative for White, Lukacs-Sidorov, Budapest 1994.

c) 6...♗e4 7 0-0 ♗xc3 8 bxc3 ♗xd3 9 ♕xd3 0-0 10 e4 d6 11 ♗g5 ♕e8!? 12 ♗xf6 gxf6 13 ♘h4 ♔h8 14 f4 ± Vyzhmanavin-P.Nikolić, New York rpd 1994.

d) 6...♗xc3+ 7 bxc3 and now:

d1) After 7...♘e4, White can transpose to the note to Black's 7th move in Line A with 8 ♕c2, and note 'b' to Black's 7th move in Line B with 8 0-0.

d2) 7...♗e4 8 ♗e2 0-0 9 0-0 c5 10 ♘d2 ♗b7 11 f3 d5 12 dxc5 bxc5 13 ♖b1 ♕c7 14 ♕b3 (Taimanov-Gulko, USSR Ch (Leningrad) 1974) and now Taimanov gives 14...♗c6 ± as best.

d3) 7...d6 8 0-0 ♘bd7 (8...0-0 9 ♘d2 e5 10 e4 ♘c6 transposes to note 'b21' to Black's 7th move in Chapter 13) 9 ♘d2 e5 10 e4 0-0 (10...♕e7 11 ♖e1 0-0-0 12 ♘f1 ♔b8 13 a4 a5, Visier-Debarnot, Nice OL 1974, 14 ♘e3 ±) 11 ♖e1 ♖e8 12 f3 ♘f8 13 ♘f1 ♘e6 14 ♗e3 ♘h5 15 ♕d2 ♕f6 and Black has fully equalized, Ibragimov-Lavrov, Budapest 1993.

We now return to 6...♘e4 *(D)*:

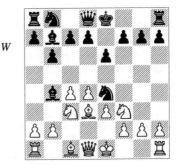

Here we have it, the position that is the starting position of the Dutch Variation. The name isn't a result of this line being invented or played by Dutch players, but rather that this line after Black's next move, 7...f5, resembles the Dutch Defence.

In one of the very first games with this line, Capablanca won very instructively as Black against Winter in

Ramsgate 1929 in a game that has been publicized in several instructional manuals.

However, the line has never really caught on among the strongest players in the world, although several have tried it once or twice.

Now there are the following main lines:

A: 7 ♕c2　　　182
B: 7 0-0　　　186

Or:

a) 7 ♗xe4?! ♗xe4 (7...♗xc3+ 8 bxc3 ♗xe4 is also good for Black) 8 0-0 ♗b7 9 d5 0-0 10 ♗d2 ♗e7 11 ♘d4 (A.Schneider-Müller, Budapest 1993) 11...c5!?, answering both 12 ♘c2 and 12 ♘de2 with 12...f5!? with chances for both sides.

b) 7 ♕b3 c5 (another interesting attempt is 7...♗xc3+ 8 bxc3 ♘g5!?, after which White's best appears to be 9 ♘d2!? with a complicated struggle ahead) 8 0-0 ♗xc3 9 bxc3 0-0 10 a4 d6 with chances for both sides, Panagop-oulos-Zimmermann, Amsterdam OL 1954.

c) 7 ♗d2!? was used as far back as 1946. Black obtains an OK position after 7...♗xc3 8 ♗xc3 ♘xc3 (8...♕e7 9 ♗xe4 ♗xe4 10 ♘d2!? ♗g6 11 ♕f3 c6 12 0-0 0-0 13 e4 is slightly better for White, F.Portisch-Dgebuadze, Loh-mar 1999) 9 bxc3 0-0 (or 9...f5 10 0-0 0-0 11 ♕e2 ♕f6 12 e4 fxe4 13 ♗xe4 ♗xe4 14 ♕xe4 ♘c6 with approxi-mately equal chances, Purdy-Tartako-wer, radio game 1946) 10 h4 f5 11 ♕e2?! (11 ♖b1 is equal) 11...c5 12 ♘g5?! h6 13 ♘f3 ♘c6 and Black is in control, A.Calvo-Galliamova, Oviedo rpd 1993.

A)
7 ♕c2 (D)

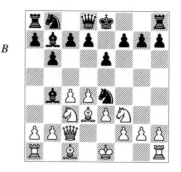

7...f5

The signature move of the Dutch Variation. However, another continua-tion is also noteworthy: 7...♗xc3+ 8 bxc3, and here:

a) 8...♘g5 9 ♘xg5 ♕xg5 10 f3 (10 ♗e4!?) 10...♕h4+ 11 ♔f1 ♘c6 12 e4 ♗a6 13 ♗e3 ♘a5 14 ♕e2 d6 = Ole-sen-I.Ivanov, Philadelphia 1992.

b) 8...f5 will usually transpose to the main line after 9 0-0, but in Con-quest-Emms, British Ch (Eastbourne) 1990, White tried 9 a4. After 9...♘g5 10 ♘xg5 ♕xg5 11 f3 ♕h4+ 12 ♕f2 ♕xf2+ 13 ♔xf2 ♘c6, the chances were equal.

8 0-0

The natural continuation, as White continues his development. Other tries:

a) 8 a3?! makes no sense and Black easily obtains the better game after 8...♗xc3+ 9 bxc3 0-0 10 0-0 c5 11 a4 ♕c7, Minev-Langeweg, Leipzig OL 1960.

b) 8 ♗d2 ♘xd2 (or 8...♗xc3 9 ♗xc3 0-0 10 ♗e2 d6 11 0-0 ♘d7 = Romani-Keene, Lugano OL 1968) 9 ♕xd2 0-0 10 a3 ♗xc3 11 ♕xc3 d6 12

0-0-0 ♘d7 with an equal position, L.Cooper-I.Ivanov, London Lloyds Bank 1987.

8...♗xc3

8...♘xc3 was Capablanca's choice in the stem game of this variation: 9 bxc3 ♗xf3 10 gxf3 ♕g5+ (the immediate 10...♗d6 has also been tried in this position) 11 ♔h1 ♗d6 12 f4 ♕h6 13 ♖g1 ♘c6 14 ♕e2 ♕f6 15 ♕f3 0-0 16 ♗d2 g6 and even though White has a slight initiative at this point, in Winter-Capablanca, Ramsgate 1929 Black went on to win in impressive fashion.

9 bxc3 *(D)*

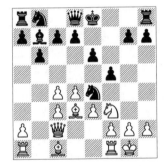

B

9...0-0

Black has two alternatives, of which the latter is especially noteworthy:

a) 9...d6?! 10 ♘e1 ♘d7 11 f3 ♘ef6 (Florea-Keller, Dortmund 1997) 12 g4! g6 (12...fxg4 13 fxg4 leaves too much in White's hands) 13 e4!? with an initiative for White.

b) 9...c5!? 10 ♘d2 (10 ♘e1 0-0 transposes to note 'e1' to White's 10th move) 10...♘xd2 (10...♕h4 can also be tried; for example, 11 f3 {11 ♗xe4 ♗xe4 12 ♘xe4 ♕xe4 =} 11...♘xd2! {11...♘g5?! 12 f4 ♕g4 13 d5 ♘f7 14 e4 ± Milić/Bozić} 12 ♗xd2 0-0 =) 11

♗xd2 ♘c6 12 f3 0-0 = Leal-Ratcu, São Paulo 1998.

10 ♘d2

White has tried several other things, but none of the alternatives really test Black:

a) 10 ♗a3, as recently played by GM Kožul, seems best countered with 10...♖f6!? 11 ♖ad1 c5 12 ♘e1?! ♖h6, when Black had the initiative in Zamfirescu-Breahna, Romanian Cht 1993.

b) 10 ♗b2 c5 11 ♖ad1 d6 (Kraidman-Keene, Beersheba 1978) 12 ♘e1 = Keene.

c) 10 d5 ♘c5 (it's unclear whether White has enough for the pawn after 10...exd5 11 cxd5 ♗xd5) 11 ♗a3 ♘ba6 12 ♘d4 ♕f6 13 ♖ab1 ♖ae8 = Plachetka-Franzen, Trnava 1982.

d) 10 ♖b1 c5 11 a4 ♕c7 12 a5 d6 is equal, Uhlmann-Botvinnik, Munich OL 1958.

e) 10 ♘e1 *(D)* is White's main alternative to 10 ♘d2. White wants to kick the e4-knight away without giving him the opportunity to exchange it. Unfortunately for White, Black has no fewer than four reasonable options to pick from:

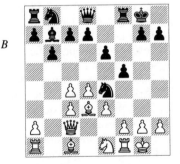

B

e1) 10...c5 11 f3 and now:

e11) 11...♘g5 is supposed to be refuted by 12 d5!; e.g., 12...♕f6 13 e4 f4 14 e5! ♕h6 15 ♗e4! ± Inkiov-Psakhis, Minsk 1982; or 12...exd5 13 cxd5 ♗xd5 14 ♗xf5 ♗c4 15 ♖f2 ♕f6 16 ♗d3 ♗xd3 17 ♕xd3 ♖f7 18 ♘c2 ♘c6 19 e4 ♘e6 20 f4 ± Fraga-Fernandez, corr. 1987. However, 12...♘f7!? may change that evaluation; for example, 13 dxe6 dxe6 14 e4 g6!? or 13 e4 ♘e5!?.

e12) 11...♘d6 and then:

e121) 12 e4?! fxe4 13 fxe4 ♖xf1+ 14 ♔xf1 e5 15 ♘f3 ♘f7 (Muir-King, British Ch (Swansea) 1987) 16 ♕f2!? d6 17 d5 ♘d7 18 ♔g1 ♘f6 19 ♘h4 ♗c8 and although Black has the long-term initiative due to the pawn-structure and piece distribution, White should be able to defend.

e122) 12 ♗a3 ♘a6 (12...♕c7 is another worthwhile move: 13 ♕e2 ♘c6 14 ♘c2 ♘a5 15 e4, Ibragimov-Grosar, Komotini 1993, and now 15...fxe4!? 16 fxe4 e5! 17 d5 ♗a6 is better for Black) 13 e4 (13 ♕e2 ♕e7 14 ♘c2 e5 15 e4 f4 16 g3 g5 and Black can be happy with the result of the opening, Psakhis-Lezcano, Copenhagen 2001) 13...fxe4! (13...♕e7?! 14 e5 ♘f7 15 f4 g5!? 16 d5 gxf4 17 ♘f3 ♘h8 18 ♖ae1 ♘g6 19 ♗c1 ♔h8 {Timman gives 19...♖ae8 as better} 20 ♕f2 ♕g7 21 h4! ± Yusupov-Timman, Tilburg Ct (1) 1986) 14 fxe4 ♖xf1+ 15 ♔xf1 (Böhle-Zlatilov, Porz 1990) 15...♕h4 16 ♘f3 ♖f8 17 ♔g1 ♕g4 18 h3 ♕g3 19 ♖f1 ♖f6! "with active counterplay for Black" – Pliester.

e2) 10...♕h4 is premature according to Pliester, but in practice Black has had good results. 11 f3 and here:

e21) 11...♘g5 and then:

e211) 12 ♕f2 is a less critical move: 12...♕xf2+ (12...♕h5?! 13 ♗e2 ♕g6 14 ♕g3 d6 15 ♘d3 ♘d7 16 h4 ♘f7 17 ♕xg6 hxg6 with a solid advantage for White, Hoffman-Wedberg, Novi Sad OL 1990) 13 ♖xf2 c5 14 ♘c2 ♖c8 15 ♘a3 ♘f7 = Filip-B.Andersen, Havana OL 1966.

e212) 12 c5! ♖f6!? (12...bxc5 13 ♖b1 ♗c6 14 ♗a3 ± Ehlvest-Vaiser, Volgodonsk 1982) 13 ♕f2 ♕xf2+ 14 ♖xf2 bxc5 15 ♖b1 ♗c8 16 e4 (Vilkov-Chernusevich, Smolensk 1992) 16...♘f7 17 dxc5 ♘e5 18 ♗c2 f4 19 ♘d3 ±.

e22) 11...♘f6 12 a4 (12 ♗a3 d6 13 c5 dxc5 14 dxc5 and now rather than the passive 14...♖e8?! 15 ♕b3 ♔h8 16 ♘c2 ± Levitt-Emms, British Ch (Swansea) 1987, 14...♖d8! improves; e.g., 15 ♕b3 ♗d5 with at least even chances for Black) 12...d6 13 d5 (13 a5!? ± ECO) 13...g6 14 e4 (Raisky-Kveinys, USSR 1982) 14...f4! with equality.

e3) 10...d6 11 f3 ♘f6 (Black can also consider 11...♘g5) 12 e4 (White has tried other moves here, including 12 c5!?) 12...fxe4 13 fxe4 ♘bd7 14 ♘f3 e5 15 c5!? ♕e7 (15...bxc5?! is worse: 16 ♕b3+ ♗d5 17 exd5 e4 18 ♘g5 exd3 19 ♘e6, Buehl-Dake, Los Angeles 1991, and here Black's best is 19...♕e7 20 ♘xf8 ♖xf8 21 ♗g5, although White is solidly better) 16 cxd6 ♕xd6?! (16...cxd6!? makes much more sense, even though White should be a little better, thanks to his bishops) 17 ♘h4?! (trying to get Black to weaken his position further, but 17 a4!? is better, leaving White with a good advantage) 17...g6? (17...exd4!? 18 ♘f5 ♕e6 19 ♘xd4 ♕f7 is OK for Black)

18 ♘f3 ♚g7 19 ♗b2 ± Rossiter-Harley, London Lloyds Bank 1987.

e4) 10...♘c6 is also met by 11 f3. Then:

e41) 11...♘f6 12 e4 (12 ♖b1!? d6 13 e4 e5 14 c5 is also interesting) 12...fxe4 13 fxe4 e5 14 ♘f3 ♕e7 and then:

e411) 15 ♗g5?! h6?! (15...exd4 is fine for Black; e.g., 16 cxd4 ♘b4 17 ♕b3 ♘xd3), Burke-Rizzitano, Chicago 1988, and now White can obtain the better game with 16 ♗xf6 ♖xf6 17 c5!? ♖af8 18 a4.

e412) 15 c5!? helps White rid himself of the doubled c-pawns, since 15...bxc5?? loses a piece to 16 ♕b3+.

e42) 11...♘g5 12 ♕e2 ♕e7 (Van der Wiel gives 12...e5 13 e4 f4 14 ♗b2 ♘f7 = as better) 13 ♘c2 e5 14 ♗a3! d6 15 c5 bxc5 16 dxc5 ♘e6 (Portisch-Van der Wiel, Wijk aan Zee 1985) and here both 17 ♗c4 and 17 ♖ab1 are better for White.

e43) 11...♘d6 12 ♗a3! ♖f6 13 c5 ♘f7 (Florea-Bunzmann, Apolda 1997) 14 e4 e5 15 ♕b2 fxe4 16 ♗xe4 exd4 17 cxd4 ♗a6 18 ♖f2 with a better game for White.

We now return to the position after 10 ♘d2 (D):

10...♕h4

This aggressive approach is not only Black's most popular option, but it also scores better percentage-wise than the alternatives, although these also have some merit:

a) 10...d5 11 cxd5 exd5 12 c4 ♘a6 13 ♗a3 ♘xd2 14 ♕xd2 c5 15 ♖ac1 (15 ♖ab1!?) favours White, Afanasiev-Nakhaenko, corr. 1991.

b) 10...♘xd2 11 ♗xd2 and then:

b1) 11...♕h4 12 f3 transposes to the main line.

b2) 11...♕f6 12 f3 ♘c6 13 e4 ♘a5 14 exf5 exf5 15 c5 ± Stigar-S.Horvath, Copenhagen 1986.

b3) 11...c5!? is very rarely played, but it seems that further tests are necessary. One line is 12 e4 ♕h4 13 exf5 ♗xg2! with a perpetual check to come, Appel-Smith, e-mail 1999.

b4) 11...♘c6 12 e4!? fxe4 13 ♗xe4 ♕h4 and now:

b41) 14 f3 ♘a5 15 ♗d3 ♗a6 16 ♗e1 ♕h6 17 ♕e2 c6 18 ♗d2 ♕f6 19 ♖fe1 ♖fe8 and Black's chances are no worse than White's, Portisch-P.Nikolić, Nikšić 1983.

b42) 14 ♖ae1!? ♘a5 15 c5 (15 ♗xb7 ♘xb7 16 ♖e4 is better, but not more than equal) 15...♗xe4 16 ♖xe4 ♕h5 17 c4 ♘c6 18 ♗e3 bxc5 19 dxc5 ♕g6 and Black has a pleasant position, Kantsler-M.Botvinnik, Tel-Aviv 1999.

b43) 14 f4 ♘a5 15 ♗d3 ♖f6!? 16 f5 ♕g4 (Pliester gives 16...exf5 as better for Black, but 17 ♗f4 d6 18 ♗xf5 is playable for White) 17 ♗e3 ♖af8 18 ♖f4 ♕h5 19 ♖af1 exf5 20 d5 and White has a pleasant game, Agdestein-Øgaard, Gjøvik 1983.

11 f3

Or:

a) 11 g3? simply weakens the light squares around the king too much. After 11...♘g5! the white king is already scrambling as 12 e4 can be met with 12...fxe4! and 12 d5 and 12 f3 are not particularly attractive either.

b) 11 ♗a3? is even worse. Black has the direct 11...♘xd2 12 ♕xd2 ♗xg2! 13 ♔xg2 (13 ♗xf8 ♗f3 14 ♖fc1 ♕h3 0-1 Blayvas-Friedrichs, Recklinghausen 1999) 13...♕g4+ 14 ♔h1 ♕f3+ 15 ♔g1 ♖f6 16 ♖fb1 ♕h3 −+. Astonishingly, this idea was missed by both *ECO* and Pliester.

c) 11 f4 ♘xd2 12 ♗xd2 ♕g4 13 ♖f2 ♕g6 14 ♖af1 d6 (14...c5!?) 15 ♖e2 ♗e4! with a comfortable position for Black, Darga-Portisch, Oberhausen Echt 1961.

11...♘xd2

11...♘g5 is another noteworthy idea:

a) 12 e4? quickly leads to a strategically lost position: 12...fxe4 13 ♘xe4 ♘xe4 14 ♗xe4 ♗xe4 15 ♕xe4 ♕xe4 16 fxe4 ♘c6 and Black can rub his hands in excitement, Eckert-Miles, Las Vegas 1997.

b) 12 ♕d1 ♖f6 (12...c5!? is an entirely different plan, but nonetheless worth considering) 13 ♕e1 ♕h5 14 e4! ♘c6 15 ♘b3 fxe4 16 ♗xg5 ♕xg5 17 ♗xe4 ♖e8 18 c5 is slightly better for White, Inkiov-Guedon, Bourbon-Lancy 1998.

c) 12 f4!? represents the sternest test of Black's knight move according to Emms. He gives 12...♕g4 13 d5 ♘f7 14 ♗a3 d6 15 e4 and 12...♘f7 13 e4, in both cases with White the one benefiting from Black's knight manoeuvre.

12 ♗xd2 d6

Or 12...♘c6:

a) 13 ♖ab1?! d6 14 e4 fxe4 15 ♗xe4 ♘a5 16 ♗xb7 ♘xb7 17 ♖be1 ♖ae8 18 ♕a4 ♘a5 19 f4 ♕h5 20 ♖f3 e5 21 dxe5 dxe5 and Black is doing better, I.Sokolov-Cu.Hansen, Novi Sad OL 1990.

b) 13 e4?! fxe4 14 fxe4 e5!? 15 d5 ♘e7 16 c5 ♘g6 (Maurer-Donaldson, Liechtenstein 1994) and here Emms gives 17 g3 as best, when he mentions 17...♕e7 18 ♗e3, although he also offers 17...♕h3!? for Black, which seems to be about equal.

c) 13 ♗e1 ♕g5 14 ♗g3 d6 (Knott-Lawson, Edinburgh 1989) 15 ♖ae1 ♕h5 16 c5!? is quite interesting.

13 ♗e1 ♕h5 14 ♕b3

14 ♗g3!?, intending c5, is another idea.

14...♘d7 15 ♗g3 ♔h8 16 ♖ae1 e5

Here in Rizantsev-Lukianenko, Moscow 1997 White went for 17 ♕b5, but 17 c5!? seems better; e.g., 17...f4 18 exf4 exf4 19 ♗f2 dxc5 20 ♕a4 ♕f7 21 ♗b5 with a complicated struggle ahead.

B)

7 0-0 *(D)*

B

7...f5

Or:

a) 7...♘xc3? ends up costing Black too much time: 8 bxc3 ♗xc3 (8...♗e7 9 e4 d6 10 ♗e3 ♘d7 11 ♘d2 0-0 12 ♕g4 with an advantage for White, Farago-Romanishin, Kiev 1978) 9 ♖b1 ♘c6 10 ♖b3 ♗a5 11 e4 h6 12 d5 ♘e7 13 ♗b2 0-0 14 ♘e5 ± Balashov-Romanishin, Lvov 1978.

b) 7...♗xc3 8 bxc3 and then:

b1) 8...0-0 9 ♘e1 f5 transposes to line 'b353'.

b2) 8...♘xc3 9 ♕c2 ♗xf3 10 gxf3 ♕g5+ 11 ♔h1 ♕h5 12 ♖g1! ♕xf3+ 13 ♖g2 f5 14 ♗a3 ♘e4 15 ♖f1 is supposed to be very nice for White, but then 15...♘c6!? (15...♖g8?! 16 ♗e2 ♕h3 17 f3 ♘f6 18 d5 ± Keres-Spassky, Riga Ct (8) 1965) 16 d5!? (16 ♗e2? is met with 16...♘xd4!) 16...♘e5 17 ♗e2 ♕h3 18 f4 ♘g6 19 dxe6 0-0-0 20 c5 ♔b8 21 e7 ♖de8 22 cxb6 axb6 23 ♖c1 ♘h4 24 ♕xc7+ ♔a8 25 ♗f1, as analysed by Nunn, looks like a probable draw.

b3) 8...f5 and here:

b31) 9 ♕c2 transposes to Line A.

b32) 9 d5 transposes to the main line.

b33) 9 ♗a3!? deserves more attention, as Black seems to have real problems equalizing: 9...d6 (Pliester suggests 9...c5 as Black's best, but 10 ♗xe4 ♗xe4 11 dxc5 wins a pawn with a good game for White) 10 d5 exd5 11 ♘d4 dxc4 12 ♗xc4 ♕g5 13 ♘e6 ♕e7 14 f3 ♘g5 15 e4 fxe4 (Schön-Wahls, Bundesliga 1987/8) and now 16 ♗b5+! is best; e.g., 16...♗c6 17 ♗xc6+ ♘xc6 18 ♕a4 ♕xe6 19 ♕xc6+ and Black is scrambling to keep the balance.

b34) 9 ♘d2 0-0 10 f3 ♘xd2 11 ♗xd2 ♘c6 12 ♕c2 ♗a6 13 e4 g6 14 ♗h6 ♖f7 15 exf5 exf5 16 ♖ae1 ♕h4 17 ♗e3 ♘a5 18 ♗f2 ♕f6 ± J.Ivanov-Sulskis, Ubeda 2001.

b35) 9 ♘e1 leads to similar play to Line A, but where White has saved a tempo by not playing ♕c2. Black has then tried:

b351) 9...♘xc3 10 ♕h5+ g6 11 ♕h6 ♘e4 (11...♕f6 has also been played and even if *ECO* claims it to be better for White, it, too, is about equal) 12 f3 ♘g5 13 e4 ♘f7 14 ♕g7 ♕e7 15 exf5 gxf5 16 ♗xf5! ♘c6 (16...exf5?! 17 ♘d3 ♔d8?! 18 ♘e5 ♖f8 19 ♖e1 d6 20 ♘d3 pretty much wins for White) 17 ♘c2 0-0-0 18 ♗a3 ♕g5 19 ♕xg5 ♘xg5 20 ♗d3 with only a very slight advantage for White, Semkov-Wilder, Saint John 1988.

b352) 9...♕h4 10 f3 ♘g5 11 ♗a3 ♘c6 12 ♖b1 ♘e7 13 d5 (13 ♗c2!? is an alternative) with a pull for White, Holm Petersen-B.Andersen, Danish Ch (Aalborg) 1965.

b353) 9...0-0 10 f3 and then:

b3531) 10...♘f6 11 ♘c2 ♕e8 12 c5 ♕h5 13 cxb6 axb6 14 c4 ♘c6 15 ♗b2 leads to an initiative for White, Gulko-Kuzmin, Lvov Z 1978.

b3532) 10...♘d6 11 ♗a3 ♖f6 12 ♕e2 ♘c6 13 ♘c2 e5 14 e4 f4 15 c5 and White's pieces wake up, Wilder-Cu.Hansen, Dortmund 1988.

b3533) 10...♘g5 11 ♖b1 d6 12 ♖b2!? ♘d7 13 ♖bf2 e5 14 c5 dxc5 15 h4 e4 16 ♕b3+ ♔h8 (Portisch-Inkiov, Cannes 1992) 17 ♗c4 is very good for White.

8 d5

With this move, White takes on the burden of a ruined pawn-structure.

White can lead the play away from this in a number of ways:

a) 8 ♕c2 transposes to Line A.

b) 8 ♗xe4 fxe4 9 ♘d2 ♗xc3 10 bxc3 0-0 11 ♕g4 ♖f5 12 d5 ♖g5 13 ♕f4 exd5 14 cxd5 ♗xd5 15 c4 ♗c6 16 ♘xe4 ♖g6 17 ♗b2 ♘a6 = Gligorić-Larsen, Havana 1967.

c) 8 ♘e5!? 0-0 (the retreat 8...♘f6 is also playable) 9 ♘xe4 (9 ♘e2 ♗e7 10 f3 ♘f6 11 ♗c2 c5!? is worth looking into for either side) 9...fxe4 10 ♗e2 ♗d6 11 f4 exf3 12 ♗xf3 ♗xf3 13 ♘xf3 ♘c6 14 e4 ♗f4 15 d5 with some initiative for White, Chatalbashev-Ciora, Nova Gorica 2000.

d) 8 ♘e2 and now:

d1) 8...0-0 9 ♘e1 (9 b3 ♗e7 transposes to line 'd3'; 9 ♘g3 ♗d6 10 ♕c2 ♗xg3! 11 hxg3 ♕e8 12 ♘d2 ♕g6 13 b4 a5 14 b5 d6 gives Black a good game, Yusupov-Kengis, Riga 1995) 9...♕h4 (after 9...♗d6!? 10 f3 ♘f6 11 ♘c3 c5 12 d5 ♗e5 Black can be happy, Semkov-Franco, Berga 1993) 10 f3 ♘f6 11 c5 ♗xe1 12 ♕xe1 ♕xe1 13 ♖xe1 ♗a6 14 cxb6 axb6 with a fairly level game, Volke-Wahls, Biel open 1993.

d2) 8...♗d6 9 b3 0-0 10 ♗b2 (10 ♘e5!? has also been played, but the untried 10...♘c5!? 11 ♗c2 ♗xe5 12 dxe5 ♘c6 13 ♗b2 a5 equalizes) 10...c5 11 dxc5 bxc5 12 ♘g3 ♗xg3 13 hxg3 d6 14 ♘d2 ♕e7 15 ♕c2 ½-½ Malaniuk-Ikonnikov, Werfen 1996.

d3) 8...♗e7 9 b3 0-0 10 ♗b2 ♗f6 11 ♕c2 c5 12 ♖ad1 ♕e7 13 ♘g3 ♘xg3 14 hxg3 ♘c6 15 ♕e2 g6 16 ♗b1 (Lautier-Adams, Wijk aan Zee 1991) and now 16...♕g7!? gives Black a decent game.

We now return to 8 d5 (D):

8...♗xc3

Taking with the knight has also been proved playable: 8...♘xc3 9 bxc3 ♗xc3 10 ♖b1 ♗f6 11 e4 0-0 12 ♖e1 ♘a6 13 exf5 exd5 14 cxd5 ♘c5 15 ♗c2 ♖e8 16 ♖e3 ♖xe3 17 ♗xe3 ♕e7 with a decent position for Black, Atalik-Grosar, Bled 1999.

9 bxc3 ♘c5

Some alternatives are:

a) 9...exd5?! 10 cxd5 ♗xd5 (after 10...♘xc3 11 ♕c2 ♘xd5 12 ♗xf5 ♘b4 13 ♕b1 ♗xf3 14 gxf3 ♕h4 15 f4 White is much better, Visier-Fernandez, Lanzarote 1974) 11 c4 ♗b7 12 ♘d4 0-0 13 f3 ♘d6 14 ♕c2 ♕f6 15 c5 ± Bolbochan-Enevoldsen, Havana OL 1966.

b) 9...0-0?! 10 ♗a3 ♖f6 11 ♕c2 exd5 12 cxd5 ♗xd5 13 ♘d4 c5 14 ♘xf5 ± Renet-Moran, Dubai OL 1986.

c) 9...♘a6 and now:

c1) 10 ♘d4 ♘ac5 (10...♘ec5 11 ♗a3 transposes to note 'b' to White's 11th move) 11 ♗xe4 fxe4 12 ♗a3 0-0 13 ♖b1! ♖b8 14 ♗xc5 bxc5 15 ♘e2 ♗a6 16 ♖xb8 ♕xb8 17 ♕a4 ♕b6 18 ♘f4 ± Gligorić-Bukić, Vrbas 1980.

c2) 10 ♗a3 will normally transpose to the main line via 10...♘ec5, but Black has also tried 10...♘ac5: 11

♗xe4 ♘xe4 (11...fxe4?! 12 ♘d2 0-0 13 ♗xc5 bxc5 14 ♖b1 ♖b8 15 ♘xe4 with a good advantage for White, Muir-Beaton, Scotland 1991) 12 ♘d4 exd5 13 f3 ♘c5 14 cxd5 ♗a6 ½-½ Scholl-Engel, corr. 1993. The chances are about equal.

10 ♗a3

Or:

a) 10 e4 looks very strange, allowing Black to fork two of White's pieces, but it isn't as simple as that: 10...fxe4 11 ♗g5 ♕c8 12 ♗c2 0-0 (12...exf3? looks tempting at first glance, but after 13 ♕xf3 d6 14 ♖ae1 e5 15 ♕h5+ ♔f8 16 f4 e4 17 ♗xe4 ♘xe4 18 ♖xe4 reality sets in and Black will end up with a lost position) 13 ♘d2 exd5 14 cxd5 (14 ♗e7 dxc4, Hernandez-Georgadze, Aceimar 1999, and here 15 ♗xf8 ♕xf8 16 ♘xc4 ♕f6 17 ♕d4 ♕e6 leaves the game balanced) 14...♖f5 (14...♕e8!?) 15 ♕g4 ♖xd5 16 ♗h6 ♕f8 17 ♘xe4 ♘ba6 18 ♖ae1 ♘d3 (18...♔h8!? is more solid and probably Black's best choice) 19 ♖e3 ♘e5 20 ♕g3 gives White more than enough compensation for the pawn, Pelletier-Wahls, Bundesliga 1999/00.

b) 10 ♖e1 ♕f6! 11 ♕c2 0-0 12 e4 fxe4 13 ♗xe4 ♘xe4 14 ♕xe4 ♘a6 15 ♗a3 and now, instead of the standard 15...♘c5 which is better for White after 16 ♗xc5 bxc5 17 ♖ab1 ♖ab8 18 ♕e3 (Muir-Farrell, Scottish Ch 1991), Black has the somewhat unusual 15...c5!?, keeping the pressure on White's centre intact; e.g., 16 ♕d3 ♘c7!? 17 ♖ab1 (17 dxe6?! is met by 17...♗xf3! 18 e7 ♖f7, followed by ...♘e6) 17...♗a6 18 dxe6 dxe6 and Black is in control.

10...♘ba6 *(D)*

11 ♖e1

Or:

a) 11 ♗c2!? has served White well on several occasions, but Black is theoretically OK: 11...0-0 (11...♕f6!? is a new try in this position: 12 ♘d4 0-0 13 f3 g6 14 ♕d2 e5 15 ♖f2 d6 16 ♘e2 ♘d7 17 ♔h1 ♘ac5 and Black has a pleasant game, G.Buckley-Ward, British Ch (Torquay) 1998) 12 ♘d4 ♖f7 (12...♖f6 13 f3 and now, instead of 13...♖h6?! 14 ♕e2 ♕f6 15 ♖ae1 ♖e8 16 ♗c1, which is much better for White, Gligorić-Cafferty, Teesside 1972, Taimanov gives 13...♕e7 as equal) 13 f3 (alternatively, 13 ♘b3 ♕e7 14 ♖e1 e5 15 f4 d6 with an equal position, Balashov-Emms, 2nd Bundesliga 1994/5) 13...♕g5 (both 13...♕e7 and 13...♕f6 seem better than the text-move) 14 ♗c1 ♕f6 15 ♗d2 ♖e8 16 e4 ± Lukacs-Medina, Szolnok 1975.

b) 11 ♘d4 0-0 12 ♖b1 (or 12 f3 g6 13 ♕e2?! {13 ♖b1, followed by ♘b3, is about even} 13...e5 14 ♘b3 d6 15 ♗xc5 ♘xc5 16 ♘xc5 dxc5 17 f4 ♕f6 with a better game for Black, Brinck-Claussen – Cu.Hansen, Silkeborg 1983) 12...♖f7 13 ♘b3 ♕e7 14 e4 fxe4 15 ♗xe4 and here, instead of 15...e5? (Chatalbashev-Hauchard, Elista OL 1998), which loses to 16 ♗xc5! ♕h4 (or 16...♘xc5 17 d6!) 17 f4 bxc5 18 ♘d2 ♖b8 19 fxe5; Black should play 15...exd5 16 ♗f3 d6 17 cxd5 ♕e5 with chances for both sides.

11...♕f6

11...0-0?! got Black into trouble in Rechlis-Brunner, Berne Z 1990: 12 e4 fxe4 13 ♗xe4 ♖f4 14 ♗c2 ♖xc4 (this is my definition of asking for it; 14...♕f6 is more appealing; e.g., 15 ♘e5 ♖f8 16 f3 exd5 17 cxd5 ♖h4 18 ♕d2 although here too White has the better chances) 15 ♘e5 ♖xc3 16 ♗xh7+! ♔xh7 17 ♕h5+ ♔g8 18 ♗b2! ♕f6 (18...♘a4 19 ♗xc3 ♘xc3 20 ♕f7+ ♔h7 21 ♖e3 +−; 18...♖c2 19 ♕f7+ ♔h7 20 ♘g4! +−) 19 ♗xc3 ♗xd5 20 ♘g6 ♕xc3 21 ♘e7+ ♔f8 22 ♘xd5 g6 23 ♕xg6 ♕g7 and although Black has survived the worst, White is clearly better.

12 ♕c2 g6

Psakhis suggests playing the immediate 12...0-0-0!?. It makes a lot of sense and is probably better than the text-move.

13 e4! fxe4 14 ♗xe4 0-0-0 15 ♘d2 ♖de8 16 ♖ad1 (D)

Now Black must somehow restrict White's increasing activity. This can be done with 16...♖hf8 17 ♗f3 (I think 17 ♘b3!? may be a more aggressive and better choice) 17...d6!? (Psakhis), after which his chances are no

worse than White's. In Sadler-Ward, Hastings 1997/8, Black failed to realize that White could force weaknesses around his king: 16...♕f7 17 d6! ♘xe4 18 ♘xe4 ♕f5 19 dxc7 ♗xe4 20 ♖xe4 ♘c5 21 ♗xc5 ♕xc5 22 ♖ed4 ♖e7 23 ♕a4 ♕xc7 24 c5! bxc5 25 ♖d6 and White's attack continued.

Conclusion

The Dutch Variation is very much in line with many players' understanding of how Black is supposed to play the Nimzo-Indian. However, this does not prevent us from establishing that White obtains good chances by playing the aggressive Line B (7 0-0). The more careful approach, 7 ♕c2 (Line A) still has many followers, but doesn't promise more than equality with best play from both sides.

13 Keres Variation and Related Systems

After 1 d4 ♘f6 2 c4 e6 3 ♘c3 ♗b4 4 e3 b6 5 ♗d3 ♗b7 6 ♘f3 0-0 7 0-0 c5 we arrive at the position that signifies the Keres Variation. As usual with these lines, it is not really the originator of the line who has had his name affixed to it, but someone who has helped develop the theory and understanding of the line. Before Keres, several players, particularly Smyslov and Bronstein, made use of this line and since then, numerous world-class players have included it in their repertoires at some point. The position after Black's 7th move was first seen in the game Alatortsev-Chekhover, Leningrad Ch 1932. It was first played amongst top players in the Botvinnik-Bronstein world championship match in 1951, where the latter used it to win the 5th match game.

Before reaching the main line, both sides have several chances to deviate:

1 d4 ♘f6 2 c4 e6 3 ♘c3 ♗b4 4 e3 b6 5 ♗d3 *(D)*

5...♗b7

5...c5 6 ♘f3 0-0 and now:

a) 7 0-0 ♗b7 transposes to the main line.

b) 7 d5!? takes the game down an independent path. 7...exd5 8 cxd5 and now:

b1) 8...♗b7 9 e4 c4 10 ♗c2 d6 11 0-0 ♖e8 12 ♖e1 ♘bd7 13 ♗g5 a6 14

a3 ♗c5 15 ♘a4 ♕c7 16 ♘xc5 ♕xc5 17 ♕d4 ± Balashov-Aseev, USSR Ch (Odessa) 1989.

b2) 8...h6 9 e4 (9 0-0 has also been played on a few occasions) 9...♘xe4! 10 ♗xe4 ♗xc3+ 11 bxc3 ♖e8 12 ♘d2 f5 13 f3 ♗a6 14 ♔f2 fxe4 15 ♘xe4 d6 16 ♗f4 ♘d7 17 ♖e1 ♘e5 18 ♖e3 ♘c4 19 ♖e2 ♘e5 20 ♖e3 ♘c4 ½-½ Gelfand-Ivanchuk, Linares 1994.

6 ♘f3 0-0

Or:

a) 6...c5 7 0-0 0-0 again transposes to the main line.

b) 6...d5 7 0-0 0-0 transposes to Chapter 14.

7 0-0 *(D)*

7...c5

Or:

a) 7...♖e8 looks somewhat strange at first glance, but the idea is either to assist with the central ...e5 push, or to

have the rook ready on the e-file after
...d5 followed by an exchange of pawns
on d5. Then:

a1) 8 ♖e1 is an interesting idea:
8...d5 (8...d6!? makes good sense here)
9 ♘e5 ♘bd7 10 f4 ♗xc3 (10...c5!?)
11 bxc3 a6 12 a4 (M.Popović-Ahnen,
Germany tt 1992) and here 12...c5!? is
best, leaving White no more than a
tiny bit better.

a2) 8 ♗d2 d6 9 a3 (9 ♖e1 e5 10
♗c2 ♘bd7 11 h3 ♗xc3 12 ♗xc3 ♘e4
13 ♗b4 c5 14 ♖a3 f5 15 ♘d2 ♘df6
gives Black a pleasant position, Ah-
lander-Wedberg, Swedish Ch (Skara)
2002) 9...♗xc3 10 ♗xc3 ♘bd7 11
♘d2 (11 b4 e5 12 ♗c2 ♕e7 13 d5 b5!?
14 cxb5 ♗xd5 15 ♗b3 ♘b6 is fine
for Black, Franić-Stocek, Pula 2002)
11...e5 and here:

a21) 12 d5 seems to make a lot of
sense as it shuts out the b7-bishop and
plans a queenside attack where the
b6-pawn will soon become a problem
for Black. However, 12...b5! 13 e4 ♘c5
gave Black a good game in Gulko-
Kuzmin, USSR Ch (Frunze) 1981.

a22) 12 ♗c2 exd4 13 ♗xd4 c5 14
♗c3 ♕c7 15 ♖a4 ♖e6 16 ♗c2 d5 17
♗f5 ♖d6 18 b3 dxc4 19 bxc4 and now,
rather than 19...♗e4?? 20 ♗xe4 ♘xe4

21 ♕f3 +– Babula-Stocek, Czech Cht
2002, Black should play 19...♖e8 followed by 20...♘e5.

b) 7...♗xc3!? is also quite popular.
After 8 bxc3 Black has several options:

b1) 8...♘e4 transposes to note
'b353' to Black's 7th move in Line B
of Chapter 12.

b2) 8...d6 and here:

b21) 9 ♘d2 e5 (9...c5 transposes to
line 'b441') 10 e4 ♘c6 11 ♘b3 ♘e7
12 ♕e2 ♘g6 13 d5 ♘d7 14 g3 a5 and
Black has a fully satisfactory position,
Nenashev-G.Kuzmin, Tashkent 1987.

b22) 9 ♖e1 ♘e4 10 ♘d2 f5 11 f3
♘xd2 12 ♗xd2 ♘d7 13 ♕c2 ♘f6 14
d5 g6 = B.Lalić-Ochoa, Seville 1987.

b23) 9 ♕c2 ♘bd7 10 e4 e5 11 ♗g5
♖e8 12 ♘d2 ♘f8 (Pfleger-Root, Lone
Pine 1981) 13 f4 with a good game for
White.

b3) 8...♗e4 9 ♗e2 (9 ♕c2 doesn't
amount to much after 9...♗xf3!? 10
gxf3 c5 11 ♔h1 ♘c6 12 ♕e2 e5 13 d5
♘e7 14 ♖g1 d6 15 ♕f1 ♘e8 with a
pleasant game for Black, Balashov-
Danielsen, Aalborg 1993) and then:

b31) 9...d6 10 ♘d2 ♗b7 11 f3 c5
(11...e5 12 e4 ♘bd7 13 ♖f2 ♖e8 14
♘f1 ♘f8 is a playable alternative,
Lukacs-Barczay, Hungarian Ch (Budapest) 1977) 12 e4 ♘bd7 13 ♗d3 e5
14 ♘b3 ♖e8 15 d5 ♘f8 16 ♗e3 ♗c8
17 ♘c1 ♗d7 18 ♘e2 ♘g6 offers
chances for both sides, Radjabov-de
Firmian, Malmö 2001.

b32) 9...c5 10 ♘d2 (10 ♘e1 also
deserves attention; e.g., 10...♗b7 11
f3 d5 12 cxd5 ♘xd5 13 ♗d2 ♕c7 14
♖c1 ♘d7 15 ♘d3 f5 16 c4 ♘5f6 17
♕b3 ♖fe8 with a complicated struggle
ahead, Ibragimov-Psakhis, New York

1997) 10...♗b7 (10...♗g6 11 ♗f3 ♘c6 12 ♗a3 ♖c8 13 dxc5 ♕e7 14 ♘b3 ♘e5 15 ♗e2 ♘e4 16 ♖c1 ♘xc5 and Black has a satisfactory position, Re-shevsky-Fischer, Buenos Aires 1970) 11 f3 (11 ♗d3 transposes to 'b44' with two extra moves played by each side) 11...d5 12 dxc5 bxc5 13 ♖b1 ♕c7 14 ♕b3 (Taimanov-Gulko, USSR Ch (Leningrad) 1974) 14...♗c6 ± Tai-manov.

b4) 8...c5 and here:

b41) 9 ♖e1?! ♘e4 10 ♕c2 f5 11 ♗b2 ♕e8 12 ♖ad1 d6 13 ♘d2 ♕g6 ∓ Tal-Short, Montpellier Ct 1985.

b42) 9 ♘e1 d6 10 f3 ♘c6 11 ♘c2 (Gulko-Sharif, Marseilles 1986) 11...e5 = Wells.

b43) 9 a4 d6 10 ♗a3 ♘e4 11 ♘e1! f5 12 f3 ♘f6 13 ♘c2 ♘c6 14 e4 fxe4 15 fxe4 e5 16 d5 ♘e7 17 ♘e3 with the initiative for White, Sadler-Adams, Tilburg 1998.

b44) 9 ♘d2 and then:

b441) 9...d6 is playable; e.g., 10 e4 cxd4 11 cxd4 e5 12 d5 (rather than closing the centre, 12 ♗b2!? must be better) 12...♘fd7 13 ♘b3 ♘a6 with a pleasant game for Black, Chevallier-Renet, French Cht 1994.

b442) 9...♘c6 10 e4 (10 ♘b3 a5 11 a4 d6 12 f3 ♖c8 13 ♗a3 e5 14 d5 ♘e7 15 ♘d2 ♘e8 16 e4 ♖b8 17 ♕c2 ♗c8 18 ♖ae1, Gelfand-Adams, Biel IZ 1993, and here Black should play 18...f5 19 exf5 ♗xf5 20 ♘e4 ♕d7 21 f4 ♗xe4 22 ♗xe4 ♘f6 with chances for both sides according to Adams) 10...cxd4 11 cxd4 ♘xd4 12 e5 ♘e8 13 ♗a3 d6 14 ♖e1 f5 15 ♗f1 ♕g5 16 exd6 ♖d8, and now in Lesiège-Short, Elista OL 1998, White went for 17 ♘e4, but after 17...fxe4 18 ♕xd4 ♘f6

19 h3 ♘d7 20 ♖e3 e5 21 ♕b2 ♗c6 Black had equalized.

We now return to 7...c5 (D):

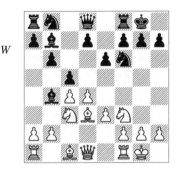

In this position, White has tried many different things. The most important continuations are:

A: 8 ♗d2   194
B: 8 ♘a4   197

Or:

a) 8 ♘e2 was used in the stem game of this variation, but is nowa-days considered harmless: 8...cxd4 9 ♘exd4 (9 exd4 allows 9...♗xf3 10 gxf3 d5 or 9...d5 10 ♗g5 dxc4 11 ♗xc4 ♘bd7 12 ♕b3 ♗e7 13 ♖fe1 ♘d5 14 ♗d2 ♖c8 15 ♖ac1 a6 = Vranesić-O'Kelly, Havana OL 1966) 9...♗e7 10 ♕e2 ♘a6 11 e4 ♘c5 12 e5 ♘xd3 13 ♕xd3 ♘e4 14 ♖d1 d5 = Letelier-Donner, Havana 1967.

b) 8 ♕e2 and now:

b1) 8...d5 can transpose into a number of different lines, most nota-bly those to be found in Chapters 1 and 2.

b2) Black can try 8...d6!?; for ex-ample, 9 ♗d2 ♘bd7 10 a3?! ♗xc3 11 ♗xc3 ♕e7 12 ♘d2 ♖ac8 13 ♖ad1 ♖fd8 14 b3 d5 = N.Rodrigues-Fernandes,

Lisbon 2001, but White's play here was hardly critical.

b3) 8...♗xc3 9 bxc3 ♗e4 10 ♘d2 ♗xd3 11 ♕xd3 d6 12 e4 e5 13 f4 ♕e7 14 fxe5 dxe5 15 ♘f3 ♘bd7 = Bobotsov-Langeweg, Wijk aan Zee 1970.

c) 8 a3 is played remarkably often, but against best play it's completely harmless. Note that Black often plays 7...♗xc3 8 bxc3 c5 with good results, which should give some sort of indication that this is nothing for Black to worry about. After 8...♗xc3 (8...cxd4 9 ♘a4 transposes to Line B1; Black can even try 8...♗a5!?) 9 bxc3, Black has tried:

c1) 9...d6 transposes to a Sämisch Variation.

c2) 9...d5 10 cxd5 exd5 11 dxc5 bxc5 12 ♖b1 ♕c7 13 c4 ± Reshevsky-Matanović, Skopje 1976.

c3) 9...♕c7 10 ♘d2 d5 11 ♗b2 ♘bd7 12 cxd5 exd5 13 f3 ♖fe8 14 ♖e1 ♖ad8 15 a4 ♖e7 with a doubleedged position which is typical of the Rubinstein Nimzo-Indian, Dydyshko-Poluliakhov, Berlin 1995.

c4) 9...♘e4!? 10 ♘e1 (10 ♕c2 f5 11 ♘d2 ♘xd2 12 ♗xd2 ♘c6 13 f3 ♘a5 = Diez del Corral-Ivkov, Palma de Mallorca 1967) 10...f5 11 f3 ♘d6 12 a4 ♘c6 13 ♘c2 (13 ♗a3 ♕c7!? is fine for Black) 13...♘a5 14 ♘a3 a6 (14...♗a6!?) 15 ♖b1 ♖c8 and Black has solved his opening problems, Lautier-Gelfand, Biel 1997.

c5) 9...♗e4 10 ♗e2 (or 10 ♘g5 ♗xd3 11 ♕xd3 h6 12 ♘h3 ♘c6 13 e4 d6 14 f4 e5 15 d5 ♘a5 16 fxe5 dxe5 17 ♖f5 ♕d6 18 ♘f2 ½-½ F.Portisch-Forintos, Hungarian Ch (Budapest) 1976) 10...♘c6 11 ♘d2 ♗g6 12 f3 d6 (12...d5 is also adequate: 13 ♘b3 ♖c8

14 cxd5 ♘xd5 15 ♕d2 cxd4 16 exd4 a5 is equal, Inkiov-Adamski, Primorsko 1977) 13 ♘b3 e5 14 e4 ♕c7 15 ♗e3 ♔h8 16 ♖f2 ♘g8 17 g4 f6 with an equal position, Ivkov-Keene, Bath Echt 1973.

A)

8 ♗d2 *(D)*

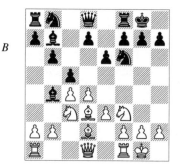

8...cxd4

Or:

a) 8...♗xc3?! makes very little sense, since White is likely to force this anyway with his next move.

b) 8...d5 usually just transposes to the main line via, for instance, 9 cxd5 cxd4 10 exd4.

c) 8...♖e8 has yet to be tested sufficiently. In Nenashev-Psakhis, Tilburg rpd 1994, White obtained slightly the better game after 9 a3 ♗xc3 10 ♗xc3 d6 11 ♖e1 ♘bd7 12 e4 cxd4 13 ♘xd4 ♘e5 14 b3 a6 15 a4 ♕c7 16 ♖c1 ♖ad8 17 ♗b1.

d) 8...d6 is a fairly popular choice:

d1) 9 ♕e2 does little for White: 9...♘bd7 10 a3 ♗xc3 11 ♗xc3 ♖c8 12 ♖fd1 ♕e7 13 ♘d2 ♖fd8 14 ♖ac1 leads only to equality, Filip-Bronstein, Zagreb 1965.

d2) 9 a3 ♗xc3 10 ♗xc3 is seen more often, but here too White has had difficulties proving an advantage:

d21) 10...♘e4 and now:

d211) 11 ♗xe4 ♗xe4 12 ♕e2 ♕e7 13 ♖fd1 ♘d7 14 b4 ♖ac8 15 ♖ac1 ♖fd8 16 ♘d2 ♗b7 17 ♕g4 ♘f6 = Kamsky-Ivanchuk, Monaco Amber blindfold 1995.

d212) 11 ♗e1 ♘d7 12 ♘d2 f5 (12...♘xd2 is also fine) 13 f3 ♘xd2 14 ♗xd2 ♕h4 15 ♗c3 = G.Buckley-Cherniaev, Coulsdon 1999.

d22) 10...♘bd7 and here:

d221) 11 ♕e2 transposes to line 'd1'.

d222) 11 ♖e1 is tame: 11...♖c8 12 e4 cxd4 13 ♘xd4 ♘c5 14 f3 ♘xd3 15 ♕xd3 ♗a6 16 b3 d5! leads to a pleasant game for Black, P.Nikolić-Larsen, Næstved 1985.

d223) 11 ♘d2 ♖c8 12 b3 ♖e8 13 ♖c1 d5 14 f3 e5!? 15 ♗f5 (Lyrberg-Wells, Copenhagen 1995) 15...exd4 16 exd4 ♕c7 is fine for Black.

9 exd4

With 9 ♘xd4, White can take the game into a Hedgehog-like position, where White has to spend another tempo playing e4 and Black therefore has nothing to worry about.

9...d5

9...♗e7 has also seen some action and here too White has not been too convincing; for example, 10 ♕e2 d6 11 ♖ae1 ♖e8 12 ♘g5 ♗f8 13 ♘ce4 ♘bd7 14 ♕f3 ♕e7 ½-½ Kharitonov-Moiseenko, St Petersburg 2001.

10 cxd5

10 ♕e2 dxc4 11 ♗xc4 and now:

a) 11...♘bd7 and here 12 ♖fd1 transposes to note 'b' to White's 12th move in Line C2 of Chapter 2, while

12 ♖ac1 is note 'c' to White's 9th move of Line C of that chapter.

b) Black can do even better with 11...♘c6!; e.g., 12 a3 ♗e7 13 ♗e3 ♖c8 ∓ Shocron-Sanguinetti, Mar del Plata 1956.

10...♘xd5

Or:

a) 10...exd5 11 ♘e5 ♘c6 12 ♗g5 ♗e7 13 ♘xc6 ♗xc6 14 ♖e1 h6 15 ♗h4 ± Gligorić-Filip, Havana 1967.

b) 10...♗xc3 11 bxc3 ♕xd5 (the alternative 11...exd5 12 ♗g5 is very pleasant for White) and here:

b1) 12 c4 ♕d6 (or 12...♕h5 13 ♘e5 ♕xd1 14 ♖fxd1 ♘c6 15 ♘xc6 ♗xc6 16 f3 ♗a4 17 ♖e1 ♖fd8, Van der Sterren-Seul, Antwerp 1999, 18 ♗e3!? ±) 13 ♗c3 ♘bd7 (13...♖d8 14 ♖e1 ♕f4 15 ♘e5 ♘bd7 16 g3 ♕h6 17 h4 ± V.Georgiev-Fyllingen, Bergen 2001) 14 ♖e1 ♖ac8 15 h3 ♖fd8 16 ♗e3 h6 and now instead of 17 ♕b3?! ♗xf3! 18 ♖xf3 e5 19 dxe5 ♘xe5 20 ♗xe5 ♕xe5 21 ♖b1 ½-½ Gligorić-Keres, USSR-Yugoslavia (Zagreb) 1958, White should play 17 ♖b1 with a slight initiative.

b2) 12 ♖e1 ♘bd7 (12...♗a6!? Dautov) 13 ♕e2 (13 ♗f4 ♖ac8 14 c4 ♕h5 15 ♗d6 ♖fd8 16 ♗e7 ± Browne-Andersson, Wijk aan Zee 1976) 13...♖fd8 (13...♕h5 14 a4 a6 15 ♖eb1 ♖fd8 ± Reshevsky-Smyslov, Zurich Ct 1953) 14 a4 ♗c6 (14...a6!? Dautov) 15 ♕f1 ♕d6 16 ♘e5 ♘xe5 17 ♖xe5 (Bareev-Karpov, Tilburg 1994) 17...h6! 18 ♕c1 (18 a5!? could be an improvement) 18...♘g4 19 ♖h5 e5 20 h3 (20 f3!?) 20...e4 21 hxg4 exd3 = (Ftačnik).

We now return to 10...♘xd5 *(D)*:

This position closely resembles those that often arise in the Classical

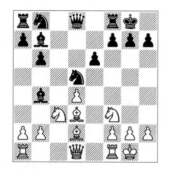

Variation (4...0-0 5 ②f3 d5 6 ♗d3 c5 7 0-0 ②c6 8 a3 cxd4 9 exd4 dxc4 10 ♗xc4) and in particular the Karpov Variation (4...0-0 5 ②f3 d5 6 ♗d3 c5 7 0-0 dxc4 8 ♗xc4 cxd4 9 exd4 b6). In this case, however, Black has already achieved the blockade of White's d-pawn. This is an essential part of playing against an IQP. Despite this, several world-class players have taken this line on as White and in some cases succeeded, which should go to show that Black's task isn't necessarily easy.

11 ♕e2

Or:

a) 11 ②xd5 ♗xd2 12 ♕xd2 ♗xd5 13 ②e5 ②d7 (Maslov-Keres, USSR Cht (Moscow) 1967) and now Kotov's 14 ♕e3 leads to equality.

b) 11 ♖e1 ②d7 (*ECO* gives the move 11...②xc3 as interesting, but after 12 bxc3 White is better) 12 a3 ♗e7 13 ♕e2 ♖e8 (*ECO* mentions 13...♖c8 = but White could easily have a little pull after 14 ♗a6!? ♗xa6 15 ♕xa6) 14 ②e4 a6 15 ♖ac1 ②f8 16 ②e5 is slightly better for White, Vaganian-Balashov, Riga 1970.

c) 11 ♖c1 and here:

c1) 11...②c6 12 ♖e1 (12 ♕e2!? – Yusupov) 12...♖c8 13 ♖e4 (13 ♗b1 is

better according to Lautier) 13...②ce7 14 ②xd5 ②xd5 15 ♖h4 g6 16 ♖xc8 ♕xc8 17 ②g5 ♗e7 18 ♕g4 (Yusupov-Ivanchuk, Brussels Ct (8) 1991) and now 18...f5!? 19 ♕h3 ♗xg5 20 ♗xg5 ♖f7 or 18...②f6! 19 ♕h3 h5, in both cases with a fine game for Black.

c2) 11...②f6 12 a3 ♗e7 13 ♖e1 ②c6 14 ♗f4 ♖c8 15 ♗b1 ②a5 16 ②e5 ②c4 17 ②xc4 ♖xc4 18 ♗e5 ♖c8 and the slight initiative White has at this point was soon neutralized in Bareev-Timman, Wijk aan Zee 1995.

d) 11 ②e5!?, intending 11...②c6?! 12 ♗a6!, was given by Kotov as '±'. This was tested in Lauber-de Firmian, Hamburg 1997: 12...♗xa6 13 ②xc6 ♕d7 14 ②xd5 ♗d6 15 ②f6+ gxf6 16 ♕g4+ ♔h8 17 ♕h4 ♗e7 18 ②xe7 ♕xe7 and here White decided to force the draw by 19 ♗b4 ♕xb4 20 ♕xf6+, but he would have had a safe advantage after 19 ♖fc1. But 11...②d7!? is OK for Black.

11...②c6 (D)

Or:

a) 11...②d7 leaves White with some initiative after 12 ♕e4!? ②7f6 13 ♕h4 ♗e7 14 ②e5 ± Bolbochan-Keres, Argentina-USSR (Buenos Aires) 1954.

b) 11...②f6 12 ♖fd1 ②bd7 13 ♗g5 ♗xc3 (13...h6 14 ♗h4 ♖c8 is about equal) 14 bxc3 ♕c7 15 ♖ac1 h6 16 ♗d2 (16 ♗h4!?) 16...♖ad8 17 c4 with a slight initiative for White, Sanguinetti-Bilek, Munich OL 1958.

White now (after 11...②c6) has three continuations, but he has failed to prove any tangible advantage with any of them:

a) 12 ②xd5 ♕xd5 13 ♗e4 ♕a5 14 ♗xb4 ♕xb4 15 ♖ac1 ♖ac8 = Tal-Keres, Riga 1968.

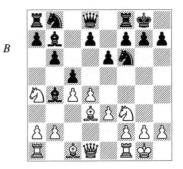

b) 12 ♖fd1 ♗e7 13 ♖ac1 ♖c8 14 a3 (or 14 ♕e4 ♘f6 15 ♕f4 ♘b4 16 ♗b1 ♘bd5 with a pleasant game for Black, Kluger-Keres, Hastings 1957/8) 14...♘xc3 15 ♗xc3 ♘b8! (clearing the path for the bishop to challenge White's build-up against Black's king) 16 ♗e4 ♗d5 = Gligorić-Keres, Moscow 1963.

c) 12 ♖ad1 ♗e7 13 a3 (or 13 ♖fe1 ♖c8 14 h4!? ♘cb4 15 ♗b1 ♗a6 16 ♕e4 ♘f6 17 ♕e3 ♗b7 and Black has no complaints, Leveille-Druet, corr. 1992) 13...♗f6 14 ♕e4 g6 15 ♘xd5 ♕xd5 16 ♕xd5 exd5 17 ♗c3 ♖fe8 18 ♖c1 ♖ac8 ½-½ Donner-Bobotsov, Skopje OL 1972.

B)

8 ♘a4 *(D)*

White sidesteps the exchange on c3 and puts the knight on the edge of the board. Note that the knight doesn't intend to return to c3 at the first chance, but will stay on a4, where it will assist in the queenside attack by supporting a c5 advance at a later juncture.

8...cxd4

Also seen are:

a) 8...♘a6 is similar to an idea championed by Ivan Sokolov in another line (4...c5 5 ♘e2 b6). Here though White quickly gains the upper hand: 9 a3 ♗a5 10 b3 ♕e7 (10...♘e4!? and the 'mysterious' 10...♖b8!?, intending 11...d5, where an exchange on c5 will leave the rook well-placed, are possible improvements) 11 ♗b2 ♖ac8 12 d5! exd5 13 cxd5 d6 14 ♘h4 with a strong initiative for White, Lesiège-I.Sokolov, Elista OL 1998.

b) 8...♕e7 used to be condemned as bad for Black, but it has recently been used by both Gelfand and Lautier. After 9 a3 ♗a5, White can try:

b1) 10 b3 d5 11 ♗b2 dxc4 12 ♗xc4 (12 bxc4 ♘bd7 is pleasant for Black) 12...♘bd7 13 ♖c1 ♖fd8 14 ♕e2 a6! 15 ♗d3 (Sadler-Lautier, Elista OL 1998) 15...cxd4! 16 exd4 ♘d5! and here Wells gives 17 ♗b1 ♘f4 18 ♕e3 ♘d5 19 ♕d3 (19 ♕e4!? f5!?) 19...♘7f6 20 b4 b5 21 ♘c5 ♗b6 and 17 b4 ♘f4 18 ♕d2 ♘xd3 19 ♕xd3 b5, in both cases with chances for both sides.

b2) 10 ♘d2 ♗c6 11 ♘c3 d5 12 ♕e2 ♕b7 13 f3 cxd4 14 exd4 ♗xc3 15 bxc3 ♘bd7 16 ♖e1 ♖fe8 ½-½ Panno-Keene, Buenos Aires OL 1978.

b3) 10 ♖b1 ♖c8! (*ECO* only mentions the line 10...♘e4?! 11 ♘e1, when 11...♗xe1 is probably Black's best, although White has a solid advantage) 11 ♕e2 (11 ♘e1, 11 ♘d2 and 11 b3 are all also best met with 11...♗c6) 11...♗c6 (Gelfand mentions 11...♗e4!? 12 ♗xe4 ♘xe4 13 ♕d3 f5, which is fine for Black) 12 ♗c2 d5 13 cxd5 (13 dxc5 dxc4!? Wells) 13...exd5 14 dxc5 bxc5 15 b4 cxb4 16 ♗d2 b3 with chances for both sides, Lautier-Gelfand, German Cup 1996/7.

We return to 8...cxd4 *(D)*:

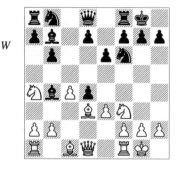

Now there are two important lines, the latter being the more popular:

B1: 9 a3   198
B2: 9 exd4   201

B1)

9 a3 ♗e7

The main line. An alternative is 9...♗d6!?, which was introduced by Korchnoi as recently as 1995. So far, the results have been encouraging for Black. His idea is to attack the white centre immediately. 10 exd4 ♗xf3! 11 ♕xf3 ♘c6 and now:

a) 12 ♗e3 e5! 13 dxe5 (both 13 d5?! e4! 14 ♗xe4 ♘e5 15 ♕f4 ♕c7 {Wells} and 13 c5!? exd4 14 cxd6 dxe3 15 ♕xe3 ♖e8 16 ♕g3 ♘e5 17 ♗f5 {Wells} 17...♘h5 18 ♕h3 g6 are

pleasant for Black) 13...♘xe5 14 ♕d1 ♕c7 15 h3 ♖fe8 16 ♖c1 ♖ac8 17 b4 ♘xd3 18 ♕xd3 ♗h2+ 19 ♔h1 ♗f4 and Black has at least equalized, Mornier-Zarnicki, Rosario 2001.

b) 12 ♖d1 ♘xd4 13 ♗xh7+ ♘xh7 14 ♖xd4 ♗e5 15 ♖e4 ♘g5 (or 15...d6 16 ♕h3 ♘g5 17 ♗xg5 ♕xg5 18 ♖d1 ♖ac8 19 ♖h4 f5 {19...g6!?} 20 g3 ♕f6 21 ♖h8+ ♔f7 22 ♕h5+ ♔e7 = Lukacs-Korchnoi, Austrian Cht 1995) 16 ♗xg5 ♕xg5 17 ♖d1 ♖ad8 (17...d6 18 b3 {18 g3!? Wells} 18...♖ac8 19 ♖e2 ♖fd8 20 g3 d5! 21 cxd5 b5 with an initiative for Black, Zilberman-Wells, Herzliya 2000) 18 ♘c3 ♕f6 19 ♕h5 ♗xc3 20 ♖h4 ♕h6 21 ♕xh6 gxh6 22 bxc3 ♔g7 23 ♖hd4 ♔f6 ½-½ Leitão-Nisipeanu, Las Vegas FIDE 1999.

10 exd4 d6

This solid and flexible approach represents Black's favourite continuation, but other moves also deserve consideration:

a) 10...♘e4 11 ♕e2 f5 12 ♘c3 ♘xc3 13 bxc3 ♗d6 14 a4 ♕e8 15 ♘e5 is slightly better for White, Lilienthal-Simagin, USSR 1954.

b) 10...d5?! 11 c5! ♘bd7 (11...bxc5 12 ♘xc5 ♗xc5 13 dxc5 ♕c7 14 b4 e5 15 ♗b2 e4 16 ♗xf6 gxf6 17 ♗c2 exf3 18 ♕xf3 ♕e5 19 ♖ae1 ♕g5 20 ♕d3 ♕h5 21 ♖e3 with some compensation for the piece, Toledo-Trinidade, São Paulo Z 1993) 12 b4 bxc5 13 ♘xc5 ♗xc5 14 dxc5 e5 15 ♗b5 a6 16 ♗a4 ♕c7 17 ♖e1 ♖fe8 18 ♗g5 ± Najdorf-Eliskases, Mar del Plata 1954.

c) 10...♗xf3!? 11 ♕xf3 ♘c6 12 ♗e3 (12 d5?! ♘e5! 13 ♕e2 ♕c7 14 ♗f4 ♗d6 15 ♘c3 ♘f3+! 16 ♕xf3 ♗xf4 is slightly better for Black, Chatalbashev-Nisipeanu, Krynica 1998)

12...e5 (12...d5 is also possible) 13 d5 e4 14 ♗xe4 ♘e5 15 ♕f4 ♗d6 16 c5 ♘g6 17 ♕f3 ♘h4 18 ♕h3 ♘xe4 19 cxd6 ♘g6 20 ♘c3 ♘xd6 with chances for both sides, Psakhis-Speelman, Monaco rpd 1992.

d) 10...♖e8 11 ♖e1 d6 (11...♕c7 is line 'e1') 12 b4 ♘bd7 transposes to the main line.

e) 10...♕c7 (D) and here:

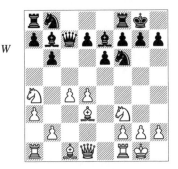

e1) 11 ♖e1 ♖e8 (11...d5 12 b3 ♘c6 13 ♘c3 ♖fd8 14 ♗b2 dxc4 15 bxc4 g6 with chances for both sides, Podgaets-Tukmakov, USSR 1977) 12 b4 a5 13 bxa5 ♖xa5 14 ♗d2? (14 ♘c3 is level) 14...♗xf3 15 gxf3 ♖h5 with an attack for Black, Muir-Norri, Pula Echt 1997.

e2) 11 ♘c3 d5 (11...d6 12 ♖e1 ♘bd7 13 d5 e5 14 b4 is slightly better for White, Gligorić-Timman, Hastings 1969/70) 12 cxd5 (or 12 ♘b5 ♕d8 13 ♗f4 ♘c6 14 ♖c1 a6 15 ♘c3 ♖c8 16 cxd5 ♘xd5 17 ♗e3 ♘a5 with a pleasant game for Black, Ibragimov-Emelin, Elista 1994) 12...♘xd5 13 ♘xd5 ♗xd5 14 ♘e5 ♘d7 15 ♗f4 ♕b7 16 ♘xd7 ♕xd7 with an equal position, Gligorić-Smyslov, Palma de Mallorca 1967.

e3) 11 b4 and then:

e31) 11...♘g4 12 g3 f5 13 ♘c3 a6 14 ♖e1 ♘c6 15 ♗f1 ♖ae8 (15...♘d8 16 ♗f4 ♗d6 17 ♗xd6 ♕xd6 18 ♗g2 with a pull for White, Botvinnik-Bronstein, Moscow Wch (5) 1951) 16 ♗f4 ♗d6 17 ♗xd6 ♕xd6 18 ♗g2 ♘d8 19 c5 ± Ordzhonikidze-Tiumen, cities corr. 1957.

e32) 11...a5 12 b5 d6 13 ♖e1 ♖e8 14 ♗f4 (or 14 ♗b2 ♘bd7 15 ♖c1 ♗f8 = Portisch-Smyslov, Mar del Plata 1966) 14...♘bd7 15 ♖c1 ♕d8 16 ♘d2 ♖c8 17 ♘b3 ♗f8 18 h3 e5 19 ♗g5 with an initiative for White, Ibragimov-Wells, Ubeda 1996.

11 b4

Or:

a) 11 ♘c3 d5 12 ♖e1 ♘c6 13 cxd5 ♘xd5 14 ♗c2 ♘xc3 15 bxc3 ♖c8 16 ♕d3 g6 17 ♗h6 ♖e8 18 ♕e3 ♗f6 = Gligorić-de Firmian, Vršac 1983.

b) 11 ♖e1 ♘bd7 and then:

b1) 12 b4 transposes to the main line.

b2) 12 b3 ♖e8 (12...d5 is another possibility: 13 ♗b2 ♖c8 14 ♕e2 ♕c7 15 ♘c3 ± Ehlvest-Aseev, USSR Ch (Lvov) 1984) 13 ♗b2 ♗f8 14 ♖c1 g6 15 b4 ♖c8 = F.Portisch-Flesch, Hungary 1966.

b3) 12 ♘c3 and here:

b31) 12...a6 13 d5! exd5 14 cxd5 ♘e5? (14...♖e8!?) 15 ♘xe5 dxe5 16 ♖xe5 ♗d6 17 ♖e3 ♘xd5 18 ♘xd5 ♗xd5 19 ♗xh7+! ± Gligorić-Adorjan, Vrbas 1980.

b32) 12...d5 13 b3 (13 cxd5 ♘xd5 14 ♗d2 ♖c8 15 ♘xd5 ♗xd5 16 ♗a6 ♖a8 17 ♖c1 ½-½ Gulko-de Firmian, USA Ch (Cambridge Springs) 1988) 13...♖c8 14 ♗f4!? ♘b8 (Dautov suggests 14...♗a6!?; e.g., 15 cxd5 ♖xc3 16 ♗xa6 ♘xd5 =) 15 ♘e5 ♘c6 16

♘b5! a6 17 ♘xc6 ♖xc6 18 ♘c3 ♖c8 19 ♕d2 ♖e8 = Gelfand-de Firmian, Biel 1995.

11...♘bd7

Most players prefer to prepare the attack on White's queenside with this move. However, the immediate 11...a5 has also been tried: 12 ♗b2 axb4 13 axb4 e5 (13...♘c6!?) 14 dxe5 dxe5 15 ♘xe5 ♗xb4 16 ♕b3 ♘a6 17 ♖fd1 ♕c7 = Schön-Grabarczyk, Pula 1998.

12 ♖e1 *(D)*

Or:

a) 12 ♗b2 ♖e8 13 ♖e1 transposes to the main line.

b) 12 ♘c3 ♖e8 13 ♖e1 ♗f8 14 h3 g6 15 ♗f4 ± Vaïsser-Röder, Las Palmas 1996.

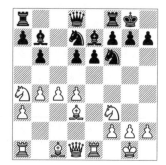

12...♖e8

There are some worthwhile alternatives:

a) 12...♖c8 13 ♗b2 ♖e8 14 ♖c1 ♗f8 15 ♗e2 g6 16 ♘d2 ♗h6!? 17 ♖c2 ♖c7 18 ♘c3 a6 = Zilberman-Bischoff, Havana 1998.

b) 12...a5!? 13 ♗b2 axb4 14 axb4 and here:

b1) 14...♖e8 15 ♘c3 (15 ♘d2?! e5 16 ♘b3 exd4 17 ♘xd4 ♗f8 18 ♖xe8 ♕xe8, Razvaliaev-Magerramov, corr.

1989, and here 19 ♘b5 ♘e5 20 f3 ♕c6 =) 15...♖xa1 16 ♗xa1 ♗f8 17 ♗f1 ♕a8 18 ♘d2 g6 19 ♗b2 ♘h5 20 ♕c2 (20 d5!?) and now, rather than the mechanical 20...e5? (this ruins the dynamics of the black game) 21 d5 f5 22 ♖a1 ♕b8 23 ♕a4 with a solid advantage for White, Schön-Weih, Bundesliga 1986/7, Black should continue 20...♕b8, intending to play ...d5 at some point.

b2) 14...b5!? 15 cxb5 ♘b6 16 ♘d2 ♘fd5 17 ♕b3 ♘xa4 18 ♖xa4 ♕b6 19 ♖ea1 ♖xa4 20 ♖xa4 ♘f4 21 ♗f1 ♗f6 with fairly balanced chances, Lein-de Firmian, USA Ch (Estes Park) 1986.

13 ♗b2

Or:

a) 13 ♘c3 transposes to note 'b' to White's 12th move.

b) 13 ♗f4 a5 14 b5 d5 (Black has solved his opening problems) 15 ♘e5 dxc4 16 ♘xc4 ♘d5 = Ibragimov-Tiviakov, Russian Ch (Elista) 1997.

13...♗f8

13...♖c8 transposes to note 'a' to Black's 12th move.

14 ♘c3

Or:

a) 14 ♖c1 ♖c8 15 ♘g5 (15 ♘c3!? makes more sense) 15...g6 16 ♗c3 ♗g7 17 ♗d2 h6 18 ♘h3 ♘f8 19 ♗e3 (19 ♘c3!? is again the right way to go) 19...e5 20 d5 b5! 21 cxb5 ♘xd5 with a complicated game ahead, Markovich-Eriksen, corr. 1987.

b) 14 ♗f1 ♖c8 15 ♘c3 ♕c7 16 ♘d2 (16 d5!? has been suggested as leading to a slight advantage for White, but after 16...exd5 17 ♖xe8 ♖xe8 18 ♘xd5 ♕d8!? 19 ♖c1 ♘e5 Black has a decent game) 16...♕b8 (Wirthensohn-Spassky, Zurich 1984) 17 ♘b3 d5 18 c5 e5 is unclear according to Peter Wells.

14...a6

Black continues with a Hedgehog-like set-up that has proved quite dependable in this line too.

Other moves include:

a) 14...♖c8 15 d5 (15 ♘d2 g6 16 ♘b3 ♗a6 17 b5 ♗b7 18 ♘a4 ♖c7 19 ♕d2 ♕a8 = Nadyrkhanov-Shneider, Barnaul 1988) 15...e5 16 ♘d2 g6 17 ♘f1 ♘h5 18 ♘b5 a6 19 ♘a7 ♖c7 20 b5 axb5 21 ♘xb5 ♖c8 ½-½ Garcia Palermo-Stoica, Dubai OL 1986.

b) 14...g6 15 ♗f1 ♗g7 16 ♖c1 a6 17 ♖c2 ♖c8 18 ♘b1 ♕c7 19 ♘bd2 e5 = W.Schmidt-Tomaszewski, Porabka 1986.

15 ♗f1

Now:

a) After 15...g6, Volzhin-Djurić, Canberra 2001 continued 16 ♘d2 d5!? 17 c5 bxc5 18 dxc5 (18 bxc5 e5 is also fine for Black) 18...e5 19 ♘b3 d4 ½-½.

b) A different plan for Black was shown in Ravi Sekhar-Toth, Malta OL 1980: 15...♖c8 16 ♖c1 ♕c7 17 ♘d2 g6 18 ♖c2 ♗g7 19 ♘b3 ♕b8 with chances for both sides.

B2)

9 exd4 *(D)*

9...♖e8

Aside from this move having transpositional qualities (to Line B1), it also makes a lot of sense to clear the path for the return of the dark-squared bishop to f8. Nonetheless, Black has tried several other moves, some of which are fairly interesting:

a) 9...d5? 10 c5! bxc5 11 a3 c4 12 ♗xh7+ (12 axb4 is also good for White: 12...cxd3 13 ♘c3 ♗c6 14 ♕xd3,

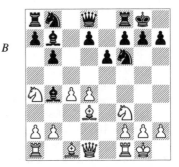

Kozma-Kolarov, Kapfenberg Echt 1970) 12...♘xh7 13 axb4 ♗c6 14 ♘c5 ♗b5 15 ♘e5 c3 (15...♘c6!?) 16 ♖e1 cxb2 17 ♗xb2 followed by the rook-lift ♖a3-h3 gives White the advantage, Korchnoi-Iordachescu, Calcutta 2000.

b) 9...♘e4? 10 c5 bxc5 11 a3 ♗a5 12 ♘xc5 ♘xc5 13 dxc5 ♗c7 14 ♗g5 ♕e8 15 ♘d4 ± Antoshin-Keres, USSR Ch (Moscow) 1957.

c) 9...♗xf3 10 ♕xf3 ♘c6 11 ♗e3 e5 (11...d5 12 ♖ac1 e5 13 cxd5 ♘xd4 14 ♗xd4 exd4 15 ♖c4 and Black loses his d-pawn, Portisch-Lengyel, Beverwijk 1965) 12 d5 ♘e7 13 a3 ♗d6 14 ♘c3 ♘g6 15 ♖ad1 h6 16 g3 ♖c8 17 ♖fe1 ♖e8 18 ♘e4 ♘xe4 19 ♕xe4 and White has a slight advantage, Radjabov-Kallio, Leon Echt 2001.

d) 9...♕c7 often transposes to note 'e' to Black's 10th move in Line B1 via 10 a3 ♗e7, but 10 ♗g5 is interesting: 10...♘g4 11 d5 b5 12 h3 ♘e5 13 cxb5 ♗xd5 14 ♖c1 ♘xf3+ 15 ♕xf3 ♕a5 16 ♕h5 (16 ♕g3!?) 16...f5 with a complicated position and fairly even chances, Babula-Timman, Bundesliga 1998/9.

e) 9...♗e7 and here:

e1) 10 a3 transposes to Line B1.

e2) 10 ♘c3 d5 11 cxd5 ♘xd5 12 ♕e2 ♘d7 13 ♖d1 ♘7f6 14 ♗g5 ♘h5 15 ♕e5 ♗f6 16 ♗xf6 ♘hxf6 17 ♕g3 ♘h5 18 ♕e5 = Gligorić-Petrosian, Siegen OL 1970.

e3) 10 ♗f4!? is a noteworthy idea that deserves more tests. In Petrosian-Keres, Gothenburg IZ 1955, Black continued with 10...♘e4 (10...d5 is met by 11 c5 with a good game, while 10...d6 allows White to save a tempo with 11 b4, not having to support it with a3) 11 ♘c3 d5 12 cxd5 ♘xc3 13 bxc3 ♕xd5 14 ♖e1 with a better game for White.

e4) 10 ♖e1 (D) and then:

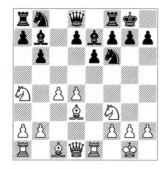

e41) 10...d5?! 11 c5 bxc5 (alternatively, 11...♘bd7 12 b4 ♘e4 13 ♗f4! ± Øgaard-Karlsson, Gausdal 1982) 12 ♘xc5 ♗xc5 13 dxc5 ♘bd7 14 b4 a5 15 ♘d4 ♕c7 16 ♗g5! e5 (16...axb4 17 c6! is a disaster for Black) 17 ♘b5 ♕b8 18 ♘d6 axb4 19 ♗xf6 ♘xf6 20 ♖xe5 ♗c6 21 ♖g5 with an initiative for White, Iskusnykh-Ibragimov, Russian Ch (Elista) 1995.

e42) 10...♖e8 often ends up transposing to Line B1 after White plays a3 on this or one of the next few moves. However, in 11 ♗f4 White has a worthy

alternative: 11...d6 12 ♘c3 a6 13 b4 ♘bd7 14 a4 (14 a3 may be better) 14...♗f8 (14...e5!?, to break White's dominance in the centre and on the queenside, should be tried; e.g., 15 ♗g3 a5 16 b5 exd4 17 ♘xd4 ♘e5 with a complicated struggle ahead) 15 ♗g3 ± Lukacs-Csom, Budapest 1977.

e43) 10...d6 11 ♗f4 (11 b4 is best met with 11...a5, when 12 a3 ♘bd7 transposes to note 'b' to Black's 12th move in Line B1) 11...♘bd7 12 ♘c3 ♖e8 (12...d5 can be tried) 13 h3 ♘f8 (13...♖c8!? – Chekhov) 14 d5! e5 15 ♗d2 ♘6d7 16 b4 ♘g6 17 ♖c1 with a more pleasant game for White, Najdorf-Golombek, Moscow 1956.

e44) 10...♘a6!? 11 a3 d5 12 cxd5 ♘xd5 13 ♘c3 ♘ac7 14 ♘e4 ♘f6 15 ♘xf6+ ♗xf6 16 ♗f4 ♘d5 17 ♗e5 ♗xe5 18 dxe5 ♘f4 = Iskusnykh-Budnikov, Vladivostok 1995.

We now return to the position after 9...♖e8 (D):

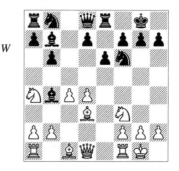

10 a3

Or:

a) 10 ♗f4 ♗f8 11 ♖c1 d6 12 ♖e1 ♘bd7 13 ♘c3 a6 14 a3 h6 with a fairly level game, Gulko-Matanović, Biel IZ 1976.

b) 10 c5?! is an attempt to take advantage of the b4-bishop: 10...♗xf3 (or even 10...bxc5 11 a3 c4 12 ♗xh7+ ♘xh7 13 axb4 ♗xf3 14 ♕xf3 ♘c6 ∓ Ree-Langeweg, Dutch Ch (Hilversum) 1983) 11 ♕xf3 ♘c6 12 ♗e3 (12 ♕d1?! ♘xd4 13 ♗xh7+ ♘xh7 14 ♕xd4 bxc5 15 ♘xc5 ♕b6 leaves Black with a better centre and a better game, Korchnoi-Ivanchuk, Monaco rpd 1993) 12...e5 (12...bxc5 13 dxc5 ♘e5 is also possible) 13 dxe5 (13 d5 was suggested by Den Broeder, who continued his analysis with 13...e4, but 13...♘d4! is better; e.g., 14 ♗xd4 exd4 15 c6 dxc6 16 dxc6 b5 17 c7 {17 ♗xb5? ♕a5 −+} 17...♕xc7 18 ♗xb5 ♖ed8 ∓) 13...♘xe5 14 ♕d1 ♘fg4 is better for Black, Øgaard-Adorjan, Gjøvik 1983.

c) 10 ♗g5 and here:

c1) 10...♗e7 11 ♖e1 d6 12 ♖c1 ♘bd7 13 ♘c3 ♖c8 14 a3 h6 15 ♗f4 d5 16 ♘e5 dxc4 17 ♘xc4 ♘d5 18 ♘xd5 ♗xd5 ½-½ Kengis-Stoica, Timisoara 1987.

c2) 10...h6 11 ♗h4 ♗xf3 12 ♕xf3 ♘c6 13 ♗xf6 (13 ♕e3 is a suggestion of Kotov's, but Black is still OK after 13...d5!?) 13...♕xf6 14 ♕xf6 gxf6 15 d5 ♘e5 16 ♗e2 ♖ac8 17 a3 ♗f8 18 ♖ac1 ♘g6 = Gligorić-Kaplan, Lone Pine 1979.

10...♗f8 (D)

10...♗e7 to some extent defeats the purpose of Black's previous move. It transposes to note 'd' to Black's 10th move in Line B1.

11 b4

Or:

a) 11 ♗g5 h6 (this is *ECO*'s suggested improvement over 11...d6 12 ♘c3 ♗e7 13 ♖e1 ♘bd7 14 ♕e2 h6 15 ♗h4 ♘h5 16 ♗xe7 ♕xe7 17 ♕e3 ±

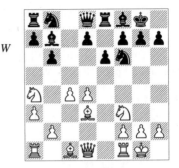

W

Kharitonov-Chernin, USSR Ch (Lvov) 1984) 12 ♗h4 ♗xf3 13 ♕xf3 ♘c6 ('unclear' in *ECO*) and now 14 ♗xf6 ♕xf6 15 ♕xf6 gxf6 16 d5 ♘d4 17 ♘c3 f5 is fairly level.

b) 11 ♘c3 d6 (or 11...d5 12 ♗g5 dxc4 13 ♗xc4 ♗e7 14 ♖c1 ♘c6 15 ♖e1 ½-½ Bischoff-Huss, Beersheba 1985) 12 ♖e1 ♘bd7 13 ♗g5 ♖c8 14 ♖c1 h6 15 ♗h4 a6 16 ♘d2 ♕c7 = Babula-Seul, Bundesliga 1998/9.

c) 11 ♖e1 ♗xf3!? (11...d6 12 ♘c3 ♘bd7 13 d5! e5 14 ♗f1 g6 15 b4 ♘h5 16 ♕b3 with a pull for White, Azmaiparashvili-Lerner, Kuibyshev 1986) 12 ♕xf3 ♘c6 13 ♗e3 e5 14 dxe5 ♘xe5 15 ♕d1 d5 16 cxd5 ♘xd3 17 ♕xd3 ♕xd5 ½-½ Lukacs-Tolnai, Austrian Cht 1998.

11...d6 12 ♗b2

Or 12 ♖e1 ♘bd7 13 ♗b2 ♖c8 14 ♘c3 e5 15 dxe5 dxe5 16 ♘e4 ♗xe4 17 ♗xe4 ♕c7 (17...♖xc4 18 ♗d3 ♖c6 19 ♗b5 gives White more than sufficient compensation according to Yusupov), Yusupov-Korchnoi, Vienna 1996, and here Yusupov gives 18 ♗f5! g6 19 ♗h3 ♖cd8 20 ♕c2 ±.

12...♘bd7 13 ♖e1 ♖c8

The more direct approach based on 13...a5 leaves White with an advantage after 14 ♘c3 axb4 15 axb4 ♖xa1 16 ♗xa1 g6 17 ♗b2 e5 and now, instead of 18 d5?! (Iskusnykh-Lomineishvili, Moscow 1996), which allows 18...b5!, White should play 18 ♗f1 with some advantage.

14 ♖c1 g6 (D)
14...♘h5!? 15 ♘c3 ♘df6 is another idea.

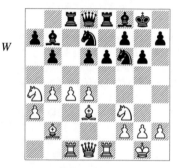

15 ♘c3 ♕c7 16 ♗f1 ♕b8 17 d5 e5 18 ♘d2 ♗g7 19 ♘b3

White has a lasting initiative, R.Hernandez-Vilela, Havana 1985.

Conclusion

Overall, Black seems to be doing OK in the Keres Variation, especially in Lines A and B1, where the problems seem to have been dealt with.

In Line A, White has had big problems showing any advantage and in my view this is not likely to change.

Aside from the main line in B1, Black may also consider 9...♗d6!?, which has so far only been tried on a relatively small number of occasions, but with very decent results. Line B2 currently represents the biggest threat to Black in the Keres Variation. White leaves the b4-bishop alone to start with, and thereby lets Black decide how long he feels confident having it there. Often Black will retreat and let White play b4 without the support of a3, saving White a full tempo.

14 Classical Fianchetto Variation

The Classical Fianchetto Variation, or the Tal Variation, as it is sometimes also called, is characterized by the position that arises after 1 d4 ♘f6 2 c4 e6 3 ♘c3 ♗b4 4 e3 b6 5 ♗d3 ♗b7 6 ♘f3 0-0 7 0-0 d5 *(D)*.

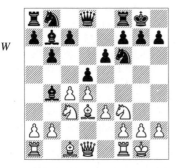

This position can also arise via a few different move-orders, some of which are quite important as it is possible for either side to deviate prior to arriving at the position after Black's 7th move. The most important is probably 4...0-0 5 ♗d3 d5 6 ♘f3 b6 7 0-0 ♗a6, and we consider 7th move alternatives for both White and Black in Line A. In Line B we discuss the main line.

1 d4 ♘f6 2 c4 e6 3 ♘c3 ♗b4 4 e3
Now:
A: 4...0-0 5 ♗d3 d5 6 ♘f3 b6   205
B: 4...b6 5 ♗d3 ♗b7 6 ♘f3 0-0
   7 0-0 d5   206

A)
4...0-0 5 ♗d3 d5 6 ♘f3 b6 7 0-0
White can deviate with the following moves:

a) 7 ♗d2 ♗b7 (7...dxc4 is also possible) 8 cxd5 exd5 (8...♘xd5 is by transposition Mason-Blackburne, Paris 1878! White is better after both 9 0-0 and 9 e4) 9 ♖c1 (9 0-0 transposes to note 'd' to White's 9th move in Line B1) 9...a6 10 ♘e2 ♗d6 11 ♘g3 ♖e8 12 ♘f5 ♗f8 13 ♘e5 c5 = Pelletier-Baklan, Istanbul OL 2000.

b) 7 ♕b3 ♗e7 8 0-0 ♘c6 9 cxd5 exd5 10 ♘e5 ♗b7 11 ♖d1 a6 (Poluga-evsky-Shamkovich, USSR Ch (Leningrad) 1960) 12 ♘xc6 ♗xc6 13 ♗d2 = (Yudovich).

c) 7 cxd5 exd5 and here:

c1) 8 a3 ♗d6 9 0-0 ♗b7 transposes to Line B22.

c2) 8 0-0 ♖e8 (8...♗b7 transposes to Line B1) 9 ♘e5 ♗b7 10 ♕a4 ♗d6 11 f4 c5 12 ♗d2 a6 13 ♗e1 b5 with chances for both sides, Conquest-Schandorff, Copenhagen 1988.

d) 7 a3 ♗xc3+ (7...♗d6?! is less interesting: 8 e4 dxe4 9 ♘xe4 ♘bd7 10 0-0 ♗b7 11 ♘xd6 {Timman suggests 11 ♘c3!?} 11...cxd6 12 ♗g5 h6 13 ♗h4, Korchnoi-Timman, Horgen 1995, 13...♕c7 14 ♖c1 ± Korchnoi) 8 bxc3 ♗a6!? (8...♗b7 9 0-0 dxc4 10 ♗xc4 c5 11 ♗d3 ♘bd7 transposes to note 'f2' to White's 9th move in Line C of Chapter 2) 9 cxd5 (9 ②e5 ②fd7!? = Knaak-Lukacs, Wijk aan Zee 1988) 9...♗xd3 10 ♕xd3 ♕xd5 (10...exd5 is also fully playable) 11 0-0 (or 11 c4 ♕b7 12 ♗b2 ②bd7 13 ♖d1 ♖fd8 14 0-0 ♖ac8 15 ♖fe1 ♕e4 16 ♕c3 c5 17 d5!? exd5 18 ♖xd5 with a slight initiative for White, Granda-Tal, Buenos Aires 1991) 11...c5 (11...②bd7!?) 12 ♖e1 c4!? 13 ♕c2 ♕e4 14 ♕e2 ②bd7 15 ♕xc4 ♖fc8 16 ♕b3 ♕d5 17 ♖b1 ②e4 18 ♗d2 g5 with compensation for the pawn, Kupreichik-Vitoliņš, Severodonetsk 1982.

7...♗a6

7...♗b7 is Line B, of course.

8 ♕e2

8 cxd5 ♗xc3 (8...exd5 and 8...♗xd3 have also been tried) 9 ♗xa6 ②xa6 10 bxc3 ♕xd5 (Lukacs-Kurajica, Sarajevo 1981) 11 ♕e2 = (*ECO*).

8...②bd7 9 ♖d1 ♕c8 10 ♗d2

Now 10...♕b7? 11 ②xd5 exd5 12 ♗xb4 dxc4 13 ♗xc4 ♗xc4 14 ♕xc4 ± was Plachetka-Csom, Lucerne OL 1982, but 10...c5!? improves.

B)

4...b6 5 ♗d3 ♗b7 6 ②f3 0-0 7 0-0 d5

Here, White has two main options:

B1: 8 cxd5   206
B2: 8 a3   211

Alternatives include:

a) 8 ②e5 ♗d6 9 f4 c5 10 ♕f3 ②c6 is pleasant for Black, Tsevremes-Arnason, Katerini 1993.

b) 8 ②e2 dxc4 9 ♗xc4 ②bd7 10 b3 ♕e7 11 ②g3 ♖fd8 12 ♕e2 c5 is equal, Garcia Gonzalez-Ljubojević, Linares 1981.

c) 8 ♕e2 ②bd7 (8...dxc4 9 ♗xc4 c5 transposes to note 'd33' to Black's 8th move in Chapter 2) and now:

c1) 9 ♗d2 ♗d6 10 cxd5 exd5 11 ♗a6 ♕c8 12 ♗xb7 ♕xb7 13 ♖ac1 a6 with chances for both sides, Korchnoi-Dautov, Bad Homburg 1998.

c2) 9 a3 ♗e7 (9...♗xc3 10 bxc3 dxc4 11 ♗xc4 c5 12 ♗d3 transposes to note 'f22' to White's 9th move in Chapter 2) 10 b3 (Yudovich gave 10 e4 ±, but Black seems to be doing fine after 10...dxe4 11 ②xe4 c5!?) 10...c5 11 ♗b2 ♖c8 12 ♖ac1 ♕c7 13 ♖fd1 (or 13 cxd5!?) 13...♕b8 14 cxd5 exd5 15 ♗f5 ♖cd8 16 ♕c2 g6 17 ♗h3 ± Soffer-Grünfeld, Givatayim 1997.

d) 8 ♗d2 and then:

d1) 8...c5 9 cxd5 cxd4 (9...exd5 transposes to note 'd2' to White's 9th move in Line B1) 10 exd4 transposes to Line A of Chapter 13.

d2) 8...♗d6 9 cxd5 (9 ♕c2!? is another idea) 9...exd5 transposes to note 'd3' to White's 9th move in Line B1.

d3) 8...②bd7? 9 ②xd5! ②xd5 10 cxd5 ♗xd2 11 dxe6 ♗xf3 12 gxf3 fxe6 13 ♕xd2 ♕h4 14 ♗e4 ♖f6 15 f4 is much better for White, Zilberman-Liss, Tel-Aviv 1991.

d4) 8...♗e7 9 ♕e2 ②bd7 10 ♖fd1 c5 (10...②e4!?) 11 ♖ac1 ♖c8 12 cxd5 exd5 13 ②e5 is slightly better for White, Donner-Bobotsov, Noordwijk 1965.

B1)

8 cxd5 exd5 *(D)*
9 ②e5

This is clearly White's most aggressive and interesting choice. The following options are also worthy of attention:

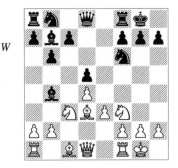

a) 9 a3 &d6 transposes to Line B22.

b) 9 &e2 &d6 10 b3 (the alternative 10 &g3 g6 11 b3 &bd7 12 &b2 We7 13 &c1 was played in Granda-Onishchuk, Wijk aan Zee 1997 and now Yudasin suggests 13...a6!? intending ...&e4 and ...f5) 10...&e8 11 &b2 &bd7 12 &g3 g6 13 &d2 h5 = Malaniuk-Lerner, Swidnica 1997.

c) 9 Wc2 &e8 10 &e5 &d6 11 f4 c5 12 &f3 cxd4 13 exd4 &c6 14 &xc6 &xc6 15 &d2 &e4 with a good game for Black, Or.Rodriguez-G.Georgadze, Spanish Cht 2001.

d) 9 &d2 and then:

d1) 9...a6 prepares the retreat of the bishop to d6, but since White isn't really up to playing &b5, this loss of time favours White.

d2) 9...c5 10 dxc5 (10 &e5 transposes to note 'c2' to Black's 9th move; 10 a3 &xc3 11 &xc3 &e4 12 &c1 &xc3 13 &xc3 c4 14 &b1 b5 15 b3 f5 16 &e5 &d7 {16...&c6!? 17 Wh5 We8 appears fine for Black} 17 Wh5 ± Bukić-Matanović, Belgrade 1968) 10...bxc5 11 a3 &a5 12 &a4 &xd2 13 Wxd2 &bd7 14 b4 &e4 15 Wb2 &b8 16 &xe4 dxe4 17 &e5 &xe5 ½-½ Babula-Bareev, Bundesliga 1999/00.

However, White is slightly better after 18 Wxe5 cxb4 19 axb4 &c6 20 &fb1.

d3) 9...&d6 and here:

d31) 10 &e5 c5 11 f4 &c6 12 Wf3 transposes to the note to White's 12th move.

d32) 10 &b5 &e7 11 &c1 c5 (the alternative 11...c6 has also tested OK for Black) 12 &e5 &bd7 13 &xd7 Wxd7 14 &c3 &e4 15 dxc5 &xc5 16 &e2 (Yusupov-Kachiani, German Ch (Bremen) 1998) 16...&ac8 is approximately equal.

d33) 10 &c1 a6 (or 10...c5 11 dxc5 bxc5 12 &e2 &bd7 13 &c3 We7 14 &g3 g6 15 &e1 &fd8 16 Wa4 &e4 17 &xe4 dxe4 18 &d2 &b6 = Babula-Lutz, Batumi Echt 1999) 11 &e5 c5 12 f4 &c6 (12...&bd7 is also playable) 13 Wf3 cxd4 14 &xc6 &xc6 15 exd4 Wd7 16 f5 &fe8 17 &fe1 b5 leads to an equal position, Radev-Mittitelu, Dečin 1975.

d4) 9...&bd7 and here:

d41) 10 &e5 &xe5 11 dxe5 &xc3 (11...&d7 also leads to an even game) 12 &xc3 &e4 13 &xe4 dxe4 14 Wg4 We7 15 &fd1 We6 16 Wh4 &fe8 17 &d4 h6 = A.Schneider-Volosin, Hungarian Cht 1993.

d42) 10 Wc2 a6 (10...c5 has also been tried) 11 &e5 &xe5!? 12 dxe5 &e4! 13 &xe4 dxe4 14 &fd1 &xc3 15 &xc3 We7 16 &d2 (16 b4!? – Dautov) 16...&ad8 17 &ad1 a5 = Yusupov-Dautov, Dresden Z 1998.

d43) 10 &c1 a6 11 &e5 &xe5 12 dxe5 &d7 13 a3 &e7 14 Wc2 &xe5 15 &xh7+ &h8 16 f4 &g4 17 &f5 &h6 18 &e2 c5 = Gligorić-Tal, Oberhausen Echt 1961.

We now return to the position after 9 &e5 (D):

B

9...Åd6

With White aiming so directly at his king, Black has to be fairly attentive at this point. The text-move takes a look at the e5-knight in order to remove him if necessary. A number of other moves have been tested here:

a) 9...a6?! is again a waste of time. White has essentially two options: 10 Åd2, after which 10...Åd6 11 f4 is very pleasant for White; or the slower 10 ②e2 Åd6 11 b3 ②bd7 12 Åb2 罝e8 13 f4 ②e4 14 Åxe4 dxe4 15 ②g3 ± Donner-Van Scheltinga, Beverwijk 1965.

b) 9...Åe7 10 f4 c5 11 豐f3 ②c6 12 豐h3 and instead of 12...②xe5 13 fxe5 ②e4 14 Åxe4 dxe4 15 d5 罝e8 16 b3 ± Pinter-Renet, Haifa Echt 1989, Black can try 12...h6!?; e.g., 13 罝f3 ②e4 14 Åxe4 dxe4 15 罝g3 ②xe5 16 dxe5 ✿h8 with fairly even chances.

c) 9...c5 and then:

c1) 10 f4 ②bd7 transposes to line 'd34'.

c2) 10 Åd2 ②c6 (10...cxd4 11 exd4 ②c6 12 Åg5!?, intending 12...Åd6 13 ②xc6 Åxc6 14 豐f3 ± or 12...Åe7 13 Åa6! 豐c8 14 Åxb7 豐xb7 15 罝e1 with an initiative for White) 11 ②xc6 Åxc6 12 a3 Åxc3 13 Åxc3 c4 14 Åc2

罝e8 15 豐e2 b5 = Bareev-Sakaev, Russian Ch (Elista) 1995.

c3) 10 ②e2 c4 11 Åf5 (this has proved stronger than the more common 11 Åc2) 11...g6 12 Åh3 b5 (Bareev-Salov, Tilburg 1994) and here White should try either 13 ②c3!? 豐b6 14 f4 (Dautov) or Bareev's 13 f4! ②c6 14 ②g3 with an initiative for White according to Dautov.

d) 9...②bd7 is Black's most important alternative to the main line. Now:

d1) 10 Åd2 transposes to note 'd34'.

d2) 10 豐a4 Åd6 (10...②xe5?! 11 dxe5 Åxc3 12 bxc3 ②d7 13 Åa3 c5 14 f4 豐e7 15 c4! f6 16 Åf5 罝fd8 17 cxd5 fxe5 18 e4 ②f8 19 Åb2 ± Furman-Antoshin, Rostov-on-Don 1953) 11 ②xd7 (11 f4 is harmless in this position) 11...②xd7 (11...豐xd7 12 豐xd7 ②xd7 13 ②b5 ± *ECO*) 12 Åb5 (or 12 b4 a6 13 豐b3 豐h4 14 g3 豐h5 15 ②e2 ②f6 with a pleasant game for Black, Hráček-Dautov, Nîmes 1991) 12...②b8 13 Åd2 a6 14 Åd3 ②d7 15 罝ac1 ②f6 and now 16 ②e2 seems best. Then 16...罝e8 17 Åb4 was good for White in Arpiainen-Kosonen, corr. 1989, but Black can improve with 16...②e4, when 17 Åb4 (17 Åxe4 dxe4 18 Åb4 Åxb4 19 豐xb4 a5 =) 17...c5 18 Åxe4 cxb4 leads to chances for both sides, although I'd prefer to play White's side.

d3) 10 f4 and now:

d31) 10...②e4 11 ②xe4 dxe4 12 Åc4 ②xe5 13 fxe5 ± Liptay-Varnusz, Hungarian Ch (Budapest) 1965.

d32) 10...a6 11 豐f3 b5 12 豐h3 ②b6 13 Åd2 Åd6 14 Åe1 ②e4 is equal, F.Portisch-Kushnir, Wijk aan Zee 1975.

d33) 10...♗xc3!? has only been seen a few times, but the positions that have arisen appear encouraging for Black: 11 bxc3 c5 12 ♗a3 ♖c8 13 ♕e2 ♘e4 14 ♗xe4 dxe4 15 ♖ad1 ♕e8 16 ♘xd7 ♕xd7 = Piket-Illescas, Wijk aan Zee 1997.

d34) 10...c5 and then:

d341) 11 ♖f3?! ♘e4 12 ♖h3 ♘xe5 13 ♕h5 h6 14 dxe5 ♗xc3 15 bxc3 f6! 16 c4 d4 ∓ Tolush-Antoshin, USSR Ch (Leningrad) 1956.

d342) 11 ♗f5 g6 12 ♗h3?! (12 ♗c2!?) 12...♗xc3 13 bxc3 ♘xe5 14 dxe5 ♘e4 15 ♕c2 ♗a6 ∓ Portisch-Rogoff, Las Palmas 1976.

d343) 11 ♕f3 ♖e8 12 ♕h3 ♘f8 13 ♗d2 ♖c8 14 a3 ♗xc3 15 ♗xc3 c4 16 ♗c2 ♘e4 offers chances for both sides, Cherepkov-Kholmov, USSR Ch (Alma-Ata) 1968.

d344) 11 ♗d2 ♘e4 (both 11...a6 and 11...♖e8 have been tried here as well, both with decent play for Black) 12 ♘xe4 dxe4 13 ♗c4 ♘xe5 14 fxe5 ♗xd2 15 ♕xd2 ♗d5 16 b3 (16 ♗a6 ♕e7 17 dxc5 ♕xe5 18 ♖fd1 ♗c6 19 ♖ac1 ♖ab8 and although White has the initiative, Black should be able to defend, Sadler-Polugaevsky, Hastings 1992/3) 16...cxd4 17 exd4 ♖c8 18 ♖ac1 ♕d7 19 ♕e3 h6 20 ♖fe1 ♖fd8 21 ♗xd5 ♖xc1 22 ♗xf7+ ♔xf7 23 e6+ ♕xe6 24 ♖xc1 ½-½ Sadler-Speelman, Hastings 1992/3.

d345) 11 ♘e2 cxd4 12 exd4 ♘e4! 13 ♕a4 ♘xe5 14 fxe5 ♗e7 15 ♘f4 a6 16 ♗e3 ♗g5 17 ♖ae1 ♖c8 with chances for both sides, Popov-Gorniak, corr. 1983.

We now return to the position after 9...♗d6 (D):

10 f4

A more positional approach is 10 ♘b5, after which Black has a few interesting but untried ideas in 10...♖e8!? 11 ♘xd6 cxd6 12 ♘f3 ♘e4 (Pliester) and 10...a6!? 11 ♘xd6 cxd6 (Yudovich). Both options need testing. So far, 10...♗e7 is the only move tried by Black: 11 b3 (11 ♕c2 c5 12 b3, Kozma-Korchnoi, Luhačovice 1969, 12...♘bd7 13 ♗b2 a6 14 ♘c3 cxd4 15 exd4 b5 = Korchnoi) 11...c5 (an interesting alternative is 11...a6 12 ♘c3 c5 13 dxc5 bxc5 14 ♘e2 ♗d6 15 ♗b2 ♕e7 16 ♘f3 ♘bd7 with chances for both sides, Letić-Brilla Banfalvi, corr. 1975) 12 ♗b2 ♘bd7 13 ♖c1 a6 14 ♘c3 cxd4 15 exd4 ♖e8 16 f4 b5 17 ♗f5 ♘f8 18 ♘e2 ♘e4 19 ♘g3 ♘xg3 20 hxg3 ♗d6 21 ♕f3, with more space and play for White, M.Gurevich-Bareev, Moscow 1990.

10...c5

This attack on White's centre is not only Black's most popular continuation – it is also his best chance. By putting pressure on the centre, Black forces some exchanges, which is also in his interest. Other options:

a) 10...a6!? 11 ♕f3 b5 12 a3 c5 13 ♗d2 (13 g4!?) 13...♕b6 14 ♘e2 (14 dxc5 ♗xc5 15 b4 ♗d6 16 ♖ac1 is quite interesting) 14...♘e4 15 ♗xe4 dxe4 16 ♕h3 ♗c8 17 ♕h5 ♘d7 18 ♘xd7 ♗xd7 = Van Buskirk-Grünfeld, Philadelphia 2001.

b) 10...♘bd7 11 ♕f3 c5 12 ♗d2 a6 13 a4 ♖e8 14 ♗e1 ♘f8 15 ♗h4 ♗e7 16 ♖ad1 cxd4 17 exd4 with an initiative for White, Lugovoi-Z.Szabo, Hungarian Cht 1997.

11 ♕f3

Or:

a) 11 ♗d2 will usually transpose to the note to White's 12th move via 11...♘c6 12 ♕f3.

b) The 11 ♖f3 rook-lift looks like a lot of fun:

b1) 11...♘e4 has been suggested as best in several places, but has yet to be tested. Then 12 ♕c2! seems best. Since 12...f5? does not work on account of 13 ♘xe4 fxe4 14 ♗xe4! +– dxe4? 15 ♕c4+ ♔h8 16 ♘g6+ mating, Black is forced to retreat: 12...♘f6 13 ♗d2 with a better game for White.

b2) 11...♘c6 12 ♘xd5 ♗xe5 (not 12...♘xd5?? losing to 13 ♗xh7+) 13 fxe5 ♕xd5 14 exf6 g6 (Brinck-Claussen – Pokojowczyk, Copenhagen 1981) and now 15 ♖f4 (*Junior*) seems best (15 ♕e1? ♘e5! ∓ or 15 ♕e2 {Ftáčnik} 15...♖fe8! ∓): 15...cxd4 16 ♗e4 ♕e6 17 exd4 ♖ad8 with chances for both sides.

b3) 11...♘bd7 12 ♗d2 ♘e4 13 ♗e1 ♘df6 14 ♗h4 ♗e7 15 ♖h3 g6 with chances for both sides, Niklasch-Portisch, Biel 1998.

b4) 11...g6 12 ♗d2 ♘c6 13 ♖h3 cxd4 14 ♘xc6 ♗xc6 15 exd4 ♘e4 16 f5 ♕f6 17 ♗xe4 dxe4 18 ♕g4 ♕xf5 (Knaak-Petrosian, Tallinn 1979) 19 ♕xf5 gxf5 20 ♖f1 = Petrosian.

11...♘c6 (*D*)

W

12 ♕h3

White goes for the throat. An important alternative is 12 ♗d2 cxd4 13 ♘xc6 ♗xc6 14 exd4, and then:

a) 14...♖e8 15 f5 (15 ♖ae1 ♕c7 16 g3 ♕b7 17 f5 b5 18 ♗g5 ♘e4 with chances for both sides, Knaak-Lukacs, Leipzig 1986) 15...♘e4 16 ♗f4 (16 ♗xe4 dxe4 17 ♕f2 {this is assessed as slightly better for White by Pliester} 17...♕f6 followed by 18...♖ad8 ∓) 16...♗xf4 17 ♕xf4 ♕f6 18 ♘e2 ♖e7 ½-½ Knaak-Lukacs, Leipzig 1986.

b) 14...♕d7 15 f5 ♖fe8 16 ♗f4 ♘e4 (16...♖e7, as suggested by Byrne, is best met with 17 ♗g5 ♖ae8 18 ♗xf6 gxf6 19 ♕g4+ ♔h8 20 ♕h4 ♔g7 21 ♖ae1 ±) 17 ♗xd6 ♕xd6 18 ♗xe4 dxe4 19 ♕e3 f6 (allowing White to play f6 isn't without problems either: 19...♖ad8 20 ♖ad1 ♗d5 21 f6) 20 d5! ♗d7 21 ♖ad1 ♖e5 (Garcia Palermo-Karpov, Mar del Plata 1982) 22 g4! ±.

12...g6

Other moves:

a) 12...♘e7?? 13 ♘d7! +– Simagin-Razuvaev, USSR 1967.

b) 12...h6 13 ♖f3!? cxd4 14 exd4 (14 ♘xc6 ♗xc6 15 exd4 =) 14...♘xd4 15 ♖g3 ♘e4 (15...♔h8!?) 16 ♗xe4 dxe4 17 ♗e3 ♗c5 18 ♕g4 with some but perhaps not full compensation for the pawn, Utasi-Sisniega, Havana 1985.

c) 12...♘b4!? 13 ♗b1 ♖e8 14 a3 ♘a6 15 ♗d3 ♘c7 with a complicated game, Morris-Alvarez, corr. 1994.

13 ♔h1

13 ♗d2 has long been condemned based on 13...cxd4 14 ♘xc6 ♗xc6 15 exd4 ♘e4 16 ♗xe4 dxe4 17 f5 ♗c5!. However, instead of 18 ♗e3 ♗xd4 19 ♖ad1 ♗xe3+ 20 ♕xe3 ♕e7! ∓ Farago-Lerner, Kiev 1978, 18 dxc5 ♕xd2 19 ♖ad1 ♕g5 20 ♖d6 ♖ac8 gives both sides chances, Bielecki-Preziuso, corr. 1986.

A third move is 13 ♘e2 ♘b4 14 ♗b5 a6 15 ♗a4 b5 16 dxc5 ♗xe5 17 fxe5 ♘e4 18 ♗b3 ♕e7 = I.Zaitsev-Spasov, Albena 1970.

13...a6

13...♖e8 also deserves attention: 14 ♗d2 ♗f8 15 ♗b5 ♕c8 16 ♗xc6 ♗xc6 17 f5 ♗g7 18 ♕h4 ♖f8 (Sadler-Ehlvest, Groningen FIDE 1997) and here 19 ♖ac1!? could be considered.

14 ♗d2 b5 15 ♖ad1 cxd4 16 ♘xc6 ♗xc6 17 exd4 b4 18 ♘e2 ♗b5!?

18...♗d7!?.

19 f5 ♗xd3 20 ♕xd3 ♘e4 21 ♗f4 ½-½ Sadler-Korchnoi, Tilburg 1998.

B2)

8 a3 *(D)*
8...♗d6

This retreat is not only Black's most popular choice, but it also makes a lot of sense when Black has to generate counterplay. Other options include:

a) 8...♗xc3 9 bxc3 dxc4 10 ♗xc4 c5 11 ♗d3 ♘bd7 transposes to note 'f2' to White's 9th move in Line C of Chapter 2.

b) 8...dxc4 and now:

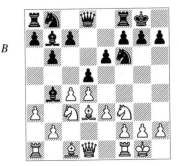

b1) 9 ♗xc4 usually transposes to other lines covered in this chapter; e.g., 9...♗d6 10 b4 is Line B21. With this move-order Black has prevented 8...♗d6 9 cxd5 (Line B22), which is generally considered more problematic for Black. Alternatively, Black can play 9...♗xc3 10 bxc3 c5 11 ♗d3 ♘bd7, transposing to note 'f2' to White's 9th move in Line C of Chapter 2.

b2) A noteworthy idea is 9 ♗xh7+!? ♔xh7 10 axb4 which, according to Pliester, is nothing for Black to worry about after 10...a6 as "White cannot easily get in e3-e4", but White can in fact play 11 e4!? ± due to the fact that 11...♘xe4?? 12 ♘xe4 ♗xe4 13 ♘g5+ costs Black a piece.

c) 8...♗e7 is somewhat more passive than the text-move. Often the bishop soon ends up on d6 anyway, so the value of this move can be questioned. In reply, White has tried:

c1) 9 b4 c5 10 bxc5 dxc4 11 ♗xc4 bxc5 12 ♖b1 ♕c8 13 d5!? exd5 (the alternative 13...♖d8 looks obvious and good, but after 14 e4 ♘xe4 15 ♘xe4 exd5 16 ♘fg5!, White has an attack; e.g., 16...h6 17 ♘xf7 ♔xf7 18 ♕f3+ ♔g8 19 ♖d1! ♔h8 {or 19...dxc4 20 ♖xd8+ ♕xd8 21 ♖xb7 ±} 20 ♕f7 ±)

14 ♘xd5 ♗xd5 15 ♗xd5 ♘xd5 16 ♕xd5 ± Portisch-Bobotsov, Beverwijk 1965.

c2) 9 cxd5 exd5 10 b4 (10 ♘e5 c5 11 ♕f3 ♘c6 12 ♕h3 g6 13 ♗d2 ♘xe5 14 dxe5 ♘e4 15 ♖ad1 ♕c8 = Shamko-vich-Ree, Amsterdam 1968) and then:

c21) 10...♘bd7 11 ♕b3 a6 12 ♗b2 ♗d6 13 a4 ♕e7 14 b5 c5 15 bxc6 ♗xc6 16 ♖fc1 ± Geller-Lisitsyn, USSR Ch (Kiev) 1954.

c22) 10...♘e4 11 ♗b2 ♘d7 (the alternative 11...♘xc3 12 ♗xc3 ♗d6 13 ♕c2 g6 can be met by 14 h4!? ± or 14 b5 ± Gligorić-Donner, Wijk aan Zee 1971) 12 ♘e2 (12 ♕c2!?) 12...c5 (12...♖e8!? is a more solid alternative) 13 bxc5 bxc5 (Ovseevich-G.Kuzmin, Alushta 1999) 14 dxc5!? ♘dxc5 15 ♖b1 may favour White.

c23) In Hjartarson-G.Georgadze, Tilburg rpd 1993, Black managed to equalize without too many problems after 10...c6 11 ♗b2 ♘bd7 12 ♕b3 a5 13 ♖ac1 axb4 14 axb4 b5!? 15 e4 dxe4 16 ♘xe4 ♘d5 17 ♘c5 ♘xc5 18 bxc5 (18 dxc5 is given by Pliester as an improvement, but after 18...♘xb4 19 ♗xb5 {19 ♗xh7+! =} 19...cxb5 20 ♕xb4, instead of 20...♕d5, Black can play 20...♗xf3 21 gxf3 ♗g5!?, securing at least equal chances) 18...♘f4 19 ♖fe1 ♘xd3 20 ♕xd3 ♗f6 21 ♕b3 ♗c8 with a pleasant position for Black.

We return to 8...♗d6 (D).
Now:
B21: 9 b4   213
B22: 9 cxd5   215

Less critical are:
a) 9 ♕e2 c5 (9...♘bd7!? 10 ♖d1 ♖e8 11 b4 a5 12 b5 ♕e7 = Gofshtein-Salov, Beltsy 1979) 10 dxc5 bxc5 11

W

♖d1 (11 e4?! d4! was satisfactory for Black in the game Djurić-Khalifman, Bled/Rogaška Slatina 1991) 11...♘bd7 12 b3 (Mecking-Polugaevsky, Lucerne Ct (2) 1977) 12...♕e7 = Bagirov.

b) 9 ♘b5 and here:
b1) 9...dxc4 10 ♗xc4 ♗e7 11 ♕e2 ♘bd7 12 ♖d1 ♘e4 13 ♘c3 ♘df6 (13...♘xc3 14 bxc3 ♘f6 15 ♘d2 ♘d5 16 ♗b2 ♗d6 17 g3!?, intending e4, is more pleasant for White) 14 ♘e5 ♕c8 15 f3 ♘xc3 16 bxc3 c5 17 e4 with a better game for White, Ibragimov-Sha-riyazdanov, St Petersburg 1997.

b2) 9...♗e7 and then:
b21) 10 cxd5 exd5 11 ♕c2 c5 (11...c6!? is another idea) 12 b3 ♘bd7 13 ♗b2 a6 14 ♘c3 ♖c8 15 ♕e2 ± Gomez Esteban-G.Georgadze, Mon-dariz Balneario 1999.

b22) 10 b3 ♘bd7 transposes to line 'c3'.

c) 9 b3 and here:
c1) 9...c5 10 ♕e2 ♘c6 11 ♖d1 ♕e7 12 ♘b5 ♗b8 13 ♗b2?! (13 cxd5 exd5 is equal) 13...a6 (the immediate 13...♘a5!? is also good for Black) 14 ♘c3 ♘a5! and Black is better, Kam-sky-Lautier, Monaco rpd 1995.

c2) 9...a6 10 ♗b2 ♘bd7 11 ♖e1 ♘e4 12 ♘e2 ♕e7 13 ♘g3 f5 14 b4

♘df6 15 cxd5 (Scherbakov-Rantanen, Jyväskylä 1994) 15...♗xd5 =.

c3) 9...♘bd7 10 ♘b5 ♗e7 11 ♗b2 dxc4 (11...c5 is considered better for White; 11...a6 12 ♘c3 ♗d6 13 ♕e2 gives Black a choice between 13...♘e4 = Ibragimov-Yakovenko, Russian Ch (Elista) 2001, and 13...dxc4 14 bxc4 ♖e8, intending ...e5, which is interesting) 12 bxc4 c5!? 13 ♕e2 ♖e8 14 ♖ad1 (14 a4!?) 14...a6 15 ♘c3 cxd4 16 exd4 ♕c7 17 ♖fe1 (Lukacs-Z.Almasi, Hungarian Cht 1994) 17...♖ad8!?, intending ...♕f4 and ...♘f8-g6, with a better game for Black according to Lukacs.

B21)
9 b4 dxc4

9...a5 is rare. Then:

a) 10 b5 and now:

a1) Black can deviate by playing 10...♘bd7, but after 11 cxd5 exd5 12 ♕b3 ♖e8 13 a4, with 14 ♗a3 to follow, White is slightly better, Cifuentes-Polaczek, Antwerp 1999.

a2) 10...dxc4 11 ♗xc4 transposes to note 'b' to Black's 10th move.

b) 10 c5!? axb4 11 ♘a4 ♗e7 12 axb4 ♘e4 13 ♗b2 and now Black may be able to improve over *ECO*'s line 13...f5 14 ♘e5 ± Zukhovitsky-Sokolsky, USSR 1958 with the provocative 13...♘c6 or the more solid 13...♘d7!?.

10 ♗xc4 *(D)*
10...♘bd7

Again 10...a5 will usually transpose to the main line, but play can also continue independently:

a) 11 bxa5 is completely harmless; e.g., 11...♖xa5 12 ♗b2 ♘bd7 13 ♘b5 ♗e7 14 a4 c6 15 ♘c3 ♕a8 16 ♗e2 c5 17 ♘b5 cxd4 18 exd4 ♘d5 19 g3 and here a draw was prematurely agreed

B

in Yermolinsky-Piket, Wijk aan Zee 1999. Black is slightly better in the final position.

b) 11 b5 ♘bd7 and here:

b1) 12 ♗b2 transposes to the main line.

b2) 12 ♖e1 e5 13 e4 h6 14 ♗b2 ♕e7?! (14...exd4 =) 15 ♕c2 ♖ae8 (Taimanov-Buslaev, USSR Cht (Moscow) 1963) 16 ♘h4!? ±.

b3) 12 ♘e2 ♘e4 13 ♗b2 ♕f6?! (13...♕e7 =) 14 ♘g3 ♖ad8 15 ♗d3 ♘xg3 16 hxg3 (Torre-Bisguier, New York 1985) 16...♖fe8 17 ♕c2 ±.

11 ♗b2

Or:

a) 11 ♖e1 a5 12 b5 transposes to note 'b2' to Black's 10th move.

b) 11 ♘b5 is not particularly threatening: 11...a6 (11...♗e7 = has also been played) 12 ♘xd6 cxd6 13 ♗b2 (13 a4!?) 13...b5 14 ♗d3 ♘b6 15 ♖c1 ♗e4! 16 ♗e2 ♕e7 17 ♘d2 ♗g6 18 f3 ♖ac8 19 e4 d5 and Black has a slight initiative due to the weakness on the light squares and in particular c4, Morović-Korchnoi, Santiago 1991.

11...a5

As we have seen in a few examples above, this move is a popular idea. The reason for this is that Black forces

White to push his b-pawn to b5, where it occupies the square that he would otherwise have for his knight; e.g., 11...e5?! 12 ♘b5! ±. Some alternatives:

a) 11...♕e7 12 ♘b5 a6 13 ♘xd6 cxd6 14 a4 ♖fc8 15 ♗e2 ♘e4 16 b5 axb5 17 axb5 ♖xa1 18 ♕xa1 ♖a8 19 ♗a3 is slightly better for White, Psakhis-Lerner, USSR Ch (Moscow) 1983.

b) 11...a6 12 ♕e2 (12 ♖e1 e5 13 e4 ♕e7 14 d5 a5!? =) 12...e5 13 ♖ad1 e4 14 ♘e5 ♕e7 15 ♘xd7 ♕xd7 16 h3 ♖fe8 = Kamsky-Speelman, New York PCA 1994.

12 b5

This is in accordance with Black's plan; the queenside pawn-structure gets locked and play in the centre can begin. Alternatively, White can play 12 bxa5 ♖xa5 13 ♘b5 ♗e7 14 a4 (14 ♕e2 ♘e4 15 ♖fc1, Neverov-Brodsky, Alushta 1994, 15...♘df6 16 ♘e5 ♘d6 = Brodsky) 14...c5 15 ♘e5 cxd4 16 ♗xd4 ♘xe5 17 ♗xe5 ♕xd1 (a more aggressive and possibly better continuation is 17...♕a8!?; e.g., 18 f3 ♖c8 19 ♕b3 ♘d7!? with a nicely coordinated position for Black) 18 ♖fxd1 ♖fa8 19 ♗b3 ♗d5 = Gulko-Tal, USSR Ch (Erevan) 1975.

12...e5 (D)

The logical follow-up to his previous moves, as Black challenges White in the centre. Alternatives:

a) 12...♕e7 13 ♗e2 ♖ad8 14 ♕c2 e5 15 a4 ♖fe8 16 ♖ad1 e4 17 ♘d2 ♘d5 18 ♘xd5 ♗xd5 19 ♘c4 ♘f8 (19...f5!?, intending ...♕e6 – Cu.Hansen) 20 ♖de1 ♘g6 21 f4 exf3 22 ♗xf3 ♗xf3 23 gxf3! gives White a slight advantage, Shabalov-Benjamin, USA Ch (Los Angeles) 1993.

b) 12...♖a7!? was used successfully in Neverov-Zagrebelny, St Petersburg 1994: 13 ♖e1 ♕a8 14 ♕e2 e5 15 e4 ♖e8 16 ♖ad1 exd4 and here Zagrebelny gives 17 ♖xd4 ♖e7!? as best, with chances for both sides.

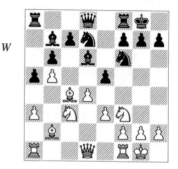

13 ♖e1

This move looks a bit odd as the e-file has yet to open and, as we shall see, generally doesn't open later. Although it is seen more frequently than other move, White has yet to prove an advantage with it. Therefore it may be worth considering 13 a4 ♕e7 14 h3 ♖ad8 15 ♕e2, as played in Spassky-Tal, Moscow 1975. Tal then gave two lines where he claimed equality, but improvements for White are fairly easy to find:

a) 15...e4 16 ♘h2 ♖fe8 was one of Tal's lines. Then 17 ♗a2, followed by ♘g4, leaves White slightly better.

b) 15...exd4 16 ♘xd4 ♘e4 17 ♘xe4 and now Tal gave 17...♗xe4, but then White plays 18 ♘c6!? and after 18...♗xc6 19 bxc6 ♘e5 20 ♗b5 he has a small plus. However, Black may be able to improve by 17...♕xe4!? 18 f3 ♕g6, with a different type of position.

It should also be mentioned that White is not interested in playing d5 in this type of position as the c5-square will then be entirely under Black's control.

13...e4

This is both necessary and good. White wants to play e4 to gain space in the centre, which is now prevented. Furthermore, Black can now start a kingside initiative.

14 ♘d2 ♕e7

After 14...♖e8, 15 ♗f1 h5 16 h3 ♘f8 17 ♘c4 h4 18 ♕b3 ♕e7 19 a4 ♕e6 gave Black a good game in Portisch-Bolbochan, Stockholm IZ 1952, but White can improve with 15 ♗e2, followed by f4 and ♘d2-c4-e5.

15 ♗e2!?

White follows the plan that I just outlined to meet 14...♖e8.

15 f3!? is a very different plan, immediately attacking the black e-pawn. 15...exf3 16 gxf3 and then:

a) 16...♖ad8 17 ♕e2 ♖fe8 18 ♕f2 ♘f8 19 ♘de4 ♘g6 20 ♘xd6 cxd6!? 21 ♗f1 ♘h5 22 e4 ♘hf4 with a complicated game, but Black cannot be worse, Hübner-Khalifman, Bundesliga 1991/2.

b) However, in 16...♗xh2+ Black has an alternative that should make White avoid this option; e.g., 17 ♔xh2 ♘g4+ and then:

b1) Not 18 fxg4?? ♕h4+ 19 ♔g1 ♕g3+ 20 ♔f1 ♕g2#.

b2) 18 ♔g3 (Neverov-Stocek, Lazne Bohdanec 1996) 18...♘xe3 19 ♕e2 ♕d6+ 20 ♔f2 ♘c2 21 ♘de4 ♕h2+ with a perpetual.

b3) White's best seems to be 18 ♔g1!?; e.g., 18...♘xe3 19 ♕e2 ♕g5+ 20 ♔f2 ♘c2 21 ♘de4 ♗xe4 22 ♘xe4

♕f4 23 ♖h1 with a complicated struggle ahead.

15...♖ad8 16 f4

Cementing White's control over the e5-square. White has also tried 16 ♕c2 ♖fe8:

a) 17 f3?! exf3 18 ♗xf3 ♗xf3 19 ♘xf3?! (19 gxf3 is the right move, even if Black is better after 19...♘f8) 19...♘e4 20 ♘xe4 ♕xe4 21 ♕xe4 ♖xe4 22 ♘d2 ♖e6 ∓ 23 e4?! ♘c5! and Black wins a pawn, Portisch-Petrosian, Lone Pine 1978.

b) Byrne's suggestion of 17 ♘c4!? seems worth a try.

16...♘d5 17 ♘xd5 ♗xd5 18 ♘c4 f5 19 ♘e5 ♕e6 20 ♔h1 h6 21 ♖g1 ♘xe5 22 dxe5 ♗c5

The chances are approximately equal, Portisch-Hübner, Abano Terme Ct (8) 1980. White would like to attack on the kingside by playing g4, while Black hopes to exchange the light-squared bishops to gain access to d3.

B22)

9 cxd5 exd5 *(D)*

10 b4

This move is the natural follow-up to the previous move; White wants to acquire some space on the queenside, while making it harder for Black to achieve the liberating ...c5.

On occasion White has also tried 10 ♘e5?! which leaves White a full tempo down on the lines covered in Line B1. Black obtains a good game after 10...c5 11 f4 ♘c6 12 ♕f3 cxd4 13 ♘xc6 ♗xc6 14 exd4 ♖e8, as in Sher-Palac, Bled 1992.

10...a6

This prevents ♘b5, but other noteworthy moves have been tried at this point:

a) 10...♖e8 11 ♕b3 and now 11...a6 transposes to note 'c' to Black's 11th move, while 11...♘e4 is line 'c1'.

b) 10...a5? 11 b5 ♘bd7 12 ♕b3 ♕e7 13 a4 ♖fe8 14 ♗a3 ♗xa3 15 ♕xa3 g6 16 ♕xe7 ♖xe7 17 ♖fc1 ± Gligorić-Delaune, Saint John 1988.

c) 10...♘e4!? has proved a tough nut for White to crack: 11 ♕b3 (11 ♘b5 ♗e7 12 ♕c2, Yusupov-Hübner, Bundesliga 1995/6, 12...c6!? 13 ♘c3 f5 14 ♘e5 ♘d7 = Hübner) and then:

c1) 11...♖e8 12 ♗b2 ♖e6!? leads to very interesting play: 13 ♖ad1 ♖h6 14 ♘e5 ♘xc3 15 ♗xc3 ♗xe5 16 dxe5 ♕h4 17 h3 d4 18 ♗c4 dxc3 19 ♗xf7+ ♔h8 20 ♗d5 c6 21 ♗f3 ♕e7 22 ♗g4 c5 23 b5 a6 24 a4 axb5 25 axb5 ♖g6 26 ♕xc3 with some, if not full, compensation for the piece, Polugaevsky-A.Sokolov, French Cht 1992.

c2) 11...♘xc3 12 ♕xc3 ♕e7 (or 12...♘d7 13 ♗b2 ♖e8 14 ♖ac1 ♖e6 15 b5 ♖h6, Reynolds-Shteinsapir, corr. 1981, 16 a4!? ±) 13 ♗b2 ♘d7 14 b5 a6 15 a4 axb5 16 axb5 ♘f6 17 ♘e5 ♘e4 18 ♕c2 with at best a minimal advantage for White, Gavrikov-Salov, Irkutsk 1986.

d) 10...c6 will often transpose to other lines. 11 ♗b2?! (11 ♕b3!?, intending a4-a5, is better according to Pliester) 11...♖e8 12 ♖e1 ♘bd7 13 ♕b3 a5 14 ♖ad1?! (Pliester gives 14 bxa5 ♖xa5 15 a4 as better) 14...axb4 15 axb4 ♗f8 16 ♗f5 g6 17 ♗h3 ♕e7 18 ♗a3 ♗a6 19 ♘d2 ♗c4 20 ♕b2 b5 and Black is clearly in control, Muir-Milošević, Berne 1990.

e) 10...♘bd7 (D) and here:

e1) 11 ♕c2 c5!? (11...♖e8 12 ♗b2 transposes to line 'e2', while 11...a6 is also possible) 12 bxc5 bxc5 13 ♖b1 ♗c6 14 ♘b5?! (14 dxc5 ♘xc5 15 ♘d4 ♗d7 and now 16 ♖d1 or 16 ♘db5 looks a bit better for White) 14...♗xb5 15 ♖xb5 c4 16 ♗e2 ♕c7 and Black is better, Lugovoi-Sakaev, Tallinn 2001.

e2) 11 ♗b2 ♖e8 12 ♕c2 a6 13 b5 a5 14 a4 ♘e4 15 ♗a3 ♖c8 16 ♖fc1 ♘df6 17 ♕b2 ♘g4 18 ♘d1 h6 19 h3 ♘gf6 20 ♖c2 with a small plus for White due to his pressure along the c-file, Ivanchuk-Piket, Monaco rpd 1999.

e3) 11 b5!?, attempting to fix the black queenside, worked well for White in Knaak-Beliavsky, Novi Sad 1979: 11...♘e4 12 ♕b3 ♖e8 13 a4

♘df6 14 ♗a3 a5 15 ♗xd6 cxd6 16
♘e2 h6 17 ♖a2 ♕d7 18 ♘e1 ♖e7 19
f3 ♘g5 20 ♘g3 g6 21 ♖e2 and White
was dynamically better.

e4) 11 ♕b3 and then:

e41) 11...a6 transposes to the main
line.

e42) 11...♖e8 12 a4 c6 (12...a6
transposes to note 'a' to Black's 12th
move) 13 ♗a3 ♘f8 14 ♘e2 ♘e4 15
♘g3 ♕d7 (15...a5!? could be considered) 16 ♖fd1 f5 17 ♗b2 ♘g6 18 a5 ±
Ehlvest-Slipak, Villa Martelli 1997.

e43) 11...c6 12 ♖e1 (12 a4 ♕e7 13
♗a3 ♖ab8 14 h3 ♖fe8 15 ♘d2 c5!? 16
bxc5 bxc5 17 ♘b5 ♗c6 18 ♕c2 ♗xb5
19 axb5 c4 with a pull for Black,
Volke-Smirin, Munich 1993) 12...♖e8
13 ♗b2 ♖b8 14 ♕c2 ♖c8 15 ♖ad1 a6
16 ♗f5 ♖c7 17 ♘a4 h6 18 ♘e5 with
some initiative for White, Timman-Van
der Vliet, Dutch Ch (Hilversum) 1983.

11 ♕b3 *(D)*

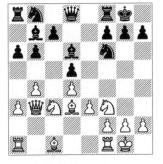

B

We are now at one of the more important crossroads for this line.

11...♘bd7

A number of other moves have been
tested:

a) 11...♘c6?! 12 ♗b2 ♖e8 13 ♖fc1
♗f8 14 ♕c2 g6 15 ♘e2 ♗d6 16 ♘f4

♘e7 17 ♘e5 ♖c8 (Kantsler-Rechlis,
Israeli League 2000) 18 ♕e2, intending ♕f3, with an advantage for White.

b) 11...♘e4 12 ♗b2 ♘xc3 13 ♕xc3
♖e8 14 a4 ♘c6?! (14...♘d7, aiming
for e4, is better) 15 b5 ♘b4 16 ♗e2 a5
17 ♘e5 f6 18 ♘d3 ♕d7 19 ♗a3 and
the c7-pawn is gradually becoming
softer, Semkov-Genov, Bulgarian Ch
(Bankia) 1992.

c) 11...♖e8 doesn't have the best
reputation, but will often just transpose to our main line below. White has
a few good moves:

c1) 12 ♗b2 and then:

c11) 12...♘e4!? 13 a4 ♖e6!? 14 b5
♖h6 and now 15 g3?! ♕d7 16 ♘xd5
♕g4 (Engers-Hoerner, corr. 1964) 17
♘e5! ♗xe5 18 ♗xe4 ♗xg3 19 ♘e7+!
♔h8 20 fxg3 ♕xe4 21 d5 might be
good for White, but 15 h3 followed by
♖fc1 ± is simpler.

c12) 12...♘bd7 13 ♖ac1 (Taimanov
suggests 13 a4 followed by ♗a3 and
b5) 13...c6 14 ♕c2 ♕e7 15 ♗f5 a5 16
b5 c5 is fully OK for Black, Boleslav-
sky-Taimanov, USSR Ch (Leningrad)
1956.

c2) 12 a4 ♘c6 (12...♘bd7 transposes to note 'a' to Black's 12th move)
13 ♗a3 a5 14 ♗b5 (14 b5 ♘b4 15
♗xb4 ♗xb4 16 ♘e5 ± Taimanov)
14...axb4 15 ♗xc6 ♗xc6 16 ♗xb4
♗xb4 (16...♘e4 17 ♖fc1 ♗xb4 18
♕xb4 is ± according to *ECO*, Silman-
Kane, USA 1981) 17 ♕xb4 ♕e7 18
♕b3 ♖a5 19 ♘e5 ♗b7 20 ♖fc1 ♖c8
21 h3 ± Cu.Hansen-Sigurjonsson,
Reykjavik 1985.

d) 11...♕e7 and here:

d1) 12 b5 axb5 (or 12...a5 13 a4
♘bd7 14 ♗a3 ♖ac8 15 ♖fc1 ♖fe8 16
♗f5 g6 17 ♗h3 ± Yusupov-Korchnoi,

Garmisch Partenkirchen rpd 1994) 13 Nxb5 Nbd7 (13...Nc6!? 14 Nxd6 Qxd6 15 a4 Na5 16 Qc2, Knaak-Rantanen, Jyväskylä 1994, 16...Qc6 17 Qb1 Nc4 is OK for Black) and now:

d11) 14 Nxd6 Qxd6 15 a4 Ba6 16 Rd1 Bxd3 17 Qxd3 c5 18 dxc5 bxc5 is equal, Agdestein-Lutz, Bundesliga 1999/00.

d12) 14 a4 c5 15 Ba3 (or 15 Nxd6 Qxd6 16 Ba3 Ba6 17 Rfd1 Bxd3 18 Qxd3 Qc6 ∓ Semkov-Nikčević, Rome 1990) 15...Ba6!? (also adequate is 15...Bc6 16 Qc2 Rfc8 17 Rfc1 Bxb5 18 Bxb5 Ne4 19 dxc5 bxc5 20 Qd1 Ndf6 21 h3 Qe6 = Handke-Chuchelov, Fürth 1999) 16 Rfb1 g6 17 Qd1 Bxb5 18 Bxb5 c4 19 Bxd6 Qxd6 20 Nd2 Rfc8 = Beliavsky-Hraček, Polanica Zdroj 1996.

d13) 14 Bb2 c5 15 dxc5 (15 Nxd6 Qxd6 16 Bf5 c4 17 Qc2 g6 18 Bxd7 Nxd7 19 Ne5 Rfe8 20 Bc3 Bc6 21 Qb2, Yusupov-Timman, Linares Ct (5) 1992, and here 21...f6 = has been suggested) 15...bxc5 (15...Nxc5 16 Qd1 Nxd3 17 Qxd3 Bc5 18 Nfd4 Qe4 19 Rfd1 Qxd3 ½-½ Malaniuk-Chuchelov, Hamburg 1995) 16 Nxd6 Qxd6 17 Qc3 Ba6! 18 Rfd1 Bxd3 19 Rxd3 Rfb8 (Yusupov-Dautov, Nussloch 1996) 20 Rad1 Qb6! 21 Ra1 Qa5 22 Ne5 Qxc3 23 Bxc3 Rxa3 24 Nxd7 Nxd7 25 Rxd5 Rxc3 26 Rxd7 = Dautov.

d2) 12 Rb1 Nbd7 13 a4 Ne4 (or 13...Rfe8 14 b5 a5 15 Ra1 Nf8 16 Ba3 Rad8 17 Bxd6 Rxd6 18 Rac1 ± Muir-Rechlis, Novi Sad OL 1990) 14 Nxd5!? (14 Bb2 Ndf6 15 b5, Petrosian-Browne, Tilburg 1982, 15...Nxc3 16 Bxc3 axb5 17 axb5 Ra7 with chances for both sides – Petrosian)

14...Bxd5 15 Qxd5 Nc3 16 Qb3 Nxb1 17 Qxb1 g6 18 b5 axb5 19 axb5 Qe6 20 e4 Be7 21 Qc2 Nf6 22 Ne5 Ra2 23 Qb1 Ra4 24 Nc6 and White has excellent control over the position, Onishchuk-Yermolinsky, Las Vegas 2001.

12 a4

12 Bb2 Qe7 13 b5 axb5 14 Nxb5 transposes to note 'd13' to Black's 11th move.

12...Qe7

Black has three alternatives:

a) 12...Re8 13 Ba3 and here:

a1) 13...g6 14 b5 a5 15 Rfc1 Rc8 16 Rc2 Nf8 17 g3 Ne6 18 Rac1 with pressure down the c-file and a slight advantage for White, Muir-Engqvist, Budapest 1995.

a2) 13...c6 14 b5 Qe7 15 bxc6 Bxc6 16 Bxd6 Qxd6 17 Rfc1 ± Zilberman-Hübner, Havana 1998.

a3) 13...Qe7 14 b5 a5 15 Bxd6 cxd6 16 Rac1 Nf8 (16...Rac8 17 Rc2 Rc7 18 Rfc1 ± Yerofeev-Bertino, corr. 1997) 17 Bf5 Ne6 18 Rc2 Rac8 19 Rfc1 ± Lesiège-Vasquez, New Delhi 2000.

b) 12...c6 13 a5 b5 14 e4 dxe4 15 Nxe4 Nxe4 16 Bxe4 Nf6 17 Bc2 Nd5 18 Bd2 Re8 19 Rae1 Rxe1 20 Rxe1 Qf8 21 Ng5 (Gligorić-Ionescu, Sochi 1986) 21...h6 =.

c) 12...Ne4!? 13 Nxd5 Ng5 14 Nxg5 (14 Ne1 looks better at first sight, but Black is OK after 14...Qh3+! 15 Kh1 {Timman} 15...Qg5 16 e4 Bxd5 17 exd5 Nf4 18 Bxf4 Qxf4) 14...Qxg5 15 e4 Bxd5 16 Qxd5 Qxd5 17 exd5 Bxb4 18 Bf4 Nf6 19 Rab1 Nxd5 = Ftačnik-Ligterink, Wijk aan Zee 1985.

13 Ba3 (D)

13 b5 a5 transposes to Yusupov-Korchnoi in note 'd1' to Black's 11th move.

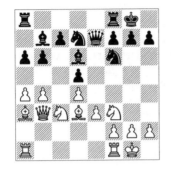

B

13...♖fb8

Black prepares to play ...c5 and therefore protects his bishop. He has two other moves at hand:

a) 13...c6 is a suggestion of Dautov's that has yet to be tried. A possible continuation is 14 a5 b5 15 ♖fc1 ♖fe8 =.

b) 13...♖fd8 and then:

b1) 14 ♖fc1 c6 15 a5 b5 16 ♖e1 ♘e4 17 ♗xe4 dxe4 18 ♘d2 ♘f6 19 f3 exf3 20 ♘xf3 ♗c8 21 e4 and now, instead of 21...♗c7 22 e5 ♘d5 23 ♘e4 ♗e6 24 ♕c2 ± Handke-Ravi, Biel 2000, Black should play 21...♗e6 22 ♕b1 ♗c7 23 e5 ♘d5 24 ♘e4 ♗f5 with a pleasant position.

b2) 14 b5!? ♗xa3 (Ftačnik gives 14...a5 15 ♖fc1 ♖e8 as unclear, but this type of position usually favours White and this one is no exception) 15 bxa6 ♗xa6 16 ♗xa6 ♖xa6 17 ♖xa3 c6 18 ♖a2 ♖c8 19 ♖c1 h6 20 ♖ac2 ♕d6 (20...♕e6 immediately makes more sense) 21 ♘d2 ♕e6 22 h3 is slightly

better for White, Yusupov-Benjamin, Amsterdam 1994.

14 ♗f5

14 ♖fe1 also has some logic to it: 14...c6 (14...h6!?, to keep e4 better guarded, is probably best) 15 a5 (15 e4!?) 15...b5 16 ♗f5 ♘f8 and now instead of the tame 17 ♖ec1 ♗c8 18 ♗c2 ♗g4 = Gligorić-Portisch, Moscow 1999, 17 e4!? gives White livelier play and the better prospects.

Another possibility is 14 b5!?, which has yet to be tried.

14...♘f8 15 ♖fc1 g6 16 ♗h3 c6 17 g3 ♗c8 18 ♗g2 ♗b7

The position is balanced, Polugaevsky-Lautier, French Cht 1992.

Conclusion

Although these lines are fairly complicated, with White holding some sort of initiative in the early stage of the game, it appears that Black has adequate defensive resources and should be able to maintain the balance.

In Line B1, White usually tries to build up a kingside initiative, but Black can relatively easily fend off the worst threats. The old main line is 9...♗d6, but 9...♘bd7 is gaining popularity, even though I believe that White has better chances for an advantage after this move.

In Line B2 White also has problems presenting Black with difficulties. In Line B21, Black equalizes in the main line, but White should have a look at 13 a4, which deserves further attention. Line B22 seems more promising for White and in particular his options on move 14 deserve further study.

15 Hübner Variation

1 d4 ♘f6 2 c4 e6 3 ♘c3 ♗b4 4 e3 c5 5 ♗d3 ♘c6 6 ♘f3

6 ♘e2 is covered in note 'e' to Black's 4th move in Chapter 16.

6...♗xc3+ 7 bxc3 d6 (D)

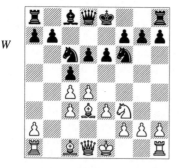

This is the starting position of the Hübner Variation, which was first invented by Belgian GM Alberic O'Kelly de Galway, who played it on several occasions with reasonable results. The first game of his dates back to 1949. However, the variation has been named after German GM Robert Hübner who played it in the late 1960s and early 1970s. That was when it caught the attention of a new audience, including Bobby Fischer, who used it to spectacular effect in game 5 of his 1972 world championship match against Boris Spassky in Reykjavik.

Black's idea is to close the centre, after which his knights will be stronger than White's bishops. Furthermore, the doubled c-pawns prevent White from carrying out a pawn-storm on the queenside, where it otherwise would have been logical to do so.

White now has three main options:

A: 8 e4   220
B: 8 0-0   226
C: 8 ♘d2   230

White has also tried:

a) 8 ♕e2?! e5 9 ♘d2 transposes to note 'c' to White's 9th move in Line C.

b) 8 ♕c2 e5 (8...♕c7!?) 9 dxc5 (9 0-0 transposes to note 'd' to White's 9th move in Line B) 9...dxc5 10 ♘g5 h6 11 ♘e4 ♘xe4 12 ♗xe4 ♗e6 13 ♖b1 0-0 = Atalik-Kalesis, Karditsa 1994.

c) 8 ♖b1!? 0-0 9 0-0 e5 10 ♘g5 ♕e7 11 ♕c2 h6 12 ♘h7 ♘xh7 13 ♗xh7+ ♔h8 14 ♗e4 ♘a5?! (Christiansen-Seirawan, Buenos Aires 1981; 14...exd4 is OK) and now 15 dxc5 dxc5 16 ♕a4 ♕c7 17 ♖b5 ♘c6 18 ♖xc5 ♗d7 19 ♖d1 means an extra pawn for White.

A)

8 e4 e5 (D)
9 d5
Or:
a) 9 0-0 used to be considered an error, but this isn't evident any longer: 9...cxd4 10 cxd4 ♗g4 11 d5 ♘d4 12 ♔h1 0-0 13 ♗e3 ♘xf3 14 gxf3 ♗h3 15 ♖g1 ♘h5 16 c5 with chances for both sides.

b) 9 h3 is a reasonably popular alternative:

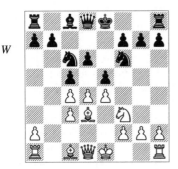

b1) 9...0-0 10 0-0 h6 (10...b6!?) 11 ♗e3 b6 12 d5 ♘e7 13 ♔h2!? g5!? (this kind of move is designed to prevent White from playing f4, a theme we will meet several times in this chapter; alternatively, 13...♘h7 14 ♕c2 ♔h8 15 ♘h4 ♗d7 16 ♘f5 ♘xf5 17 exf5 ♖e8 18 ♗e4 ♘f6 19 g4 ♘xg4+ 20 hxg4 ♕h4+ 21 ♔g2 ♕xg4+ 22 ♔h2 ½-½ Mukhaev-Kiseliov, Moscow 1995) 14 ♘g1 ♘h7 15 ♘e2 f5 16 exf5 ♗xf5 17 ♘g3 ♗g6 18 ♕c2 ♗xd3 19 ♕xd3 ♕d7 20 a4 ♘f5 is equal, Yusupov-Gomez Esteban, Oviedo rpd 1993.

b2) 9...h6 10 ♗e3 (10 0-0 0-0 is line 'b1') 10...b6 (or 10...♕a5 11 0-0 0-0 12 ♗d2 ♕c7 13 d5 ♘e7 14 ♘e1 ♘g6 = Van der Sterren-P.Nikolić, Rotterdam 1998) and now:

b21) 11 ♕e2 ♕c7 12 d5 ♘e7 13 ♘h4 g5 14 ♕f3 ♘fg8 15 ♘f5 ♘xf5 16 exf5 ♘f6 with chances for both sides, Ibragimov-Serper, Kherson 1991.

b22) 11 0-0 ♕c7 (11...0-0 transposes to line 'b1') 12 d5 ♘e7 13 ♘h4 g5 14 ♕f3 ♘fg8 15 ♘f5 ♘xf5 16 exf5 ♘f6 17 g4 ♕e7 (an interesting plan worth noting since it is often an idea in positions of this type; 17...♗a6 and 17...♗b7 are also possible) 18 ♖fe1

♔d8! 19 ♕g3 ♕f8 20 f3 ♔c7 21 ♕f2 a5 22 ♔g2 ♗a6 23 ♕d2 ♕g7 24 ♖h1 ♖ae8 25 ♖ae1 ♖hg8 ½-½ Ibragimov-Csom, Budapest 1995.

b23) 11 d5 ♘e7 12 ♘d2 (D) (or 12 g3 ♗d7 13 ♔f1 ♕c8 14 ♔g2 ♘h7 15 ♘h4 g5 16 ♘f3 f5 17 exf5 ♗xf5 18 ♕b1 ♘f6 19 ♘d2 ♗xd3 20 ♕xd3 ♕f5 and Black has a comfortable game, Lugovoi-Ibragimov, Russian Ch (Elista) 1995) and here:

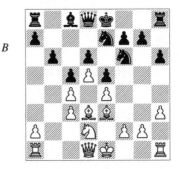

b231) 12...g5 13 ♘f1! (13 h4 gxh4! 14 ♖xh4 ♘g6 15 ♖h1 ♘g4 16 ♘f1 ♘f4 17 g3 ♘g2+ 18 ♔e2 ♘4xe3 19 ♘xe3 ♘xe3 20 ♔xe3 ♕g5+ 21 ♔e2 ♔e7 = Yusupov-Karpov, Dortmund 1994) 13...♘g6 14 g3 ♗d7 15 ♗d2 ♕e7 16 ♘e3 0-0-0 17 ♕f3 ♘e8 18 0-0-0 ± Yusupov-B.Lalić, Erevan OL 1996.

b232) 12...♘h7 13 ♘f1 (13 h4 ♘f6!? 14 ♘f1 ♗d7 15 ♗d2 ♕c8 16 ♘e3 ♔d8 17 h5 ♔c7 = Yusupov-Timman, Madrid 1995) 13...0-0 (13...♘g6?! 14 g3 0-0 15 h4 ♗d7 16 h5 ♘e7 17 g4 f6 18 ♘g3 ± Yusupov-Hall, Bundesliga 1998/9) 14 ♘g3 f5 15 exf5 ♘xf5 16 ♘xf5 ♗xf5 17 ♗xf5 ♖xf5 18 a4 ♘f8 19 ♕g4 ½-½ Sturua-Damljanović, Leon Echt 2001.

b233) 12...♘g6 13 g3 ♗d7 (13...0-0 14 ♔f1 ♘e8 15 ♔g2 ♘e7 16 f3 f5 = Portisch-Browne, Tilburg 1982) 14 f4 (14 ♕c2!?, as suggested by Wells, is probably better) 14...exf4 15 gxf4 ♘h7! 16 ♕h5 ♕f6 17 e5 dxe5 18 ♗xg6 (Lugovoi-Sammalvuo, Myyrmanni 1999) 18...exf4 19 ♗xh7 ♖xh7 20 0-0 ♕g5+! 21 ♕xg5 hxg5 22 ♗f2 ♗xh3 23 ♖fe1+ ♔d7 and Black's kingside pawns provide him with the better chances.

b234) 12...0-0 13 g4 ♘g6 14 g5 hxg5 15 ♗xg5 ♕e8 16 ♗xf6 gxf6 17 ♔f1 ♔g7 ½-½ Yusupov-Torre, Moscow OL 1994.

9...♘e7 (D)

This is where the knight belongs. It can proceed to g6 or remain on e7, where it both supports an ...f5 break and prevents invaders from entering the f5-square.

9...♘a5, on the other hand, is completely wrong, although Black was only slightly worse after 10 ♘d2 b6 11 ♘f1 ♗a6 12 ♘e3 ♗d7 13 0-0 ♔c7 14 f4 ♘d7 15 f5 in Hort-Spiridonov, Slančev Brjag 1974.

W

10 ♘h4

This was Spassky's choice against Fischer in their world championship match. It opens the path for the f-pawn and was also intended to take the g6-square away from Black's knight. White has tried several other moves:

a) 10 g3 intends to meet 10...♘g6 with 11 h4, which nonetheless is playable for Black. Even better, however, is 10...h6 11 ♘h4 g5 12 ♘g2 ♕a5 13 ♕b3 ♗h3 14 0-0 0-0-0 15 ♖b1 ♕c7 16 f3 ♔b8 17 ♖f2 ♖hg8 with fairly even chances, Najdorf-Hübner, Wijk aan Zee 1971.

b) 10 h3 h6 (10...♘g6 11 g3 ♕a5 12 ♗d2 h5 13 ♘h4!? ♘xh4 14 gxh4 ♗d7 15 ♕f3 0-0-0 16 0-0 ♖df8 = Spassky-Hort, Manila IZ 1976) 11 ♗e3 (11 ♘d2 0-0 12 ♘f1 ♘e8 13 ♘e3 f5 14 exf5 ♘xf5 15 ♘xf5 ♗xf5 16 ♗xf5 ♖xf5 17 ♕g4 ♕f6 18 0-0 h5 19 ♕e4 ♕g6 and Black has solved his opening problems, Lugovoi-Shaposhnikov, St Petersburg 2000) 11...♕a5 12 ♕b3 ♕c7 13 ♘d2 ♘h5 14 g3 g5 15 0-0-0 ♘g6 16 ♗e2 ♘f6 17 ♖df1 ♕e7 18 ♕b1 ♔d8 19 ♘f3 ♔c7 and Black's king holds the queenside together; the chances are fairly balanced, Kamsky-Karpov, Linares 1991.

c) 10 ♖b1 h6 (10...♕c7 11 ♘h4 h6 12 g3 ♗h3 13 f4 0-0-0 14 fxe5 dxe5 and now, instead of 15 ♖b2?! ♔b8 16 ♘f3 ♔a8 17 ♕b3 ♘c8! ∓ Gligorić-Van der Wiel, Vršac 1983, White should play 15 ♘f3!? according to Cebalo) and then:

c1) 11 0-0 transposes to line 'd31'.

c2) 11 h4 0-0 12 ♘h2 ♘h7 13 g4?! (13 ♘f1 ♘g6!? is approximately balanced) 13...♘g6 14 g5 ♘xh4 15 gxh6 g6 16 ♖g1 ♔h8 17 ♖g3 b6 18 ♖b2 f5 ∓ Gligorić-Adorjan, Sarajevo 1983.

c3) 11 ♘d2 ♘g6 12 g3 0-0 13 ♘f1 ♕a5 14 ♕c2 ♕c7 15 ♘e3 ♖e8 16 f3

罝b8 17 0-0 ♗h3 18 罝f2 h5 with approximate equality, Bandza-Brodsky, Miedzybrodzie 1991.

c4) 11 ♘h4 0-0 12 g3 罝b8 13 0-0 ♗h3 14 ♘g2 ♘h7 15 f4 f5 16 fxe5 dxe5 17 exf5 ♗xf5 18 ♗e3 ♕d6 19 ♗xf5 罝xf5 20 罝xf5 ♘xf5 with an equal position, Safin-P.Nikolić, Moscow FIDE 2001.

d) 10 0-0 *(D)* and now:

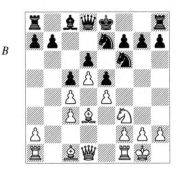

B

d1) 10...♘g6 11 ♘e1 0-0 is Tegelidis-Kalesis in line 'd2'.

d2) 10...0-0 11 ♘h4 (11 ♘d2 transposes to note 'b' to White's 11th move in Line C; 11 ♘e1 ♘g6 12 g3 ♘e8 13 ♘g2 f5 14 f3 f4 15 g4, Tegelidis-Kalesis, Greece 1998, 15...♕g5 ∓) and here:

d21) 11...♘g6 12 ♘f5 罝e8 13 罝b1 h6 14 ♕f3 罝b8 15 g3?! (Pliester's 15 g4 is probably stronger) 15...♘h7 16 h4 ♘e7 leaves the initiative in Black's hands, Yusupov-Epishin, Dortmund 1994.

d22) 11...h6 and then:

d221) 12 f4 ♘g6 13 ♘xg6 fxg6 transposes to the main line.

d222) 12 f3 g5 13 ♘f5 ♘xf5 14 exf5 ♗d7 15 ♗d2 ♔g7 (15...罝b8!? Ftačnik) 16 g4 罝h8 (16...a6 17 a4 b5!?

is another suggestion of Ftačnik's) 17 罝b1 罝b8 18 ♔g2 a6 19 a4 (Gelfand-Short, Dos Hermanas 1997) and now 19...b5!? 20 cxb5 axb5 21 ♗xb5 ♗xb5 22 axb5 ♘xd5 23 ♗xg5 ♘xc3 24 ♗xd8 ♘xd1 25 罝fxd1 罝hxd8 with even chances (Ftačnik).

d223) 12 ♕f3!? (preventing ...g5) 12...♘g6 13 ♘f5 ♗xf5 14 ♕xf5 ♘h7 15 罝b1 ♕e7 16 g3 罝ac8 17 h4 and Black is struggling for counterplay, Hort-J.Adamski, Polanica Zdroj 1977.

d3) 10...h6 and here:

d31) 11 罝b1 ♕c7 12 ♘e1 ♗d7 13 ♘c2 ♘h7 14 f4 exf4! 15 ♗xf4 ♘g6 16 ♗g3 0-0! with even chances, Gligorić-Andersson, Bugojno 1980.

d32) 11 ♘e1 g5 12 g3 (12 罝b1 ♘g6 13 g3 ♗h3 14 ♘g2 ♕d7 15 ♕b3?? {15 罝e1 is better} 15...♗xg2 16 ♔xg2 ♘h4+ 17 ♔h1 ♕h3 −+ Sebih-Hmadi, Dubai OL 1986) 12...♗h3 13 ♘g2 ♕d7 14 f3 0-0-0 15 罝f2 ♔b8 16 罝b1 ♔a8 17 ♘e3 ♕c7 and Black is doing fine, Glianets-Brodsky, Kazan 1995.

d33) 11 ♘h4 is an idea we have seen a few times. Black has now tried:

d331) 11...0-0 transposes to line 'd22'.

d332) 11...g5 12 ♕f3 (or 12 ♘f5 ♘xf5 13 exf5 e4 14 ♗c2 ♗xf5 15 f3 ♗g6 16 fxe4 ♗d7 ∓ Dautov) 12...♘h7 (12...♘fg8 13 ♘f5 ♗xf5 14 exf5 ♘f6 15 ♕h3 ♔d7 16 g3 ♔c7 17 f4 e4 18 ♗e2 g4! 19 ♗xg4 h5 20 ♗d1 ♕d7 21 ♕h4 ♕xf5 ∓ Milanović-B.Knežević, Yugoslav Cht (Cetinje) 1993) 13 ♘f5 ♘xf5 14 exf5 ♗d7 15 罝b1 b6 16 ♗c2 罝b8 17 a4 a5 18 h4 ♕f6 and Black is at least equal, Vaganian-Short, Horgen 1995.

e) 10 ♘d2 *(D)* gives Black a handful of options:

B

e1) 10...0-0?! is premature; the black king should remain in the centre for the time being to await any developments. In the game Petrosian-Ivkov, Nice OL 1974, White obtained excellent chances after 11 ♘f1 ♕a5 12 ♗d2 ♘e8 13 ♘g3 f5 14 exf5 ♘xf5 15 ♕c2 g6 16 0-0 ♗d7 17 ♘e4 ♘f6 18 ♘g5! ♖ae8 19 f3! ♘g7 20 g4! ♕a4 21 ♕b3!.

e2) 10...h6 11 h4 ♗d7 12 ♘f1 ♕a5 13 ♗d2 0-0-0 14 ♘e3 h5 (Knaak-Vaganian, Sochi 1980) 15 f3 leaves White somewhat better.

e3) 10...♘g6 11 h4 (or 11 g3 ♗h3 12 f3 h5 13 ♘f1 ♗xf1 14 ♔xf1 h4 15 ♔f2 hxg3+ 16 hxg3 ♖xh1 17 ♕xh1 ♕a5 18 ♕e1 0-0-0 19 ♗e3 ♖h8 20 ♔g2 ♕a4 21 ♕d2 ♘d7 22 ♕c2 ♖xc2+ ½-½ Kharitonov-Raaste, Lodz 1980) 11...h5 12 g3 ♕a5 13 ♕c2 ♗d7 14 a4 ♘e7 15 ♘f1 0-0-0 16 ♗g5 ♘fg8 17 ♘d2 ♖f8 18 f3 ½-½ Hraček-Aseev, Brno 1991.

e4) 10...♕a5 11 ♕b3 (Black does not have the same kind of problems after 11 ♕c2; for example, 11...h5! 12 h4 ♗d7 13 g3 0-0-0 14 a4 ♘g4 15 ♘b3 {15 ♘f1!?, intending f3, is better according to *ECO*} 15...♕c7 16 f3 ♘h6 17 a5 ♖df8 18 ♕a2 f5 19 ♗g5

fxe4 20 fxe4 ♘eg8! and Black starts penetrating the white kingside on the light squares, Gligorić-Larsen, Bugojno 1980) 11...0-0 12 0-0 ♘h5 13 g3 ♗h3 14 ♖e1 ♕c7 15 ♕d1 g6 16 ♘f1, Gligorić-Timman, Tilburg 1977. According to Ugrinović, Black should now continue 16...f5 17 exf5 ♗xf5 18 ♗xf5 ♘xf5 19 ♘e3 with chances for both sides.

10...h6

Or:

a) 10...0-0 11 0-0 h6 transposes to note 'a' to White's 11th move.

b) 10...♘g6 is inaccurate according to *ECO*, which gives 11 ♘f5 '± with initiative'. This has been tested: 11...♗xf5 12 exf5 e4 13 fxg6 exd3 14 gxf7+ ♔xf7 15 0-0 ♖e8 16 ♕xd3 ♕e7 and after 17 ♗f4? ♕e4 18 ♕xe4 ♖xe4 Black had taken over the initiative in Lesiège-Zarnicki, Matanzas 1993, but 17 f3 improves, leaving White with the better chances.

11 f4

This advance is the logical follow-up to White's previous move and it is also the way to counter Black's pawn-structure. Other moves are somewhat slower and give Black a choice of replies:

a) 11 0-0 transposes to note 'd33' to White's 10th move.

b) 11 g3 and here:

b1) 11...♗h3 12 f4 ♘g6 13 ♕f3 ♗g4 14 ♕f2 exf4 15 ♘xg6 fxg6 (Donner-Sosonko, Amsterdam 1977) and now 16 e5! is quite problematic for Black.

b2) 11...0-0?! is premature; there is no reason to decide where the king is going just yet. Nonetheless, Black was OK after 12 0-0 ♗h3 13 ♘g2 ♕a5

14 ♖b1 ♕xa2 15 ♖xb7 ♘g6 16 ♖b3 ♕a4 17 ♕c2 ♕d7 = in Tukmakov-M.Gurevich, Leningrad 1987.

b3) 11...g5 12 ♘g2 ♕a5 (the alternative 12...♗h3!? is also good) 13 ♕b3 (or 13 ♗d2 ♗h3 14 ♘e3 h5 15 a4 0-0-0 16 ♕b3 ♖hg8 17 ♔e2 ♔b8 with chances for both sides, Tukmakov-Averkin, USSR 1972) 13...♗h3 14 0-0 0-0-0 15 ♖b1 ♕c7 16 f3 ♔b8 17 ♖f2 ♖hg8 18 ♘e3 ♗c8 19 ♔f1 ♖df8 ∓ Najdorf-Hübner, Wijk aan Zee 1971.

c) 11 f3 and now:

c1) 11...g5 12 ♘f5 ♗xf5 13 exf5 ♖g8 (13...♕a5!?) 14 g4 ♕e7 15 ♕e2 ♗d7 16 h4 0-0-0 17 hxg5 hxg5 18 ♔f2 ♖de8 = Vasilevich-Tunik, Yalta 1996.

c2) 11...♘h5 12 g3 g5 13 ♘f5 ♘xf5 14 exf5 ♕f6 15 ♕c2 ♔d8 16 ♗e3 ♔c7 17 0-0-0 ♗d7 = Gerusel-Hoffmann, Bundesliga 1991/2.

c3) 11...♕a5 and then:

c31) 12 ♕c2 g5 13 ♘f5 ♘xf5 14 exf5 ♗d7 15 h4?! (15 g4 0-0-0 16 h4 e4! is pretty bad too, although it is given as an improvement by *ECO*; 15 0-0 is safest) 15...g4! 16 fxg4?! ♘xg4 17 ♗e2 ♖g8! is slightly better for Black, Donner-Portisch, Skopje OL 1972.

c32) 12 ♗d2 g5 13 ♘f5 ♘xf5 14 exf5 ♗d7 15 h4 (15 g4!? *ECO*) 15...g4 16 fxg4 e4 17 ♗e2 e3! 18 ♗xe3 ♕xc3+ (Donner-Timman, Amsterdam 1981) 19 ♗d2 ♕g3+ 20 ♔f1 is unclear – *ECO*.

11...♘g6! *(D)*

This is Fischer's invention and is also Black's only reasonable way to continue. After 11...exf4? 12 ♗xf4 g5 13 e5!, Black's position has crumbled on more than one occasion; e.g.,

13...♘g4 14 e6 ♘f6 15 0-0 fxe6 16 ♗e5 dxe5 17 ♖xf6 gxh4 18 ♕h5+ ♔d7 19 ♖xe6 ♖g8 20 ♕xe5 1-0 Lukacs-Szomlai, Budapest 1991.

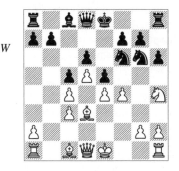

12 ♘xg6 fxg6 13 0-0

In Spassky-Fischer, Reykjavik Wch (5) 1972, Spassky played the illogical 13 fxe5? and soon got himself into more trouble than he could have imagined at this point: 13...dxe5 14 ♗e3 b6 15 0-0 0-0 16 a4? (16 ♔h1!?) 16...a5! (fixing the white a-pawn) 17 ♖b1 ♗d7 18 ♖b2 ♖b8 19 ♖bf2 ♕e7 20 ♗c2 g5 21 ♗d2 ♕e8! 22 ♗e1 ♕g6 23 ♕d3 ♘h5 (aiming for f4) 24 ♖xf8+ ♖xf8 25 ♖xf8+ ♔xf8 26 ♗d1 ♘f4 27 ♕c2?? ♗xa4! 0-1.

13...0-0 14 ♖b1

This move was first played in Spassky-Hort, Tilburg 1979. Other moves have proved less effective at combating the black set-up:

a) 14 fxe5 dxe5 15 ♗e3 b6 16 ♕f3 ♕d6 17 ♕g3 g5 18 h4 g4 and Black is in the driving seat, Van der Marel-Evseev, Groningen 1996.

b) 14 f5 was the main line for a long time, but Black has scored too well in this line for White to keep playing it. Black can choose from:

b1) 14...gxf5 15 exf5 ♕e7 (Black can also play 15...♕a5!? 16 ♗d2 ♗d7 17 a4 ♖ae8 18 ♕c2 e4 19 ♗e2 e3 20 ♗e1 ♕d8 21 ♗h4 ♕c7 = Lugovoi-Ionov, St Petersburg 1996) 16 ♕e2 b6 17 ♗d2 ♗a6 18 ♗e4 ♖f7 19 ♖f2 ♖af8 20 g4 ♘xe4 21 ♕xe4 ♕h4 22 ♖af1 h5 with a pleasant game for Black, Knaak-Csom, Amsterdam 1974.

b2) 14...♗d7 15 ♗e3 ♕e8 16 ♖b1 ♖b8 17 g4 b6 18 ♖f2 a6 19 ♕f3 b5! 20 ♖fb2 ♖a8! 21 ♕g2 bxc4 22 ♗xc4 ♗b5! ∓ Vaidya-Miles, British Ch (Brighton) 1984.

b3) 14...b5!? is reminiscent of the Benko Gambit:

b31) 15 g4 bxc4 (15...♕a5 16 ♗d2 bxc4 17 ♗c2 g5 18 ♖f2 ♖b8 19 a4 ♗d7 20 h3 {20 ♖a2!? Pliester} 20...♖b2 and White's position is deplorable, Saltis-Markauss, corr. 1991) 16 ♗c2 g5 17 ♕f3 ♗d7 18 ♖f2 ♖b8 19 ♗d1 ♖b7 20 ♗e2 ♕b8 and once again Black is much better, Langerak-Etmans, corr. 1986.

b32) 15 cxb5 c4! 16 ♗c2 gxf5 17 exf5 ♕b6+ 18 ♔h1 ♕xb5 ∓ Unzicker-Timman, Wijk aan Zee 1981.

c) 14 ♕e1!? ♗d7 (14...♕e7?! leads to a better game for White after 15 ♕g3 ♔h7 16 f5 ± Larsen-Ivkov, Manila 1973) 15 h3 ♕e7 16 ♖b1 b6 17 ♖b2 ♘h5 18 f5 g5 19 g3 ♘f6 20 g4 ♘h7 21 ♗e3 ½-½ G.Georgadze-Gavrikov, Erevan Z 1982.

14...b6

Or 14...♕e7 15 ♕e1 b6 16 h3 ♗a6 17 ♖b2 exf4 18 ♗xf4 (Zilberman-Van der Wiel, Leeuwarden 1994) and now 18...♖ae8 looks quite appealing to me.

15 ♖b2

15 f5 gxf5 16 exf5 e4 17 ♗e2 ♘h7 18 g4 ♘g5 19 ♔g2 ♕f6 20 ♕e1 ♗a6

gave Black the better game in Azmai-parashvili-Andersson, Panormo ECC 2001.

15...♕e7 16 h3 ♗d7

Or 16...♗a6 17 f5 gxf5 18 exf5 e4 19 ♗e2 ♖ae8 20 ♗e3 ♕e5 21 ♕e1 ♘d7 = Zilberman-Medvegy, Tel-Aviv 2001.

17 f5 gxf5 18 exf5 e4 19 ♖e2 ♕e5 20 ♕e1 ♗xf5 21 ♗f4 ♕e7 22 ♗g5 ♕d7!

½-½ Spassky-Hort, Tilburg 1979.

B)

8 0-0 *(D)*

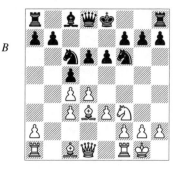

B

8...e5

Or:

a) 8...b6 9 e4 e5 10 h3 h6 11 ♗e3 transposes to note 'b22' to White's 9th move in Line A.

b) 8...0-0 usually transpose elsewhere; e.g., 9 e4 e5 10 h3 transposes to note 'b1' to White's 9th move in Line A, 9 ♘d2 e5 is Line C, and 9 ♘g5 e5 transposes to the main line.

9 ♘g5

Otherwise:

a) 9 ♘d2 transposes to Line C.

b) 9 e4 h6 and then: 10 d5 ♘e7 transposes to note 'd3' to White's 10th move in Line A; 10 h3 0-0 is note 'b1' to White's 9th move in Line A.

c) 9 d5 ♘e7 10 ♕c2 (10 ♘d2 0-0 is Line C; 10 e4 transposes note 'd' to White's 10th move in Line A) 10...0-0 11 ♘e1 (11 ♘d2 transposes to note 'a' to White's 11th move in Live C) 11...♕e8 12 f3 ♘g6 13 ♗d2 e4 14 fxe4 ♘g4 15 ♘f3 b6 16 e5 ♘4xe5 17 ♘xe5 ♕xe5 18 a4 a5 19 ♖fb1 and now, somewhat prematurely, Portisch-Seirawan, Lucerne OL 1982 was agreed drawn.

d) 9 ♕c2 gives Black a choice of good lines:

d1) 9...♕e7 10 ♘g5 transposes to note 'b2' to Black's 9th move.

d2) 9...h6 10 d5 ♘e7 11 ♘d2 0-0 12 ♖b1 b6 13 h3 ♘e8 (13...♕d7 14 f4 exf4 15 exf4 ♘f5 with chances for both sides, Ibragimov-Giddins, Bad Wiessee 2000) 14 f4 f5 15 e4 exf4 16 exf5 ♗xf5 17 ♖xf4 ♕d7 18 g4 ♗xd3 19 ♖xf8+ ♔xf8 20 ♕xd3 ♘f6 and Black has neutralized any white initiative, Brynell-Cu.Hansen, Års 1995.

d3) 9...0-0 and here White has tried numerous moves, the most important of which are:

d31) 10 ♘g5 transposes to note 'a' to White's 10th move.

d32) 10 d5 ♘e7 11 ♘d2 transposes to note 'a' to White's 11th move in Line C.

d33) 10 dxc5 dxc5 11 ♘g5 h6 12 ♘e4 ♘xe4 13 ♗xe4 ♗e6 14 ♖d1 ♕c7 15 ♗d5 ♘a5 16 ♖b1 ♖ad8 17 e4 b6 18 ♕a4 ½-½ Van Wely-Stohl, Bundesliga 1998/9.

d34) 10 ♖b1 ♕e7 11 dxe5 ♘xe5 12 ♘xe5 dxe5 13 ♗e4 ♘xe4 14 ♕xe4 ♖b8 and Black is doing very well since his bishop has more active influence

on the game than its counterpart on c1, Yurtaev-Kovalev, Simferopol 1988.

9...0-0

With White intending to open the centre, it now makes sense for Black to get his king into safety. Alternatively:

a) 9...h6 10 ♘e4 0-0 11 f4 (11 ♕c2 transposes to note 'a2' to White's 10th move) 11...exd4 12 cxd4 cxd4 13 ♘xf6+ ♕xf6 14 ♗b2 ♗f5 15 exd4 ♘b4 16 ♗xf5 ♕xf5 17 ♕d2 ± Knaak-Vaïsser, Berlin 1992.

b) 9...♕e7 is again a popular move:

b1) 10 ♘e4 0-0 11 dxc5?! dxc5 12 ♘xf6+ ♕xf6 13 ♕c2 g6 14 ♗e4 ♗f5! and White ends up with a wrecked pawn-structure and a bad bishop versus a strong knight, J.C.Fernandez-Yusupov, Cienfuegos 1979.

b2) 10 ♕c2 and here:

b21) 10...♗d7 11 f4 0-0-0 12 fxe5 dxe5 13 d5 ♘a5 14 e4 h6 15 ♘f3 ♘e8 16 ♕f2! b6 17 ♘d2! ♘d6 18 ♘b3 ♘ab7 19 a4 and Black's position is becoming critical, Sande-Tiller, Norwegian Ch (Oslo) 1980.

b22) 10...h6 11 ♘e4 ♘xe4 12 ♗xe4 0-0 13 dxc5 dxc5 14 ♗d5 ♗e6 15 e4 ♖ac8 16 f4 exf4 17 ♗xf4 ♘a5 18 ♕d3 ♖fe8 19 ♖ae1 b6 20 ♖e3 is slightly better for White, Danner-Spiridonov, Albena 1983.

We now return to the position after 9...0-0 (D):

10 f4

This is a very forcing option that challenges Black across the whole board and in particular on the kingside. White's main alternatives are:

a) 10 ♕c2 and here:

a1) 10...g6 11 d5 ♘e7 12 f4 exf4 13 ♖xf4 ♘g4 14 e4 f6 15 ♘h3 ♔g7 16

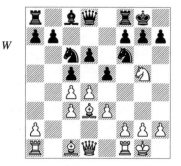

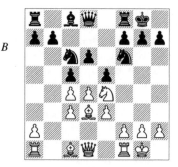

罝f1 ♘g8 17 ♘f4 ♘e5 18 ♗e2 ♕e7 19 ♗d2 ½-½ Volke-Womacka, Biel open 1993.

a2) 10...h6 11 ♘e4 (11 ♘h7 ♘xh7 12 ♗xh7+ ♔h8 13 ♗e4 ♕c7 14 dxc5 dxc5 15 ♗d5 f5 16 f3 ♘e7 17 ♗d2 ♗d7 = Keene-Shamkovich, New York 1981) and then:

a21) 11...♘xe4 12 ♗xe4 ♕c7 13 dxc5 dxc5 14 ♗d5 ♘e7 15 e4 ♘g6 with roughly equal chances, Brynell-Lindberg, Swedish Cht 1995.

a22) 11...b6 12 ♘xf6+ ♕xf6 13 ♗e4 ♗b7 14 dxe5 dxe5 15 ♗d5 罝ad8 (15...♘a5 16 e4 ♕g6 17 f4, Yusupov-Ivanchuk, Brussels Ct rpd (10) 1991, 17...exf4 18 ♗xf4 罝ad8 ∓ Yusupov) 16 e4 ♘a5 17 f4 (Yusupov suggests 17 ♗e3!?, while 17 罝d1 ♗a6 18 ♕e2 = is given as best by Csom) 17...exf4 18 ♗xf4 ♕g6 ∓ Sande-Csom, Malta OL 1980.

b) 10 ♘e4 (D) gives Black a broad selection of interesting moves:

b1) 10...♘xe4 11 ♗xe4 ♕e7 12 ♗d5 ♗d7 13 dxc5 dxc5 14 e4 b6 15 f4 exf4 16 ♗xf4 ♔h8 17 ♕h5 罝ae8 with chances for both sides, Soppe-Rosita, Villa Martelli 2001.

b2) 10...b6!? 11 ♕f3 ♗b7 (Anand-Kamsky, Sanghi Nagar FIDE Ct (1)

1994) 12 ♘xf6+ ♕xf6 13 ♕xf6 gxf6 14 f4! ♘a5 15 e4 ♗a6 16 罝f3 is OK for White, despite dropping the c4-pawn, according to Anand.

b3) 10...exd4 11 cxd4 ♗f5 12 ♘xc5 dxc5 13 ♗xf5 cxd4 14 罝b1 b6 15 ♕f3 ♕d6 16 罝b3 罝fe8 17 ♕h3 h6 18 罝d3 (Knaak-Garcia Gonzalez, Cienfuegos 1984) 18...罝ad8 19 exd4! ♘xd4 20 ♗xh6 and now Knaak's analysis continued with 20...gxh6(?), but this loses after 21 罝g3+. Therefore 20...♕e5 is best.

b4) 10...♗f5 11 ♘xf6+ (11 ♘g3 ♗g6 12 d5 e4 13 ♘xe4 {13 dxc6 exd3 14 cxb7 罝b8 15 f4 ♗e4 16 ♘xe4 ♘xe4 17 ♕xd3 ♕e7 is very good for Black} 13...♗xe4 14 ♗xe4 ♘xe4 15 dxc6 bxc6 16 f3 ♘f6 17 e4 罝e8 18 ♗g5 h6 19 ♗h4 罝e6 = Tella-Yakovich, Stockholm 1999) 11...♕xf6 12 e4 ♗d7 13 d5 ♘e7 14 罝b1 b6 15 f3 ♕g6 16 a4 f5 17 a5 fxe4 18 ♗xe4 ♗f5 and Black has at least equalized, Garcia Martinez-Tiviakov, Linares 1999.

10...exd4

10...exf4 11 罝xf4 h6 12 罝xf6 ♕xf6 13 ♘h7 ♕h4 14 ♘xf8 ♗g4 15 ♕f1 罝xf8 16 ♗d2 ± Knaak-Grünberg, Leipzig 1983.

11 cxd4 cxd4

Instead of the almost automatic additional exchange on d4, Black can also play the immediate 11...h6!?; e.g., 12 ♘f3 ♖e8 13 d5 ♘b4 14 ♗b1 ♘e4 (14...b5!? 15 a3 ♘a6 16 cxb5 ♘c7 17 a4 ♘cxd5 18 ♖a3 ♗b7 19 ♖e1 ♘b4 ∓ Villeneuve-Boudre, Val Maubuée 1988) 15 ♗b2 ♗f5 16 a3 ♘a6 17 ♘d2 ♘xd2 (Babula-Haba, Czech Ch (Zlin) 1997) 18 ♕xd2 ♗xb1 19 ♕c3 f6 20 ♖axb1 ♖e4 21 ♖f3 ♕d7 22 ♖g3 ♖f8 ∓ (Psakhis). This possibility is clearly a problem for White, who seriously needs an improvement to be able to continue playing this line.

12 exd4 (D)

12...h6

Or:

a) 12...♘xd4? 13 ♗b2 (13 ♘xh7 leads to massive exchanges and a drawn endgame: 13...♘xh7 14 ♗xh7+ ♔xh7 15 ♕xd4 ♕b6 16 ♕xb6 axb6 17 ♖d1 ♖d8 18 ♗e3 ♗e6 = Christiansen-de Firmian, USA Ch (Berkeley) 1984) 13...♘f5 14 ♕c2 ♘e3 15 ♗xh7+ ♔h8 16 ♕d3 ♘xf1 17 ♖xf1 d5 (17...♗g4 isn't any better: 18 ♗e4! ♕a5? 19 ♗d5 ♕b6+ 20 ♗d4 ♗f5, Pliester-Bergström, Andorra 1986, 21 ♗e4! ♗xe4 22 ♘xe4 ♕d8 23 ♘xf6 gxf6 24

♕h3+ ♔g7 25 ♕g4+ ♔h7 26 ♖f3 +–) 18 ♔h1! ♗g4 19 c5 ♕e7 20 ♕d4 ♖fe8 21 h3 ♗h5 22 ♗b1 ± Kuuksmaa-Uogele, corr. 1983.

b) 12...d5!? 13 ♗a3 ♖e8 and here:

b1) 14 cxd5 ♕xd5 15 ♖c1 ♕xd4+ 16 ♔h1 gives White sufficient compensation (Browne).

b2) 14 ♕b1 ♘e4 15 cxd5 ♘xg5 16 dxc6 ♕xd4+ 17 ♔h1 ♘h3 (Flear-Lobron, Paris 1983) and here Danner gives 18 ♕c2 ♘f2+ 19 ♔xf2 ♕xd3 20 ♖fe1 with chances for both sides.

b3) 14 ♕c2 g6 and then:

b31) 15 cxd5 ♘xd5 16 ♘xf7!? ♔xf7 17 f5 g5 and here:

b311) 18 f6 ♘f4 (18...♘xd4? 19 ♕d1! g4 20 ♗c4! b5 21 ♗e7 ♕d7 22 ♕xd4 bxc4 23 ♕e5 +–) 19 ♗c4+ ♔xf6 20 ♕xh7, Schön-Przewoznik, Netanya 1987. Although White went on to win this game, the line should not be repeated, since Black should be winning here with correct play.

b312) 18 ♗c4 ♔f6 19 ♗b2 ♕d6! (Black can also play 19...♘a5!?, but 19...♘e3? 20 ♕e2 ♘xc4 21 ♕xc4 ♕b6 22 ♖f2 ♗d7 23 ♖b1 ♕a6, Clarizza-Looeoe, corr. 1984, 24 d5+! ♔f7 25 ♕g4! lands Black in serious trouble, as White's attack crashes through) 20 ♕d3 ♘f4 21 ♖xf4 (White can try 21 d5+ ♘e5 22 ♕d4 b5, but this still looks good for Black) 21...gxf4 22 ♗e6 ♗xe6 23 d5+ ♘e5 24 fxe6 ♖ad8 gave Black a decisive advantage in Zöbisch-Polak, Austrian Cht 1995. This line seems too speculative for White and cannot be recommended.

b32) 15 f5 ♘xd4 16 fxg6 ♘xc2 17 gxf7+ ♔g7 18 ♗xc2 ♖h8 19 ♖ae1 dxc4! (A.Schneider-Grünberg, Hungary-East Germany 1980) and here 20

♗e7 ♕d4+ 21 ♔h1 ♗g4 has been given as unclear, but I have my doubts that White's play is sufficient.

13 ♘f3

Dropping the knight back to f3 has proved to be White's best choice since other moves have given him little hope of obtaining an advantage:

a) 13 ♘e4 ♘xe4 14 ♗xe4 ♕b6 15 ♗a3 ♘xd4 ½-½ A.Schneider-Cvetković, Stary Smokovec 1983.

b) 13 d5!? hasn't proved terribly effective in the past, but it prevents ...d5 and is definitely worth looking into. 13...♘e7 (13...hxg5 14 fxg5 is too dangerous for Black) 14 ♘f3 and then:

b1) 14...♗g4 15 ♗b2 ♘g6 16 ♕d2 ♗xf3 17 ♖xf3 ♖e8 (Frieser-Kaiser, Bavaria 1993) and now 18 ♗d4 leaves White with two strong bishops and not too many worries.

b2) Nor does 14...♗f5 offer Black any relief; e.g., 15 ♖b1 b6 16 ♗b2 ♗xd3 17 ♕xd3 ♘d7 18 ♕c3 favours White thanks to his spatial advantage.

b3) 14...♘f5 15 ♖b1 ♖e8 (Spycher-Titz, Zurich 1988) and now, as pointed out by Jonathan Berry, 16 ♖b3!? gives White good chances of obtaining an advantage; e.g., 16...♕a5 17 ♕d2 ♕c5+ 18 ♔h1 followed by ♗a3.

13...d5

13...♗g4?! gives White yet another chance to play 14 d5; e.g., 14...♘d4 15 ♗b2 ♘xf3+ 16 gxf3 ♗h3 (Benjamin-Browne, USA Ch (Greenville) 1983) and at this point Pliester gives 17 ♔h1!, continuing his analysis with 17...♗xf1 18 ♕xf1 ♔h8 (or 18...♘h5 19 ♕g2 f5 20 ♖g1 with a strong attack) 19 ♕h3 ± ♘d7? 20 ♕xh6+ gxh6 21 ♗xf6+ ♔g8 22 ♖g1+ with mate to follow.

14 c5

I hate to say it, but at this point White more than anything else needs to focus on damage limitation. The text-move closes the centre and therefore has a significant advantage compared to White's other possibilities; for example:

a) 14 ♘e5 dxc4 15 ♗xc4 ♗e6 16 ♗xe6 fxe6 17 ♗a3 ♖e8 18 ♖b1 ♕d5 19 ♕a4 ♘xd4 and White is a pawn down for next to no compensation, Slipak-Zarnicki, Saint Martin 1994.

b) 14 ♗a3 ♖e8 15 ♘e5 dxc4 16 ♗xc4 ♗e6 17 ♗xe6 ♖xe6 18 f5 ♖e8 (Pliester-Mednis, Amsterdam 1986) and now 19 ♘xc6 bxc6 20 ♗c5 gives White a defensible position, but it certainly isn't an attractive way for White to have to play.

14...♗g4 15 ♕a4 ♕d7 16 ♗b5 ♗xf3 17 ♖xf3 ♖fe8 18 ♗e3 ♕f5 19 ♖d1 ♘e4 20 ♕a3 ♖e6 21 ♗c1 ♖ae8

Black is clearly having too much fun compared to White, Strand-Ambrož, corr. 1987.

C)

8 ♘d2 *(D)*

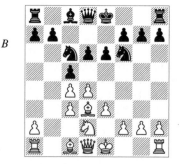

8...e5 9 0-0

At this early stage, White's alternatives tend to transpose to other lines; e.g.:

a) 9 ♘b3 is very likely to transpose to note 'd' to White's 10th move.

b) 9 d5 ♘e7 10 ♕c2 (10 0-0 0-0 transposes to the main line) 10...0-0 11 0-0 transposes to note 'a' to White's 11th move.

c) 9 ♕e2?! is best answered with 9...cxd4! 10 cxd4 0-0 11 d5 ♘b4 12 ♗b1 ♘a6 13 0-0 ♗g4! 14 f3 ♗h5 ∓ Knaak-Csom, E.Berlin 1979.

9...0-0

It's also worth taking a brief look at the alternatives:

a) 9...h6 10 ♘e4 transposes to note 'a' to Black's 9th move in Line B.

b) 9...♕e7?! is premature and lets White force the queen's knight to a sub-par square: 10 d5 ♘b8 11 e4 ♘bd7 12 ♖e1 0-0 13 ♘f1 ♘e8 14 ♘g3 g6 15 ♗h6 ♘g7 16 ♕d2 ± Vaganian-Yusupov, Barcelona 1989.

c) 9...♕c7 10 ♕c2 ♗d7 11 f4 exd4 12 exd4 0-0-0 13 d5 ♘e7 14 ♘f3 ♗g4 15 ♘g5 ♖df8 16 f5 h6 17 ♘e4 ♘xe4 18 ♗xe4 f6 is unclear, Farago-Govedarica, Belgrade 1984.

10 d5

Despite White closing the centre in a way we have seen in other lines, this position is quite different since he does not have to follow up by playing e4, but can instead try to take advantage of his space advantage in other ways. White has several alternatives:

a) 10 ♘e4 transposes to note 'b' to White's 10th move in Line B.

b) 10 ♖e1 cxd4 11 cxd4 exd4 12 exd4 ♗g4! 13 f3 ♗h5 14 ♘e4 ♘xe4 15 ♗xe4 ♖c8 ∓ Beliavsky-Adorjan, Thessaloniki OL 1988.

c) 10 ♗b2 h6 11 ♖e1 ♖e8 12 f3 b6 13 ♘f1 e4 14 fxe4 ♘xe4 15 ♕f3 ♕e7 = Najdorf-Szabo, Palma de Mallorca 1969.

d) 10 ♘b3 and here:

d1) 10...e4 11 ♗c2 ♕e7 12 f3 ♖e8 13 ♔h1 h6 14 ♘d2 exf3 15 gxf3 cxd4 16 cxd4 ♕xe3 17 ♘e4 ♕xd4 18 ♕xd4 ♘xd4 19 ♘xf6+ gxf6 20 ♖g1+ ♔f8 21 ♗xh6+ ♔e7 22 ♗e4 ♗e6 23 ♖ab1 offers White compensation for the pawn, F.Olafsson-Andersson, Reykjavik 1972.

d2) 10...b6 11 f3 ♗a6 12 ♖f2 ♖c8 13 ♗f1 ♘e7 14 ♖d2 ♕e8 15 e4 h6 16 a4 ♖c7 17 a5 ± F.Olafsson-Csom, Bad Lauterberg 1977.

d3) 10...♕e7 11 f4 ♗g4 12 ♕e1 e4 13 ♗e2 h5 14 h3 is slightly better for White, Garcia Palermo-Sisniega, Bayamo 1983.

e) 10 ♖b1 and now:

e1) 10...h6 11 h3 b6 12 d5 ♘e7 13 ♕c2 transposes to note 'd2' to White's 9th move in Line B.

e2) 10...b6 11 h3 ♗b7 12 d5 ♘e7 13 f4 exf4 14 exf4 ♘g6 15 ♘f3 ♕d7 16 ♗d2 ♖ae8 17 ♕c2 ♗c8 and although White has more space, Black's position is solid and the chances are about equal, Li Wenliang-Xu Jun, Beijing 1996.

e3) 10...♖e8 11 d5 ♘e7 12 f3 ♗f5!? 13 e4 ♗c8 14 g3 h6 15 ♖f2 b6 16 ♘f1 ♘h7 17 ♘e3 and for now Black's intended counterplay with ...f5 has been stopped and White's position is a little better, Djurhuus-Cu.Hansen, Reykjavik 1997.

10...♘e7 *(D)*

11 f3

This line bears a Hungarian stamp of approval – it is primarily played by

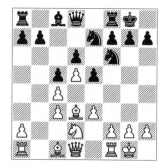

W

Farago, Lukacs and Pinter. Alternatives also deserve a look:

a) 11 ♕c2 and here:

a1) 11...h6 transposes to note 'd2' to Black's 9th move in Line B.

a2) 11...♘g6 12 f4 ♘g4 13 ♘f3 f5 14 h3 e4 15 hxg4 exd3 16 ♕xd3 fxg4 17 ♘g5 ♕f6 with a good game for Black, Wessman-Kiik, Helsinki 1997.

a3) 11...g6 12 f4 ♘g4! 13 ♘f3 exf4 14 exf4 ♘f5 15 ♖e1 h5! 16 ♘g5 ♘g7 17 ♗d2 ♗f5 18 ♘e4 ♘f6 19 ♘g3 ♗xd3 20 ♕xd3 h4 21 ♘f1 ♕d7 ∓ Donner-Stean, Marbella Z 1982.

b) 11 e4 and then:

b1) 11...♘e8 12 ♕c2 ♘g6 13 g3 ♗h3 14 ♖e1 ♕d7 15 ♘f1 f5 16 exf5 ♗xf5 17 ♗xf5 ♖xf5 18 ♗e3 ♘f6 19 ♘d2 and White's chances are preferable, Gligorić-Andersson, Nikšić 1978.

b2) 11...♘g6 12 g3 ♗h3 13 ♖e1 ♘e8 14 ♖b1 ♕d7 15 ♖b2 b6 16 f3 h6 17 ♕e2 f5 18 exf5 ♗xf5 19 ♘e4 ♘e7 is equal, Taimanov-Vyzhmanavin, Leningrad 1984.

b3) 11...h6 12 ♖e1 ♘h7 13 ♘f1 f5 14 exf5 ♗xf5 15 ♘g3 ♗xd3 16 ♕xd3

♕d7 17 a4 ♖f7 18 a5 ♖af8 19 f3 ♘f5 is slightly better for Black, Balashov-Vaganian, USSR Ch (Odessa) 1989.

11...♘e8

Or:

a) 11...♗f5 12 e4 ♗d7 13 ♖f2 ♘e8 14 ♕c2 h6 15 ♖b1 b6 16 g3 f5 17 exf5 ♗xf5 18 ♘e4 ± Inkiov-Lalev, Varna 1983.

b) 11...♘g6 12 g3 ♘e8 13 e4 ♗h3 14 ♖f2 ♖c8 with chances for both sides, Farago-Csom, Budapest 1979.

c) 11...h6 12 ♖f2 ♘h7 13 e4 f5 14 exf5 ♗xf5 15 ♘e4 ♘f6 16 ♘g3 ♗xd3 17 ♕xd3 ♕d7 is equal, Pinter-Nenashev, Recklinghausen 1998.

12 e4 h6

Or:

a) 12...f5 13 exf5 ♗xf5 14 ♘e4 h6 15 ♕c2 ♘f6 16 ♘g3 ♗xd3 17 ♕xd3 ♕e8 with an equal position, Lukacs-Yrjölä, Sochi 1984.

b) 12...♘g6 13 g3 f5 14 exf5 ♗xf5 15 ♘e4 ♕d7 16 ♕c2 ♘f6 = 17 ♘xc5?! ♗xd3 18 ♘xd3 ♖ac8 19 ♘b2 b5 20 ♗g5 bxc4 with better prospects for Black, Lukacs-Stohl, Austrian Cht 1994.

13 ♕c2 ♘g6

13...g5 14 ♖f2 ♘g7 15 g3 ♘g6 16 ♗b2 f6 17 ♘f1 f5 18 exf5 ♗xf5 19 ♘d2 ♗xd3 20 ♕xd3 ♕e8 21 ♘e4 ♖d8 is level, Pinter-Khuzman, Pula Echt 1997.

14 g3 ♗h3 15 ♖f2 ♕d7 16 ♗a3 a6 17 ♔h1 b5 18 ♖g1 f5

In this position there are chances for both sides, Farago-Sosonko, Amsterdam 1979.

16 Modern Variation and Related Systems

This chapter is devoted to the lines where White chooses a set-up that involves ♗d3 and ♘ge2, with the exception of those lines covered in Chapter 6 (4...0-0 5 ♗d3 d5 6 a3 ♗xc3+ 7 bxc3 and now 7...c5 8 cxd5 exd5 9 ♘e2 or 7...dxc4 8 ♗xc4 c5 9 ♘e2) or that fall under the Taimanov System (lines involving an early ...♘c6 without ...c5), which is covered in Chapter 18.

The lines covered in this chapter are becoming increasingly popular for White amongst grandmasters, a popularity that I expect will soon spread to players of lower strength.

White's idea is to avoid the doubled c-pawns, while at the same time taking care of the development of the light-squared bishop. The problem with this set-up is that White's knight on e2 doesn't have much influence in the centre and it is pretty much up to Black how he wants to open the game. As we will see from the theoretical coverage below, the e2-knight often continues its journey to either g3 or f4 to address this problem.

1 d4 ♘f6 2 c4 e6 3 ♘c3 ♗b4 4 e3 0-0

4...c5 5 ♗d3 *(D)* can also lead to a number of lines that fall under the subject of this chapter:

a) 5...0-0 6 ♘e2 (the alternative 6 a3 ♗xc3+ 7 bxc3 transposes to the

Sämisch Variation, which is not a part of this book) 6...d5 transposes to the main line.

b) 5...d6 6 ♘e2 ♘c6 7 0-0 0-0 (7...♗xc3 8 bxc3 transposes to line 'c2') and here:

b1) 8 a3 ♗a5 (8...♗xc3 9 bxc3 transposes to the Sämisch Variation, which is not covered by this book) 9 ♕c2 ♕e7 10 ♖b1 ♗xc3 11 ♕xc3 e5 12 d5 with an advantage for White, Knaak-Espig, East German Ch (Freiberg) 1970.

b2) 8 d5!? ♘e5 9 e4 ♘e8 (another idea is 9...exd5!?) 10 f4 ♗xc3 11 ♘xc3 ♘xd3 12 ♕xd3 e5 13 f5 with potential for a good kingside attack for White, Neverov-Tregubov, Pardubice 1992.

b3) 8 ♘e4 ♘xe4 9 ♗xe4 ♗a5 10 dxc5 dxc5 11 ♗xc6 bxc6 12 ♕xd8 ♖xd8 13 e4 e5 14 ♗e3 with a slight advantage for White, Stoltz-Ragozin, Saltsjöbaden IZ 1948.

c) 5...♗xc3+ 6 bxc3 d6 (6...♘c6 7 ♘e2 d6 is the same) 7 ♘e2 ♘c6 and now:

c1) 8 e4 e5 9 0-0 (9 f3 and 9 d5 are both liable to come to the same thing) and then:

c11) 9...h6 10 f4 (10 d5 ♘e7 11 f3 g5 12 ♔h1 ♘g6 is good for Black, Kadymova-Kakhiani, Debrecen wom Echt 1992) 10...cxd4 11 cxd4 exd4 12 ♘g3 ♘g4 13 ♕f3 (Norri-Kiik, Helsinki 1996) 13...0-0 14 h3 ♘f6 =.

c12) 9...0-0 10 d5 (10 f3 h6 11 d5 ♘a5 12 ♘g3 ♖e8 13 h3 ♘d7 = Guseinov-Daly, Pula Echt 1997) 10...♘e7 11 ♗g5 ♘e8 12 ♗h4 f6 13 f3 g5 14 ♗f2 ♘g6 15 ♗e3 ♘g7 16 ♕d2 ♕e7 with equality, Volke-Socko, Groningen 1995.

c2) 8 0-0 e5 9 ♘g3 (9 e4 transposes to line 'c1', as most likely will 9 f3 followed by 10 e4) 9...0-0 10 f4 (10 ♘e4 transposes to note 'b' to White's 10th move in Line B of Chapter 15) 10...exd4 11 exd4 cxd4 12 cxd4 ♕b6 and Black should not be any worse.

d) 5...b6 6 ♘e2 and now:

d1) 6...♗b7 7 0-0 0-0 transposes to note 'c21' to Black's 5th move.

d2) 6...cxd4 7 exd4 ♗b7 8 0-0 ♗e7 9 d5 ♘a6 10 ♘g3 0-0 11 ♖e1 ♖e8 12 ♗f4 ♗b4 13 d6 ♗xc3 14 bxc3 ± Taimanov-Panno, Palma de Mallorca IZ 1970.

d3) 6...♘c6 7 0-0 and then:

d31) 7...cxd4 8 exd4 ♗xc3!? (after 8...0-0 9 ♘e4 we transpose to line 'd32') 9 bxc3 (Keres recommended 9 ♘xc3 ♘xd4 10 ♗g5 with an initiative and sufficient compensation for the pawn) 9...♘a6 10 ♗a3 (10 ♗g5!? can

also be considered) 10...♖c8 (Kavnatsky-D.Gurevich, Chicago 1986) and here White should continue with 11 ♖e1 or 11 ♗d6; in either case he is doing quite well.

d32) 7...0-0 8 ♘e4 (8 d5!?) 8...cxd4 9 exd4 ♗e7 10 ♘xf6+ ♗xf6 11 ♗e4 ♗b7 12 a3 ♖c8 13 ♕d3 g6 14 ♗h6 ± Piskov-Anastasian, Belgorod 1989.

d33) 7...♗a6 8 ♕a4 ♗b7 9 ♖d1 a6 10 d5 and now 10...♘e5?! 11 e4 ♗xc3 12 ♘xc3 b5 (Torre-Van der Wiel, Bochum 1981) should be punished with 13 ♕b3 ♘xd3 14 ♖xd3 b4 15 e5 ±. Instead Black should try 10...b5!? 11 cxb5 axb5 12 ♕c2 exd5 13 ♘xb5 d6 14 a3 ± (Van der Wiel).

e) 5...♘c6 6 ♘e2 (6 a3 ♗xc3+ 7 bxc3 transposes to a Sämisch Variation, which is not covered in this book) and here:

e1) 6...0-0 is possible.

e2) 6...d5 and then:

e21) 7 0-0 0-0 transposes to note 'b' to Black's 7th move in Line C.

e22) 7 a3 ♗xc3+ 8 bxc3 and now 8...dxc4 9 ♗xc4 0-0 is note 'd' to Black's 9th move in Line B2 of Chapter 6, while 8...0-0 9 cxd5 exd5 transposes to note 'd' to Black's 9th move in Line B1 of that chapter.

e23) 7 cxd5 (D) and here:

e231) 7...exd5 8 a3 (8 0-0 0-0 transposes to note 'b3' to Black's 7th move in Line B) 8...cxd4 9 axb4 (9 exd4 should be compared with note 'b332' to Black's 7th move in Line B) 9...dxc3 10 b5 ♘e5 11 ♘xc3 (an interesting gambit line is 11 ♗c2!? cxb2 12 ♗xb2 ♘c4 13 ♗d4 0-0 14 ♕d3 ♖e8 15 ♗xf6 ♕xf6 16 ♕xh7+ ♔f8 17 0-0 with a better game for White, Matveeva-Chepukaitis, St Petersburg 1994) and then:

B

e2311) 11...0-0 12 ♗e2 b6 13 0-0 ♗b7 14 b3 ♖e8 15 ♗b2 ♕d6 16 ♖a4 ♘ed7 17 ♖d4 ♘c5 18 ♗f3 ± J.Horvath-Enders, Balatonbereny 1988.

e2312) 11...♘xd3+ 12 ♕xd3 0-0 13 b3 ♗e6 14 ♘e2 ♘e4 15 ♗b2 ♕g5 16 0-0 ♘c5 17 ♕c2 ♖fc8 18 ♗d4 ♗f5 19 ♕d1 ♗e4 20 ♘f4 ♘e6 21 f3 ♗c2 22 ♘xe6 fxe6 23 ♕e1 and although the chances are about even at this point, I prefer White's position, as it is somewhat easier to play, Miles-Romanishin, USSR-Rest of the World (London) 1984.

e2313) 11...♗g4!? 12 f3 ♘xd3+ 13 ♕xd3 ♗e6 14 ♕d4 a6!? (14...b6 has also been played; for example, 15 0-0 0-0 16 b3 ♕d7 17 ♗b2 ♖fd8 18 ♖fc1 ♘e8 19 ♖a4 f6 20 ♖ca1 ♕f7 21 ♘e2 leads to a slight advantage for White) 15 bxa6 bxa6 16 ♗d2 0-0 17 ♘e2 ♖e8 18 ♗c3 ♗d7 19 ♘f4 ♗b5 20 ♔f2 and White has at best a minimal advantage, Bareev-Akopian, Dortmund 2000.

e2314) 11...d4 12 exd4 ♕xd4 13 ♗e2 ♕xd1+ 14 ♘xd1! ♗f5 (14...♘d5 15 ♘c3 ♗e6 16 f4 ♘xc3 17 bxc3 ♘c4 18 f5 ♗d5 19 ♖a4 ♘b6 20 ♖g4 g6 21 fxg6 hxg6 22 0-0 and thanks to his dark-squared bishop, White has the better chances, Knaak-Grünberg, Potsdam 1985) 15 ♖a3!? 0-0 16 ♗f4 ♖fe8 17 ♘e3 ♘g6 18 ♗g3 ♗d7 19 0-0 ♘e4 20 ♖d1 ♘xg3 21 hxg3 is much better for White, Sashikiran-Plaskett, Hampstead 1998.

e2315) 11...♕c7!? 12 ♗e2 0-0 13 0-0 ♖d8 14 ♕d4 b6 15 b3 (15 h3!? Wells) 15...♘eg4 16 ♗xg4 ♘xg4 17 f4 ♗b7 18 ♗b2 f6 19 ♖a4 ♕e7 20 ♖f3 with chances for both sides, Cebalo-Gligorić, Budva 1986.

e232) 7...♘xd5 8 a3 (8 0-0 cxd4 9 exd4 0-0 transposes to Line B) and now:

e2321) 8...♘xc3 9 bxc3 ♗a5 10 0-0 0-0 11 c4 ♗c7 12 ♗b2 (D.Gurevich-Wedberg, Eksjö 1982) and now 12...cxd4 13 exd4 ♕h4 14 g3 ♕h5 15 f4 leaves White only slightly better according to ECO.

e2322) 8...cxd4 9 axb4?! dxc3 10 bxc3 and then:

e23221) 10...0-0 11 e4 ♘b6 12 f4!? ♕h4+ 13 ♘g3 ♖d8 (Pliester's suggestion of 13...f5 leads to a very pleasant position for White after 14 exf5 exf5 15 ♕b3+ ♔h8 16 0-0) 14 0-0 and now instead of the very passive continuation 14...♗d7, J.Horvath-A.Schneider, Debrecen 1988, Black can play 14...a5 with some counterplay, although I still tend to prefer White's chances.

e23222) 10...♘e5! 11 ♗e4!? (11 ♗b5+ ♗d7 12 ♗xd7+ ♕xd7 13 e4 ♘b6 is quoted in ECO as equal, but I agree with Pliester that this piece of analysis by Blumenfeld leads to a favourable game for Black) 11...0-0 12 0-0 ♘f6 13 ♗c2 ♕c7 14 ♕d4 (14 f4!?) 14...♖d8 15 ♕h4 ♘g6 16 ♗xg6 hxg6 = Borbjerggaard-Knežević, Budapest 1996.

e2323) 8...&a5 9 0-0 (9 dxc5 is weaker; for example, 9...&xc3 10 &xc3 &xc3+ 11 bxc3 &e5 12 &b5+ &d7 13 &xd7+ ₩xd7 14 ₩d4 &d3+ 15 &e2 0-0-0 with a pull for Black, Rai-čević-Am.Rodriguez, Pančevo 1985) 9...cxd4 10 exd4 0-0 11 &c2 &c7 12 ₩d3 g6 13 &d1 &xc3 14 bxc3 b6 15 &g3 &b7 16 &e4 with approximately equal chances, Glek-Neverov, Blago-veshchensk 1988.

e3) 6...cxd4 7 exd4 d5 *(D)* and then:

e31) 8 0-0 dxc4 9 &xc4 0-0 trans-poses to Line C.

e32) 8 &g5 &e7 9 0-0 0-0 10 c5 b6 11 ₩a4 &d7 12 &b5 ₩e8 13 b4 a6 14 &xc6 &xc6 15 ₩c2 bxc5 16 bxc5 &d7 = Schwartz-Yermolinsky, New York 1994.

e33) 8 a3 dxc4 9 &xc4 and here:

e331) 9...&e7 10 0-0 0-0 trans-poses to Line C1.

e332) 9...&d6 10 0-0 0-0 trans-poses to Line C2.

e333) 9...&xc3+ 10 bxc3 h6 11 &f4 0-0 12 &g3 &e4 13 &d3 &xg3 14 hxg3 e5 15 d5 &b8 offers chances for both sides, Agdestein-Sosonko, Haninge 1988.

e34) 8 c5 0-0 9 0-0 e5 10 a3 &xc3 11 bxc3 h6 12 ℤb1 ℤe8 13 h3 b6 14 cxb6 axb6 15 &b5 &d7 16 a4 exd4 17 cxd4 &e7 is equal, F.Portisch-Mini-böck, Austrian Cht 1997.

e35) 8 cxd5 ₩xd5 (8...exd5 9 a3 should be compared with note 'b332' to Black's 7th move in Line B; 8...&xd5 9 0-0 0-0 transposes to Line B) 9 0-0 ₩h5 (9...₩d8 10 &c2 0-0 transposes to note 'b' to Black's 10th move in Line B2) 10 &e4 (10 &f4 has been played several times recently, but Black's best play remains 10...0-0 11 ₩b3 &e7 12 ℤad1 b6 13 &g3 &b7, Bagirov-M.Gurevich, Baku 1986, and now White should settle for 14 &f4 ₩g5 15 d5 =) and now:

e351) 10...&xe4 11 &xe4 0-0 trans-poses to note 'b222' to Black's 8th move in Line B.

e352) The retreat 10...&e7 is also playable: 11 &e3 (11 a3!? ₩d5 12 &xf6+ &xf6 13 &e3 0-0 14 ₩c2 g6 15 ℤfd1 ₩d8 16 &e4 ± Lerner-Rash-kovsky, USSR 1986) 11...0-0 12 &xf6+ &xf6 13 ℤc1 &b4 (13...ℤd8?! is less accurate: 14 ℤc5 e5 15 ₩b1! ₩h4 16 dxe5 &xe5 17 &e4 &g4 18 &f4 &e7 19 &g3 ₩h6, Kruppa-Yudasin, St Pe-tersburg 1998, 20 ℤb5!? ±) 14 &e4 &d5 15 ₩d3 &d7 16 &f3 ₩g6 17 ₩xg6 hxg6 18 &xd5 exd5 19 &f4 &c6 20 &d3 a5 = Fedorowicz-Carlier, Brussels 1987.

5 &d3 *(D)*
5...d5
Or:

a) 5...&xc3+ 6 bxc3 d6 (6...b6 7 e4 d6 8 &e2 e5 9 0-0 ℤe8 10 &g3 c5 11 d5 h6, Tella-Salmensuu, Finnish Ch (Espoo) 1995, 12 h3 ±) 7 &e2 e5 8 e4 ℤe8 9 f3 &bd7 10 0-0 &f8 11 &e3 b6

B

12 a4 c5 13 a5 ♗a6 14 d5 ± Ki.Georgiev-Stefanov, Bulgarian Ch (Sofia) 1984.

b) 5...d6 transposes to note 'g2' to Black's 4th move in Chapter 18.

c) 5...c5 and here:

c1) 6 d5 b5!? (6...♗xc3+!? is also noteworthy; e.g., 7 bxc3 d6 8 ♘e2 ♘bd7 9 ♘g3 ♕a5 10 ♗b2 ♘b6 11 e4 ♘a4 and Black has a pleasant game, Appleberry-Nisipeanu, Budapest 1996) 7 dxe6 bxc4! (7...fxe6 8 cxb5 a6 9 ♘e2 d5 10 0-0 e5 11 a3 axb5 12 ♗xb5 ± Korchnoi-Karpov, Baguio City Wch (7) 1978) 8 exf7+ ♔h8 9 ♗xc4 d5 10 ♗e2 ♘e4 11 ♗d2 ♘xd2 12 ♕xd2 d4 13 0-0-0 (White may be able to improve with 13 ♗f3!? ♘c6 14 ♘ge2) 13...♘c6 14 ♕c2 ♕a5 15 ♘b1 ♗e6 16 ♘f3 ♗xf7 and Black has more than adequate compensation for the pawn, Venglovsky-Goncharenko, corr. 1984.

c2) 6 ♘e2 b6 7 0-0 and then:

c21) 7...♗b7 is risky; for example, 8 d5!? ♗xc3 9 ♘xc3 exd5 10 cxd5 d6 11 e4 ♘bd7 12 ♗g5 and White is slightly better, Donner-Damjanović, Palma de Mallorca 1967.

c22) 7...cxd4 8 exd4 ♗b7 9 ♗g5 (9 a3 ♗xc3 10 ♘xc3 d5 11 ♗g5 dxc4 12 ♗xc4 ♘c6 13 d5 ♘e5 14 ♗a2 exd5

= V.Georgiev-Galego, Andorra 1999) 9...♗e7 10 ♖c1 ♘c6 11 ♗b1 d5 12 cxd5 ♘xd5 13 ♕d3 g6 14 ♗h6 ♖e8 15 ♖cd1 ♘cb4 16 ♕h3 ♖c8 17 ♖fe1 is slightly better for White, Ravikumar-Ree, Thessaloniki OL 1984.

6 ♘e2

Or:

a) 6 a3 is considered in Line C2 of Chapter 18.

b) 6 cxd5 exd5 7 ♘e2 *(D)* and now Black has a number of options, the last of which is currently quite popular at GM level:

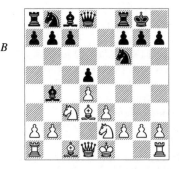

B

b1) 7...c5 transposes to note 'b' to Black's 7th move in Line B.

b2) 7...♘bd7 8 0-0 c6?! (8...♗d6!?) 9 f3 c5 10 a3 cxd4 11 exd4 ♗e7 12 ♘f4 ♘b8 13 g4 with a definite initiative and the better game for White, Kasparov-Yurtaev, Moscow tt 1981.

b3) 7...c6 8 0-0 ♘a6 (this is a bit passive; so is 8...♘bd7, which transposes to line 'b2', while 8...♖e8 transposes to line 'b744') 9 f3 ♘c7 10 a3 ♗e7 11 ♔h1 ♘e6 12 ♗c2 b6 13 e4 ♗a6 14 e5 ♘e8 15 f4 f5 16 ♗e3 g6 17 ♖g1 gives White a promising attack, Fedorowicz-Hraček, Novi Sad OL 1990.

b4) 7...b6 transposes to note 'd1' to Black's 6th move.

b5) 7...♘c6?! has a poor reputation for a good reason: 8 0-0 ♘e7 9 a3 (9 f3 ♘g6 10 ♗c2 c6 11 ♔h1 is slightly better for White, I.Sokolov-Andersson, Reggio Emilia 1988/9) 9...♗d6 10 ♘b5 is a suggestion of Sokolov's, which was vindicated in Gudmundsson-G.Thorhallsson, Icelandic Cht (Reykjavik) 1995: 10...♗f5 11 ♘xd6 ♕xd6 12 ♗xf5 ♘xf5 13 ♕d3 ♕d7 14 f3 ±.

b6) 7...♗d6 and now:

b61) 8 a3 a5 (8...♖e8 transposes to line 'b73', while 8...c6 is best answered by 9 0-0 ♖e8 10 ♘f4 with chances for both sides) 9 ♕c2 ♘a6 10 ♗d2 c6 11 ♘g3 ♖e8 12 ♘ce2 ♘c7 13 f3 ♘e6 14 ♘f5 ♗f8 15 0-0 (Chernin-Kavalek, Subotica IZ 1987) and here 15...g6! followed by ...c5 equalizes – Chernin/Dvoretsky.

b62) 8 ♘b5 ♗e7 9 0-0 ♖e8 and then:

b621) 10 a3 a5?! (10...a6!? = Pliester) 11 ♔h1 ♘a6 (*ECO* mentions 11...♘bd7!?, intending ...♘f8-g6) 12 f3 and now 12...c5 was given a '?' by Pliester, while *ECO* awards it an '!'. I tend to agree with Pliester, as the b5-square is now permanently weakened: 13 ♘ec3 ♗d7 14 g4 ♘c7 15 a4 ♘e6 16 ♖g1 with the better chances for White, M.Gurevich-Dizdar, Reykjavik 1988.

b622) 10 ♕c2 c6 11 ♘bc3 ♗d6 12 ♔h1 (J.Horvath-Ionov, Budapest 1989) and Horvath claims that 12...♗xh2 13 ♔xh2 ♘g4+ 14 ♔g3 ♕g5 15 f4 ♕h5 should lead to a draw by repetition after 16 ♘g1 ♕h2+ 17 ♔f3 ♕h5, but 16 ♗d2!? looks good for White.

b63) 8 f3 c5 9 0-0 ♘c6 10 ♖f2 (other options include 10 ♔h1, 10 ♕e1 and 10 g4) 10...a6 (Pliester gives 10...cxd4 11 exd4 ♘e7 12 g4 ♘e8 intending ...f5 as an alternative) 11 g4 b5 (this may not be Black's best; he could consider 11...♖e8!? to help contain White's pawn expansion) 12 g5! ♘e8 13 dxc5 ♗xc5 14 ♘xd5 ♕xg5+ 15 ♖g2 with a promising attack for White, Fedorowicz-Arnason, Groningen 1990.

b64) 8 0-0! ♘g4 (8...♖e8 transposes to line 'b746') 9 g3 ♖e8!? (9...c6 is more solid) 10 ♘xd5 ♗xg3 11 fxg3 ♕xd5 and now, rather than 12 ♕c2 ♘xe3 13 ♗xe3 ♖xe3 14 ♘c3 ♕xd4 15 ♗xh7+ ♔h8 16 ♔g2 (Aleksandrov-J.Polgar, Batumi Echt 1999) 16...♕c4 with the better chances for Black, White should play 12 ♘f4!?.

b7) 7...♖e8!? is currently the most popular line for Black after 6 cxd5 exd5. White has now tried:

b71) 8 ♕c2 ♗f8 9 0-0 ♘bd7 10 b3 c6 11 f3 c5 12 ♗d2 b6 13 ♖ae1 ♗b7 with chances for both sides, Shamkovich-Sunye, Moscow 1989.

b72) 8 ♗d2 b6 9 f3 ♗b7 10 0-0 ♘bd7 11 g4 ♘f8 12 a3 ♗d6 13 ♕e1 c5 with a complicated struggle ahead, Bischoff-Van der Sterren, Bundesliga 1999/00.

b73) 8 a3 ♗d6 9 b4 c6 10 ♖a2 ♘bd7 11 f3 a5 12 0-0 axb4 13 axb4 ♖xa2 14 ♘xa2 ♘f8 15 ♕c2 ♕e7 and it is clear that Black has solved his opening problems, D.Gurevich-de Firmian, USA Ch (Chandler) 1997.

b74) 8 0-0 (D) and then:

b741) 8...♘c6!? 9 f3 ♗f8 10 a3 g6 11 ♗c2 ♗g7 12 b4 a6 13 ♖e1 ♘a7 14 ♘f4 ♘b5 = Barbeau-Hébert, Quebec 1988.

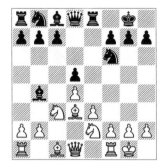

B

b742) 8...♘bd7 9 f3 c5 10 a3 cxd4 11 axb4 dxc3 12 bxc3 ♘e5 13 ♗c2 ♗d7 14 ♘f4 ♗b5 15 ♖e1 a6 16 ♕d4 ± D.Gurevich-Peters, USA Ch (Berkeley) 1984.

b743) 8...b6 9 f3 ♗b7 10 g4 ♗f8!? (or 10...c5 11 ♘f4 h6 12 ♘ce2 ♘c6 13 a3 ♗a5 14 ♖f2 ♘h7 15 ♕f1 ♖c8 16 ♖g2 ♖c7 with chances for both sides, Ulko-Loginov, St Petersburg 2000) 11 ♘g3 c5 12 g5 ♘fd7 13 f4 ♘c6 14 ♗xh7+!? ♔xh7 15 ♕h5+ ♔g8 16 f5 ♘e7 17 g6 fxg6 18 fxg6 ♘xg6 19 ♕xg6 ♕e7 and it is far from clear who should be happier, Makarov-Govasheishvili, corr. 1991.

b744) 8...c6 9 f3 b6 (Piket mentions 9...h5!? as a noteworthy idea; 9...♘bd7 10 ♔h1 ♗f8 11 ♕e1 b5 12 ♕f2 b4 13 ♘a4 c5 14 ♗d2 ♗b7 15 b3 ♖c8 16 ♖fc1 g6 = Aleksandrov-Bauer, Bastia rpd 1999) 10 g4 ♗a6 11 ♗c2 (11 ♘g3!? Piket) 11...♘bd7 12 ♖f2 ♘f8 13 ♘g3 ♘e6 14 f4!? ♗xc3 15 bxc3 ♘c7! with fairly even chances, G.Georgadze-Piket, Istanbul OL 2000.

b745) 8...♗f8 is the move which was prepared by 7...♖e8. White has many options:

b7451) 9 f3 is harmless if met by 9...c5! 10 ♕e1 b6 11 ♕f2 ♗a6 12

♗xa6 ♘xa6 13 dxc5 ♗xc5 14 ♖d1 ♘c7 15 ♘f4 ♕d6 16 ♘a4 ♘e6 17 ♘xc5 bxc5 with a pleasant game for Black, Kacheishvili-Lerner, Berlin 1995.

b7452) 9 a3 a5 10 ♔h1!? (another set-up for White is 10 ♗c2 b6 11 ♘f4 ♗b7 12 ♗b3 c6 13 f3 b5 14 ♖e1 ♘bd7 15 ♗d2 ♘b6 and Black is doing fine, Supatashvili-Dgebuadze, Georgian Ch (Tbilisi) 1996) 10...b6!? (or 10...♘a6 11 f3 c5 12 ♘f4 ♘c7 13 dxc5 ♗xc5 14 e4 dxe4 15 ♘xe4 ♘xe4 16 ♗xe4 ♕xd1 17 ♖xd1 ♘b5 18 ♘d3 and White has a pull thanks to his better coordinated pieces, Kramnik-Leko, Dortmund rpd 2001) 11 ♘f4 ♗a6 12 f3 ♗xd3 13 ♕xd3 ♘a6 14 e4 dxe4 15 fxe4 c5! 16 ♘fd5 ♘xd5 17 exd5 cxd4 18 ♕xd4 ♘c5 and Black has fully solved his opening difficulties, Yusupov-Prusikhin, Altenkirchen 2001.

b7453) 9 ♕c2!? g6 (9...c6 10 ♗d2 transposes to line 'b7455') 10 a3 ♘c6?! 11 f3 ♗g7 12 ♔h1 b6 13 ♗d2 ♗b7 14 ♖ae1 a6 15 b4 ± Torre-Speelman, London 1984.

b7454) 9 ♘f4 b6 10 f3 ♗b7 11 ♗c2 g6 12 ♖e1 ♘a6 13 ♗a4 ♖e7 14 ♘d3 (14 ♗d2!? is possible) 14...c5 15 ♘e5 ♖c8 with chances for both sides, Galliamova-Timoshenko, Naberezhnye Chelny 1993.

b7455) 9 ♗d2 looks fairly harmless, but is presently causing Black plenty of headaches; e.g., 9...c6 (neither 9...b6 10 ♖c1 ♗b7 11 ♘f4 ± nor 9...a5 10 ♕c2 ♘a6 11 a3 c5 12 ♘g3 b6 13 ♖ad1 ♗b7 14 ♗e2!? ♘c7 15 ♗f3 cxd4 16 exd4 ± Epishin-Ikonnikov, Vlissingen 2001, is particularly interesting for Black) 10 ♕c2 a5 11 ♖ad1 (preparing a central break with f3 followed by e4) 11...♞a6 12 a3 b5 13 ♗c1 b4 14 ♞a4 ♗d7 15 ♞g3 c5 16 ♗xa6 ♗xa4 17 ♕xa4 ♖xa6 18 dxc5 ♗xc5 19 axb4 ♗xb4 20 b3 ♕d7 21 ♗b2 and Black's problem with his isolated d-pawn becomes evident, Epishin-Belikov, Dortmund 2001.

b746) 8...♗d6 and then:

b7461) 9 ♗d2 has received some attention at grandmaster level. Black's best answer appears to be 9...c5; e.g., 10 dxc5 ♗xc5 11 ♖c1 ♞c6 12 ♞b5 ♗b6 13 ♞bd4 ♗d7 14 ♗c3 ♞e4 15 ♞xc6 (15 ♗xe4!? =) 15...bxc6 16 ♗d4 ♕g5 17 ♗xe4 ♖xe4 18 ♞g3 ♖h4 19 f4 ♕h6 20 h3 ♖e8 21 ♖f3 ♕d6 22 a4 ♕b4 and although Black has the initiative at this point, White eventually went on to win in Piket-Gelfand, Wijk aan Zee 2002.

b7462) 9 f3 c5 10 ♕e1 (10 ♗d2 ♞c6 11 ♖c1 a6 12 ♗b1 h6 {Tisdall also mentions 12...♕e7!? intending ...b5-b4} 13 ♔h1 cxd4 14 exd4 ♞a5 15 ♖e1, Djurhuus-P.H.Nielsen, Gausdal 1995, and here Tisdall gives the continuation 15...♞c4! 16 ♞xd5 ♞xd5 17 ♖xc4 ♕h4 18 ♞g3 ♗d7, when Black's initiative compensates for the sacrificed pawn) 10...♞c6 11 ♕h4 ♗e7 12 ♕f2 a6 13 g4 b5 14 ♞g3 b4 15 ♞ce2 a5 16 g5 ♞d7 17 f4 ♗a6 18 ♗xa6 ♖xa6 19 ♗d2 ♞b6 20 ♖ad1 ♕d7 21 ♗c1 (G.Georgadze-Almasi, Erevan OL 1996) 21...cxd4 22 exd4 f5! 23 gxf6 ♗xf6 24 f5 ♞e7! 25 ♞f4!? ♞xf5 26 ♞fh5 with chances for both sides – Almasi.

We now return to 6 ♞e2 *(D)*:
6...c5
There are some minor alternatives:
a) 6...♞c6 should be compared with Line D of Chapter 18.

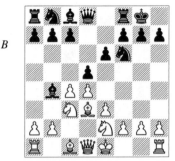

B

b) 6...e5 7 cxd5 exd4 8 exd4 ♞xd5 9 0-0 ♞c6 transposes to note 'b1' to Black's 6th move in Line D2 of Chapter 18.

c) 6...♞bd7 7 a3 ♗e7 8 cxd5 exd5 9 0-0 ♖e8 and now instead of 10 f3 c5 11 ♔h1 ♞f8 12 ♞g3 ♞e6 13 dxc5 ♗xc5 with equality, Chekhov-Kharitonov, Leningrad 1991, White should try 10 ♕c2, ♗d2, ♖ad1 and only then f3.

d) 6...b6!? and here:
d1) 7 cxd5 exd5 8 a3 and then:
d11) 8...♗e7 is note 'b' to White's 6th move in Line B of Chapter 18.
d12) 8...♗xc3+ 9 ♞xc3 c5 10 dxc5 bxc5 11 b4! d4 12 ♞e4 cxb4 13 axb4 with a better game for White, Ehlvest-Cherniaev, Port Erin 1998.
d13) 8...♗d6 9 b4 ♖e8 10 ♕b3 (10 ♕c2!? *ECO*) 10...a6 (Cebalo-Djurić, Titograd 1984) and here *ECO* suggests 11 ♗d2!? ♗b7 12 ♞g3!? with unclear play.
d2) 7 0-0 and now:
d21) 7...♗a6!? is interesting: 8 b3 ♞bd7 9 ♗b2 ♗xc3 10 ♞xc3 dxc4 11 bxc4 c5 12 ♖c1 (12 ♕a4!? *ECO*) 12...cxd4 13 exd4 e5! with a double-edged position, Gulko-Vitolinš, USSR Cup 1984.

d22) 7...♗b7 8 cxd5 (8 ♗d2 dxc4
9 ♗xc4 ♘bd7 10 a3 ♗d6 11 ♖c1 c5
12 dxc5 ½-½ Scherbakov-Balashov,
Russian Cht (Omsk) 2001) 8...exd5 9
f3 (also seen is 9 ♘g3 ♖e8 10 a3 ♗d6
11 ♕f3 ♘bd7 12 ♖d1 c5 13 ♘f5 ♗f8
{13...♗b8!?} 14 ♕g3 ± Martynov-
Renaze, Val Maubuée 1990) 9...♖e8
(9...c5!? is, as we know, the standard
way of meeting a white set-up that in-
cludes f3 and should therefore be considered at this point) and then:

d221) 10 g4!? is also worth noting,
although at first glance it looks somewhat premature: 10...c5 11 a3 cxd4 12
exd4 ♗f8 13 ♘g3 g6 14 ♗f4 ♖e6 15
♔g2 ♘c6 16 ♘ge2 ♘a5 (16...♗g7!?
followed by ...h5!? is also interesting)
17 b3 ♖c8 with a decent game for
Black, Sokolov-Granda, Amsterdam
1996.

d222) 10 a3 ♗f8 11 b4 c5 12 bxc5
bxc5 13 ♖b1 ♕c8 14 ♕b3 (Sokolov
gives 14 dxc5 ♗xc5 15 ♘b5 ± with a
blockade of Black's isolated d-pawn)
14...♗c6 15 ♕a2 ♘bd7 16 a4! ♕d8 17
a5 ♖b8 18 ♗d2 ♖xb1 19 ♖xb1 ±
I.Sokolov-Sunye, New York 1996.

d3) 7 a3 ♗e7 (with the situation in
the centre still unresolved, the e7-
square is usually a better place for the
bishop than d6, where it blocks the
queen's scope) 8 0-0 (other moves
give Black nothing to worry about: 8
cxd5 exd5 9 b4 c5!? 10 bxc5 bxc5 11
dxc5 ♗xc5 12 ♗b2 ♘bd7 = *ECO*; 8
e4 dxe4 9 ♘xe4 ♗b7 10 ♘xf6+ ♗xf6
11 0-0, Magerramov-Antoshin, Baku
1980, 11...g6!? 12 ♗h6 ♖e8 13 ♗c2
c5!? 14 dxc5 and now 14...bxc5 and
14...♗xb2 are both fine) 8...♘bd7 9
cxd5 exd5 10 ♘f4 ♗b7 11 b4 ♖e8 12
♕b3 (12 b5!?) 12...♘f8 13 ♗d2 (13

e4!? is interesting, but probably not
sufficient for an advantage; for example, 13...♘xe4 14 ♘xe4 dxe4 15 ♗c4
♘e6 16 ♘xe6 fxe6 17 ♗xe6+ ♔h8 18
♗e3 ♗f6 and Black has things under
control) 13...♘g6 14 g3 (*ECO* gives
14 ♗xg6!? hxg6 15 ♘d3 as unclear,
but after 15...c6 followed by ...♗d6,
Black looks pretty comfortable to me)
14...a6 15 ♖fe1 ♖b8 and with the
preparations for ...c5 in order, Black
has equalized, Qi Jingxuan-Hübner,
Thessaloniki OL 1984.

e) 6...dxc4 7 ♗xc4 e5 (D) (7...c5 8
0-0 cxd4 9 exd4 transposes to Line C,
while 7...b6 is a reasonable alternative; e.g., 8 a3 ♗e7 9 e4 ♗b7 10 e5
♘d5 11 0-0 ♘xc3 12 ♘xc3 and now
instead of 12...♗a6?! 13 ♗xa6 ♘xa6
14 ♕g4 ♔h8 15 ♖d1, which left White
with the initiative and better chances
in Wiedenkeller-Rogers, Berlin 1986,
Black should opt for 12...c5!? intending
13 d5 exd5 14 ♗xd5 ♗xd5 15 ♘xd5
♘c6 with chances for both sides) and
here:

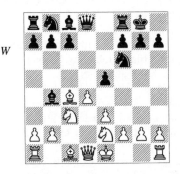

e1) 8 ♕b3 exd4 9 ♘xd4 (9 ♕xb4?!
♘c6 10 ♕c5 dxc3 11 ♘xc3 has been
claimed to be equal, but 11...♘d7! is
quite pleasant for Black; e.g., 12 ♕h5

♘de5 13 ♗e2 ♘d3+ 14 ♗xd3 ♕xd3)
9...c5 10 ♘f3 (Black is better after 10
♘c2 ♘c6 11 ♗e2 ♗f5 12 0-0 ♘a5!?
13 ♕a4 ♗d7 14 ♗b5 ♗xb5 15 ♕xb5
{15 ♘xb5?? a6 would be embarrass-
ing for White} 15...♗xc3 16 bxc3
♘e4) 10...♘c6 11 ♕c2 ♗g4 12 ♗d2
♕d7 13 a3 ♗a5 14 0-0-0 ♗f5 (Suba-
Sax, Budapest Z 1993) and now the
best continuation for White is 15 e4,
which leads to exciting play after both
15...♘d4!? and 15...♗g6.

e2) 8 a3 and now:

e21) 8...♗a5!? 9 b4 exd4 10 ♕xd4
♕xd4 11 ♘xd4 ♗b6 12 ♘f3 a5 = is
given in *ECO*, Sanguinetti-Eliskases,
Mar del Plata 1947.

e22) 8...exd4 9 axb4 dxc3 10 ♕xd8
♖xd8 11 bxc3 ♘bd7 12 ♘d4 c5 13
bxc5 ♘xc5 and despite the early queen
exchange, there is a complex struggle
ahead, Zarubin-Loginov, Russian Cht
(Kazan) 1995.

e23) 8...♗d6 9 dxe5 (9 ♘b5 ♘c6
10 ♘xd6 ♕xd6 11 0-0 ♖d8 is fine for
Black, Mascariñas-Christiansen, Thessaloniki OL 1988) 9...♗xe5 10 ♕xd8
♖xd8 11 e4 h6 12 f3 ♘c6 13 ♗e3 ♘a5
14 ♗a2 ♗e6 15 ♗xe6 fxe6 16 ♖d1
♘c4 17 ♗c1 c5 with a comfortable
game for Black, Tatai-Sax, Rome 1985.

e3) 8 0-0 and here:

e31) 8...♗d6 9 ♘b5 e4 10 ♘xd6
♕xd6 11 ♘f4 ♘c6 12 ♗d2 ♘e7 13 a3
♘ed5 14 ♘xd5 ♘xd5 15 ♕b3 c6 16
♗xd5 ♕xd5 17 ♕xd5 cxd5 = Mur-
shed-Tiviakov, Dhaka 1997.

e32) 8...exd4 9 exd4 (9 ♘xd4 a6
10 ♕c2 c5 11 ♘f3 ♗g4 12 ♗e2 h6 13
♗d2 ♘c6 14 a3 ♗a5 15 ♖ad1 ♕e7 16
♖fe1 b5 = G.Schwartz-Dautov, Bad
Wiessee 1997) 9...♘c6 10 h3 ♗f5 11
a3 ♗d6 12 ♗g5 h6 13 ♗h4 ♗e7 14

♖e1 (Alterman-Wells, Groningen FIDE
1997) and here Psakhis recommends
14...♕d7!? 15 ♘g3 ♗e6 16 ♗xe6
fxe6 with unclear play.

e33) 8...♘c6 *(D)* and here:

W

e331) 9 d5 ♘e7 10 e4 (10 a3 ♗c5
{10...♗d6 transposes to 'e3322'} 11
b4 ♗b6 12 ♕b3 ♘e8 13 ♘a4 ♘d6 14
♘xb6 axb6 15 ♗d3 ♗d7 16 ♘c3 f5 =
Rabascall-Kosten, La Réunion 1997)
10...♘g6 11 a3 ♗c5 12 b4 ♗b6 13
♗g5 ♗d7 14 ♕d2 h6 15 ♗e3 ♘h5
with chances for both sides, Grosz-
peter-Rohde, New York 1988.

e332) 9 a3 ♗d6 and then:

e3321) 10 ♘b5 e4 (10...♗e7 11 d5
♘a5 12 ♗a2 is given as '±' in *ECO*,
but matters are not that clear; for example, 12...c6 13 ♘bc3 cxd5 14 ♘xd5
♘xd5 15 ♗xd5 ♗e6!? {15...♘c6!? is
another option} 16 ♗xe6 ♕xd1 17
♖xd1 fxe6 and although Black has an
inferior pawn-structure, he is doing
fine thanks to his greater piece activity, O.Rodriguez-Winants, Barcelona
1991) 11 ♘xd6 ♕xd6 12 h3 ♗e6 13
b3 (Cebalo-Suba, Vršac 1983) and
now *ECO* gives 13...♖fe8 14 a4 a5 15
♗a3 ♘b4 16 ♘f4 ♘fd5 17 ♘xe6
♖xe6 =.

e3322) 10 d5 ♘e7 11 e4 (11 ♘g3 ♘g6 {11...♘f5 can also be considered} 12 h3 ♘e8 13 e4 ♘f4 14 ♘f5 ♕g5 15 ♕g4 ♕f6 16 ♕h4 g5 17 ♕h6 ♕g6 18 ♕xg6+ hxg6 19 ♘xd6 ♘xd6 20 b3 ♗d7 = D.Ilić-Mitkov, Vienna 1990) 11...♘g6 12 f3 ♘h5 13 ♗e3 ♘hf4 (*ECO* gives 13...f5 as unclear, but this looks very unconvincing after 14 exf5 ♘gf4 15 g4) 14 g3 ♘xe2+ (14...♗h3!? 15 ♖f2 ♘xe2+ 16 ♗xe2 a6 is also worth a try) 15 ♕xe2 a6 16 ♗d3 ♗d7 17 ♖ac1 ♖c8 18 ♘b1 c6 (18...h5!? intending 19...h4 can also be considered) 19 dxc6 ♖xc6 20 ♘c3 ♗e6 21 ♘a4 with at best a tiny pull for White, Suba-Szekely, Tallinn 1983.

We return to 6...c5 (*D*):

W

Now:

A)

7 a3 cxd4

Alternatively:

a) 7...♗a5 8 0-0 dxc4 9 ♗xc4 ♕e7 10 ♕c2 ♗d7 11 ♗d3 cxd4 12 exd4 h6 13 ♗f4 ♖c8 14 ♖ad1 ♗c6 15 b4 ♗b6 16 b5 ♗d7 17 ♕b3 ♗e8 (Sadler-Suba,

London 1991) and now both 18 d5!? and 18 ♖fe1 leave White somewhat better.

b) 7...dxc4 8 ♗xc4 and then:

b1) 8...♗a5 9 0-0 transposes to 'a'.

b2) 8...♗xc3+ should be compared with line 'c'.

b3) 8...cxd4 9 axb4 (9 exd4 transposes to the main line) 9...dxc3 10 ♘xc3 ♕d1+ (10...♘c6 is another popular move, but if Black wants an alternative, he can try 10...♕e7 or 10...e5!?) 11 ♔xd1 ♖d8+ 12 ♔c2 e5 13 f3 e4!? 14 fxe4 ♘c6 15 b5 ♘b4+ 16 ♔b3 ♘d3 17 ♗xd3 ♖xd3 and Black has obtained approximate equality, Rogers-Lutz, Biel 1996.

c) 7...♗xc3+ and then:

c1) 8 bxc3 dxc4 9 ♗xc4 transposes to Line B2 of Chapter 6.

c2) 8 ♘xc3 cxd4 9 exd4 dxc4 10 ♗xc4 ♘c6 11 ♗e3 b6 12 0-0 ♗b7 13 ♕d3 (13 ♗d3 h6 14 ♖c1 ♖c8 15 ♗b1 ♕d7 16 ♕a4 a6 17 ♖fd1 b5 with a pleasant game for Black, Muttoni-Galvao, corr. 1997) 13...h6 (13...♕d6 14 f3 ♖ac8 15 ♖ad1 ♘e7 16 ♗f2 ♘fd5 is equal, Semkov-Geller, Sochi 1982) 14 ♖ad1 ♘e7 15 ♗a2 ♘ed5 16 ♗c1 ♖c8 17 ♖fe1 ♕c7 18 ♘b5 ♕b8 19 ♕g3 ♕xg3 20 hxg3 ♗a6 with chances for both sides, Zaichik-Dokhoian, Moscow 1989.

8 exd4 (*D*)
8...dxc4

The alternatives are:

a) 8...♗e7 9 cxd5 ♘xd5 10 0-0 ♘c6 11 ♗c2 transposes to note 'c1' to Black's 10th move in Line B2.

b) 8...♗xc3+ 9 bxc3 (9 ♘xc3 transposes to note 'c2' to Black's 7th move in Line A) 9...dxc4 10 ♗xc4 b6 11 0-0 ♗b7 12 a4 ♘bd7 13 ♗a3 ♖e8 14 ♖c1

B

♖c8 15 ♗d3 ♘f8 16 ♘f4 e5 with chances for both sides, Hort-Ribli, Tilburg 1980.

9 ♗xc4 ♗e7

Or:

a) 9...♗xc3+ and then 10 bxc3 transposes to note 'b' to Black's 8th move, while 10 ♘xc3 ♘c6 11 ♗e3 is Line B11 in Chapter 17.

b) Black can also try 9...♗d6; e.g., 10 ♕d3 ♘c6 11 ♗g5 b6 12 ♖d1 ♗b7 13 ♗a2 ♗e7 14 ♗b1 g6 15 0-0 ♖e8 16 ♗a2 ♘d5 17 ♗h6 ♘xc3?! (17...♗f6!?) 18 ♘xc3 ♗g5 (Ionescu-Hjartarson, Moscow 1987) and now 19 ♗xg5 ♕xg5 20 d5 maintains a certain initiative.

10 0-0 a6

Or:

a) 10...♘bd7 transposes to note 'd5' to Black's 9th move in Line C.

b) 10...♘c6 transposes to Line C1.

11 ♘f4

This particular position hasn't been played terribly often, but it is evident that White is ready to play d5 with the initiative. However, Black can attempt to throw a spanner in the works by attacking the f4-knight; e.g., 11...♕c7 12 ♗b3 and now 12...♗d6 13 ♕f3 ♘bd7 or 12...♖d8!? 13 d5 ♘c6 14

♕d3 e5 15 ♘fe2 ♕b6 and Black need not worry too much.

B)

7 cxd5 *(D)*

B

7...cxd4

There are some alternatives to consider:

a) 7...♘xd5 normally just transposes to the main line via 8 0-0 cxd4 9 exd4.

b) 7...exd5 is a reasonably popular alternative that has proved quite durable. White has now tried:

b1) 8 dxc5 ♗xc5 9 a3 ♘c6 10 0-0 a6 11 ♘g3 ♖e8 12 ♕c2 ♗a7 13 ♘ce2 ♘e5 14 ♗f5 g6 15 ♗xc8 ♖xc8 with a pleasant game for Black, Watanabe-Moussa, Istanbul OL 2000.

b2) 8 a3 cxd4 (8...♗xc3+ 9 bxc3 transposes to Line B1 of Chapter 6) and now:

b21) 9 exd4 should be compared with line 'b332'.

b22) 9 axb4 dxc3 10 ♘xc3 (10 bxc3 ♘c6 11 f3 ♘e5 12 ♗c2 ♗d7 13 ♕d4 ♕c7 14 0-0 ♗b5 15 ♖f2 ♗xe2 16 ♖xe2 a6 = D.Gurevich-Unzicker, Beersheba 1984) 10...d4 (10...♗g4 11 f3 ♗h5 12 ♗e2 ♗g6 13 b5 ♕d6 14

♖a4 ♘bd7 15 ♖d4 ± Bareev-Agde-stein, Gausdal jr Wch 1986) 11 exd4 ♘c6 12 0-0 ♗g4 13 ♕d2 ♘xd4 with chances for both sides, D.Gurevich-Farago, Hastings 1982/3.

b3) 8 0-0 ♘c6 and now:

b31) 9 f3 ♖e8 10 ♖f2!? h5!? (Spraggett mentions 10...cxd4 11 exd4 h6!?) 11 a3 ♗xc3 12 bxc3 ♕d6 13 ♘g3 h4 14 ♘f5 ♗xf5 15 ♗xf5 with chances for both sides, but I prefer White, Spraggett-Rivas, Manila OL 1992.

b32) 9 dxc5 ♗xc5 10 b3 a6 11 ♗b2 ♕e7 12 ♖c1 ♖d8 13 ♘g3 ♗a3 14 ♗xa3 ♕xa3 15 ♘h5 ♘e8 16 ♕e2 ♕e7 = Prins-Matanović, Amsterdam OL 1954.

b33) 9 a3 cxd4 *(D)* (9...♗xc3 10 bxc3 transposes to note 'd2' to Black's 9th move in Line B1 of Chapter 6, but 9...c4 has also been seen; for example, 10 ♗c2 ♗d6 11 f3 ♗c7 12 h3 ♕d6 13 f4 a6 14 ♕e1 ♖e8 15 g4 and White builds up a kingside attack, Ornstein-Sjöberg, Swedish Ch (Borlange) 1995) and here:

W

b331) 10 axb4 dxc3 11 b5 (11 bxc3 makes much less sense; e.g., 11...♘e5 12 ♗c2 ♗d7 intending ....♗b5 is excellent for Black, Goldberg-Taimanov,

USSR Ch (Moscow) 1949) 11...♘e5 (11...cxb2? leaves Black too far behind in development and is therefore too risky; e.g., 12 ♗xb2 ♘e7 13 ♘d4 with much the better game for White – *ECO*) 12 ♘xc3 (12 bxc3 is according to *ECO* best met with 12...♘e4 13 ♗c2 ♕c7 =) and then:

b3311) 12...♘xd3 13 ♕xd3 ♗e6 and now rather than 14 ♘e2 ♕b6 15 ♗d2 ♗d7 16 ♘d4 ♖fc8 17 f3 ♘e8 = Speelman-Short, British Ch (Brighton) 1984, 14 ♖a4!? intending ♗d2 and ♖fa1 seems like a good try for an edge.

b3312) 12...♗g4 13 f3 d4 (the alternative 13...♗h5?! 14 ♗e2 is very pleasant for White, M.Gurevich-Tal, Saint John blitz 1988) 14 ♗xh7+ ♘xh7 15 ♕xd4 ♕xd4 16 exd4 ♘xf3+ 17 gxf3 with a better endgame for White, Ki.Georgiev-Spassov, Bulgarian Ch (Sofia) 1984.

b3313) 12...♕c7!? 13 ♗e2 ♖d8 14 ♖a4 b6 15 ♖d4 ♗b7 16 f3 ♖ac8 17 ♕a4 ♘ed7 18 ♖fd1 ♘c5 19 ♕a3 h6 20 ♗f1 ♖e8 = Salov-Gligorić, Belgrade 1987.

b3314) 12...♕d6 13 ♗c2 ♖e8 14 ♕d4 ♘eg4 15 f4 ♕e7 with approximately equal chances, Semkov-Maksimović, Sumen 1985.

b332) 10 exd4 ♗d6 (somewhat more passive is 10...♗e7, which led to a better game for White after 11 ♕c2 ♗g4 12 ♗e3 ♖c8 13 f3 ♗h5 14 ♘g3 ♗g6 15 ♘f5 ♖e8 16 ♖fe1 ♕d7 17 g4 in Skembris-Kotronias, Greek Ch (Athens) 1988) and here:

b3321) 11 h3 h6 12 ♗c2 ♖e8 is the same as 'b3322'.

b3322) 11 ♗c2 ♖e8 12 h3 h6 13 ♕d3 ♗e6 14 ♗e3 ♘e7 15 ♘g3 ♘g6

16 ♘f5 ♗c7 = Korchnoi-Pinter, Haninge 1988.

b3323) 11 ♗f4 ♗g4 12 ♕d2 ♗xe2 13 ♘xe2 ♖e8 14 ♖fe1 ♘e4 15 ♗xe4 ♖xe4 16 ♗xd6 ♕xd6 = Cebalo-Velimirović, Yugoslav Ch (Vrbas) 1982.

b3324) 11 f3 h6 (11...♖e8 12 ♗g5 h6 13 ♗h4 ♗e6 14 ♕d2 ♗f8 15 ♖ae1 g6 16 ♘f4! ± Granda; 11...♘h5?! gives Black nothing but headaches: 12 g4 ♕h4 13 ♖f2 ♘f6 14 ♗f4! ♗xf4 15 ♘xf4, Shariyazdanov-Sax, Bosnian Cht 2001, 15...♗e6 16 ♕d2 ♖ac8 17 ♗b5 a6 18 ♗xc6 ♖xc6 19 ♖e1 ± Shariyazdanov) 12 ♗e3 (both 12 ♔h1 ♘h5! 13 ♕e1 f5 14 ♘xd5 ♗xh2 15 ♔xh2 ♕xd5 16 ♕h4, Tal-Sax, Subotica IZ 1987, 16...♕f7 followed by ...g5 = {Tal} and 12 g4!? ♗e6 13 ♗c2 ♖e8 14 ♕d3 ♖c8 15 ♖f2 a6 16 ♖g2 ♔f8 17 ♔h1 b5 18 b4 ♕c7, Sutkus-Rumiantsevas, corr. 1988, are perfectly OK for Black) 12...♘e7 13 ♗f2 ♗f5 14 ♗h4 ♗xd3 15 ♕xd3 ♘g6 16 ♗xf6 ♕xf6 17 ♘xd5 ♗xh2+ 18 ♔xh2 ♕d6+ 19 f4 ♕xd5 and once more Black has equalized, W.Arencibia-J.Arencibia, Cuba 1988.

8 exd4 *(D)*

White generally doesn't bother with 8 ♘xd4 as Black equalizes smoothly after 8...exd5 9 0-0 ♘c6 and he may even consider 8...♕xd5 or 8...e5.

8...♘xd5

This move is usually Black's preference, but obviously he has two other options that deserve a look:

a) 8...exd5 9 a3 should be compared with note 'b332' to Black's 7th move.

b) 8...♕xd5 9 0-0 and then:

b1) 9...♕d8 is slightly passive, but at the same time fairly logical as it

continues to target White's isolated d-pawn. White can play in a number of ways, but one safe road to an edge is 10 a3 (or 10 ♗g5 ♗e7 11 ♗c2 ♘c6, transposing to note 'b1' to Black's 10th move in Line B2) 10...♗e7 11 ♗c2 b6 12 ♕d3 ♗b7 13 ♗g5 ♘bd7 14 ♖ad1 g6 15 ♗b3 ♘d5 16 ♗xd5 ♗xd5 17 ♗xe7 ♕xe7 18 ♘xd5 exd5 19 ♘c3 ± Timoshchenko-Khuzman, USSR Army Ch (Tashkent) 1987.

b2) 9...♕h5 and here:

b21) 10 ♗f4 isn't particularly difficult to deal with; e.g., 10...♘c6 11 ♕b3 (or 11 ♘e4 ♗e7 12 ♖c1 ♘b4 13 ♗b1 ♘bd5! = ECO) 11...♗e7 12 ♖ad1 b6 13 ♖fe1 ♗b7 14 ♗b1 ♘b4 15 ♘g3 ♕g4 16 ♗e5 (Tabatadze-Yuferov, Moscow 1991) and now 16...♘bd5 seems to offer fairly balanced chances, although the black queen looks somewhat oddly placed on g4.

b22) 10 ♘e4 ♘xe4 (10...♘bd7 was tried out fairly recently: 11 ♕b3 ♕a5 12 a3 ♗e7 13 ♕c2 ♘xe4 14 ♗xe4 ♘f6 ½-½ V.Georgiev-G.Georgadze, Aceimar 1999) 11 ♗xe4 and then:

b221) 11...♗d6 12 ♗f4 ♗xf4 13 ♘xf4 ♕xd1 (13...♕g5 14 ♕f3 ♘d7 15 ♖ac1 ♕b5 16 b3 ♘f6 17 ♖c5 ± Lerner-Benjamin, Moscow 1987) 14

♖fxd1 ♘d7 (note that 14...♘c6? is a bad positional mistake on account of 15 ♗xc6! bxc6 16 ♖ac1 ♖b8 17 b3 ♗d7 18 f3 ♖fd8 19 ♔f2 ♖b4 20 ♔e3, and Black is positionally lost, V.Georgiev-Dinstuhl, Bundesliga 1999/00) 15 ♖ac1 ♘f6 16 ♗f3 ♖d8 17 h4 ♖b8 18 g4 ♗d7 19 g5 ♘e8 20 d5 e5! 21 ♘d3 f6 and Black seems to be over the worst, Lempert-Arkhipov, Naberezhnye Chelny 1993.

b222) 11...♘c6 and then:

b2221) 12 ♘f4!? offers an early exchange of queens; e.g., 12...♕xd1 13 ♖xd1 ♖d8 14 ♗e3 ♗d6 15 d5 exd5 16 ♖xd5 ♗g4 17 f3 ♗xf4 18 ♗xf4 ♖xd5 19 ♗xd5 ♗e6 20 ♗xe6 fxe6 21 ♖d1 with a clearly better endgame for White, Milov-Macieja, Las Vegas FIDE 1999.

b2222) 12 ♕d3 ♗d6 (12...♖d8!? 13 ♘f4 ♕h4 14 g3 ♕e7 15 ♗xh7+ ♔h8, Karason-Åkesson, Reykjavik 1988, and now, according to Wells, White can obtain the better game with 16 ♗e4!? ♘xd4 17 ♕d1 ♔g8 18 a3 ♗c5 19 ♗e3) 13 ♗f4!? (13 ♘f4 doesn't seem as strong: 13...♗xf4 14 ♗xf4 ♖d8 15 ♕e3 ♘e7 16 ♕b3 ♘d5 17 ♗e5 b6 18 ♖fd1 f6 19 ♗g3 ♗b7 20 ♖e1 ♖ac8 21 ♖ad1 = Peshina-Komarov, USSR 1987) 13...♗xf4 14 ♘xf4 ♕h6 15 ♕e3 ♗d7 16 ♘d3! ♖fd8 17 ♘c5 ♖ab8 18 ♕xh6 gxh6 19 ♖fd1 ♗e8 20 d5 exd5 21 ♗xd5 with a slight plus for White, Se.Ivanov-Kveinys, Polish Cht (Glogow) 2001.

We now return to the position after 8...♘xd5 *(D)*:

9 0-0

The main line. On occasion, White tries other moves, but so far with unconvincing results:

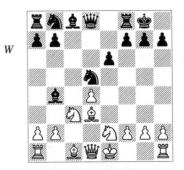

W

a) 9 ♗b1 ♖e8 10 ♕d3 g6 11 0-0 ♘xc3 12 bxc3 ♗f8 13 ♕g3 ♗g7 14 ♗g5 ♕a5 15 ♘f4 ♘d7 16 ♗c2 ♘f8 with chances for both sides, I.Sokolov-Gausel, Oslo rpd 1996.

b) 9 a3 ♗e7 (9...♘xc3!? also deserves attention; e.g., 10 bxc3 ♗d6 11 ♗e4 ♘c6 12 ♕d3 h6 which was played in I.Sokolov-Van der Wiel, Wijk aan Zee 1989, and here Sokolov gives 13 0-0 ♕c7 as 'unclear') 10 ♗c2 (10 0-0 should be compared with the main line) 10...♘c6 (Gavrikov once suggested 10...♘d7 11 ♘xd5 exd5 12 ♕d3 ♘f6 =) 11 ♕d3 g6 12 h4!? (12 ♗h6 can also be played) 12...♘xc3 (the premature central break 12...e5?! gets Black into trouble: 13 dxe5 ♘xc3 14 ♕xc3 ♗g4 15 f3 ♖c8 16 fxg4 ♘xe5!?, Knaak-Christiansen, Thessaloniki OL 1988, 17 ♕xe5 ♖xc2 18 ♗h6 ♗f6 19 ♕e4 +−) 13 bxc3 e5! 14 ♕g3 exd4 15 h5 ♗d6! 16 ♗f4 ♗xf4 17 ♘xf4 g5 with a complicated struggle, Marin-Gavrikov, Tallinn 1989.

c) 9 ♗c2 b6 (9...♘c6 10 0-0 transposes to Line B2) 10 ♕d3 g6 11 h4 ♗a6 12 ♕h3 ♗xe2 13 ♔xe2 h5 14 ♔f1 ♘c6 15 ♗g5 ♕c8 16 ♕d3 ♗e7 17 ♗b3 ♖d8 18 ♘xd5 exd5 19 ♖c1 ♗xg5 20 hxg5 ♘e5! 21 ♕d2 ♘c4 and

Black has solved his opening problems, Milov-Beliavsky, Essen 2000.

9...♘c6 *(D)*

Black has two other options, both of which transpose to other lines:

a) 9...♘f6 is note 'b1' to Black's 8th move.

b) 9...♖e8 10 ♗c2 ♘c6 transposes to Line B2.

This is an important point in the Modern Variation. White has a number of options, of which two deserve 'main line' status:

B1: 10 a3   250
B2: 10 ♗c2   253

Several of the alternatives are also significant:

a) 10 ♗e3 ♘xe3 11 fxe3 e5!? 12 ♕b3 exd4 13 exd4 ♗g4 14 h3 ♗xe2 15 ♘xe2 ♕e7 (Nogueiras-Ribli, Lucerne OL 1982) and here 16 ♖ad1 gives White a reasonable game.

b) 10 ♗b1 and then:

b1) 10...♗d6 11 ♘e4 ♗e7 12 a3 ♖e8 13 ♕d3 g6 14 ♗a2 b6 15 ♗h6 ♗b7 16 ♘2c3 ♘xc3 17 ♘xc3 ♗g5 18 ♗xg5 ♕xg5 19 d5 ♘e5 with an equal position, Marin-Beliavsky, Thessaloniki OL 1988.

b2) 10...♖e8!? (intending to play ...g6 and ...♗f8-g7) 11 ♕d3 g6 12 ♕f3! ♗f8 13 ♗e4 ♘xc3 14 bxc3 ♗g7! 15 ♗xc6 (15 ♖b1 is met by 15...e5! 16 ♗d5 ♕c7 with chances for both sides – Shipov) 15...bxc6 16 ♕xc6 ♗d7 17 ♕f3 (Shipov suggests 17 ♕d6!?, but after 17...e5!? Black should have sufficient compensation for the pawn), Lugovoi-Shipov, St Petersburg 1994 and now Shipov gives 17...♖c8, when after 18 ♘g3(?!) ♗c6 Black has compensation for the pawn, but 18 ♗f4 may be more to the point; after 18...♗c6 19 ♕g3 ♗b5 20 ♖fe1 ♕a5 Black should be OK.

c) 10 ♕c2 isn't considered particularly critical for Black:

c1) 10...g6 11 a3 (11 ♖d1 ♖e8 12 ♗c4 ♗f8 13 ♘f4 ♘xc3 14 bxc3 ♗g7 15 ♗e3 ♘a5 16 ♗e2 b6 17 ♖ac1 ♗b7 gives roughly equal chances, Øgaard-Psakhis, Gausdal 1994) 11...♗e7 12 ♖d1 ♗f6 13 ♗e4 ♘ce7 14 ♕b3 b6 15 ♘xd5 ♘xd5 16 ♗h6 ♖e8 17 ♕f3 ♗b7 18 ♖ac1 ♗g5 = Hort-Ribli, Bundesliga 1991/2.

c2) 10...♘f6 11 a3 ♗d6!? (11...♗e7 isn't right in this position; after 12 ♖d1 h6 13 ♗f4! ♖e8 14 ♗c4! ♗f8 15 h3 ♘d5 16 ♗g3 ♗d6, Speelman-Salov, Linares 1992, Salov gives 17 ♗xd5!? exd5 18 ♕b3 ±) 12 ♘e4 (Kiseliov and Gagarin mention that 12 ♗g5 can be met by 12...h6 13 ♗h4 g5 14 ♗g3 ♗xg3 15 fxg3 ♘xd4 16 ♘xd4 ♕xd4+ 17 ♔h1 with compensation for the pawn) 12...♘xe4 13 ♗xe4 h6 14 ♖d1 ♗d7 (I think 14...♕c7 deserves preference over this slow move) 15 ♗f4 ♗xf4 16 ♘xf4 ♖c8 and now rather than 17 ♕d2?! ♘a5 with equality, Scherbakov-Kiseliov, Cheliabinsk 1993,

White should try something like 17 ♕d3!? or 17 ♕e2!? with good chances of an advantage – Kiseliov/Gagarin.

c3) 10...h6 has been established as a good way for Black to meet White's set-up:

c31) 11 ♖d1 also looks acceptable, but Black has had an easy time after 11...♗d6 12 ♘h7+ (12 a3 ♘ce7 is great for Black) 12...♔h8 13 ♗e4 ♕h4 14 g3 ♕h5 15 ♕d3 ♘xc3 (15...♘cb4!? may even improve) 16 ♘xc3 e5 17 ♘b5 ♖d8 18 d5 ♘e7 19 ♘xd6 ♖xd6 20 ♗e3 ♗f5 with chances for both sides, Lerner-Alekseev, Maccabia 2001.

c32) 11 a3 ♗e7 (11...♗d6!? can also be considered: 12 ♘e4 ♗c7 13 ♖d1 ♕h4 14 g3 ♕h5 15 ♘4c3 ♘xc3 16 ♘xc3 e5!? 17 ♗e2 ♗f5 offers chances for both sides, Speelman-M.Gurevich, Munich 1992) 12 ♖d1 ♗f6 13 ♗c4 ♘ce7 14 ♕e4 ♖e8 15 ♘f4 (Dolmatov mentions that 15 ♗b5 ♗d7 16 ♗d3 ♘g6 17 ♘xd5 exd5 18 ♕xd5 is met by 18...♗a4! 19 ♕xd8 ♖axd8 =) 15...♘xc3 16 bxc3 ♘f5 17 ♗a2 (Vyzhmanavin-Dolmatov, Irkutsk 1986) and at this point Dolmatov gives 17...g6!? 18 ♘d3 ♕c7 ('unclear') as Black's best continuation, although I wouldn't mind playing White in this position after 19 ♘c5!?.

d) 10 ♗e4 *(D)* and now:

d1) 10...♘xc3 11 bxc3 ♗d6 12 ♕d3 h6 13 ♗f4!? is slightly better for White – Nisipeanu/Stoica.

d2) 10...♘ce7 11 ♗g5 ♕a5 12 ♕d3 ♘xc3 13 bxc3 ♕xg5 14 cxb4 g6?! (14...h6!?) 15 ♖ac1 ♘d5 (Lempert-Zlochevsky, Moscow 1994) and here White can obtain a solid positional advantage with 16 ♗xd5! ♕xd5 (or 16...exd5 17 ♖c7) 17 ♖c5.

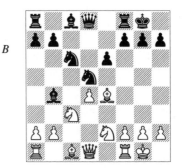

d3) 10...♗d6 11 ♕d3 (a less convincing continuation is 11 ♗xd5 exd5 12 ♗f4 ♗b4! 13 a3 ½-½ Vyzhmanavin-M.Gurevich, Burgas 1994; Ftačnik gives 13...♗xc3 14 ♘xc3 ♗e6 = as a possible continuation) 11...♕h4!? 12 g3 ♕h5 13 ♗f3 ♘db4 14 ♕e4 ♕g6 15 ♕xg6 hxg6 16 ♖d1 ♘e7 17 ♗f4 (17 ♗d2!? is suggested in *Informator* and is worth a try as it keeps some of the tension on the board) 17...♗xf4 18 ♘xf4 ♖d8 and a draw was soon agreed in the game Vaïsser-Nisipeanu, French Cht 2000.

d4) 10...♖e8 11 ♕d3 (11 ♕b3 ♗f8 12 ♖d1 ♘a5 13 ♕c2 g6 14 ♘f4 ♘f6 15 ♗f3 ♗d7 16 a3 ♗c6 17 ♗e2 ♖c8 18 b4 ♗e4 19 ♕b2 ♘c4 20 ♕b3 ♗d5 and Black has equalized without too much effort, Zlotnik-A.Sokolov, Moscow 1991) 11...♘f6 12 ♗g5 h6 13 ♗h4 (13 ♗xf6 ♕xf6 14 ♕b5 a6 15 ♕c4 ♖b8 16 a3 ♗d6 17 ♗xc6 bxc6 18 b4 ♕g6 19 ♘g3 e5 20 ♖ac1 ♗f8 with a pleasant game for Black, Shariyazdanov-Aleksandrov, Krasnodar 1997) 13...♗e7 14 ♗xf6 ♗xf6 15 ♗xc6 bxc6 16 ♘e4 e5 17 ♘xf6+ ♕xf6 18 dxe5 ♕xe5 and due to his bishop being stronger than the knight, Black should have at least equal chances despite his isolated pawns on the queenside, Matveeva-Brodsky, Moscow 1995.

d5) 10...♘f6 11 ♗f3 h6 12 ♖e1 ♕d7 (12...♘e7 13 ♗f4 ♘fd5 14 ♗d2 ♗a5 15 ♖c1 ♘xc3 16 bxc3 ♘f5 17 ♗e4 ♘d6 18 ♗b1 ♗d7 19 ♕c2 f5 20 ♘f4 ♖e8 21 ♕b3 ♕f6 22 ♘d3 with a better game for White, Yrjölä-Solozhenkin, Jyväskylä 1991) 13 ♗f4 ♖d8 14 ♗e5 ♗e7 15 ♖c1 ♘xe5 16 dxe5 ♕xd1 17 ♖cxd1 ♘d7 18 ♘c1 ♖b8 19 ♘b5 ♗c5 20 ♘b3 ♗b6 21 a4 (21 ♖d6!? is another idea) gives White the initiative, Groszpeter-Mascariñas, Kusadasi 1990.

e) 10 ♘xd5 *(D)* and now Black obviously has two ways to recapture:

B

e1) 10...exd5 11 ♘f4 and then:

e11) 11...♗e7 is too passive and allows White to obtain an advantage without any difficulty: 12 ♗e3 ♗f6 13 ♖c1 g6 14 ♖c5 and Black's problems with his d-pawn are already clear; after 14...♘b4 15 ♗b1 (15 ♖b5!?, 15 ♕b3!? and 15 a3!? are all worthy of consideration) 15...b6 16 ♖c3 ♗b7 17 a3 ♘c6 18 ♗a2 ♘e7 19 ♕f3, with better chances for White, V.Georgiev-Sulskis, Cappelle la Grande 1999.

e12) 11...♗d6 12 ♖e1 (or 12 ♗e3 g6 13 ♖c1 ♘e7 14 ♕f3 ♗e6 15 ♖c3 ♕d7, V.Georgiev-Psakhis, Batumi Echt 1999, 16 ♘xe6 fxe6 17 ♕g4 ♘f5 = Psakhis) 12...g6 (12...♕f6 13 ♘xd5 ♕xd4 14 ♗e3 ♕h4 {14...♕xb2!?} 15 g3 ♕d8 16 ♕c2 h6 17 ♖ad1 ♗g4 18 ♗e2 ♗xe2 19 ♖xe2 ♖e8 20 ♕b3 and White's more active pieces easily compensate for the missing pawn, Chiburdanidze-S.B.Hansen, Lippstadt 1997) 13 ♗c2 ♘b4 14 ♗b1 ♕f6 15 g3 (15 a3 ♗xf4 16 ♗xf4 ♕xf4 17 axb4 ♗g4 18 f3 ♗e6 and Black has obtained a good position without a real fight, Lerner-Razuvaev, Moscow 1986) 15...♗e6 16 ♗e3 ♘c6 17 ♘xe6 fxe6 18 a3 ♗c7 19 ♕d3 ♗b6 ∓ V.Georgiev-Stohl, Bundesliga 1998/9.

e2) 10...♕xd5 11 a3 (11 ♗e3 allows Black a reasonable position without too many complications: 11...♘e7!? 12 ♘f4 ♕a5 13 ♕f3 ♖b8 14 h4 ♗d7 15 h5 ♗c6 16 ♕g4 f5 with chances for both sides, Hurme-Farago, Järvenpää 1982) 11...♗d6 (11...♗e7 and 11...♗a5 have also been played on several occasions with decent results) 12 ♘c3 ♕a5 13 ♗e3 ♘e7 14 b4 ♕d8 15 ♘e4 ♘d5 16 ♕h5 f5 17 ♘xd6 ♕xd6 18 ♕f3 b6 19 ♗c4 ♗b7 ½-½ Kacheishvili-Milov, Linares 2001. Note the remarkable ease with which Black obtained a satisfactory position.

B1)

10 a3 *(D)*
10...♗d6
Or:

a) 10...♗e7 and then:

a1) 11 ♕c2 should be compared with note 'c' to White's 10th move in Line B.

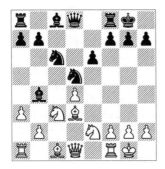

B

a2) 11 &c2 transposes to note 'c1' to Black's 10th move in Line B2.

b) 10...②xc3!? 11 bxc3 &d6 12 ②g3 f5! 13 f4 &d7 14 &e3 ②e7 15 c4 b5! 16 d5 exd5 17 cxb5 &c7! 18 ②e2 &b6 with a pleasant position for Black, who intends to follow up with ...&h8 and ...②g8-f6, Bykhovsky-Tunik, Russia 1992.

11 ②e4

Alternatively:

a) 11 &c2?! transposes to note 'd2' to Black's 10th move in Line B2.

b) 11 ②xd5 exd5 12 &f4 (another plan is 12 ②f4 罩e8 13 &c2 &xf4 14 &xf4 營f6 15 &e3 &f5 16 &b3 罩ad8 17 營d2 h6 18 罩ac1 b6 19 &a4 &d7 20 罩c3 ②a5 21 &c2, Epishin-P.H.Nielsen, Malmö 2002, and here Nielsen gives 21...&b5!? as best, with fairly even chances) and then:

b1) 12...&xf4 is another try: 13 ②xf4 營f6 14 ②xd5 營d6 (14...營xd4? is a mistake due to 15 ②e7+! &h8 16 ②xc6 and White is much better) 15 ②c3 ½-½ Iz.Jelen-Sher, Ptuj 1991, but after 15...②xd4 16 &e4 罩d8 17 罩e1 White has a slight pull.

b2) 12...&g4 13 f3 &h5 14 &xd6 營xd6 15 營d2 &g6 16 &b5 ②e7 17 罩fe1 ②c8 18 ②f4 ②b6 and White is at

most very slightly better, Stempin-King, Haifa Echt 1989.

b3) 12...&e7 is positionally correct: 13 營c2 g6 14 罩ad1 &f6 15 &b5 &f5 16 營d2 罩c8 17 &xc6 罩xc6 18 ②c3 罩e8 19 罩fe1 ½-½ Wessman-Serper, Tunja jr Wch 1989.

11...&e7

11...&c7!? has also been seen on a few occasions: 12 ②g5 (12 &c2?! is worse; e.g., 12...營h4! 13 h3 h6 14 營d3, Korchnoi-Yusupov, Ubeda 1997, and here Psakhis gives 14...f5 15 ②4c3 ②f6 16 &b3 &h8 intending ...罩d8 and ...e5 ∓) 12...②f6 13 &c2 h6 14 ②f3 罩e8 15 營d3 e5 with equality – Arkhipov.

12 &c2 *(D)*

12 &b1 transposes to note 'b1' to White's 10th move in Line B.

B

12...b6

Or:

a) 12...罩e8 13 營d3 g6 14 &h6 b6 transposes to the main line.

b) 12...營b6?! 13 營d3 g6 14 罩d1 罩d8 15 營f3 (Salov-Timman, Sanghi Nagar FIDE Ct (3) 1994) and here 15...&d7 is forced, although White has the initiative after 16 b4 a5 17 &b3 &e8 18 &h6 – Salov.

c) 12...♘f6 13 ♕d3 ♘xe4 14 ♕xe4 g6 15 ♖d1 ♗f6 16 ♗f4 ♕d5 (another possibility is 16...♕b6!?) 17 ♕e3 ♗g7 (17...♕b5!?) 18 ♘c3 ♕c4 19 b3 ♕a6 20 ♗h6 ♘e7 21 ♗xg7 ♔xg7 (Malishauskas-Itkis, Miedzybrodze 1991) and now 22 d5!? ♘xd5 23 ♘xd5 exd5 24 ♖xd5 ♗e6 25 ♕d4+ ♔g8 26 ♖d6 leaves White with the initiative.

d) 12...♗d7 13 ♕d3 g6 14 ♗h6 ♖e8 15 ♖ad1 ♖c8 16 ♗b3 a6 17 ♕g3 ♘f6 18 ♘2c3 ♕b6 offers chances for both sides, Milov-Andersson, Biel 1996.

e) 12...♕c7 13 ♕d3 ♖d8 *(D)* and here:

e1) 14 ♖d1 b6 15 ♘4c3 g6 16 ♘xd5 ♖xd5 17 ♗f4 ♗d6 18 ♗xd6 ♖xd6 and it is White who has to search for equality, Yashtlov-Grigoriants, Vladimir jr 2002.

e2) 14 ♘4c3 g6 15 ♗h6 ♘xc3 16 bxc3?! (16 ♕xc3 = Rogers) 16...e5! 17 ♗b3 ♗f5 18 ♕e3 ♗f6 19 ♖ac1 (Hübner-Rogers, Polanica Zdroj 1996) and here Hübner gives 19...♕e7! ∓.

e3) 14 ♘g5 g6 15 ♕f3 (15 ♗b3 has been tested in a few Karpov games: 15...♘f6 16 ♖d1 ♗f8 17 ♗f4 ♕e7 18 ♕e3 ♘d5 19 ♗xd5 exd5 20 ♘f3

♕xe3 21 fxe3 f6 22 ♖ac1 ♗f5 ∓ Kamsky-Karpov, Elista FIDE Wch (14) 1996; 15...♗f8 16 ♕h3 ♘f6 17 ♘f3 ♕b6 18 ♗a2 ♗g7 19 ♕h4 ♘d5 20 ♘c3 ♘ce7 21 ♘xd5 ♘xd5 22 ♗h6 f6 = V.Milov-Karpov, Biel 1997) 15...♗f8 16 ♗b3 ♗g7 17 ♖d1 h6 18 ♘e4 ♘ce7 (Rogers-Ivanchuk, Moscow OL 1994) and here White should try either 19 ♘2c3 or 19 ♕h3!? e5 20 ♕f3 ♗f5 = Dautov.

e4) 14 ♘2c3 g6 15 ♗h6 f5?! (the alternatives 15...♘f6!? and 15...♕b6!? can both be considered) 16 ♘xd5 exd5 17 ♘d2 ♘f6 18 ♘f3 ♗e6 19 b4 with a positional plus for White thanks to his better pawn-structure and stronger bishops, Shariyazdanov-Shestoperov, Russian Cht (Briansk) 1995.

f) 12...e5 *(D)* and then:

f1) 13 ♗b3 ♘f6 14 ♘xf6+ ♗xf6 15 d5 ♘d4 16 ♘xd4 exd4 17 ♗f4 (Savon mentions that 17 ♕f3 ♕b6 18 ♗c2 ♗d7 is about equal) 17...♗f5 18 ♖c1 d3! and now instead of 19 ♖c7? ♗xb2 20 a4 ♗a3! ∓ Dumitrache-Savon, Baku 1988, Savon gives 19 ♕d2 ♕b6 20 ♕b4 as White's best, when 20...♗xb2 21 ♖c7 gives him compensation; however, 20...♕xb4! 21

axb4 ♖ac8 looks comfortably better for Black.

f2) 13 dxe5 ♘xe5 14 ♘f4 (14 ♕d4 ♘g6 15 ♖d1 ♗e6 16 ♘2c3 ♘b6 17 ♕xd8 ½-½ Tisdall-S.B.Hansen, Reykjavik 1995) 14...♘xf4 15 ♗xf4 ♘g6 (15...♕xd1 doesn't bring much excitement either: 16 ♖fxd1 ♘c4 17 ♗d6 ♘xd6 18 ♘xd6 ♖d8 ½-½ Sadler-Winants, French Cht 1992) 16 ♗e3 ♗e6 17 ♕h5 ♕d5 18 ♕xd5 ♗xd5 19 ♖fd1 ♗c6 is dead equal, Malishauskas-Serper, Miedzybrodze Zyw. 1991.

13 ♕d3 g6

13...a5!? is an interesting idea of Helgi Olafsson's: 14 ♘d6 (14 ♖d1?! ♗a6 15 ♕f3 ♖c8 16 ♗b3?! ♗b7 17 ♕g3 ♗h4 18 ♕d3 ♘ce7 19 ♘f4?? ♖xc1 0-1 F.Olafsson-H.Olafsson, Reykjavik 1995) 14...g6 15 ♘xc8 ♖xc8 16 ♗h6 ♖e8 17 ♗a4 ♗f8 18 ♗xf8 ♖xf8 19 ♖fd1 ♕d6 and Black is in control, Carleson-H.Olafsson, New York 1989; it is rather remarkable that this idea isn't seen more often – it certainly deserves more tests.

14 ♗h6 ♖e8 *(D)*

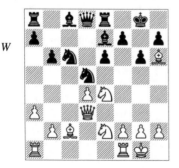

15 ♖ad1

15 ♖ac1 ♗b7 16 ♗a4 (16 ♖fd1 can also lead to an interesting struggle:

16...♖c8 17 ♕g3!? ♘f6 18 ♘g5 ♕d6 19 ♕h4?! ♘a5 20 ♘f4 ♖c4!, Semkov-Psakhis, Erevan 1988, and here 21 ♗b1? fails to 21...♕xd4!, while 21 ♘xg6 fxg6 22 ♘xh7 ♖xh7 23 ♕g4 e5 is none too convincing for White either) 16...♖c8 17 ♖fd1 a6 18 ♗xc6 ♖xc6 19 ♖xc6 ♗xc6 20 ♕xa6 ♕a8 21 ♕xa8 ♖xa8 and Black's bishop-pair compensates for the pawn deficit, Gelfand-Anand, Shenyang 2000.

15...♗b7 16 ♖fe1 ♖c8

Now:

a) 17 ♘2c3 is harmless: 17...♘a5! 18 ♕g3 ♘c4 19 ♗a4 ♗c6 20 ♗b3 ♘xc3 (Shirov-Psakhis, Klaipeda 1988) 21 ♘xc3 ♗d6 22 ♗f4 ♗xf4 23 ♕xf4 ♕d6 = Pliester.

b) 17 ♗b3!? and then:

b1) 17...a6?! 18 ♘2g3 ♘b8 19 ♕f3 ♖c7 20 ♘h5 ♘d7 21 h4 ♘7f6? 22 ♘hxf6+ ♘xf6 23 d5! ♘xe4 24 dxe6 f5 25 ♖xd8 ♖xd8 26 ♖d1 1-0 Kamsky-Short, Linares PCA Ct (5) 1994.

b2) 17...♘a5 18 ♗a2 ♘f6 19 ♘xf6+! ♗xf6 20 ♘f4 ♗g5 21 ♘xe6 ♖xe6 22 ♖xe6 fxe6 23 ♗xe6+ ♔h8 24 ♗xc8 ± Reilly-Wright, Melbourne 2002. This game followed analysis by Hübner.

b3) Black's best continuation is probably 17...♖c7!? intending ...♖d7, which is a suggestion of Seirawan's.

B2)

10 ♗c2 *(D)*
10...♖e8

This odd-looking sidestep prepares the retreat of the bishop to f8 as well as the potential counter in the centre with ...e5. Other tries include:

a) 10...♘xc3?! 11 bxc3 ♗d6 12 ♕d3 g6 13 ♘g3 b6 14 ♘e4 ♗e7 15

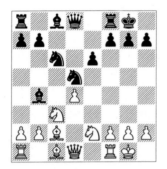

B

♗h6 ♖e8 16 ♗a4 ♗b7 17 ♕g3 is slightly better for White, Dumitrache-Kalesis, Cappelle la Grande 1995.

b) 10...♘f6 and then:

b1) A lot can be said in favour of 11 ♗g5!? ♗e7 12 a3 b6 (12...♘d5 13 ♕d3 g6 14 ♗h6 ♖e8 15 ♖ad1 ♗f6 16 ♘e4 ± Kuzmin-Vilela, Polanica Zdroj 1984) 13 ♕d3 g6 14 ♖ad1 ♗b7 15 ♖fe1 ♖e8 16 h4 ♘h5 17 ♕e3, which gives White a slight advantage, Bagirov-Aseev, USSR 1986.

b2) 11 ♕d3 ♗e7 12 a3 b6 (not 12...g6?! 13 ♗h6 ♖e8 14 ♗a4 a6 15 ♕f3 ♗d7 16 ♖ad1 ♘a5 17 ♗xd7 ♘xd7 18 d5! e5 19 d6 and Black is in bad shape, Jelen-Sher, Ptuj 1991) 13 ♖d1 (13 ♗g5!?) 13...♗b7 14 ♕h3 g6 15 ♗h6 ♖e8 16 ♗a4 a6 17 b4 ♘d5 18 ♘xd5 exd5 19 ♕f3 ♗f6 20 ♗e3 ♖e6 21 ♗b3 ♘e7 22 ♘f4 ♖d6 and while White has a slight pull, the black position is solid, Gligorić-Pikula, Yugoslav Ch (Nikšić) 1997.

c) 10...♗e7 is a reasonably popular option. White now has:

c1) 11 a3 and then:

c11) 11...♖e8 is possible.

c12) 11...g6 12 ♖e1 ♗f6 13 ♗h6 ♖e8 14 ♘e4 ♗g7 15 ♕d2 b6 16 ♗g5 f6 17 ♗h4 ♘ce7 18 ♘4c3 with no more than a slight initiative for White, Sashikiran-Egiazarian, Calcutta 2002.

c13) 11...b6 12 ♕d3 g6 13 ♗h6 (13 ♘e4!? has also been tried) 13...♖e8 14 ♖ad1 ♗b7 15 ♖fe1 ♖c8 16 ♕g3 ♘xc3 17 bxc3 ♗f6 18 ♘f4 ♘xd4! 19 ♗xg6 hxg6 20 cxd4 ½-½ Schipkov-Siklosi, Kecskemet 1993. Schipkov gives the possible continuation 20...♔h7! 21 ♕h3 ♗h4 22 d5! ♔xh6 23 dxe6 ♕f6 24 g3 with an assessment of 'unclear'; most of all it is unclear how White will find sufficient compensation after a move like 24...♖c4 or even 24...g5.

c14) 11...♘xc3 12 bxc3 b6 (the alternative is 12...e5?! 13 d5 ♘a5 14 f4! exf4 15 ♗xf4 ♗d6 16 ♘g3 g6 17 ♗xd6 ♕xd6 18 ♘e4 ♕b6+ 19 ♔h1 ♗f5, Timoshchenko-Vyzhmanavin, Novosibirsk tt 1986, 20 ♖b1 ♕d8 21 ♕d4 ± Vyzhmanavin) 13 ♕d3 g6 14 ♖e1 ♗b7 15 ♘f4 ♗f6 16 ♘h5!? ♗g5 17 ♗b2 with some initiative for White, Knaak-Stohl, Potsdam 1985.

c2) 11 ♕d3 g6 and then:

c21) 12 a3 b6 is line 'c13'.

c22) 12 ♕f3 ♘xc3 13 bxc3 ♗d7 14 ♗h6 ♖e8 15 ♘g3 ♖c8 16 ♖ad1 ♘a5 17 ♖fe1 ♗c6 18 ♗e4 (Renet-Gavrikov, Swiss Cht 1996) and here Black can easily equalize by means of 18...♗xe4 19 ♘xe4 ♘c4.

c23) 12 ♗b3 ♘xc3 13 bxc3 ♘a5 14 ♘g3 (or 14 ♗h6 ♖e8 15 ♖ac1 ♗d7 16 ♘g3 ♘xb3 17 axb3 ♗c6 18 c4 with a position that is slightly easier to play as White, Tisdall-Ashley, San Francisco 1995) 14...b6 15 ♖d1 ♗b7 16 c4 ♕d7 17 ♗b2 ♗f6 18 ♖ac1 ♖fd8 19 ♗c3 ♘xb3 20 axb3 ♗g7 = Podgaets-Novikov, Ukrainian Ch (Kiev) 1986.

d) 10...♗d6 *(D)* and here:

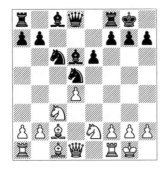

W

d1) 11 ♘e4 ♗e7 12 a3 transposes to Line B1.

d2) 11 a3?! ♛h4 12 g3 ♘xc3 13 bxc3 ♛h5 14 ♘f4?! (Pliester gives this as wrong and instead suggests 14 ♗e3 with equal chances, but after 14...e5!? Black certainly doesn't have any problems; therefore it may be White's 11th move that is to blame as it doesn't contribute anything positive to his game) 14...♛xd1 15 ♖xd1 e5 16 ♘d5 ♗g4 17 ♖d2 ♗f3 18 ♘e3 ♖fd8 19 ♗b2 ♗c5 with a good game for Black, Magai-Itkis, Frunze 1989.

d3) 11 ♛d3 ♛h4 12 g3 ♛h5 13 ♘xd5 exd5 14 ♗f4 (with 14 ♘f4 White wants to win the bishop-pair, but after 14...♗xf4 15 ♗xf4 ♗h3 16 ♛d1 ♗g4 17 f3 ♗h3 18 ♖f2 ♖fe8 19 ♖c1 ♗e7 20 ♛d2 f6 21 b4 ♖ae8 Black is firmly in control, Tulegren-Bjuhr, corr. 1989) 14...♗e7 15 ♗d2 ♛g6 (15...♗d6 16 ♗f4 ♗e7 17 ♗d2 ♛g6 18 ♔g2 ♛xd3 19 ♗xd3 ♗f6 20 ♗c3 ♖d8 21 ♖ac1 ♗d7 22 ♖fd1 g6 is also adequate for equality, Lautier-M.Gurevich, Marseilles 1988) 16 ♛xg6 (16 ♔g2 ½-½ Korchnoi-Portisch, Brussels 1988 doesn't tell us much except that Korchnoi couldn't have been pleased with the outcome of the opening to

offer a draw this early on) 16...hxg6 17 ♗b3 ♖d8 18 ♗c3 ♗f6 19 ♔g2 g5 20 h3 ♘e7 21 ♖fe1 ♗e6 22 ♘g1 ♘c6 is equal, Lukov-Schandorff, Thessaloniki OL 1988.

d4) 11 ♘xd5 exd5 12 ♗f4 ♗e7!? (note Black's decision to avoid the exchange of the dark-squared bishops; this is due to Black's light-squared bishop not being as strong as its white counterpart because of the d5-pawn being fixed on a light square) 13 ♖c1 (after 13 ♗e3 ♗g4! 14 f3 ♗h5 15 ♗b3 f6! 16 ♘f4 ♗f7 17 ♗f2 ♗d6 18 ♘d3 ♛c7 19 g3 ♘a5 Black is in control, Rivas-Chernin, New York 1989) 13...♗g4 14 f3 ♗e6 15 ♛d3 g6 16 ♗b3 ♛b6 17 ♔h1 ♖fd8 18 ♖fd1 ♗f6 and Black has equalized, Lutz-Karpman, Budapest 1989.

11 ♛d3 g6 12 ♖d1

There are two minor alternatives:

a) 12 ♛f3 ♛f6 (12...♗f8 13 ♗b3 ♘xc3 14 bxc3 ♘a5 15 ♗f4 ♘xb3 16 axb3 ♛d5 = Kantsler-Ruban, Podolsk GMA 1989) 13 ♛xf6 ♘xf6 14 ♗g5 ♗e7 15 ♖fd1 ♖d8 16 ♖ac1 ♗d7 = Gligorić-Shaked, Cannes 1998.

b) 12 a3 doesn't make much sense; after 12...♘xc3!? (12...♗f8 leads to a position that often occurs, where Black doesn't have anything to be worried about either) 13 bxc3 ♗f8 14 f4?! (14 ♖d1!?) 14...♗g7 15 ♗e3 b6 16 ♘g3 ♘e7 17 ♘e4 ♗b7 Black is better, Yashtylov-Tunik, Togliatti 2001.

12...♗f8

12...b6!? 13 a3 ♗f8 14 ♛f3 ♗g7 15 ♗e4 ♗a6 16 ♗e3 ♛d6 17 ♘xd5 (17 ♘f4!? is better, although Black should be OK after 17...♘xc3 18 bxc3 ♗b7) 17...exd5 18 ♗d3 ♗xd3 19 ♖xd3 ♖ac8 = Santoro-Breazu, corr. 1991.

13 ♕f3 (D)

13 ♕g3!? ♗g7 14 h4 and now, rather than 14...♕c7?! 15 ♕f3 ♘xc3 16 bxc3 b6 17 ♗g5 ♗b7 18 ♕h3 ♖ac8 19 h5 ± McClintock-Browne, Chicago 1988, Black can equalize with 14...♗f6! – *ECO*.

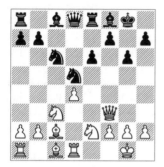

13...♗g7

This is considered the most solid continuation for Black, who puts pressure on the d4-pawn, while completing the delayed fianchetto of the dark-squared bishop. The alternatives include:

a) 13...♕f6 14 ♗e4 ♕xf3 15 ♗xf3 ♘xc3 16 bxc3 e5 17 g3 exd4 18 cxd4 ♗f5 and now the careless 19 ♘c3? ♘xd4! 20 ♖xd4 ♖e1+ 21 ♔g2 ♗g7 22 ♘b5 a6 23 ♗b2 ♖xa1 24 ♗xa1 axb5 25 ♖d1 ♗xa1 26 ♖xa1 ♗e6 led in due course to a victory for Black in Iskusnykh-Yudasin, Kemerovo 1995. However, with 19 ♗e3!? White can put a bid in for an advantage.

b) 13...♘xc3 14 bxc3 ♗d7 (alternatively, 14...♗g7 15 ♘g3! f5 16 ♘e2 ♗d7 17 ♕g3 ♕f6 18 ♖b1 ± M.Gurevich-Razuvaev, Moscow 1987) 15 ♘g3! f5 16 ♘e2 (the idea behind White's previous move is simply to

provoke another weakening of the dark squares in the black camp, to which Black must unfortunately acquiesce) 16...♕h4! (taking the g3-square away from White's queen) 17 ♘f4 ♖ac8 18 ♖b1 ♘a5 and while White hopes to take advantage of Black's compromised dark squares, Black is now taking aim at the light squares in White's camp, and the chances are about equal, Rivas-Benjamin, New York 1989.

14 ♗e4

Alternatives:

a) 14 ♗e3 ♘ce7 15 ♗g5 ♕b6 16 ♘a4 ♕d8 17 ♘ac3 ♕b6 18 ♗b3 (18 ♘a4 accepts Black's invitation to a repetition of moves and a draw) 18...♗d7 (Hjartarson-Pigusov, Biel IZ 1993) and here Ambrož gives 19 ♘e4 ♗c6 20 ♕h3 ♗b5!? 21 ♘2c3 ♗c6 with about equal chances, which isn't far from the truth.

b) 14 ♗b3 ♘xc3 15 bxc3 ♘a5 16 ♗f4 and here 16...♗d7 is solid, but 17 ♗e5!? f6 18 ♗f4 ♘xb3 19 axb3 ♗c6 20 ♕g3 ♕b6 (Timoshchenko-Rashkovsky, Sverdlovsk 1987) 21 ♘c1 should promise White a slight pull. However, Black can equalize by playing 16...♘xb3 17 axb3 ♕d5.

c) 14 ♘e4 h6 (14...♕b6!?) 15 ♕g3 (White should avoid both 15 ♗d2 ♘ce7 ∓ Shirov-Ulybin, Klaipeda 1988 and 15 ♗b3 ♘a5 16 ♗a4 ♗d7 17 ♗xd7 ♕xd7 18 ♘2c3 ♘xc3 19 bxc3 f5! ∓ Hjartarson-Andersson, Szirak IZ 1987) 15...♘f6 16 ♗e3 ♘b4 17 ♘xf6+ ♕xf6 18 ♗e4 ♘d5 (Dumitrache-Chernin, Cappelle la Grande 1994) and here 19 ♘c3!? is an interesting idea; e.g., 19...♘xe3 20 fxe3 e5 21 ♖f1 and White holds the initiative.

14...♘xc3

The older move 14...♕e7 seems to have been abandoned on account of 15 ♕g3 ♗d7 16 h4 (16 ♗g5 ♕b4 17 a3 ♕b6 18 ♕h3 ♘ce7 19 ♗h6 ♖ad8 = Fedorowicz-Riemersma, Wijk aan Zee 1988) 16...♕f8 17 ♗g5 ♘ce7 18 ♗xe7 ♖xe7 19 ♗xd5 exd5 20 ♘f4 with a pull for White, Parker-Hoffmann, London 1997.

15 bxc3 *(D)*

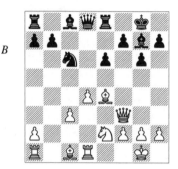

15...e5
Or:

a) It should be mentioned that the continuation 15...♘e5 16 ♕g3 ♘c4 17 ♗d3 (Timoshchenko-Arnason, Helsinki 1986) 17...♘d6 18 ♗g5 ♕a5 is equal according to Pliester.

b) 15...♗d7 16 ♖b1 f5!? 17 ♗c2 b6 18 ♕g3 ♖c8 has been considered sufficient for equality (e.g. in *ECO*) based on 19 ♗g5 ♗f6, Vasiljević-Am.Rodriguez, Pančevo 1987. However, the dark squares in Black's camp are terribly weak and deserve a closer look. A new idea achieved complete success in Bern-Pioch, corr. 1994: 19 h4 ♕e7 20 h5 ♕f7 21 hxg6 ♕xg6 22 ♕d6 ♕f7 23 ♕h2 ♘e7 24 ♖d3 ♘d5 25 ♖g3 ♔h8 26 ♗d2 ♗f6 27 ♗b3 ♗b5 28 ♘f4 ♘xf4 29 ♗xf4 ♗c4 30

♖e1 b5 31 ♖h3 ♖g8 32 ♗xc4 bxc4 33 ♖h6 1-0. 34 ♖xf6 looms.

16 ♗e3 exd4 17 cxd4
Now:

a) 17...♕h4 18 ♗d5!? ♗e6 19 ♗xe6 fxe6 20 ♖ab1 ♕e7 21 h4 ♗f6 22 h5 is gives White a slight advantage, Kaspi-Shmuter, Kharkov 1988.

b) 17...♕e7 18 ♘c3 ♗d7 (18...h5 19 h3 ♗d7 20 ♖ac1 ± Kaspi-Khasin, Rishon le Zion 1997) 19 ♖ab1 ♖ab8 20 h3 a6 ½-½ Dumitrache-Belikov, Enakievo 1997. However, there is plenty left to play for; a good start is 21 ♗d5!? with excellent pressure on Black's position.

c) 17...♗e6 18 ♗xc6 bxc6 19 ♕xc6 ♕a5 20 ♕c3 (20 ♘f4!?) 20...♕a6 21 ♕d2 ♖ac8 22 a4 ♗b3 23 ♖dc1 ♖xc1+ 24 ♘xc1 ♗c4 gives Black adequate compensation for the pawn, Baklanov-Drwikowski, corr. 1998.

C)

7 0-0 cxd4
Or:

a) 7...dxc4 8 ♗xc4 ♘bd7 (8...cxd4 9 exd4 transposes to the main line, as does 8...♘c6 9 a3 cxd4 10 exd4) 9 a3 ♗xc3 10 bxc3 transposes to note 'a' to Black's 9th move in Line B2 of Chapter 6.

b) 7...♘c6 8 a3 (8 cxd5 exd5 transposes to note 'b3' to Black's 7th move in Line B) and here:

b1) 8...cxd4 9 exd4 ♗e7 (9...dxc4 10 ♗xc4 transposes to the main line) 10 cxd5 ♘xd5 11 ♗c2 transposes to note 'c1' to Black's 10th move in Line B2.

b2) 8...♗xc3 9 bxc3 dxc4 10 ♗xc4 transposes to note 'd4' to Black's 9th move in Line B2 of Chapter 6.

b3) 8...dxc4 9 ♗xc4 cxd4 10 exd4 transposes to the main line.

8 exd4 dxc4

Or:

a) 8...♘c6 9 a3 and now 9...dxc4 10 ♗xc4 transposes to the main line, while 9...♗e7 10 cxd5 ♘xd5 is note 'a' to Black's 10th move in Line B1.

b) 8...b6 9 ♗g5 ♗e7 10 ♕c2 ♘bd7 11 cxd5 exd5 12 ♘g3 h6 13 ♗f4 ± Spraggett-Taylor, Montreal Z 1981.

9 ♗xc4 (D)

9...♘c6

Black has tried several other things, some of which are more aimed at restraining White's isolated d-pawn:

a) 9...♗d6 10 ♘g3 a6 11 a3 b5 12 ♗a2 ♗b7 13 ♗g5 h6 14 ♗xf6 ♕xf6 15 d5 ♗e5 16 dxe6 fxe6 17 ♕g4 and White has the initiative, Reshevsky-Burger, Lone Pine 1981.

b) 9...b6!? is played surprisingly rarely, which seems unjustified as Black seems to equalize smoothly after, for example, 10 ♕d3 ♗b7 11 ♗g5 ♘c6 12 a3 ♗e7 13 ♖ad1 ♘d5 = Bagirov-Zaichik, Yaroslavl 1982.

c) 9...a6 10 ♕d3 (10 ♗g5 b5 11 ♗b3 ♗b7 12 ♕d3 ♗e7 13 ♖ad1 ♘bd7 leads to equality, Toshkov-Guseinov,

Baku 1983) 10...♘bd7 transposes to line 'd4'.

d) 9...♘bd7 is another perfectly logical move, aiming at blockading the d-pawn with ...♘b6-d5.

d1) 10 ♗g5 ♘b6 11 ♗b3 ♗e7 12 ♕d3 ♗d7 13 ♘f4 ♗c6 14 ♗c2 g6 15 ♗b3 ♘fd5 16 ♗xe7 ♘xe7 17 ♖ad1 ½-½ Kantsler-Kholmov, Frunze 1989.

d2) 10 ♘f4 ♘b6 11 ♗b3 ♗d7 12 d5 exd5 13 ♘fxd5 ♘bxd5 14 ♘xd5 ♘xd5 15 ♕xd5 ♗e6 = Ki.Georgiev-Polugaevsky, Thessaloniki OL 1984.

d3) 10 ♗b3 b6 (10...♘b6 has also been tried) 11 ♗f4 ♗a6 12 ♖e1 ♖c8 13 ♖c1 ♖e8 14 a3 ♗f8 15 ♘g3 ♗c4 16 ♗c2 ♘d5 and Black has equalized, Volke-Pieniazek, Bundesliga 1994/5.

d4) 10 ♕d3 a6 11 a4 ♘b6 12 ♗b3 ♗d7 (12...♘bd5 13 ♖d1 b6 14 ♗g5 ♗e7 {14...♕d6!?} 15 ♘xd5 ♘xd5 16 ♗xd5 exd5 17 ♗xe7 ♕xe7, Ehlvest-Arnason, Tallinn 1983, 18 ♘c3 ♗b7 19 ♕f5 with a slight pull for White) 13 ♗g5 ♗c6 14 ♗c2 g6 15 ♖fd1 ♗e7 ½-½ Day-Nurmi, Montreal Z 1981.

d5) 10 a3 ♗e7 (or 10...♗d6 11 ♗a2 ♘b6 12 ♘f4 ♗d7 13 d5 ♗xf4 14 ♗xf4 ♘fxd5 15 ♘xd5 exd5 16 ♗xd5 ♕f6 17 ♗c7 ♘xd5 18 ♕xd5 ♗c6 19 ♕e5 ½-½ Hübner-Hort, Wijk aan Zee 1985) and here:

d51) 11 ♕d3 b6 (or 11...♘b6!?) 12 ♗f4 ♗b7 13 ♖ac1 a6 14 a4 ♖e8 15 ♖fd1 ♘f8 16 ♗g3 ♘g6 17 f4 ♕d7 = Cherepkov-Aleksandrov, St Petersburg 1994.

d52) 11 ♗a2 ♘b6 12 ♗g5 ♗d7 13 ♕d3 ♖c8 14 ♖fe1 ♘a4 15 ♘xa4 ♗xa4 16 ♘c3 ♗c6 = Panczyk-Barbulescu, Polanica Zdroj 1984.

d53) 11 ♘f4 ♘b6 12 ♗a2 ♗d6 13 ♘d3 ♘fd5 14 ♘xd5 ♘xd5 15 ♗xd5

exd5 16 ♗f4 ♗f5 17 ♗xd6 ½-½ Bertok-Tolush, USSR-Yugoslavia (Leningrad) 1957.

10 a3

This is a very natural follow-up to Black's last move: White kicks the bishop away, makes room on a2 for the light-squared bishop and prevents ...♘b4, the latter two aiming at setting up the familiar ♕d3 + ♗c2(b1) line-up towards the black king. Naturally White has tried other moves, but most of them have failed to kick up a storm:

a) 10 h3 b6 11 ♗e3 ♗b7 12 a3 ♗xc3 13 ♘xc3 h6 14 ♕d3 ♘e7 15 ♖ad1 ♘ed5 16 ♗a2 ♖c8 = Vaganian-Tukmakov, Reggio Emilia 1987/8.

b) 10 ♕d3 b6 11 ♖d1 ♗b7 12 ♕h3 ♗e7 13 ♗g5 ♘b4 14 a3 ♘bd5 15 ♘xd5 exd5 16 ♗d3 h6 17 ♗h4 ♗c8 is equal, Plachetka-T.Horvath, Kecskemet 1983.

c) 10 ♗e3 is a fairly harmless continuation: 10...a6 (10...b6 11 h3 transposes to line 'a') 11 a3 ♗e7 12 ♖c1 ♗d7 13 ♗a2 ♖c8 14 ♘f4 e5 15 dxe5 ♘xe5 16 ♘cd5 ♘xd5 17 ♘xd5 ♗d6! = Byrne-Zaltsman, USA Ch (Greenville) 1980.

d) 10 ♗g5 *(D)* is a major alternative:

d1) 10...h6!? is interesting: 11 ♗h4 (11 ♗e3 b6 12 ♕d3 ♗d6 13 a3 ♗b7 14 ♖ad1 ♕b8 15 ♘g3 a6 16 ♗a2 ♘e7 is very pleasant for Black, Mikhalchishin-Psakhis, USSR Ch (Frunze) 1981) 11...♗e7 12 ♖c1 e5 13 ♗xf6 ♗xf6 14 d5 ♘d4 15 ♘e4 ♗f5 16 ♘xf6+ ♕xf6 = ½-½ Groszpeter-Garcia Gonzalez, Lucerne Wcht 1989.

d2) 10...♗e7 and here:

d21) 11 a3 and then:

d211) 11...b6?! 12 ♕d3 ♗b7 and now:

d2111) 13 ♖fd1 ♘d5 14 ♗d2 ♘xc3 15 ♗xc3 ♗f6 16 d5 ½-½ Høi-Mortensen, Danish Ch (Odense) 1980. This seems a little premature, as White holds a reasonably firm initiative after 16...exd5 17 ♗xd5 ♗xc3 18 ♘xc3.

d2112) 13 ♖ad1 ♖c8 14 ♕h3 e5 15 ♕g3 exd4 16 ♘xd4 ♘xd4 17 ♖xd4 was played in Inkiov-Mirallès, Bulgaria-France 1985, and now 17...♘h5 18 ♕h4 ♗xg5 19 ♕xg5 ♘f6 20 ♖fd1 ♕c5 21 ♕xc5 bxc5 22 ♖4d2 gives White a slight advantage according to Ki.Georgiev.

d212) 11...a6 12 ♕d3 (12 ♖c1 {12 ♗a2 b5 13 ♖c1 is the same} 12...b5 13 ♗a2 ♗b7 14 ♕d3 ♘e5 15 ♕c2 ♘c4 16 ♖fd1 ♖c8 17 h3 ♘d5 18 ♗xe7 ♘xe7 19 ♖d3 ♕d6 20 ♖cd1 ♖fd8 with chances for both sides, Bronstein-Kosten, London 1989) 12...b5 13 ♗b3 (or 13 ♗a2 transposing to note 'b' after White's 12th move in Line C1) 13...♘e5 (not the only move; *ECO* suggests 13...♗b7 as being equal and that 13...b4!? is to be considered) 14 ♕g3 ♘c4 15 ♗h6 ♘e8 16 a4 ♗d6 17 ♕f3 ♖b8 18 ♗c1 ♕h4! 19 g3 ♕h3 with chances for both sides, Cebalo-M.Gurevich, Vršac 1985.

d213) 11...♘d5 12 ♗xe7 ♘cxe7
13 ♘xd5 ♘xd5 14 ♕b3 ♘b6 15 ♖fd1
♗d7 16 ♘c3 ♖c8 17 ♗b5 ♖c7 18 a4
♗c6 19 ♗xc6 bxc6 20 ♘e4 ♖d7 21 a5
♘c8 22 ♕a4 ♘e7 and Black has at
least equalized, Stanec-Beliavsky, Graz
1986.

d22) 11 ♖c1 ♕a5!? (11...b6 is also
fully playable; e.g., 12 a3 ♗b7 13 ♕d3
♘d5 14 ♗e3, Bellon-Gomez Esteban,
Barcelona 1984, 14...♘xc3 15 ♖xc3
♗d6 =) 12 ♕d2 ♖d8 13 a3 ♗d7 14
♖fd1 ♗e8 15 ♗a2 (Kamsky-Beliav-
sky, Linares 1994) and here Dautov
suggests 15...♖ac8!?, Kasparov gives
15...a6!?, while Beliavsky recommends
15...b5, which I think may be met with
the d5 advance, either here or in the
next few moves.

We now return to the position after
10 a3 *(D)*:

Now:
C1: 10...♗e7   260
C2: 10...♗d6   263
The former is more standard, but
Black has scored strikingly well with
the latter.

Black has also tried 10...♗xc3 11
bxc3:

a) 11...e5?! 12 ♗g5! ♕d6 13 ♖e1
(13 ♗a2 ♖e8 14 d5 ♘a5 15 ♗xf6
♕xf6 16 ♕a4 ♕d8 17 ♘g3, Chekhov-
Makarychev, Moscow 1986, 17...b6 is
approximately equal – Makarychev)
13...♗g4!? 14 f3 ♗e6 15 ♗xe6 fxe6
16 ♗xf6! ♖xf6 17 ♘g3! ♕c7 18 ♘e4
♖h6 (18...♖g6 is better according to
Salov) 19 d5! exd5 20 ♕xd5+ ♕f7 21
♖ad1 ♖f8 22 c4 ± Korchnoi-Salov,
New York 1996.

b) 11...b6 12 ♗g5 ♗b7 13 ♗a2
♖c8 14 c4?! (the c-pawn will get in
trouble on this square and for that reason 14 ♖e1 is to be preferred) 14...h6
15 ♗h4 ♘a5 16 ♖c1 g5 17 ♗g3
♘xc4! 18 ♖xc4 ♕d5 19 f3 ♖xc4 20
♗e5 ♘d7 and Black is simply a pawn
up, Bozinović-Shariyazdanov, Zadar
1998.

c) 11...h6 12 ♘f4 (12 ♕d3!? is
given as '±' in *ECO*, while Pliester
says that "Black has nothing to fear",
which is a bit of an exaggeration, but
Black has good chances to equalize
after 12...a6 13 a4 ♘a5 14 ♗a2 ♗d7
15 ♕g3 ♔h8 followed by ...♖c8 and
...♗c6) 12...♗d7 13 ♗a2 ♖c8 14 ♖e1
♖e8 15 ♖e3 e5 16 ♘h5 = Panczyk-
Yusupov, Warsaw 1985.

C1)
10...♗e7 *(D)*
11 ♕d3
Alternatively:
a) 11 ♗g5 transposes to note 'd21'
White's 10th move in Line C.
b) 11 ♗e3 a6 (11...b6 is also satisfactory for Black) 12 ♗a2 b5 13 ♘f4
b4 14 axb4 ♘xb4 15 ♕f3 ♖b8 16 ♗b1
♗d6 with a pleasant game for Black,
Schukin-Kiriakov, St Petersburg Ch
1997.

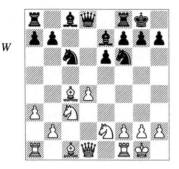

c) 11 ♗a2 a6 12 ♗f4 (12 ♕d3 transposes to the main line) 12...b5 13 d5 exd5 14 ♘xd5 ♘xd5 15 ♗xd5 ♗b7 16 ♘g3 ♔h8 17 ♘f5 ♕d7 18 ♗e4 ♖fd8 19 ♕g4 ♗f6 20 ♖ae1 ♘d4 ½-½ Agdestein-Van der Wiel, Lyons 1988.

d) 11 ♗f4 ♗d6 (11...b6 12 d5 ♘a5 13 ♗a2 exd5 14 ♘xd5 ♘xd5 15 ♗xd5 ♗b7 16 ♘c3 ♖c8 {16...♗f6! =} 17 ♗xb7 ♘xb7 18 ♕f3 ♘c5 19 ♖ad1 ♕e8 20 ♘d5 {20 ♖fe1!?} ½-½ Skembris-Grivas, Karditsa 1996; however, White holds the initiative) 12 ♕d2 ♗xf4 13 ♕xf4 b6 14 ♖ad1 ♘e7 15 ♕f3 ½-½ Balashov-Shamkovich, Baku 1972.

e) 11 ♖e1 b6 12 ♗d3 ♗b7 13 ♗c2 ♘a6 14 ♗e3 ♖c8 15 ♘f4 ♗d6 16 ♕f3 e5 17 dxe5 ♘xe5 18 ♕h3 ♘g6 = Kouatly-Danailov, France-Bulgaria 1985.

11...a6

Or:

a) 11...♕d7!? looks funny, but is nonetheless an interesting idea, with which Black intends to follow up with 12...♖d8 and ...♘d5. The one example I have found with it is quite old: 12 ♗f4 ♖d8 13 ♖ad1 ♘d5 14 ♕g3 ♘xf4 15 ♘xf4 ♗d6 (15...♘xd4 seems too risky for Black due to 16 ♘h5 g6 17

♘e4) 16 d5 exd5 17 ♖xd5 and now rather than 17...♕g4 18 ♖fd1 ± Castaldi-Plater, Hilversum Z 1947, Black should play 17...♕e7!? with good chances of equalizing.

b) 11...b6 and then:

b1) 12 ♗e3 ♗b7 13 ♖fd1 (the alternative 13 ♖ac1?! e5! is simply inferior for White, Hort-Miles, Indonesia 1982) 13...♗d6 14 h3 h6 15 ♖ac1 ♘e7 16 ♗a2 ♘ed5 17 ♗b1 ♕d7 = Letrefuilly-J.Lopez, French Cht 1998.

b2) 12 ♗g5!? transposes to note 'd211' to White's 10th move in Line C.

b3) 12 ♖d1 ♗b7 13 ♕h3 (D) and then:

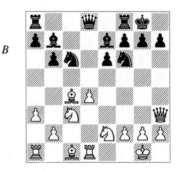

b31) 13...♘d5 14 ♗d3 g6 15 ♗h6 ♖e8 16 ♘e4 ♖c8 17 ♖ac1 ♘b8 18 ♕g3 ± Scheeren-Andersson, Wijk aan Zee 1983.

b32) 13...♖e8 has a poor reputation. 14 ♗a2 and then:

b321) 14...♘b8?! 15 ♘f4 ♗d6 16 d5 e5 17 ♘h5 ♘xh5 18 ♕xh5 ♘d7 19 ♗g5 with a big advantage for White, Petrosian-Miles, Tilburg 1981.

b322) 14...♗d6 15 ♗g5 h6 (after 15...♖c8?! 16 d5 exd5 17 ♗xd5 White has an unpleasant initiative) 16 ♗xf6

♕xf6 17 ♘e4 ♕e7 18 d5 exd5 19 ♘xd6 ♕xd6 20 ♗xd5 leaves White with a slight pull.

b323) 14...♗f8 15 ♗g5 h6 16 d5! exd5 and now 17 ♗xd5 ♕e7!? (after 17...hxg5 18 ♗xc6 ♗xc6 19 ♖xd8 ♖axd8 20 ♕g3 White is a little better thanks to his slight material advantage, D.Gurevich-Dzindzichashvili, Lone Pine 1981) 18 ♗xf6 ♕xf6 19 ♖d3 ♗e7 20 ♖ad1 ♖ae8 gives Black a playable position. However, White can improve: 17 ♖xd5!? ♕c8 (17...♕e7? runs into 18 ♗xf6 ♕xf6 19 ♖f5 +–) 18 ♕xc8 ♖axc8 19 ♗xf6 gxf6 20 ♖d7 ♖e7 21 ♖ad1 gives him a solid advantage.

b33) 13...♘a5 *(D)* and then:

b331) 14 ♗d3!? is an interesting idea that has been tested on a few occasions; e.g., 14...♖c8 15 ♗g5 g6 16 ♗h6 ♖e8 17 ♗b5 ♘c6 (17...♖c6?! 18 ♗a6 ♖c7 19 b4 ♘b7 20 ♘b5 and Black's position is pretty bad, Blees-Schüssler, Berlin 1984) 18 d5!? exd5 19 ♘xd5 ♘xd5 20 ♘c3 ♗c5 21 ♘xd5 and White has the initiative.

b332) 14 ♗a2 ♖c8 (14...♘d5 15 b4!? ♘xc3 16 ♘xc3 ♘c6 17 d5! exd5 18 ♗xd5 ♕c8, Nalepa-Jasinski, corr. 1990, and here Jasinski gives 19 ♕h5

as unclear, but after a plausible continuation such as 19...♗f6 20 ♗b2 ♘e7 21 ♖ac1 White seems to hold the better chances) 15 ♘f4 (*ECO* also mentions 15 ♖d3 ♘c4 16 b3 ♘d6 {Black might even consider playing 16...♘xa3!?, after which White has to find sufficient compensation for the pawn} 17 ♗f4 ♘de4 'unclear', but this is unconvincing because Black's position is comfortable, if not better) 15...♗d6 (15...♘c4? is answered by 16 ♘xe6! and 15...♖e8?! by 16 d5!) and here:

b3321) 16 ♘h5 ♘xh5 17 ♕xh5 ♘c4 (Chekhov-Oll, USSR 1986) and now White can try 18 d5!? exd5 (18...e5!? is mentioned by Pliester, but I think 18...g6!? is even stronger; e.g., 19 ♕f3 exd5 20 ♘xd5 ♗e5) 19 ♘xd5 ♖c5 20 ♗xc4 ♖xc4 21 ♗g5 f6 with chances for both sides – Chekhov.

b3322) 16 d5 ♗xf4 (16...exd5 17 ♘fxd5 ♘xd5 18 ♘xd5 ♘c4 19 ♘e3 ♘xe3 20 ♗xe3 ♕e7 = Glek-Gagarin, Moscow 1989) 17 dxe6?! (here Chekhov gives 17 ♗xf4 ♘xd5 18 ♗b1 f5 as 'unclear') 17...♕c7 18 exf7+ ♔h8 19 ♘b5 ♕b8 20 ♗xf4 ♕xf4 21 ♘xa7 (21 ♘d4 has also been suggested, but 21...♘e4! leaves White with inadequate compensation) and now 21...♖c5 is entirely possible, since 22 b4? loses to 22...♖g5!, while Black can also counterattack with 21...♖c2!, leaving White to exchange queens with 22 ♕g3 ♕xg3 23 hxg3 and now 23...♖xb2 asks White why he sacrificed the piece.

12 ♗a2

Or:

a) 12 ♗g5 transposes to note 'd212' to White's 10th move in Line C.

b) 12 ♖d1 b5 13 ♗a2 b4 (alternatively, 13...♗b7 14 ♗g5 ♘d5 15 ♗xd5 exd5 {15...♗xg5!?} 16 ♗xe7 ♘xe7 17 ♘c1 ♗c6 18 ♘b3 ♘c8 19 ♘c5 ♘d6 20 ♖e1 ± Lein-Christiansen, USA Ch (Greenville) 1983) 14 ♘e4 (after 14 ♘a4? ♕a5 15 ♗b3 ♕b5! White faces major difficulties on the queenside, Chekhov-Dorfman, Lvov 1984) 14...a5 15 ♗b1 g6 16 axb4 ♘xb4 17 ♕f3 ♖a7 18 ♗h6 ♖e8 19 ♗f4 ♗b7 with an equal position, Mester-Sarosi, Hungarian Cht 1998.

Now (after 12 ♗a2):

a) 12...♘e5!? 13 ♕d1 ♘g6!? (the line 13...♘c6 14 ♕d3 ♘e5 15 ♕d1, with a draw to come, has been tried more than once; e.g., Podgaets-Chernin, Sverdlovsk 1984) 14 ♘f4 ♕d6 15 ♘xg6 hxg6 16 ♗e3 ♖d8 17 b4 ♗f8 18 ♕f3 ♗d7 19 d5 exd5 20 ♗f4 ♕e6 21 ♗c7 ♖dc8 22 ♘xd5 with an initiative for White, V.Kostić-Barlov, Vrnjačka Banja 1982.

b) 12...b5 13 ♗g5 b4 (13...♘e5!? 14 ♕h3 ♘c4 is another interesting option) 14 ♗b1 g6 15 axb4 ♘xb4 16 ♕d2 ♖a7 17 ♘a4 a5 18 ♘c5 ♗a6 19 ♖d1 ♗c4 with chances for both sides, Vaganian-Ki.Georgiev, Lvov 1984.

C2)

10...♗d6 *(D)*

This non-standard move doesn't do anything with respect to blocking White's IQP's march to d5. However, on d6, it is an excellent blockading piece: it helps control some important central squares and points directly towards the white king. Black's idea is in fact to push his own e-pawn ...e5-e4 regardless of what White is doing with his d-pawn. By doing so, Black hopes

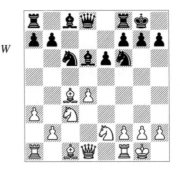

to gain the initiative on the kingside. Statistically, this approach has also paid off: Black has scored 67% with 10...♗d6.

11 ♕d3

As we have seen in several of the other lines, this is more or less the standard set-up. But on occasion, White tries something different:

a) 11 f4? prevents Black from playing 11...e5, but unforgivably weakens the light squares: 11...♘e7 12 ♘g3 ♗d7 13 ♘ce4 ♘xe4 14 ♘xe4 ♗c6 15 ♗d3 ♗c7 ∓ Schulze-Ionov, Dortmund 1992.

b) 11 ♗a2 b6 12 ♕d3 ♗b7 13 ♖d1 ♖c8 (13...♘e7!? is another worthwhile idea; e.g., 14 ♗g5 ♘g6 15 ♕h3 h6 16 ♗e3 ♖e8 17 ♖ac1 ♖c8 18 ♗b1 ♘f8 19 ♘f4 ♘8h7 20 ♘h5 ♘xh5 21 ♕xh5 ♘f6 22 ♕h3 ♗f8 with at least equal chances for Black, Stanec-Hjartarson, Moscow OL 1994) 14 ♘g3 g6 15 ♘ge4 ♘xe4 16 ♕xe4 ♘a5 17 ♕g4 ♕f6 18 ♘e4 ♗xe4 19 ♕xe4 ♖fd8 and Black has again obtained a very agreeable position, Agdestein-de Firmian, Oslo 1984.

c) 11 h3 and here:

c1) 11...h6 12 ♗e3 ♘e7 13 ♗d3 ♘ed5 14 ♗c2 ♗d7 15 ♘xd5 ♘xd5 16

♕d3 ½-½ Høi-N.J.Fries Nielsen, Danish Ch (Aalborg) 1989.

c2) 11...b6 12 ♗g5 ♗e7 13 ♕d3 h6 14 ♗h4 ♗b7 15 ♖ad1 ♘d5 16 ♗g3 ♗f6 17 ♘e4 ♗e7 18 ♘4c3 ♗f6 (Korchnoi-Salov, Madrid 1996) and here Salov gives 19 ♘e4 (repeating) as White's best.

11...e5

Amongst the alternatives, these moves are the most important:

a) 11...a6!? is seen very rarely, but deserves attention; e.g., 12 ♗b3 ♕c7 13 ♗c2 h6 14 ♘g3 ♖d8 15 ♗e3 b5 with a good game for Black, E.Pedersen-Larsen, Danish Ch (Åbybro) 1952.

b) 11...b6 12 ♖d1 ♗b7 (12...h6!? 13 ♘e4 ♗b7 14 ♘xd6 ♕xd6 15 ♗f4 ♕d7 16 ♕h3 ♘d5, Korchnoi-Ivanchuk, Yalta rpd 1995, and here 17 ♕g3!? leaves everything open) 13 ♕h3 ♘a5 14 ♗a2 ♖c8 15 ♗g5 h6 (after 15...♗e7, White can obtain an edge: 16 ♘f4 ♘d5 17 ♗xe7 ♘xe7 18 d5 exd5 19 ♘fxd5 ♘xd5 20 ♘xd5 ♗xd5 21 ♗xd5 ± Ki.Georgiev-Short, Lvov 1984) 16 ♗h4 ♘c4 17 ♘b5 ♗b8 18 ♖ac1 (Ki.Georgiev-Langeweg, Amsterdam 1985) and here according to Georgiev Black can maintain the balance with 18...♘xb2 19 ♖xc8 ♗xc8 20 ♖d2 ♘a4 21 ♕b3 a6 22 ♕xa4 axb5 23 ♕xb5.

12 d5 e4!?

As described above, Black pushes his e-pawn forward and opens lines for his pieces, minor as well as major.

13 ♘xe4 ♘e5 14 ♕d4 ♘xe4 15 ♕xe4 ♗g4 *(D)*

Black may also consider 15...♖e8!? 16 ♘g3 ♘g4 17 ♕c2 ♗d7 18 ♗e2 ♖c8 19 ♕d1 ♕h4 20 ♗xg4 ♗xg4 21 ♕a4 b5!?. Here White went astray

with 22 ♕xb5? ♗e2! and soon lost in Flear-Grooten, Copenhagen 1983. The proposed improvement 22 ♕xa7 'with unclear play' doesn't ring right after 22...♗e2! either, as 23 ♖e1? can be answered by 23...♗c5, after which White has to give up his queen since otherwise 24...♗xf2+ 25 ♔xf2 ♕d4+ mates. Best seems 22 ♕a6!?, which should leave White with good chances of obtaining a long-term advantage.

White now has several options to choose from and many ways to go wrong:

a) 16 f3? f5 17 ♕c2 ♖c8 18 b3 b5 19 fxg4 bxc4 20 b4 ♘xg4 21 ♘f4 ♕f6 22 ♖a2 ♖fe8 and White is in trouble, Petran-Herzog, Budapest 1982.

b) 16 f4? ♘xc4 17 ♕xc4 ♖c8 is much better for Black, Meulders-Kasparov, Brussels 1987.

c) 16 ♗d3?! (Bareev-Podlesnik, Ljubljana 1989) 16...g6 17 ♘g3 f5 18 ♕d4 f4 19 ♘e4 ♘f3+! 20 gxf3 ♗xf3 21 ♗d2 ♖f5 22 ♗c3 ♗e5 −+ Bareev.

d) 16 ♘g3 f5 17 ♕d4 h5! 18 ♔h1 (18 h3 h4 19 hxg4 hxg3 is dangerous for White) 18...h4 19 ♘e2 (Borbjerggaard-Engqvist, Stockholm 1996) and here Engqvist gives 19...♖c7!?:

d1) 20 f3?! ♕xc4 21 ♕xc4 ♘xc4 22 fxg4 fxg4 was assessed by Engqvist as clearly better for Black, but this seems somewhat exaggerated as 23 ♗f4 ♖ae8 24 ♗xd6 ♖xf1+ 25 ♖xf1 ♘xd6 26 ♘f4 leaves Black at the very best with a slight edge.

d2) White may consider 20 ♗b5 a6 21 f3 axb5 22 fxg4 ♘xg4 23 ♗f4, when he appears to be doing quite well.

e) 16 ♗f4 f5! (16...♘xc4 17 ♗xd6 ♕xd6 18 ♕xc4 ♗xe2 ½-½ Haugseth-Stigar, corr. 1989) 17 ♕d4 ♘xc4 18 f3 *(D)* and now:

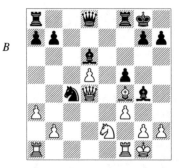

e1) 18...♖c8 19 ♗xd6 ♘xd6 20 fxg4 ♖c4 21 ♕xa7 ♖xg4 22 h3 is given as unclear by Van der Wiel, but after 22...♖e4 23 ♘f4 White seems comfortably better.

e2) 18...♘xa3?! 19 ♗xd6 ♘b5 20 ♕b4 ♘xd6 21 fxg4 ♖e8 22 ♘g3! fxg4

23 ♕xg4 ♕b6+ 24 ♔h1 ♕xb2 25 ♘h5 ♖e7 26 ♘f6+ ♔h8 27 ♘xh7 ♕e2 (Sakharov-Vaiser, Stavropol 1985) and here 28 ♕g6 gives White an ongoing attack.

e3) 18...♘a5! 19 ♗xd6 ♕xd6 20 fxg4(?) is given as '±' in *ECO*, but Black has 20...♘b3!, which puts a question mark not only to this little line, but also White's play after 11...e5.

17 Rubinstein Variation

1 d4 ♘f6 2 c4 e6 3 ♘c3 ♗b4 4 e3 c5 5 ♘e2 *(D)*

The Rubinstein Variation in the Rubinstein Nimzo-Indian... It sounds a little too much, but this variation was invented at a later date than the Rubinstein complex itself. It was first tried out in the game Rubinstein-Maroczy, Hamburg OL 1930, which was won by Rubinstein in just 25 moves.

Just like in the Reshevsky Variation, White wants to avoid the doubled c-pawns.

5...cxd4

Other moves:

a) 5...b6 is covered in Line A of Chapter 11.

b) 5...0-0 transposes to note 'd' to Black's 5th move in Chapter 10.

c) 5...♘e4 has the reputation of being a solid move:

c1) 6 ♗d2 ♘xd2 7 ♕xd2 b6 (after 7...cxd4 8 exd4, 8...d5 9 c5 transposes to Line B2, while 8...0-0 9 c5 is note

'c' to White's 7th move in Line A) 8 a3 ♗a5 9 ♖b1 ♘a6 10 g3 ♗b7 11 d5 0-0 12 ♗g2 e5 13 0-0 d6 14 e4 ♗c8 15 f4 f6 16 ♕e3 ± Garcia Palermo-Garcia Gonzalez, Havana 1983.

c2) 6 ♕c2 cxd4 (6...f5 7 a3 ♗xc3+ 8 ♘xc3 ♘xc3 9 ♕xc3 ♕f6 10 ♗d2 is somewhat better for White) 7 exd4 d5 8 a3 ♘xc3 9 ♘xc3 ♗e7 (9...♗xc3+ also leads to problems for Black: 10 bxc3 ♘c6 11 ♖b1! 0-0 12 ♗d3 h6 13 0-0 b6 14 cxd5 ♕xd5 15 ♖b5 ♕d7 16 ♖h5 ♗b7 17 ♖e1, M.Gurevich-Yudasin, Lvov 1984, and here Black's best move 17...♘e7 is met with 18 ♗f4! ± followed by ♗e5 – Chernin/Gurevich) 10 cxd5 exd5 11 ♘xd5 ♘c6 12 ♘xe7 ♘xd4 13 ♕c3 ♕xe7+ 14 ♗e3 ♘e6 15 ♗e2 0-0 16 0-0 ± Borik-Miles, Bundesliga 1981/2.

d) 5...♘c6 6 a3 ♗xc3+ (6...cxd4 7 exd4 ♗xc3+ 8 ♘xc3 d5 transposes to note 'b' to Black's 8th move in Line B11) 7 ♘xc3 and then:

d1) 7...cxd4 8 exd4 d5 is again note 'b' to Black's 8th move in Line B11.

d2) 7...d6 8 d5 ♘e7 9 ♗e2 (another idea is 9 dxe6!?) 9...0-0 10 0-0 a6 11 a4 exd5 12 cxd5 ± Züger-Kovačević, Geneva 1988.

d3) 7...b6 8 d5 ♘e5 9 e4 0-0 10 ♗e2 exd5 11 cxd5 d6 12 0-0 ♗g4 13 f3 ♗d7 14 ♗g5 ± Estremera Panos-Moreno Latorre, Zaragoza 1999.

e) 5...d6 is a fairly rare continuation that is occasionally tried by GMs, most recently Winants and Chiburdanidze. White's best moves are:

e1) 6 dxc5 dxc5 7 ♕xd8+ ♔xd8 8 ♗d2 ♔e7 9 ♘f4 (intending ♘d3) 9...b6 10 a3 ♗a5?! 11 b4 cxb4 12 axb4 ♗xb4 13 ♘cd5+ ♘xd5 14 ♘xd5+ exd5 15 ♗xb4+ with an ongoing initiative, Smyslov-Stoltz, Bucharest 1953.

e2) 6 a3 ♗a5 (6...♗xc3+ is a bit passive: 7 ♘xc3 0-0 8 ♗e2 ♕e7 9 0-0 e5 10 b4 ± Shulman-Voloshin, Pardubice 1996) and here:

e21) 7 ♖b1 0-0 (7...♘c6 8 b4 ♗c7 9 g3 a5?! {9...0-0 10 ♗g2 ± ECO} 10 bxc5 dxc5 11 ♗g2 cxd4 12 exd4 0-0 13 0-0 ± Evans-Keres, San Antonio 1972) 8 b4 ♗c7 9 ♘g3 ♘bd7 (or 9...cxb4 10 axb4 a5!? 11 b5 {11 ♗d2 is worse in view of 11...axb4 12 ♖xb4 e5 with ...♗a5 to come} 11...b6 12 e4 ♗b7 and while Black's position is a bit cramped at this point, it has dynamic potential) 10 ♗e2 a6 (10...cxd4!?) 11 0-0 ± Saidy-Bronstein, Tallinn 1971.

e22) 7 g3 0-0 (7...d5 8 dxc5 dxc4 9 ♕xd8+ ♗xd8 10 ♘d4 ♘bd7 11 ♗xc4 ♘xc5 ±) 8 ♗g2 ♘c6 9 0-0 ♗d7 10 b3 ♕e7 11 ♗b2 ♖fd8 12 ♘f4 ♖ab8 13 ♘h5 ♗e8 14 ♘xf6+ ♕xf6 15 ♘e4 ♕g6 16 d5 ♘e7 17 a4 exd5 18 cxd5 ♗d7 ½-½ G.Georgadze-Garcia Ilundain, Ampuriabrava 1997.

f) 5...d5 usually just transposes to the main lines covered below; here we will look at the exceptions. 6 a3 *(D)* and now:

f1) 6...cxd4 7 axb4! (7 exd4 is Line B1) 7...dxc3 8 ♘xc3 dxc4 (8...0-0 transposes to note 'd2' to Black's 5th move in Chapter 10) 9 ♕xd8+ ♔xd8 10 ♗xc4 ♘bd7 11 0-0 ♔e7 12 e4 b6 13 f3 ± Uhlmann-Larsen, East Germany-Denmark 1957.

B

f2) 6...♗xc3+ 7 ♘xc3 cxd4 8 exd4 transposes to Line B11.

f3) 6...♗a5 is comparable to the lines discussed in Chapter 3. White has two options:

f31) 7 cxd5 ♘xd5 8 ♗d2 cxd4 9 ♘xd5 ♕xd5 10 ♗xa5 (10 ♕a4+ ♘c6 11 ♗xa5 ♕xa5+ 12 ♕xa5 ♘xa5 13 ♘xd4 ♗d7 = Veresagin-Tunik, Krasnodar 1998) 10...♕xa5+ 11 b4 ♕g5 12 h4 ♕e7 13 ♘xd4 0-0 = Wade-Donner, Havana 1964.

f32) 7 dxc5 dxc4 8 ♕xd8+ ♔xd8 (in Aleksandrov-Tunik, St Petersburg 1998, Black instead went for 8...♗xd8 and after 9 ♘d4 ♘bd7 10 c6 ♘e5 11 ♘cb5 0-0 12 ♘d6 ♗a5+ 13 ♗d2 c3 {13...♗xd2+ 14 ♔xd2 ♘xc6 is also worth looking into} 14 ♗xc3 ♗xc3+ 15 bxc3 ♘xc6 16 ♘xc6 bxc6, the chances were about even) 9 ♗d2 e5 10 ♘e4 ♘c6 11 ♘2c3 (11 ♘2g3 ♗xd2+ 12 ♔xd2 ♘a5 13 ♔c3 ♘d5+ 14 ♔c2 ♔e7 15 ♘d6 ♗e6 16 ♘gf5+ ♔f8 with approximately equal chances, D.Gurevich-L.Schneider, Reykjavik 1982) 11...♗xc3 12 ♘xc3 ♗e6 13 f3 ♘d7 14 ♘e4 f5 15 ♘d6 ♘xc5 16 ♘xc4 ♘b3 17 ♖d1 ♘xd2 18 ♘xd2 ♔e7 19 ♗c4 ♖ac8 20 ♗xe6 ♔xe6 21 ♔e2 ½-½ Lautier-Tkachev, Enghien-les-Bains 2001.

6 exd4 *(D)*

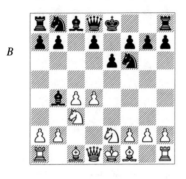

Now:
A: 6...0-0   268
B: 6...d5   278

Several other things have been tried at this juncture, but these two are the most interesting:

a) 6...♘e4 7 a3!? ♘xc3 8 ♘xc3 ♗xc3+ 9 bxc3 b6 10 ♕f3 ♘c6 11 d5 ± Korchnoi-Timman, Las Palmas 1981.

b) 6...a6 7 a3 ♗e7 8 g3! 0-0 9 ♗g2 d6 10 0-0 ♘bd7 (Lautier-Short, Tallinn/Pärnu 1998) 11 h3, intending ♗e3, gives White a pleasant edge – Short.

A)

6...0-0 7 a3

7 c5!? is a very recent idea of Scherbakov's that so far has fared quite well. The idea is to take charge of the dark squares.

a) 7...d5 transposes to note 'b' to Black's 7th move in Line B2.

b) 7...d6 8 a3 ♗xc3+ 9 ♘xc3 dxc5 10 dxc5 ♕c7 (after 10...♕xd1+!?, 11 ♘xd1 ♘bd7 12 ♗e3 ♘d5 appears pleasant for Black, so 11 ♔xd1!? may be White's best) 11 ♕d6 ♕xd6 12 cxd6 ♖d8 13 ♘b5 ♘c6 14 ♗g5 and

the passed d-pawn provides White with a solid advantage, Sadler-Van der Sterren, Wattenschied 2000.

c) 7...♘e4!? 8 ♗d2 ♘xd2 9 ♕xd2 d6 10 a3 ♗xc3 11 ♘xc3 b6 12 ♘b5?! (12 ♕f4!? =) 12...dxc5 13 dxc5 ♘d7 leaves Black with a lead in development, Lesiège-Macieja, Elbow Beach 2001.

7...♗e7 *(D)*

Now:
A1: 8 ♘f4   269
A2: 8 d5   273

Also seen with some frequency are:

a) 8 ♘g3 is quite tame: 8...d5 9 ♗e3 b6 10 ♗e2 ♗a6 11 cxd5 ♗xe2 12 ♕xe2 ♘xd5 and Black has a pleasing position, T.Plachetka-Frolov, Trnava 1989.

b) 8 g3 d5 (8...a6 transposes to note 'b' to Black's 6th move) 9 cxd5 (9 c5 is probably better, but transposes via 9...b6 10 b4 to Line B12) 9...♘xd5 10 ♗g2 ♘xc3 11 bxc3 (11 ♘xc3?! ♗f6 12 ♗e3 ♘c6 13 ♗xc6 bxc6 14 0-0 a5 is a clear failure for White, Gyimesi-Shipov, Budapest 1992) 11...♘c6 12 0-0 ♘a5 (12...♗d7 13 ♘f4 ♖c8 14 d5 exd5 15 ♘xd5 ♗e6 16 ♗f4 ♗f6 17

置b1 ②a5 18 ②xf6+ 豐xf6 19 豐d4 豐xd4 20 cxd4 b6 ± Borik-Kinder-mann, Bundesliga 1982/3) and now:

b1) 13 置b1 ②d7 14 c4 (14 ②f4 is line 'b3') 14...②xc4 15 置xb7 ②a5 16 置b1 置b8 17 置xb8 豐xb8 18 d5 e5 is slightly better for Black, Hébert-Vag-anian, Toronto 1990.

b2) 13 ②e4 ②d7 14 豐d3 h6 15 c4 置c8 16 c5 ②c6 17 置b1 b6 with a pleasant game for Black, Hraček-Stohl, Stary Smokovec 1990.

b3) 13 ②f4 ②d7 14 置b1 置c8 15 置e1 b6 16 d5 ②c5!? 17 豐h5 ②c4 18 dxe6 ②xe6 19 ②xe6 fxe6 20 ②f4 ②xf2+!? 21 ②xf2 置c5 22 豐g4 e5 ∓ Korchnoi-Greenfeld, Beersheba 1997.

b4) 13 ②f4!? ②d7 14 c4 (14 豐c2!?) 14...置c8 (my silicon friend suggests 14...g5!?; e.g., 15 ②c1 ②xc4 16 ②xb7 置b8 17 ②g2 豐a5 with an edge for Black) 15 c5 ②c6 16 ②xc6 ②xc6 17 置b1 b6 again with a good game for Black, Korchnoi-H.Olafsson, Reykja-vik 2000.

A1)
8 ②f4 *(D)*

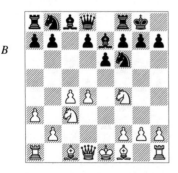

8...d5
Or:

a) 8...b6?! 9 ②e2 ②b7 10 d5! 置e8 11 0-0 ②f8 12 ②e3 d6 13 豐d2 e5 14 ②d3 ②bd7 15 f4 ± Kristinsson-Bjar-nason, Reykjavik 1984.

b) 8...置e8!? 9 ②e3 d6 10 ②e2 ②bd7 11 0-0 ②f8 12 b4 ②g6 13 豐b3 ②h4 14 置ad1 ②d7 15 f3 b6 16 ②f2 ②g6 17 ②xg6 hxg6 = Bu Xiangzhi-Short, Reykjavik 2000.

c) 8...d6 has a solid reputation:

c1) 9 ②e3 ②bd7 (9...e5!? is possi-bly better: 10 dxe5 dxe5 11 豐xd8 置xd8 12 ②fd5 ②xd5 13 ②xd5 ②c6 14 0-0-0 ②f8 = V.Milov-Beliavsky, Leon Echt 2001) 10 ②e2 a6 11 0-0 豐c7 12 置c1 b6 13 b4 ②b7 14 d5 e5 15 ②d3 置ac8 with a spatial advantage for White, but Black's position is very solid, Gulko-Fedorowicz, USA Ch (Seattle) 2002.

c2) 9 ②e2 is the most common move:

c21) 9...置e8 10 0-0 ②f8 11 ②e3 g6 12 置c1 a6 13 c5 (13 b4!? ± Kas-parov) 13...②g7 14 ②a4 ②c6 15 ②b6 置b8 16 b4 d5 17 豐b3 g5 18 ②h3 h6 19 置cd1 leads to an advantage for White, G.Georgadze-Kasparov, Debre-cen Echt 1992.

c22) 9...a6 10 ②e3 ②bd7 11 b4 b6 12 0-0 ②b7 13 豐b3 置e8 14 置ac1 ②f8 15 ②a4 ②6d7 16 置fd1 ②g6 17 ②xg6 hxg6 with a solid position for Black, but with more space for White, Gutov-Tunik, St Petersburg 1998.

c23) 9...e5 10 ②fd5 (10 dxe5 dxe5 11 ②fd5 ②xd5 12 cxd5 a6 13 0-0 f5 14 ②e3 ②d6 15 b4 ②d7 is equal, Bareev-Dorfman, Bundesliga 2000/1) 10...②xd5 11 ②xd5 ②c6 12 dxe5 dxe5 13 ②e3 ②g5 14 0-0 ②xe3 15 ②xe3 豐g5 = Hort-Van der Wiel, Amsterdam 1983.

9 cxd5

This way of fixing the pawn-structure makes the most sense in this position. Alternatively, White has played 9 ♗e3, which usually leads to transpositions after 9...♘c6:

a) 10 cxd5 ♘xd5 11 ♘cxd5 exd5 12 ♗d3 ♗f6 (12...♗g5 13 0-0 is note 'a' to Black's 12th move) 13 0-0 transposes to the main line.

b) 10 ♗e2 dxc4 11 ♗xc4 e5!? 12 dxe5 ♘xe5 13 ♗e2 ♘eg4 14 ♕xd8 ♖xd8 and Black has grabbed the initiative, Liavdansky-Sanakoev, corr. 1997.

9...♘xd5 *(D)*

The immediate 9...exd5?! leaves Black with more problems: 10 ♗e2 ♗f5 (10...♘c6 11 0-0 ♖e8 12 ♗f3 ♗e6, S.Bekker Jensen-E.Berg, Aviles jr Wch 2000, 13 ♘xe6 fxe6 14 ♖e1 ±) 11 g4!? ♗e6 12 ♗f3 ♘c6 13 0-0 ♗d6 14 ♖e1 ♕b6 15 g5 ♗xf4 16 ♗xf4 ♕xd4 (Keene-Karlsson, Esbjerg 1981) and here *ECO* gives 17 ♗g3 ♘d7 18 ♘xd5 ♘de5 19 ♗g2! ±.

10 ♘cxd5

The exchange on d5 should be made with this knight as his colleague on f4 is better placed, putting pressure on d5

as well as contributing to kingside play. Other moves:

a) 10 ♗c4?! makes no sense and immediately leaves White scrambling to equalize: 10...♘xc3 11 bxc3 ♕c7 12 ♕d3 ♘d7 13 ♗a2 ♘f6 14 ♘e2 b6 15 ♗f4 ♕c6 ∓ Alzata-Yusupov, Thessaloniki OL 1984.

b) 10 ♘fxd5 exd5 11 ♕b3 (11 ♗d3 leads to a nearly symmetrical position and equal chances) 11...♘c6 12 ♗e3 ♗f6 13 ♕xd5 ♗e6! 14 ♕e4 ♖e8 15 ♗d3 g6 and Black has seized the initiative, M.Gurevich-Van den Doel, 2nd Bundesliga 1998/9.

10...exd5 11 ♗d3

11 ♗e2 is more timid. Black should not then experience any major problems:

a) 11...♘c6 12 ♗f3 ♗e6 13 0-0 ♗g5 14 b4 ♗xf4 15 ♗xf4 transposes to line 'b'.

b) 11...♗g5 12 0-0 ♘c6 13 ♗f3 ♗xf4 14 ♗xf4 ♗e6 15 b4 ♕b6 16 ♗e3 a5 = Varga-Adorjan, Hungarian Ch (Budapest) 1993.

11...♘c6

11...♗f6 12 0-0 ♘c6 transposes to the main line, while 11...♗g5 12 0-0 ♘c6 is the note to Black's 12th move.

12 0-0 *(D)*

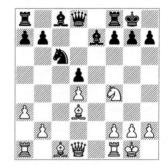

12...♗f6

Black has a popular alternative in 12...♗g5. His aim is to liquidate the f4-knight, which is causing some pain by constantly threatening the d5-pawn. Although the position is fairly open, the strength of the bishop-pair is relatively minor in this type of position. White's two main options are then:

a) 13 ♗e3 ♗xf4 14 ♗xf4 ♕f6 (the move 14...♕b6!? is suggested in *ECO*, and is yet to tested, but there doesn't seem to be any obvious way to prove an advantage against it) and now:

a1) 15 ♕h5 is *ECO*'s recommendation, but after 15...g6 16 ♗e5, rather than 16...♕e7 17 ♕d1 ♘xe5 18 ♖e1 ± Cebalo-Velimirović, Yugoslav Ch (Subotica) 1984, Black should play 16...♕e6!?. Then 17 ♕d1 ♘xe5 18 ♖e1 can be answered with 18...f6 19 f4? ♕b6!.

a2) 15 ♗e3 ♗f5 16 ♗e2 (neither 16 ♗b5 a6 17 ♗xc6 ♕xc6 ½-½ Gelfand-Anand, Shenyang 2000, nor 16 ♖c1 ♗xd3 17 ♕xd3 ♖fe8 18 ♕b5 ♘xd4 19 ♗xd4 ♕xd4 20 ♖fd1 ♕f6 ½-½ Kozlov-Aseev, Frunze 1988, creates a lasting impression) 16...♖fe8 17 ♖e1 h6 18 ♖c1 ♖ad8 19 ♕d2 a6 20 b4 ♕g6 (20...♖c8!?) 21 a4 (G.Georgadze-Supatashvili, Panormo Z 1998) and now 21...♖c8 is roughly equal.

b) 13 ♖e1 and then:

b1) 13...♗xf4 makes less sense now that White hasn't invested a tempo in ♗e3. White is better after 14 ♗xf4 ♕f6 (14...♕h4 15 ♗e3 ♗e6 16 ♕d2 ♕f6 17 f3 ♗f5 18 ♗f1 h6 19 b4 ± Epishin-Khenkin, Bundesliga 2000/1) 15 ♗e5 ♘xe5 16 ♖xe5 ♗e6 17 ♕d2 ♖ad8 18 ♖ae1 h6 19 ♖1e3, Kramnik-Leko, Budapest rpd 2001.

b2) 13...h6 14 ♗c2 ♕d6 15 g3!? ♖d8 16 h4 ♗xf4 17 ♗xf4 ♕f6 18 ♗c7 ♗e6! 19 ♗e5 (Black offers, and White declines, the chance to win the exchange, thanks to the numerous weak squares surrounding the white king) 19...♘xe5 20 dxe5 ♕e7 21 ♕d3 g6 22 ♕d4 ½-½ Khalifman-Anand, New Delhi FIDE 2000. A somewhat premature decision if you ask me.

b3) 13...♕d6 is preferred by *ECO* and may also be the best move: 14 ♘e6!? (14 ♕h5 h6 15 ♘e2 ♕e7 16 ♗xg5 ♕xg5 17 ♕xg5 hxg5 18 ♗b5 ♗d7 19 f4 gxf4 20 ♘xf4 a6 21 ♗xc6 ♗xc6 ½-½ Chiburdanidze-Supatashvili, Perm 1997) 14...♗xe6 15 ♗xg5 ♕d7 16 ♖c1 ♖fe8 (16...a6!? Psakhis) 17 ♗b5 ♗f5 18 ♖xe8+ ♖xe8 19 b4 ♖c8! = I.Sokolov-Epishin, Groningen FIDE 1997.

13 ♗e3 g6 *(D)*

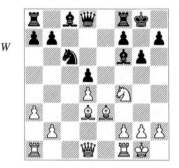

14 ♖c1

Aside from this logical continuation, White has some other interesting moves available:

a) 14 ♗c2 ♕d6 (other moves like 14...♖e8 and 14...b6 are also fully playable) 15 ♕d2 a5 16 ♗b3 ♘e7 17 ♖ac1 b6 18 ♖c3 ♗b7 19 ♖fc1 ♖ac8 and Black has neutralized White's initiative, Beliavsky-Ljubojević, Madrid 1988.

b) 14 ♗b5 ♘e7 15 ♖c1 ♘f5 16 ♖c5 ♗e6 17 ♗d3 ♘xe3 18 fxe3 ♗e7 19 ♖c2 ♕d7 20 ♕f3 ♖ac8 = Sloth-Bang, corr. 1970.

c) 14 ♗b1 ♕d6 15 ♕d2 ♘e7 16 ♗a2 ♗e6 17 ♖ac1 ♖ac8 18 ♘e2 ♘f5 19 ♗f4 ♕e7 = G.Georgadze-Smagin, Amantea 1995.

14...♗g7 (D)

Alternatively:

a) 14...♗e6?! 15 ♘xe6 fxe6 16 ♕g4 ♕e7 17 ♖fe1 ♕f7 18 ♗b5 ♖ac8 19 ♗xc6 ♖xc6 20 ♖xc6 bxc6 21 b4 with a solid advantage for White, G.Georgadze-Egiazarian, Erevan OL 1996.

b) 14...♕d6 15 ♖c5 (15 ♗b1 ♗e6 16 ♖e1 ♖fe8 17 ♕d2 ♖ac8 doesn't grant White much of an edge, Timman-Ravi, Antwerp 2000) 15...♗e6 (15...♗xd4?! is risky; e.g., 16 ♖xd5 ♕f6 17 ♗xd4 ♘xd4 18 ♗xg6 ♘e6 19 ♖f5 and Black is in severe trouble) 16 ♘xe6 and then:

b1) 16...♕xe6 17 ♗b5 ♘e7 (alternatively, 17...♖ac8 =) 18 ♖e1 ♕b6 19 b4 a5 20 bxa5 ♕xa5 21 a4 ♖fd8 22 g4 is slightly better for White, Babula-J.Hall, Panormo ECC 2001.

b2) 16...fxe6 17 ♕a4 (17 ♕g4 has proved harmless since after 17...e5!, White's best is to take a draw with 18 ♗xg6 hxg6 19 ♕xg6+ ♔h8 20 ♕h5+ ♔g8 = Psakhis) 17...♘xd4 18 ♗xd4 ♕f4 19 ♕d7 ♗xd4 20 ♕xe6+ ♔h8 21 ♖c2 ♖ad8 22 g3 ♕f3 23 ♕e2 ♖de8 and Black has at least equalized, G.Georgadze-Gomez Esteban, Elgoibar 1997.

15 ♖c5

W

This move is White's most frequent choice in this position, but it is not necessarily his best. There are two very interesting alternatives:

a) 15 ♗b1 is a recent idea of Timman's: 15...♘e7 16 ♖e1 ♖e8 17 ♕f3 ♕b6?! (17...♗f5!? seems to equalize, although it isn't mentioned by Timman in his analysis in *Informator*; e.g., 18 ♗xf5 ♘xf5 and the weak pawns on d4 and d5 balance each other out) 18 b4 ♗e6 19 h4 (19 ♘xe6!? Timman) 19...♗d7 20 ♗a2 with a solid advantage for White, Timman-Anand, Wijk aan Zee 2000.

b) 15 ♗b5 ♘e7 16 ♕b3 ♕b6 (the idea 16...a6 17 ♗e2 ♕d6!? is worth considering) 17 ♕b4 ♗f6 18 ♕c5 ♕xc5 19 ♖xc5 with a small but clear advantage for White, Gligorić-Matanović, Tel-Aviv 1966.

15...♘e7 16 ♕b3 b6 17 ♖c3 ♕d6

Or 17...♗f5 18 ♗xf5 ♘xf5 19 ♘xd5 ♘xd4 20 ♗xd4 ♗xd4 21 ♖d3 ♗g7 22 ♖e1 ♕h4 23 g3 ♕h3 24 ♖e4 ± Paramos-Eslon, Zaragoza 1996.

18 ♖fc1 ♗xd4 19 ♗xd4 ♕xf4 20 ♗e3

White achieves less after the alternative 20 ♕b4 ♘f5 21 ♗f6 ♕xb4 22 axb4 ♗d7 23 ♗a6 ♖ae8 24 ♖c7 ♗a4

25 ♖xa7 ♖e6, Lautier-P.Nikolić, Moscow 2001. White has won his pawn back, but most of his initiative has vanished; the chances are about even.

20...♕d6 21 ♖c7 d4 22 ♗h6 ♗e6 23 ♕a4 ♖fd8 24 h3

White's excellently coordinated pieces give him full compensation for the pawn, Paramos-Nava, Spanish Ch (Cordoba) 1995.

A2)

8 d5 (D)

This line was played a few times by the young Kasparov, but is quite unpopular nowadays. At the expense of his development, White increases his space advantage.

8...exd5

This is played almost exclusively, but on rare occasions Black tries the more passive 8...d6; for example, 9 ♘g3 e5 10 ♗d3 ♘bd7 11 0-0 ♘e8 12 f4 exf4 13 ♗xf4 and White's position is clearly preferable, Guliev-Gaprindashvili, Moscow 1998.

9 cxd5 ♖e8

When I was younger, I didn't understand this invitation from Black to kick the bishop back to f8. However,

what I didn't realize was just how vulnerable the pawn becomes once at d6. If this invitation is not to your taste, Black has two alternatives:

a) 9...d6!? 10 ♘d4 ♘bd7 (10...♖e8 isn't as accurate: 11 ♗e2 ♘bd7 12 0-0 a6, Lautier-Andersson, Malmö 1998, 13 h3 ♗f8 14 ♗g5 ♘e5 15 f4!? ♘ed7 16 ♔h1 ± Lautier) 11 ♗e2 ♘b6 12 ♗f3 ♖e8 13 0-0 ♗f8 14 ♕d3 ♘bd7 15 ♗f4 ♘e5 and Black has equalized, Saborido-O'Kelly, Malaga 1966.

b) 9...♗c5 takes the bishop out on open grass again:

b1) 10 ♘d4 d6 11 ♗e2 a6 12 0-0 ♘bd7 13 ♗g5 ♖e8 14 b4 (14 ♘b3 ♗a7 15 ♘d2 h6 16 ♗h4 ♘e5 17 ♘de4 g5 18 ♘xf6+ ♕xf6 19 ♗g3 ♗f5 20 ♔h1 ♘g6 and Black has at least equalized, Sadler-Short, British Ch (Torquay) 1998) 14...♗a7 15 ♖c1 (15 h3 h6 16 ♗h4 ♘f8 17 ♕d3 ♘g6 18 ♗g3 ♘e5 is comfortable for Black, Volkov-Yakovich, Samara 1998) 15...h6 16 ♗h4 ♘f8 17 h3 ♗d7 18 ♗g3 ♖c8 19 ♗f3 (19 ♗xd6?! ♗xd4 20 ♕xd4 ♖xc3 21 ♖xc3 ♖xe2 is better for Black) 19...♕b6 20 ♘b3 ♘g6 21 ♘a5 ♘e5 = Lautier-Anand, Monaco rpd 1997.

b2) 10 ♘a4 is seen more frequently. White wants to eliminate Black's only active piece so far:

b21) 10...♗b6 will normally transpose to line 'b32' via 11 b4.

b22) 10...b6!? invites White to alter the pawn-structure, but with the d-pawn utterly isolated on d5, this is best left undone: 11 b4 (11 ♘xc5?! bxc5 12 ♘c3 ♖e8+ 13 ♗e2 ♗a6 14 0-0 ♗xe2 15 ♘xe2 ♕b6 16 ♘c3 d6 17 ♖b1 ♘bd7 leaves Black with a comfortable game, Gallego-B.Lalić, Benasque 1996) 11...♗d6 12 ♘ec3 ♗e5

13 ♗e3 ♖e8 14 ♗e2 ♗a6 15 ♖c1 ♗xe2 16 ♕xe2 d6 17 0-0 ♘bd7 with about even chances, Shulman-Ulybin, Gothenburg 1999.

b23) 10...d6 is another solid option: 11 ♘xc5 (11 b4? b5! 12 ♘ac3 ♗b6 is terrible for White, while 11 ♘ec3 a6 12 ♘xc5 dxc5 13 ♗e2 b5 14 0-0 ♗b7 15 ♗f3 ♘bd7 16 ♖e1 ♖e8 17 ♗g5 ♖xe1+ 18 ♕xe1 ♕b6 is about equal, Shulman-Engqvist, Stockholm 1996) 11...dxc5 12 ♘c3 b6 13 ♗e2 ♗b7 (13...♗a6!?) 14 0-0 ♘bd7 15 ♗f4 ♖e8 16 ♖e1 a6 17 a4 ♘e5 18 ♗xa6 ♖xa6 19 ♖xe5 ♖xe5 20 ♗xe5 ♘xd5 leaves the chances balanced, Chernin-Shereshevsky, USSR 1984.

b3) 10 b4 (D) and here:

b31) 10...♗d6 looks odd, but it is a rather natural idea given the fact that White has just weakened the a1-h8 diagonal. 11 g3 (or 11 ♗b2 ♗e5 12 ♘g3 a5 13 b5 d6 14 ♗e2 ♘bd7 15 0-0 ♘c5 16 f4 ♗xc3 17 ♗xc3 a4 18 f5 ♗d7 19 ♖b1 ♖e8 with sufficient counterplay for Black, Knaak-Piket, Bundesliga 1997/8) 11...♖e8 12 ♗g2 ♗e5 13 0-0 a5! 14 b5 d6 15 h3 ♘fd7 16 f4 ♗f6 17 ♖a2! ♘c5 18 g4 g6 19 ♖c2 ♗g7 and after completing an exhausting bishop

tour (f8-b4-e7-c5-d6-e5-f6-g7), Black has obtained a good game, Sadler-Topalov, Tilburg 1998.

b32) 10...♗b6 11 ♘a4 and now:

b321) 11...d6?! 12 ♘xb6 axb6 (not 12...♕xb6?! 13 ♗e3 ± ECO) 13 ♘c3 (White achieves far less after 13 ♘g3?! ♕e7+! 14 ♗e2 ♕e5 15 ♗e3 ♗g4! 16 ♗d4 ♗xe2 17 ♘xe2 ♕xd5 18 ♗xf6 ♕xd1+ 19 ♖xd1 gxf6 20 0-0 ♖d8 ∓ Cu.Hansen-Winants, Antwerp 1993) 13...♗f5 14 ♗e2 ♘e4 15 ♘xe4 ♗xe4 16 0-0 ♕f6 17 ♖a2 ♕g6 18 f3 ♗b1 19 ♖d2 ♘d7 20 ♗b2 ♗f5 21 ♕e1 ± Gligorić-P.Nikolić, Yugoslav Ch (Subotica) 1984.

b322) 11...♖e8 12 ♘xb6 axb6 (or 12...♕xb6 13 ♗e3 ♕d6 14 ♘c3 b6 15 ♖c1 ♗a6 16 ♗xa6 ♘xa6 17 0-0 ± Cu.Hansen-Plachetka, Kerteminde (5) 1985/6) and here:

b3221) 13 d6?! ♘e4 (ECO mentions two interesting alternative ideas: 13...♘c6!?, intending to play ...♖e6, and 13...b5!?) 14 ♗b2 b5 15 ♕d4 ♕g5 16 f3 (16 h4?! ♕h6 and here White prematurely resigned in Davidović-Maksimović, Niš 1985) 16...♘c6 17 ♕xg7+ ♕xg7 18 ♗xg7 ♔xg7 19 fxe4 ♖xe4 20 ♔d2 (Kastek-T.Horvath, Harkany 1986) 20...♖xb4 21 ♘g3 ♖b3 and Black is better.

b3222) 13 h3 d6 14 ♗e3 ♘e4 15 ♕d4 ♘d7 16 ♘c3 ♘xc3 17 ♕xc3 ♘f6 18 ♗c4 ♗d7 = Goormachtigh-Van Gisbergen, Sas van Gent 1992.

b3223) 13 g3 d6 14 ♗g2 ♗g4 15 ♗e3 ♘bd7 16 h3 ♗f5 17 0-0 ♘e5 18 ♘d4 ♗e4 19 ♗xe4 ♘xe4 20 ♕c2 (Muir-Zelčić, Pula Echt 1997) and now 20...♘f6!? seems best, offering approximately equal chances.

We now return to 9...♖e8 (D):

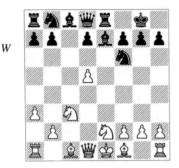

W

10 d6

White picks up the gauntlet and accepts the challenge. The d-pawn is likely to drop off at some point, but the investment in time that Black has to put in should allow White to gather enough compensation in the meantime. Alternatively, White can try:

a) 10 h3 &c5 11 b4 &b6 12 g4 (12 ♘a4 d6 13 ♘xb6 axb6 14 &e3 &f5 15 ♘g3, Guliev-Papaioannou, Agios Nikolaos 1995, and here Black can mobilize his forces with 15...&d7!? 16 &c4 &a4 17 ♕d4 ♘bd7) 12...a5 13 b5 d6 14 &g2 h5! 15 g5 ♘h7 with a good game for Black, Dukić-Csom, Niš 1984.

b) 10 g3 &c5 and then:

b1) 11 ♘a4?! d6! is an old recommendation of Fridrik Olafsson's. 12 ♘xc5 (12 b4 ♘e4 13 bxc5 ♕a5+ 14 &d2 ♘xd2 15 ♕xd2 ♕xa4 is much better for Black, Molo-Nalepa, corr. 1984) 12...dxc5 13 &g2 &g4 14 &e3 ♕a5+ (14...♘a6!?) 15 ♕d2 ♕a6 16 f3 (Fuller-Ver Nooy, e-mail 1995) 16...&f5!? is quite problematic for White.

b2) 11 b4 scores absolutely horribly for White on my database: 1/9. Peter Wells writes that "the b4 pawn

merely presents something of a target": 11...&b6 (11...♘g4?! 12 bxc5 ♕f6 13 &e3 ± D.Gurevich-Van der Sterren, Manchester 1981) and then:

b21) 12 h3? is, in my humble opinion, a horrible move: 12...a5 13 b5 ♕c7 14 &b2 (Timman suggested 14 &d2, but 14...&d4! 15 ♖c1 ♕c5 16 ♖h2 is a positional disaster for White, and Black can pick up several pawns) 14...♕c5 15 ♖h2 a4 16 ♕d3 d6 17 ♖c1 ♘bd7 (17...&a5!?) 18 ♘e4 ♘xe4! 19 ♖xc5 ♘exc5 with more than sufficient compensation for the queen, Gligorić-Timman, Nikšić 1983.

b22) 12 &g2 a5 (12...d6 has also been tested with adequate results for Black) 13 ♖b1 axb4 14 axb4 d6 15 0-0 &f5 16 ♖b3 (G.Mohr-Sher, Belgorod 1990) 16...♘bd7 with a better game for Black.

b3) 11 &g2 d6 12 h3 (12 0-0 a6 13 &f4 &g4 14 ♕d2 ♘bd7! 15 b4 &a7 16 &xd6 &xe2 17 ♘xe2 ♘g4 18 ♖ac1 ♘e3! 19 ♖fe1 ♘xg2 20 ♔xg2 ♘f6 = Beliavsky-Movsesian, Polanica Zdroj 1996) 12...a6 (after 12...&f5 13 0-0, Kasparov-Csom, Baku 1980, Black should play 13...♘e4! 14 ♘a4 ♘d7 15 ♘xc5 ♘exc5 followed by ...♘e5 – Gufeld/Chiburdanidze) 13 0-0 ♘bd7 14 ♘d4 ♘e5 15 ♔h1 (15 ♘ce2 &d7 ∓ Chandler-Andersson, Malta OL 1980) 15...&d7 16 b3 h6 17 &b2 ♖c8 18 ♘ce2 a5 ∓ Alterman-Yu Shaoteng, Beijing 1995.

c) 10 &e3 ♘g4 (10...d6 11 h3 &f8 12 g4 ♘e4 13 ♘xe4 ♖xe4 14 &g2 {14 ♕d2 ♖e8 is also fine for Black} 14...♖xe3 15 fxe3 ♕h4+ 16 ♔d2 ♘d7 17 ♘d4 ♘e5 with a double-edged position, Lukov-Vilela, Cienfuegos 1983) 11 &d4 and here:

c1) 11...d6 12 ♘g3 ♗f6+ 13 ♗e2 ♘d7 14 0-0 ♗xd4 15 ♕xd4 ♘gf6 16 ♖fe1 ± Ki.Georgiev-P.Littlewood, Plovdiv Echt 1983.

c2) 11...♗f6 12 h3 ♗xd4 13 ♕xd4 ♘e5 14 f4 ♘g6 15 g3 d6 16 ♗g2 ♘d7 (16...♘e7!?, intending ...♘f5, is another idea) 17 0-0 ♘c5 18 ♖ad1 ♗f5 19 ♘c1 h5 (19...a5!?) 20 ♔h2 ± Seirawan-Karlsson, Lucerne OL 1982.

c3) 11...♘h6! (D) is a beautiful idea masterminded by Hungarian GM Andras Adorjan:

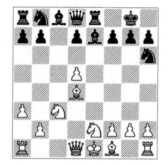

c31) 12 g4? d6 13 h3 f5! ∓ Groszpeter-Adorjan, Hungary 1983.

c32) 12 ♘g3? ♗xa3+ 13 ♗e2 ♗xb2 14 ♘b5 ♗xd4! ∓ Ree-Ligterink, Wijk aan Zee 1984.

c33) 12 g3? ♘f5 13 ♗g2 ♘xd4 14 ♕xd4 ♗f6 15 ♕d2 ♗xc3! ∓ ECO.

c34) 12 d6? ♗xd6 13 ♗xg7 ♘f5! 14 ♗h6 ♕h4 15 ♗c1 ♗c5 ∓ ECO.

c35) 12 ♕d3 d6 (12...♗f6 is also playable; e.g., 13 g3 d6 14 ♗g2 ♗f5 15 ♕d1 ♗xd4 16 ♕xd4 ♘d7 17 0-0 ½-½ Durnopianov-Kaplun, Kherson 1990; I think Black has a quite comfortable position after 17...♘e5 18 ♖ac1 a5) 13 ♘g3 ♘d7 (13...♗f6+ 14 ♗e2 ♗xd4 15 ♕xd4 ♘f5 16 ♕f4,

Ki.Georgiev-Qi Jingxuan, Thessaloniki OL 1984, 16...♖e5 17 0-0 ♘a6 ± Ki.Georgiev) 14 ♗e2 ♘c5 15 ♗xc5 (15 ♕c2?! ♗f6 16 ♗e3 ♘g4 is simply good for Black, Semkov-Dzindzichashvili, Saint John 1988) 15...dxc5 16 0-0 a6 17 ♗f3 ♗d6 18 ♖fe1 f5 19 ♕d2 ♗d7 with a pleasant game for Black, Shulman-Nikolenko, Moscow 1995.

10...♗f8 11 g3 b6
Or:

a) 11...♘c6 12 ♗g2 b6 transposes to the main line.

b) 11...♕b6 12 ♗g2 ♗xd6 13 ♗e3 (Korchnoi-Miles, Wijk aan Zee 1984) 13...♕c7! 14 0-0 ♗e5 15 ♘b5 ♕d8 16 ♘d6 ± Korchnoi.

c) 11...♖e6 is Black's main alternative. Black takes the time to pick up the d6-pawn:

c1) 12 ♗g2 ♖xd6 13 ♕c2 ♘c6 (13...♖e6 14 0-0 usually comes to the same thing after 14...♘c6, but 14...d5!? is independent: 15 ♖d1 ♘c6 16 ♘xd5 ♘xd5 17 ♖xd5 ♕e8 18 ♗e3 is somewhat better for White) 14 0-0 ♖e6 and now:

c11) 15 ♘f4 ♖e8 16 b4 d6 17 ♗b2 ♗d7 (Gligorić-Karpov, Bugojno 1980) and here Karpov gives 18 b5 ♘a5 19 ♕d3 ♖c8 20 ♘cd5 ♘xd5 21 ♗xd5 with an unclear position.

c12) 15 ♗g5 h6 16 ♗xf6 ♖xf6 17 ♘f4 d5!? 18 ♘fxd5 ♖d6 19 ♖ad1 ♗e6 20 ♖fe1 ♖c8 21 ♕a4 a6 22 ♘f4 ♗g4 with an equal position, M.Gurevich-Chernin, USSR Ch playoff (Vilnius) 1985.

c13) 15 b4 a6 16 ♘f4 ♖e8 17 ♘fd5 ♘xd5 18 ♘xd5 d6 19 ♗e3 ♖b8 20 ♗e4 (Tal-Andersson, Tilburg 1980) 20...♗h3!? 21 ♗xh7+ ♔h8 22 ♖fe1

♘e5 23 ♗e4 (Tal) 23...b5 with chances for both sides.

c2) 12 ♗f4 ♘h5 13 ♗e3 ♖xd6 14 ♕c2 (14 ♕b3 ♘c6 15 ♗g2 ♘f6 16 0-0 ♖e6 17 ♘d4 ♘xd4 {17...♖e8!?} 18 ♗xd4 ♕a5 19 ♘d5 ♘e4 20 ♕a2 ± Atalik-Golod, Iraklion 1995) 14...♖e6 (14...♘c6 15 ♗g2 ♖e6 comes to the same thing) 15 ♗g2 ♘c6 16 0-0 ♘f6 17 ♖ad1 d6 18 ♘d4 ♘xd4 19 ♗xd4 (19 ♖xd4 ♕c7 20 ♖c1 ♗d7 21 ♘d5 ♕xc2 22 ♘xf6+ ♖xf6 23 ♖xc2 ♖b8 24 ♖c7 ♗e6 25 ♖xb7 ♖xb7 26 ♗xb7 ♖f5 27 b4 ♗d7 28 ♗d5 ♖xd5 29 ♗xd5 a6 30 ♔f1 ♗e7 31 ♗d4 leaves White much better in the endgame, Webb-Franzen, corr. 1994) 19...♖e8 20 ♖c1 ♘d7 21 ♘b5 ♘c5 22 ♘xd6 (Makarov-Xu Jun, Belgrade 1988) and now Xu Jun gives 22...♕xd6 23 ♗xc5 ♕xc5 24 ♕xc5 ♗xc5 25 ♖xc5 ♖e7 as 'unclear', although after 26 ♖fc1 it looks like White has a solid advantage.

12 ♗g2 ♘c6 *(D)*

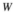

13 b4

White has a few alternatives:

a) 13 ♘b5?! ♗a6 14 a4 ♖c8 15 0-0 was played in Fedorowicz-Sosonko, New York 1984, but presumably both players had missed the neat win of a pawn by 15...♗xd6!, based on the pin of the b5-knight.

b) 13 0-0 ♗a6 and then:

b1) 14 a4 ♖c8 15 ♘b5 transposes to line 'a'.

b2) 14 ♖e1 ♖c8 15 ♗f4 transposes to line 'b4'.

b3) 14 b4 ♗c4 15 ♖e1 ♖c8 16 ♗f4 ♘e5 17 ♕d4 ♘d3 18 ♖ed1 ♘xf4 19 ♘xf4 (Dzindzichashvili-Kiriakov, Dos Hermanas Internet 2002) 19...g5!? 20 ♘h3 ♗g7 activates Black's remaining pieces with beautiful coordination.

b4) 14 ♗f4 ♖c8 15 ♖e1 ♘e5 16 ♕a4 ♗c4 (16...♗xe2?! 17 ♖xe2 ♘d3 18 ♖d2 ♘xf4 19 ♕xf4 ± Csom-Adorjan, Hungarian Ch (Budapest) 1984) 17 ♖ed1 ♘g6 18 ♖d2 a5 19 ♕d1 b5 = Miles-Csom, Esbjerg 1984.

13...♗b7

Black can also decide to postpone the decision about where to put his light-squared bishop with 13...♖b8: 14 0-0 h6 15 ♗f4 (or 15 ♘b5 ♗a6 16 ♘ec3 ♖e5 17 a4 ♖e6 18 ♘d5 ♗xd6 19 ♗b2 ♗e5 20 ♗xe5 ♖xe5 21 ♘xf6+ ♕xf6 22 ♕xd7 ♘xb4 with approximately equal chances, Vaïsser-Adrian, French Cht 1999) 15...♗b7 16 ♘b5 g5!? 17 ♗e3 ♖e6 18 ♘ed4 ♘xd4 19 ♘xd4 ♖xd6 20 ♗xb7 ♖xb7 21 ♕f3 ♕a8 22 ♘b5 ♖c6 23 ♘d4 ♖d6 24 ♘b5 ♖c6 25 ♘d4 ½-½ Khalifman-Cu.Hansen, Munich 1992.

14 0-0 ♖b8

Or:

a) 14...♕b8 15 ♘b5 ♗a6 16 ♘ec3 (Rosenberg-Moskow, New York 1992) 16...♖e5!? leads to a double-edged position according to Hjartarson, although 17 ♘c7 ♗xf1 18 ♕xf1 seems to give Black more than his share of headaches.

b) Again 14...♖e6!? is an obvious move to look at. 15 ♗f4 and now:

b1) 15...♕b8?! is OK for Black according to *ECO*, but in Muir-Martin, British Ch (Eastbourne) 1990, White showed the right way: 16 ♘b5 ♘h5 17 ♗d5! ♘xf4 18 ♘xf4 ♖h6 19 ♗xf7+! ♔xf7 20 ♕b3+ (*ECO* only mentions 20 ♕d5+ ♖e6 21 ♕f5+ ♖f6 22 ♕d5+ with a perpetual check) 20...♖e6 21 ♖fe1 ♕c8 22 ♘xe6 dxe6 23 d7! ♕xd7 24 ♖ad1 ♕c8 25 ♘c7! and Black was busted.

b2) 15...♘h5 16 ♗e3 ♖xd6 17 ♕b3 ♘f6 18 ♖ad1 ♖xd1 19 ♖xd1 d6 20 ♗f4 ½-½ Muir-Hakki, Novi Sad OL 1990.

15 ♘b5 a5

15...♗a6 16 ♘ec3 ♖e5 (M.Gurevich-Kengis, Lvov 1984) and now 17 ♕a4 ♗xb5 18 ♘xb5 a6 19 ♘c3 b5 20 ♕d1 ± Kengis.

16 ♘c7 ♖e5 17 b5 ♘a7 18 ♗xb7 ♖xb7 19 ♗f4 ♗xd6 20 ♕xd6 ♖xe2

Aleksandrov-Hjartarson, Groningen FIDE 1997. Now, according to Hjartarson, White should play 21 a4! ♘c8 22 ♕d3 ♕e7 23 ♖ac1 ♕e4 24 ♕xe4 ♘xe4 with an 'unclear' position, but 25 ♘d5 seems to favour White: 25...♘c5 26 ♘xb6 or 25...♘a7 26 ♗e3.

B)
6...d5 *(D)*
Now:
B1: 7 a3   278
B2: 7 c5   286

B1)
7 a3
Here Black has to decide which type of position to play:
B11: 7...♗xc3+   278
B12: 7...♗e7   283

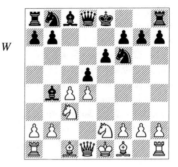

B11)
7...♗xc3+ 8 ♘xc3 *(D)*

8...dxc4
Black immediately makes sure to leave White with an IQP. This method has proved more reliable than the alternatives, which nonetheless have seen their share of action:

a) 8...0-0 and now:
a1) 9 ♗g5 dxc4 10 ♗xc4 ♘c6 11 d5 (11 ♗e3 looks odd here, but transposes to Line B11 in Chapter 17) 11...exd5 12 ♘xd5 ♖e8+ (12...♕e8+ is also fine for Black; e.g., 13 ♗e3 ♘xd5 14 ♗xd5 ♗e6) 13 ♔f1 ♗e6 14 ♗xf6 gxf6 15 ♖c1 ♖c8 16 ♗b3 ♗xd5 17 ♗xd5 ♘e5 and Black is better due

to his lead in development, J.G.Nielsen-Iskov, Copenhagen 1985.

a2) 9 ♗e3 ♘c6 10 c5 e5 11 ♗e2 exd4 12 ♗xd4 ♘e4 13 ♘xe4?! (13 0-0 is safer, although Black is comfortably equal after 13...♘g5 14 f3 ♘e6 followed by ...d4 and an attack on the c5-pawn) 13...dxe4 14 ♗c3 (14 ♗e3 ♕f6 15 ♕b3 ♕g6 is also better for Black) 14...♕g5 15 ♕d6 ♕xg2 16 0-0-0 ♕g5+ 17 ♔c2 ♖d8 (Najer-Filippov, St Petersburg 1998) 18 ♖hg1 ♖xd6 19 ♖xg5 ♖g6 is better for Black, although White has some compensation for his pawn in the form of his bishop-pair.

a3) 9 c5 and now:

a31) 9...♘c6 transposes to line 'b'.

a32) 9...a5?! is merely weakening: 10 ♗f4 ♗d7 11 ♗d3 a4?! (11...♘c6 ±) 12 0-0 ♗c6 13 ♗d6 ± Scherbakov-T.Ivanov, Moscow 1999.

a33) 9...b6 10 b4 (10 ♗e2 a5 11 ♗f4!? ± Petursson-Baquero, Philadelphia 1989) 10...bxc5 11 dxc5 e5 (11...♕c7 12 ♗e2 ♘c6 13 0-0 gives White a slight advantage; 11...a5?! 12 b5 d4 13 ♘a4 ♗b7 14 f3 and the two strong pawns on the queenside leave Black struggling, Rechlis-Fauland, Berne Z 1990) 12 ♗g5 ♗b7 13 ♘b5 d4 and now 14 ♘d6 ♗d5 15 f3 ± is the line given in *ECO*, but 14 ♗xf6 ♕xf6 15 ♘c7 ♖d8 16 ♘xa8 ♗xa8 17 ♖a2 e4 18 ♗c4 may be even better for White.

a34) 9...♘e4!? 10 ♘xe4 dxe4 11 ♗f4?! (White should play 11 ♗e3!? f5 12 ♕d2 ± or 11 b4!?) 11...♘c6 12 ♗d6 ♖e8 13 ♕d2 (Shulman-Nemtsev, Russia Cup (Nizhny Novgorod) 1998) 13...e5! and now neither 14 dxe5 ♘xe5 15 0-0-0 ♗g4 nor 14 d5 ♘d4 is particularly enjoyable for White.

b) 8...♘c6 9 c5 0-0 *(D)* is generally considered to be slightly better for White, who has a handful of options here:

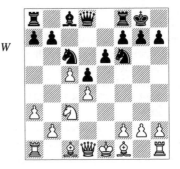

b1) 10 ♗e3 transposes to line 'a2'.

b2) 10 ♗g5?! h6! 11 ♗h4 e5 12 dxe5 ♘xe5 13 ♗e2 d4 14 ♗xf6 (Torre-Larsen, Tilburg 1982) 14...♕xf6 15 ♘d5 ♕g5 16 ♕xd4 ♘c6 ∓.

b3) 10 ♗f4 ♘e4 (10...♘e8 is too passive; after 11 b4 ♕f6 12 ♗e3 followed by ♗d3, White is comfortably better) 11 ♘xe4 dxe4 12 ♗d6 (12 ♗e3 f5 13 ♕d2 ♕f6 is fine for Black) 12...♖e8 13 ♕c2 (13 ♕d2 has been tried a few times, but after 13...e5 14 d5 ♘d4 15 ♖d1? {15 ♕c3 =}, Black should play 15...♕h4! with the nasty threat of 16...e3) 13...♕h4 14 ♖d1 e5 (14...e3 15 ♗g3 exf2+ 16 ♕xf2 ±) 15 dxe5 ♘xe5 16 ♗b5 ♗d7 17 ♗xd7 ♘xd7 18 0-0 ±.

b4) 10 ♗e2 ♘e4 11 ♘xe4 dxe4 12 ♗e3 f5 13 ♕d2 ♕f6 14 g3 e5 15 dxe5 ♘xe5 16 0-0-0 ± M.Gurevich-Zaid, USSR 1984.

b5) 10 ♗b5 e5 11 dxe5 (not 11 ♗xc6?! bxc6 12 dxe5 ♘d7 13 ♗e3 ♘xe5 14 ♕d4 ♘c4 15 0-0, Gulko-Landenbergue, Berne 1994, 15...♖e8!?

∓) 11...♘xe5 12 ♗f4 ♘c4 13 0-0 ♘xb2 14 ♕e2 d4 (Volkov-Filippov, Krasnoiarsk 1998) 15 ♘a2!? a6 16 ♗d6 axb5 17 ♗xf8 ♕xf8 18 ♕xb2 ±.

9 ♗xc4 ♘c6

After 9...0-0 10 0-0, 10...♘c6 11 ♗e3 transposes to the main line, but Black can instead try 10...♘bd7. In Yrjölä-Korhonen, Finnish Ch (Helsinki) 1984, White quickly obtained a better game: 11 ♗g5 ♕a5 12 ♕d2 a6 13 b4 ♕c7 14 ♗a2 ♖d8 15 ♖fd1 ±.

10 ♗e3

10 d5 (or this advance on the next move) takes the tension out of the position, which as a whole is quite drawish.

10...0-0 11 0-0 (D)

11...b6

This is the most logical continuation for Black, who must aim to control d5 in order to prevent White from pushing his d-pawn forward at an advantageous moment. Other tries:

a) 11...♘d5 12 ♕h5! ♘xc3 13 bxc3 ♕a5 14 ♕xa5 ♘xa5 15 ♗a2 ± Henneberke-Rellstab, Zevenaar 1961.

b) 11...a6 12 ♗a2 b5?! (12...♖e8!?, preparing to meet an eventual d5 advance from White, is more to the point)

13 d5! ♘xd5 14 ♘xd5 exd5 15 ♗xd5 ♕f6 16 ♕f3 ♕xf3 17 ♗xf3 ♗b7 18 b4 gives White a slight advantage, Semkov-Stefanov, Varna 1982.

c) 11...♘e7 12 ♗g5 ♗d7 and now 13 ♖e1 ♗c6 14 ♗xf6 gxf6 15 ♕d2 ♔h8 16 ♖ad1 ½-½ Züger-Grün, Berlin 1988 doesn't tell us a lot, but improving on it isn't too difficult; e.g., 13 ♗xf6 gxf6 14 d5 leaves White with a solid advantage.

d) 11...h6 and now:

d1) 12 d5 exd5 13 ♘xd5 ♗e6 14 ♘xf6+ ♕xf6 15 ♗xe6 ♕xe6 16 ♕a4 a6 17 ♖ac1 ♖ad8 18 ♖fe1 ♖fe8 19 h3 ½-½ Akopian-Oll, Dos Hermanas 1992.

d2) 12 ♖e1 and then:

d21) 12...b6 13 ♕f3 ♗b7 and now:

d211) 14 ♕g3 ♘e7 15 ♗d3 ♔h8 16 ♕h3 (16 ♖ac1!?) 16...♘h7 17 ♗f4 (17 ♖ac1!? and 17 ♖ad1!? can both be considered) 17...♘d5 18 ♗e5 (18 ♘xd5 ♕xd5 =) 18...f6 19 ♗g3 ♘g5 20 ♕h5 ♘xc3 21 bxc3 ♕d5 22 ♗f1 ♖ac8 23 ♖ac1 ♕a5! 24 ♕g4 ♖xc3 and Black is a pawn up for nothing, Mascarenhas-Hébert, corr. 1997.

d212) 14 ♗a2! ♖b8 15 ♕h3 ♘e7 16 ♖ad1 ♘fd5 17 ♗b1 ♖e8 18 ♗c1 ♕d7 19 ♕g3 ♔h8 20 ♘e4 ♖bd8 21 ♕h3! ♘g8 22 ♘g5 with an initiative for White, M.Gurevich-Andersson, Leningrad 1987.

d22) 12...♘e7 13 ♗f4 ♗d7 14 ♗e5 ♘ed5 15 ♕d3 (15 ♘xd5 ♘xd5 16 ♗xd5 exd5 17 ♖c1 also leaves White with a slight plus) 15...♗c6 16 ♗a2 ♘g4 17 ♗g3 (Nenashev-Boshku, Katerini 1993) 17...♖c8 18 ♖ac1 with a slight initiative for White.

d3) 12 ♕d3 and here:

d31) 12...b6 is possible.

d32) 12...♗d7 13 ♖ad1 ♘e7 transposes to line 'd33'.

d33) 12...♘e7 13 ♖ad1 (13 ♗f4 ♗d7 14 ♗e5 ♘g6 15 ♖ad1 ♗c6 16 f4 ♘d5 17 ♗xd5 ♗xd5 18 ♕g3 ♖e8 19 f5 exf5 20 ♖xf5 ♗e6 21 ♖h5 ♗b3 22 ♖d2 ♕a5 is equal, Barlov-Bönsch, Sochi 1984) 13...♗d7! 14 ♗a2 (14 f3 ♘ed5 {14...♗c6!?} 15 ♗f2 ♖c8 16 ♗a2 ♕a5 = G.Flear-Matanović, Graz 1984) 14...♗c6 15 ♗f4 ♘g6 16 ♗g3 ♘d5 17 ♕d2 ♖c8 18 ♖c1 ♕d7 19 ♘e4 ♖fd8 = Gligorić-Barlov, Yugoslav Ch (Subotica) 1984.

d4) 12 f3 b6 (*ECO* only quotes 12...♘e7 13 ♗f2 ♗d7 14 ♖e1 ♗c6 15 ♕d3 ♖c8 16 ♗a2 ♖c7 17 ♖ad1 ♖d7 18 ♘e4 ± W.Schmidt-Klinger, Polanica Zdroj 1985) 13 ♗f2 ♗b7 14 ♕d3 ♘e7 15 ♖ad1 (Garcia Palermo-Cvitan, Polanica Zdroj 1985) 15...♘fd5!? =.

d5) 12 ♗a2 ♘e7 13 ♕f3 ♘fd5 14 ♖ac1 b6 15 ♗b1 ♗b7 16 ♕g3 ♔h8 17 ♕h3 ♘g8 18 ♖fe1 ♕d7 (18...♖c8!?) 19 ♗d2 (19 ♘xd5!? ♗xd5 20 ♗f4, intending ♗e5, is an interesting idea) 19...♖ac8 20 ♖e5 and now instead of the positionally ugly 20...f5?!, Avrukh-Hulak, Pula 2000, Black can safely continue 20...♖fd8 with roughly equal chances.

12 ♕f3

This queen move is the most aggressive option available to White. From f3, the queen can continue to g3 and h3, attempting to inflict harm upon Black. White has other moves at his disposal though:

a) 12 ♗a2 is frequently seen in conjunction with other moves. After 12...♗b7, 13 ♖c1 transposes to line 'c' and 13 ♖e1 to line 'd', but 13 d5 leads to independent play: 13...exd5 14 ♘xd5

♘e5 15 ♗f4 ♗xd5 16 ♗xd5 ♕xd5 17 ♕xd5 ♘xd5 18 ♗xe5 = Ghitescu-Parma, Lugano OL 1968.

b) 12 d5 is fairly tame if Black knows what he is doing: 12...♘e5 (or 12...exd5 13 ♘xd5 ♗e6 14 ♘xf6+ ♕xf6 15 ♗xe6 ♕xe6 16 ♖e1 ♕f5 17 ♕b1 ♕b5 18 b4 h6 19 h3 ♖fd8 20 ♕e4 ½-½ Ki.Georgiev-Andersson, Thessaloniki OL 1984) 13 ♗a2 exd5 14 ♗d4 (14 ♘xd5 ♗a6 is fine for Black) 14...♘c6 15 ♗xf6 ♕xf6 16 ♗xd5 ♗d7 17 ♕f3 ♕xf3 18 ♗xf3 ♖ac8 = Tempone-Urday, Mar del Plata 1997.

c) 12 ♖c1 ♗b7 13 ♗a2 ♘e7 (after 13...♖c8 White can play 14 d5, which is uncomfortable for Black, but not devastating; e.g., 14...♘xd5 15 ♘xd5 exd5 16 ♗xd5 ♕d7 17 ♗f3 ♕e7 18 ♖e1 ♘e5 19 ♗xb7 ♕xb7 20 ♖xc8 ♖xc8 21 ♗d4 with a very slight initiative for White, Chernin-Miles, Rome 1990) 14 ♗b1 ♘ed5 15 ♗g5 ♖c8 (Nabholz-Bonin, New York 1991) 16 f3 h6 is more or less equal.

d) 12 ♖e1 ♗b7 13 ♗a2 ♘e7 14 ♗g5 ♘g6 15 h4!? (15 d5 is also fine, Cebalo-Hulak, Zagreb (2) 1982) 15...h6 16 h5 ♘e7 17 ♗xf6 gxf6 ± *ECO*.

e) 12 ♕d3 is a very popular choice for White. The idea is to connect the rooks, centralize the queen's rook and then redeploy the light-squared bishop to wherever it creates most possible unrest for Black. After 12...♗b7 13 ♖ad1, Black has tried:

e1) 13...♘e7?! 14 ♗g5! ♘g6 15 f4 h6 16 f5 exf5 17 ♗xf6 ♕xf6 18 ♖xf5 ♕d6 19 ♖df1 ♘h8 (Balashov-Gipslis, USSR Ch (Riga) 1970) 20 ♘e4 with an ongoing initiative for White.

e2) 13...♕c7 14 ♕e2 ♘e7 15 ♘b5 ♕c6 16 f3 ♘fd5 and Black is in equal territory, Knaak-Siegel, Bundesliga 1995/6.

e3) 13...h6 and then:

e31) 14 ♗f4 ♘e7 15 ♖fe1 ♘fd5 16 ♗g3 ♘g6 17 f3 ♖c8 18 ♘xd5 ♗xd5 19 ♗a6 ♖a8 20 ♖c1 h5 with an equal position, Korchnoi-Cu.Hansen, Biel 1992.

e32) 14 ♖fe1 ♘e7 15 ♗f4 ♖c8 16 ♗e5 ♘fd5 17 ♘b5 ♗a6 18 a4 ♘f5 is pleasant for Black, Petrosian-Olafsson, Bled Ct 1959.

e33) 14 ♗a2 ♘e7 15 f3 ♘fd5 16 ♗f2 ♘f5 17 ♘e4 a5 18 ♖fe1 ♗a6 with chances for both sides, D.Gurevich-Kogan, USA Ch (Estes Park) 1985.

e34) 14 f3 ♘e7 (14...♖c8 allows White a dangerous initiative: 15 ♗a2 ♖c7 16 ♗b1 ♖d7 17 ♘e4 ♖e8 18 ♘xf6+ ♕xf6 19 ♕h7+ ♔f8 20 ♗e4 ♘e7 21 d5!, Gligorić-Djurić, Vršac 1983) 15 ♗f2 ♘fd5 16 ♗a2 ♖c8 and now, instead of 17 ♗b1?! ♘g6 18 ♗g3 ♘xc3 19 bxc3 (D.Gurevich-Seirawan, USA 1985) 19...♕d5 20 ♖c1 b5 21 a4 a6 ∓ (Gurevich), White should play 17 ♘e4!? with chances for both sides – Seirawan.

12...♗b7 (D)

13 ♗d3

White maintains the pin a little bit longer while targeting the bishop towards the black kingside. However, White has two other very direct options:

a) 13 ♕g3 ♘e7 14 ♗d3 ♘g6 15 ♖ad1 ♕b8!? 16 f4?! ♘d5 17 ♘xd5 ♗xd5 18 ♖c1?! f5 ∓ Wells-Chernin, Odorheiu Secuiesc 1993.

b) 13 ♕h3 ♘e7 14 ♖ad1 ♘fd5 15 ♗g5 (15 ♗d3 ♘g6 looks reasonably solid for Black, but has yet to be tested) 15...h6 16 ♗d3 f5 17 ♗c1 ♖c8 18 ♖fe1 ♖f6 19 ♗f1 ♘g6 = Utasi-Am.Rodriguez, Havana 1986.

13...♕d7

Or:

a) 13...♖b8 14 ♕g3 ♘e7 15 ♗f4 ♖c8 16 ♗e5 ♘g6 17 ♖ad1 ± Beliavsky-Andersson, Bugojno 1984.

b) 13...♖c8 14 ♖ad1 ♖c7 15 ♕h3 ♘e7 16 ♗g5! ♘g6 17 ♕g3!? ♖d7 18 d5! exd5 19 ♗f5 ♖e7 20 h4! ♕c7 21 ♕xc7 ♖xc7 22 ♖fe1! (Kasparov-Psakhis, La Manga (6) 1990) 22...h6 ± (Psakhis).

14 ♕h3 ♘e7 15 ♗g5

Also worth considering is 15 ♖ad1 ♘g6 16 f4 ♘d5 17 f5 exf5 18 ♗xf5 ♕c7 19 ♘xd5 ♗xd5 20 ♖c1 ♕e7 21 ♕g3 ♕h4 22 ♗f4, which favours White due to his bishop-pair, Sadler-Karpov, Monaco Amber rpd 1998.

15...♘g6 16 ♗xf6 gxf6 17 ♖ad1

17 d5 has been used to great effect – at least result-wise – on a few occasions: 17...♗xd5 18 ♖ad1 ♖ad8 (18...♕c7!? has yet to be tried out, but after 19 ♘xd5 exd5 20 ♕h5 ♖ad8, despite his pawn-structure not being the model of positional understanding, Black should be OK) 19 ♗e4 ♕b7 20 ♕f3 ♔g7 21 ♗xd5 exd5 22 ♘xd5 ♖d6 23 ♖d4 with

an obvious advantage for White, Vaganian-A.Petrosian, Telavi 1982.

17...♖ad8 18 ♗e4!?

18 ♖fe1 ♔g7 19 ♗c2 ♖g8 20 ♖e3 ♕c7 = Cu.Hansen-Agdestein, Gausdal Z 1985.

18...♗xe4 19 ♘xe4 ♕e7 20 ♖fe1 f5 21 ♘c3 ♕g5 22 d5

White has an advantage thanks to Black's weakened king position, Najer-Mitenkov, Moscow 1996.

B12)

7...♗e7 *(D)*

W

8 c5

With this move White tries to close the centre and make a clamp on the black queenside. Otherwise:

a) 8 cxd5 ♘xd5 9 ♘xd5 (9 ♘f4 0-0 transposes to Line A1) 9...♕xd5 10 ♘c3 ♕d8 11 ♗c4 0-0 12 0-0 ♘c6 13 d5 exd5 14 ♘xd5 ♗d6 = Ermenkov-Kolev, Bulgarian Ch 1998.

b) 8 ♘f4 mostly transposes to other lines:

b1) 8...♘c6 9 cxd5 ♘xd5 10 ♘cxd5 exd5 11 ♗e3 0-0 transposes to note 'a' to White's 9th move in Line A1.

b2) 8...0-0 9 cxd5 ♘xd5 10 ♘cxd5 exd5 transposes to Line A1.

b3) 8...dxc4 9 ♗xc4 ♘bd7 (9...♘c6 10 ♗e3 0-0 11 0-0 ♗d6 12 ♘h5 ♘xh5 13 ♕xh5 g6 14 ♕h6 ± M.Gurevich-Yudasin, Lvov 1987) 10 0-0 0-0 11 ♗e3 ♘b6 12 ♗a2 ♗d7 13 d5 ♘bxd5 14 ♘cxd5 exd5 15 ♘xd5 ♘xd5 16 ♗xd5 ♗f6 with some initiative for White, Supatashvili-Tsichlis, Panormo Z 1998.

8...b6

This is the main move. In the coverage below, you will notice the ample opportunities both sides have to transpose back and forth between main lines and side-lines. Black has also tried:

a) 8...♘c6 9 b4 e5 10 dxe5 ♘xe5 11 ♘d4 0-0 12 ♗e2 ± Gligorić-Broadbent, Birmingham 1951.

b) 8...0-0 is seen quite often and it often transposes to the main line. Now:

b1) 9 b4 b6 transposes to the main line.

b2) 9 ♗f4 b6 10 b4 transposes to note 'b' to White's 10th move.

b3) 9 ♘g3 b6 10 b4 a5 11 ♗b2 bxc5 12 bxc5 ♘c6 13 ♗b5 ♗d7 14 0-0 ♖b8 15 a4 ♘e8 16 ♕d2 ♘c7 is equal, Solmundarson-Mednis, Reykjavik 1982.

b4) 9 g3 and then:

b41) 9...b6 10 b4 transposes to the main line.

b42) 9...♘c6?! 10 ♗g2 e5 11 dxe5 ♘xe5 12 b4 ♗g4 (Flear-Speelman, British Ch (Edinburgh) 1985) 13 0-0! ♗f3 14 ♗f4 ♗xg2 15 ♔xg2 ♘c4 16 ♕b3, intending ♖ad1, is clearly better for White according to Langeweg.

b43) 9...a5 10 ♗f4 ♘c6 11 ♖c1 b6 12 cxb6 ♕xb6 13 ♘a4 ♕b7 14 ♗g2 ♗d7 = D.Gurevich-Smyslov, Palma de Mallorca 1989.

9 b4 0-0 *(D)*

Or:

a) 9...a5 10 ♘a4 ♘fd7 11 ♘ec3 axb4 12 axb4 0-0 13 ♗e3 ± Hort-Garcia Gonzalez, Novi Sad 1976.

b) 9...bxc5 10 dxc5 (10 bxc5 ♗a6 11 g3 0-0 12 ♗g2 ♘c6 13 0-0 e5 is pleasant for Black, Noteboom-Euwe, Amsterdam (2) 1931) 10...e5 (10...0-0 11 g3 transposes to the main line) 11 f4 was first played in the game Rubinstein-Maroczy, Hamburg OL 1930. After 11...♘c6 (11...a5!? *ECO*) 12 fxe5 ♘xe5 13 ♘d4 0-0 14 ♗e2 ♘e4 15 ♘xe4 dxe4 16 0-0 ♗f6 17 ♗e3 ♘d3 18 ♖xf6 ♕xf6 19 ♗xd3 exd3 20 ♕xd3, White has compensation for the exchange, Zilberman-Cherepkov, USSR 1963.

W

10 g3

This way of developing the kingside appears to be the best way to retain control over the centre while developing the remaining pieces. Some alternatives:

a) 10 ♘g3 transposes to note 'b3' to Black's 8th move.

b) 10 ♗f4 and now:

b1) 10...bxc5 11 dxc5 ♘c6 12 ♘d4 ♘xd4 13 ♕xd4 ♘d7 14 ♗g3 ♗b7 15 ♕d2 ♗g5 16 f4 ♗f6 17 ♗d3 favours White, Torre-Ree, Bangalore 1981.

b2) 10...a5 11 ♖b1 axb4 12 axb4 bxc5 13 dxc5 ♘c6 14 ♘d4 ♘xd4 15 ♕xd4 ♘g4 16 ♗e2 with at the very best a minimal advantage for White, Yurenko-Shaposhnikov, Russian U-16 Ch (Kaluga) 1996.

10...bxc5

Or 10...a5, and now:

a) 11 ♖b1 axb4 (11...bxc5 12 dxc5 transposes to the main line) 12 axb4 bxc5 13 dxc5 transposes to the note to Black's 12th move.

b) 11 ♘a4?! axb4 12 ♘xb6 ♖a7 13 ♗e3 ♖xa3 14 ♖xa3 bxa3 15 ♘c3?! (15 ♕a4 ♗b7 is merely pleasant for Black), Granda-Morović, New York 1997, and now 15...♘bd7! 16 ♘xd7 ♗xd7 is plainly awful for White.

11 dxc5 a5

11...♗a6 is also worth a go; e.g., 12 f4 ♘c6 13 ♘d4 ♘xd4 14 ♗xa6 ♘f5 15 ♕d3 h5 16 ♗d2 g6 with chances for both sides, Corral Blanco-Rivas, Spanish Cht (Cala Galdana) 1994.

12 ♖b1 ♘c6

12...axb4 13 axb4 will normally transpose, but there are some independent lines as well:

a) 13...♘a6 14 ♘d4 highlights the problems with Black's position; in Evans-Pilnik, Lone Pine 1975, Black became desperate and went for 14...♘xb4 (14...♗d7!? is only slightly better for White) 15 ♖xb4 ♗xc5 16 ♖b5 ♕c7 17 ♗e3 ♗xd4 18 ♕xd4 ±.

b) 13...♗a6!? 14 b5?! ♗xc5! 15 bxa6 ♘g4 16 ♘d4 ♘xf2! 17 ♔xf2 ♕f6+ 18 ♔g2 ♗xd4 19 ♘xd5 exd5 20 ♗d3 (Grotnes-Bern, Norwegian Ch 1992) and now 20...♖xa6! looks good for Black.

13 ♗g2 *(D)*

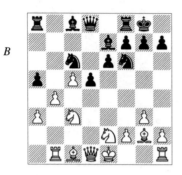

13...axb4

13...♖b8 is possibly more accurate than the text-move, as it doesn't allow White's dark-squared bishop to get to a3, from where it can support the passed pawns' further march down the board. Now:

a) 14 ♗f4?! axb4 15 ♗xb8 bxc3 (Salov-M.Gurevich, Leningrad 1987) and here Gurevich's suggestion of 16 ♗d6 is relatively best, although Black has an advantage after 16...♗xd6 17 cxd6 ♕a5! 18 0-0 ♕xa3 19 ♕c2 ♕xd6 (M.Gurevich).

b) 14 ♘d4?! ♘xd4 15 ♕xd4 ♘d7 16 0-0 ♗a6 17 ♖d1 ♗f6 18 ♕d2 axb4 19 axb4 ♘e5 ∓ Marin-Portisch, Szirak IZ 1987.

c) 14 b5?! ♗xc5! 15 bxc6 ♖xb1 16 ♘xb1 ♕b6 17 ♗e3 ♗xe3 18 fxe3 ♘g4 19 ♕c1 ♘xe3 20 ♗f3 ♗a6 gives Black superb compensation for the piece, Thompson-Vehre, corr. 1989.

d) 14 ♕a4 axb4 15 axb4 ♗d7 16 b5 ♘e5 17 ♕d4 ♗xc5! 18 ♕xe5 ♗xf2+ 19 ♔f1 ♗a7 and again Black has excellent compensation for the piece, Lugovoi-Womacka, Hamburg 2001.

14 axb4 ♖b8 15 ♗a3

As mentioned above, this is the extra option that is available to White due to the early exchange on b4. Two other options:

a) 15 ♕a4 transposes to note 'd' to Black's 13th move.

b) 15 b5? was played recently by Avrukh, but his opponent didn't play the critical line. I wonder what he had in mind after 15...♗xc5 16 bxc6 ♖xb1 17 ♘xb1 ♕b6 18 ♗e3 ♗xe3 19 fxe3 ♘g4 20 0-0 ♕xe3+ 21 ♔h1 ♗a6 22 ♘bc3 (Zilberman-Kaiumov, Cheliabinsk 1975), when *ECO* rates 22...♖c8 as '–+', which is a gross exaggeration, but nonetheless it is the best move, leaving Black with a solid advantage.

15...♗d7

ECO prefers 15...♗a6!? 16 0-0 ♗c4 17 ♖e1 (or 17 ♕c2 ♘g4 18 h3 ♘ge5 19 ♖fd1 ♕c7 20 ♘f4, Garcia Palermo-Adorjan, Szirak 1986, 20...♖fd8 ∓ Garcia Palermo) 17...♖a8! (17...♕c7 18 ♘d4! ♖fd8 with chances for both sides, M.Gurevich-Lerner, Tallinn 1987) 18 ♗c1 ♘g4!? (this is a rather inventive idea that appears to work) 19 ♘f4 ♘xf2 20 ♔xf2 ♘xb4 (this is the idea behind Black's sacrifice on f2) 21 ♗e3 ♕a5 22 ♖a1 ♕xa1 23 ♕xa1 ♖xa1 24 ♖xa1 ♗f6 and Black's pawns and active pieces outweigh the sacrificed piece, D.Gurevich-Whitehead, New York 1987.

16 0-0 ♘a7

16...♘e8 is similar to the main line. The idea is for Black to blockade White's passed pawns on the light squares and then start rolling with his central pawns. Chernin-Novikov, USSR Ch (Lvov) 1984 went as follows: 17 ♕c2 (17 ♖e1 ♘a7 transposes to the main line) 17...♘c7 18 ♖fd1 ♘a7 19

♗c1 ♘cb5 20 ♘xb5 ♘xb5 21 ♗b2 ♗f6 and Black had equalized fully.

17 ♖e1 ♘e8 18 ♘d4 ♘c7

Now we are getting to crunch time. The battle is between Black's attempts to blockade the queenside pawns on the light squares, and White's efforts to blockade Black's central pawns on the dark squares. There are now two lines of interest:

a) 19 f4 (or 19 ♕d2 ♗f6 20 f4) 19...♗f6 20 ♕d2 and here:

a1) 20...♕c8?! 21 ♘ce2 ♖d8 22 ♗b2 ♘e8 23 ♖ec1 ± Garcia Palermo-Pinter, Lucerne Wcht 1985.

a2) 20...♖e8 21 ♘ce2 ♘cb5 22 ♗b2 ♘c6 23 ♘xb5 ♖xb5 24 ♗f1! ± Marin-Ki.Georgiev, Warsaw Z 1987.

a3) 20...♗xd4+ (despite this only being played in a relatively obscure game, it appears to be Black's best bid for equality) 21 ♕xd4 ♘ab5 22 ♘xb5 ♘xb5 23 ♕d3 ♘xa3 24 ♕xa3 ♗b5 25 ♕b2 ♕d7 and the chances are about equal, Wastney-Barrance, New Zealand Ch 1994.

b) 19 ♗c1!? (avoiding the risk of getting this bishop exchanged for a black knight) 19...♗f6 (19...♘cb5 and now 20 ♘dxb5 ♘xb5 21 ♘xb5 ♗xb5 is about equal, but 20 ♘cxb5 ♘xb5 21 ♗f4!? may improve) 20 ♗f4 ♗xd4 21 ♕xd4 ♘cb5 22 ♘xb5 ♘xb5 23 ♕d2 ♖a8 24 ♗e5 and despite the closed nature of the position, White has an advantage due to his strong bishops, Eingorn-Kharitonov, Riga 1980.

B2)

7 c5 *(D)*

With this move, White grabs space on the queenside, enabling him to start an early attack on this wing. White's

B

overall space advantage may also give him attacking chances against the black king. This move also prevents Black's dark-squared bishop from retreating to e7.

Black has to play actively in order to keep chances of counterplay. Therefore, we will often see Black playing ...a5-a4 or ...b6, or a combination of both. Another pawn break is ...e5, but this thrust has to be timed accurately if Black is not to end up in an inferior position.

7...♘e4

The alternatives are:

a) 7...♘c6 8 a3 ♗a5 (8...♗xc3+ 9 ♘xc3 0-0 transposes to note 'b' to Black's 8th move in Line B11) 9 b4 ♗c7 10 g3 e5 11 ♗g2 a5!? 12 ♗g5!? ♗g4 13 f3 axb4 14 axb4 ♖xa1 15 ♕xa1 ♗f5 16 dxe5 ♗xe5 17 f4 (17 0-0!? may improve) 17...♗xc3+! 18 ♕xc3 0-0 19 ♗xf6 ½-½ Gligorić-Spassky, Linares 1981.

b) 7...0-0 8 a3 and here:

b1) 8...♗a5 looks like it wastes too much time: 9 g3 ♗c7 10 ♗g2 a5?! (10...b6!? seems safer) 11 0-0 ♗d7 12 b3 b6 13 ♖b1 bxc5 14 dxc5 ± Gomez Esteban-Hernando Pertierra, Barbera del Valles 1995.

b2) 8...♗xc3+ 9 ♘xc3 transposes to note 'a3' to Black's 8th move in Line B11.

c) 7...a5 looks truly bizarre at first glance, but the strategic idea is to attack White's c5-pawn with ...b6 without allowing White to play b4 to protect it: 8 a3 ♗xc3+ 9 ♘xc3 b6 10 ♗f4 bxc5 11 dxc5 0-0 12 ♗d6 ♖e8 13 ♗e2 ♘c6 14 0-0 (14 ♘b5!? also looks attractive) 14...♗d7 15 ♖b1 e5 16 f4 ± Dvoirys-Averkin, Sochi 1982.

d) 7...e5 *(D)* scores very badly for Black, but it isn't that clear. White now has two options:

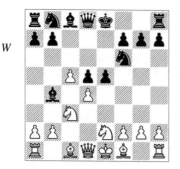

W

d1) 8 dxe5 ♘g4 (8...♘e4 9 a3 ♘xc3 10 ♘xc3 ♗xc3+ 11 bxc3 ♕a5 12 ♗d2 ♕xc5 13 ♗d3 ♘c6 14 0-0 ♗e6 15 ♕e2 ± Anapolsky-Popov, Leningrad 1991) 9 ♘d4 0-0 10 e6 ♘f6 11 exf7+ ♖xf7 12 ♗e2 ♘e4 13 0-0 ♗xc3 14 bxc3 ♘xc3 15 ♕d2 ♘xe2+ 16 ♘xe2 ♘c6 17 ♗b2 b6 with chances for both sides, Onishchuk-Browne, Las Vegas 2001.

d2) 8 a3 ♗xc3+ 9 ♘xc3 exd4 10 ♕xd4 0-0 (10...♘c6 11 ♗b5 0-0 12 ♗xc6 bxc6 13 0-0 ± Semkov-Tejero, Badalona 1993) 11 ♗b5 ♗d7 12 0-0 ♗xb5 13 ♘xb5 ♘c6 14 ♕d3 ♘e4 15

♗e3 ♘e5 (15...a6?! is worse: 16 ♘c3 ♘xc3 17 bxc3 with a solid advantage for White according to Knaak, Knaak-Browne, Palma de Mallorca 1989) 16 ♕d4 ♘c6 17 ♕d1 (17 ♕a4 {Knaak} is better; e.g., 17...♕e7 18 ♖ac1 ± Pliester) 17...♖e8 18 ♖c1 a6 19 ♘d4 ♕f6 = Christiansen-Browne, USA Ch (Jacksonville) 1990.

8 ♗d2

A much less frequently seen option is 8 a3 ♗xc3+ 9 ♘xc3 ♘xc3 10 bxc3 0-0 11 ♗f4 b6 12 ♗d6 ♖e8 13 ♗b5 ♗d7 (Martinez Martin-Yakovich, Seville 1999) 14 ♗d3 = Yakovich.

8...♘xd2

This is safest and probably best. Other options:

a) 8...a5 9 ♘xe4! dxe4 10 a3 ♗xd2+ 11 ♕xd2 0-0 12 ♕e3 b6 13 ♕xe4 (13 ♘c3!?) 13...♖a7 14 ♘c3 ± Miles-Van der Wiel, Wijk aan Zee 1984.

b) 8...♗xc3!? (this move deserves more attention on the basis of this game) 9 ♘xc3 0-0 10 ♘xe4 dxe4 11 ♗f4 ♘c6 12 ♗d6 ♖e8 13 ♕d2 e5!? 14 dxe5 ♘xe5 15 0-0-0 ♗g4!? 16 ♖e1 ♗f5 and Black is at least equal, Avrukh-Aseev, Beersheba-St Petersburg 1999.

c) 8...♘c6 9 ♘xe4 dxe4 and then:

c1) 10 a3 ♗xd2+ 11 ♕xd2 0-0 12 ♖d1 f5 13 ♘c3 ♔h8 14 ♗e2 (14 ♗c4!?) 14...♕h4 15 g3 ½-½ Cummings-Dive, London 1994.

c2) 10 g3 ♗xd2+ 11 ♕xd2 ♕d5 12 ♕e3 ♘b4 13 ♔d2 (Granda-Zarnicki, Buenos Aires 1992) 13...f5 14 ♘f4 ♕d8 with a better game for Black.

c3) 10 ♗xb4 ♘xb4 11 ♘c3 f5 (11...♕xd4?! is weaker; e.g., 12 ♕xd4 ♘c2+ 13 ♔d2 ♘xd4 14 ♘xe4 ± Polugaevsky-Taimanov, USSR Ch (Tbilisi)

1959) 12 ♗b5+ ♗d7 13 0-0 ♗xb5 (13...♘d5 14 ♕h5+ g6 15 ♕h6 is comfortably better for White) 14 ♘xb5 0-0 15 f3 e3 16 f4 ♕f6 17 ♕a4 a6 18 ♘c7 e2 19 ♖f2 ♕xd4 (Bareev-Aseev, USSR Ch (Leningrad) 1990) and now 20 ♘xa8 ♕d2 21 ♖xe2 ♕xe2 22 ♕xb4 ♖xa8 23 ♖e1 ♕c2 is unclear according to Kharitonov, but as far as I can judge White is solidly better after 24 ♕d4.

9 ♕xd2 *(D)*

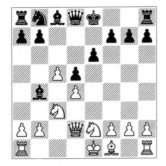

9...a5

This is by far Black's most popular move. Black aims at restricting White's queenside pawn expansion or, if White proceeds along this path, to have more space for his pieces given the room left by the pawn exchanges on b4 and possibly also c5 after a black ...b6. Black has tried a great number of other things:

a) 9...♘c6 10 a3 and now:

a1) 10...♗xc3 11 ♘xc3 0-0 12 f4 b6 (12...♕f6 is a good idea) 13 b4 e5?! (13...♕f6 is preferable) 14 dxe5 bxc5 15 bxc5 ♕a5?! (15...♗e6 ±) 16 ♘b5 ± I.Sokolov-Ashley, New York 1996.

a2) 10...♗a5 11 b4 ♗c7 12 g3 b6 13 ♗g2 bxc5 14 dxc5 ♖b8 15 ♖b1 0-0

16 0-0 ♗e5 17 ♖fd1 ± Korchnoi-Spassky, USSR Ch (Moscow) 1973.

b) 9...0-0 10 a3 ♗xc3 (10...♗a5 11 g3 ♘c6 12 b4 ♗c7 is similar to line 'a2') 11 ♘xc3 and now: 11...♘c6 is line 'a1'; 11...a5 is note 'a' to Black's 11th move; 11...b6 transposes to line 'f1'.

c) 9...e5!? has only been tried a few times in correspondence games that are over 40 years old, but have since been forgotten:

c1) 10 dxe5 ♗e6 11 0-0-0 (11 ♘f4 d4 12 ♘xe6 fxe6 13 0-0-0 ♘c6 is highly unclear) 11...♘c6 12 f4 ♖c8 (12...♗xc5 is also fine for Black) 13 g3 0-0 14 ♗g2 ♘e7 15 ♔b1 ♖xc5 and Black has equalized, Tanner-Dannberg, corr. 1958.

c2) 10 a3 is probably a better idea: 10...♗xc3 11 ♘xc3 e4 12 ♗b5+ ♘c6 13 0-0 0-0 14 f3 with an initiative for White.

d) 9...♕e7!? (Black clears the d8-square for his dark-squared bishop) 10 a3 ♗a5 11 g3 ♗d8 12 b4 b6 13 ♗g2 a5 14 0-0 0-0 and now instead of 15 f4 bxc5 16 bxc5 (or 16 dxc5 ♘c6 =) 16...g6 with balanced chances, Muir-Csom, Mendrisio 1989, White should try the more aggressive 15 b5!?, intending 15...bxc5 16 dxc5 ♕xc5 17 ♘xd5 exd5 18 ♖fc1 ♕xb5 19 ♖xc8, when White has the initiative.

e) 9...♕f6 10 a3 ♗a5 11 g3 (11 b4 ♗d8 12 g3 ♕f3 13 ♖g1 ♕f6 14 ♕e3 0-0 15 g4 g6 16 g5 ♕g7 ½-½ Vaïsser-Van der Wiel, Brussels Z 1993; 11 f4 0-0 12 g3 ♘c6 13 b4 ♗d8 14 ♗g2 g6 15 0-0 ♕g7 16 ♖fd1 ♖b8 17 ♖ac1 h5 18 ♔h1 ♗f6 = Van Kooten-Van der Wiel, Amsterdam 2001) 11...♕f3 12 ♖g1 ♘c6 13 b4 ♗c7 14 ♗g2 ♕f6 15 f4 0-0 16 ♖f1 ♘e7 17 ♖c1 ♗d7 18 ♖f2 (Knaak-Van der Wiel, Palma de Mallorca 1989) 18...h5, followed by ...♘f5, with a decent game for Black.

f) 9...b6 10 a3 ♗xc3 11 ♘xc3 (D) and now:

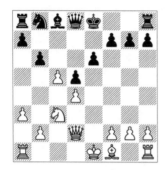

B

f1) 11...0-0 12 b4 (12 ♗e2 promises White less: 12...bxc5 13 dxc5 a5 14 0-0 a4 15 ♖ac1 ♕a5 = Ivkov-Andersson, Hilversum 1973) 12...bxc5 13 dxc5 d4?! (13...a6 is more solid and better) 14 ♘b5 e5 15 ♗e2 ♗b7 16 0-0 ♗d5 17 f4 with a better game for White, Vaiser-Lengyel, Sochi 1981.

f2) 11...bxc5 and here:

f21) 12 dxc5 a5 13 ♖c1 (13 ♗b5+ ♗d7 transposes to 'f22') 13...a4!? (or 13...♘c6 14 ♗b5 ♗d7 15 0-0 0-0 16 ♘a4 ± Kasparov-Tal, Brussels blitz 1987) and now:

f211) 14 ♘xa4!? is also worth looking into: 14...♖xa4 15 ♗b5+ ♗d7 16 ♗xa4 (16 c6? ♖e4+ 17 ♔f1 ♘c6 18 ♗xc6 ♗xc6 19 ♖xc6 ♕b8 favours Black) 16...♗xa4 17 ♕d4 ♗b5 18 ♕xg7 ♖f8 19 f3 ♘c6 with chances for both sides.

f212) 14 ♘b5 0-0 15 c6 ♕b6 16 ♕e3 ♕a5+ 17 ♕d2 ♕b6 18 ♕e3 ♕a5+ ½-½ Yrjölä-Ornstein, Helsinki 1984.

f22) 12 ♗b5+ ♗d7 13 dxc5 a5 14 0-0 a4 15 ♗xd7+ ♕xd7 16 f4 ♕e7 (Bu Xiangzhi-Shaposhnikov, Athens jr Wch 2001) 17 ♕d4! ♕f6 18 ♕d1 leaves Black with problems regarding his a-pawn.

g) 9...♕d7 10 a3 ♗a5 and then:

g1) 11 b4 ♗d8 12 ♘g1 (quite similar is 12 f4 0-0 13 ♘g1 b6 14 ♘f3 bxc5 15 ♗b5 ♕c7 16 dxc5 ♗f6 17 0-0 with an initiative for White, Erykalov-Khasin, Novosibirsk 1995) 12...♘c6 13 f4 0-0 14 ♘f3 f6 (14...a6, followed by ...f6, may be more accurate) 15 ♗b5 a6 16 ♗a4 ♕f7 17 0-0 ♗d7 = Nenashev-Budnikov, USSR Army Ch (Khabarovsk) 1990.

g2) 11 g3 ♗d8 (or 11...0-0 12 ♗g2 ♘c6 13 0-0 ♗d8 14 b4 ♗f6 15 b5 ♘e7 16 ♖ab1 ♕c7 = Liogky-Oll, Antwerp 1996) and now:

g21) 12 ♗g2 a5!? (12...b6 13 0-0 0-0 14 f4 ♘c6 15 b4 bxc5 16 dxc5 ♖b8 17 ♖ab1 ± Lautier-Garcia Ilundain, Terrassa 1991) 13 b3 b6 14 0-0 0-0 15 b4 ♗a6 16 ♖fb1?! (16 ♖ab1 ♗c4 is double-edged) 16...♗xe2 17 ♘xe2 ♕a7! = Knaak-Skembris, Dortmund 1990.

g22) 12 b4 0-0 13 ♗g2 b6 14 0-0 ♗e7 15 ♖ab1 a5 16 ♖fc1 axb4 17 axb4 ♖d8 (Levitt-M.Gurevich, Tel-Aviv 1989) and here Pliester claims an advantage for White after 18 b5! bxc5 19 dxc5 ♗xc5 20 ♘xd5 ♗xf2+ 21 ♔xf2 ♗b7 22 ♖c7 ♕xc7 23 ♘xc7 ♖xd2 24 ♘xa8 ♗xg2 25 ♖c1.

10 a3 ♗xc3 11 ♘xc3 a4

Two inferior alternatives are:

a) 11...0-0 12 ♘a4 ♗d7 13 ♘b6 ♖a7 14 ♗d3 ♘c6 15 0-0 ♗e8 (the alternative 15...♘xd4 16 ♗xh7+ ♔xh7 17 ♕xd4 is also better for White) 16

♝c2 ♜a6 17 ♜ad1 f6 18 ♜fe1 ± Yako-
vich-Frog, Russian Ch (Elista) 1995.

b) 11...♝d7 12 ♝d3 (*ECO* gives
12 b3! ±) 12...a4 transposes to the note
to Black's 12th move.

12 ♝d3

Again White has a choice:

a) 12 ♜c1 ♝d7 13 ♝d3 b6 14 0-0
0-0 15 f4 ♛f6 16 ♚h1 bxc5 17 dxc5
g6 and Black has the better chances,
Yrjölä-Dolmatov, Tallinn 1985.

b) 12 f4 will normally just trans-
pose; e.g., 12...0-0 13 ♝b5 ♝d7 14
0-0 transposes to line 'c', but 12...b6!?
is worth looking into.

c) 12 ♝b5+ ♝d7 13 0-0 0-0 14 f4
(D) (14 ♜ac1 is best met by 14...♝xb5
15 ♞xb5 ♞c6 16 f4 g6 17 ♜f3 ♛f6 18
♜d1 ♜fb8 with a comfortable game,
Bensi-Rivola, corr. 1988) and here:

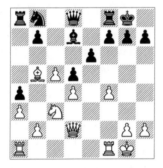

B

c1) 14...♝xb5 15 ♞xb5 g6 16 g4
♞c6 17 f5 ♛h4 18 ♛f4 exf5 19 gxf5
♛xf4 20 ♜xf4 b6! = Levitt-Björnsson,
Hafnarfirdi 1992.

c2) 14...f5 15 ♜fe1 ♝xb5 16 ♞xb5
♛d7 17 ♞c3 ♞c6 18 ♛d1! ♞d8 19
♜c1 ♜f6 = Korchnoi-Seirawan, Bad
Kissingen 1981.

c3) 14...b6 15 f5 bxc5 (15...exf5
leaves White with the better chances:

16 ♝xd7 ♛xd7 17 cxb6 ♞c6 18 ♛f4
g6 19 ♜ac1 ♜a5 20 ♛c7! ± Gligorić-
Lein, Lone Pine 1981) 16 f6!: gxf6 17
♛h6 ♚h8 and here:

c31) 18 ♝d3 f5 19 ♞xd5 f6 20
♞f4 cxd4 (20...♜g8?! 21 ♝c4! ♛e7
22 ♜ae1 is good for White) 21 ♞g6+
♚g8 22 ♞xf8 ♛xf8 23 ♛h4 ♞c6 24
♝b5 with a solid advantage for White.

c32) 18 ♞xd5 ♝xb5 19 ♞xf6 ♝d3
20 ♜f3 ♛xd4+ 21 ♚h1 ♞d7 22 ♞xd7
♜g8 23 ♜xd3 ♛xd3 24 ♛f6+ ♜g7 25
♞e5 ♛e4 ½-½ Khlusevich-Loginov,
corr. 1988.

c4) 14...g6 15 ♜ac1 (15 ♜ae1?!
♝xb5 16 ♞xb5 b6 17 g4 bxc5 18 f5
exf5 19 dxc5 ♞a6! 20 gxf5 ♞xc5 ∓
Miles-Short, Esbjerg 1985) and then:

c41) 15...♛a5 16 ♝d3 (16 ♝xd7
♞xd7 17 g4 b6! = Guliev-Belozerov,
St Petersburg 1994) 16...♞c6 17 ♝b5
(Utasi gives 17 ♝c2 ♞e7 18 g4 with
an initiative for White) 17...♞b8 18 f5
(Utasi-Klinger, Szirak 1985) and now
18...♝xb5 19 f6 ♞d7 20 ♛h6 ♞xf6
21 ♜xf6 ♝d3 is best, with chances for
both sides – Utasi.

c42) 15...♝xb5 16 ♞xb5 ♞c6 17
♜f3 (or 17 ♜c3 ♛f6 18 ♜d3 ♜fb8 19
♜f2 ♜a5 20 ♞c3 b6 = W.Schmidt-
Stempin, Prague Z 1985) 17...♛f6 18
♜d1 ♜fb8 19 ♞c3 b6 20 cxb6 ♜xb6
and Black doesn't have any problems,
Züger-Hellers, New York 1987.

Now we return to the position after
12 ♝d3 *(D)*:

12...b6

This is the critical line. Black attacks White's front pawn and thereby
forces him to make a decision.

12...♝d7 also deserves special attention. After 13 0-0, Black has the
following options:

B

a) 13...b6 14 cxb6 ♕xb6 and now 15 ♗c2 and 15 ♖fe1 0-0 16 ♗c2 both transpose to the main line.

b) 13...0-0 14 f4 g6 15 ♔h1 ♘c6 16 ♗c2 ♘e7 17 ♖ae1 with an initiative for White, Korchnoi-Karpov, Baguio City Wch (3) 1978.

c) 13...♘c6?! and then:

c1) 14 ♖ae1?! just leaves Black a pawn up after 14...♘xd4 15 ♘xd5 ♗c6 16 ♘b6 ♖a5!! 17 ♖d1 (obviously 17 ♕xa5?? is met with the showstopper 17...♘f3+!; e.g., 18 ♔h1 ♕h4 19 h3 ♕f4 −+) 17...♖xc5 18 ♗e4!? ♕xb6 19 ♕xd4 0-0 20 ♖c1 ♖b5, Ivanchuk-Seirawan, Tilburg 1992.

c2) 14 ♗c2 ♘e7 and here:

c21) 15 ♖fe1 b6 (or 15...0-0 16 ♕d1 ♕a5 17 ♕h5 g6 18 ♕h6 ♔h8 19 ♖e3 ♘g8 20 ♕f4 with a solid initiative for White, Bareev-Yudasin, Kranevo 1996) and now:

c211) 16 ♕d1 bxc5 17 dxc5 ♕a5 18 ♘xd5!? (a very aggressive reaction; 18 ♕d4!? is also worth considering) 18...exd5 19 ♕xd5 ♗e6 20 ♕g5 ♘g6 21 ♖e4 0-0 22 ♖xa4 with three connected passed pawns for the piece, Rechlis-Portisch, Manila IZ 1990.

c212) 16 ♕g5! 0-0 17 cxb6 ♘g6 18 ♕xd8 ♖fxd8 19 b4! axb3 20 ♗xg6

hxg6 21 ♖eb1 ♖db8 22 ♖xb3 ♖a6 23 ♖ab1 ± Nenashev-Yudasin, Kemerovo 1995.

c22) 15 ♖ae1 b6 (after 15...0-0, Shirov's 16 ♕d1 ♕a5 17 ♖e3!? looks pleasant for White) 16 ♕g5!? (16 ♕d1 bxc5 17 dxc5 ♕a5 18 ♕d4 0-0 19 ♖e3, Shirov-Yudasin, Moscow OL 1994, 19...♖fc8 20 ♖h3 ♘g6 21 ♗xg6 hxg6 22 ♕h4 f6 23 ♕h7+ ♔f7 24 ♖h6! ♖g8 25 ♖xg6 ♕xc5 26 ♕h5! ♖ac8! leads to a double-edged position − Shirov) 16...0-0 17 cxb6 ♘g6? (17...h6!?) 18 ♕xd8 ♖fxd8 19 b7 ♖a7 20 ♗xa4! ♗xa4 21 ♘xa4 ♖xa4 22 ♖c1 ♖c4?! (22...♘e7!?) 23 b3 ♖xc1 24 ♖xc1 ♘e7 25 a4 ♖b8 26 ♖c7 1-0 Scherbakov-Ramesh, Linares 1996.

c23) Last but not least is Yudasin's suggestion 15 ♕d1!?. His analysis continues 15...♕a5 16 ♕g4 g6 17 ♕g5 ♕d8! 18 ♕h6 ♘g8! with an unclear position (Yudasin). However, this appears a bit optimistic on Black's part; White has a solid lead in development and a good initiative after 19 ♕e3.

We now return to 12...b6 *(D)*:

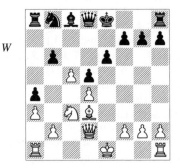

W

13 cxb6

This is not White's only possibility, but is the most logical one. However,

White's other tries are also worthy of attention:

a) 13 ♘xa4 ♖xa4 14 ♗b5+ ♗d7 15 ♗xa4 ♗xa4 16 ♕b4 b5! 17 b3 ♘c6 18 ♕c3 b4 (18...♕f6 19 bxa4 ♘xd4 20 ♖b1 ±) 19 ♕d3 ♕a5 20 bxa4 b3+ 21 ♔e2!? ♕xa4 22 ♖hd1 0-0 23 ♕c3! ♖b8 (Ziatdinov-Yudasin, USSR 1985) 24 ♖ab1 g6 25 ♖d3 e5!? 26 dxe5 ♕e4+ 27 ♔f1 ♘xe5 28 ♖dd1 ♕c4+ = (Yudasin).

b) 13 0-0 and now:

b1) 13...bxc5 14 dxc5 ♕a5 15 ♖ac1 0-0 16 ♖fe1 ♘d7 17 ♕c2 ♘f6 18 ♘a2 ♗a6 19 ♗xa6 ♕xa6 20 ♘b4 ♕b5 21 f3 with a slight initiative for White, Miles-Torre, London 1984.

b2) 13...♗a6 leads to an interesting game after 14 f4 bxc5 15 f5!. Then 15...0-0 16 dxc5 ♘d7 17 fxe6 fxe6 18 ♗xa6 ♖xa6 19 ♘xd5 ♘xc5 20 ♖xf8+ ♕xf8 21 ♖f1 ♕d6 22 ♕f2 ♖a7! gave White just a very slight advantage in Bagirov-Yusupov, USSR 1979, but after 15...cxd4!? White needs to prove the value of his pawn sacrifice.

13...♕xb6 14 ♗c2!

The most precise move-order. After 14 0-0, 14...♗d7 and 14...0-0 are both likely to transpose to the main line, but Black's strongest move, 14...♘c6!?, equalizes smoothly: 15 ♗b5 ♗a6 16 ♗xc6+ ♕xc6 17 ♖fe1 0-0 18 ♖e3 ♕d7 = Shulman-Shaposhnikov, St Petersburg 1997.

14...♗d7 15 0-0 0-0

On occasion Black has preferred 15...♘c6, but without the dominating threat to d4, this move makes less sense and the knight is better off being sent to f6 via d7. White's best is then 16 ♖fd1 ♘e7 17 h4 f6 18 ♖ab1 0-0 19 ♖e1 ♖fe8 (this is the wrong plan, but

19...♖fc8 20 ♕d3 g6 21 h5 also leaves White with a strong initiative) 20 ♖e3 e5 21 dxe5 d4 (Pieniazek-Macieja, Polish Cht (Lubniewice) 1994) and now 22 ♖e4 ♘f5 23 exf6 ♕xf6 24 ♖d1 is strongest.

16 ♖fe1 (D)

Gligorić's suggestion of 16 ♖ae1 also deserves attention. Gomez Esteban-Sanz, Spanish Ch (Zamora) 1996 continued 16...f5 (16...♖c8!?) 17 ♖e3 ♖f7 (the acid test of White's approach is 17...♕xb2!?, which doesn't have any obvious refutation) 18 ♖b1 f4 19 ♖h3 g6 20 ♖h4 ♘c6 21 ♗a4 ♘xd4 22 ♗xd7 ♖xd7 23 ♕xf4 with about equal chances. Black's active pieces and central pawns compensate for the pawn deficit.

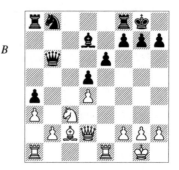

Black has now tried a number of moves:

a) 16...g6?! 17 ♖e3! ♖c8 18 ♖d1 ♗c6 19 ♖f3 ♘d7?! (Lautier gives 19...♖a7 as better, even though 20 h4 leaves White with the initiative) 20 ♕f4 is much better for White, Lautier-Yudasin, Manila IZ 1990.

b) 16...♖a7 17 ♖ad1 ♕d8 18 ♖e3 g6 19 ♖f3 f5 20 ♖e1 ♕f6 21 ♖d3! (preventing Black's idea of ...♘c6)

21...♖c8 22 ♕d1 ♖c4 23 b3 axb3 24 ♗xb3 ♖c8 25 ♗xd5 (Scherbakov-Mitenkov, Russian Ch (Elista) 1995) 25...♖xa3 26 ♗b3 ± Dautov.

c) 16...♘c6 ('?' in *ECO*, which simply gives White's next move without any evaluation) 17 ♗xa4 ♘xd4 18 ♗xd7 ♘b3 19 ♕e2 ♘xa1 20 ♖xa1 ♖fb8 21 a4 ♕xb2 22 ♕xb2 ♖xb2 23 ♖c1 leads to an endgame favourable for White, but his bishop and knight coordinate poorly, reducing his winning chances, Jelling-Berg, Silkeborg 1988.

d) 16...♖c8 17 ♖ad1 (17 ♖e3 ♖c4 18 ♖d1 ♘c6 19 ♘e2 ♖b8? {19...♘e7} 20 ♗d3 ♘a5 21 ♖g3 g6, Makarov-Karpman, USSR Cht (Naberezhnye Chelny) 1988, 22 ♕h6! gives Black serious problems) and now:

d1) 17...♕d8?! 18 ♖e3 ♕f8 19 h4! ♖c4 20 ♗d3 ♖c7 21 ♗b1 ♖b7 22 h5 ♘c6 23 ♘xa4! ♘xd4 (23...♖xa4 24 ♕c2 ♕a8 25 ♕xh7+ ♔f8 26 ♖g3 wins for White) 24 ♕xd4 ♖xa4 25 b4 is much better for White, Knaak-Lerner, Lugano 1989.

d2) 17...♖c4 18 ♗d3 ♖c8 19 ♖e3 ♘c6 20 ♖g3 ♘e7 21 h4 ♕d8 22 ♖e1 ♔h8 23 ♖e5 f5 ± Bareev-Dolmatov, Irkutsk 1986.

e) 16...♗c6 *(D)* and now:

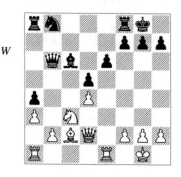

W

e1) 17 ♕d3 g6 18 h4 ♘d7 19 h5 ♖fe8 20 ♖ab1 ♘f8 (Pliester mentions 20...♕d8, intending ...♕f6, as an interesting possibility) 21 ♕d1 ♕a7 22 ♕g4 ♖ec8 with chances for both sides, Gligorić-Seirawan, Nikšić 1983.

e2) 17 ♖e3 ♘d7 18 ♖g3 ♖fc8 (or 18...♖fb8!? 19 ♖b1 ♕d8 20 ♕h6 g6 21 h4 ♕f6 with a complicated struggle ahead, Smith-Cabana, corr. 1995) and now instead of 19 ♖d1?! ♘f8 20 h4 ♕c7 21 h5 h6! 22 ♖e1 ♔h8 23 ♕d1 ♕d7 24 ♘e2 ♗b5 25 ♘c3 ♗c6 with equality, Speelman-Khalifman, Reykjavik 1981, White should play 19 h4!?, when he has some initiative according to Speelman.

18 Taimanov Variation and Odds and Ends

In this chapter, I will take a close look at the Taimanov Variation as well as the minor lines that are not played very regularly, but still turn up in competitions from time to time.

1 d4 ♘f6 2 c4 e6 3 ♘c3 ♗b4 4 e3

Now:

A: 4...c5	296
B: 4...d5	297
C: 4...0-0	298
D: 4...♘c6	306

With the exception of Line D, all of these moves can transpose into the main lines we have covered in the other chapters. In this chapter, however, we look at the side-lines that do not transpose but follow their own independent path.

a) 4...c6 (Grob's move) is best used to transpose to a line of the Semi-Slav: 5 ♗d3 d5 6 ♘f3 ♘bd7. Otherwise ...c6 does not make any sense.

b) 4...a6 5 ♘f3 c5 6 ♗d3 0-0 7 0-0 ♘c6?! (7...d5 ± Keene/Chandler) 8 d5 ♘e7 (Speelman-Short, London 1980) 9 e4! ♗xc3 10 bxc3 d6 11 ♖b1 ± Keene/Chandler.

c) 4...♕e7 5 ♘e2 b6 6 a3 ♗xc3+ 7 ♘xc3 ♗b7 8 d5 d6 9 ♗e2 ♘bd7 10 0-0 0-0 11 e4 ± Botvinnik-Ragozin, Moscow 1947.

d) 4...♘e4 is for some reason not even mentioned in *ECO* despite it

having been played more than 60 times according to my database! The main line is 5 ♕c2 (or 5 ♘e2!?) 5...f5 (5...♗xc3+ and 5...d5 have also been played) 6 ♗d3 and now:

d1) 6...♗xc3+ was played by GM Rashkovsky on one occasion: 7 bxc3 0-0 8 ♘f3 (8 ♗xe4 deserves a look) 8...b6 9 ♗a3 (9 ♗xe4!?) 9...♘d6 10 0-0 ♗b7 11 ♘d2 ♖f6 12 f3 ♖h6 with chances for both sides, Mitenkov-Rashkovsky, Moscow 1995.

d2) 6...d5 7 ♘e2 0-0 8 0-0 c6 9 f3 ♘xc3 10 bxc3 ♗d6 11 ♗d2 and with White ready to break open the centre with e4, he is – with the bishop-pair and better development – better prepared for the middlegame, Muir-Dunworth, British Ch (Swansea) 1987.

e) 4...♗xc3+ 5 bxc3 and now:

e1) 5...c5 and now 6 ♘f3?! ♘c6 7 ♗d3 d6 transposes to Chapter 15, while 6 ♗d3 transposes to note 'c' to Black's 4th move in Chapter 16.

e2) 5...d6 6 ♗d3 e5 7 e4 ♕e7 8 f3 ♘bd7 9 ♘e2 c5 10 0-0 0-0 ±.

e3) 5...0-0 6 ♗d3 d6 (after 6...c5, 7 ♘e2 is similar to lines covered in Chapter 16, while 7 ♘f3 d6 8 0-0 ♘c6 is note 'b' to Black's 8th move in Line B of Chapter 15; 6...b6 7 e4 d6 8 ♘e2 h6 9 0-0 ♗b7 10 ♘g3 c5 11 d5 exd5 12 cxd5 ♖e8 13 c4 ± F.Portisch-Bodo, Nagykanizsa 1994) 7 ♘e2 ♘c6 8 0-0 e5 9 ♘g3 b6 10 f4!? favours White, Šahović-Vincent, Montpellier 1988.

e4) 5...♕e7 6 ♘f3 d6 7 ♗e2 0-0 8 0-0 b6 9 ♘d2 ♗b7 10 f3 ♘bd7 11 e4 e5 12 ♖e1 ♖fe8 13 ♘f1 ± Gligorić-Cekro, Yugoslav Cht (Zlatibor) 1989.

e5) 5...b6 6 ♗d3 ♗b7 7 f3 d6 8 ♘e2 ♘c6 9 e4 ♘a5 10 ♗g5 h6 11 ♗h4 g5?! (Shulman gives 11...♕d7 12 ♘c1 c5 13 ♘b3 ♕a4 14 ♘xa5 ♕xa5 15 ♕d2 ♖c8 16 ♖d1 with chances for both sides) 12 ♗f2 ♕d7 13 ♘c1 0-0-0 14 ♘b3 with better chances for White, Shulman-Yudasin, St Petersburg 1998.

f) 4...b6 leads to a number of the main lines that are covered in the previous chapters. Here, however, we will look at only the lines not covered in other chapters:

f1) 5 a3 ♗xc3+ 6 bxc3 is a Sämisch Variation, which falls outside the scope of this book.

f2) 5 ♘f3 will usually transpose to the previous chapters; e.g., 5...♘e4 6 ♕c2 ♗b7 7 ♗d3 is Line A of Chapter 12.

f3) 5 ♕f3 ♘c6 6 ♗d3 ♗a6 7 ♗d2 ♘a5 8 ♕e2 d5 9 cxd5 ♗xd3 10 ♕xd3 ♗xc3 11 ♗xc3 ♕xd5 and Black has equalized without further problems, Tolush-Estrin, USSR 1954.

f4) 5 f3 bears a resemblance to 4 f3, the Gheorghiu Variation, but here it is only played *after* 4 e3, so White will often lose a tempo on e3-e4 compared to a regular 4 f3. Black's two most interesting moves are now:

f41) 5...♘h5 6 ♘h3 f5 7 e4 0-0 8 ♗g5 ♕e8 9 exf5 exf5+ 10 ♗e2 ♘c6 11 d5 (Mikhalchishin-A.Ivanov, Frunze 1979) and now Pliester's continuation 11...♘e5 should leave Black with a decent game.

f42) 5...c5 6 d5 0-0 7 ♘h3 b5 8 dxe6 fxe6 9 cxb5 d5 with chances for both sides, Miles-de Firmian, Reykjavik 1986.

g) 4...d6 *(D)* and here:

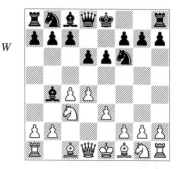

g1) 5 ♘e2 c6 (Black doesn't want to rid himself of the bishop just yet and instead spends some time making a nest for it) 6 a3 ♗a5 7 b4 ♗c7 8 ♘g3 (8 e4 a5 9 ♖b1 axb4 10 axb4 ♘bd7 11 ♘g3 e5 = Altanoch-Kurajica, Elista OL 1998) 8...h5!? 9 ♗d3 h4 10 ♘ge2 e5 (10...h3!?) 11 h3 ♕e7 12 ♕c2 a5 13 b5 with somewhat better chances for White, Supatashvili-Kogan, Mlada Boleslav 1993.

g2) 5 ♗d3 0-0 (other moves have been tried here, including 5...♘c6, which should be compared with Lines D2 and D3) and now:

g21) 6 ♘f3, although played relatively often, is not the most accurate:

g211) 6...♘c6!? is similar to note 'a' to Black's 5th move in Line D3.

g212) 6...♕e7 7 e4 e5 8 d5 ♗xc3+ 9 bxc3 ♗g4 10 h3 ♗h5 11 g4 ♗g6 12 ♗g5 ♘bd7 13 ♘d2 a5 = Uddenfeldt-Raaste, Nice OL 1974.

g213) 6...c5 transposes to note 'f54' to Black's 5th move in Line C1.

g214) 6...♘bd7 7 ♕c2 e5 8 0-0 ♗xc3 9 bxc3 ♖e8 10 e4 b6 11 ♘d2 ♗b7 12 f3 ♘f8 = Portisch-Szabo, Hungarian Ch (Budapest) 1964.

g22) 6 ♘e2 e5 (6...c5 7 0-0 ♘c6 8 a3 ♗xc3 9 ♘xc3 e5 10 dxc5 dxc5 11 ♕c2 gives White a solid advantage due to his bishop-pair and Black's light-squared weakness, Babula-Phiri, Istanbul OL 2000) 7 0-0 *(D)* (or 7 ♕c2!? c6 8 a3 ♗a5 9 b4 ♗c7 10 0-0 ♘bd7 11 d5 cxd5 12 cxd5 ♖e8 13 ♗d2 ♘f8 14 ♖ac1 with a solid advantage for White, D.Gurevich-Spraggett, San Francisco 1987) and then:

B

g221) 7...♘c6 8 d5 ♘b8 9 a3 ♗xc3 10 ♘xc3 ± Botvinnik-Kholmov, Moscow 1947.

g222) 7...exd4?! 8 exd4 d5?! 9 cxd5 ♘xd5 10 ♕c2 ♘f6 (10...h6 loses only a pawn and so is better) 11 ♗g5! ♗xc3 (Black's position is falling apart; Pliester gave 11...h6 as 'necessary', but 12 ♗xf6 gxf6 {12...♕xf6 13 ♘d5 ±} 13 ♕c1! ♔g7 14 ♘g3 is a disaster for Black) 12 ♗xh7+ (12 ♘xc3! is even better) 12...♔h8 13 bxc3 g6 14 ♗xg6 fxg6 15 ♘f4 ♗f5 16 ♘xg6+ ♗xg6 17 ♕xg6 ♕d6 18 ♖ae1 with a nasty attack, Lerner-Raičević, Geneva 1989.

g223) 7...c5?! 8 ♘e4! ♕e7 9 ♘xf6+ ♕xf6 10 d5 ♕e7 11 e4 ± Ragozin-Keres, Moscow 1947.

g224) 7...♗xc3 8 ♘xc3 ♘c6 9 d5 ♘e7 (9...♘b8!?) 10 ♕c2 ♘g6 11 f4 exf4 12 exf4 c6 13 dxc6 bxc6 14 h3 d5 15 cxd5 cxd5 16 ♕f2 with a clear positional advantage for White, Kasparov-L.Jones, Cannes simul 1988.

g225) 7...♖e8 8 a3 ♗xc3 9 ♘xc3 ♘bd7 10 ♗c2 h6 11 d5 ♘f8 12 f3 ± Chekhov-Kuzmin, Leningrad 1991.

g226) 7...c6 8 ♕c2 ♖e8 9 a3 ♗a5 10 b4 ♗c7 11 ♗b2 ♘bd7 12 ♖ad1 ♕e7 13 ♘g3 ♘f8 14 d5 ♗d7 15 ♘f5 ± Taimanov-Golombek, Moscow 1956.

g227) 7...h6 8 ♘e4 ♘xe4 9 ♗xe4 c6 10 ♕a4 ♗a5 11 dxe5 dxe5 12 ♖d1 ♘d7 13 ♗f5 ± Shabtai-Svidler, Tel-Aviv 1991.

A)

4...c5 5 ♘f3

Aside from 5 ♗d3, followed by 6 ♘e2 or 6 ♘f3, which are covered in Chapters 16 and 15 respectively, White can also try 5 a3, which is best met with 5...♗xc3+ 6 bxc3, transposing to a Sämisch Variation.

5...♘c6

Several other moves can be considered:

a) 5...♘e4 6 ♕c2 cxd4 7 exd4 ♕a5 8 ♕xe4 ♗xc3+ 9 ♘d2 f5 10 ♕d3 ♗b4 11 ♗e2 ♗e7 12 0-0 0-0 13 ♘f3 ± Lugovoi-Fusthy, Hungarian Cht 1997.

b) 5...♗xc3+ 6 bxc3 d6 7 ♗d3 ♘c6 is a Hübner Variation, covered in Chapter 15.

c) 5...d5 transposes to note 'd' to White's 5th move in Line B.

d) 5...cxd4 6 exd4 d5 is a Caro-Kann, Panov Attack.

6 ♗d2
Or:

a) 6 ♗d3 transposes to the Hübner Variation (Chapter 15).

b) 6 d5 ♘e7! 7 d6?! (*ECO* gives 7 dxe6 as equal) 7...♘f5! 8 ♕d3 b5 9 cxb5 ♗b7 10 ♗e2 ♖c8 11 0-0 c4 12 ♕c2 ♘xd6 and Black has every reason to be happy with the outcome so far, Christiansen-Browne, USA Ch (South Bend) 1981.

6...cxd4 7 exd4

In Hort-Timman, Amsterdam 1983, Black didn't face any obstacles after 7 ♘xd4 0-0 8 ♗e2 d5 9 cxd5 ♘xd4 10 exd4 exd5 11 0-0 ♗f5 =.

7...0-0 8 a3 ♗xc3 9 ♗xc3 b6 10 ♗d3 a5 11 a4 ♗a6 12 0-0 ♖c8 13 ♖c1 ♕e7

= Jakobsen-Adorjan, Plovdiv Echt 1983.

B)
4...d5 *(D)*

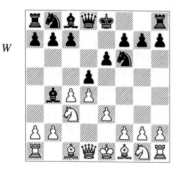

5 a3
Or:

a) 5 ♗d3 and then: 5...♘c6 transposes to note 'c' to Black's 5th move in Line D2; 5...0-0 leads to various main lines considered elsewhere in

this book (Chapters 3, 6 and 16, and Line A of Chapter 14).

b) 5 ♗d2 0-0 6 ♘f3 transposes to Line C1.

c) 5 ♕b3 ♗e7 6 ♘f3 0-0 7 cxd5 exd5 8 ♗d3 b6 9 0-0 c5 10 ♗b1 ♘c6 with a pleasant game for Black, Konings-Ljubojević, Dutch Cht 1997.

d) 5 ♘f3 c5 (5...♘c6 transposes to note 'b' to Black's 5th move in Line D3; 5...0-0 leads to various main lines considered elsewhere in this book: Chapters 1, 2, 4, 5, 7, 8 and 9) 6 ♗d2 (6 a3 ♗xc3+ 7 bxc3 0-0 transposes to note 'e24' to White's 6th move in Line C1) 6...0-0 transposes to Line C1.

e) 5 ♕a4+ ♘c6 6 ♗d2 (6 cxd5 ♘xd5 7 ♗d2 ♘b6 8 ♕c2 e5 9 dxe5 ♘xe5 = Marinelli-Dizdar, Makarska 1994) 6...0-0 7 ♘f3 a6 (7...♗e7!?) 8 a3 ♗xc3 9 ♗xc3 ♘e4 10 ♕c2 ♘xc3 11 ♕xc3 ± Hjartarson-Bator, Eupen ECC 1994.

f) 5 cxd5!? ♘xd5 (not 5...exd5?! 6 ♕a4+ ♘c6 7 ♗b5 ± *ECO*) 6 ♗d2 0-0 7 ♖c1 c5 8 ♘xd5 ♕xd5 9 ♗xb4 cxb4 10 ♕c2 ♘c6 11 ♕c4 (Skembris suggests 11 ♘f3!? ♕xa2 12 ♘g5 with compensation for the pawn) 11...♕a5 12 ♕b3 e5 13 d5 ♘e7 14 e4 ♗d7 15 ♗c4 ♘c8 16 ♘f3 ♘d6 17 ♘d2 (Skembris-Djurić, Istanbul 1988) and here 17...f5!? leads to an unbalanced game with chances for both sides.

g) 5 ♘e2 dxc4! (5...0-0 transposes to Chapter 10) 6 a3 and now:

g1) 6...♗a5 7 ♕a4+ c6 8 ♕xc4 0-0 9 ♘g3 ♘bd7 10 f4 ♘b6 11 ♕d3 c5 is equal, Euwe-Capablanca, Amsterdam (3) 1931.

g2) 6...♗d6 7 e4 e5 8 f4 exd4 9 ♕xd4 ♘c6 10 ♕xc4 0-0 11 ♗e3 (after 11 e5 ♗xe5 12 fxe5 ♘xe5 13 ♕d4

♘d3+ 14 ♔d2 Black has at least a draw with 14...♘c5) 11...♗e6 12 ♕d3 ♘a5 with a good game for Black, Fine-Fischer, New York blitz 1963.

g3) 6...♗e7 7 ♕a4+ ♘bd7 8 ♕xc4 0-0 9 g3 e5! 10 ♗g2 exd4 11 exd4 ♘b6 12 ♕d3 c6 13 ♘f4 ♗d6 14 0-0 ♗xf4! 15 ♗xf4 ♗e6 with a pleasing position for Black, Zaja-Dizdar, Pula 1998.

5...♗e7

5...♗xc3+ is obviously also possible, but this is a Sämisch Variation and therefore not covered in this book.

6 ♘f3

Or:

a) 6 cxd5 exd5 7 ♘ge2 0-0 transposes to Line B of Chapter 10.

b) 6 ♗d3 0-0 7 ♘ge2 (7 ♘f3 transposes to Line C2) 7...b6 8 cxd5 exd5 9 b4 c5!? 10 b5 a6 11 0-0 axb5 12 ♗xb5 ♗b7 13 ♘g3 g6 14 ♗b2 ♘c6 = Petrosian-Antoshin, USSR Ch (Moscow) 1957.

6...0-0 7 b4 *(D)*

White has also tried several other moves at this point, most importantly:

a) 7 ♗d3 transposes to Line C2.

b) 7 b3 c5 8 ♗d3 b6 9 0-0 transposes to Line C2.

c) 7 ♕c2 b6 (or 7...♘bd7 8 ♗e2 c5 9 dxc5 ♘xc5 10 0-0 dxc4 11 ♗xc4 a6 12 b4 ♘cd7 13 ♗b2 b5 14 ♗d3 ♗b7 = Pilnik-Rabar, Bled 1950) 8 cxd5 (8 e4!? dxe4 9 ♘xe4 ♗b7 10 ♗d3 ♘bd7 11 ♗g5 ♘xe4 12 ♗xe7 ♕xe7 13 ♗xe4 ♗xe4 14 ♕xe4 c5 = Korchnoi-Ljubojević, Amsterdam 1991) 8...exd5 9 ♘e5 c5 10 ♗d3 c4 11 ♗e2 a6 12 0-0 b5 13 ♗d2 ♖a7 14 f4 ♖c7 15 ♗f3 ♗b7 with chances for both sides, Volkov-G.Georgadze, Frankfurt 1999.

7...b6

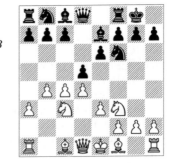

Or:

a) 7...♘bd7?! 8 ♗b2 c6 9 ♕c2 ♖e8 10 ♗d3 dxc4 11 ♗xc4 a5 12 b5 ♘b6 13 ♗d3 cxb5 14 ♘xb5 ♗d7 15 ♘e5 ± Botvinnik-Lipnitsky, USSR Ch (Moscow) 1951.

b) 7...a5 8 b5 c5 9 bxc6 (9 ♗b2!? can also be considered) 9...bxc6 10 c5 ♘bd7 11 ♕c2 ♕c7 12 ♗e2 e5 13 0-0 exd4 14 exd4 ♖e8 15 ♗d3 ♗f8 16 ♗d2 ♗a6 = Furman-Kholmov, USSR 1953.

8 ♗e2

8 cxd5 exd5 9 ♗b2 c5 10 bxc5 bxc5 11 dxc5 ♘a6 12 ♘d4! gave White some advantage in Smyslov-Serper, Tilburg 1992.

8...dxc4 9 ♗xc4 ♗b7 10 0-0 ♘bd7 11 ♖b1 ♘e4 12 ♘xe4 ♗xe4 13 ♗d3 ♗xd3 14 ♕xd3 c5

Black has equalized, Taimanov-Averbakh, Leningrad 1985.

C)

4...0-0

Now we round up the few lines that weren't covered in Chapters 1-10.

5 ♘e2 is covered in Chapter 10.

C1)
5 ♘f3 *(D)*

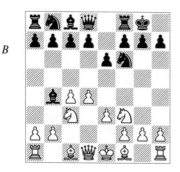

B

5...d5

Black has a number of lesser lines to choose from as well:

a) 5...d6 6 ♗d3 transposes to note 'g21' to Black's 4th move.

b) 5...b6 6 ♗d3 ♗b7 is the subject of Chapters 13 and 14.

c) 5...♘c6 transposes to Line D3.

d) 5...♘e4 6 ♕c2 f5 7 ♗d3 ♘f6 8 ♗d2 h6 9 a3 ♗e7 10 h3 ± O'Kelly-Ortega, Havana 1964.

e) 5...♕e7 is seen very rarely and since it is by no means clear that the queen belongs on this square, even if Black intends ...e5, it should not be played this early on. That said, it is impossible to find a straightforward refutation, so let me just show a classic Nimzowitsch example: 6 ♗d2 d6 7 ♗e2 b6 8 0-0 ♗b7 9 ♕c2 ♘bd7 10 ♖ad1 ♗xc3 11 ♗xc3 ♘e4 12 ♗e1 f5 13 ♕b3 c5!? with a pleasant game for Black, who went on to crush his opponent in just 29 moves in Vidmar-Nimzowitsch, New York 1927.

f) 5...c5 will normally end up transposing to lines covered in other chapters. However, White has some ways

of keeping the game off the beaten track:

f1) 6 ♗d2 d5 transposes to the main line.

f2) 6 a3?! makes very little sense until Black has committed himself to ...d5. 6...♗xc3+ 7 bxc3 d6 (7...d5?! transposes to note 'e24' to White's 6th move) 8 ♗d3 ♘c6 is a good version of the Hübner Variation for Black.

f3) 6 d5 b5!? 7 dxe6 fxe6 8 cxb5 a6 9 a3 axb5 10 ♗d2 ♗xc3 11 ♗xc3 (Hort-Geller, Warsaw 1975) and here Hort gives 11...♕b6 12 b4 as unclear.

f4) 6 ♗e2 is a fairly logical move but doesn't fight for the e4-square and therefore is less interesting than putting the bishop on d3. Black has now tried:

f41) 6...d5 transposes to note 'd4' to White's 6th move.

f42) 6...♗xc3+!? 7 bxc3 d6 8 0-0 b6 9 ♘d2 ♗b7 10 f3 ♘c6 11 ♗b2 e5 12 d5 ♘e7 13 e4 ♘g6 with chances for both sides, Zilberman-Krumbacnik, Oberwart 1998.

f43) 6...b6 7 0-0 and here:

f431) 7...♗xc3 8 bxc3 ♗b7 9 ♘d2 ♘c6 10 ♘b3 (10 ♗f3 can also be tried) 10...d6 11 f3 e5 12 e4 h6 13 ♖b1 ♕c7 14 ♗e3 ♘e7 and the chances are about even, Shestoperov-Osnos, Moscow 1963.

f432) 7...♗b7 8 ♘a4!? (8 ♕b3 is as harmless as it looks: 8...cxd4 9 ♕xb4 ♘c6 10 ♕a3 dxc3 11 ♕xc3 ♘e4 12 ♕c2 f5 13 a3 = Geller-Petrosian, Zurich Ct 1953) 8...cxd4 9 exd4 ♗e7 10 a3 d6 (10...♘e4?! is worse; e.g., 11 d5! b5 12 cxb5 ♗xd5 13 ♗e3 f5 14 ♖c1 ♕e8 15 ♖e1 ± Korchnoi-Mecking, Palma de Mallorca 1969) 11 b4 ♘bd7 12 ♗f4 ♖e8 13 ♖e1 and now, instead of 13...♘f8 14 h3 ♘g6 (Ivanov-Korchnoi, USSR 1973) 15 ♗e3 ± (Korchnoi), Black should continue 13...♘e4!?, intending 14 ♗d3 f5 15 ♗xe4 fxe4 16 ♘d2 d5 with chances for both sides. This is yet to be tested in practice, but as far as I can judge, it has some merit and isn't as passive as 13...♘f8.

f5) 6 ♗d3 (D) is White's natural follow-up. Black has tried various replies, of which the most important are:

B

f51) 6...d5 is the subject of Chapters 1-5 and 7-9.

f52) 6...cxd4 7 exd4 d5 8 0-0 dxc4 9 ♗xc4 transposes to Chapter 1.

f53) 6...♗xc3+ 7 bxc3 d6 should be compared with the Hübner Variation (Chapter 15), although Black has castled rather early.

f54) 6...d6 7 0-0 (7 ♗d2 b6 8 a3 ♗xc3 9 ♗xc3 ♗b7 10 ♕c2 ♘bd7 11 0-0-0 ♖c8 is equal, A.Schneider-Hraček, Stara Zagora Z 1990) 7...♗xc3 8 bxc3 ♕e7!? (8...♘c6 transposes to note 'b' to Black's 8th move in Line B of Chapter 15, while 8...♘bd7 9 e4 e5 10 d5 is a Hübner Variation with a misplaced knight on d7, which Black has to play ...♖e8 to activate; e.g.,

10...♖e8 11 ♕e2 ♘f8 12 ♘e1 ♘g6 13 g3 ♗h3 14 ♘g2 h6 with chances for both sides, Kalesis-Gogolis, Mitilini 1996) 9 e4 e5 10 h3 h6 11 ♖e1 ♘c6 12 d5 ♘d8 13 ♘h2 ♘e8 14 f4 exf4 15 ♗xf4 f6 16 ♘f1 ♘f7 17 ♘e3 g5 18 ♗g3 ♘g7 19 ♗e2 ♘e5 20 ♗g4 ♗d7 21 ♗xe5 ½-½ Parker-Ward, British League (4NCL) 1996/7.

f55) 6...♘c6 7 d5 (7 0-0 and then: 7...♗xc3 8 bxc3 d6 transposes to note 'b' to Black's 8th move in Line B of Chapter 15; 7...d5 is the subject of Chapters 3, 4, 5 and 7) and now:

f551) 7...♘e7 8 e4 ♗xc3+ 9 bxc3 d6 10 ♘h4 e5 11 g3 ± Taimanov-Short, Baku 1983.

f552) 7...exd5 8 cxd5 ♘xd5 9 ♗xh7+ ♔xh7 10 ♕xd5 ♔g8 11 0-0 ♗xc3 12 bxc3 d6 13 e4 ♗g4 14 ♘g5 ♕e7 15 h3 (15 f4!? is best met by 15...♖fe8) 15...♗e6 16 ♘xe6 fxe6 17 ♕g5 (ECO's 17 ♕b3!? fails to impress after 17...♖ad8 =) 17...♕xg5 18 ♗xg5 d5 = Gligorić-Larsen, Nikšić 1983.

f553) 7...♗xc3+ 8 bxc3 and now:

f5531) 8...♘e7?! 9 d6 ♘g6 10 h4 e5 11 h5 ± Furman-Cherepkov, USSR 1956.

f5532) 8...♘a5!? may be worth trying: 9 e4 d6 10 0-0 h6 11 h3 (11 ♘e1, as given in ECO, is best met with 11...b6!?, when Black has the better chances after 12 f3 ♗a6!? or 12 f4 exd5 13 exd5 {13 cxd5 ♖e8} 13...♗a6) 11...b6 12 ♗e3 ♖e8 13 ♘d2 ♗a6 14 ♕c2 ♕d7 15 ♖fe1 ♖e7 with an equal position, Dueball-Hertneck, Bundesliga 1985/6.

f5533) 8...♘b8!? 9 e4 d6 10 0-0 e5 11 ♘e1 ♘bd7 12 f4 ♕a5 13 ♕c2 ♘e8 14 f5 f6 15 g4 ♘b6 16 h4 ♗d7 17 ♘g2

♖c8 (this looks truly mysterious, but the idea becomes clear after Black's next six moves) 18 ♖b1 ♔f7 (rather than await execution on the kingside, Black's king heads for safety on the queenside) 19 ♖f3 ♔e7 20 ♖g3 ♔d8 21 g5 ♔c7 22 ♘e3 ♔b8 23 ♗d2 ♔a8 and White must be better at this point, although Black went on to win in Norri-Hölzl, Pula Echt 1997.

f56) 6...b6 7 d5 (7 0-0 ♗b7 transposes to Chapter 13) 7...exd5 8 cxd5 h6 (the only proper way to proceed; e.g., 8...♘xd5 9 ♗xh7+ ♔xh7 10 ♕xd5 ♗xc3+ 11 bxc3 ♕f6 12 0-0 ♘c6 13 e4 ± Geller-Smyslov, Moscow Ct (3) 1965, or 8...♖e8 9 0-0 ♗b7 10 e4 ♗xc3 11 bxc3 ♘xe4 12 ♗xe4 ♖xe4 13 ♘g5 ♖e5 14 ♕h5 h6 15 ♕xf7+ ♔h8 16 f4 ± Donner-O'Kelly, Palma de Mallorca 1967) and now:

f561) 9 d6 ♗xc3+ 10 bxc3 ♗b7 11 c4 ♘e4 12 ♗xe4 ♗xe4 13 ♗b2 ♘c6 14 0-0 ♕e8 15 ♕e2 ♕e6 with a pleasant game for Black, Vaïsser-Bauer, French Ch (Auxerre) 1995.

f562) 9 0-0 ♗xc3 10 bxc3 ♘xd5 11 e4 ♘c7 12 e5 ♗a6 13 c4 f5 14 exf6 ♕xf6 15 ♖b1 ♘c6 16 ♗b2 ♕f7 17 ♘e5 ♘xe5 18 ♗xe5 (Knaak-Chernin, Palma de Mallorca 1989) 18...d5 19 ♗xc7 ♕xc7 20 cxd5 ♗xd3 21 ♕xd3 ♖f4 ∓ (Chernin).

f563) 9 e4 ♘xe4!? (or 9...♖e8 10 0-0 ♗xc3 11 bxc3 ♘xe4 12 ♖e1 ♘f6 13 ♖xe8+ ♘xe8 14 ♗f4 d6 15 ♕d2 ♗g4! 16 ♗xh6 ♗xf3 17 gxf3 gxh6 18 ♕xh6 ♕f6 19 ♗h7+ ♔h8 20 ♗g6+ ♔g8 21 ♗h7+ ½-½ Timman-Gelfand, Moscow 1992) 10 ♗xe4 ♗xc3+ 11 bxc3 ♖e8 12 ♘d2 f5 13 f3 ♗a6! 14 ♔f2 fxe4 15 ♘xe4 d6 16 ♗f4 ♘d7! 17 ♖e1 ♘e5 18 ♖e3 ♘c4 19 ♖e2 ♘e5 20

♖e3 ♘c4 ½-½ Gelfand-Ivanchuk, Linares 1994.

We now return to 5...d5 (D):

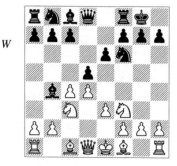

6 ♗d2

Naturally, there are several alternatives to discuss:

a) 6 ♗d3 and then:

a1) 6...♘c6 transposes to Line D3.

a2) 6...b6 is Line A of Chapter 14.

a3) 6...dxc4 7 ♗xc4 c5 8 0-0 is covered in Chapters 1 and 2.

a4) 6...c5 is the subject of Chapters 1-5 and 7-9.

b) 6 ♕b3 c5 7 a3 can be met by 7...♗a5 8 dxc5 ♘bd7 or 7...♗xc3+ 8 ♕xc3 cxd4 9 exd4 ♘c6, in both cases with a pleasant game for Black.

c) 6 ♕c2 b6 (or 6...c5 7 a3 ♗xc3+ 8 bxc3 ♘c6 with a standard Nimzo-Indian position where White has prematurely placed his queen on c2) 7 cxd5 exd5 8 ♗d3 c5 9 dxc5 bxc5 10 0-0 ♗b7 11 ♖d1 ♕e7 12 ♗d2 ♘c6 13 a3 ♗a5 14 ♘a4 ♗b6 15 ♖ac1 ♘e4 with chances for both sides, Kraidman-G.Georgadze, Gausdal 1992.

d) 6 ♗e2 and here:

d1) 6...♘c6 7 0-0 dxc4 8 ♗xc4 transposes to the note to Black's 7th move in Line D3.

d2) 6...a6 followed by ...♘c6 should be compared with Line D3.

d3) 6...b6 7 0-0 ♗b7 8 cxd5 (8 a3 ♗d6 9 cxd5 exd5 10 b4 ♖e8!? {the solid 10...c6 is also fully playable} 11 ♕b3 ♘e4 12 a4 ♘c6 13 ♗a3 ♖e6! with a good game for Black, Lugovoi-A.Sokolov, St Petersburg 1998) 8...exd5 9 ♗d2 (9 a3 ♗d6 10 b4 c6 11 ♕b3 ♘bd7 12 a4 ♖e8 13 ♖d1 ♖c8 14 a5 ♘e4 15 axb6 axb6 16 ♘xe4 dxe4 = Vaïsser-Relange, French Ch (Méribel) 1998) 9...a6 10 ♘e5 ♗d6 11 f4 c5 12 ♗e1 ♘c6 (Bobotsov-Korchnoi, Sochi 1966) and here *ECO* gives 13 ♗h4 cxd4 14 ♘xc6 ♗xc6 15 exd4 as '±', but Black is doing reasonably well after 15...b5.

d4) 6...c5 and here:

d41) 7 cxd5 cxd4 (7...exd5 8 dxc5 ♗xc5 9 0-0 ♘c6 transposes to a Tarrasch Queen's Gambit, while 7...♘xd5 8 ♕c2?! {8 ♗d2 =} 8...cxd4 9 exd4 ♕c7 10 ♗d2 ♘f4 is pleasant for Black, Vistaneckis-Antoshin, Erevan 1955) 8 exd4 exd5 9 0-0 ♗xc3 10 bxc3 ♘e4 11 ♗b2 b6 12 c4 ♗b7 13 ♖e1 ♘d7 is equal, Balashov-Makarychev, Moscow Ch 1982.

d42) 7 a3 and here:

d421) 7...♗xc3+ 8 bxc3 dxc4 9 ♗xc4 and then: 9...b6 10 0-0 transposes to note 'd41' to Black's 8th move in Chapter 2; 9...♘bd7 10 0-0 b6 is note 'f2' to White's 9th move in Line C of Chapter 2; 9...♘c6 10 0-0 transposes to Line A of Chapter 6.

d422) 7...cxd4 8 axb4 dxc3 9 bxc3 ♕c7 10 ♕b3 ♗d7 11 ♗b2 ♖c8 12 cxd5 exd5 13 0-0 ♗e6 14 ♘d4 ♘bd7 15 ♖a5 a6 16 ♖fa1 with chances for both sides, Korchnoi-Tal, Wijk aan Zee 1968.

d43) 7 0-0 ♘c6 (7...b6 is playable, while 7...dxc4 8 ♗xc4 transposes to Chapters 1 and 2) 8 cxd5 exd5 (the alternative 8...cxd4 9 dxc6 dxc3 10 ♕b3 was played in Bronstein-Szabo, Zurich Ct 1953 and here Bronstein gives 10...♕b6!? as Black's best) 9 dxc5 ♗xc3!? (against 9...♗xc5, Schwarz gives 10 a3 a6 11 b4 ♗d6 12 ♗b2 ♗g4 13 ♖c1 ♗c7 14 ♘a4 ♕d6 15 g3 ♘e4 16 ♘c5 ±) 10 bxc3 ♕a5 11 ♘d4 ♕xc5 12 ♘b5 ♖d8 13 ♗a3 ♕b6 14 ♖b1 ♗f5 15 ♖b2 ♕a5! 16 ♕b3 ♖d7 17 ♘d6 ♗e6 18 ♕c1 ♖b8 19 ♕b2 ♕c7 20 ♘b5 ♕d8 21 ♘d4 ♘a5! 22 ♖b5 ♖c8 with approximately equal chances, Speelman-Abramović, Biel IZ 1993.

e) 6 a3 *(D)* and here:

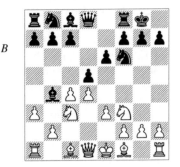

e1) 6...♗e7 transposes to Line B.

e2) 6...♗xc3+ 7 bxc3 and now:

e21) 7...♘c6 8 ♗d3 transposes to note 'a' to White's 7th move in Line D3.

e22) 7...c6 8 ♗d3 (or 8 a4 ♖e8 9 ♗b2 b6 10 cxd5 ♕xd5 11 ♕c2 ♗b7 12 ♗d3 c5 13 e4!? ♘xe4 14 c4 ♕f5 15 0-0 ♘a6 16 ♗a3, Korchnoi-Chabanon, Enghiens les Bains 1997, 16...♕f4 17 ♗c1 ♕f5 18 ♗a3 =) 8...b6 9 0-0 ♗a6 10 cxd5 ♗xd3 11 ♕xd3 cxd5 12 c4

♘c6 13 cxd5 ♕xd5 = Smyslov-Serper, Tilburg 1992.

e23) 7...b6 8 cxd5 exd5 9 ♗b2 ♘c6 10 c4 ♗a6 11 ♖c1 ♘a5 12 cxd5 ♗xf1 13 ♔xf1 ♕xd5 14 ♕d3 c5 with a pleasant game for Black, Graf-Milov, Ohrid 2001.

e24) 7...c5 and here:

e241) 8 ♗d3 and 8 ♗e2 are met by 8...dxc4 9 ♗xc4; see line 'd421' for the details of the possible transpositions from there.

e242) 8 ♕c2 as mentioned above doesn't lead anywhere for White, as he wastes a tempo on the at present useless ♕c2.

e243) 8 cxd5 exd5 9 ♗e2 ♘e4 10 ♗b2 cxd4 11 ♘xd4 ♘d7 12 0-0 ♘b6 13 a4 ♖e8 14 a5 ♘c4 15 ♗xc4 ± Boleslavsky-Rabar, Vienna 1957.

e244) 8 ♗b2 has been used occasionally by Korchnoi:

e2441) 8...♕a5 9 ♘d2 ♘bd7 10 cxd5 exd5 11 ♗d3 cxd4 12 cxd4 (the alternative 12 ♘b3 ♕c7 13 cxd4 ♘b6 14 a4 ♖e8 15 0-0 ♘g4 16 g3 ♕d6 17 ♗c1 ♕h6 18 h4 ♕h5 19 ♕f3 ♘c4 20 ♖e1 ♘d6 21 ♕g2 ♘f6 with chances for both sides, Agdestein-Richardson, Reykjavik 1998) 12...♘b6 13 0-0 ♘a4 14 ♕c2 ♗d7 15 ♘b3 ♕d8 16 ♘c5 ♖c8 17 ♕b3 ♘xc5 18 dxc5 is slightly better for White, F.Olafsson-Medina, Wijk aan Zee 1969.

e2442) 8...♘c6 9 ♕c2 cxd4 10 cxd4 ♗d7 11 ♗d3 dxc4 12 ♕xc4 ♖c8 13 ♕a2 ♕a5+ 14 ♔e2 ♘e7 15 ♖ac1 ♘ed5 16 ♕b1 ♗b5 = Korchnoi-Palac, Val Maubuée 1990.

6...c5 *(D)*

Black has a long list of other moves that have been tried out at this point. The most important are these:

a) 6...b6 7 ♗d3 transposes to note 'a' to Black's 7th move in Line A of Chapter 14.

b) 6...♘c6 7 ♖c1 (7 ♗d3 should be compared with Line D3) 7...a6 8 a3 ♗d6 9 c5 ♗e7 10 ♗d3 ♖e8 11 b4 e5 12 ♘xe5 ♘xe5 13 dxe5 ♘g4 14 0-0 d4 15 ♘e4 ♘xe5 with chances for both sides, Hort-Novak, Havirov 1970.

c) 6...♘bd7 7 ♕c2 c6 (7...c5 is also playable) 8 a3 ♗d6 9 0-0-0 (White can also castle kingside if this move seems a little too bold) 9...c5 10 ♔b1 cxd4 11 ♘xd4 a6 12 ♗c1 ♕c7 13 cxd5 exd5 14 ♘f5 ♘b6 15 ♘xd6 ♕xd6 = Borisenko-Kholmov, USSR 1965.

W

7 dxc5

I don't believe this is the kind of move that should keep you up at night. However, the alternatives are not particularly impressive either:

a) 7 cxd5 cxd4 (or 7...exd5 8 dxc5 ♗xc5 9 ♗e2 ♘c6 10 0-0 a6 11 ♖c1 ♗a7 with an advantage for Black, Pleimer-Balinov, Raiffeisen 1997) 8 ♘xd4 ♘xd5 9 ♖c1 ♘f6 10 ♗e2 e5 11 ♘b3 ♘c6 12 0-0 ♗e6 13 ♕c2 ♖c8 14 ♖fd1 ♕e7 with a somewhat more pleasant game for Black, Høi-P.H.Nielsen, Danish Ch (Tåstrup) 1998.

b) 7 a3 ♗xc3 (7...cxd4 8 exd4 ♗xc3 9 ♗xc3 dxc4 10 ♗xc4 b6 11 ♕e2 ♗b7 12 0-0 ♘c6 13 ♖fe1 ♘d5 14 ♗d2 ♕d6 and despite the chances being about equal, handing White the bishop-pair can easily become a liability in the long run, Slipak-Zarnicki, Buenos Aires 1995) 8 ♗xc3 ♘e4 9 ♖c1 ♘xc3 10 ♖xc3 cxd4 11 ♘xd4 a6 12 cxd5 ♕xd5 13 ♕c2 ♘d7 14 f3 ♘f6 15 ♗c4 ♕h5 16 0-0 ♗d7 17 ♗e2 ♖ac8 ½-½ Velikov-Semkov, Bulgarian Ch (Pernik) 1983.

7...♗xc5 8 ♖c1

8 ♗d3 ♘c6 9 0-0 dxc4 10 ♗xc4 e5 11 ♕c2 ♗g4 = Gerusel-Pachman, West German Ch (Bad Neuenahr) 1978.

8...♘c6 9 cxd5 exd5 10 ♘a4 ♗e7 11 ♗c3 ♘e4 12 ♗e2 ♘xc3 13 ♘xc3 ♗e6

The chances are equal, Varga-Lyrberg, Budapest 1993.

C2)
5 ♗d3 d5 6 a3

This move forces Black to make an immediate decision regarding the future of his dark-squared bishop. Two lines with ♘e2, viz. 6 ♘e2 and 6 cxd5 exd5 7 ♘e2, are discussed in Chapter 16.

6...♗e7 (D)
Or:

a) 6...♗xc3+ 7 bxc3 transposes to Line B of Chapter 6.

b) 6...dxc4 and then:

b1) 7 ♗xc4 is quite tame. 7...♗d6 and now:

b11) 8 ♘f3 and here:

b111) 8...♘c6 transposes to note 'b' to White's 7th move in Line D3.

b112) 8...♘bd7 leads to a better game for White according to Botvinnik,

who gives 9 b4 e5 10 ♗b2 a5 11 b5 exd4 12 ♘xd4 ♘b6 13 ♗e2 ±.

b12) 8 f4 c5! 9 dxc5 ♗xc5 10 b4 ♗b6 11 ♕xd8 ♖xd8 12 ♘f3 ♗d7! 13 ♗d2 ♖c8 and Black has equalized, although White won in the end in Botvinnik-Balashov, Hastings 1966/7.

b2) 7 ♗xh7+ ♘xh7 (7...♔xh7 8 axb4 ♘c6 9 b5 ♘b4 10 ♖a4 a5 11 ♘f3 ♗d7 12 e4 ♘d3+ 13 ♔f1 ± Jelen-Farago, Sas van Gent 1992) 8 axb4 and then:

b21) 8...e5 9 ♘f3 and now 9...exd4 10 ♘xd4 ♘d7 11 b5! was better for White in Gulko-Benko, Aruba 1992, while 9...♗g4 10 h3 ♗xf3 11 ♕xf3 ♘c6, as quoted in *ECO*, is best met with 12 0-0 exd4 13 exd4 ♕xd4 14 b5, when White has the initiative – Dautov.

b22) 8...♘c6 9 b5 ♘b4 10 ♘f3 ♘d3+ 11 ♔f1 ♘f6 12 ♘d2 (12 b3 used to be considered better for White, but in *NCO* Emms refutes this move with 12...♘g4! 13 ♕c2 ♘gxf2 14 bxc4 e5 ∓) 12...e5 13 ♘xc4 exd4 14 ♕xd3 dxc3 15 ♕xc3 gives Black sufficient compensation for the pawn – Ernst.

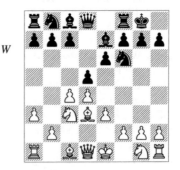

7 ♘f3 b6
Or:

a) 7...dxc4 8 ♗xc4 c5 9 0-0 transposes to line 'c2'.

b) 7...♘bd7 8 0-0 c5 9 cxd5 exd5 10 ♘e5 ♕c7 11 f4 b6 12 ♕f3 ♗b7 13 ♗d2 ♖ad8 14 ♖ac1 ± Van Scheltinga-Bouwmeester, Wageningen 1958.

c) 7...c5 8 0-0 (White has a noteworthy alternative in 8 cxd5 exd5 9 dxc5 ♗xc5 10 0-0 ♘c6 11 b4 ♗b6 12 ♗b2 ♖e8 13 h3 ♗e6 14 ♘a4 with a better game for White, Van der Sterren-Sosonko, Brussels Z 1993; Black badly needs an improvement here to avoid too much pain) and then:

c1) 8...b6 transposes to the main line.

c2) 8...dxc4 9 ♗xc4 a6 10 ♕e2 b5 11 ♗d3 (after 11 ♗a2 cxd4 12 exd4 b4 13 axb4 ♘c6 14 ♗c4 ♘xb4 15 ♗e3 ♗b7 16 ♖fc1 ♖c8 17 ♘e5 ♘d7 Black has neutralized most of White's initiative, Sadler-I.Sokolov, Dutch Cht 2000) 11...♘bd7 12 dxc5 ♗xc5 13 e4 e5 14 ♗g5 h6 15 ♗xf6 ± Szabo-Dely, Hungarian Ch (Budapest) 1951.

8 0-0

White can deviate by playing 8 e4: 8...dxe4 9 ♘xe4 ♗b7 10 ♕c2 (10 ♕e2, as given in *ECO*, isn't as problematic for Black: 10...c5 11 dxc5 bxc5 12 0-0 ♘xe4 13 ♗xe4 ♗xe4 14 ♕xe4 ♘d7 15 ♗d2 ♕b6 16 ♖ab1 a5 = Baranov-Antoshin, Moscow Ch 1953) 10...♘bd7 11 0-0 c5 (11...♘xe4 12 ♗xe4 ♗xe4 13 ♕xe4 c5 is about equal) 12 ♖d1 cxd4 13 ♘xd4 ♕c7 14 ♗g5 h6 15 ♗h4 with an initiative for White, Sashikiran-Hoang Hai, Vung Tau City 1999.

8...c5 *(D)*

8...♗b7 transposes to note 'c' to Black's 8th move in Line B2 of Chapter 14.

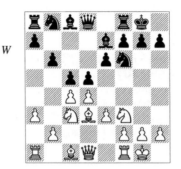

9 b3
Or:

a) 9 cxd5 exd5 10 dxc5 bxc5 11 e4 dxe4 12 ♘xe4 ♗a6 13 ♗xa6 ♘xa6 14 ♘g3 ♘c7 = Smyslov-Keres, USSR Ch (Moscow) 1949.

b) 9 ♕e2 ♘c6 10 dxc5 bxc5 11 ♖d1 ♗b7 12 ♕c2 d4 13 ♘e2 e5 14 ♘g3 ♖e8 15 exd4 ♘xd4 and it's clear that Black has solved his opening problems, Filip-Keres, Curaçao Ct 1962.

9...♘c6 10 ♗b2 ♗b7
Or 10...cxd4 11 exd4 ♗a6 12 ♖e1 ♘a5 13 ♘e5 ♖c8 14 ♘b5 dxc4 15 bxc4 ♘xc4 16 ♗xc4 ♖xc4 17 ♘xc4 ♗xb5 18 ♘e5 ♕d5 19 ♕c2 ♗d6 20 ♖ac1 ♗a6 21 ♕c6 ♗b5 22 ♕xd5 ♘xd5, with some but perhaps not completely full compensation for the exchange, Gligorić-F.Olafsson, Varna OL 1962. Black has a good grip of the light squares and it will be quite difficult for White to penetrate Black's solid position.

11 cxd5 exd5
Ftačnik calls this a mistake and instead gives 11...♘xd5 12 ♘xd5 ♕xd5 13 ♕c2 ♕h5 =.

12 ♘e2!? ♘e4
Ftačnik isn't impressed with this move either, calling 12...a5 the better

move, although I think White has the upper hand after 13 dxc5 bxc5 14 ♕c2.

13 dxc5 bxc5 14 ♕c2 ♕b6 15 ♘g3 f5 16 ♘h5 ♖f7

This position is called equal by *ECO*, but White seems able to obtain an advantage with 17 ♘f4 (in the game Bronstein-Furman, USSR Ch (Moscow) 1948, White continued 17 ♖ab1, which should have been answered with 17...♗d6 =) 17...♖d8 18 ♖ac1 with pressure against Black's hanging pawns.

D)
4...♘c6 *(D)*

W

This is the Taimanov Variation, named after the strong Russian GM and great theoretician Mark Taimanov who participated in two candidates cycles, but who in many people's minds is nowadays unjustifiably only remembered for his 0-6 loss to Fischer in 1971. Taimanov is still an active player after whom several other opening lines are named, notably the Taimanov Sicilian (1 e4 c5 2 ♘f3 e6 3 d4 cxd4 4 ♘xd4 ♘c6) and the Taimanov Benoni (1 d4 ♘f6 2 c4 c5 3 d5 e6 4

♘c3 exd5 5 cxd5 d6 6 e4 g6 7 f4 ♗g7 8 ♗b5+). He is also the author of several opening manuals, including one on the Nimzo-Indian.

The Taimanov Variation of the Nimzo-Indian is a very flexible system which allows a choice of plans for Black, making it difficult for White to prove a simple path to an advantage.

White must now choose how to proceed:

D1: 5 ♘e2   306
D2: 5 ♗d3   309
D3: 5 ♘f3   310

White can also consider:

a) 5 a3 ♗xc3+ 6 bxc3 0-0 transposes to a line of the Sämisch Variation (4 a3 ♗xc3+ 5 bxc3 0-0 6 e3 ♘c6), which is not covered in this book.

b) 5 ♕b3 is a Spielmann Variation (4 ♕b3 ♘c6 5 e3) and thus also outside the scope of this book.

c) 5 ♕c2 is the Zurich Variation of the Classical Nimzo-Indian (4 ♕c2 ♘c6 5 e3) which is not covered here either.

d) 5 ♗d2 d5 (or 5...♗xc3!? 6 ♗xc3 d6 7 ♗d3 e5 8 d5 ♘e7 9 ♕c2 c6 10 e4 cxd5 11 cxd5 ♘d7 {11...♗d7!?} 12 ♘e2 ± Anikaev-Rashkovsky, USSR Ch (Minsk) 1979) 6 ♘f3 (6 ♗d3 e5 7 cxd5 ♘xd5 = Danchez-Barcza, Stockholm IZ 1952) 6...0-0 7 a3 ♗xc3 8 ♗xc3 ♘e4 9 ♕c2 a5 with an equal position, Pachman-Fischer, Buenos Aires 1960.

D1)
5 ♘e2 *(D)*
5...d5
Or:

B

a) 5...♘e4 6 ♕c2 d5 7 a3 ♘xc3 8 ♘xc3 ♗xc3+ 9 ♕xc3 0-0 (Bosbach-Goldberg, Bundesliga 1996/7) 10 ♗d3 ±.

b) 5...e5 6 a3 ♗xc3+ 7 ♘xc3 exd4 8 exd4 d5 9 c5 h6 10 ♗b5 0-0 11 0-0 ♗f5 12 f3 ♖e8 13 g4 and White is taking control over the game, Botvinnik-Sokolsky, USSR Ch (Moscow) 1944.

6 a3

This is the logical follow-up to White's previous move, but he has also tried:

a) 6 ♘g3 e5 7 a3 exd4 8 axb4 dxc3 9 bxc3 0-0 10 cxd5 ♘xd5 11 ♕c2 ♖e8 12 ♗d3 ♕h4 13 0-0 ♘e5 14 ♖d1 ♘xd3 15 ♕xd3 ♗e6 (Azmaiparashvili-Rashkovsky, Volgodonsk 1981) and although *ECO* has this as equal, I prefer White's chances after 16 e4!?.

b) 6 cxd5 exd5 7 a3 ♗d6 8 g3 ♗f5 9 ♗g2 ♕d7 10 h3 0-0-0 11 g4 ♗g6 (Toshkov-Rashkovsky, Baku 1983) 12 b4!? ±.

6...♗e7

This retreat is the most obvious continuation, but Black has also tried:

a) 6...♗xc3+?! 7 ♘xc3 0-0 8 f4 ± Kluger-Barcza, Hungary 1966.

b) 6...♗f8 (the idea behind this paradoxical move is to use the e7-square

as a transfer point for the c6-knight on its way to f5) 7 cxd5 (the main line, but in my database, White has a 100% score with 7 ♘g1, 7 ♘g3 and 7 ♘f4, despite none of them being particularly convincing) 7...exd5 8 ♘f4 (8 g3!? has been tried on a few occasions; 8 b4!? ♘e7 9 g3 ♘f5 10 ♗g2 ♗e7 11 0-0 0-0 12 f3 ± Geller-Taimanov, Budva 1967) 8...♘e7 9 b4 a6 10 g3 c6 11 ♗g2 ♘f5 12 0-0 ♗d6 (Osnos-Taimanov, USSR Ch (Tbilisi) 1966) 13 ♘d3 0-0 14 a4 with a slight advantage for White thanks to his queenside initiative – *ECO*.

c) 6...♗d6!? is Black's latest try in this line and has done quite well: 7 c5 (7 ♘g3 is answered by 7...h5!? 8 cxd5 exd5 9 ♗d3 h4 10 ♘f1 ♕e7 11 ♗e2 ♗f5, when Black is doing very well, Kharlov-Rashkovsky, Moscow 1992) 7...♗e7 8 f4!? a5 9 ♖b1 b6 10 b4 axb4 11 axb4 bxc5 12 bxc5 0-0 13 ♘g3 ♗a6 14 ♗xa6 ♖xa6 15 ♕d3 ♖a8 = Milov-Rashkovsky, Moscow 2002.

7 cxd5

7 ♘g3 is also seen relatively often, but Black is doing fine in this line: 7...h5! 8 cxd5 (8 ♗d3 h4 9 ♘ge2 h3 10 g3 e5 11 cxd5 ♘xd5 12 ♘xd5 ♕xd5 13 e4 ♕a5+ {or 13...♕d6!? =} 14 ♗d2 ♕b6 15 d5 ♘b8 16 ♘c3, Jelen-Gostiša, Slovenian Ch 1992, 16...♗d7 =) 8...exd5 9 ♗d3 h4 10 ♘f1 h3 11 g3 0-0 12 ♘d2 ♗g4 13 f3 ♗c8 with a pleasant position for Black, Botvinnik-Taimanov, USSR Ch (Moscow) 1951.

7...exd5 *(D)*

8 ♘f4

Or:

a) 8 ♘g3 0-0 (8...h5!? transposes to the note to White's 7th move) 9

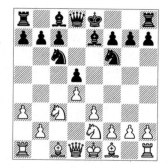

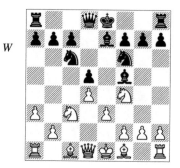

♗d3 g6 10 ♕c2 ♖e8 11 ♗d2 a6 12 0-0-0 b5 with chances for both sides, Podgaets-Gulko, USSR 1970.

b) 8 g3 0-0 (the standard 8...h5!? can also be considered; e.g., 9 ♗g2 ♗d6 10 h3 ♗f5 11 ♘xd5 ♘xd5 12 e4 ♗xe4 13 ♗xe4 ♘ce7 14 ♕b3 ♖b8 15 ♗g5 ♕d7 16 0-0-0 c6 with a complicated struggle ahead, Gavrikov-Rashkovsky, USSR Ch (Kiev) 1986) 9 ♗g2 ♘a5 10 0-0 c6 11 ♘a4 b6 12 ♘ac3 ♗a6 with roughly equal chances, Botvinnik-Taimanov, USSR Ch (Moscow) 1952.

8...♗f5 *(D)*

After 8...0-0, White has a choice:

a) 9 ♗e2 ♘a5 (9...♗f5 and 9...♖e8 can also be considered) 10 b4 ♘c4 11 ♘cxd5 ♘xd5 12 ♗xc4 ♘xf4 13 exf4 a5 14 b5 ♗g4! with compensation for the pawn, Taimanov-Stobik, San Augustin 1990.

b) 9 ♗d3 ♖e8 10 0-0 ♗f8 11 h3 ♘e7 12 ♕f3 c6 13 ♗d2 (Korchnoi-Mukhutdinov, Sverdlovsk 1957) 13...♘g6 14 ♘h5 ♘xh5 15 ♕xh5 a5 = (*ECO*).

9 ♗e2

White has a few other moves at his disposal:

a) 9 b4 ♕d7 10 ♕b3 ♖d8 11 ♗d3 0-0 12 ♗d2 ♖fe8 13 0-0 ♗xd3 14 ♘xd3

♕f5 15 ♘f4 (Ivkov-Pachman, Beverwijk 1965) 15...♗d6 16 ♘cxd5 ♘xd5 17 ♕xd5 ♕xd5 18 ♘xd5 ♗xh2+ 19 ♔xh2 ♖xd5 =.

b) 9 ♕b3 ♘a5 10 ♕a4+ (not 10 ♕a2?! g5 11 ♗d3 ♗xd3 12 ♘xd3 c6 13 ♘e5 ♘d7 14 0-0 f6 15 ♘xd7 ♕xd7 and Black is slightly better, O'Kelly-Borisenko, corr. 1957) 10...♘c6 11 ♗a6 bxa6 12 ♕xc6+ ♗d7 13 ♕xa6 ♗d6 14 ♘fe2 0-0 15 f3 ♖e8 with excellent compensation for the pawn, Mohrlok-Hecht, Büsum 1968.

9...♕d7 10 b4

White's latest try in this line. Previously, White preferred 10 ♗f3 ♗e4 11 ♗xe4 dxe4 12 ♕c2 (12 ♘h5 ♘xh5 13 ♕xh5 g6 14 ♕b5 0-0-0 = Polugaevsky-Borisenko, USSR 1958) 12...♗d6 13 ♘fe2 ♗g4 (13...♕e7!?) 14 ♘g3 ♗xg3 15 fxg3 0-0 = Kuzmin-Rashkovsky, USSR 1971.

10...0-0 11 ♗d2 ♖fe8 12 0-0 ♗f8 13 f3 g6 14 ♘d3 b6 15 g4

A very aggressive approach from White, but Black's defensive resources are in place.

15...♗xd3 16 ♗xd3 ♘d8 17 b5 c5 18 bxc6 ♘xc6 19 ♕c2 ♖ed8

½-½   G.Georgadze-Rashkovsky, Ubeda 1996.

D2)

5 ♗d3 *(D)*

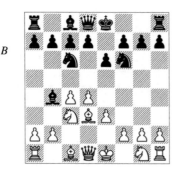

5...e5

Or:

a) 5...d6 is possible, but gives Black fewer active possibilities.

b) 5...0-0 6 ♘ge2 (6 ♘f3 transposes to Line D3) and now:

b1) 6...♖e8 7 0-0 d5 8 cxd5 exd5 9 f3 b6 10 a3 ♗f8 11 b4 ♗b7 12 ♗c2 and White has the better chances, D.Gurevich-Benko, New York 1987.

b2) 6...e5 7 0-0 ♖e8 8 d5 ♘b8 9 e4 a5 10 a3 ♗f8 11 ♘g3 ± Reshevsky-Tolush, Leningrad/Moscow 1939.

b3) 6...d5 7 a3 ♗d6 8 c5 ♗e7 9 f4 a5 10 ♕c2 b6 11 ♘a4 bxc5 12 ♘xc5 ♗xc5 13 ♕xc5 ♗a6! 14 ♗xa6 ♖xa6 is comfortable for Black, Pähtz-Reeh, Bundesliga 1991/2.

c) 5...d5 and here:

c1) 6 ♘e2 0-0 is line 'b3'.

c2) 6 ♘f3 0-0 transposes to Line D3.

c3) 6 cxd5 ♕xd5 (6...exd5 7 ♘ge2 0-0 8 f3 ♘e7 9 g4 c5 10 a3 cxd4, Rechlis-Johansen, Novi Sad OL 1990, and now 11 axb4 dxc3 12 bxc3 is better for White) 7 ♘f3 e5 8 dxe5 ♘xe5 9 ♘xe5 ♗xc3+ 10 bxc3 ♕xe5

11 ♕c2 0-0 = Zifroni-Wojtkiewicz, Graz 1997.

c4) 6 a3 dxc4 (6...♗xc3+!? 7 bxc3 e5 8 ♘e2 e4 9 ♗b1 dxc4 10 ♘g3 ♘a5 {10...♕d5 is possibly better} 11 ♘xe4 ♘b3 12 ♘xf6+ ♕xf6 13 ♖a2 ± I.Sokolov-Eslon, Stockholm 1987) 7 ♗xc4 ♗d6 8 f4!? (8 ♘f3 0-0 transposes to note 'b' to White's 7th move in Line D3) 8...♘d5 9 ♘f3 ♘xc3 10 bxc3 ♘a5 11 ♗d3 c5 12 0-0 (Keene-Fedorowicz, New York 1981) and at this point 12...0-0 keeps White's advantage within limits.

6 ♘e2

Now and again, White has tried 6 d5, but this is harmless: 6...♗xc3+ 7 bxc3 ♘e7 8 e4 (8 ♘e2 d6 9 ♕c2 ♘d7 10 ♘g3 ♘c5 11 e4 ♘g6 = Andersson-Borisenko, Varna 1972) 8...d6 9 ♘e2 0-0 10 0-0 b6 (10...♘d7 is also perfectly playable) 11 ♘g3 h6 12 ♗e3 ♗d7 13 ♗c2 ♕c8 14 ♗a4 ♗xa4 15 ♕xa4 ♕d7 = Lomineishvili-Balashov, Schwäbisch Gmünd 1998.

6...d5!?

This move appears to be Black's best, since other moves seem to leave White with the better chances:

a) 6...0-0 transposes to note 'b2' to Black's 5th move.

b) 6...exd4 7 exd4 d5 and here:

b1) 8 cxd5 is an unconvincing move: 8...♘xd5 9 0-0 0-0 10 ♕c2 g6 11 a3 ♗e7 12 ♗h6 ♖e8 13 ♖ad1 ♘xc3 14 ♕xc3 ♗f6 15 ♕b3 ♘xd4 16 ♘xd4 ♗xd4 17 ♗c4 ♗e6 18 ♗xe6 ♖xe6 19 ♕xb7 c5 = Cebalo-Popović, Yugoslav Ch (Novi Sad) 1985.

b2) 8 c5 0-0 9 0-0 ♗xc3 10 bxc3 h6 (or 10...♘e7 11 ♕c2 ♘g6 12 ♗g5 h6 13 ♗d2 ± Mileika-Tal, Latvian Ch (Tallinn) 1953) 11 ♘g3 b6 12 ♗a3

♖e8 13 ♕f3 ♗g4 14 ♕f4 ♘e7 15 ♖ae1 ± Gligorić-Pachman, Havana OL 1966.

7 cxd5

In recent years, White has scored very well with 7 0-0, which has otherwise been considered reasonably harmless. Black seems able to equalize: 7...dxc4 8 ♗xc4 exd4 9 ♘xd4 (or 9 exd4 0-0 10 h3 h6 11 ♗e3 ♘e7 12 ♘g3 c6 13 ♕f3 ♘fd5 14 ♘xd5 ♘xd5 15 ♘h5, Jeremić-Kyriakidis, Khalkidhiki U-16 Ech 2001, 15...♕d6!? =) 9...♘xd4 10 exd4 0-0 11 ♗g5 c6 (11...♗e7!? = ECO) 12 ♖e1 ♕d6 13 ♕d2 ♗f5 14 ♗f4 ♕d7 and White has at most a tiny plus thanks to his bishop-pair, Høi-Pachman, Lucerne 1979.

7...♘xd5 (D)

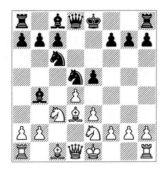

8 e4

Or:

a) 8 a3 exd4 (8...♗a5 is also sufficient for equality) 9 exd4 ♗e7 10 0-0 0-0 11 ♗e4 ♘f6 12 ♗f3 ♗g4 13 ♗xg4 ♘xg4 14 h3 ♘f6 = Jelen-Rashkovsky, Bled 1992.

b) 8 0-0 exd4 and then:

b1) 9 ♘xd5 ♕xd5 10 exd4 0-0 11 ♗e3 ♗f5! 12 ♗xf5?! (Chekhov gives 12 ♘f4!? ♕d7 13 d5 ♘e7 14 ♕b3 ♗d6 15 ♖ad1 without any evaluation, but 15...♗xd3 is more than adequate for Black) 12...♕xf5 13 ♕b3 a5! 14 ♖ac1 a4 15 ♕c4 ♗d6 is pleasant for Black, Levenfish-Mikenas, USSR Ch (Moscow) 1940.

b2) 9 exd4 0-0 10 ♕c2 h6 11 a3 ♗e7 12 ♘xd5 ♕xd5 13 ♗e3 ♗d6 14 ♖fd1 ♗g4 15 h3 ♗xe2 16 ♗xe2 ♘e7 17 ♗f3 ± Lerner-Gurgenidze, Kharkov 1985.

8...♘b6 9 d5

In Levitt-Madl, London 1990, White tried 9 a3!? and quickly obtained the better position after 9...exd4 10 axb4 dxc3 11 bxc3 ♘e5 12 ♘d4. Therefore, 9...♗d6 is probably best, when 10 d5 ♘e7 transposes to note 'a' after Black's 9th move.

9...♘e7

Now:

a) 10 a3 ♗d6 11 ♗g5 h6 12 ♗h4 c6 13 dxc6 bxc6 = Lipnitsky-Borisenko, USSR Ch (Moscow) 1950.

b) 10 0-0 0-0 11 a4 a6 12 ♗e3 c6 13 ♕b3 a5 14 ♖fd1 cxd5 15 exd5 ♗d7 = Lempert-Rashkovsky, Cappelle la Grande 1995.

c) 10 ♗g5!? h6 11 ♗h4 a6 12 0-0 g5 13 ♗g3 ♗d6 14 f3 h5 15 ♗f2 h4 16 h3 ♘g6 17 ♕c2 ♘f4 18 ♘d1 ± Scherbakov-Rashkovsky, Linares 1996.

D3)

5 ♘f3 (D)
5...0-0

Black has a few important alternatives:

a) 5...d6 and now:

a1) 6 ♗d2 0-0 7 ♕c2 e5 8 dxe5 dxe5 9 a3 ♗xc3 10 ♗xc3 e4 11 ♘d4 ♘e5 12 ♖d1 ♕e7 = Luckis-Foguelman, Buenos Aires 1952.

a2) 6 ♕c2 e5 7 ♗d2 0-0 8 0-0-0 ♗g4 9 dxe5 dxe5 10 ♗d3 ♕e7 11 ♗f5 e4 12 ♗xg4 ♘xg4 13 ♘d5 ♕c5 14 ♘d4 ♘ge5 with chances for both sides, Iskusnykh-Rashkovsky, Russian Ch (Elista) 1995.

a3) 6 ♗e2 e5 7 0-0 ♗xc3 8 bxc3 0-0 9 ♘d2 ♖e8 10 f3 d5 11 ♘b3 b6 12 ♗d2 ♗a6 13 cxd5 ♗xe2 14 ♕xe2 ♕xd5 15 e4 ♕d7 16 ♗e3 ± Avrukh-Rashkovsky, Biel 2001.

b) 5...d5 and here:

b1) 6 ♗d3 0-0 transposes to the main line.

b2) 6 a3 ♗xc3+ 7 bxc3 0-0 8 ♗d3 dxc4 9 ♗xc4 e5 10 0-0 e4 11 ♘d2 b6 12 f3 ♘a5 13 ♗a2 exf3 14 gxf3 c5 = Norri-Pulkkinen, Finnish Ch (Helsinki) 1994.

b3) 6 ♕c2 0-0 7 a3 ♗xc3+ 8 ♕xc3 ♗d7 9 ♗d3 ♘e4 10 ♕c2 f5 11 0-0 ♖f6 12 b4 ♖h6 13 cxd5 exd5 14 b5 ± Ostojić-Djosić, Tivat open 1995.

6 ♗d3 d5 7 0-0
White has an additional option in 7 a3, when Black has to decide whether to exchange his bishop or retreat it:

a) 7...♗xc3+!? 8 bxc3 ♘a5 9 ♘d2 c5 10 0-0 b6 11 cxd5 exd5 12 f3 ♖e8 = Reshevsky-Fischer, Los Angeles (7) 1961.

b) 7...dxc4 8 ♗xc4 (8 ♗xh7+ ♔xh7 9 axb4 ♘xb4 10 0-0 c5 11 ♘e5 ♔g8 12 dxc5 ♘d7 13 ♘xd7 ♗xd7 14 ♕g4 b5 15 cxb6 ♕xb6 16 e4 ♘d3 17 ♗h6 ♕d4 18 ♗e3 ♕d6 ½-½ Petursson-Tal, Reykjavik 1988; the position is still interesting though) 8...♗d6 and then:

b1) 9 h3 a6 10 0-0 h6 transposes to the main line.

b2) 9 0-0 e5 10 h3 ♗f5 11 d5 ♘b8 12 ♘h4 ♗c8 13 ♘f3 e4 14 ♘d2 ♕e7 and Black's chances are to be preferred, Kuzmin-Gulko, USSR Ch (Tbilisi) 1978.

b3) 9 e4 e5 10 d5 ♘e7 11 0-0 (11 h3 a6 12 0-0 and now, instead of 12...h6 13 ♖e1 ♘g6 14 ♗f1 ♗d7 15 ♗e3 ♕e7 16 ♘d2 ± Lerner-A.Sokolov, USSR Ch (Lvov) 1984, Sokolov suggests 12...b5 13 ♗e2 c5 'unclear' as an improvement) 11...♘g6 (11...a6 12 ♖e1 seems a tiny bit better for White: 12...♘g6 13 ♗f1 h6 14 h3 ♘h7 15 ♗e3, Callergaard-Knežević, Budapest 1990) 12 ♖e1 ♗d7 13 b4 a5 14 ♖b1 axb4 15 axb4 ♕e7 16 ♕b3 h6 is equal, Ilivitsky-Averbakh, Sverdlovsk 1951.

b4) 9 ♗b5 e5 10 0-0 exd4 11 exd4 h6 12 ♖e1 a6 13 ♗xc6 bxc6 14 ♘e5 c5 15 dxc5 ♗xc5 16 ♕f3 ♗e6 17 ♗f4 with a pull for White, Vaganian-Mitkov, Istanbul OL 2000.

b5) 9 b4 e5 (9...a6!? can also be considered; e.g., 10 ♗b2 e5 11 ♗e2 ♖e8 12 dxe5 ♘xe5 13 ♕c2 ♕e7 14 h3 ♗d7 15 ♘d4, which is ± according to ECO, but I'm leaning towards equality, Botvinnik-Hecht, Belgrade 1969) 10 ♗b2 (10 d5 ♘e7 11 ♗b2 ♗g4 12 ♕c2, Christiansen-Garcia Gonzalez, Moscow IZ 1982, 12...♗h5! = Christiansen) 10...♗g4 11 d5 ♘e7 12 h3

&d7 13 ©g5 and now, instead of 13...©g6?, which was met with the energetic 14 ©e6! in Botvinnik-Tal, Moscow Wch (3) 1961, Black should play the much safer 13...h6 14 ©ge4 ©xe4 15 ©xe4 &f5 16 ©xd6 cxd6 = Schwarz.

b6) 9 ©b5 is best met with 9...e5 (on occasion, Black plays 9...&e7, intending 10 0-0 a6 11 ©c3 &d6 12 e4 e5) 10 ©xd6 ©xd6 11 dxe5 ©xd1+ 12 ©xd1 ©g4 which has been tried out several times, but the verdict remains equality, Botvinnik-Tal, Moscow Wch (1) 1961.

7...a6
This move prevents White from playing ©b5 and mainly &b5.

Black may also consider 7...dxc4 8 &xc4:

a) 8...a6 comes to the same thing as 7...a6 followed by 8...dxc4.

b) 8...©e7!? has been tried, but has yet to be met with 9 &b5!? ±. Then 9...&d6 transposes to Petrosian-Nei in line 'c4'.

c) 8...&d6 (D) is an attempt to do without ...a6. Now:

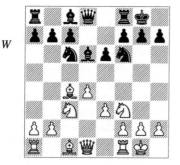

c1) 9 a3 transposes to note 'b2' to White's 7th move.

c2) 9 ©b5 is one of the reasons why Black usually plays ...a6 before ...&d6, but it normally just transposes back into the main line after 9...&e7! followed by 10...a6 11 ©c3 &d6.

c3) 9 e4 e5 10 d5 (10 dxe5?! ©xe5 11 ©xe5 &xe5 12 f3 ©e7 13 ©h1 c6 14 ©e1 b5 ∓ Vokač-Blatny, Lazne Bohdanec 1995) 10...©e7 11 ©e1 a6 12 a4 ©g6 13 &e2 ©e7 14 ©d3 h6 15 &e3 &d7 16 f3 ©ae8 17 ©b3 &c8 18 ©fc1 ©f4 19 &f1 ©d7 20 ©e2 and White's spatial advantage and pressure on the queenside promise him a small but clear advantage, Gavrilov-Blatny, Pardubice 1995.

c4) 9 &b5!? e5 (9...©e7?! is too slow: 10 &xc6 bxc6 11 e4 e5 12 dxe5 &xe5 13 ©xe5 ©xe5 14 ©f3 ©e8 15 &f4 ©e6 16 ©fe1 ± Petrosian-Nei, Tallinn 1983) 10 &xc6 exd4 11 exd4 (11 ©xd4 attempts to win a pawn, but after 11...bxc6 12 ©xc6 ©e8 13 ©d4 &b7 Black has ample compensation for it; e.g., 14 ©f5 &e5 15 f3 g6 16 ©g3 h5, Norwood-Blatny, Groningen jr Ech 1984/5) 11...bxc6 12 &g5 and here:

c41) 12...&f5 13 ©e1 h6 14 &h4 ©e8 15 ©xe8+ ©xe8 16 &xf6 gxf6 17 ©h4 ± Moiseev-Kozma, Moscow 1954.

c42) 12...©e8 13 ©e1 ©xe1+ 14 ©xe1 &e6 15 ©e5 ©e8 16 &xf6 gxf6 17 ©d3 ©f8 18 ©e3 ± Teschner-Dückstein, Wageningen Z 1957.

c43) 12...h6 13 &h4 ©e8 (White gets the better of it after 13...&g4 14 h3 &h5 15 g4 &g6 16 ©e5 &xe5 17 dxe5 ©xd1 18 ©axd1 ©d5 19 ©xd5 cxd5 20 ©xd5 ± Portisch-Andersson, Prague Z 1970, or 13...©b8 14 ©c2 ©b6, Furman-Kopylov, Leningrad 1954, 15 ©e5

±) 14 ♕d3 c5!? 15 ♗xf6 ♕xf6 16 ♘e4 ♕f4 17 dxc5 ♗f8 18 ♘g3 ♗g4 19 ♖ac1 ♖ad8 20 ♕c4 ♕xc4 21 ♖xc4 ♗e6 = Michenka-Gipslis, Ostrava 1993.

8 h3

Or:

a) 8 a3 is met by 8...dxc4 9 ♗xc4 ♗d6.

b) 8 c5 ♗xc3 9 bxc3 ♕e7 10 ♖b1 e5 11 ♘d2 ♖e8 12 ♕c2 ♖b8 with chances for both sides, Grigorian-Gulko, Moscow 1974.

c) 8 cxd5 exd5 9 h3 (9 ♘e5 ♗d6 10 f4 ♘e7 11 f5?! gets White into trouble: 11...g6! 12 e4 dxe4 13 fxg6, Janošević-V.Sokolov, Yugoslav Ch (Kraljevo) 1967, 13...♘xg6 ∓) 9...♖e8 10 ♕c2 h6 11 ♗d2 ♗e6 12 a3 ♗f8 13 b4 with at best a very slight pull for White, Barsov-Berenyi, Budapest 1990.

d) 8 ♕e2 and then:

d1) 8...dxc4 9 ♗xc4 ♗d6 10 ♖d1 (10 e4 is harmless; e.g., 10...e5 11 dxe5 ♘xe5 12 ♘xe5 ♗xe5 13 f4 ♗g4 14 ♕d3 ♕xd3 15 ♗xd3 ♗d4+ = Lokvenc-Taimanov, Marianske Lazne 1962) 10...♕e8 11 ♘g5! (11 e4 e5 12 dxe5 ♘xe5 13 ♘xe5 ♗xe5 14 f3 b5 15 ♗b3 ♗e6 = Relange-Mitkov, Nice 1994) 11...e5 12 d5 (12 ♘ge4 also suffices for an edge; e.g., 12...♘xe4 13 ♘xe4 ♗f5!? 14 ♘xd6 cxd6 15 dxe5 dxe5 16 ♗d2 and White has a slight advantage, Donner-Lengyel, Beverwijk 1964) 12...♘e7 13 ♘ge4 ♘xe4 14 ♘xe4 f5 15 ♘xd6 cxd6 16 f3 ♗d7 (16...♘g6 17 ♗d2 ♕e7 18 ♖ac1 ♗d7 19 ♗a5 favours White, Ionov-Vasiljević, Budapest 1989) 17 ♗d2 ♖c8 18 ♖ac1 with a minimal pull for White.

d2) 8...♕e8!? 9 ♗d2 dxc4 10 ♗xc4 ♗d6 11 ♖ac1 (Donner-Gipslis, Havana 1971) 11...e5 (Kotov) 12 dxe5

♘xe5 13 ♘xe5 ♕xe5 14 f4 ♕e7 with chances for both sides.

e) 8 ♕c2 dxc4 9 ♗xc4 ♗d6 10 ♖d1 ♕e7 (or 10...♕e8 11 ♘g5 h6 12 ♘ge4 ♘xe4 13 ♘xe4, Vaiser-Knežević, Trnava 1983, 13...b5 ±) 11 a3 h6 12 h3 e5 (12...♖e8 transposes to note 'a' to Black's 8th move) 13 b4 (13 d5 ♘b8 14 ♘d2 ♘bd7 15 ♘de4 ♘xe4 16 ♘xe4 ♘f6 17 ♘xd6 cxd6 18 ♗d2 ♗d7 = Balashov-Gulko, USSR Ch (Riga) 1985) 13...♗d7 14 ♗b2 ♖ae8 15 b5 axb5 16 ♘xb5 e4 17 ♘d2 ♘a5 18 a4 ♗b4 19 d5 ♗f5 20 ♘b3 ± Kakageldiev-Miladinović, Elista OL 1998.

We now return to 8 h3 *(D)*:

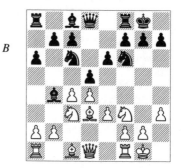

8...h6

Other than creating some *luft* for the king, this move doesn't have a lot of sense to it, since only relatively rarely does White make use of the g5-square in this line (with note 'd1' to White's 8th move as the exception that confirms the rule). Therefore, it isn't surprising that Black has tried other moves:

a) 8...♖e8 9 a3 dxc4 10 ♗xc4 ♗d6 11 ♕c2 (or 11 e4 e5 12 d5 ♘e7 13 ♖e1 ♘g6 14 ♗f1 ± Anton-Webb, corr.

1988) 11...h6 12 ♖d1 ♕e7 13 b4 e5 14 d5 e4 15 ♘xe4 ♕xe4 16 ♗d3 ♘xb4 17 ♗xe4 ♘xc2 18 ♗xc2 ♗d7 19 ♗b2 ♘e4 20 ♘d4 ± Ki.Georgiev-Johansen, Thessaloniki OL 1984.

b) 8...dxc4 9 ♗xc4 and here:

b1) 9...♕e8 10 ♖e1 e5 11 e4 exd4 12 e5 dxc3 13 exf6 c2 14 ♕d5 is given as ± in *ECO*, but this evaluation is probably based too much on the result of a game that ended in a quick win for White. After 14...♕d8 15 fxg7 ♔xg7 16 ♕h5 ♕d6 17 ♖e3 ♕g6 18 ♕h4, instead of 18...♖d8? (Gligorić-Kovačević, Sarajevo 1983), Black should opt for 18...♗d6, although White has the initiative after a move like 19 ♘d4!?.

b2) 9...♗d6 10 e4 (10 a3 ♖e8 transposes to line 'a') 10...e5 11 ♗e3 and now:

b21) 11...exd4?! 12 ♘xd4 ♗d7 13 ♖e1 ± Taimanov-Fischer, Buenos Aires 1960.

b22) 11...b5?! 12 ♗b3 ♗b7 13 d5 ♘a5 14 ♘d2 ♘xb3 15 ♕xb3 ♗c8 16 a4 ♗d7 17 ♖fc1 ♕e7 18 ♕d1 ± Panno-Reshevsky, Palma de Mallorca IZ 1970.

b23) 11...h6 12 ♖e1 transposes to the note to White's 9th move.

9 a3

9 ♖e1 dxc4 10 ♗xc4 ♗d6 11 e4 e5 12 ♗e3 is quite similar to the main line. Then:

a) 12...exd4 13 ♗xd4 ♘xd4 14 ♕xd4 b5 15 ♗b3 b4 16 ♘a4 ♗e7 17 ♕e3 with a better game for White, Åkesson-Karlsson, Swedish Ch (Uppsala) 1985.

b) 12...♗d7 13 a3 ♕c8 (13...exd4 14 ♗xd4! ± Gligorić-Kovačević, Yugoslavia 1981) 14 ♖c1 ♖e8 15 d5 (15 ♕b3!?) 15...♘e7 16 ♗f1 ♕d8 17 ♘d2

♘g6 18 a4 ♕e7 19 ♘c4 with at best a minimal plus for White, Lautier-Mitkov, Batumi Echt 1999.

c) 12...b5 13 ♗b3 (13 dxe5!? ♘xe5 14 ♗b3 ♗b7 15 ♗d4 ♘fd7 = Viaud-Diaconescu, corr. 1984) 13...♗b7 14 dxe5 (14 d5 ♘e7 15 ♘d2 c6 16 dxc6 ♗xc6 17 ♗c2 ♖c8 = Atalik-Miladinović, Ano Liosia 1995) 14...♘xe5 15 ♗d4 (15 ♘xe5 ♗xe5 16 ♗c5 ♖e8 = Rotshtein-Mitkov, French Cht 1994) 15...♘fd7 16 ♘xe5 ♗xe5 17 a4 c6 18 ♖e3 ♕f6 19 ♖f3 ♕e7 = Wanatabe-Mitkov, Merida 2000.

9...dxc4 10 ♗xc4 ♗d6 11 e4

11 ♕c2 ♕e7 12 ♖d1 transposes to note 'e' to White's 8th move.

11...e5 12 ♗e3 *(D)*

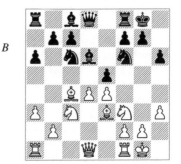

12...b5

Or:

a) 12...♖e8 13 ♖e1 exd4 14 ♗xd4 ♘xd4 15 ♕xd4 ♗f8 16 e5 ♘h7 17 ♕f4 ♗e6 18 ♗xe6 fxe6 19 ♖ad1 ± Portisch-Pachman, Stockholm IZ 1962.

b) 12...♕e7!? 13 ♖e1 exd4 14 ♗xd4 ♘xd4 15 ♕xd4 ♗c5 16 ♕d2 ♖d8 17 ♕c2 ♗e6 18 ♗xe6 ♕xe6 19 ♘d5 ♗b6 is equal, Vaiser-Gulko, Sochi 1985.

13 ♗a2

Or 13 ♗b3 ♗b7 14 d5 ♘e7 15 ♕d3 ♘g6 16 ♖ac1 ♘h5 17 ♘e2 ♕f6 18 ♔h2 ♗c8 19 ♕d2 ♗d7 20 ♘fg1 ½-½ Iskusnykh-Zemerov, Russian Cht (Omsk) 2001.

13...♗b7 *(D)*

14 d5

The alternative 14 ♖e1 has not been especially convincing in recent games:

a) 14...exd4 15 ♗xd4 ♘xd4 16 ♕xd4 c5!? (16...♘h7 17 ♕e3 ♖e8 18 e5! ♗xf3 19 ♗xf7+! ♔xf7 20 ♕xf3+ is slightly better for White, Farago-Knežević, Polanica Zdroj 1978) 17 ♕d2 ♖e8 18 ♖ad1 ♗c7 19 ♕e3 ♕e7 20 ♗d5 ♗xd5 21 ♘xd5 ♘xd5 22 ♖xd5 c4 with chances for both sides, Lesiège-Mitkov, Istanbul OL 2000.

b) 14...♖e8!? 15 d5 ♘e7 16 ♘h4 ♗c8 17 g4 ♘g6 18 ♘f5 ♘h7 with a pleasant game for Black, Danner-Mitkov, Leon Echt 2001.

14...♘e7 15 ♘d2

15 ♕d3 ♘g6 16 ♘e2 ♘h5 ½-½ Averbakh-Knežević, Polanica Zdroj 1976.

15...♘g6

15...c6!? is an interesting option; e.g., 16 dxc6 ♗xc6 17 ♖c1 ♖c8 with chances for both sides.

16 ♘b3 ♗c8 17 ♘a5 ♘h7 18 ♕h5

This move is the first of several pre-emptive strikes against Black's upcoming kingside play. However, focusing on the queenside may work just as well; one such move is 18 ♕c2, although Black's chances are not worse after 18...♘f4.

18...♕f6 19 g3 ♘g5 20 h4 ♘f3+ 21 ♔g2 ♘e7 *(D)*

Now:

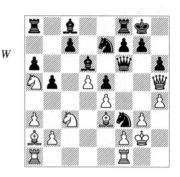

a) White obviously can't take on f3 as 22 ♕xf3? is met effectively with 22...♗h3+!.

b) After 22 ♘c6, Black continued 22...♖e8?! and ended up in an inferior position in the game Farago-Knežević, Kiev 1978. However, with 22...♘xc6!? 23 dxc6 ♘d4 24 ♘d5 ♕e6, threatening ...♕h3+ and ...♕g4, Black would be doing fine.

Conclusion

In Lines A-C, White's unusual options don't present Black with many problems. Against the Taimanov Variation, Line D2 currently appears to offer White the best chances of an advantage, while the traditional main line, D3, gives Black good chances of obtaining equal chances.

Index of Variations

Chapter Guide

1 d4 ♘f6 2 c4 e6 3 ♘c3 ♗b4 4 e3

B

Now:

A: 4...b6
B: 4...0-0

Or:
a) Miscellaneous 4th moves for Black – Chapter 18
b) 4...d5 – Chapter 18
c) 4...♘c6 – Chapter 18
d) 4...c5:
d1) 5 ♘e2 – Chapter 17
d2) 5 ♗d3 (intending ♘e2) – Chapter 16
d3) 5 ♗d3 ♘c6 6 ♘f3 ♗xc3+ 7 bxc3 d6 – Chapter 15
d4) All other lines – Chapter 18

A)

    4 ...   b6
    5 ♗d3

5 ♘e2 – Chapter 11

    5 ...   ♗b7

5...c5 6 ♘f3 0-0 – Chapter 13

    6 ♘f3

Other moves – Chapter 12

    6 ...   0-0

6...♘e4 – Chapter 12

    7 0-0

Now:
a) 7...c5 – Chapter 13
b) 7...d5 – Chapter 14
c) Other moves – Chapter 13

B)

    4 ...   0-0

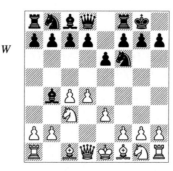

W

    5 ♘f3

Or:
a) 5 ♘e2 – Chapter 10
b) 5 ♗d3 (intending ♘e2) – Chapter 16
c) 5 ♗d3 d5:
c1) 6 ♘f3 – *see 5 ♘f3 d5 6 ♗d3*
c2) 6 a3 ♗xc3+ (other moves – Chapter 18) 7 bxc3 – Chapter 6

    5 ...   d5

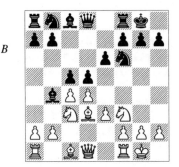

B

1: Karpov Variation
1 d4 ♘f6 2 c4 e6 3 ♘c3 ♗b4 4 e3 0-0
5 ♘f3 d5 6 ♗d3 c5 7 0-0 dxc4 8 ♗xc4
cxd4 9 exd4 *7* 9...b6 10 ♗g5 ♗b7 *11*

A: 11 ♘e5 *11*
B: 11 ♖e1 *13*
C: 11 ♖c1 *16*
D: 11 ♕e2 *18*

2: Parma Variation and Related Systems
1 d4 ♘f6 2 c4 e6 3 ♘c3 ♗b4 4 e3
0-0 5 ♘f3 d5 6 ♗d3 c5 7 0-0 dxc4 8
♗xc4 *21*

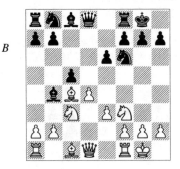

B

A: 8...♕e7 *23*
B: 8...♗d7 *26*
C: 8...♘bd7 *27* 9 ♕e2 b6 *32*
C1: 10 d5 *35*
C2: 10 ♖d1 *39*

3: ...♗a5 Systems
1 d4 ♘f6 2 c4 e6 3 ♘c3 ♗b4 4 e3
0-0 5 ♘f3 d5 6 ♗d3 c5 7 0-0 ♘c6 8
a3
A: 8...♗a5 *43*
B: 8...dxc4 9 ♗xc4 ♗a5 *49* 10 ♕d3
a6 11 ♖d1 b5 12 ♗a2 *52*

4: Nimzowitsch Variation
1 d4 ♘f6 2 c4 e6 3 ♘c3 ♗b4 4 e3
0-0 5 ♘f3 d5 6 ♗d3 c5 7 0-0 ♘c6 8
a3 ♗xc3 9 bxc3 b6 *56* 10 cxd5! exd5
11 ♘e5!? ♕c7 12 ♘xc6 ♕xc6 13 f3
58

5: Khasin Variation
1 d4 ♘f6 2 c4 e6 3 ♘c3 ♗b4 4 e3
0-0 5 ♘f3 d5 6 ♗d3 c5 7 0-0 ♘c6 8
a3 ♗xc3 9 bxc3 ♕c7 *59* 10 cxd5!
exd5 *61*
A: **11 ♘h4** *63*
A1: 11...♘e7!? *64*
A2: 11...♕a5! *67*
B: **11 a4** *69*

6: Main Variation
1 d4 ♘f6 2 c4 e6 3 ♘c3 ♗b4 4 e3
0-0 5 ♗d3 d5
A: **6 ♘f3 c5 7 0-0 ♘c6 8 a3 ♗xc3 9
bxc3 dxc4 10 ♗xc4** *73* **10...♕c7** *73*

W

A1: **11 ♗e2** *75*
A2: **11 ♗d3** *77* 11...e5 12 ♕c2 ♖e8
77
A21: 13 e4 *79*
A22: 13 ♘xe5 *81*
A3: **11 ♗a2** *83*
A4: **11 ♗b2** *86*
A5: **11 ♗b5** *87*
B: **6 a3 ♗xc3+ 7 bxc3** *89*
B1: 7...c5 *90*
B2: 7...dxc4 *94*

7: Classical Variation
1 d4 ♘f6 2 c4 e6 3 ♘c3 ♗b4 4 e3
0-0 5 ♘f3 d5 6 ♗d3 c5 7 0-0 ♘c6 8

a3 dxc4 *99* 9 ♗xc4 cxd4 10 exd4 *99*
10...♗e7 11 ♖e1 b6 *102*

8: Averbakh Variation
1 d4 ♘f6 2 c4 e6 3 ♘c3 ♗b4 4 e3
0-0 5 ♘f3 d5 6 ♗d3 c5 7 0-0 ♘bd7
105
A: 8 a3 *105*
B: 8 cxd5 *107*

9: Delayed Fianchetto Variation
1 d4 ♘f6 2 c4 e6 3 ♘c3 ♗b4 4 e3
0-0 5 ♘f3 d5 6 ♗d3 c5 7 0-0 b6 *111*
8 cxd5 exd5 9 dxc5 bxc5 *113*

10: Reshevsky Variation
1 d4 ♘f6 2 c4 e6 3 ♘c3 ♗b4 4 e3
0-0 5 ♘e2 *115* 5...d5 6 a3 ♗e7 7
cxd5 *119*
A: 7...♘xd5 *121*
B: 7...exd5 *124*

11: Fischer Variation and Related Systems
1 d4 ♘f6 2 c4 e6 3 ♘c3 ♗b4 4 e3
b6 5 ♘e2 *132*

B

A: 5...c5 *132*
B: 5...♗b7 *145*
C: 5...♗a6 *150*
C1: 6 ♘g3 *151*

12: Dutch Variation
**1 d4 ♘f6 2 c4 e6 3 ♘c3 ♗b4 4 e3
b6 5 ♗d3 ♗b7** *180* **6 ♘f3 ♘e4** *181*

13: Keres Variation and Related Systems
**1 d4 ♘f6 2 c4 e6 3 ♘c3 ♗b4 4 e3
b6 5 ♗d3 ♗b7** (5...c5 6 ♘f3 0-0
191) **6 ♘f3 0-0 7 0-0** *191* **7...c5** *191*

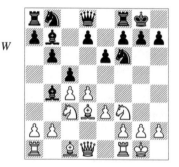

14: Classical Fianchetto Variation
1 d4 ♘f6 2 c4 e6 3 ♘c3 ♗b4 4 e3

15: Hübner Variation
**1 d4 ♘f6 2 c4 e6 3 ♘c3 ♗b4 4 e3 c5
5 ♗d3 ♘c6** *220* **6 ♘f3 ♗xc3+ 7
bxc3 d6** *220*

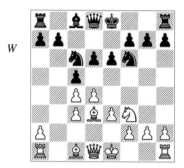

16: Modern Variation and Related Systems
**1 d4 ♘f6 2 c4 e6 3 ♘c3 ♗b4 4 e3
0-0** (4...c5 5 ♗d3 *233*) **5 ♗d3** *236*
5...d5 6 ♘e2 c5 *240*

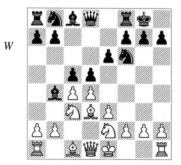

Index of Named Variations